# The Art of War

The complete and fully illustrated edition
of Sun Tzu's philosophical masterpiece

with four other classics in the ancient warrior tradition

Foreword by Paul Couch

SWEETWATER
PRESS

SWEETWATER
PRESS

Published in 2008 by Sweetwater Press
© 2008 Sweetwater Press

Excerpts from *Shinkendo, Japanese Swordsmanship* and *Shinkendo Tameshigiri: Samurai Swordsmanship & Test-Cutting*, by Toshishiro Obata, © Toshishiro Obata; used by permission.

Photograph and illustration copyrights noted on pages 582–584

Created and produced by Cliff Road Books, Inc.

ISBN−13:978−1−49244−394−0

Printed in China

Front cover: Ceremonial *huang* (reproduction) intricately carved in jade. China. Circa Warring States period.
Back cover: Samurai Chosyu during the Boshin War period. Felice Beato. Japan. 1860s. Hand-colored albumen silver print.

*Production staff*
Publishing Director: Ellen Sullivan
Project Manager: Holly Smith
Designers: Miles G. Parsons and Maria Mann
Cover Design: Pat Covert
Mon Illustrations: Pat Covert
Production Assistance: Dottie Barton
Editors: Trinket Shaw and Larisa Lovelady
Proofreaders: Trinket Shaw, Laura Vann, Carla Jean Whitley, Nick Phillips, Margo Spotswood, Lesley Messer, and Katie Finley
Contributors: Dean Calbreath, Linda Romine, Lisa Harris, Megan Roth, Russ Mitchell, Larisa Lovelady, Rachel Horton, Laura Hendrix, Trinket Shaw, Pat Covert, Paul Couch, and Toshishiro Obata
Translator: William Ridgeway
Photo Research: Larisa Lovelady, Chuck Evans, and Staci Wilson
Photography: Karim Shamsi-Basha, Paul Couch, Pat Covert, and Kazuhiro Tsuruta of the Asian Art Museum of San Francisco
Mapping: Pat Covert and Mapping Specialists
Fact Checking: Ashlea Denham, Chelsea Dean, and Matt Dexter
Asian History Research Consultant: Pat Covert
Martial Arts Consultants: Paul Couch, Ray Deadman, and Toshishiro Obata
Index: Stacey Baggett

Special thanks to: Sensei Toshishiro Obata and the International Shinkendo Foundation, Paul Couch, Jasa Kazuo Moriya (Japanese American Society of Alabama), Trinity United Methodist Church, Birmingham Botanical Gardens, Blake Pogue and CAS Hanwei, Clive Sinclair, Stephen Selby, Scott Fuller, Heather Stripling, Dragonfly Sword Supplies, and especially to Mr. Don Wood, Chief Curator at the Birmingham Museum of Art, and Mr. Ray Deadman for their kind permission and assistance in photographing weapons, armor, and artifacts from the Ray Deadman Collection.

# CONTENTS

---

# FOREWORD

In times of peace or of war, accomplishing the safety and well-being of any society is tied to the martial arts way of thinking and acting. When war is ongoing, coping with life-threatening situations is a reality that every soldier faces constantly. Having served in law enforcement and the military for more than forty years, I can say without a doubt that martial arts are equally important off the battlefield; they have sustained me and given me tools to deal with every imaginable circumstance. The ability to protect myself and, often, others has been ever useful in my career, as well as in my life. To avoid confrontations, to de-escalate volatile situations, and to calm fears, experience in martial arts has always given me the mental and physical training to persevere.

This book shows how and why ancient martial arts have transcended time and place to survive today, not only in terms of their relevance to military applications, but also to the strategies needed to master every kind of challenge in work and in life. The Asian warriors of old were trained in the use of various weapons; but certainly the most powerful weapon of all, then and now, is the mastery of the mind. Using physical weapons as his tools, the warrior recognized his own mind as the force that ultimately vanquished the enemy. The mental disciplines, as well as the vast arsenal at the disposal of the ancient Asian warrior, are documented in the pages of this book, albeit far from completely—that would require a set of volumes to rival the *Encyclopedia Britannica*. The entries that follow are purely for educational purposes, to invite the reader's further study of the martial arts, ancient and modern.

Law enforcement is a good example of how study of the martial arts can be helpful in modern life. Why must law enforcement recruits attend intensive training? That training is, of course, based on today's needs for protecting and serving the citizenry. Throughout history, law enforcement has been necessary because there are always those who would harm others and those who would take what is not legitimately theirs.

I began my martial arts training in the United States Marine Corps at Parris Island, South Carolina, as part of "boot camp." All the training I received while in the Marine Corps on active duty was based on warfare and preparation for it. The reading list for Marines includes such titles as *The Art of War* by Sun Tzu for a very good reason. Training is never over in the military establishment, and this includes reading for the knowledge that those who have been there, done that can impart, which can give a clearer understanding of both warfare and keeping peace. To know one's enemy as well as one's self is the key. I continued my Marine Corps career in the active reserve, which develops skills in updated and current methods, weapons, and strategies. I retired after twenty-five years, but my law enforcement career had run concurrently. At present, I am the director of training for a large, urban police force, the Jefferson County Sheriff's Office in Birmingham, Alabama.

The more years one spends in the literal application of the martial arts, the clearer it is that these disciplines carry over into everything in life that has stringent requirements. That includes any area that challenges one never to give up but to persevere in studies to attain one's goal, as in sports or business. For instance, if one were to check the recommended reading list for the various branches of the armed forces in the United States, one would find ancient works that would inspire members of the business world also, where intelligence and counterintelligence are huge assets. The essence of strategy and success lies in these books. The ability to win in an often dog-eat-dog business can hinge on one's clear

*Opposite page: A Large Panel of Golden Yellow Silk Satin Woven in Colored Silks and Gilt Threads With Nine Dragons Chasing Flaming Pearls. China. Circa 19th century.*
*Above: Bronze ritual axe head from the early Western Zhou period. Circa 1000 BCE.*

understanding of the competitor and his strategies. In many arenas one can certainly benefit from the spirit of martial arts. Being the best one can and being a role model are worth pursuing and can be directly tied to the many lessons contained in Sun Tzu's *The Art of War* and the other ancient military philosophy classics.

Today's world is not different in many ways from ancient times, but man's essential nature and his innate ability to wage or avoid war have taken a unique turn as the world has seemed to grow much smaller than it was hundreds of years ago. Modern strategy and planning, however, are virtually unchanged. Based on their experiences of actual incidents or circumstances, the ancients tell us to "Know your enemy, his strengths and weaknesses, as well as your own," and this is the maxim by which plans can be formalized. Today, surveillance and intelligence are continually kept up to date by spying, either by men on the ground and in the air or by satellite from space. Success or failure may very well depend on understanding the adversary, which includes knowing the opponent's abilities of leadership, planning, and implementation. Reading the books contained herein with an open mind will show that they all have one thing in common: preserving one's way of life and that of one's family or institution. What motivates the successful soldier, law enforcement officer, athlete, student, or businessman can be found within the covers of this book in the time-proven wisdom of these ancient warriors and scholars.

Some of the boundless books concerning the mystique of the ancient warrior may not be totally factual because the essence of these tales is connected to the spirit of the warrior and his code. In every country throughout history, there have been heroes and heroines who are culturally intertwined with the national persona and immortalized in legend, mythology, poetry, and song. However, the five ancient writings contained in this book should be taken as fact, in the way it was known and written at the time, based on the authors' experiences. Of all the books presented here, perhaps the most recognized and the most widely read are *The Art of War* by Sun Tzu and *The Book of Five Rings* by Miyamoto Musashi. While *The Art of War* is especially popular with military and business establishments and is required or recommended reading worldwide, *The Book of Five Rings* has been almost the bible for martial artists for years. Musashi was famous as a swordsman and is the subject of many books, movies, and television series in Japan. One other book that has inspired many present-day martial artists is Munenori's *The Sword and the Mind*, which concerns techniques and strategies representing *shinkage ryu* swordsmanship along with with the mental and spiritual discipline that accompanies this art.

Today's traditional martial arts, or *budo*, are those directly descended from an earlier time, primarily coming to us from Japan by way of China. Whether it is karate, aikido, swordsmanship, or myriad other martial practices, it will always be traceable back to those origins. As an example, traditional Japanese swordsmanship can be seen in many styles, or *ryuha*, today. One of those styles, *shinkendo* ("true sword way"), is introduced in this volume. This art is directly descended from family heritage and training, which includes shinkage ryu swordsmanship, covered in the book *The Sword and the Mind*. The founder and chief instructor of shinkendo, Toshishiro Obata Kaiso, has spent a lifetime studying, training in, and teaching this ancient samurai martial art. For him, it is much more than how to wield a sword; it is a way of life.

I have been a student of Kaiso Obata for eighteen years and am an instructor now, holding the position of *hanshi*. I have also been a student of karate for more than forty years and am *shihan*, fifth-degree black belt in the World Oyama Karate Organization. I have taught both shinkendo and karate in colleges and private dojo. All of my training has been a blessing, and sharing these martial arts with others is an honor and privilege.

Almost every child will some day want to try martial arts, and will probably think the martial arts are about fighting. Martial arts can best be thought of as a constant consciousness of one's own abililites. The most successful martial artists know how to avoid a fight without a show of cowardice. Some of the most notable samurai, such as Musashi, avoided confrontation whenever possible, and only when necessary fought with all available advantages to win. These teachings are solemnly respected by those of us who have combined our efforts to publish this book. We wish all readers well in their goals, whatever may be their sport, business, or other endeavors requiring guidance from the martial arts.

Paul Couch
*Hanshi, International Shinkendo Federation*

*Shihan, World Oyama Karate Organization*

*Deputy Chief, Jefferson County, Alabama, Sheriff's Office*

*United States Marine Corps Reserve, Retired, Gy/Sgt*

*Collector and Scholar of Japanese Samurai Arms and Armor*

*Top Left: Spearhead. Late Shang, Circa 1200 BCE.*
*Top Right: Dagger-axe. Western Zhou. Circa 1000 BCE. Bronze.*

# CRITICAL ASIAN MILITARY WRITINGS

Sun Tzu's *Art of War* is one of the world's most widely read works on military strategy. Required reading by military officers, politicians, and businesspeople alike, these writings have been studied and dissected ever since the author recorded them more than 2,500 years ago. Written during one of the most turbulent times in Chinese history, the Warring States period, Sun Tzu's classic built the platform for wars to come, not just in Asia, but internationally. *The Art of War* also laid the groundwork for a host of writers to further expound on military strategies and codes of conduct during Japan's many centuries of war, when the samurai rose to prominence.

But *The Art of War* reigns as the most influential written work. The author's thoughts on planning, tactical disposition, evaluation of one's opponent, maneuvering, the use of spies, and assessment of terrain are all still applicable to the modern day. Sun Tzu said, "In all fighting, the direct method may be used for joining the battle, but indirect methods will be needed to secure victory." This comment alone would cause any leader, ancient or modern, to carefully consider all his options before engaging in conflict.

Although not as broad in terms of military strategy, the writings of Japanese authors Yagyu Munenori and Miyamoto Musashi can also be applied to many aspects of life in today's world. Both of these warriors were accomplished swordsmen who lived and fought during the early seventeenth century, in the waning of the samurai era.

Munenori's *The Sword and the Mind*, a blend of Zen thinking and sword-fighting strategy, shares the warrior's insight on how to defeat an opponent by merging the mind, body, and sword into one. "First see with your mind, then with your eyes, and finally with your body."

Miyamoto Musashi, author of *The Book of Five Rings* and a contemporary of Munenori, is considered by many to be the most mentally acute and physically adept swordsman who ever lived. Throughout *The Book of Five Rings*, Musashi draws on his experience as a consummate combat technician and strategist, often stressing mental clarity and preparedness divined from his devotion to the meditative aspects of Buddhism.

Japanese authors Inazo Nitobe and Yamamoto Tsunetomo never fought a battle but are known for writing the two most widely read books on the samurai code of ethics. Nitobe's work, *Bushido*, lays out the tradition and responsibilities of the samurai in detail, stressing the positive attributes of strong discipline, integrity, and loyalty. Yamamoto Tsunetomo, author of *Hagakure*, spent thirty years as a samurai under the retainership of Nabeshima Mitsushige, ruler of Japan's Saga prefecture. After his master's death in 1700, Tsunetomo became a Zen monk, living in seclusion until his death in 1720. *Hagakure* is a younger samurai's compilation of Tsunetomo's oral recollections, many of which emphasize the theme of death with honor. Like Inazo Nitobe's works, Tsunetomo's writings have been embraced for their philosophical values.

From Sun Tzu's broad but succinct strategies on warfare to Tsunetomo's incantations on the fundamentals of a virtuous life, all of these influential writings were the by-products of thousands of years of Asian warfare. Ironically, these words out of Asia have probably given Western military leaders much insight into defeating the nations of the Far East in the wars that were to come.

*Above: A 16th-century example of the armor (do) known as haramaki, with murasaki-ito odoshi or deep purple lacing, complete with sode.*

# The Art of War

Sun Tzu

# CONTENTS

*Preceding pages: Nine dragons detail (ink and color on paper),*
*Chen Rong, Chinese, first half of the 13th century.*
*Photograph © 2008 Museum of Fine Arts, Boston.*
*Opposite page: Emperor Wu Ti (156–87 BCE) welcoming a*
*man of letters, from a history of Chinese Emperors. China.*
*17th century. Color on silk.*

# Laying Plans

## 1

*Sun Tzu said:*

### 1

The art of war is of vital importance to the State. It is a matter of life and death, a road either to safety or to ruin. Hence it is a subject of inquiry which can on no account be neglected.

### 2

The art of war, then, is governed by five constant factors, to be taken into account in one's deliberations, when seeking to determine the conditions obtaining in the field.

### 3

These are: The Moral Law; Heaven; Earth; The Commander; Method and Discipline.

### 4

The Moral Law causes the people to be in complete accord with their ruler, so that they will follow him regardless of their lives, undismayed by any danger.

### 5

Heaven signifies night and day, cold and heat, times and seasons.

### 6

Earth comprises distances, great and small; danger and security; open ground and narrow passes; the chances of life and death.

### 7

The Commander stands for the virtues of wisdom, sincerity, benevolence, courage, and strictness.

### 8

Method and Discipline are the marshaling of the army in its proper subdivisions, the graduations of rank among the officers, the maintenance of roads by which supplies may reach the army, and the control of military expenditure.

*Opposite page: The Capture of the Mountain at Ko Hu Chu So Lung, from a series depicting scenes from the Quinlong Campaign in Sichuan 1772–6. Engraving.*

### 9

These five heads should be familiar to every general: he who knows them will be victorious; he who knows them not will fail.

### 10

Therefore, in your deliberations, when seeking to determine the military conditions, let them be made on the basis of a comparison, in this wise:

### 11

Which of the two sovereigns is imbued with the Moral Law? Which of the two generals has the most ability? With whom lie the advantages derived from Heaven and Earth? On which side is discipline most rigorously enforced? Which army is stronger?

### 12

On which side are officers and men more highly trained?

### 13

In which army is there the greater constancy both in reward and punishment?

### 14

By means of these seven considerations I can forecast victory or defeat.

### 15

The general that hearkens to my counsel and acts upon it, will conquer: let such a one be retained in command! The general that hearkens not to my counsel nor acts upon it, will suffer defeat: let such a one be dismissed!

### 16

While heeding the profit of my counsel, avail yourself also of any helpful circumstances over and beyond the ordinary rules. According as circumstances are favorable, one should modify one's plans.

## 17

All warfare is based on deception.

## 18

Hence, when able to attack, we must seem unable; when using our forces, we must seem inactive.

## 19

When we are near, we must make the enemy believe we are far away; when far away, we must make him believe we are near.

## 20

Hold out baits to entice the enemy. Feign disorder, and crush him.

## 21

If he is secure at all points, be prepared for him. If he is in superior strength, evade him.

## 22

If your opponent is of choleric temper, seek to irritate him.

## 23

Pretend to be weak, that he may grow arrogant.

## 24

If he is taking his ease, give him no rest.

## 25

If his forces are united, separate them.

## 26

Attack him where he is unprepared, appear where you are not expected.

## 27

These military devices, leading to victory, must not be divulged beforehand.

## 28

Now the general who wins a battle makes many calculations in his temple before the battle is fought. The general who loses a battle makes but few calculations beforehand. Thus do many calculations lead to victory, and few calculations to defeat: how much more no calculation at all! It is by attention to this point that I can foresee who is likely to win or lose.

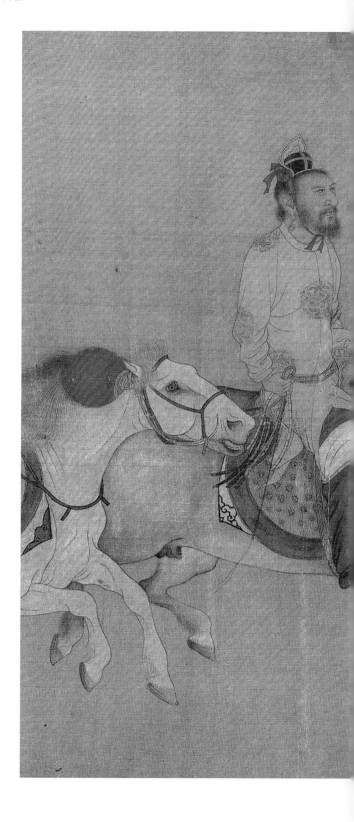

*Nomads with a tribute horse. Li Zanhua, 899–936. China. 11th–12th century. Ink, color, and gold on silk. Photograph © 2008 Museum of Fine Arts, Boston.*

# SETTING THE STAGE
# PREDYNASTIC CHINA

China is one of the world's oldest and most continuous civilizations. Nomadic hunter-gatherers inhabited the vast area of Asia now known as China during the Old Stone Age, or the Paleolithic period, around 2.5 million to 10,000 BCE. Prehistoric remains—teeth, skulls, and skeletal fragments of human beings discovered near modern-day Beijing (formerly Peking)—indicate that people inhabited the area more than half a million years ago. Archaeologists called these ancestors of *Homo sapiens* Peking Man, or *Homo erectus pekinensis*. Historians tell us that Peking Man, who lived between two periods when glaciers covered the Earth, knew how to use fire and worked with stone tools.

Around 10,000 BCE, China began to grow as people learned to farm the land. Then, during the Neolithic period, about 5000 BCE, agricultural settlements began to spring up throughout China. The heartland of Chinese civilization developed in the forested river valleys in the modern-day provinces of Shaanxi, Shandong, and Henan. Millet was the main crop cultivated in the north and northwest, along the high, terraced banks of the Yellow River. The Yangshao people, who farmed the fine loess soils in the highlands, developed one of the most extensive early settlements, building plaster-floored houses supported by wooden beams. Farther south, in the fertile jungles of the Yangtze River basin, rice paddies became increasingly prominent.

The ancient Chinese supplemented their diet with fish and aquatic plants. The earliest methods of farming began with the burning of wooded areas so that the soil could be tilled. Animals also provided dietary sustenance for the ancient Chinese as, around 3000 BCE, farmers began to raise pigs and other livestock, including sheep in the northern areas and water buffalo in the southern areas.

One of the most advanced farming civilizations was that of the Longshan, in the north. Regarded as the first great

engineers, they developed flood control and irrigation projects that greatly increased agricultural production. But they also were the first Chinese to weave silk and to create pottery using a potter's wheel and high-temperature kilns. The Longshan practiced the art of scapulimancy, in which the cracks in heated animal bones were used for interpretation. The Longshan's legendary leader, Yu, founded the Xia dynasty about 2000 BCE.

Many other important developments had occurred during the Neolithic period. One was the making of pottery in which to store food and drink. The types varied by region: in the northwest, near Yangshao village, red-clay pots were decorated with black pigment swirls, spirals, and stick figures; in the northeast area of the Longshan, smooth black pottery was common; and deep, three-legged vessels were found in eastern areas. Another discovery was jade, a lustrous, green gemlike mineral. This extremely hard material became highly prized for use in ritual objects and decorative ornaments and for shaping into blades. In terms of architectural engineering, the ancient Chinese took another step forward when they discovered how to build bricks made of blocks of stamped earth. These blocks were used to build walls and other fortifications.

The next significant period in China's development occurred during the Bronze Age, when legendary rulers such as Huang Di, the Yellow Emperor, are credited with creating key elements of civilization, including agriculture, silk, boats, carts, the calendar, and the bow and arrow. The last of these rulers was a king named Yu. The people later chose his son to be their leader, a precedent that established the concept of dynastic or hereditary rule. Yu's descendants created the Xia dynasty (ca. 2000 to ca. 1500 BCE), which is said to have survived for fourteen generations.

Archaeological evidence for the Xia dynasty is inconclusive, but its mythical origins are well-known by the

*Above: Look carefully at the design incised on the surface of this small plaque. The animal it represents might be the predecessor of the one depicted in monster masks (taotie) found on vessels of the early Bronze Age. Three-pronged plaque with animal masks. China. 3300–2200 BCE. Nephrite.*
*Opposite page: Three-legged pots like this one were common in eastern areas of China during the Neolithic period. Single-handled tripod. China. 2800–2000 BCE. Earthenware with stamped decoration.*

Chinese people. According to their mythology, the god Pan Ku created the universe. The world was compared to an egg that after 18,000 years, split into two parts. The yolk, or bright part of the egg, created the heavens, while the white part formed the Earth below. Over the next 18,000 years, the worlds grew farther apart.

When Pan Ku died, his body gave life to the earthly elements. As the legend goes, Pan Ku's eyes became the sun and moon, his blood the rivers, and his skin the soil. Thunder came from his voice, and the wind and clouds were his breath. Mountains that rippled across the land were Pan Ku's fingers; his arms and legs encompassed the corners of the square earth. The god's hair sprouted trees and plants, and his sweat caused rain. The parasites in his body eventually became human beings.

Many gods ruling heaven, earth, and mankind followed, as did a succession of wise rulers. One of these sages, Huang Di, the Yellow Emperor, is credited with creating Chinese civilization. Another mythical figure, Kun, tried

unsuccessfully to dam the rivers when floods threatened the land. For his failure, the gods killed him, but three years later, another leader, Yu, came to life from his corpse. Yu discovered how to dig channels to divert floodwaters. He was said to have taken on animal form; some say a turtle, a fish, a dragon, or a bear. In any case, the gods designated Yu as the first king of China, the leader of the Xia dynasty.

While there are no written records of the Xia, it is believed to have coincided with the beginnings of the Chinese Bronze Age (ca. 2000 to ca. 771 BCE). These civilizations devised a class system, religious order, and writing. Another significant development was metallurgy. During the Bronze Age, copper and tin were mined to create bronze, which was used to manufacture tools and artifacts. Large-scale production of bronze allowed for the creation of weaponry, as well as ritual objects for use by rulers. Bronze work would reach its culmination during the Shang dynasty (ca. 1523 to ca. 1027 BCE), which is the first documented and archaeologically proven dynasty of ancient China.

武皇帝劉秀

# EMPERORS AND DYNASTIES
## A TIMELINE

### Predynastic China

The dates for the ancient dynasties of China are inexact at best. Some scholars consider only the specific dates of events to delineate the changing dynasties, while others feel that such dating policies are inappropriate for the earliest eras and choose to see the changeover as a fluid line of events over time. So, several dates for the earliest dynasties are used.

### Neolithic Period (ca. 5000 to ca. 1500 BCE)

The early Chinese farmed around the Yellow River valley, where they grew such crops as millet, rice, and wheat. Using stone tools for agriculture and for weapons, they also raised livestock such as cows and chickens and lived in pit dwellings.

### The Bronze Age (ca. 2000 to ca. 771 BCE)

Tools and weapons began to be made from bronze, replacing stone implements. As the population grew, cities emerged, class structure developed, and territorial disputes began. Agriculture was still prominent, and the only remnants of art were from clay pots.

### Earliest Dynasties
#### Xia (ca. 2000 to ca. 1500 BCE)

Though this dynasty was previously thought to be mythological, recent discoveries have proved its existence. According to legend, a man named Yu drained the waters of a monumental flood threatening his village and was rewarded with the first kingship of the Xia dynasty.

### Shang (ca. 1523 to ca. 1027 BCE)

The Shang dynasty, based in the Yellow River valley region, controlled what is now part of northern and central China. From about 1384 BCE, the capital city was located at Anyang near the border of Henan. It was an agrarian society concentrating on millet, wheat, and barley, but silkworms, pigs, sheep, and oxen were also raised. The Shang dynasty was also advanced in metallurgy. Bronze ships, weapons, and tools from that era have been found. The Shang created a universal writing system, which led to the first historical records. Their society also began to divide into upper and lower classes as the horse and chariot appeared and created a power imbalance among the barbarian tribes and other small city-states around it. Ancestor worship was coupled with deity worship, in that ancestors interceded with the supreme god, Deity Above, on behalf of the people. There were also lesser gods of nature, such as the water, the sun, the wind, and the moon. When the Shang army became occupied during a northern barbarian uprising, the Zhou, under the leadership of Wu Wang, rallied all of the other Shang enemies and succeeded in attacking and defeating the Shang, destroying the capital of Anyang.

### Zhou (ca. 1027 to 256 BCE)

The exact origins of the Zhou are unknown, but the earliest record of their existence is in the Wei Valley. The Zhou dynasty is divided into two sections: the Western or Early Zhou, between 1027 and 771 BCE, and Eastern or Later Zhou, between 771 and 256 BCE.

The Western Zhou, believing that the Shang had lost the support of the Deity Above, created the so-called Mandate of Heaven and therefore claimed legitimacy. This mandate stated that the king rules by the authority of the Deity Above only to the extent that the king remains just, equitable, and worthy of his people. The Mandate of Heaven effectively ended the hereditary succession system, and for centuries to come, all kings would claim that the supreme god supported their rule. In the meantime, as the population grew even further, a social structure similar to that of Europe in the Middle Ages developed, with upper-class rulers,

*Above: In China, bats are foremost among auspicious decorative motifs based on visual puns because "bat" (fu) sounds like both "blessings" (fu) and "riches" (fu). In this nephrite pendant four bats surround a coin (qian), the word for which sounds like "before" (qian). Circular plaque with four bats surrounding a coin. China. 1800–1900. Nephrite.*

*Opposite page: The thirteen emperors (detail). Yan Liben. 600–673. China. Second half of the seventh century. Ink and color on silk. Photograph © 2008 Museum of Fine Arts, Boston.*

middle-class scholars and officials, and lower-class peasants. When northwestern nomads attacked, the Western Zhou were forced to move their capital eastward to Luoyang.

The Eastern Zhou were also divided into two time frames. The first, the Spring and Autumn period, also known as the One Hundred Schools of Thought, lasted from around 771 to 481. Iron was discovered, bringing advances

*Head of an arhat. China. 1368–1644. Wood with traces of pigments.*

in agricultural technology and massive population growth but resulting in conflict among the city-states. During the time, at the end of the Spring and Autumn period and the beginning of the Warring States period, many scholars were pursuing knowledge through philosophy, the most influential of which were Taoism and Confucianism. As the Warring States period (480 to 221 BCE) progressed, the growing settlements clashed against one another in long, drawn-out battles, as indicated by Sun Tzu's *Art of War*. Though the smallest city-states formed alliances to avoid being swallowed up by the more powerful city-states, only one large city-state finally emerged victorious, and the Qin united all of China for the first time.

## The First Imperial Age
### Qin (221 to 206 BCE)

With the Qin as the first dynasty to control all of China, for the first time people from outside acknowledged the existence of another race of people, aptly naming the nation China after the Qin, or the Chin. The Qin Empire extended China's borders south to current-day Vietnam and Korea, with the central kingdom remaining in the area of the Yellow River valley.

First Emperor Qin Shihuangdi, a very strict legalist who believed that all people were inherently bad and needed laws to guide them, instituted the first bureaucracy and state spy systems to maintain his position of complete authority. The Great Wall was begun, or continued, depending on the historical point of view, and the forced labor used to build it was comprised of anyone who criticized Qin or the system he employed to exact control over his subjects. In a positive vein, he introduced written language and a unified system of weights and measures.

## Han (206 BCE to 220 CE)

A centralized government was established, but feudal lords no longer had the power to challenge the emperor's reign. The peace and prosperity of this dynasty allowed the new religion of Buddhism to be introduced. The creation of paper, among many such innovations, advanced Chinese culture past that of other civilizations, and was also evidence of the level of literacy, education, and governmental organization.

When Liu Bang proclaimed himself emperor in 206 BCE, he established the longest of the imperial dynasties, the Early or Western Han, which ruled until 9 CE. The Han Empire was established using the Qin system with a few modifications. Taxes were sharply reduced, and the government played a smaller role in the economic policies. The emperors chose leaders using a merit system to replace the old hereditary system, and written exams were instituted to identify the most qualified people for the job. Education was stressed, and in the second century BCE, an imperial university was established to teach students the five classics of the Confucian school, the official dogma, to prepare them to become bureaucrats. The Han distinguished themselves by making scientific discoveries, many of which were not known to Westerners until centuries later. The Han were particularly advanced in astronomy but also invented sundials and water clocks, divided the day equally into ten and then into twelve periods, recorded sunspots, and devised the lunar calendar that was used as late as 1912. In mathematics, the Han were the first to use the place value system. Other innovations included wheelbarrows, locks to control water levels in streams and canals, compasses, a crude seismograph, and advances in acupuncture. Today, the Chinese show pride in their heritage by referring to themselves as the Han people.

Emperor Wudi, who ruled from 140 to 87 BCE, expanded the kingdom again and, in doing so, bankrupted the country.

Taxes and the old legalist policies of the Qin dynasty were reinstated, which led to a revolt and overthrow of his reign. Emperor Wang Mang, who usurped the throne and ruled from 9 to 23 CE, attempted to limit the control of the large, powerful families and made enemies of most of them. His slow pace in implementing welfare reforms angered the poor, and he was murdered. A succession of regional leaders then took turns naming themselves emperor and fought among one another.

From the Liu family came the new ruler for the Late or Eastern Han dynasty, Guangwudi, the Shining Martial Emperor, who lasted until 57 CE. The Later Han recovered lost territories and, in 73 CE, a great diplomat-general, Ban Chao, eventually led an army almost to the borders of eastern Europe. Ban Chao returned to China in 101 CE with information about the Roman Empire, but the Romans had already known of China as a silk producer. Within a century, the peasant rebellions of 184 and the general's uprising of 190 had led to the destruction of the capital and the rule of one dictator after another over China. By 207, General Chao had become the dominant dictator in the north. When he died in 220, his son established the kingdom of Wei, so that the Han Empire was divided into the three kingdoms of Wei, Shu, and Wu. Subsequently, because China was no longer unified under one emperor, a series of dynasties or kingdoms ruled over the various regions.

## Period of Disunity
### Three Kingdoms (220 to 280 CE)

Three dynasties in three different regions ruled over China simultaneously during this period: the Wei, located in the north and ruled by the Chao family; the Shu, ruling in the southwest; and the Wu, ruling in the southeast. These landowning rulers, who gained their power by creating armies of serfs and vassals, fought constantly and finally fell to northern invaders.

### Chin (265 to 420 CE)

When a Wei general overthrew the throne in 265 CE to found the Chin dynasty in northern China, he had reunited both northern and southern China, but unification fell apart when he died. For the first time, Northern non-Chinese tribes now controlled the former Chin dynasty. Non-Chinese rule lasted until the Northern Wei dynasty reclaimed China in 420.

Even though foreign tribes had conquered the Chinese, the native peoples still had influence on their new rulers. So, during the second half of the fifth century, the Northern Wei adopted a policy of Sinification, in which foreign invaders were forced to adopt Chinese clothing, customs, and language. The non-Chinese rebelled against this policy, and in 534 CE, the dynasty fell. For the next half century, non-Chinese ruled northern China.

*The Second Sui Emperor, Yangdi (569–618) with his fleet of sailing craft, from a history of Chinese emperors. China. 17th century. Color on silk.*

### Southern and Northern Dynasties (420 to 588 CE)

After the barbarians destroyed the Three Kingdoms, they set up new dynasties, in which the north and the south were dominated by a series of kingdoms. The most permanent of these kingdoms was the northern kingdom of Wei, established by the Toba tribe, which adopted the Chinese form of bureaucratic government and thus survived longer than any of the others.

## The Second Imperial Age
### Sui (581 to 618 CE)

Emperor Wendi reunited China under one ruler by consolidating the north and then taking the south from the leaders of the Hou Liang dynasty and the Chin dynasty. Wendi established a new form of administration with a governing body, the censorate, to hold the bureaucracy and court system in check. A census was instated for tax purposes. Expensive canal projects begun in the early seventh century were built with the taxes and labor of the poor. When the poor protested the taxes, the Turks began causing trouble to the east, and the Sui emperor withdrew to the south.

## Tang (618 to 907 CE)

Having wrested the throne from Gaozong, his retired father, Taizong ruled for more than two decades. During that time, civil service exams were improved, paper money was developed, and port cities thrived, as did the middle class. Tang society allowed many new religions, including Islam, Judaism, and a heretical form of Christianity, though Buddhism remained the principal religion. Another dominant force in the Tang dynasty was Madame Wu, who ruled first as regent for her two sons and then as empress until 705 CE, when she was removed from power. She was a strong supporter of Buddhism and lived in a monastery for several years.

Husan Zong took control soon after Empress Wu, though he ignored his country's affairs to spend his time with his favorite concubine, a situation that resulted in a series of rebellions. By the time the rebellions had finally been stopped, the central government had lost a great deal of power and could not maintain order.

Later in the ninth century, a man named Chao began one of the worst rebellions in China, leading peasants against the government in hopes of overthrowing the ruling dynasty. After doing a great deal of damage to the country, the peasants were stopped by the head of the Turkish army, Li Koyong, who was employed by the Tang emperor. These battles resulted in a divided China led by five Chinese army generals, a period known as the Five Dynasties and spanning the years between 907 and 960 CE.

## Song (960 to 1279 CE)

Emperor Taizu used a centralized army to establish the unification of China once again, strictly controlling the army so that the generals could not gain too much power, as they had at the end the Tang dynasty. During the Song dynasty, Chinese culture and technology reached its height. With the invention of the printing press, for instance, literature was more widely distributed and literacy was easier to attain. The monetary system of paper money was extended, and the concept of credit was also developed. Su Dongpo, the poet, calligrapher, and painter, was one of the most talented artists of this period. His and other paintings from the time show humans as miniscule compared to landscapes that seem to overwhelm them.

As powerful barbarians began to surround the borders of China, the Song emperors were forced to pay them off with trade and incentives to keep the peace,. At last, the Song devised a plan to subdue these Mongols by employing another northern barbarian tribe, the Jurchen, to fight for them. However, the Jurchens aligned themselves with the Mongols and turned on the Song to attack from the northeast. The Song tried to reestablish themselves as rulers but had already lost much of their power and never regained it. The Mongols, under Kublai Khan, overthrew and replaced the Song dynasty in 1279.

## Yuan (1279 to 1368)

Genghis Khan's grandson, Kublai Khan, defeated the Song dynasty in 1279, thereby creating the second non-Chinese empire. The capital was located in Peking (present-day Beijing), so that he could be near Mongolia to the north. In short work, he made the Mongols the upper class, gave them minority power over the Chinese, and kept his countrymen from assimilating through intermarriage. In matters of spiritual philosophy, the Mongols were often atheists but were very tolerant and accepting of many religions, including Tibetan Buddhism, Christianity, Islam, Taoism, and Confucianism, among others. Most Chinese, however, held on to Chinese Buddhism.

In the meantime, Italian explorer and trader Marco Polo had left Italy in 1260, after hearing rumors of great wealth to the east. Having served in Kublai Khan's court for a few years, Polo collected information on the Chinese and other nearby cultures and published a book, *Discovery of the World*.

After less than a hundred years, the Mongol Empire of Yuan was fractured by internal strife and external pressures from the other Khanates surrounding China. Eventually, the independent armies of the other regions fought among themselves and brought down the Yuan with them. Finally, the Chinese marched on the capital of Peking and ran the Mongols out of China.

## Ming (1368 to 1644)

The first emperor, Zhu Yanzhang (later Taizu), divided China into fifteen provinces but still kept most of the power centralized. Zhu was a cruel leader with a tendency to kill officials who upset him. Nevertheless, the Chinese concepts of Confucianism and Buddhism were supported and flourished, as their leaders took on ever-increasing roles in society. In fact, one Confucian philosopher, Wang Yangming, became quite famous. Because more Chinese were literate, the novel became popular; however, the Confucian leaders of the country discouraged the composition of novels. In trade, Silk Road trafficking thrived and Chinese markets experienced unparalleled wealth, while resistance from private merchants prevented the Chinese government from gaining control of commerce.

But internal rebellions, caused by unfair tax practices,

weakened the Ming government. Meanwhile, the Manchus, descendants of the Jurchen barbarians, breeched the Great Wall to invade and topple the Ming dynasty.

*A Rare Imperial Embroidered Yellow Silk Twelve-Symbol Dragon Robe, Ji Fu. China. Qianlong period. 1735–1796. Silk.*

## Qing (1644 to 1912)

The empire now included the regions of Mongolia, Tibet, and Korea, so the Manchu emperors instituted tax and land reform and gave refugees abandoned land for farming. With irrigation and flood control systems repaired, the agricultural output increased dramatically.

Early in the dynasty, the Jesuits had practiced freely and had been successful in winning converts. However, when the pope publicly condemned Confucianism as a pagan religion, the leaders of China outlawed Christian missions. This external conflict turned to internal strife as the Chinese merchants and the Chinese government began to refuse to trade with the West. At first, only the port of Canton was open, but then even Canton closed as a result of anti-Western sentiment. As the West pushed the Chinese to open trade doors, conflict began, producing the Opium Wars between western Europe and China.

The first Opium War, from 1839 to 1842, was won by the West because of its superior war technology. After years of

diplomacy, China and Western officials agreed, in 1860, that China would open other ports to trade. Throughout the country, numerous revolts caused a great deal of destruction and mayhem. The largest, the Taiping Rebellion, from 1850 to 1864, almost succeeded; however, the West intervened by providing weapons to the Manchu leaders. Elsewhere, the yearlong Sino-Japanese War of 1894 weakened China and won further trade concessions.

Western influences and modernization soon fueled social dissatisfaction and began a push for more rights. The Boxer Rebellion, which broke out in China's capital of Peking with the intent to rid China of Western influence, was eventually supported by Manchu leaders. In 1900, the Boxers attacked foreigners in Peking, and this revolution brought an end to centuries of imperial rule. By 1911, the dynastic system of government had finally collapsed, and a new republican government was established.

# DYNASTIES GEOGRAPHY

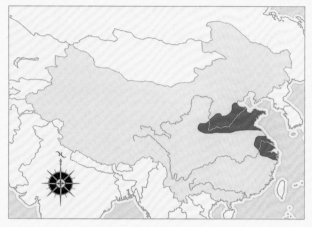

Neolithic Era circa 5000–1500 BCE. The early Chinese were skilled in agriculture, farming areas around the Yellow River.

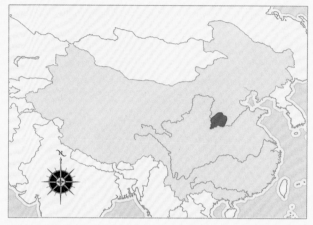

Xia Dynasty circa 2000–1500 BCE. The Xia dynasty was once thought to be legendary, but recent discoveries have proved its existence.

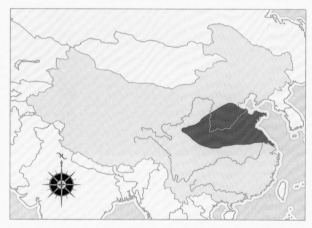

Shang Dynasty circa 1523–1027 BCE. The Shang dynasty controlled what is now part of northern and central China.

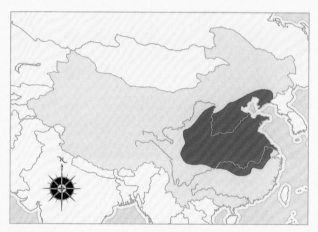

Zhou Dynasty circa 1027–256 BCE. During this time period, a social structure developed, with upper-class rulers, middle-class scholars and officials, and lower-class peasants.

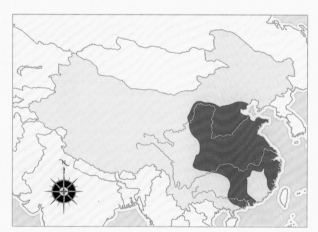

Qin Dynasty circa 221–206 BCE. The Qin dynasty extended China's borders south to current-day Vietnam and Korea, with the central kingdom remaining in the Yellow River valley.

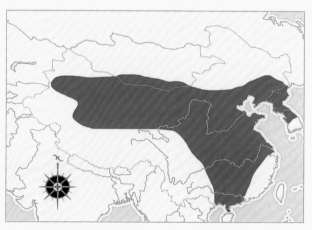

Han Dynasty 206 BCE–220 CE. During the Han dynasty, a centralized government was established.

# A TIMELINE

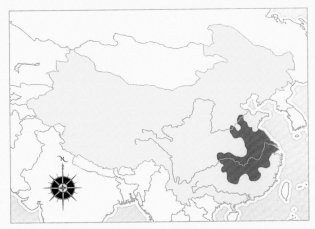

*Sui Dynasty 581–618 CE. Emperor Wendi of the Sui dynasty reunited China by consolidating the north and then taking the south from the leaders of the Hou Liang dynasty and the Chin dynasty.*

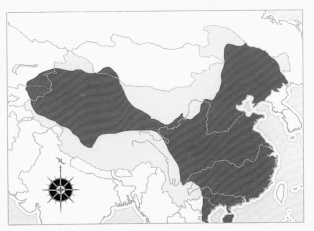

*Tang Dynasty 618–907 CE. The middle class thrived during the Tang dynasty.*

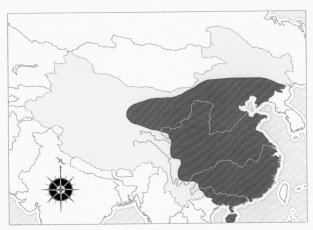

*Song Dynasty 960–1279 CE. During the Song dynasty, Chinese culture and technology reached new heights.*

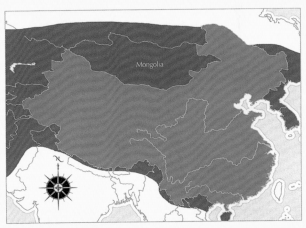

*Yuan Dynasty 1279–1368. Mongol ruler Kublai Khan defeated the Song dynasty and created the second non-Chinese empire.*

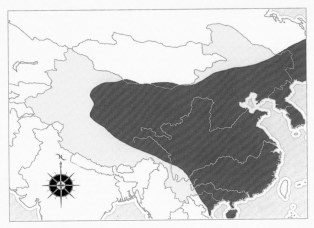

*Ming Dynasty 1368–1644. Trade along the Silk Road brought Chinese markets unparalleled wealth during the Ming dynasty.*

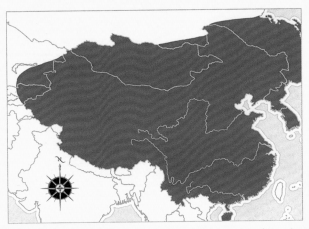

*Qing Dynasty 1644–1912 The Qing dynasty included the regions of Mongolia, Tibet, and Korea.*

*Statues in Xian, China. Tomb of the Terra-cotta Army—showing a rank of courtiers (rather than soldiers) in partial excavation.*

# Waging War 2

## Sun Tzu said:

### 1

In the operations of war, where there are in the field a thousand swift chariots, as many heavy chariots, and a hundred thousand mail-clad soldiers, with provisions enough to carry them a thousand *li*, the expenditure at home and at the front, including entertainment of guests, small items such as glue and paint, and sums spent on chariots and armor, will reach the total of a thousand ounces of silver per day. Such is the cost of raising an army of a hundred thousand men.

### 2

When you engage in actual fighting, if victory is long in coming, then men's weapons will grow dull and their ardor will be damped. If you lay siege to a town, you will exhaust your strength.

### 3

Again, if the campaign is protracted, the resources of the State will not be equal to the strain.

### 4

Now, when your weapons are dulled, your ardor damped, your strength exhausted and your treasure spent, other chieftains will spring up to take advantage of your extremity. Then no man, however wise, will be able to avert the consequences that must ensue.

### 5

Thus, though we have heard of stupid haste in war, cleverness has never been seen associated with long delays.

### 6

There is no instance of a country having benefited from prolonged warfare.

### 7

It is only one who is thoroughly acquainted with the evils of war that can thoroughly understand the profitable way of carrying it on.

*Terra-cotta soldier found in Xian.*

**8**

The skillful soldier does not raise a second levy, neither are his supply wagons loaded more than twice.

**9**

Bring war material with you from home, but forage on the enemy. Thus the army will have food enough for its needs.

**10**

Poverty of the State exchequer causes an army to be maintained by contributions from a distance. Contributing to maintain an army at a distance causes the people to be impoverished.

**11**

On the other hand, the proximity of an army causes prices to go up; and high prices cause the people's substance to be drained away. When their substance is drained away, the peasantry will be afflicted by heavy exactions.

**12**

With this loss of substance and exhaustion of strength, the homes of the people will be stripped bare, and three-tenths of their income will be dissipated; while government expenses for broken chariots, worn-out horses, breastplates and helmets, bows and arrows, spears and shields, protective mantles, draught oxen and heavy wagons will amount to four-tenths of its total revenue.

**13**

Hence a wise general makes a point of foraging on the enemy. One cartload of the enemy's provisions is equivalent to twenty of one's own, and likewise a single *picul* of his provender is equivalent to twenty from one's own store.

**14**

Now in order to kill the enemy, our men must be roused to anger; that there may be advantage from defeating the enemy, they must have their rewards.

**15**

Therefore in chariot fighting, when ten or more chariots have been taken, those should be rewarded who took the first. Our own flags should be substituted for those of the enemy, and the chariots mingled and used in conjunction with ours.

**16**

The captured soldiers should be kindly treated and kept.

**17**

This is called using the conquered foe to augment one's own strength.

**18**

In war, then, let your great object be victory, not lengthy campaigns.

**19**

Thus it may be known that the leader of armies is the arbiter of the people's fate, the man on whom it depends whether the nation shall be in peace or in peril.

*Right: Found in the ancient capital of China, Xian. Dagger. China. 1300–1050 BCE. Nephrite.*

# THE GEOGRAPHY OF CHINA
# DIVERSE LANDSCAPES TO CONQUER

China, the fourth-largest country in the world after Russia, Canada, and the United States, lies on the eastern coast of Asia and the western coast of the Pacific Ocean. In terms of sheer size and expanse, the country is so massive that spring planting in the south often coincides with winter blizzards in the north. Numerous countries border China: North Korea to the east; Russia to the northeast and northwest; Mongolia to the north; Kazakhstan, Kyrgyzstan, and Tajikistan to the northwest; Afghanistan, India, Pakistan, Myanmar, and Nepal to the west and southwest; and Burma, Laos, and Vietnam to the south. Unlike some of its landlocked neighbors, China also includes more than 5,000 islands, including Taiwan, which in modern times asserted its independence by claiming to be the True Republic of China.

Nearly two-thirds of China's land mass is mountainous. The five major mountain ranges in China form steps from west to east leading down to the sea. The westernmost, the Himalayas, are referred to as the rooftop of the world. A line of mountains stretching from the Greater Khingan Range in the northeast to the Yunnan-Guizhou Plateau in the south creates a natural boundary. East of this line are the densely populated plains, where the vast majority of cultivation takes place. A major north-south boundary within China is the Qinling Range of the Kunlun Mountains, which divides the North China Plain to play an important role in influencing the location of customs and language. South of the Qinling divide are the populous lower and middle plains. From these mountains spring all of China's rivers.

China is a nation of rivers. Dozens of them slice the diverse terrain, promoting navigation, creating trade routes, and providing the country's people with nourishment and raw material. The two largest rivers in China, the Yangtze and the Huang He, played significant roles in the development of Eastern society, and do so to this day.

The world's third-largest river, the Yangtze, begins its great journey in western China, a result of large sheets of ice melting high in the Tanggula Mountains of the Qinghai province. The river cuts an immense path across the provinces of China, winding nearly 4,000 miles until it reaches its end in the East China Sea. While flowing rapidly at first, the Yangtze begins to slow, and for centuries, it has

*Mountain motifs are commonly found in Chinese art. The lofty Mount Song. Lan Ying. 1585–after 1664. China. 1627. Ink and color on silk. Photograph © 2008 Museum of Fine Arts, Boston.*

provided the bank's inhabitants with salmon and rice. The river played a large role in the early settlements, including

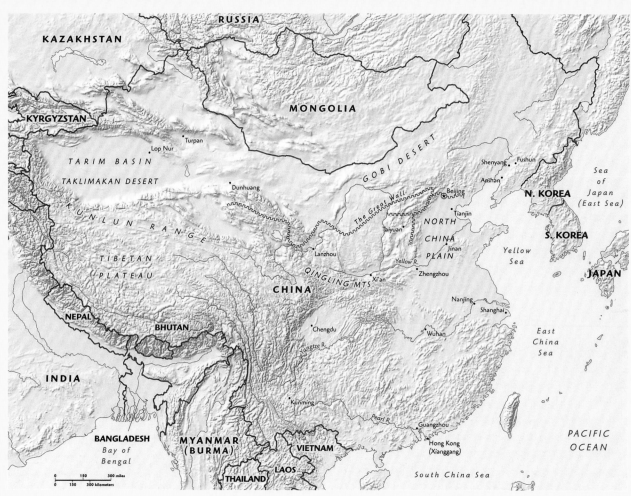

*Topographical map of China.*

that of the province known as Shu during Sun Tzu's era, and known today as Sichuan. Modern cities lining the river include not only Jingzhou and Yangzhou, cities founded during Sun Tzu's lifetime, but also the eighth-largest city in the world, Shanghai.

Prior to the life of Sun Tzu, farmers settled along the banks of the Yangtze to raise rice crops and livestock. Most historians believe that Sun Tzu spent his final years in the state of Wu, a province that straddled the mouth of the Yangtze River. The people of the river worked and traded peacefully together, enjoying the times of abundance and praying to their ancestors to keep the river peaceful.

Over the years, the people living along the river learned to survive the river's swings of fortune and hardship. Unfortunately, the peace could not last. During Sun Tzu's life, the people living far north of the river began to attack the villages along the river. Although it did not occur in time for Sun Tzu to witness it, the violent quibbling over the riverfront eventually led to the various Chinese states' joining in 221 BCE to become the Chinese Empire.

The Huang He, recognized throughout the world as the Yellow River, is known as the cradle of Chinese civilization.

The Yellow River passes through nine provinces or autonomous regions: Shaanxi, Qinghai, Sichuan, Gansu, Ningxia, Inner Mongolia, Henan, Shandong (home to the powerful states of Qi and Lu during the era of Sun Tzu), and Shanxi. Archaeologists have discovered evidence along its banks that indicates that fishing and the cultivation of cereal crops occurred as far back as 5000 BCE. At its lower reaches, the river wets the Shandong province, an area known during Sun Tzu's lifetime as the state of Qi. It is here that the strategist began his life as a member of the *shi*, a group of landless aristocrats. The massive amount of erosion that occurs along the river's course is thought to be largely due to centuries of heavy farming. There is a saying in China that "if you fall into the Yellow River, you may never get clean again." Years of silt deposits have caused the waterway to pour above the contiguous farmland, making flooding a continual problem. In Sun Tzu's time, flooding created turmoil within the ruling dynasties. Put into place during the dynastic period, the flood control system of embankments required constant repair, and early emperors were judged on their ability and willingness to deal with this serious problem.

# THE LIFE OF SUN TZU

Much controversy surrounds the reputed author of *The Art of War*. There are theories that Sun Tzu did not actually exist, that he was fabricated to protect the privacy of the actual author. Whether he is a mythical character or a real person who was also a brilliant combat strategist does not detract from the universality of *The Art of War* and its philosophical and military genius. Legend has it that Mao Zedong and Joseph Stalin, among others, applied its wisdom for fighting strategies and tactics during wartime. Its theories have been studied in martial realms as well as in the areas of management, sports, investments, politics, and personal relationships.

Written works were often named after the author in ancient China; therefore, *The Art of War* was originally referred to as the *Sun Tzu*. Evidence that Sun Tzu was, in fact, the famed general of legend is first noted in the *Huainanzi*, another work known by its author's name, which states, "When sovereign and ministers show perversity of mind, it is impossible even for a Sun Tzu to encounter the foe." Since Huainanzi died in 122 BCE, this places the career of Sun Tzu at a prior time.

Supposedly, Sun Tzu, originally Sun Wu, was born to a family of minor nobility in the state of Qi during the Warring States period. He was a counterpart of Confucius, who would have lived in a nearby region. The later name,

*Most experts agree that The Art of War was written during the early part of the Warring States period. Sun Tzu. China. 6th–5th century BCE.*

## *Let your plans be dark and impenetrable as night, and when you move, fall like a thunderbolt.*

meaning "Master Sun," reflects a sign of status. As a mercenary, he presented his text of thirteen chapters to King Helu of Wu, hoping to gain employment from the monarch. As the tale goes, he then, immediately trained an "army" of the king's concubines to perform simple commands in order to illustrate the reliability of the principles in his book. He so impressed the king that he was hired as a general. According to tradition, Sun Tzu's military conquests included the powerful Chu state, as well as the Qi and the Qin. Yeh Shui-hsin is quoted as saying that the commonly understood record of Sun Tzu's military achievements "is not authentic matter, but the reckless fabrication of theorizing pundits," and that the story of Sun Tzu training concubines "is utterly preposterous."

The early Warring States period (ca. 480 to 221 BCE)

seems to be the most accepted date of the book. In support of the theory that Sun Tzu wrote sometime after 400 BCE, the *Shiji*, a Chinese history, gives the last record of the general. In this account, Sun Tzu, referred to as Sun Wu, advises King Helu wisely, and the army successfully takes the city of Ying to defeat that state of Chu. But the time and circumstances of Sun Tzu's death are unknown. "Ten miles outside the city gate of Wu Hsieh, there is a large tomb of the strategist Sun Tzu," the *Yueh chueh shu* text declares. No further evidence of either the location of his remains or his life after the conquest of the Chu has been found.

The text of *The Art of War* is composed of short thoughts or theories and is often presented with commentaries from scholars and critics. There is also much discussion regarding a possible total of eighty-two chapters rather than the thirteen we have today; however, despite historical references to these additional chapters, no record of them has been unearthed. Forgeries, or perhaps ancient commentaries on the original work, may have been the source of these references.

# Attack By Stratagem

## 3

*Sun Tzu said:*

**1**

In the practical art of war, the best thing of all is to take the enemy's country whole and intact; to shatter and destroy it is not so good.

**2**

So, too, it is better to recapture an army entire than to destroy it, to capture a regiment, a detachment or a company entire than to destroy them.

**3**

Hence to fight and conquer in all your battles is not supreme excellence; supreme excellence consists of breaking the enemy's resistance without fighting.

**4**

Thus the highest form of generalship is to balk the enemy's plans;

**5**

the next best is to prevent the junction of the enemy's forces;

**6**

the next in order is to attack the enemy's army in the field;

**7**

and the worst policy of all is to besiege walled cities. The rule is not to besiege walled cities if it can possibly be avoided.

**8**

The preparation of mantlets, movable shelters, and various implements of war will take up three whole months; and the piling up of mounds over against the walls will take three months more.

**9**

The general, unable to control his irritation, will launch his men to the assault like swarming ants, with the result that one-third of his men are slain, while the town still remains untaken. Such are the disastrous effects of a siege.

**10**

Therefore, the skillful leader subdues the enemy's troops without any fighting; he captures their cities without laying siege to them; he overthrows their kingdom without lengthy operations in the field.

**11**

With his forces intact he will dispute the mastery of the Empire, and thus, without losing a man, his triumph will be complete. This is the method of attacking by stratagem.

**12**

It is the rule in war, if our forces are ten to the enemy's one, to surround him;

**13**

if five to one, to attack him;

*Right: Lancer. 265–317 CE. Painted earthenware.*

*Opposite page: The first section of the earliest existent manuscript of The Art of War from Yinqueshan, Lin Yi, Shandong. It was excavated in 1972 and dates from the Western Han period.*

孫子曰：兵者，國之大事也，死生之地，存亡之道，不可不察也。

一曰道，二曰天，三曰地，四曰將，五曰法。道者，令民與上同意也，故可與之死，可與之生，而不畏危也。

天者，陰陽、寒暑、時制也，順逆、兵勝也。地者，遠近、險易、廣狹、死生也。將者，智、信、仁、勇、嚴也。法者，曲制、官道、主用也。凡此五者，將莫不聞，知之者勝，不知者不勝。

故校之以計，而索其情，曰：主孰有道？將孰有能？天地孰得？法令孰行？兵衆孰強？士卒孰練？賞罰孰明？吾以此知勝負矣。

將聽吾計，用之必勝，留之；將不聽吾計，用之必敗，去之。計利以聽，乃為之勢，以佐其外。勢者，因利而制權也。兵者，詭道也。

故能而示之不能，用而示之不用，近而示之遠，遠而示之近。利而誘之，亂而取之，實而備之，強而避之，怒而撓之，卑而驕之，佚而勞之，親而離之。攻其無備，出其不意。此兵家之勝，不可先傳也。

夫未戰而廟算勝者，得算多也；未戰而廟算不勝者，得算少也。多算勝，少算不勝，而況於無算乎！

## 14

if twice as numerous, to divide our army into two.

## 15

If equally matched, we can offer battle;

## 16

if slightly inferior in numbers, we can avoid the enemy;

## 17

if quite unequal in every way, we can flee from him. Hence, though an obstinate fight may be made by a small force, in the end it must be captured by the larger force.

## 18

Now the general is the bulwark of the State; if the bulwark is complete at all points, the State will be strong; if the bulwark is defective, the State will be weak.

## 19

There are three ways in which a ruler can bring misfortune upon his army:

## 20

By commanding the army to advance or to retreat, being ignorant of the fact that it cannot obey. This is called hobbling the army.

## 21

By attempting to govern an army in the same way as he administers a kingdom, being ignorant of the conditions which obtain in an army. This causes restlessness in the soldier's minds.

## 22

By employing the officers of his army without discrimination, through ignorance of the military principle of adaptation to circumstances. This shakes the confidence of the soldiers.

## 23

But when the army is restless and distrustful, trouble is sure to come from the other feudal princes. This is simply bringing anarchy into the army, and flinging victory away.

## 24

Thus we may know that there are five essentials for victory:

## 25

He will win who knows when to fight and when not to fight.

## 26

He will win who knows how to handle both superior and inferior forces.

## 27

He will win whose army is animated by the same spirit throughout all its ranks.

## 28

He will win who, prepared himself, waits to take the enemy unprepared.

## 29

He will win who has military capacity and is not interfered with by the sovereign.

## 30

Hence the saying: If you know the enemy and know yourself, you need not fear the result of a hundred battles.

## 31

If you know yourself but not the enemy, for every victory gained you will also suffer a defeat.

## 32

If you know neither the enemy nor yourself, you will succumb in every battle.

*Military officer. China. 386–581 CE. Molded and hand-sculpted earthenware with traces of paint.*

# THE FIVE CONSTANT FACTORS

Sun Tzu's ancient military treatise, *The Art of War*, offers a detailed examination of how and when to wage warfare. One of the world's oldest books on military tactics, it consists of thirteen concise chapters, the first of which is titled "Laying Plans." In that chapter, the author outlines his "five constant factors" for determining the conditions of all war. Furthermore, he outlines how these five key elements—mortal law, heaven, earth, the commander, and methods and discipline—can be evaluated to gain competitive strength against the enemy.

Although *The Art of War* was not translated into a Western language until the late eighteenth century, its influence has been far-reaching. Military leaders from France's Napoléon Bonaparte, to America's General Douglas MacArthur and China's Mao Zedong are said to have been inspired by this text from the fifth century BCE. Moreover, modern-day business leaders who model managerial strategies on his ideas have also embraced the principles Sun Tzu lays out in his treatise.

The first of the five governing factors is mortal law, or the importance of maintaining a sense of mutual agreement. Whether within a military regiment or a group of corporate coworkers, shared purpose is critical if people are going to develop passion, patriotism, focus, and a successful sense of team spirit.

Timing and weather are the key considerations of the climate, second of Sun Tzu's five factors, which he calls heaven. It is logical that generals manipulating actions on the battlefield must assess environmental elements such as the time of day, the season of the year, and the availability of daylight or the advantage of darkness when planning to execute their war strategies. Failure to calculate the implications of any of these variables may make the all-important difference between success or defeat, between life or death.

Unlike environmental conditions, which are beyond human control, the third factor concerning war involves assessment of the earth. Properly analyzed in the context of military strategy, the earth can provide tactical advantages in terms of distance and terrain. For example, being able to properly gauge an army's distance from the enemy is a crucial consideration. How much space separates the

*Ax (yue). China. 1300–1050 BCE. Bronze.*

opponents is as important as the ground itself. In war, lands that are flat or hilly, dry or wet can influence outcomes.

Courage and superior intelligence are core characteristics needed for the commander, the fourth factor of Sun Tzu's *The Art of War*. To be effective, military leaders must possess both of these qualities, as well as strictness tempered with compassion. The fierce but wise commander who judiciously balances all of these qualities has the greatest chance of earning credibility among his troops.

Finally, the fifth condition that affects war considers both method and discipline. While taking into account all four of the previous factors, victory rests on the ability (or inability) of a commander to effectively measure, plan, and implement his military strategies. The methods used are as critical as the discipline with which those tactics are effectively executed.

# JADE IN CHINESE CULTURE
# THE MEASURE OF WEALTH

*The position in which excavated examples of this type of object have been found indicates that they were used to hold the hair of the deceased. Ornament in the shape of a hoof. China. 4700–2920 BCE. Nephrite.*

*Costume accessories, such as this belt buckle, were adorned with images of dragons to indicate high social status. Buckle and hook. China. 1850–1940. Glass.*

The word "jade" connotes the creamy-textured, pale or milky green hard stone that is commonly used in polished pieces of jewelry or sculpture. However, in the ancient world, jade had a more practical application: bodily protection.

The name jade comes from the Spanish *piedra de ijada*, "loin stone." It was valued over gold by the Mayan and Aztec people and was thought to have restorative powers, mainly to heal kidney ailments. Jade is either of two distinct minerals, nephrite or jadeite, which are generally pale green or white and are today used mainly as gemstones or in decorative or religious carvings. Primitive societies almost universally devised tools, weapons, and decorative objects of jadelike stone,

*This carved jade disk is one example of the immense skill of Chinese artists. Disk. China. 1644–1911. Nephrite.*

but after the Stone Age, most stopped using the material. Only in China did the long tradition of jade work continue to flourish.

Unfazed by sharp metals, tough, durable jade must be shaped using abrasives such as sandstone (crushed quartz). Because of these properties, the ancient Chinese had difficulty working with the material. Yet as early as 5000 BCE, the Chinese were producing sophisticated sculpted objects with high levels of detail. Many scholars believe that hand- or foot-powered tools were created and used for this purpose. Jade craftsmanship was a laborious process, but the results created a high-priced market for the green gem. Over time, advancements in carving, cutting, drilling, and polishing techniques developed. But in ancient China, because of the skill required in shaping jade, it was rarely used for ordinary objects: instead, it was used for decorative and ceremonial objects, for furnishings in the royal court, and for accoutrements in elaborate burial tombs.

*Yu* was the general Chinese term for many semiprecious gemstones, including nephrite, or greenstone, and jadeite, a tremolite-actinolite mineral found as pebbles or boulders in greens and white, along with agate, onyx, serpentine, amber, and lapis lazuli. In fact, as early as 3000 BCE, jade was referred to in China as *yu*, "royal gem." Throughout China's vast history, jade has held a venerable place in its arts and culture, as highly prized as gold and diamonds have been in the West. Although other materials such as gold, silver, and bronze were also used for decorations, none of these ever attained the spiritual position that jade acquired in the Chinese mind. Jade is eternally associated with the five cardinal virtues of charity, courage, justice, modesty, and wisdom.

In Chinese written language, the linguistic connotation of yu, referring to jade, also extends to moral character. The Chinese aphorism, "Unpolished jade never shines," is another way of saying that an uneducated person can never be a useful person.

The highly favored concubine of Emperor Xuanzong in the Tang dynasty 618 to 907 CE), Yang Yuhuan, or had the coveted term as part of her name, means "jade ring." Many girls in ancient times received names relating to the word as a way for their parents to show their love.

Jade was prized in China as the most beautiful of all stones. A single piece could be worth more than a man's life. Ancient records tell the story of Bian He, who possessed a priceless piece of jade locked inside a coarse stone. Not wishing to carve the stone himself, he dedicated it to the King of Chu. For some unstated reason, the King had Bian He's legs cut off. When the jade was finally cut from the stone encasing it, the court was amazed at its exquisite qualities, and it quickly became a national treasure. In fact, it was deemed so precious that the question of its custody precipitated a war between the states of Qin and Zhao.

Many fine examples of jade work have been unearthed in ancient burial sites throughout China. At Yongcheng in the Henan province, burial clothes of high-ranking officials were found to have been made by tying jade pieces together with gold, silver, or copper wire, according to each nobleman's rank. One such suit was the garment of King Liang of the Western Han dynasty. It used 2,008 pieces of jade sewn together with gold wire. The complete suit comprises a head cover, face cover, upper garment, sleeves, gloves, trousers, and foot covers.

Other jade burial objects were purely ceremonial and symbolic in nature. The cicada, for example, symbolized rebirth and might be buried with an individual, usually placed in the mouth. As the dynasties progressed, the symbolic spectrum of jade objects increased along with the skill of the artist, so that by the subject of the design as well as its intricacy, the social class of the owner or wearer would be readily evident. Animal figures, mythical creatures, fruit, and flowers were some of the commonly wrought symbols that found their way into personal ornaments, ceremonial objects, and costume accessories such as belt buckles and hair ornaments. The images of the phoenix and dragon were used only by the nobility, while the general populace used animals from real life to signify their clan membership and level of status.

Not until the modern dynasties (Ming, 1368 to 1644; and Qing, 1644 to 1912) did jade artists begin to create works that were culturally self-referencing, illustrating popular aspects of the country's artistic, literary, and historical heritage or imitating earlier works that were originally created in ceramic or bronze.

Although jade is found in many regions of China, including Liaoning, Shaanxi, and Henan provinces, the most well-known is probably that from Hetian in Xinjiang province. An enormous piece of this jade, so hard it will scratch glass, weighs 5,350 kg (11,795 pounds) and features a carved scene of Yu the Great fighting to save his people from a flood. This enormous jade carving can be seen on exhibit in the Forbidden City.

*Butterflies and bats have the same symbolic significance in some areas of China. This motif represents blessings and happiness. Circular plaque with butterflies flanking the character for happiness. China. 1700–1800. Nephrite.*

*Hair clasp. China. 1900–1949. Nephrite.*

*Pendant in an ancient style with dragon heads. China. 1850–1940. Nephrite.*

# Tactical Dispositions 4

## Sun Tzu said:

### 1

The good fighters of old first put themselves beyond the possibility of defeat, and then waited for an opportunity of defeating the enemy.

### 2

To secure ourselves against defeat lies in our own hands, but the opportunity of defeating the enemy is provided by the enemy himself.

### 3

Thus the good fighter is able to secure himself against defeat, but cannot make certain of defeating the enemy.

### 4

Hence the saying: One may know how to conquer without being able to do it.

### 5

Security against defeat implies defensive tactics; ability to defeat the enemy means taking the offensive.

### 6

Standing on the defensive indicates insufficient strength; attacking, a superabundance of strength.

### 7

The general who is skilled in defense hides in the most secret recesses of the earth; he who is skilled in attack flashes forth from the topmost heights of heaven. Thus on the one hand, we have the ability to protect ourselves; on the other, a victory that is complete.

### 8

To see victory only when it is within the ken of the common herd is not the acme of excellence.

### 9

Neither is it the acme of excellence if you fight and conquer and the whole Empire says, "Well done!"

*Taiping Rebellion, contemporary painting of Imperial Chinese troops putting the rebels to flight at Tai Ping fort, Tientsin. Circa 1850.*

### 10

To lift an autumn hare is no sign of great strength; to see the sun and moon is no sign of sharp sight; to hear the noise of thunder is no sign of a quick ear.

### 11

What the ancients called a clever fighter is one who not only wins, but excels in winning with ease.

### 12

Hence his victories bring him neither reputation for wisdom nor credit for courage.

### 13

He wins his battles by making no mistakes. Making no mistakes is what establishes the certainty of victory, for it means conquering an enemy that is already defeated.

### 16

The consummate leader cultivates the moral law, and strictly adheres to method and discipline; thus it is in his power to control success.

### 17

In respect of military method, we have, firstly, Measurement; secondly, Estimation of quantity; thirdly, Calculation; fourthly, Balancing of chances; fifthly, Victory.

### 18

Measurement owes its existence to Earth; Estimation of quantity to Measurement; Calculation to Estimation of quantity; Balancing of chances to Calculation; and Victory to Balancing of chances.

### 19

A victorious army opposed to a routed one, is as a pound's weight placed in the scale against a single grain.

### 20

The onrush of a conquering force is like the bursting of pent-up waters into a chasm a thousand fathoms deep.

*Ceremonial tablet in the shape of an axe. China. 2500–2000 BCE. Nephrite.*

*Left: Chinese dragon in the Forbidden City. As with every mythological creature, dragons are perceived in different ways by different cultures. They are commonly portrayed as serpentine or reptilian, hatching from eggs and possessing extremely large, typically scaly bodies; they are sometimes portrayed as having large eyes, a feature that is the origin of the word for dragon in many cultures, and are often (but not always) portrayed with wings and fiery breath. Some dragons do not have wings at all, but look more like long snakes. Dragons can have a variable number of legs: none, two, four, or more when it comes to early European literature. Chinese dragons are usually seen as benevolent.*

*Dragons are particularly popular in China, and along with the phoenix, the dragon was a symbol of the Chinese emperors. Dragon costumes manipulated by several people are a common sight at Chinese festivals.*

*Dragons are often held to have major spiritual significance in various religions and cultures around the world. In many Eastern and Native American cultures dragons were, and in some cultures still are, revered as representative of the primal forces of nature and the universe. They are commonly said to possess some form of magic or other supernormal power, and are often associated with wells, rain, and rivers.*

### 14

Hence the skillful fighter puts himself into a position which makes defeat impossible, and does not miss the moment for defeating the enemy.

### 15

Thus it is that in war the victorious strategist only seeks battle after the victory has been won, whereas he who is destined to defeat first fights and afterwards looks for victory.

# THE WARRING STATES PERIOD
## LIFE IN SUN TZU'S TIME

Following the Spring and Autumn period of the Zhou dynasty, the Warring States period (ca. 480 to 221 BCE) began peacefully enough but quickly degraded into all-out warfare. In keeping with the tenor of the age, *The Art of War*, written during the early Warring States period by Sun Tzu, is recognized today as perhaps the oldest, and certainly one of the most influential, known military strategy guides.

After the initial round of wars, several states enjoyed relative calm for a while, namely, the Qi, the Chu, the Yan, the Han, the Zhao, the Wei, and the Qin. Each state had its own king, along with several dukes who controlled outlying areas on behalf of their respective kings. Eventually, though, the dukes of the earlier Zhou dynasty began to call themselves kings, claiming they were on an equal footing with the Zhou king.

Military tactics also changed. In 307 BCE, King Wuling of Zhao revolutionized warfare by adopting a cavalry and, as a corollary, superior non-Chinese clothing called trousers. The horse-driven chariots used in the Spring and Autumn period meanwhile gave way to the combined use of infantry and cavalry. Arms and weapons used by the soldiers also changed, as bronze production gave way to iron, particularly for dagger-axes, an extremely popular weapon in various kingdoms, especially for the Qin, who produced pikes as long as eighteen feet.

Various kingdoms in China competed with each other by amassing huge armies of soldiers, and as a result the nobles in China remained a literate rather than warrior class. Eventually, one after another, the rival states fell to each other. Decisive battles at Guiling, Maling, and Yique began a shift that saw the assimilation of the states into a unified China. The defining moment in this transformation occurred in 260 BCE, at the battle of Changping, which resulted in a Qin victory and final dominance over the disputing states.

On the domestic front, even though increased trade produced a powerful merchant class, prevailing conditions during Sun Tzu's lifetime reflected those of a largely agrarian society. Among China's earliest crops was millet, which had been grown in the upper Yellow River valley for around 2,500 years, as had rice, which was common in the wet, tropical landscape of southern China. Farming methods varied over time. Until this period, wooden and stone tools were used to cultivate the earth and to harvest food, which the early Chinese revered for its importance in establishing good health. Around 400 BCE, though, with the use of domesticated animals and iron plows, cultivation became easier as well as more efficient and productive. Oxen were used in the rocky terrain of northern fields and plains, while hardy water buffalo were better suited to the wet, humid rice paddies in the southern parts of the country. Regardless of this helpful addition of working livestock, men did most of the agricultural work. They cut wheat with sickles, separated the wheat grain from the chaff by beating it with sticks, and carried bagged grains by poles hung across their shoulders.

For early Chinese farmers, the most complex tool used in farming was the irrigation system. Rice was, and still is, a mainstay of southern Chinese agriculture. While rice grows much more easily in marshy areas than in drier landscapes, it can be difficult to harvest when wet. The early Chinese solved this problem by developing a system of foot pumps, powered by hundreds of people, to help drain the fields. Other techniques also contributed to improved agricultural production during Sun Tzu's time. In order to ensure good crops and long-term use of the land, the ancient Chinese developed fertilizer from ashes and manure and implemented planned crop rotation to ensure that they could maintain rich soil quality.

Along with rice and millet, the Chinese also grew hundreds of other crops. These included cabbage, soybeans, peas, and bamboo shoots. Foods common to this period included steamed buns, noodles or pancakes with vegetables, soybean products for protein, and pickles. Meat, eggs, and fish were eaten only occasionally, most often at celebratory meals. Meals and customs varied according to wealth and status. For example, wealthy Chinese augmented their diets of cooked grains and vegetables with eggs and meat, including shark fin, wild boar, and bear. Interestingly enough, warm rice beer was the prevalent drink during the period, while tea, the hot beverage most closely identified with ancient China, wasn't widely popularized until the Han dynasty several hundred years later.

In spite of the relative simplicity of the overwhelmingly agrarian society, sophisticated systems of

intellectual thought appeared. In fact, several philosophies that developed in this era would later greatly influence China and the world. In his travels, Confucius spread the ideas that soon dominated Chinese rulers' methods and became known as Confucianism. Concurrently, Lao Tzu's philosophy was transcribed into the *Tao Te Ching*, the classic Taoist text. Meanwhile, Buddhism was being taught in India and, by means of the Silk Road, arrived in China, where the teachings were revised and called Zen Buddhism. The country's widely varying philosophies evolved into the so-called Hundred Schools of Thought, which included Confucianism, Taoism, and, to a lesser extent, the Zhuangzi argument, Legalism, and Mohism.

*Opposite page: Ancient Chinese huang, a ceremonial object meticulously carved using abrasion technique and drilled for hanging. The exact significance of the huang is not known, but typically such objects featured mythological beasts and other symbolism, probably to bring good luck and increased powers to the object's owner. Note the dragon heads at each end of this piece, the translucence of the delicate jade, and the immaculate detail of the fine cutout work and surface decoration. Probably from the Warring States period or slightly later.*

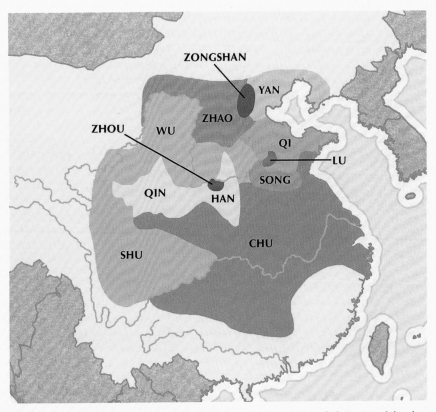

The Warring States period (480–221 BCE) was an isolated moment in time, during which Sun Tzu is believed to have written his masterpiece of military philosophy, discipline, and strategy.

# THE MONGOLS
## OF THE YUAN DYNASTY

While on a campaign against the Southern Song dynasty of China, Kublai Khan, grandson of the great Mongol leader Genghis Khan, built a city near present-day Beijing, calling it Dadu, or "great capital." By 1272, Dadu had become the capital of what was to become known as the Yuan dynasty for the next hundred years.

Although Kublai Khan maintained his Mongol title of khan and ruled China as one of several khanates of the Mongol Empire, which already included eastern Asia, Russia, and Europe, his successors all claimed status as emperor of China. Kublai Khan was under intense pressure from his advisors to expand his large territory, but incursions into Japan, Myanmar, Vietnam, and Java all failed.

The Khan's early years imposed immense looting, with much of China's wealth being sent to the Mongolian homeland. Trade along the Silk Road never slowed, however, and Western contact was first made during Kublai Khan's reign. Though the Yuan dynasty was relatively short-lived, Kublai Khan served as a true emperor by reforming many of China's institutions over the course of several decades. He centralized the government, reformed the tax code, extended the Grand Canal, improved highways, and built granaries throughout the provinces to guard against famine. He promoted science and religious tolerance, built hospitals and orphanages, suspended taxes during hardship, and even went so far as to distribute food to the hungry. Marco Polo's visit was during this time, and the Venetian explorer commented in his journal on the benevolence of Kublai Khan toward his people. His rule was not without controversy, however.

As is common with conquering armies, all the important posts were held by Mongols, with the conquered Han given jobs in faraway non-Chinese regions. There were four distinct classes in Yuan culture. First were the Mongols, who had all the privileges; second were the so-called "color-eyed," or central Asians; third were the Han; and fourth were the Southern Song and other ethnic groups. By the time of Kublai Khan's death in 1294 at an advanced age, the Mongol Empire had broken into various khanates.

Zhenjin, Kublai's son and stated successor, died in 1285, nine years before Kublai, so Zhenjin's son, Kublai's grandson, ruled as Emperor Chengzong from 1294 to 1307. Chengzong

*Majestic warrior enters the fight during a Genghis Khan reenactment, Mongolian steppes.*

continued his grandfather's works, but corruption gained a foothold and effectively ended many of his attempts. Matters further declined with Yuan's third emperor, Wuzong, who was particularly incapable, rejecting all of Kublai's work and sending China into massive debt and popular unrest. Renzong, the fourth and probably the last competent Mongol emperor, was mentored by a Confucian academic and embraced mainstream Chinese culture, much to the discontent of the elitists in the Mongol Empire. Among Renzong's accomplishments was the abolishment of the Department of State Affairs, which implemented examinations for state officials and codified much of the law.

Because of the Yuan connection with the Mongol Empire, there was an extensive amount of cultural exchange between western Asia and Europe. Writing, literature, Western-style musical instruments, and drama developed, along with saltpeter, printing techniques, porcelain production, playing cards, and advances in cartography, geography, and scientific education. A diverse influx of religious thought dates from the Yuan dynasty. Islam, Nestorianism, Roman Catholicism, Tibetan Buddhism, and Confucianism, all based on long-forgotten philosophical classics, enjoyed wide latitude, while, curiously, Taoism was persecuted. It is possible that this freedom was allowed so as to placate the Han society and avoid confrontation. In an aesthetic move, the city of Dadu, present-day Beijing, was completely renovated, with artificial lakes, hills, mountains, and parks on the new palace grounds. The Grand Canal was revitalized and extended to the city.

By the last years of the Yuan dynasty, Kublai Khan's successors had become increasingly assimilated into the life and culture of China and were thus seen as too Chinese by the Mongols beyond China. Eventually, the Yuan emperors lost all confidence in the Chinese people and army. China became dissected and lawless. Emperor Yingzong lasted only two years and was replaced in a coup, as was his successor, Taidingdi. Zhu Yuanzhang threw out the ninth and final Kublai Khan successor in 1368 and founded the Ming dynasty.

With the birth of the Ming dynasty, what was left of the Mongols returned to Mongolia, where they carried on the Yuan dynasty. Modern historians refer to this as the Northern Yuan. It would seem that there were now competing Chinese dynasties. However, according to Chinese political orthodoxy, there can only be one legitimate empire, so the Ming denied the Northern Yuan, and the Northern Yuan denied the Ming. However, the Ming did recognize the Yuan in Beijing as legitimate and considered it a previous dynasty.

The Ming army invaded Mongolia and, in 1388, overran and destroyed the Northern Yuan capital of Karakorum. Border conflicts continued for several centuries until 1634, when the last Mongol khan died while traveling to Tibet. His son, Ejei Khan, surrendered the great seal of the Yuan emperor to the Manchu ruler, Hong Taiji, who then established the Qing dynasty.

*Preceding pages: Marco Polo (1254–1324) before the Grand Khan of the Tartars. Tranquillo Cremona (1837–1878). Italy. 1863.*

*Right: Kublai Khan's grandfather, the great Mongol leader Genghis Khan, is depicted fighting a battle alongside his troops in this painting. Genghis Khan (1162–1227) Fighting a Battle in a Mountain Pass. China. Ink on vellum.*

# Energy

### 1

Fighting with a large army under your command is nowise different from fighting with a small one: it is merely a question of instituting signs and signals.

### 2

To ensure that your whole host may withstand the brunt of the enemy's attack and remain unshaken—this is effected by maneuvers direct and indirect.

### 3

That the impact of your army may be like a grindstone dashed against an egg—this is effected by the science of weak points and strong.

### 4

In all fighting, the direct method may be used for joining battle, but indirect methods will be needed in order to secure victory.

### 5

Indirect tactics, efficiently applied, are as inexhaustible as Heaven and Earth, unending as the flow of rivers and streams; like the sun and moon, they end but to begin anew; like the four seasons, they pass away to return once more.

### 6

There are not more than five musical notes, yet the combinations of these five give rise to more melodies than can ever be heard.

### 7

There are not more than five primary colors (blue, yellow, red, white, and black), yet in combination they produce more hues than can ever been seen.

### 8

There are not more than five cardinal tastes (sour, acrid, salt, sweet, bitter), yet combinations of them yield more flavors than can ever be tasted.

### 9

In battle, there are not more than two methods of attack—the direct and the indirect; yet these two in combination give rise to an endless series of maneuvers.

### 10

The direct and the indirect lead on to each other in turn. It is like moving in a circle—you never come to an end. Who can exhaust the possibilities of their combination?

### 11

The onset of troops is like the rush of a torrent which will even roll stones along in its course.

### 12

The quality of decision is like the well-timed swoop of a falcon which enables it to strike and destroy its victim.

### 13

Therefore the good fighter will be terrible in his onset, and prompt in his decision.

### 14

Energy may be likened to the bending of a crossbow; decision, to the releasing of a trigger.

### 15

Amid the turmoil and tumult of battle, there may be seeming disorder and yet no real disorder at all; amid confusion and chaos, your array may be without head or tail, yet it will be proof against defeat.

### 16

Simulated disorder postulates perfect discipline; simulated fear postulates courage; simulated weakness postulates strength.

### 17

Hiding order beneath the cloak of disorder is simply a question of subdivision; concealing courage under a show

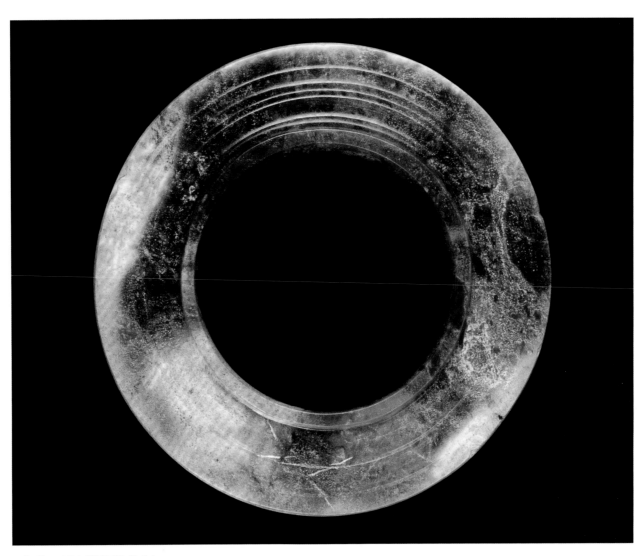

*Disk. China. 1600–1050 BCE. Nephrite.*

of timidity presupposes a fund of latent energy; masking strength with weakness is to be effected by tactical dispositions.

### 18

Thus one who is skillful at keeping the enemy on the move maintains deceitful appearances, according to which the enemy will act. He sacrifices something, that the enemy may snatch at it.

### 18

By holding out baits, he keeps him on the march; then with a body of picked men he lies in wait for him.

### 20

The clever combatant looks to the effect of combined energy, and does not require too much from individuals.

Hence his ability to pick out the right men and utilize combined energy.

### 21

When he utilizes combined energy, his fighting men become as it were like unto rolling logs or stones. For it is the nature of a log or stone to remain motionless on level ground, and to move when on a slope; if four-cornered, to come to a standstill, but if round-shaped, to go rolling down.

### 22

Thus the energy developed by good fighting men is as the momentum of a round stone rolled down a mountain thousands of feet in height. So much on the subject of energy.

# RELIGION IN ANCIENT CHINA
# THE GUIDING DOCTRINES

The integrated belief systems of ancient China, which most Westerners would refer to as religion, should be viewed as complex combinations of philosophy and spirituality. The Chinese have no exact equivalent for the term *religion* in their native language. In its stead, the term used to describe the structured and traditional belief systems common in Chinese culture is *chiao*, which best translates to "guiding doctrine."

Although strangers to the Far East may assume that Buddhism has long been the dominant chiao of the nation, this is far from correct. Buddhism is not even of Chinese origin. It emerged in China about the same time that Christianity appeared, coming from India sometime in the fifth century CE. Nearly a millennium before, during the time of Sun Tzu, the Chinese doctrines to which most of the populace adhered were Confucianism and Taoism. Together these two traditions, developed during the Warring States period of Chinese history, stress harmony between man and nature and thus have constructed the foundation of Chinese values and morality. Long before the Chinese began following the chiao of Confucius and Lao Tzu, however, the spiritual and philosophical leanings of the populace were found within one of China's oldest practices.

## Ancestor Worship

To this day, ancestor worship continues to be the most widespread religious practice in China. Using the term *worship* in its Judeo-Christian sense in reference to the Chinese practice is misleading because, although Western ancestors are admired and honored, they are rarely worshipped as deities. For centuries, the Chinese believed that the spirits of a person's ancestors demanded respect from their offspring, and they viewed ritual and sacrifice to be the greatest method of demonstrating such respect. What sociologists refer to as an ancestral cult developed in the years that the rituals spread across Asia, and these cults became the strongest ties between families and their ancestors.

During Sun Tzu's lifetime, it would have been necessary to adhere to strict procedures following the death of a family member. A son appointed to the ritualistic tasks would perform animal sacrifices after the death, ensuring that the grave was interred with good *feng shui*, a configuration that allowed for a balanced flow of spiritual energy. If a family succeeded in providing the proper rites, the Chinese

*Portrait of Confucius (551–479 BCE). China. 17th century. Gouache on paper scroll.*

believed that the ancestors would act as guardians and bless the family. If, on the other hand, the son failed to provide a proper flow of energy, the family was certain to experience the ancestors' dissatisfaction through a barrage of curses.

Aside from planning and maintaining a proper burial ground, most families also kept a small ancestral shrine within their homes. The shrine often contained wooden tablets inscribed with the family members' personal information, including names and the dates in which they lived. Throughout the year, the family would place on the shrine small offerings of wine and food, that they believed the ancestor to have enjoyed while among the living.

## Confucianism

Although ancestor worship played a crucial role in the cultural developments of the people of China, no practice influenced the Chinese as much as that of Confucianism. The centuries-old values of China originate directly from the philosophical teachings of Kongfuzi, more commonly known as Confucius (551 to 479 BCE). The ancient teachings of Confucius provided the structure for the mainstream thinking of the Chinese people. The doctrine called Confucianism in the West was referred to by most native followers as *kong-chiao*. The kong-chiao existed purely as a philosophy of morality and social behavior. Unlike most Western religions, and many Eastern ones as well, Confucianism included neither deities nor priests. Instead, the teachings of Confucius focused on the attainment of harmony achieved principally through a strict social order. Confucius stressed the love of parents and children, explaining that those who show respect and reverence to their parents will follow suit when engaged with neighbors and friends. Confucius also believed that men would consistently view their ruler as a parental figure and would therefore remain loyal to him.

Confucius, like Sun Tzu, did not deny the occasional necessity of war but did feel that it was extremely undesirable. In times of division and endless war between feudal states, Confucius wanted a return of the Mandate of Heaven, which could unify the world (that is, China) and bestow peace and prosperity on the people. The Mandate of Heaven stated that rulers were not selected on the basis of heredity but by their own competence or worthiness. Once a ruler was considered unworthy, whether or not it was through a fault of his own or through an act of nature that had devastating repercussions on the people, the leader was seen as being weak and ineffective. Rulers could legally and quite simply be overthrown for being unworthy.

Students of kong-chiao will now find the teachings of Confucius in several texts, the most prominent of which is the *Analects*. The text, which was the fundamental course of study for Chinese scholars for centuries, stresses propriety, righteousness, loyalty, and filial piety. Emphasizing the importance of ritual, the text's transcription of Confucian wisdom demonstrates how such ritual implies order. By following the rituals that inevitably become duties, the followers develop structure and self-discipline.

Other texts imperative to followers of Confucianism are collectively known as the Five Classics. These documents, viewed by the Chinese as the unassailable authority on morality and intellect, were memorized by students and used as test material for anyone aspiring to enter any civil office. Combining several pre-Confucian works as well as his own teachings, the canon is thought to comprise five visions: metaphysical, poetic, social, historical, and political. In short, Confucian ethics have had a stronger influence on the moral fabric of Chinese society than have either Taoism or Buddhism, also prevalent at the time. Consider that one of Confucius' most famous teachings was a negative form of the Golden Rule, called the Silver Rule. When asked if there is any one word that could guide a person throughout life, Confucius replied, "*Shu*—never impose on others what you would not choose for yourself."

*Lao Tzu (circa 604–531) on his buffalo, followed by a disciple. China. 18th century. Watercolor on paper.*

## Taoism

As with Confucianism, the teachings of Lao Tzu (604 to 531 BCE), referred to as Taoism, existed as more of a philosophy than a religion during the life of Sun Tzu. A major difference in the two philosophies is the Taoist emphasis on passive resistance. Within an all-encompassing tradition where all beings and all things are fundamentally one, harmony with the natural universe through inaction is a purposeful goal in the pacifist philosophy. Where Confucianism demands social order to attain accord, the *tao-jia* suggested an internal transformation to achieve such harmony. Lao Tzu taught his followers that in order to achieve *tao*, "the way," one must realize the *te*, the peaceful inner nature of man.

The Taoist philosophy, as described in Lao Tzu's manuscript the *Tao te ching*, greatly impacted the people of China. Its magnitude was so great that it eventually developed into a more complex system known as *tao-qiao*. Tao-qiao, which was more religious in nature than tao-jia, influenced later spiritual movements, particularly the Buddhist philosophy of India. Even so, the rapid ascendancy of Buddhism into the homes of the Chinese eventually transformed the culture to such an extent that Buddhism became the predominant belief system of the Chinese people.

## Zen Buddhism

The natural leanings of Taoism and the societal focus of Confucianism blended with Indian philosophy to form a framework for Zen Buddhism. The name *Zen* is derived from the Sanskrit word *dhyana*, or "meditation." In China, this name was taken literally, and the school there practiced

*Above: Buddhist carvings in Feilai Feng Caves.*
*Opposite page: Portrait of Posou Fairy. China. 1279–1368. Wall painting.*

meditation over all other principles, including scripture or doctrine. In its earliest form, both Taoism and the elements of Buddhism, focusing on wisdom, influenced Zen. When Bodhidharma came to China from India in the late fifth century CE to found Zen Buddhism, he taught the practice called "wall-gazing."

The two trains of spiritual thought that sprang from Bodhidharma's original teachings were the ideas of gradual enlightenment and sudden enlightenment. Gradual enlightenment taught intense meditation and patience to attain the desired state, or Buddha. Sudden enlightenment accepted the immediate transformation to intuitive thought that did not require adherence to strict meditation.

Chinese Zen was eventually led by Hui Neng (638 to 713 CE), who, though illiterate, claimed leadership by his mastery of the intuitive grasp of the truth of enlightenment. Hui Neng defined enlightenment as the direct seeing of one's original mind or original nature, which is Buddha, a concept that remained a staple of Chinese Zen and was passed down from generation to generation. During the Golden Age of Zen Buddhism, masters such as Huang Po, Lin Chi, and Chao Chou developed a unique teaching style that stressed oral instruction and, in some cases, the use of physical violence to jolt the student out of the old habits of

ordinary forms of thought. In fact, Zen rejected the ideals of scholarly knowledge, ritual, and performing good deeds as having comparatively little spiritual value.

Somehow, Zen escaped the general persecution of Buddhism in 845 CE to become the dominant sect, mainly because of its popularity and location in isolated centers such as mountain monasteries, far from the political turmoil of the cities. However, very few of the holdouts of Zen Buddhism, or of Taoism, for that matter, survived the rise of communism during Mao's Cultural Revolution of the 1960s, which led to the dismantling of religious culture within China. Conformists to the old ways experienced a forced change away from their age-old beliefs. Revolutionaries destroyed anything they viewed as feudal or religious, including temples, monasteries, and public shrines, and the ordinary Taoist or Buddhist was given no option but to renounce his or her beliefs.

However, the roots of the practices common during the time of Sun Tzu's life go deeper than any Western concept of religion. The centuries of tradition affect everyday life to the extent that, although the people may not consider their behaviors acts of religion, their values and principles deeply reflect the beliefs of ancient ages.

# Weak Points and Strong

## 6

### 1

Whoever is first in the field and awaits the coming of the enemy, will be fresh for the fight; whoever is second in the field and has to hasten to battle will arrive exhausted.

### 2

Therefore the clever combatant imposes his will on the enemy, but does not allow the enemy's will to be imposed on him.

### 3

By holding out advantages to him, he can cause the enemy to approach of his own accord; or, by inflicting damage, he can make it impossible for the enemy to draw near.

### 4

If the enemy is taking his ease, he can harass him; if well supplied with food, he can starve him out; if quietly encamped, he can force him to move.

### 5

Appear at points which the enemy must hasten to defend; march swiftly to places where you are not expected.

### 6

An army may march great distances without distress if it marches through country where the enemy is not.

### 7

You can be sure of succeeding in your attacks if you only attack places which are undefended. You can ensure the safety of your defense if you only hold positions that cannot be attacked.

### 8

Hence that general is skillful in attack whose opponent does not know what to defend; and he is skillful in defense whose opponent does not know what to attack.

### 9

O divine art of subtlety and secrecy! Through you we learn to be invisible, through you inaudible; and hence we can hold the enemy's fate in our hands.

### 10

You may advance and be absolutely irresistible, if you make for the enemy's weak points; you may retire and be safe from pursuit if your movements are more rapid than those of the enemy.

### 11

If we wish to fight, the enemy can be forced to an engagement even though he be sheltered behind a high rampart and a deep ditch. All we need do is attack some other place that he will be obliged to relieve.

### 12

If we do not wish to fight, we can prevent the enemy from engaging us even though the lines of our encampment be merely traced out on the ground. All we need do is to throw something odd and unaccountable in his way.

### 13

By discovering the enemy's dispositions and remaining invisible ourselves, we can keep our forces concentrated, while the enemy's must be divided. We can form a single united body, while the enemy must split up into fractions. Hence there will be a whole pitted against separate parts of a whole, which means that we shall be many to the enemy's few. And if we are able thus to attack an inferior force with a superior one, our opponents will be in dire straits.

### 14

The spot where we intend to fight must not be made known; for then the enemy will have to prepare against a possible attack at several different points; and his forces being thus distributed in many directions, the numbers we shall have to face at any given point will be proportionately few.

*Preceding pages: Large Handscroll Painted Depicting A Battle Scene. China. 19th century. Ink and colors on silk. Right: Finial. China. 1300–1050 BCE. Bronze.*

## 15

For should the enemy strengthen his front, he will weaken his rear; should he strengthen his rear, he will weaken his front; should he strengthen his left, he will weaken his right; should he strengthen his right, he will weaken his left. If he sends reinforcements everywhere, he will everywhere be weak.

## 16

Numerical weakness comes from having to prepare against possible attacks; numerical strength, from compelling our adversary to make these preparations against us.

## 17

Knowing the place and the time of the coming battle, we may concentrate from the greatest distances in order to fight. But if neither time nor place be known, then the left wing will be impotent to succor the right, the right equally impotent to succor the left, the front unable to relieve the rear, or the rear to support the front. How much more so if the furthest portions of the army are anything under a hundred li apart, and even the nearest are separated by several *li!*

## 18

Though according to my estimate the soldiers of Yueh exceed our own in number, that shall advantage them nothing in the matter of victory. I say then that victory can be achieved.

## 19

Though the enemy be stronger in numbers, we may prevent him from fighting.

## 20

Scheme so as to discover his plans and the likelihood of their success.

## 21

Rouse him, and learn the principle of his activity or inactivity.

## 22

Force him to reveal himself, so as to find out his vulnerable spots.

## 23

Carefully compare the opposing army with your own, so that you may know where strength is superabundant and where it is deficient.

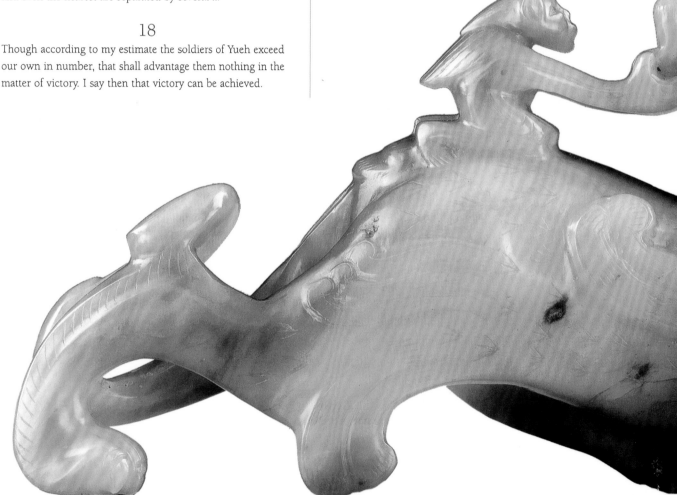

## 24

In making tactical dispositions, the highest pitch you can attain is to conceal them; conceal your dispositions, and you will be safe from the prying of the subtlest spies, from the machinations of the wisest brains.

## 25

How victory may be produced for them out of the enemy's own tactics—that is what the multitude cannot comprehend. All men can see the tactics whereby I conquer, but what none can see is the strategy out of which victory is evolved.

## 26

Do not repeat the tactics which have gained you one victory, but let your methods be regulated by the infinite variety of circumstances.

## 27

Military tactics are like unto water; for water in its natural course runs away from high places and hastens downward. So in war, the way is to avoid what is strong and to strike at what is weak.

## 28

Water shapes its course according to the nature of the ground over which it flows; the soldier works out his victory in relation to the foe whom he is facing.

## 29

Therefore, just as water retains no constant shape, so in warfare there are no constant conditions.

## 30

He who can modify his tactics in relation to his opponent and thereby succeed in winning, may be called a heaven-born captain.

## 31

The five elements (water, fire, wood, metal, earth) are not always equally predominant; the four seasons make way for each other in turn. There are short days and long; the moon has its periods of waning and waxing.

*Chimera (bixie) with Rider. Eastern Han dynasty, circa 25–220. China. Pale yellowish-green jade with grey-brown patches. HxWxD: 8.1 x 13.9 x 3.8 cm (3 3/16 x 5 1/2 x 1 1/2 in). Origin: China.*

# MASTERS OF BRONZE
## TAKING WEAPONRY FORWARD

The appetite for war precipitated unprecedented technological developments during the Warring States period of Sun Tzu's lifetime, and for the most effective weapons, the ancient Chinese preferred bronze. The material, whose name is taken from the Persian word *birinj*, "copper," is any of an extensive range of alloys, though the Chinese experimented with different proportions of copper, lead, and tin to make weapons of varying rigidity and temper. One of the most useful alloys of man's creation, bronze was manipulated in the creation of innumerable items ranging from ornamentations, weapons, armor, and tools starting before 3000 BCE, an era presently referred to as the Bronze Age.

The extensive occurrence of bronze smelting in ancient China implies a settled and orderly society, as the process requires locating, protecting, mining, and smelting the ores that contain the copper and tin used in the process. It also implies a large organized labor force and proficient craftsmen. Made possible by China's steadily improving cultural, societal, and technological conditions, the Bronze Age greatly affected China's continued development as a civilized culture, demonstrating the population's unceasing advancement in sophistication and ingenuity.

China's involvement with bronze metallurgy is thought to have begun during the Erlitou culture, somewhere around 2000 BCE, based on an archaeological site discovered at Erlitou in Yanshi, Henan province. But because no written records exist that succeed in linking that site with a specific dynasty, most Western archaeologists refute the connection their Chinese counterparts make between the Erlitou culture and the Xia dynasty of that same time frame.

In Europe, artifacts plainly demonstrate that bronze replaced stone and was then afterward replaced by iron. Complications arise in the placement of specific dates for the Bronze Age in China, however, and historians disagree on the actual dates that should be applied to the age. Two factors complicate the attempt to assign definite dates for China's Bronze Age: the early arrival of iron smelting technology and the persistence of bronze in weapons, tools, and sacred vessels, regardless of iron's emergence in metallurgy.

Iron in China is found to date back to the Zhou period (1027 to 256 BCE), and some historians believe that it may have even been a Chinese invention. The era of time in Chinese history referred to as the Iron Age corresponds with the Spring and Autumn and the Warring States periods, spanning the dates of 770 to 221 BCE, but artifacts from the era indicate that its use was nominal. Because archaeological finds record that a majority of Chinese vessels and weapons were created from bronze until well into the Han period (206 BCE to 220 CE), one may assume that the alloy remained the preferred material for the Chinese up to that time.

As the medium of choice, bronze underwent three stages, the first of which is known as the forming period, here referring to a portion of the Neolithic period. The forming period was eventually followed by the thriving period, which began sometime in the eleventh century BCE, with astonishing artistic achievements in vessels, musical instruments, and weapons. During the Spring and Autumn period, China existed as a violent and tumultuous conglomerate of

*Above: The ancient Chinese produced a bounty of masterfully crafted bronze weapons, such as this dagger. Dagger-axe (ge). China. 771–225 BCE. Bronze. Opposite page: Bronze was used to make weapons as well as ritual objects, such as this bell. Ritual bell (yongzhong). China. 560–500 BCE. Bronze.*

warring states. Because warfare was an almost constant affair in China during this time, military campaigns greatly depended on weapons. As a result, the states all strove to create effective and practical devices to give their armies the upper hand in times of conflict. Because of its durability, bronze was the obvious material for weapons production. The commitment of the Chinese nobility to producing forces armed with such weaponry ultimately resulted in a bounty of beautiful and masterfully crafted swords and daggers. However, the last of the three periods, the turning period, saw the end of bronze's reign as China's most precious metal. It was during this time that the Chinese of the Han dynasty began creating steel.

Examples of the weaponry developed in the Bronze Age abound. The dagger-axe, which was the essential and typical weapon of the soldier, was used throughout the age. It features a conveniently hooked blade with a directly fixed handle and is shaped somewhat like a modern-day sickle. The spear, used to stab in a straight, forward motion, consisted of a metal spearhead and handle. It was usually five to seven feet in length, although there were exceptions ranging to twelve feet. The halberd, a dangerous spear and dagger-axe combination, gradually replaced these two. With its metal blade and wooden handle joined, the halberd could reach a length of nine feet and could function as both an infantry and cavalry weapon for thrusting, hooking, and cleaving.

The sword, with its long, sharp-edged blade, was ideal for fighting in close combat. Its strengths were its flexibility and durability, along with its length, which offered advantages both for attack and for self-defense. During the Spring and Autumn period, the length of the Chinese sword was gradually extended, and as a result its durability improved. Craftsmanship had also evolved to a high standard of casting techniques and artisanship, and many displayed blades with unique engraved patterns and a long-lasting, polished sheen.

Aside from these four pieces of weaponry, bronze augmented the effectiveness of other devices. The shield, for example, while decorated with the alloy at its center, could also be equipped with blades to create sharp, lethal edges. For use with different types of bows, the bronze-tipped arrows began to be reconfigured with three-sided heads instead of two-sided heads.

Weapons made during the Zhou dynasty, around 1000 BCE, are the earliest known examples of iron work in the world. With refinement of the process, iron weapons became supreme during the following Warring States period and endured through the Qin dynasty and into the Han dynasty around the turn of the millennium. However, since few of the discovered iron weapons had exterior processes, they were corroded when excavated. The weapons of the Bronze Age have been protected by a thin layer of oxidation, and have been better preserved.

From among the bronze relics that have been unearthed, the most famous sword is believed to have been crafted and owned by Goujian. The king of the state of Yue from 496 to 465 BCE, Goujian built an army with a strange but effective

*The jue is a vessel with a long tradition in Neolithic ceramics. Its combination of a body with a spout and a tail, three legs, and a handle was awkward to cast in bronze using the piece-mold process, and eventually the shape was dropped. Ritual wine vessel (jue). China. 1300–1050 BCE. Bronze.*

intimidation strategy. According to legend, the army's officers were infamous for forcing the men of their front lines to commit suicide by decapitation in an effort to frighten their foes before going into battle.

Goujian's sword, discovered by archaeologists working along the Zhang River Reservoir in Jingzhou, Hubei, is almost two feet long and slightly less than two inches broad. The artifact is decorated with black patterns and characters that scholars believe to read "King Goujian of Yue, made for his personal use." When the sword was found, its condition was so pristine that one researcher reportedly cut his finger on the blade's edge. It is alleged that such unbelievable preservation resulted not only from the airtight black-lacquered wooden scabbard in which it was housed, but also from its chemical composition. The blade's brilliant composition, of course, gives credence to the mastery of bronze work among the Chinese during this period.

Another celebrated bronze relic from the Spring and Autumn period is the spear belonging to the last king of Wu, King Fuchai (495 to 473 BCE). Each a thorn in the other's side, Fuchai and Goujian were sworn mortal enemies, so it seems poetic justice today that such fine specimens of bronze weapons have been discovered from these two ancient kings. The Fuchai artifact, found in Jiangling, Hubei, supposedly includes an inscription translated by linguists specializing in the period's characters as being a weapon "used by Fuchai in his wars against Yue."

In 1974, a group of peasant farmers stumbled upon another illustration of ancient China's preference for bronze in its weapon manufacturing. The farmers were digging a well in the Shaanxi province when they uncovered some unusual pottery. The find promptly secured the attention of archaeologists, who descended upon the area in hordes to explore it. What the team found startled and amazed the world. The find, which has since been named the Terra-cotta Army, included more than 7,000 life-size Chinese warriors accompanied by weapons, horses, and chariots. Each of the soldiers was created in the stances they would have assumed while preparing for battle, and many of them held bronze swords, daggers, and spears. More than 10,000 bronze weapons have been discovered in the three pits that make up the site. Experts in the field associate the Terra-cotta Army with the short five-year reign of the Qin dynasty, immediately following the Warring States period. Researchers agree that large portions of the weapons were cast in molds for the purpose of ensuring a standardized model, a find that helps reinforce the theory that, by this point in China's mastery of bronze work, the people had established well-principled scientific standards for their bronze weapon construction.

*Rattle, one of a pair. China. 1300–1050 BCE. Bronze.*

*Ritual vessel (zun or gui) in the shape of a rhinoceros. China. 1100–1050 BCE. Bronze.*

# Maneuvering

*Sun Tzu said:*

---

## 1

In war, the general receives his commands from the sovereign. Having collected an army and concentrated his forces, he must blend and harmonize the different elements thereof before pitching his camp.

## 2

After that comes tactical maneuvering, than which there is nothing more difficult. The difficulty of tactical maneuvering consists in turning the devious into the direct, and misfortune into gain.

## 3

Thus, to take a long and circuitous route, after enticing the enemy out of the way, and though starting after him, to contrive to reach the goal before him, shows knowledge of the artifice of *deviation*.

## 4

Maneuvering with an army is advantageous; with an undisciplined multitude, most dangerous.

## 5

If you set a fully equipped army in march in order to snatch an advantage, the chances are that you will be too late.

## 6

On the other hand, to detach a flying column for the purpose involves the sacrifice of its baggage and stores.

## 7

Thus, if you order your men to roll up their buff-coats, and make forced marches without halting day or night, covering double the usual distance at a stretch, doing a hundred *li* in order to wrest an advantage, the leaders of all your three divisions will fall into the hands of the enemy. The stronger men will be in front, the jaded ones will fall behind, and on this plan only one-tenth of your army will reach its destination.

## 8

If you march fifty *li* in order to outmaneuver the enemy, you will lose the leader of your first division, and only half your force will reach the goal. If you march thirty *li* with the same object, two-thirds of your army will arrive.

## 9

We may take it then that an army without its baggage train is lost; without provisions it is lost; without bases of supply it is lost.

## 10

We cannot enter into alliances until we are acquainted with the designs of our neighbors. We are not fit to lead an army on the march unless we are familiar with the face of the country—its mountains and forests, its pitfalls and precipices, its marshes and swamps.

## 11

We shall be unable to turn natural advantage to account unless we make use of local guides.

## 12

In war, practice dissimulation, and you will succeed. Whether to concentrate or to divide your troops, must be decided by circumstances.

## 13

Let your rapidity be that of the wind, your compactness that of the forest. In raiding and plundering be like fire, in immovability, like a mountain. Let your plans be dark and impenetrable as night, and when you move, fall like a thunderbolt.

## 14

When you plunder a countryside, let the spoil be divided amongst your men; when you capture new territory, cut it up into allotments for the benefit of the soldiery.

*Opposite page: Emperor Qianlong's review of the grand parade of troops. 18th century. Handscroll, ink and color with gold on silk.*

*Blade with handle. China. 1300–1000 BCE. Nephrite and bronze.*

*Opposite page, top: Sword pommel. China. 206 BCE–220 CE. Nephrite.*
*Opposite page, bottom: Sword. China. 771–255 BCE. Bronze.*

### 15

Ponder and deliberate before you make a move.

### 16

He will conquer who has learned the artifice of deviation. Such is the art of maneuvering.

### 17

*The Book of Army Management* says: On the field of battle, the spoken word does not carry far enough: hence the institution of gongs and drums. Nor can ordinary objects be seen clearly enough: hence the institution of banners and flags.

### 18

Gongs and drums, banners and flags, are means whereby the ears and eyes of the host may be focused on one particular point. The host thus forming a single united body, is it impossible either for the brave to advance alone, or for the cowardly to retreat alone. This is the art of handling large masses of men.

### 19

In nightfighting, then, make much use of signal fires and drums, and in fighting by day, of flags and banners, as a means of influencing the ears and eyes of your army.

### 20

A whole army may be robbed of its spirit; a commander-in-chief may be robbed of his presence of mind.

### 21

Now a soldier's spirit is keenest in the morning; by noonday it has begun to flag; and in the evening, his mind is bent only on returning to camp.

### 22

A clever general, therefore, avoids an army when its spirit is keen, but attacks it when it is sluggish and inclined to return. This is the art of studying moods.

### 23

Disciplined and calm, to await the appearance of disorder and hubbub amongst the enemy—this is the art of retaining self-possession.

### 24

To be near the goal while the enemy is still far from it, to wait at ease while the enemy is toiling and struggling, to be well-fed while the enemy is famished—this is the art of husbanding one's strength.

### 25

To refrain from intercepting an enemy whose banners are in perfect order, to refrain from attacking an army drawn up in calm and confident array—this is the art of studying circumstances.

### 26

It is a military axiom not to advance uphill against the enemy, nor to oppose him when he comes downhill.

### 27

Do not pursue an enemy who simulates flight.

### 28

Do not attack soldiers whose temper is keen.

### 29

Do not swallow bait offered by the enemy.

### 30

Do not interfere with an army that is returning home.

### 31

When you surround an army, leave an outlet free.

### 32

Do not press a desperate foe too hard.
Such is the art of warfare.

# THE TACTICAL STRATEGIES OF SUN TZU

For Sun Tzu, knowing the enemy and knowing oneself summarized the strategy of war. An effective leader specialized in adaptability based on up-to-date information about the enemy, which could be obtained by men knowledgeable of the enemy's situation. Such foreknowledge, Sun Tzu proclaims, is the "treasure of a sovereign"; that is secret agents and their effective use were pivotal to gaining the necessary data to ensure success. The deceitful and covert means of obtaining information through spies would have been horrifying to those who followed Confucian thought. But Sun Tzu himself never comments on what today's psychologists would recognize as a classic case of cognitive dissonance.

An important area of knowledge that spies would have secured for Sun Tzu involved the enemy's terrain. Sun Tzu discouraged battles not fought on enemy land. Positioning troops in the land of the enemy decreased desertion, allowed the army to live off the land of the enemy (rather than sap the resources of the homeland), and also disrupted the mobilization plans of the enemy. But knowledge of foreign terrain was an indispensable component of developing a battle plan. In his words, "conformation of the ground is of the greatest assistance in battle." Sun Tzu classifies the land as accessible, entrapping, indecisive, constricted, precipitous, and distant, and tactical plans would have been changed based on the type of terrain his spies discovered.

Horses, chariots, and troops are all mentioned by Sun Tzu, although their specific tactical use is not explained. However, he does say that reliance should not be placed on "hobbled horses or buried chariot wheels," the assumption being that these resources should be used wisely within the context of the circumstances of war.

According to Sun Tzu, the length of deployment should be examined and a study of human nature should be conducted in order to promote victory.

A strategy based on human nature involved torches, drums, gongs, banners, and flags, which were important for strategic visual and auditory communication and would serve as a morale booster for the army and as an intimidation and distraction factor for the enemy. Their use made troop location easier, so that members of the army were not confused by their surroundings.

Information on the weaknesses and vices of commanders would have been invaluable and would have been used against them. The study of the troops as they rested and their organization as they prepared for battle would also give insight into the state of mind and plans of the enemy.

Weighted mathematical calculations regarding the strengths of the enemy were made to determine whether war should be pursued. If war was deemed necessary, speed was essential for maintaining momentum and morale for the troops and for surprising the enemy.

As the above points indicate, offensive strategy was important to Sun Tzu. His preference was that the army should attack the weaknesses of the enemy and determine the scope of the attack, rather than defend its own position and allow the enemy to decide the timing and circumstances of battle.

The combination of *zheng* (extraordinary) and *qi* (normal) forces in battle again illustrates Sun Tzu's view that war tactics should be fluid and versatile. The qi forces were to be used directly to engage the enemy, while the zheng forces were to be used indirectly to surprise the enemy.

Another element that Sun Tzu encouraged as an effective strategy of war was the proper use of fire. The first four methods of fire attack were to burn personnel, stores, equipment, and arsenals, while the fifth was "to use incendiary missiles," which scholars explain as the firing of flame-tipped arrows into the enemy's camp or barracks by strong crossbowmen.

阿玉錫者伊何人準噶爾屬司牧臣其
法獲眾應劉臀何不即斬犯顏尊徒步
為眾三司七青一裏卜

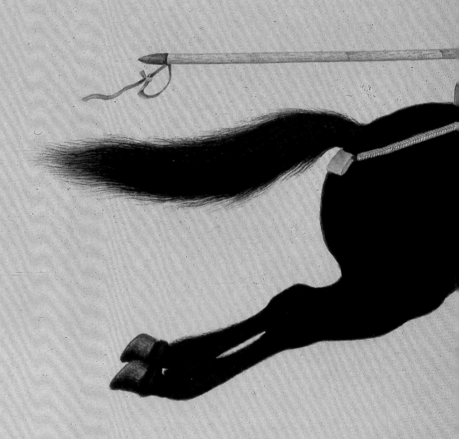

# THE WARHORSE
## LIVING WEAPON

China's progress in warfare during ancient times came in various forms. Much of the nation's impressive military theory, finely crafted weapons, impregnable armor, and masterfully constructed walls and fortresses were developed during the years that the eastern and western empires coexisted with minimal interaction. During the years of Sun Tzu's life, China experienced nearly constant warfare. Rivalries between kingdoms and invasions from northern tribes kept the continent in turmoil, and consequently, the Chinese people became dangerously skilled in what became Sun Tzu's pet subject: the art of warfare. Among the numerous military advances of the era, one of the most noteworthy developments involved a creature that was not concerned with conquest and certainly had no interest in the power struggles between this king and that king. Since the early days of its

*Above: Forgery of a Saddled Horse by the Prince of Dongdan. Zhang Daqian (Chang Dai-chien), 1899–1983. Forgery after Li Zanhua, Prince of Dongdan. Chinese. 899– 936. 20th century. Colors and ink on paper. H x W: 35.7 x 37.5 cm (14 1/16 x 14 3/4 in). Origin: China.*
*Preceding pages: Horse. National Palace Museum, Taipei, Taiwan, Republic of China.*

*Above: The woman depicted here is suitably attired in riding trousers and a tight-fitting tunic, and has tied-up hair. Women of the Tang court were involved in a variety of equestrian sports, including a version of polo. Horse and rider. China. 650–700 CE. Earthenware.*

*Above left: Alongside the army of 7,000 terra-cotta warriors stand life-size horse sculptures, indicating the important role the animals played in battle.*

domestication, the horse had been utilized in warfare, and China's adoption of the beast of burden significantly altered the scenes of battle across the land.

Although historians remain uncertain as to when the Chinese began using horses in battle, it seems that the rulers of the individual kingdoms embraced the equestrian concept sometime before the years in which Sun Tzu lived. The Chinese, like Westerners, used the horse to draw chariots for combat and carriages for daily use outside of violent conflict. The northern tribes, which included the Mongols and were thought by the inhabitants of the states and cities to be barbarians, used a single mount to carry a solitary warrior into combat. These nomadic groups are thought to have been the first involved in the domestication of the horse, sometime around 4000 BCE. The type of horse most often used by the Chinese was the Mongolian horse with short, stocky build and stout hooves. Accordingly, it is likely that the Chinese adoption of the animal as a tool of warfare resulted from the Mongols' use of them. One may assume that the unforgettable sight of vicious attackers galloping on horseback triggered the idea of employing the horse in the mind of the warlord under siege. In fact, the barbaric northern tribes literally beat the concept into the heads of their foes, as the mounts provided the attackers with the capacity to carry out their hit-and-run assaults on the kingdoms prospering along the banks of China's rivers.

China developed the chariot with the invention of efficient horse trappings. For centuries, the only means of harnessing a horse was by the cruel throat-and-girth method, which choked the horse even as it exerted itself. Pulling a chariot often resulted in the death of the beast, and individual riders did sometimes inadvertently strangle their horses. Doubtlessly the carnage and all the confusion of battle was ballooned by this highly ineffective method. Sometime during the fourth century BCE, the Chinese began using a yoke across the horse's chest to control the animal, and the warlords quickly abandoned the throat-and-girth harness in favor of the hard yoke. Eventually, these were also replaced by a breast strap, or trace harness, which allowed the weight of the animal's burden to be borne by the chest and collarbones.

The use of chariots in China reached its peak during the life of Sun Tzu. The vehicles, usually drawn by two or four horses, generally held a driver, a ranging archer, and sometimes a warrior armed with melee weapons such as spears or swords. Several centuries earlier, at some point in the Spring and Autumn period, a sort of "chariot culture" had emerged, and by the time of Sun Tzu, it was common for the owners of chariots to be buried with their vehicles.

During the Spring and Autumn period, almost all of the Chinese states made use of chariots in their military campaigns. The most famous example of the employment of horse-drawn chariots is the battle of Chengpu. The encounter involved the state of Chu in a three-cornered contest with the state of Jin to the north and the state of Wu to the east. Between the two of them, King Cheng of Chu and Duke Wen of Jin utilized greater than 1,000 chariots, most of which were drawn by at least four horses.

Sun Tzu's observation that "all war is based on deception" proved accurate in this battle. The Jin right wing faked a riotous withdrawal. As was expected, the Chu pursued. Upon witnessing the anticipated pursuit, a band of Jin dragging tree boughs crossed the path of the chase, stirring up an

*Above: Horse. China. 206 BCE–9 CE. Earthenware.*

immense dust cloud that blinded the Chu. Before the swirling earth settled, the confused and impeded Chu found that they were now face-to-face with an overwhelming counterattack. The trick resulted in a victory for the Jin and a loss of more than a hundred chariots for the Chu.

After the eclipse of chariot warfare by mounted cavalry during the later years of the Warring States period, the horse once again forced a change in battle methods across the expanse of China. Like the nomadic barbarian tribes who had been riding horseback for centuries, the more civilized armies began following suit. Although it is possible Sun Tzu may have witnessed the devastating hit-and-run of the nomads, it is unlikely that he saw his own people utilizing horses in this way. But while the nomadic tribes were incapable of organization, the Chinese developed ingenuous strategies for one-man horses grouped together in cavalries, continuing to pave the way for their own unique contributions to warfare.

*Horse. China. First half of 8th century. Earthenware with three-color glaze and applied motifs. Photograph © 2008 Museum of Fine Arts, Boston.*

## The Rise and Fall of the Chariot

Archaeological evidence places the first chariots during the Shang period. Though the dating of the period is difficult to determine, it is generally accepted that the first chariots appeared in China around 1200 BCE.

The earliest chariot burial site in China, discovered in the Hougang area of Anyang in the Henan province, dates to the rule of King Wu Ding of the late Shang dynasty. During the Shang dynasty, members of royalty were buried with a complete household and servants, including a chariot, horses, and a charioteer. Two horses often drew the Shang chariots, but four are occasionally found in burials. The crew consisted of an archer, a driver, and sometimes a third, armed with a spear or dagger-axe.

In battle, the chariot was used mainly as a shock weapon, meaning that the charioteers would ride ahead of the main forces, attack the enemy at great speed, and try to disrupt their movements and positions. Sometimes, the chariot wheels would have spikes attached. These would spin menacingly as the chariot passed by and had a devastating effect on both infantry and cavalry who ventured too close to the chariot while trying to attack. At other times, Chinese generals used chariots to keep themselves mobile enough to survey the battlefield and move quickly from one point to another.

Between the eighth and fifth centuries BCE, the Chinese use of chariots in warfare reached its peak, but though they often appeared in greater numbers, the infantry nonetheless defeated them in battle. The chariot became obsolete during the later years of the Warring States period, due to the invention of the crossbow and the adoption of cavalry, which was more effective in rough terrain.

Still, the Chinese royalty continued to use the chariot as a status symbol, with larger and more elaborate chariots and horses belonging to higher-ranking members. New evidence to support this claim is found frequently. For example, an archaeological dig is ongoing at the site of the last emperor of the Chu dynasty. Preliminary results are encouraging, and this site may even be bigger than that of the Terra-cotta Army. The tomb is the largest and the best preserved found to date from the state of Chu in the Warring States period. Since 1979, three comprehensive surveys have been made of the tomb, with a formal excavation launched in August 2006. More than thirty horse-and-chariot pits have been found arranged in a row, making it the largest archaeological find of its kind from the Warring States period.

The tomb's occupant is still unknown but is thought to be a Chu noble, because a large amount of treasures, particularly jade items, have been unearthed from the tomb's burial chambers. More than 1,300 pieces have been put on display in Jingzhou in the Hubei province. Many scholars suspect that the master of the tomb was one of the eleven kings of the state of Chu. The great probability is that the tomb is of King Zhao of Chu, named Xiong Zhen, who was the last king of the state. The king's name is also linked with the name of the tomb, Xiongjiazhong, which literally means "the tomb of the Xiong family." According to sources within the Jingzhou city government, the tomb is expected to become a museum, like the one built around the tomb of the terra-cotta warriors in the mausoleum of the Qin emperor Shihuangdi in Shaanxi.

*Above: Pair of axle caps with pins, one of a pair. China. 1050–771 BCE. Bronze.*

*Left: The first horse-drawn chariots appeared in China around 1200 BCE. Terra-cotta Army, horses and carriage. China. 210 BCE.*

# *Variations in Tactics* 8

## 1

In war, the general receives his commands from the sovereign, collects his army, and concentrates his forces.

## 2

When in difficult country, do not encamp.

## 3

In country where high roads intersect, join hands with your allies.

## 4

Do not linger in dangerously isolated positions.

## 5

In hemmed-in situations, you must resort to stratagem.

## 6

In desperate positions, you must fight.

## 7

There are roads which must not be followed, armies which must be not attacked, towns which must not be besieged, positions which must not be contested, commands of the sovereign which must not be obeyed.

## 8

The general who thoroughly understands the advantages that accompany variation of tactics knows how to handle his troops.

## 9

The general who does not understand these may be well acquainted with the configuration of the country, yet he will not be able to turn his knowledge to practical account.

*Opposite page: Zhang Yichao, Governor of Western Gansu on Excursion to Fight the Tibetans. China. 850–907. Wall painting.*

## 10

So, the student of war who is unversed in the art of war of varying his plans, even though he be acquainted with the Five Advantages, will fail to make the best use of his men.

## 11

Hence, in the wise leader's plans, considerations of advantage and of disadvantage will be blended together.

*Bactrian camel. China. 581–700. Glazed earthenware.*

## 12

If our expectation of advantage be tempered in this way, we may succeed in accomplishing the essential part of our schemes. If, on the other hand, in the midst of difficulties we are always ready to seize an advantage, we may extricate ourselves from misfortune.

### 13

Reduce the hostile chiefs by inflicting damage on them; make trouble for them, and keep them constantly engaged; hold out specious allurements and make them rush to any given point.

### 14

The art of war teaches us to rely not on the likelihood of the enemy's not coming, but on our own readiness to receive him; not on the chance of his not attacking, but rather on the fact that we have made our position unassailable.

### 15

There are five dangerous faults which may affect a general:

### 16

Recklessness, which leads to destruction;

### 17

cowardice, which leads to capture;

### 18

a hasty temper, which can be provoked by insults;

### 19

a delicacy of honor which is sensitive to shame;

### 20

oversolicitude for his men, which exposes him to worry and trouble.

### 21

These are the five besetting sins of a general, ruinous to the conduct of war.

### 22

When an army is overthrown and its leader slain, the cause will surely be found among these five dangerous faults. Let them be a subject of meditation.

*Emperor Yang Ti (581–618) strolling in his gardens with his wives, from a history of Chinese emperors (color on silk). Chinese. 17th century.*

# KEY BATTLES
# OF THE WARRING STATES PERIOD

Prior to the beginning of the Warring States period (ca. 480 to 221 BCE), China was made up of small individual kingdoms vying for supremacy. These opposing states were the Chu, Han, Qi, Qin, Shu, Song, Wei, Yan, Yue, Zhao, and the Zhou dynasty. No state was able to gain control until after this period, when only one great state remained, that of the Qin.

After Wu of Wei died in 371 BCE, leaving no successor, the state fell into civil war. Three years later, with the Wei still embroiled in fighting among themselves, the Zhao and Han invaded. However, for no clear reason, the two armies fell back at the point of destroying the Wei, and King Hui of Wei assumed the throne. Apparently in retaliation for the attack on the Wei, King Hui launched a major offensive against the Zhao in 354 BCE. The capital city of Handan in Zhao was besieged and losing badly when the Qi decided to step in and help Zhao. This worked mostly as a result of the strategy employed by the brilliant tactician Sun Bin, a descendant of Sun Tzu. The idea was to attack the Wei homeland, forcing the Wei armies to defend their home and therefore relieving the siege of Zhao's capital. As the retreating Wei army rushed to defend their home, they were ambushed by the waiting Qi forces and were defeated in the battle of Guiling. A saying attributed to this battle, "surrounding Wei to save Zhao," is still used in modern China to refer to attacking an enemy's vulnerable spots to relieve the pressure that the enemy is applying to an ally.

Qi once again interfered in Wei's ambitions after the Wei attacked the Han in 341 BCE. The battle of Maling ensued, with the same generals and the same result as the previous battle of Guiling. A year later, the Qin entered the picture and defeated the Wei, who were forced to lose a significant portion of their lands to end the conflict. At this point, the Qi and the Qin were the most powerful states in China.

Elsewhere, the Chu had been one of the strongest states in China early in the Warring States period. The state had risen to power around 389 BCE, when the famous reformer Wu Qi was named prime minister. Chu rose again to its

*Blade. China.*
*1300–800 BCE.*
*Nephrite.*

power in 334, when it gained vast amounts of territory. The series of events leading up to this began when the Yue prepared to attack the Qi. The king of Qi persuaded the king of Yue to attack the Chu instead. Though the Yue initiated a large-scale attack on the Chu, they were defeated by Chu's counterattack. The Chu then proceeded to conquer the Yue, thus expanding its borders eastward to the Pacific Ocean.

Toward the end of the Warring States period, the Qin became disproportionately powerful compared to the other six states, and began defeating them one by one.

In 316 BCE, the Qin conquered the Shu, and a few years later, the Qi were decimated by a coalition of five states, including the Qin, who then defeated the Wei and the Han in the battle of Yique in 293. After a relatively quiet couple of decades, the Qin attacked the Chu, managed to capture their capital city, Ying, and went on, some years later, to fight the Zhao at the battle of Changping. Although both sides were devastated, the Qin recovered and continued their conquest of China.

After the defeat of the Zhao by Qin armies, the small state of Han feared an onslaught. King An sent emissaries to Qin to surrender the kingdom without a fight. With typical cunning, the Qin, during the siege of Kaifeng in Wei in 225 BCE, realized that the city walls were too massive to attack and used the power of a local river to flood the city, resulting in massive destruction and the king's surrender. Only one year later, in a battle that included more than a million soldiers, the Qin defeated the Chu army by feigning complacency in their preparations. When the Chu forces decided to stand down, Qin attacked and overran their foes.

Turning their attention to the state of Yan, the Qin army responded to a failed assassination attempt on their emperor by increasing their number of troops to decimate their enemies. Meanwhile, the Qi were conquered when they followed the example of the Han and surrendered all of their cites. With that capitulation, the unification of China was complete and the Qin dynasty began.

# The Army on the March

## 9

### 1

We come now to the question of encamping the army, and observing signs of the enemy. Pass quickly over mountains, and keep in the neighborhood of valleys. Camp in high places, facing the sun.

### 2

Do not climb heights in order to fight. So much for mountain warfare.

### 3

After crossing a river, you should get far away from it.

### 4

When an invading force crosses a river in its onward march, do not advance to meet it in mid-stream. It will be best to let half the army get across, and then deliver your attack.

### 5

If you are anxious to fight, you should not go to meet the invader near a river which he has to cross.

### 6

Moor your craft higher up than the enemy, and facing the sun. Do not move upstream to meet the enemy. So much for river warfare.

### 7

In crossing salt marshes, your sole concern should be to get over them quickly, without any delay. If forced to fight in a salt marsh, you should have water and grass near you, and get your back to a clump of trees. So much for operations in salt marshes.

### 8

In dry, level country, take up an easily accessible position with rising ground to your right and at your rear, so that the danger may be in front, and safety lie behind. So much for campaigning in flat country.

### 9

These are the four useful branches of military knowledge which enabled the Yellow Emperor to vanquish four sovereigns.

### 10

All armies prefer high ground to low and sunny places or dark.

### 11

If you are careful of your men, and camp on hard ground, the army will be free from disease of every kind, and this will spell victory.

### 12

When you come to a hill or a bank, occupy the sunny side, with the slope on your right rear. Thus you will at once act for the benefit of your soldiers and utilize the natural advantages of the ground.

### 13

When, in consequence of heavy rains up-country, a river which you wish to ford is swollen and flecked with foam, you must wait until it subsides.

### 14

Country in which there are precipitous cliffs with torrents running between, deep natural hollows, confined places, tangled thickets, quagmires, and crevasses, should be left with all possible speed and not approached.

### 15

While we keep away from such places, we should get the enemy to approach them; while we face them, we should let the enemy have them on his rear.

*Opposite page: The First Battle Between the Chinese Army and that of the Eleuths in 1759, detail of fighting across the river, plate 10 from a series of prints representing the conquests of Qianlong, Emperor of China, engraved by Nicolas Delauney (1739–92). English. 1772.*

*Ritual implement (cong).
China. 3300–2200 BCE.
Nephrite.*

### 16

If in the neighborhood of your camp there should be any hilly country, ponds surrounded by aquatic grass, hollow basins filled with reeds, or woods with thick undergrowth, they must be carefully routed out and searched; for these are places where men in ambush or insidious spies are likely to be lurking.

### 17

When the enemy is close at hand and remains quiet, he is relying on the natural strength of his position.

### 18

When he keeps aloof and tries to provoke a battle, he is anxious for the other side to advance.

### 19

If his place of encampment is easy of access, he is tendering a bait.

### 20

Movement amongst the trees of a forest shows that the enemy is advancing. The appearance of a number of screens in the midst of thick grass means that the enemy wants to make us suspicious.

### 21

The rising of birds in their flight is the sign of an ambush. Startled beasts indicate that a sudden attack is coming.

### 22

When there is dust rising in a high column, it is the sign of chariots advancing; when the dust is low, but spread over a wide area, it betokens the approach of infantry. When it branches out in different directions, it shows that parties have been sent to collect firewood. A few clouds of dust moving to and fro signify that the army is encamping.

### 23

Humble words and increased preparations are signs that the enemy is about to advance.

*Chariot fitting. China. 400–221
BCE. Bronze with gold inlay.*

### 24

Violent language and driving forward as if to the attack are signs that he will retreat.

### 25

When the light chariots come out first and take up a position on the wings, it is a sign that the enemy is forming for battle.

### 26

Peace proposals unaccompanied by a sworn covenant indicate a plot.

### 27

When there is much running about and the soldiers fall into rank, it means that the critical moment has come.

### 28

When some are seen advancing and some retreating, it is a lure.

### 29

When the soldiers stand leaning on their spears, they are faint from want of food.

### 30

If those who are sent to draw water begin by drinking themselves, the army is suffering from thirst.

### 31

If the enemy sees an advantage to be gained and makes no effort to secure it, the soldiers are exhausted.

### 32

If birds gather on any spot, it is unoccupied.

### 33

Clamor by night betokens nervousness.

### 34

If there is disturbance in the camp, the general's authority is weak.

### 35

If the banners and flags are shifted about, sedition is afoot.

### 36

If the officers are angry, it means that the men are weary.

### 37

When an army feeds its horses with grain and kills its cattle for food, and when the men do not hang their cooking pots over the campfires, showing that they will not return to their tents, you may know that they are determined to fight to the death.

## 38

The sight of men whispering together in small knots or speaking in subdued tones points to disaffection amongst the rank and file.

## 39

Too frequent rewards signify that the enemy is at the end of his resources; too many punishments betray a condition of dire distress.

## 40

To begin by bluster, but afterwards to take fright at the enemy's numbers, shows a supreme lack of intelligence.

## 41

When envoys are sent with compliments in their mouths, it is a sign that the enemy wishes for a truce.

## 42

If the enemy's troops march up angrily and remain facing ours for a long time without either joining battle or taking themselves off again, the situation is one that demands great vigilance and circumspection.

## 43

If our troops are no more in number than the enemy, that is amply sufficient; it only means that no direct attack can be made. What we can do is simply to concentrate all our available strength, keep a close watch on the enemy, and obtain reinforcements.

## 44

He who exercises no forethought but makes light of his opponents is sure to be captured by them.

## 45

If soldiers are punished before they have grown attached to you, they will not prove submissive; and, unless submissive, they will be practically useless. If, when the soldiers have become attached to you, punishments are not enforced, they will still be useless.

## 46

Therefore soldiers must be treated in the first instance with humanity, but kept under control by means of iron discipline. This is a certain road to victory.

## 47

If in training soldiers' commands are habitually enforced, the army will be well-disciplined; if not, its discipline will be bad.

## 48

If a general shows confidence in his men but always insists on his orders being obeyed, the gain will be mutual.

*The Military Governor of Yunnan Province in full ceremonial uniform. Circa 1890. Photograph.*

# THE JIA
# A WARRIOR'S ARMOR

Known as *jia*, or "shell," a warrior's armor underwent many transitions over the periods and dynastic movements of ancient China. Throughout history, the four major parts of a Chinese warrior's armor remained relatively constant: the helmet, or *zhou*; the shoulder cover, or *pi bo*; the chest armor, or *xiong kai*; and the skirt, or *tui qun*. During the Zhou dynasty (ca. 1027 to 256 BCE), armor was known as *zhong jia*, a term that Sun Tzu would have used.

In the early years of the Xia through the Warring States periods, a span of two millennia, most armor consisted of leather and animal skins, mostly fashioned from hides of cow, buffalo, and tiger. Leather armor was suitable for protection against the brass weaponry of the time, especially in conjunction with large shields. Armor for generals and high-ranking military officials was often made with rhinoceros hide.

Historical evidence shows that warriors of the period wore a two-piece leather armor coating their front and back sides, in addition to bronze helmets and shields. This armor advanced, as battle and weaponry increased in complexity, to a more intricate design involving many leather pieces strung together with a leather thong, a design that offered movement and an easier repair of the armor's perishable material.

Armor varied across periods of combat and was specialized to fit different warriors for their particular roles in battle. For instance, after the introduction of the chariot around 1200 BCE, the armor used by charioteers was long and restricting, because most charioteers had limited movement once fixed to their chariots. Their leather armor

*Spearhead. China. 1100–900 BCE. Bronze.*

consisted of just one or two pieces, leaving only the arms free to move. A combat warrior, however, had a more intricately designed and decorated armor consisting of many pieces of strung leather. Their legs were left unrestricted, and their tunics were cut much shorter to allow free motion and running.

When cavalry were introduced, perhaps after Sun Tzu's lifetime, tunics were cut shorter, and armor was more revealing, allowing free movement of the legs. In that period, before stirrups were created, heavy armor contributed to decreased balance and increased instability for the rider. Therefore, lighter and less restrictive armor was necessary, leaving a warrior more vulnerable to injury. Unfortunately, iron armor did not begin to replace leather until the middle of the Han dynasty, at the beginning of the new millennium, even though iron swords and weaponry had already become commonplace.

The helmet known as the *dou jian* protected both the head and neck and consisted of two sections. The area shielding the head was typically constructed from a single piece of leather or metal. The neck piece was made from either wrapped chains of metal or long strips of leather to allow movement. Two chin straps held the helmet in place to minimize jostling or the loss of the helmet during frequent rough movement.

Identified by a variety of terms, the shields of ancient China were either rectangular or round, depending upon their purpose in battle. The rectangular shield, the *bu dun*, "stepping shield," was used by the foot soldier, because it was typically large and heavy and made for specific use in ground battle. In contrast, the lighter, smaller shield, the *zi dun*, was reserved for the charioteer and was made of wood and covered with leather hide. When the concept of the cavalry was introduced, the small round shield, the *ji bing*, was invented for use on horseback. The smaller shields used by charioteers and cavalry were designed to be maneuverable for face-to-face battle, while the larger shields of the foot soldiers could be steadied on the ground and positioned to block the warrior's entire body from projectile weapons.

Also as part of his armor, the foot soldier carried a small rounded sword, the *teng pai*. This sword, featuring sharp outer edges, was made from ratta, and was used both for hand-to-hand combat as well as for chopping and slashing at the legs of his opponents' cavalry horses.

The *pang pai*, a large, square shield, was common among foot soldiers facing projectile weapons from a large opposing army. A warrior could hide his entire body behind the shield to block projectile arrows, daggers, and stones. Due to the shield's weight, it became ineffective when battle escalated to hand-to-hand combat. When an opposing army advanced enough to begin ground combat, the large shields were abandoned for smaller, more portable wooden shields. Also commonly used among ground soldiers was the *ai pai*, the leaning shield. It was constructed specifically from the wood of a white willow tree and could be propped at an angle to shield soldiers from incoming airborne weapons.

> *Leather armor was suitable for protection against the brass weaponry of the time, especially in conjunction with large shields. Armor for generals and high-ranking military officials was often made with rhinoceros hide.*

Similar in purpose to the other shields but shaped differently, the swallowtail shield, the *yan wei pai*, was a long, narrow, forked tongue shape, making it the lightest and most easily maneuverable sword of all. Constructed from the trunk of the eastern Asian wood-oil tree (*Aleurites cordata*), it was both strong and agile. Because of its slender profile, a warrior in battle needed to turn sideways to hide behind the swallowtail shield, seemingly its only limitation.

The hand shield, *shou pai*, was constructed of pine or white willow wood, two extremely strong, durable woods. The hand shield was light, and easy for a soldier to carry over long distances. At its center, where it was held, the shou pai was narrow and thin, and both ends fanned out to form a butterfly shape.

Developments in armor, both in material and size, typically addressed the issue of body protection rather than weight and flexibility. Wearing all of the armor pieces together was extremely heavy, and Chinese martial arts training directed much focus to the strength and endurance of the warrior.

*This ancient statue depicts the leather armor typically worn by Chinese soldiers. Ancient statue in front of a temple. China.*

# THE WARRIOR'S SWORDS

Much controversy surrounds the development of the sword of ancient China. Most scholars tend to believe that the true sword did not appear until the late Spring and Autumn period, just before Sun Tzu's lifetime. Prior to this period, warriors used dagger-axes and many other short weapons common in hand-to-hand combat. These short weapons were most often fashioned from bronze and eventually became more elongated, more like the form of the modern sword.

The early swords of the Zhou and the Spring and Autumn periods were designed predominately for piercing and thrusting rather than for slashing. Because the early sword developed from the spear, it therefore resembled the spear in both form and usage. As the sword concept developed, blades began to lengthen, and the double-edge sword was born. These longer, sharper swords conducive for slashing were somewhat unfit and dangerous for use by the cavalry and were primarily reserved for infantrymen or for ceremonial purposes.

With the enhancement of the military and the shift toward cavalry as the dominant battle weapon during the Han period and onward into the new millennium, swords evolved to become more useful and less hazardous on horseback. The single-edge sword, bearing a ring handle, replaced the long double-edge swords of the Warring States period. As Chinese metalworking improved over time, blades became sturdier, and a divide was created in sword making: on the military front, swords became shorter, sturdier, and more functional due to the improved technology of steel making and layering; on the artistic or aesthetic front, longer steel swords were fashioned purely for the purpose of ceremony and symbolic decoration.

One of the most common swords to develop in ancient China was the *jian*, the double-edge sword that appeared during the seventh century BCE in the Spring and Autumn period. The jian was eventually replaced by shorter steel swords, but it was still common among the infantry following the Warring States period, when it featured a straight blade of nearly three feet in length. Among the four major weapons of China—that is, the *gun* (staff), the *qiang* (spear), the *jian* (sword), and the *dao* (saber)— the jian is noted in early Chinese writings as the Gentleman of All Weapons.

The jian sported a hand guard or hilt as protection from the weapon of an opponent. The guard, like two short flaps or wings, covered the top of the hand as it gripped the sword. At the end of the handle was a pommel, designed to keep the handle from slipping through the hand. Also often featured on the jian was a tassel, which usually attached to the area between the handle and blade and could distract an opponent by blurring the motion of the sword in combat. But the tassel could also serve as a weapon of sorts, because it caused lacerations when swept across the face of an opponent.

Typically, the blade of a jian was divided into three parts. The tip, the *jianfeng*, ended in a small curve and was used for stabbing or quick cuts from a distance. The middle of the blade, the *zhongren*, was used for deflections and draw cuts, both in offensive and defensive action. The unsharpened *jiangen*, the root of the blade, was used mainly for defensive strategy, particularly for blocking an opponent. Considering those three sword parts together, it is easy to imagine that the tip might be used the most heavily in battle, and that therefore the point was often rounded from wear and aged more quickly than the other parts of the blade.

The jian was originally made from bronze, though steel technology would transform it into a sturdier weapon. In later periods, however, when steel was more prevalent, the jian had already become a sword of ceremonial value, often decorated heavily and fashioned from jade.

Another short weapon, the *dao*, was a type of single-edge sword that changed greatly over the various periods of ancient Chinese warfare. Also a member of the four major categories, the dao was known as the General of All Weapons, and the term can be used to reference any broad-bladed, single-edge sword or knife. However, in modern Chinese language, the term *dao* is used to denote a knife.

The dao has been found to date back to the Shang dynasty, during the Bronze Age. While the jian was a more common weapon during earlier periods, the dao came in handy when infantrymen were replaced by higher numbers of cavalrymen. Accordingly, it was the prevalent weapon among the cavalry of the Han dynasty and was most commonly used as a chopping weapon, with the jian being reserved for slashing and stabbing. Soon, the dao replaced the jian almost completely, becoming the foot soldier's standard weapon.

Like the jian, the dao often featured tassels or scarves, which served to distract an opponent. The guard differed somewhat from that of the jian, in that it presented a disc or cup shape, which prevented blood and water from dripping down to the handle to interfere with the traction of the grip. Often, these guards were shaped into an S curve to cover the top part of the warrior's hand and knuckles in battle.

*Scabbard slide (wei). China. 209 BCE–9 CE. Nephrite.*

*Scabbard finial (bi), commonly called a chape. China. 206 BCE–9 CE. Nephrite.*

*Center: Unfit and dangerous for use by the cavalry, double-edge swords such as this one were used primarily by infantrymen and for ceremonial purposes.*

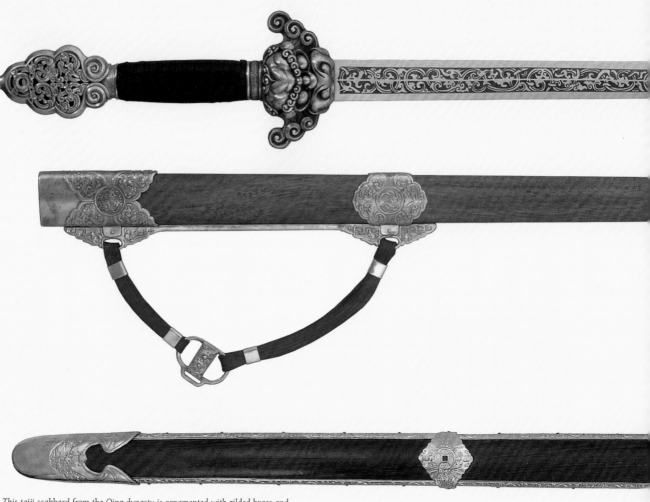

*This taiji scabbard from the Qing dynasty is ornamented with gilded brass and an intricately knotted tassel.*

*A well-proportioned and well-balanced sword, this Tang jian features an intricate engraved dragon pattern along the length of the blade, as well as a brass lion-dog guard and brass scabbard ornaments.*

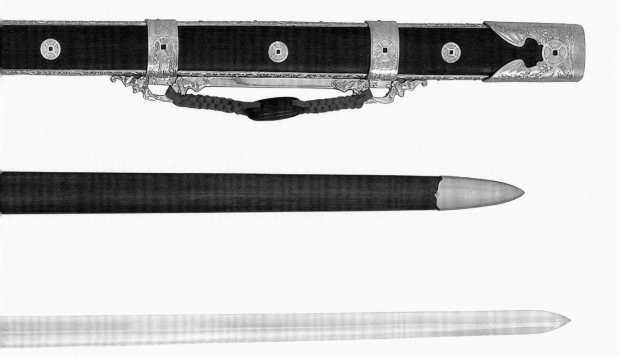

*This single-handed jian features a wooden handle with a pronounced center ridge and tapered blade for stiffness.*

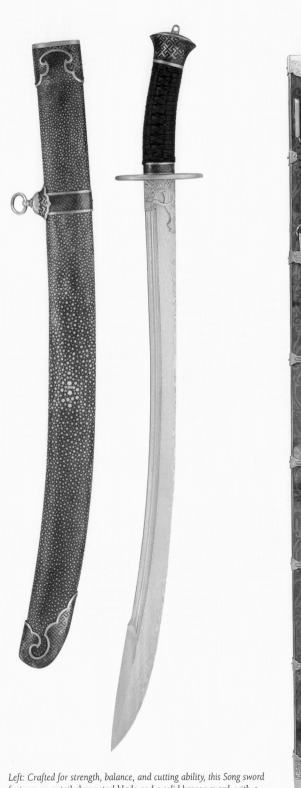

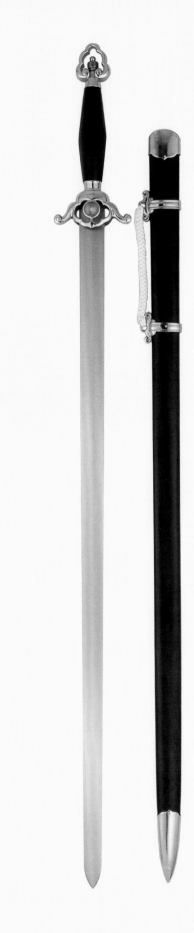

*Left:* Crafted for strength, balance, and cutting ability, this Song sword features an oxtail-shape steel blade and a solid bronze guard, with a leather-wrapped grip and sharkskin scabbard.

*Center:* This Ming sword was designed with stiffness and lightness in mind to facilitate strong thrusts and speed. It is decorated with silver-plated brass fittings.

*Right:* This sword is ideal for daily taiji practice, with a steel guard and pommel and an unsharpened blade.

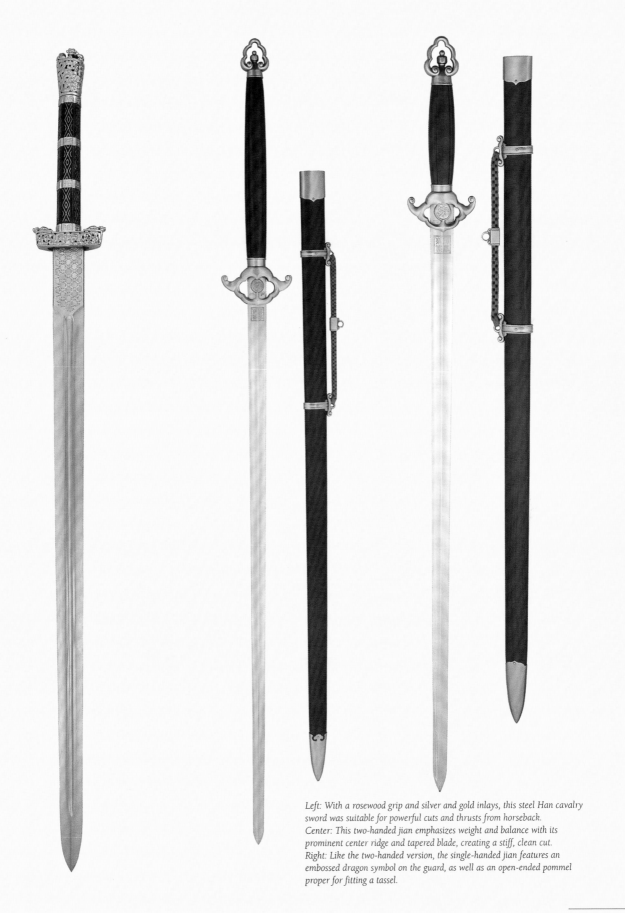

*Left:* With a rosewood grip and silver and gold inlays, this steel Han cavalry sword was suitable for powerful cuts and thrusts from horseback.
*Center:* This two-handed jian emphasizes weight and balance with its prominent center ridge and tapered blade, creating a stiff, clean cut.
*Right:* Like the two-handed version, the single-handed jian features an embossed dragon symbol on the guard, as well as an open-ended pommel proper for fitting a tassel.

# Terrain

## Sun Tzu said:

### 1

We may distinguish six kinds of terrain, to wit: Accessible ground; entangling ground; temporizing ground; narrow passes; precipitous heights; positions at a great distance from the enemy.

### 2

Ground which can be freely traversed by both sides is called accessible. With regard to ground of this nature, be before the enemy in occupying the raised and sunny spots, and carefully guard your line of supplies. Then you will be able to fight with advantage.

### 3

Ground which can be abandoned but is hard to reoccupy is called entangling. From a position of this sort, if the enemy is unprepared, you may sally forth and defeat him. But if the enemy is prepared for your coming, and you fail to defeat him, then, return being impossible, disaster will ensue.

### 4

When the position is such that neither side will gain by making the first move, it is called temporizing ground. In a position of this sort, even though the enemy should offer us an attractive bait, it will be advisable not to stir forth, but rather to retreat, thus enticing the enemy in his turn; then, when part of his army has come out, we may deliver our attack with advantage.

### 5

With regard to narrow passes, if you can occupy them first, let them be strongly garrisoned and await the advent of the enemy. Should the army forestall you in occupying a pass, do not go after him if the pass is fully garrisoned, but only if it is weakly garrisoned.

### 6

With regard to precipitous heights, if you are beforehand with your adversary, you should occupy the raised and sunny spots, and there wait for him to come up. If the enemy has occupied them before you, do not follow him, but retreat and try to entice him away.

### 7

If you are situated at a great distance from the enemy, and the strength of the two armies is equal, it is not easy to provoke a battle, and fighting will be to your disadvantage.

## 8

These six are the principles connected with Earth. The general who has attained a responsible post must be careful to study them.

## 9

Now an army is exposed to six several calamities, not arising from natural causes, but from faults for which the general is responsible. These are: Flight; insubordination; collapse; ruin; disorganization; rout.

## 10

Other conditions being equal, if one force is hurled against another ten times its size, the result will be the flight of the former.

## 11

When the common soldiers are too strong and their officers too weak, the result is insubordination. When the officers are too strong and the common soldiers too weak, the result is collapse.

## 12

When the higher officers are angry and insubordinate, and on meeting the enemy give battle on their own account from a feeling of resentment, before the commander-in-chief can tell whether or not he is in a position to fight, the result is ruin.

## 13

When the general is weak and without authority; when his orders are not clear and distinct; when there are no fixed duties assigned to officers and men, and the ranks are formed in a slovenly haphazard manner, the result is utter disorganization.

## 14

When a general, unable to estimate the enemy's strength, allows an inferior force to engage a larger one, or hurls a weak detachment against a powerful one, and neglects to place picked soldiers in the front rank, the result must be rout.

*Emperor Ming Huang's Journey to Shu. Anonymous copy of 10th century Tang period painting by Li Zhaodao. China. Song dynasty, 11th century. Silk handscroll.*

*Preceding pages: Mountains in Yunnan Province, China.*

*Vase with ascending dragons.
Jiangxi province, China.
1662–1722. Youlihong ware.*

*Ewe and lamb. China.
1644–1911. Ivory.*

*Opposite page: Zhangjiajie
National Park of China.*

## 15

These are six ways of courting defeat, which must be carefully noted by the general who has attained a responsible post.

## 16

The natural formation of the country is the soldier's best ally; but a power of estimating the adversary, of controlling the forces of victory, and of shrewdly calculating difficulties, dangers and distances, constitutes the test of a great general. He who knows these things, and in fighting puts his knowledge into practice, will win his battles. He who knows them not, nor practices them, will surely be defeated.

## 17

If fighting is sure to result in victory, then you must fight, even though the ruler forbid it; if fighting will not result in victory, then you must not fight even at the ruler's bidding.

## 18

The general who advances without coveting fame and retreats without fearing disgrace, whose only thought is to protect his country and do good service for his sovereign, is the jewel of the kingdom.

## 19

Regard your soldiers as your children, and they will follow you into the deepest valleys; look upon them as your own beloved sons, and they will stand by you even unto death.

## 20

If, however, you are indulgent, but unable to make your authority felt; kind-hearted, but unable to enforce your commands; and incapable, moreover, of quelling disorder, then your soldiers must be likened to spoilt children; they are useless for any practical purpose.

## 21

If we know that our own men are in a condition to attack, but are unaware that the enemy is not open to attack, we have gone only halfway towards victory.

## 22

If we know that the enemy is open to attack, but are unaware that our own men are not in a condition to attack, we have gone only halfway towards victory.

## 23

If we know that the enemy is open to attack, and also know that our men are in a condition to attack, but are unaware that the nature of the ground makes fighting impracticable, we have still gone only halfway towards victory.

---

*The natural formation of the country is the soldier's best ally; but a power of estimating the adversary, of controlling the forces of victory, and of shrewdly calculating difficulties, dangers and distances, constitutes the test of a great general. He who knows these things, and in fighting puts his knowledge into practice, will win his battles. He who knows them not, nor practices them, will surely defeated.*

---

## 24

Hence the experienced soldier, once in motion, is never bewildered; once he has broken camp, he is never at a loss.

## 25

Hence the saying: If you know the enemy and know yourself, your victory will not stand in doubt; if you know Heaven and know Earth, you may make your victory complete.

# THE WARRIOR'S ARSENAL

From the onset of the Shang dynasty, around 1500 BCE, bronze technology quickly made its way into the construction of weaponry. At first, only the weaponry and armor of nobles were fashioned from bronze, while the tools and devices of commoners were still crudely crafted from animal bones, rocks, and wood. Over the hundreds of years of Shang rule, however, bronze weaponry made its way into the outfit and arsenal of every Chinese warrior.

As war progressed, hand-to-hand combat required daggers and hatchets. Bronze was used for the tips of arrows and spears, as well as for the compound crossbows suitable for shooting targets at long distances. These bronze hand weapons evolved as a result of changes in military thought, terrain, and technology. Though most weapons of the period were eventually all constructed of bronze, leather armor was still considered efficient protection. Swords advanced at a much slower pace and were not introduced into the common warrior arsenal until the Warring States period, the age of Sun Tzu's *The Art of War*. Bronze weapons remained common until the end of that period, when iron began to supersede, though certainly not replace, bronze in armor, weaponry, and tools.

The most common weapon among warriors was the *ko*, the bronze dagger-axe. Soldiers carried the small weapon starting in the Shang dynasty and continuing through the Han dynasty at the turn of the millennium, though its use had decreased dramatically during the intervening Qin dynasty, when the pole arm became prevalent. The dagger-axe was used in both offensive and defensive military strategy, as well as in both hand-to-hand combat and as a projectile weapon. It is believed that the early swords were developed from the dagger-axe, lengthening over time for different military needs, such as the introduction of cavalry.

*Horseman carrying chi halberd. Wuwei, Gansu province, China. Eastern Han dynasty, 2nd century CE. Bronze.*

The pole arm was simply an extension of the dagger-axe. A sharp and often curved blade was attached to the end of a long wooden pole for close-range fighting. The extended length of the shaft allowed for increased momentum and a harder striking force. Though they are still common in martial arts practice, the pole arm was eventually rendered obsolete by the invention of firearms.

Popular among the long weapons of ancient China, the *qiang*, a spear made in a variety of shapes and lengths, evolved in conjunction with improvements in defensive battle skills. Among the four major weapons of China, the qiang is known as the King of Weapons for its ubiquitous

> *The tassels also helped absorb any blood flow from the spearhead to the shaft, a situation that could render the qiang slippery and difficult to grasp in battle. The qiang used by foot soldiers usually stretched nearly seven feet, while those carried by cavalry often towered to nearly thirteen feet.*

use in ancient Chinese battle. During the Shang dynasty, spearheads transitioned from stone to brass and commonly featured a leaf-shaped blade with tassels attached below the spearhead. The leaf shape proved aerodynamic, while the tassels were known to blur the vision of an opponent, inhibiting his defense against attack. The tassels also helped absorb any blood flow from the spearhead to the shaft, a situation that could render the qiang slippery and difficult to grasp in battle. The qiang used by foot soldiers usually stretched nearly seven feet, while those carried by cavalry often towered to nearly thirteen feet. Most were made of

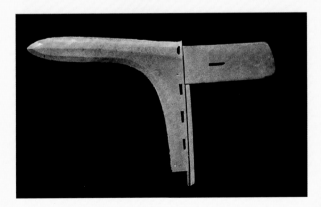

*The most common weapon among warriors was the dagger-axe. Dagger-axe (ge). China. 475–400 BCE. Bronze.*

*Bronze dagger-axe from the late Shang period (circa 1200 BCE). Note the hafting flange bears a clan emblem representing two "kui" dragons flanking a stylized sun.*

wax wood, which is strong yet flexible, bending slightly on impact to resist fractures in the wood. The bending, coupled with the blurring tassels, made the qiang difficult to follow with the eye, rendering it useful in long-distance battle.

Long before the first cavalry appeared, China experienced a turning point in military history with the development of the chariot, and new armor and weaponry had evolved to accommodate the fighting needs of charioteers, who remained relatively fixed to the vehicle, only moving their arms during battle. From the late Shang period and into the Warring States period, the chariot remained an important device in battle until replaced entirely by cavalry after the age of Sun Tzu. In an impressive display on the battlefield, a single brigade of chariots encompassed five squads of five chariots each. An individual chariot was usually surrounded by a team of infantry soldiers, brandishing both qiang and ko. Within the chariot typically rode three warriors: a driver at the center, a ko-wielding soldier on the right, and an archer on the left.

From even that slight elevation, an onslaught of arrows could prove devastating to enemy formations, as the Chinese soon learned with the advent of the war chariot—though archery had been adopted for war as far back as

*Sword guard (xun). China. 206 BCE–9 CE. Nephrite.*

*Bronze axes like this one were common in ancient China. Axe (yue). China. 1300–1050 BCE. Bronze.*

*This device was designed to pull the strings on a powerful crossbow. Crossbow crank. China. 300–221 BCE. Bronze.*

prehistoric eras some 25,000 years earlier. Those earliest bows were undoubtedly meant to replace the slinglike atlatl, which projected arrows by means of simple arm power. In spite of such a long heritage, though, the bow of the Shang dynasty had only become an effective weapon when it had morphed from a piece of bent wood to a stronger, more elastic composite of wood and horn, glued together and secured with sinew. Interestingly, the Chinese bow, unlike its counterpart in the West, sported not one but two arcs of wood, fixed as a set at the midpoint of their curves. As destructive as the bow and arrow could be as a weapon, the introduction of the crossbow as its replacement would revolutionize Chinese warfare.

Early crossbows were typically made of a single piece of strong wood, most commonly ash. Those early specimens were thought to have held the force of nearly 160 pounds, which would have made them capable of propelling arrows extremely long distances at high speeds. China is known for the repeating crossbow, a design that originated as early as the Zhou dynasty of around 1000 BCE. The design involved a wood-and-string formation that allowed the stringing, shooting, and restringing of an arrow with a single motion of one hand, while keeping the bow stationary. A warrior could fire at a faster rate this way, without having to readjust his position to reload, which would require him to simultaneously shield his body from oncoming fire. Though a material difference existed in the construction of bows after the introduction of steel and iron, the design of the bow remained relatively unchanged throughout dynastic history.

*Right: Bronze dagger. Spring and Autumn period (circa 700–500 BCE).*
*Opposite page, bottom: Lacquered wooden crossbow with bronze mechanism. China. Warring States period. Circa 250 BCE. The body of the crossbow is painted with animals and symbols related to the Taoist paradise.*

# THE CROSSBOW
# AN ORIGINAL CHINESE INVENTION

*The crossbow only became effective as a weapon after the addition of bronze parts. Crossbow mechanism. China. 206 BCE–9 CE. Bronze.*

The earliest artifact from a *nu*, the Chinese term for crossbow, dates to 400 BCE, which coincides with the supposed date for Sun Tzu's *The Art of War*. According to Chinese records, including Zhao Ye's *Romance of the Wu and Yue*, the crossbow was invented hundreds of years earlier, at the beginning of the Warring States period, in the state of Chu. However, some authorities speculate that the presumed inventor of the crossbow, Qin, was in fact simply making improvements to an existing weapon by altering the triggering assembly. Experts believe that the crossbow actually dates even farther back, with some placing its origins in the Shang dynasty (ca. 1523 to ca. 1027 BCE). In any case, the crossbow only became effective as a weapon after the addition of bronze parts sometime before 400 BCE. With the capability of mass-producing these bronze crossbows in uniform quantities, the weapon became more reliable and purportedly had a firing range of up to 650 feet.

The crossbow, which evolved from the standard archer's bow, rose to popularity during the Warring States period. Because constant brute strength was often required when drawing a bow, archers fatigued quickly. The crossbow, with its mechanical firing trigger, could hold the arrow, or bolt, in a firing position until the enemy appeared, an advancement that changed to the configuration and style of warfare. With this improvement, armies could lie in wait, crossbows ready, and ambush their rival forces without overexerting their arms. Additionally, an artifact dating back to the Warring

States period shows a safety mechanism on the trigger of the crossbow, thus enabling the archer to carry a loaded and cocked weapon without fear of accidentally sending a bolt into his own troops. The increasingly accurate and safer trigger mechanism also allowed for faster training, which resulted in more precise firing within a short amount of time. In contrast, accurate operation of the longbow used by medieval English archers took years of practice and training.

Bulky and less accurate than the single-shot crossbow, the multiple-shot *chu-ko-nu* was used primarily as a defensive weapon. Supposedly developed by the military strategist Chu Ko Liang from an earlier prototype, the repeating crossbow has possible origins from as early as 250 BCE. The chu-ko-nu was designed with a ten-bolt magazine capable of shooting seven-inch-long bolts at a rate that would empty the weapon in five seconds. The bamboo arrows, though short and light, were well made and had steel heads that were heavy in proportion to the length of their shafts. They had no feathers, so that they dropped freely one by one from the magazine when the repeating crossbow was being fired. Because the light arrow of the crossbow had little penetrative power, the arrowhead was sometimes dipped in poison to compensate for its weight.

三等侍衛克什
克巴圖魯伍克
什爾圖

預軍門選聯鑣致
青纓頭幾萬翩如
八虛達阿克蘇跰
羽及膝鉛彈在背
王今未出

恭贊

乾隆庚辰春臣劉統勳臣劉綸繪臣于敏中奉

*Preceding pages: An archery contest. China. Late 18th century. Color on silk.*
*Right: Portrait of Keshiki Batu Luwuke Shier. China. 1760. Hanging scroll. Ink and color on silk.*

# The Nine Situations

*Sun Tzu said:*

### 1

The art of war recognizes nine varieties of ground: dispersive ground, facile ground, contentious ground, open ground, ground of intersecting highways, serious ground, difficult ground, hemmed-in ground, desperate ground.

### 2

When a chieftain is fighting in his own territory, it is dispersive ground.

### 3

When he has penetrated into hostile territory, but to no great distance, it is facile ground.

### 4

Ground the possession of which imports great advantage to either side is contentious ground.

### 5

Ground on which each side has liberty of movement is open ground.

### 6

Ground which forms the key to three contiguous states, so that he who occupies it first has most of the Empire at his command, is a ground of intersecting highways.

### 7

When an army has penetrated into the heart of a hostile country, leaving a number of fortified cities in its rear, it is serious ground.

### 8

Mountain forests, rugged steeps, marshes and wetlands— all country that is hard to traverse: this is difficult ground.

### 9

Ground which is reached through narrow gorges, and from which we can only retire by tortuous paths, so that a small number of the enemy would suffice to crush a large body of our men: this is hemmed-in ground.

### 10

Ground on which we can only be saved from destruction by fighting without delay is desperate ground.

### 11

On dispersive ground, therefore, fight not. On facile ground, halt not.

### 12

On contentious ground, attack not.

### 13

On open ground, do not try to block the enemy's way.

### 14

On the ground of intersecting highways, join hands with your allies. On serious ground, gather in plunder.

### 15

In difficult ground, keep steadily on the march. On hemmed-in ground, resort to stratagem. On desperate ground, fight.

### 16

Those who were called skillful leaders of old knew how to drive a wedge between the enemy's front and rear; to prevent cooperation between his large and small divisions; to hinder the good troops from rescuing the bad, the officers from rallying their men.

### 17

When the enemy's men were united, they managed to keep them in disorder.

### 18

When it was to their advantage, they made a forward move; when otherwise, they stopped still.

### 19

Regarding how to cope with a great host of the enemy in

orderly array and on the point of marching to the attack, begin by seizing something which your opponent holds dear; then he will be amenable to your will.

## 20

Rapidity is the essence of war: take advantage of the enemy's unreadiness, make your way by unexpected routes, and attack unguarded spots.

## 21

The following are the principles to be observed by an invading force: The farther you penetrate into a country, the greater will be the solidarity of your troops, and thus the defenders will not prevail against you.

## 22

Make forays in fertile country in order to supply your army with food.

## 23

Carefully study the well-being of your men, and do not overtax them. Concentrate your energy and hoard your strength. Keep your army continually on the move, and devise unfathomable plans.

## 24

Throw your soldiers into positions whence there is no escape, and they will prefer death to flight. If they will face death, there is nothing they may not achieve. Officers and men alike will put forth their uttermost strength. Soldiers when in desperate straits lose the sense of fear. If there is no place of refuge, they will stand firm. If they are in hostile country, they will show a stubborn front. If there is no help for it, they will fight hard.

## 25

Thus, without waiting to be marshaled, the soldiers will be constantly on the ready; without waiting to be asked, they will do your will; without restrictions, they will be faithful; without giving orders, they can be trusted.

## 26

Prohibit the taking of omens, and do away with superstitious doubts. Then, until death itself comes, no calamity need be feared. If our soldiers are not overburdened with money, it is not because they have a distaste for riches; if their lives are not unduly long, it is not because they are disinclined to longevity.

## 27

On the day they are ordered out to battle, your soldiers may weep, those sitting up bedewing their garments, and those lying down letting the tears run down their cheeks.

## 28

But let them once be brought to bay, and they will display the courage of a Chu or a Kuei.

## 29

The skillful tactician may be likened to the *shuai-jan*. Now the shuai-jan is a snake that is found in the Chung mountains. Strike at its head, and you will be attacked by its tail; strike at its tail, and you will be attacked by its head; strike at its middle, and you will be attacked by head and tail both.

## 30

Asked if an army can be made to imitate the shuai-jan, I should answer yes. For the men of Wu and the men of Yueh are enemies; yet if they are crossing a river in the same boat and are caught by a storm, they will come to each other's assistance just as the left hand helps the right.

## 31

Hence it is not enough to put one's trust in the tethering of horses, and the burying of chariot wheels in the ground

## 32

The principle on which to manage an army is to set up one standard of courage which all must reach. How to make the best of both strong and weak—that is a question involving the proper use of ground.

## 33

Thus the skillful general conducts his army just as though he were leading a single man, willy-nilly, by the hand.

## 34

It is the business of a general to be quiet and thus ensure secrecy; upright and just, and thus maintain order.

## 35

He must be able to mystify his officers and men by false reports and appearances, and thus keep them in total ignorance.

## 36

By altering his arrangements and changing his plans, he keeps the enemy without definite knowledge.

## 37

By shifting his camp and taking circuitous routes, he prevents the enemy from anticipating his purpose.

## 38

At the critical moment, the leader of an army acts like one who has climbed up a height and then kicks away the ladder behind him. He carries his men deep into hostile territory before he shows his hand.

## 39

He burns his boats and breaks his cooking pots; like a shepherd driving a flock of sheep, he drives his men this way and that, and no one knows whither he is going.

## 40

To muster his host and bring it into danger—this may be termed the business of the general.

## 41

The different measures suited to the nine varieties of ground; the expediency of aggressive or defensive tactics; and the fundamental laws of human nature: these are things that must most certainly be studied.

## 42

When invading hostile territory, the general principle is that penetrating deeply brings cohesion; penetrating but a short way means dispersion.

## 43

When you leave your own country behind, and take your army across neighboring territory, you find yourself on critical ground. When there are means of communication on all four sides, the ground is one of intersecting highways.

## 44

When you penetrate deeply into a country, it is serious ground. When you penetrate but a little way, it is facile ground.

## 45

When you have the enemy's strongholds on your rear, and narrow passes in front, it is hemmed-in ground. When there is no place of refuge at all, it is desperate ground.

*Disk with clouds. China. 1850–1940. Nephrite.*

*Opposite page: Mountain village. Zhang Zeduan. 12th century. China. Hanging scroll.*

*Dancer. China. 618–906. Molded clay.*

*Cicada. China. 206 BCE–220 CE. Nephrite.*

### 46

Therefore, on dispersive ground, I would inspire my men with unity of purpose. On facile ground, I would see that there is close connection between all parts of my army.

### 47

On contentious ground, I would hurry up my rear.

### 48

On open ground, I would keep a vigilant eye on my defenses. On ground of intersecting highways, I would consolidate my alliances.

### 49

On serious ground, I would try to ensure a continuous stream of supplies. On difficult ground, I would keep pushing on along the road.

### 50

On hemmed-in ground, I would block any way of retreat. On desperate ground, I would proclaim to my soldiers the hopelessness of saving their lives.

### 51

For it is the soldier's disposition to offer an obstinate resistance when surrounded, to fight hard when he cannot help himself, and to obey promptly when he has fallen into danger.

*Xiaoqikong bridge, on the main route from Libo, Guizhou province to Yunnan province in ancient times. China.*

### 52

We cannot enter into alliance with neighboring princes until we are acquainted with their designs. We are not fit to lead an army on the march unless we are familiar with the face of the country—its mountains and forests, its pitfalls and precipices, its marshes and swamps. We shall be unable to turn natural advantages to account unless we make use of local guides.

### 53

To be ignorant of any one of the following four or five principles does not befit a warlike prince.

### 54

When a warlike prince attacks a powerful state, his generalship shows itself in preventing the concentration of the enemy's forces. He overawes his opponents, and their allies are prevented from joining against him.

### 55

Hence he does not strive to ally himself with all and sundry, nor does he foster the power of other states. He carries out his own secret designs, keeping his antagonists in awe. Thus he is able to capture their cities and overthrow their kingdoms.

### 56

Bestow rewards without regard to rule, issue orders without regard to previous arrangements, and you will be able to handle a whole army as though you had to do with but a single man.

### 57

Confront your soldiers with the deed itself; never let them know your design. When the outlook is bright, bring it before their eyes; but tell them nothing when the situation is gloomy.

### 58

Place your army in deadly peril, and it will survive; plunge it into desperate straits, and it will come off in safety.

### 59

For it is precisely when a force has fallen into harm's way that it is capable of striking a blow for victory.

### 60

Success in warfare is gained by carefully accommodating ourselves to the enemy's purpose.

### 61

By persistently hanging on the enemy's flank, we shall succeed in the long run in killing the commander-in-chief.

### 62

This is called ability to accomplish a thing by sheer cunning.

### 63

On the day that you take up your command, block the frontier passes, destroy the official tallies, and stop the passage of all emissaries.

### 64

Be stern in the council chamber, so that you may control the situation.

### 65

If the enemy leaves a door open, you must rush in.

### 66

Forestall your opponent by seizing what he holds dear, and subtly contrive to time his arrival on the ground.

### 67

Walk in the path defined by rule, and accommodate yourself to the enemy until you can fight a decisive battle.

### 68

At first, then, exhibit the coyness of a maiden, until the enemy gives you an opening; afterwards emulate the rapidity of a running hare, and it will be too late for the enemy to oppose you.

*Tomb brick. China. 25–220 CE. Clay.*

# FROZEN IN TIME
## QIN'S TERRA-COTTA ARMY

King Zheng of Qin, the self-styled Shihuangdi, "first emperor," gave himself this title once he had unified China by conquering the states of Han, Zhao, Wei, Chu, Yan, and Qi. Shihuangdi, who had taken the throne in 246 BCE as just a boy, developed a centralized monarchy that depended largely on his personal drive to completely control all aspects of life. For instance, education in China was seen as a means to further government through training of future officials, and to that end, the writings of many scholars, as well as the scholars themselves, were burned to demonstrate the emperor's power. Local forms of currency were abolished, and their use was considered an act of treason.

Daily governmental management was also controlled by the First Emperor. He personally toured and inspected the country and ordered numerous stone tablets erected to proclaim his greatness. He required himself to read a specific number of documents daily and handle their related affairs. During his reign, he also sent a large contingent of young people out to sea to look for Peng Lai, a mythical land of immortality.

More than 700,000 of his subjects were required to work on building projects such as the Great Wall, royal palaces, canals, roads, and fortifications. These subjects, a combination of lawful citizens and penal laborers, were also used to construct tombs.

*Above: Close-up of head and shoulders of 2,000-year-old terra-cotta warrior near Xian in Shaanxi Province, China. Each head was modeled on an actual live soldier. This is part of the buried Terra-cotta Army discovered in 1974 at the imperial necropolis or tomb of the first emperor of the Qin dynasty, Qin Shi Huang.*
*Opposite page: Qin's Terra-cotta Army in Xian, China.*

The emperor's own tomb was a priority, and according to *The Records of the Historian*, he began building his mausoleum soon after his enthronement; it was not complete when he died at the age of fifty. *The Records of the Historian* also gives some detailed descriptions about the tomb. It was built underground, deep, solid, and lined with stones. Groundwater was blocked off by a vermilion stone wall, which made it waterproof. Treasures and jewels, along with palaces and burial places for high officials, were included in this underground museum. Oil candles burned twenty-four hours a day. Scenes of the heavens, mountains, and rivers decorated the ceiling and ground. A ditch around the tomb was filled with quicksilver (mercury) to look like a protective river, and for further protection, robbers and looters would be met with automatic hidden arrows. The door to the tomb was closed on craftsmen and builders as they completed a section, in order to maintain secrecy regarding the tomb's interior and contents. In addition to those workmen, palace maids who had no children were buried alive with the first emperor.

According to writers of the time, the mausoleum was initially the size of a man-made mountain, and it was roughly 200 feet high when it was discovered north of Lishan Mountain in a floodplain. To protect the mausoleum from water damage and flooding, the first emperor had workers divert the river south of the mausoleum to run northwest into the Weihe River in the north. It is surmised that Zhengzhuang village, northwest of the mausoleum, was a stone-processing site for the massive building project, because iron hammers, fetters, and semifinished stones have been found there.

The emperor's tomb was discovered in 1974 by peasants who were trying to dig a well. But before it could be excavated by archaeologists, the site was looted and then burned. The remaining artifacts represent a high level of ancient craftsmanship, skill, and extensive labor. An interior and an exterior city wall had been built around the tomb to protect it. The exterior city wall included a watchtower in each of its four corners. A door was built on each of the east, west, and south sides of both the outer and inner walls. Stone and ceramic waterways, tile ridges, a post stone, a door stone, and large eave tiles have been found, along with the ruins of city gates and buildings in what is believed to be the temple and palace grounds.

Life-size terra-cotta chariots, soldiers, horses, and weapons were unearthed in three burial pits. Each of the buried warriors and horses was apparently made not from a simple mold but created individually, as if each had a distinct personality. Facial expressions, facial details, and postures are unique. Their uniforms consist mainly of short robes with waistbands and leg wrappings, although some of the leaders wear armor, including helmets. Some of their robes still hold traces of color. Swords and arrowheads were found within the pits, and most of the warriors carry bows and quivers of arrows. The weapons were primarily made of both bronze and tin with a surface chromium treatment. The chromium made the weapons rustproof, and many were sharp and ready for battle at the time of their excavation. The horses, like the warriors, are also lifelike and true to size. They, too, were individually crafted and stand with their heads up, eyes wide open, and ears erect.

Three pits surround the mausoleum site, with one to its south and two to its north. The army faces east and is in full battle array, presumably to protect the underground imperial palace and the empire that Shihuangdi planned to rule in the afterlife. Apparently, as part of that plan, the pattern that

*Terra-cotta clay soldiers of Xian, China, in a full-standing formation.*

the tomb complex was designed to mirror was that of the capital city, Xianyan. Pit 3, believed to be the headquarters commanding pits 1 and 2, is U-shaped, and the front of the pit holds a canopied chariot with four armored figures wearing long hats. Here sixty-four armored guards are contained in each of the north and south side rooms. Pit 1, the largest excavation, is rectangular and consists of a long corridor and eleven compartments. Its thousands of warriors, chariots, and horses are lined up in a formation of thirty-eight columns. This pit also includes many weapons, such as spears, bronze swords, crossbows, arrowheads, bending knives, and a type of bronze weapon called a *tongyi*. Pit 2, shaped like a carpenter's square, contains soldiers of different types, such as cavalrymen, charioteers, infantrymen, and archers. These soldiers carry various weapons, including spears, axes, swords, dagger-axes, bows, crossbows, and halberds.

Burial pits for horses and figurines associated with horse raising were found on the east and west sides of the tomb wall. Inscriptions on a manger give proper feeding portions for the horses and the name of a stable. Horses, chariots, and their drivers were also found in passageways to the emperor's underground tomb. These passageways ran north, south, east, and west of the tomb. The figures found in the passageways are half the size of the figures found in the pits. Imperial chariots found in the passageways included security and high chariots. The security chariots preceded the high chariots and were manned by drivers sitting to the rear of the chariot. Drivers of the high chariots wore uniforms that included battle robes, swallowtail caps, and swords. Four horses were harnessed to each chariot, and each had a single shaft and double wheels. Some of the chariots were bronze, and some canopied versions were painted wood.

The Chinese government has built a museum for the Terra-cotta Army at the mausoleum of Shihuangdi to house the warriors, horses, chariots, and weapons that were created to eternally guard the first emperor.

# THE SILK ROAD
## CHINA'S CONNECTION TO THE WESTERN WORLD

*The Silk Road was a 5,000-mile-long trade route that linked China to Asia Minor and the Mediterranean.*

The Silk Road, a land and sea route of more than 5,000 miles, linked China to Asia Minor and the Mediterranean. It was actually not one road but a series of interconnected ancient trade routes designed to avoid the feared, deadly Taklimakan Desert located just southwest of the better-known Gobi Desert. Divided by the Taklimakan, Eastern and Western civilizations developed independently, and contact between the two was initiated only after Zhang Qian of the Han dynasty returned to China from a trip to northern India in 125 BCE. Because of this, Zhang Qian is considered by many scholars to be the father of the Silk Road.

Trading began in earnest when Emperor Wudi of the Han dynasty learned of the existence of the strong, tall Heavenly Horses of the West and sent several emissaries each year in an effort to gain as many as he could. After the Roman conquest of Egypt in 30 BCE, regular trade between India, Southeast Asia, China, the Middle East, Africa, and Europe grew on an unprecedented scale. Roman travelers penetrated deep into the East along the Silk Road, hoping to reduce the role of Parthian middlemen. Roman records dating to the reign of Emperor Augustus (27 to 14 BCE) include descriptions of the Seres (Chinese), who in turn brought goods into Rome.

The Golden Age of the Silk Road coincides with the dates for the Byzantine Empire in the West and the Yuan dynasty in the East. Sea trade expanded to include Alexandria, Egypt, and Guangzhou, China, and resulted in Roman trading posts in India. Along with this came the trading of ideas. The Silk Road allowed Nestorian, Manichaean, Buddhist, Christian, and Islamic religions into Central Asia and China. This influx not only influenced the people of China, but also resulted in the Khazar Federation, an early Mongol khanate in what is now Russia and later a part of the great empire of the Mongols, the first non-Chinese rulers of China.

The demand for Chinese products waned with the demise of the Roman Empire in the fifth century CE. Within several hundred years, Islam had expanded within Central Asia, and the battle of Talas in 751 effectively ended the Chinese drive into the West.

Between about 1215 and 1360, the Mongol Empire revived trade and reopened the Silk Road. This is the time during which Marco Polo documented his travels, and activity along the Silk Road exploded. However, the plague and the development of gunpowder helped spell the end around 1400. Europeans began then, as they still do today, to find other ways to reach China's rich resources.

*Riding camels at Mingsha Shan (Singing Sand Dunes) in Dunhuang, China.*

# The Attack by Fire

## 12

### Sun Tzu said:

**1**

There are five ways of attacking with fire. The first is to burn soldiers in their camp; the second is to burn stores; the third is to burn baggage trains; the fourth is to burn arsenals and magazines; the fifth is to hurl dropping fire amongst the enemy.

**2**

In order to carry out an attack, we must have means available.

**3**

The material for raising fire should always be kept in readiness.

**4**

There is a proper season for making attacks with fire, and special days for starting a conflagration.

**5**

The proper season is when the weather is very dry; the special days are those when the moon is in the constellations of the Sieve, the Wall, the Wing or the Cross-bar; for these four are all days of rising wind.

**6**

In attacking with fire, one should be prepared to meet five possible developments:

**7**

When fire breaks out inside the enemy's camp, respond at once with an attack from without. If there is an outbreak of fire, but the enemy's soldiers remain quiet, bide your time and do not attack.

**8**

When the force of the flames has reached its height, follow it up with an attack, if that is practicable; if not, stay where you are.

**9**

If it is possible to make an assault with fire from without, do not wait for it to break out within, but deliver your attack at a favorable moment.

**10**

When you start a fire, be windward of it. Do not attack from the leeward.

**11**

A wind that rises in the daytime lasts long, but a night breeze soon falls.

**12**

In every army, the five developments connected with fire must be known, the movements of the stars calculated, and a watch kept for the proper days.

**13**

Hence those who use fire as an aid to the attack show intelligence; those who use water as an aid to the attack gain an accession of strength.

**14**

By means of water, an enemy may be intercepted, but not robbed of all his belongings.

**15**

Unhappy is the fate of one who tries to win his battles and succeed in his attacks without cultivating the spirit of enterprise; for the result is waste of time and general stagnation.

**16**

Hence the saying: The enlightened ruler lays his plans well ahead; the good general cultivates his resources.

*A rare imperial cinnabar lacquer "Nine-Dragons" portable tea ceremony chest. China. 1735–1796 CE.*

### 17

Move not unless you see an advantage; use not your troops unless there is something to be gained; fight not unless the position is critical.

### 18

No ruler should put troops into the field merely to gratify his own spleen; no general should fight a battle simply out of pique. If it is to your advantage, make a forward move; if not, stay where you are. Anger may in time change to gladness; vexation may be succeeded by content. But a kingdom that has once been destroyed can never come again into being; nor can the dead ever be brought back to life.

### 19

Hence the enlightened ruler is heedful, and the good general full of caution. This is the way to keep a country at peace and an army intact.

*No ruler should put troops into the field merely to gratify his own spleen; no general should fight a battle simply out of pique. If it is to your advantage, make a forward move; if not, stay where you are. Anger may in time change to gladness; vexation may be succeeded by content. But a kingdom that has once been destroyed can never come again into being; nor can the dead ever be brought back to life.*

*Four horse heads from the Xian, China, terra-cotta warriors tomb containing more than 7,000 soldier figures, 130 chariots, and nearly 700 horses.*

# THE GREAT WALL
# A HISTORY OF THE LEGENDARY BARRIER

The Great Wall of China, stretching more than 4,000 miles, is the world's longest man-made structure. It is actually several walls, made of stone and earth and built between the fifth century BCE and the sixteenth century CE to protect the northern borders of the Chinese empire during the rule of successive dynasties.

During the Warring States period, when the wall was begun, several of the larger states tried to protect their

*Stretching over 4,000 miles, the Great Wall of China is the world's longest man-made structure.*

borders by building their own extensive walls, made mostly by stamping earth and gravel between board frames. With the establishment of the Qin dynasty in 221 BCE, these individual walls were superfluous and so were destroyed in favor of a larger and stronger wall that encompassed the new northern border with the Xiongnu, or the Huns.

Local resources were used whenever possible to speed the project along and to avoid the lengthy and difficult transportation of materials over very rough terrain. Stones from the highlands were used to build the wall over

mountain ranges, while rammed earth was used for construction in the plains. Many millions of Chinese must have labored on these walls over the years, and it is estimated that approximately one million peasants died working there. Archaeologists have unearthed remains buried inside the walls, leading to its designation as the "longest cemetery in the world."

Most of these walls have eroded so that very few sections remain, and there are no records showing the length of the Qin portion of the wall or the exact placement of the missing pieces. Later, the Han, Sui, Northern, and Jin dynasties all repaired, rebuilt, or expanded sections of the Great Wall. Following a defeat at the battle of Tumu in 1449 at the hands of the Oirats, the Ming dynasty resumed building the wall in order to further fortify their new northern border with the Mongols (who now controlled the Ordos Desert), by ringing the southern edge of the desert and crossing the Yellow River.

Construction techniques had advanced to the use of bricks and stone instead of rammed earth, with fortifications being especially strong around the cities—especially, the capital of Beijing. The size and weight of the bricks made them easier to work with than earth, and stone and bricks could bear more weight and last longer than rammed earth. Because stone was harder to work with but could hold up better than brick under its own weight, it was cut into rectangular shapes and used for the inner and outer foundations, the brims, and the gateways. The wall also has watchtowers at regular intervals, which were used for smoke signal communication to warn of enemy locations and movements, as well as to store weapons and house troops. Barracks and administrative centers are located at greater

*Preceding pages: The Great Wall of China.*
*Opposite page: The Great Wall of China, as viewed from a tower on a clear day.*

*The Great Wall of China. R. I. William Simpson (1823–1899). China. 1891.*
*Pencil and watercolor.*

its way along mountains from the southeast to the northwest for several miles. Among other examples, one of the most striking sections of the Ming portion of the wall is where it climbs extremely steep slopes (seven miles long, sixteen to twenty-six feet high, ninteen feet across its base, and sixteen feet across the top). Near the eastern extremity of the wall is the so-called Number One Pass Under Heaven, the first pass of the Great Wall to be built on the Shanhaiguan and the first mountain it climbs. The only bridge section of the wall, called the Jiumenkou, is here as well. The Shanhaiguan section is called the Museum of the Construction of the Great Wall because of the Meng Jiang-Nu Temple built here during the Song dynasty.

intervals. Estimates state that more than one million men guarded the Ming portion of the wall after its completion, while two to three million died building it.

In 1644, the Great Wall was breached with the help of a disgruntled Ming general, Wu Sangui, who opened the gates at Shanhaiguan to allow the Manchu army access to Beijing. The Ming were quickly defeated, and the Qing dynasty began. The Qing soon annexed the Mongolians to the north, and so the wall, no longer used as the border, fell into disrepair. Attention was then given to the south, where the Maio threatened, and a wall was begun to keep out the barbarians coming from that direction.

Since the Great Wall was such a huge undertaking spanning many centuries, many of the older sections are now eroding quickly, and much has been lost completely. It's estimated that almost forty miles of the wall in Gansu province will disappear over the next twenty years because of erosion and sandstorms. While portions of the wall are preserved near large cities and tourist centers, others are disappearing from lack of maintenance, vandalism, use of the bricks and stones for other building projects, or just because the wall has been in the way of new construction.

The most popular sections are well preserved and even reconstructed in places around Beijing, notably, the North Pass of Juyongguon, known as the Badaling, which is made of stone and bricks from the hills (twenty-five feet high and sixteen feet wide), and the Mutianyu section of the wall, near Jinshanling, which winds

Claims that the Great Wall is visible from the moon were made even before space flight began. Considering that the Great Wall is the same color as its surroundings, the possiblity of its being visible to the human eye from such a great height is unlikely. Neil Armstrong, aboard *Apollo 11*, stated that there was no man-made object that he could see with his own eyes. Leroy Chiao, a Chinese-American astronaut, once took a photograph from the International Space Station that supposedly shows the wall. It was so indistinct that he was not certain he had actually captured it. The China *Daily* later reported that the Great Wall can be seen from space—if one knows exactly where to look.

*End of the Great Wall of China—Xinjiang Province near Jiayuguan.*

# BEIJING
# THE FORBIDDEN CITY

*The Forbidden City was the Chinese imperial palace from the mid-Ming dynasty to the end of the Qing dynasty. Located in the middle of Beijing, it now houses the Palace Museum.*

During the Warring States period (ca. 480 to 221 BCE), the capital of the state of Yan was established in present-day Beijing and was known as Ji. Beijing became the capital of the Jin dynasty in 1153 CE. It was home to approximately one million people when it was sacked by Genghis Khan's Mongol army in 1215. The Mongols, under the leadership of Kublai Khan, later established their capital there. The founder of the Ming dynasty, Zhu Yuanzhang, gained control of Beijing in 1368, but he retained Nanjing as his capital. The later ruler Chengzu moved the main capital from Nanjing back to Beijing.

The Forbidden City was the name given to the main hall of the imperial palace. Entrance was allowed only by permission of the emperor. The first Westerner to visit the Forbidden City was Italian Jesuit Matteo Ricci. At the time of his visit in 1601, Ricci would have seen hallways paved with golden bricks, marble dragons' heads, and other intricate details. The Forbidden City was the center of the Imperial City, which was the center of the government district; in turn, the Imperial City was the center of Beijing.

By 1553, Beijing covered about four square miles. The Great Wall was fortified to protect the city during this time. In 1644, the armies of the rebel Li Zicheng sacked Beijing, and the Ming emperor committed suicide. But the rebels abandoned the city to the Manchus. In another coup a half-

century later, British and French troops looted and destroyed the Summer Palace.

Following the establishment of the Chinese Republic, civil wars dictated that the city change hands repeatedly throughout 1911 and 1912. Beijing shared its status as the center of government with Guangzhou and Hankou from 1912 to 1927. The name was changed to Beiping, or "northern peace," in 1928, with the transfer of the seat of government to Nanjing. The city was again made the capital following the Japanese occupation in 1937, but it was restored to Chinese sovereignty after World War II, in 1946. Communists retained it as the capital and in 1949 restored Beijing as its name.

*Forbidden City dragon statue.*

# The Use of Spies

*Sun Tzu said:*

## 1

Raising a host of a hundred thousand men and marching them great distances entails heavy loss on the people and a drain on the resources of the State. The daily expenditure will amount to a thousand ounces of silver. There will be commotion at home and abroad, and men will drop down exhausted on the highways. As many as seven hundred thousand families will be impeded in their labor.

## 2

Hostile armies may face each other for years, striving for the victory which is decided in a single day. This being so, to remain in ignorance of the enemy's condition simply because one grudges the outlay of a hundred ounces of silver in honors and emoluments, is the height of inhumanity. One who acts thus is no leader of men, no present help to his sovereign, no master of victory.

## 3

Thus, what enables the wise sovereign and the good general to strike and conquer, and achieve things beyond the reach of ordinary men, is foreknowledge.

## 4

Now this foreknowledge cannot be elicited from spirits; it cannot be obtained inductively from experience, nor by any deductive calculation. Knowledge of the enemy's dispositions can only be obtained from other men.

## 5

Hence the use of spies, of whom there are five classes: (1) Local spies; (2) inward spies; (3) converted spies; (4) doomed spies; (5) surviving spies.

## 6

When these five kinds of spy are all at work, none can discover the secret system. This is called "divine manipulation of the threads." It is the sovereign's most precious faculty.

## 7

Having local spies means employing the services of the inhabitants of a district.

## 8

Having inward spies means making use of officials of the enemy.

## 9

Having converted spies means getting hold of the enemy's spies and using them for our own purposes.

## 10

Having doomed spies means doing certain things openly for purposes of deception, and allowing our spies to know of them and report them to the enemy.

## 11

Surviving spies, finally, are those who bring back news from the enemy's camp.

## 12

Hence it is that more intimate relations to be maintained with spies than with the remainder of the army. None should be more liberally rewarded. In no other business should greater secrecy be preserved.

## 13

Spies cannot be usefully employed without a certain intuitive sagacity. They cannot be properly managed without benevolence and straightforwardness. Without subtle ingenuity of mind, one cannot make certain of the truth of their reports.

## 14

Be subtle! be subtle! and use your spies for every kind of business.

*Opposite page: Mask, one of a pair. China. 771–255 BCE. Bronze.*

### 15

If a secret piece of news is divulged by a spy before the time is ripe, he must be put to death together with the man to whom the secret was told.

### 16

Whether the object be to crush an army, to storm a city, or to assassinate an individual, it is always necessary to begin by finding out the names of the attendants, the aides-de-camp, and doorkeepers and sentries of the general in command. Our spies must be commissioned to ascertain these.

### 17

The enemy's spies who have come to spy on us must be sought out, tempted with bribes, led away, and comfortably housed. Thus they will become converted spies and available for our service.

### 18

It is through the information brought by the converted spy that we are able to acquire and employ local and inward spies.

### 19

It is owing to his information, again, that we can cause the doomed spy to carry false tidings to the enemy.

### 20

Lastly, it is by his information that the surviving spy can be used on appointed occasions.

### 21

The end and aim of spying in all its five varieties is knowledge of the enemy; and this knowledge can only be derived, in the first instance, from the converted spy. Hence it is essential that the converted spy be treated with the utmost liberality.

### 22

Of old, the rise of the Yin dynasty was due to I Zhi, who had served under the Xia. Likewise, the rise of the Zou dynasty was due to Lu Ya, who had served under the Yin.

### 23

Hence, it is only the enlightened ruler and the wise general who will use the highest intelligence of the army for purposes of spying and thereby achieve great results. Spies are a most important element in water, because on them depends an army's ability to move.

*Warrior. China. 200–317. Bronze.*

*The enemy's spies who have come to spy on us must be sought out, tempted with bribes, led away, and comfortably housed. Thus they will become converted spies and available for our service.*

# THE INFLUENCE OF CHINA ON KOREA AND JAPAN

China's geographical proximity to Korea and Japan has allowed many Chinese influences to spread to both countries. These influences originated in a wide spectrum of daily life in China, including government, religion, art, communication, finances, family relationships, food, and the arts. Trade, political envoys, student travelers, colonization, and military conflicts among the three nations helped foster the exchange of information, symbols, and thought processes.

Evidence of the influence of the ancient Chinese systems of land division can be seen in present-day Japan, where field lines of the gridiron division system can still be traced along with ancient place-names. The ancient Japanese capital cities of Nara and Kyoto also incorporated urban Chinese design in their layouts.

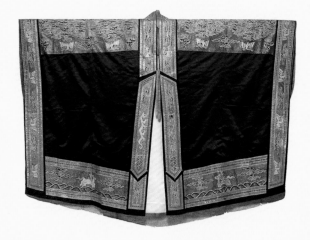

*Taoist ceremonial robe. China. 1644–1700. Silk with gold thread.*

Rice, probably introduced to Korea and Japan from the Yangtze River delta area of southern China, developed into one of the most important features of Japanese Yayoi culture. Throughout the history of the three nations, rice has been an important crop and can be found in many long-standing cultural traditions.

During the Korean period of the Three Kingdoms, Chinese and Indian medical practices were adopted in Korea. Medical texts from that time to the present reveal a continuing integration of Chinese medicinal theory and Korean herbal remedies, a diffusion of information that has spread to Japan as well.

Chinese colonies were established in the northern part of the Korean peninsula beginning in 108 BCE. These colonies acted as a conduit for Chinese culture into Korea and subsequently Japan, which is known as Wo in the Chinese chronicle of the Han dynasty. The chronicle explains the relationship between Japan and Lo-lang, one of the Chinese colonies in Korea: "In the seas off Lo-lang lie the people of Wo, who are divided into more than one hundred states, and who bring tribute at fixed intervals." This early reference is followed by many more that describe emissaries, trade exchange, and travel among the Chinese colonies in Korea and Japan.

Literature and writing in Korea and Japan were also strongly influenced by the introduction of the Chinese writing system. Until Chinese characters were first used, about the fourth century CE, Japan had no written system. Throughout its history, Korean literature was written in the native tongue and also in classical Chinese, and Korean government service required philosophical understanding of the Chinese classics. The complicated Chinese characters were only used by the educated classes of Korea and thus restricted commoners from reading and writing. In the fifteenth century, Chinese writing was supplemented by a native Korean alphabet, the *hangul*, which was developed by the Korean king Sejong the Great.

Between 421 and 478 CE, the Japanese Yamato court dispatched some ten embassies to the Chinese Southern Song dynasty. At the time, the Paekche Korean kingdom continually requested assistance from Yamato to defend itself against attacks from the other two Korean kingdoms, Koguryo and Silla. Iron was then a plentiful resource in Korea and may have been an important motivating factor for Yamato's involvement in Korean affairs during this time.

Buddhism was imported to China from Afghanistan, India, and Myanmar (Burma). Respect for ancestors and filial piety are ideas that transformed Chinese society and likewise affected both Korea and Japan, particularly in the ceremonies the Japanese hold to ensure the salvation of ancestors. Different forms of Buddhism continued to spread from China into Korean and Japanese society. For instance, two Japanese Buddhist monks, Saicho and Kukai, were sent by Emperor Kammu to China to study in the eighth century. The new sects of Japanese Buddhism that were established upon their return then became the main Buddhist sects in Japan, with Saicho founding the Tendai sect and Kukai founding the Kukai sect.

During the ninth century, iconographic pictures and previously unknown scriptures were brought to Japan from Buddhist monks traveling to China. The Chinese Tang dynasty influenced the Buddhist sculpture and paintings of Japan, and Japanese scholars and aristocracy demonstrated Chinese customs in their writing and in their daily lives.

The Chinese Tang dynasty system of governmental structure (*lu-ling*) was imitated in Japan with the *ritsuryo* system, its name coming from a combination of the words for criminal code (*ritsu*) and administrative and civil codes

*Lobed box with a scene of making tea. China. 1400–1500.*

(*ryo*). Many of the original lu-ling articles were incorporated into the Japanese ritsuryo system, but adaptations were made to customize the system to the needs of the Japanese. One of these changes concerned the role of the emperor. The emperors of China and Japan ruled their respective countries as absolute monarchs heading bureaucracies. Japan's emperor, however, simultaneously held the role and responsibility of high priest in discerning the will of the deities and paying tribute to them. Japan's adapted system, therefore, allowed for parallel government agencies in the form of the state council (*dajokan*) and the deities office (*jingikan*). Dajokan primarily headed the country's administration, while jingikan was the bureaucracy for deity worship. The final form of this Japanese system was known as the Yoro Code of 718.

During the tenth-century reign of Prime Minister Kiyomori, trade with the Song dynasty was encouraged. Chinese copper coins circulated in local Japanese markets, and Japan experienced the introduction of neo-Confucianism and Zen Buddhism from China. Confucian political and ethical thought was commonly found in religious texts and commentaries in Korea and Japan.

During the twelfth century, southeastern Korea became home to settlements begun by Japanese traders. Among those two countries and China, an exchange of practical goods and philosophical ideas ensured a similar intertwining of the arts, and Chinese influences in art and architecture can be well demonstrated by works of that particular period. Certain pottery skills and the monochromatic painting style were popular in Japan during this time, and luminous plain white porcelain vessels were favored by both the Chinese and Korean aristocracy. Prized more as precious ceremonial works of art than practical pieces were Japanese weapons, which were based on those that the Chinese had developed during the Bronze Age, especially swords and spears. A purer amalgamation was the architecture of Japanese Buddhist temples, which illustrates a blend of native Japanese and Chinese Zen styles.

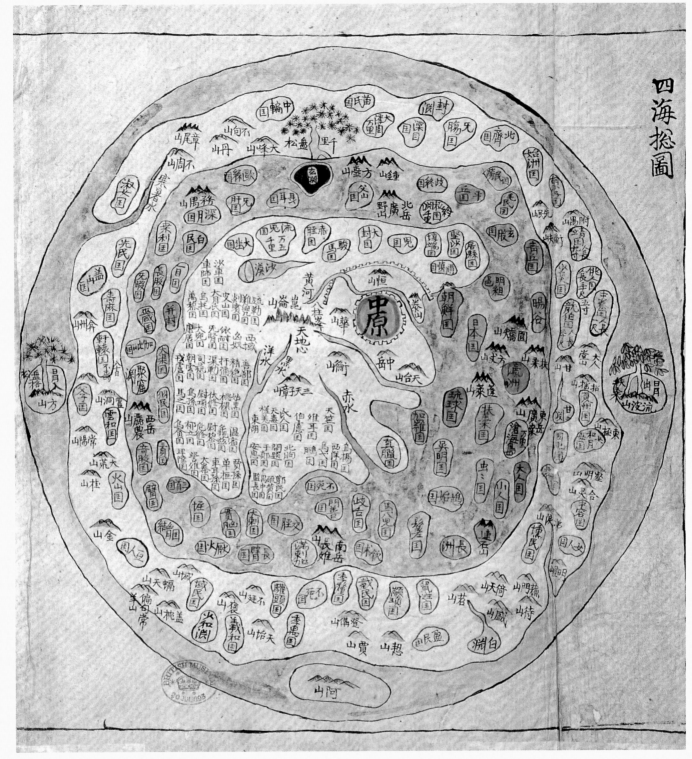

四海捴圖

*A Korean world map, printed and hand-colored, from an atlas of Korea with preliminary maps of the world, China, Japan, and Ryuku islands. Sino Korean world map. Korea. 19th century. Hand-colored print.*

As something approaching another kind of art form, the custom of tea drinking was introduced to Japan during the twelfth century and would come to greatly affect everyday life. At first practiced only by the aristocracy and the warrior classes, the tea ceremony soon became a highly cultivated ritual for all social strata.

The Chinese heavily influenced Korea and Japan, and Chinese culture absorbed numerous Korean and Japanese elements of daily life. By simple geographical closeness, the three countries have come to share integral parts of their respective world views.

# Bushido

## Inazo Nitobe

# CONTENTS

*Preceeding pages: The Story of the Archer Nasu no Yoichi, from The Tale of the Heike. Japan. 1650–1700. Six-panel folding screen, one of a pair. Ink, color, and gold on paper.*
*Opposite page: The Aoigaoka Falls in the Eastern Capital, from the series A Journey to the Waterfalls of All the Provinces. Katsushika Hokusai (1760–1849). Oban Tate-e.*

## Preface to the Tenth and Revised Edition

Since its first publication in Philadelphia, more than six years ago, this little book has had an unexpected history. The Japanese reprint has passed through eight editions, the present thus being its tenth appearance in the English language. Simultaneously with this will be issued an American and English edition, through the publishing house of Messrs. George H. Putnam's Sons, of New York.

In the meantime, *Bushido* has been translated into Mahratti by Mr. Dev of Khandesh, into German by Fräulein Kaufmann of Hamburg, into Bohemian by Mr. Hora of Chicago, into Polish by the Society of Science and Life in Lemberg—although this Polish edition has been censured by the Russian government. It is now being rendered into Norwegian and into French. A Chinese translation is under contemplation. A Russian officer, now a prisoner in Japan, has a manuscript in Russian ready for the press. A part of the volume has been brought before the Hungarian public, and a detailed review, almost amounting to a commentary, has been published in Japanese. Full scholarly notes for the help of younger students have been compiled by my friend Mr. H. Sakurai, to whom I also owe much for his aid in other ways.

I have been more than gratified to feel that my humble work has found sympathetic readers in widely separated circles, showing that the subject matter is of some interest to the world at large. Exceedingly flattering is the news that has reached me from official sources, that President Roosevelt has done it undeserved honor by reading it and distributing several dozens of copies among his friends.

In making emendations and additions for the present edition, I have largely confined them to concrete examples. I still continue to regret, as I indeed have never ceased to do, my inability to add a chapter on Filial piety, which is considered one of the two wheels of the chariot of Japanese ethics—loyalty being the other. My inability is due rather to my ignorance of the Western sentiment in regard to this particular virtue, than to ignorance of our own attitude toward it, and I cannot draw comparisons satisfying to my own mind. I hope one day to enlarge upon this and other topics at some length. All the subjects that are touched upon in these pages are capable of further amplification and discussion; but I do not now see my way clear to make this volume larger than it is.

This preface would be incomplete and unjust, if I were to omit the debt I owe to my wife for her reading of the proof-sheets, for helpful suggestions, and, above all, for her constant encouragement.

## INTRODUCTION

At the request of his publishers, to whom Dr. Nitobe has left some freedom of action concerning prefatory matter, I am glad to offer a few sentences of introduction to this new edition of *Bushido*, for readers of English everywhere. I have been acquainted with the author for over fifteen years, indeed, but, in a measure at least, with his subject during forty-five years.

It was in 1860, in Philadelphia (where, in 1847, I saw the *Susquehanna*, Commodore Perry's flagship launched), that I looked on my first Japanese and met members of the Embassy from Yedo. I was mightily impressed with these strangers, to whom *Bushido* was a living code of ideals and manners. Later, during three years at Rutgers College, New Brunswick, N.J., I was among scores of young men from Nippon, whom I taught or knew as fellow-students. I found that Bushido, about which we often talked, was a superbly winsome thing. As illustrated in the lives of these future governors, diplomatists, admirals, educators, and bankers, yes, even in the dying hours of more than one who "fell on sleep" in Willow Grove Cemetery, the perfume of this most fragrant flower of far-off Japan was very sweet. Never shall I forget how the dying samurai lad, Kusakabe, when invited to the noblest of services and the greatest of hopes, made answer: "Even if I could know your Master, Jesus, I should not offer Him only the dregs of a life." So, "on the banks of the old Raritan," in athletic sports, in merry jokes at the supper table when contrasting things Japanese and Yankee, and in the discussion of ethics and ideals, I felt quite willing to take the "covert missionary retort," about which my friend Charles Dudley Warner once wrote. At some points, codes of ethics and proprieties differed, but rather in dots or tangents than as occupation or eclipse. As their own poet wrote—was it a thousand years ago?—when in crossing a moor the dew-laden flowers brushed by his robe left their glittering drops on his brocade, "On account of its perfume, I brush not this moisture from my sleeve." Indeed, I was glad to get out of ruts, which are said to differ from graves only by their length. For, is not comparison the life of science and culture? Is it not true that, in the study of languages, ethics, religions, and codes of manners, "he who knows but one knows none"?

Called, in 1870, to Japan as pioneer educator to introduce the methods and spirit of the American public-school system, how glad I was to leave the capital, and at Fukui, in the province of Echizen, see pure feudalism in operation! There I looked on Bushido, not as an exotic, but in its native soil. In daily life I realized that Bushido, with its cha-no-yu, ju-jutsu, ("jiu-jutsu") hara-kiri, polite prostrations on the mats and genuflections on the street, rules of the sword and road, all leisurely salutations and politest molds of speech, canons of art and conduct, as well as heroisms for wife, maid, and child, formed the universal creed and praxis of all the gentry in the castled city and province. In it, as a living school of thought and life, girl and boy alike were trained. What Dr. Nitobe received as an inheritance, had breathed into his nostrils, and writes about so gracefully and forcibly with such grasp, insight, and breadth of view, I saw. Japanese feudalism "died without the sight" of its ablest exponent and most convincing defender. To him it is as wafted fragrance. To me it was "the plant and flower of light."

Hence, living under and being in at the death of feudalism, the body of Bushido, I can bear witness to the essential truth of Dr. Nitobe's descriptions, so far as they go, and to the faithfulness of his analysis and generalizations. He has limned with masterly art and reproduced the coloring of the picture which a thousand years of Japanese literature reflects so gloriously. The Knightly Code grew up during a millennium of evolution, and our author lovingly notes the blooms that have starred the path trodden by millions of noble souls, his countrymen.

Critical study has but deepened my own sense of the potency and value of Bushido to the nation. He who would understand twentieth-century Japan must know something of its roots in the soil of the past. Even if now as invisible to the present generation in Nippon as to the alien, the philosophic student reads the results of today in the stored energies of ages gone. The sunbeams of unrecorded time have laid the strata out of which Japan now digs her foot-pounds of impact for war or peace. All the spiritual senses are keen in those nursed by Bushido. The crystalline lump has dissolved in the sweetened cup, but the delicacy of the flavor remains to cheer. In a word, Bushido has obeyed the higher law enunciated by One whom its own exponent salutes and confesses his Master—"Except a grain of corn die, it abideth alone; but if it die it bringeth forth much fruit."

Has Dr. Nitobe idealized Bushido? Rather, we ask, how could he help doing so? He calls himself "defendant." In all creeds, cults, and systems, while the ideal grows, exemplars and exponents vary. Gradual cumulation and slow attainment of harmony is the law. Bushido never reached a final goal. It was too much alive, and it died at last only in its splendor and strength. The clash of the world's movement—for so we name the rush of influences and events which followed Perry and Harris—with feudalism in Japan, did not find Bushido an embalmed mummy, but a living soul. What it really met was the quickening spirit of humanity. Then the less was blessed of the greater. Without losing the best in her own history and civilization, Japan, following her own noble precedents, first adopted and then adapted the choicest the world had to offer. Thus her

opportunity to bless Asia and the race became unique, and grandly she has embraced it—"in diffusion ever more intense." Today, not only are our gardens, our art, our homes enriched by the flowers, the pictures, and the pretty things of Japan, whether "trifles of a moment or triumphs for all time," but in physical culture, in public hygiene, in lessons for peace and war, Japan has come to us with her hands gift-laden.

Not only in his discourse as advocate and counsel for the defense, but as prophet and wise householder, rich in things new and old, our author is able to teach us. No man in Japan has united the precepts and practice of his own Bushido more harmoniously in life and toil, labor and work, craft of hand and of pen, culture of the soil and of the soul. Illuminator of Dai Nippon's past, Dr. Nitobe is a true maker of the New Japan. In Formosa, the empire's new accretion, as in Kioto, he is the scholar and practical man, at home in newest science and most ancient diligence.

This little book on Bushido is more than a weighty message to the Anglo-Saxon nations. It is a notable contribution to the solution of this century's grandest problem—the reconciliation and unity of the East and the West. There were of old many civilizations: in the better world coming there will be one. Already the terms "Orient" and "Occident," with all their freight of mutual ignorance and insolence, are ready to pass away. As the efficient middle term between the wisdom and communism of Asia and the energy and individualism of Europe and America, Japan is already working with resistless power.

Instructed in things ancient and modern and cultured in the literatures of the world, Dr. Nitobe herein shows himself admirably fitted for a congenial task. He is a true interpreter and reconciler. He need not and does not apologize for his own attitude toward the Master whom he has long loyally followed. What scholar, familiar with the ways of the Spirit and with the history of the race as led by man's Infinite Friend, but must in all religions put difference between the teachings of the Founder and the original documents and the ethnic, rationalistic, and ecclesiastical additions and accretions? The doctrine of the testaments, hinted at in the author's preface, is the teaching of Him who came not to destroy, but to fulfill. Even in Japan, Christianity, unwrapped from its foreign mold and matting, will cease being an exotic and strike its roots deep in the soil on which Bushido has grown. Stripped alike of its swaddling bands and its foreign regimentals, the church of the Founder will be as native as the air.

William Elliot Griffis Ithaca, May 1905

*Above: Tsuba. Edo period.*

# Bushido as an Ethical System

Chivalry is a flower no less indigenous to the soil of Japan than its emblem, the cherry blossom; nor is it a dried-up specimen of an antique virtue preserved in the herbarium of our history. It is still a living object of power and beauty among us; and if it assumes no tangible shape or form, it not the less scents the moral atmosphere, and makes us aware that we are still under its potent spell. The conditions of society which brought it forth and nourished it have long disappeared; but as those far-off stars which once were and are not, still continue to shed their rays upon us, so the light of chivalry, which was a child of feudalism, still illuminates our moral path, surviving its mother institution. It is a pleasure to me to reflect upon this subject in the language of Burke, who uttered the well-known touching eulogy over the neglected bier of its European prototype.

It argues a sad defect of information concerning the Far East, when so erudite a scholar as Dr. George Miller did not hesitate to affirm that chivalry, or any other similar institution, has never existed either among the nations of antiquity or among the modern Orientals.[1] Such ignorance, however, is amply excusable, as the third edition of the good Doctor's work appeared the same year that Commodore Perry was knocking at the portals of our exclusivism. More than a decade later, about the time that our feudalism was in the last throes of existence, Carl Marx, writing his *Capital*, called the attention of his readers to the peculiar advantage of studying the social and political institutions of feudalism, as then to be seen in living form only in Japan. I would likewise invite the Western historical and ethical student to the study of chivalry in the Japan of the present.

Enticing as is a historical disquisition on the comparison between European and Japanese feudalism and chivalry, it is not the purpose of this paper to enter into it at length. My attempt is rather to relate, firstly, the origin and sources of our chivalry; secondly, its character and teaching; thirdly, its influence among the masses; and,

fourthly, the continuity and permanence of its influence. Of these several points, the first will be only brief and cursory, or else I should have to take my readers into the devious paths of our national history; the second will be dwelt upon at greater length, as being most likely to interest students of International Ethics and Comparative Ethology in our ways of thought and action; and the rest will be dealt with as corollaries.

The Japanese word which I have roughly rendered Chivalry, is, in the original, more expressive than Horsemanship. *Bu-shi-do* means literally Military-Knight-Ways—the ways which fighting nobles should observe in their daily life as well as in their vocation; in a word, the "Precepts of Knighthood," the noblesse oblige of the warrior class. Having thus given its literal significance, I may be allowed henceforth to use the word in the original. The use of the original term is also advisable for this reason, that a teaching so circumscribed and unique, engendering a cast of mind and character so peculiar, so local, must wear the badge of its singularity on its face; then, some words have a national timbre so expressive of race characteristics that the best of translators can do them but scant justice, not to say positive injustice and grievance. Who can improve by translation what the German "Gemüth" signifies, or who does not feel the difference between the two words verbally so closely allied as the English gentleman and the French *gentilhomme*?

Bushido, then, is the code of moral principles which the knights were required or instructed to observe. It is not a written code; at best it consists of a few maxims handed down from mouth to mouth or coming from the pen of some well-known warrior or savant. More frequently it is a code unuttered and unwritten, possessing all the more the powerful sanction of veritable deed, and of a law written on the fleshly tablets of the heart. It was founded not on the creation of one brain, however able, or on the life of a single personage, however renowned. It was an organic growth of decades and centuries of military career. It, perhaps, fills the same position in the history of ethics that the English Constitution does in political history; yet it has had nothing to compare with the Magna Carta or the

*Full-face mask. Japan. 1615–1650. Iron and lacquer.*

*December, 1904*

*To my beloved uncle
Tokitoshi Ota
who taught me to
revere the past
and
to admire the deeds of
the samurai
I dedicate
this little book.*

Habeas Corpus Act. True, early in the seventeenth century Military Statutes (Buké Hatto) were promulgated; but their thirteen short articles were taken up mostly with marriages, castles, leagues, etc., and didactic regulations were but meagerly touched upon. We cannot, therefore, point out any definite time and place and say, "Here is its fountain head." Only as it attains consciousness in the feudal age, its origin, in respect to time, may be identified with feudalism. But feudalism itself is woven of many threads, and Bushido shares its intricate nature. As in England the political institutions of feudalism may be said to date from the Norman Conquest, so we may say that in Japan its rise was simultaneous with the ascendency of Yoritomo, late in the twelfth century. As, however, in England, we find the social elements of feudalism far back in the period previous to William the Conqueror, so, too, the germs of feudalism in Japan had been long existent before the period I have mentioned.

Again, in Japan as in Europe, when feudalism was formally inaugurated, the professional class of warriors naturally came into prominence. These were known as *samurai*, meaning literally, like the old English *cniht* (knecht, knight), guards, or attendants—resembling in character the *soldurii* whom Caesar mentioned as existing in Aquitania, or the *comitati*, who, according to Tacitus, followed Germanic chiefs in his time; or, to take a still later parallel, the *milites medii* that one reads about in the history of Medieval Europe. A Sinico-Japanese word *Bu-ké* or *Bu-shi* (Fighting Knights) was also adopted in common use. They were a privileged class, and must originally have been a rough breed who made fighting their vocation. This class was naturally recruited, in a long period of constant warfare, from the manliest and the most adventurous, and all the while the process of elimination went on, the timid and the feeble being sorted out, and only "a rude race, all masculine, with brutish strength," to borrow Emerson's phrase, surviving to form families and the ranks of the samurai. Coming to profess great honor and great privileges, and correspondingly great responsibilities, they soon felt the need of a common standard of behavior, especially as they were always on a belligerent footing and belonged to different clans. Just as physicians limit competition among themselves by professional courtesy, just as lawyers sit in courts of honor in cases of violated etiquette, so must

also warriors possess some resort for final judgment on their misdemeanors.

Fair play in fight! What fertile germs of morality lie in this primitive sense of savagery and childhood. Is it not the root of all military and civic virtues? We smile (as if we had outgrown it!) at the boyish desire of the small Britisher, Tom Brown, "to leave behind him the name of a fellow who never bullied a little boy or turned his back on a big one." And yet, who does not know that this desire is the cornerstone on which moral structures of mighty dimensions can be reared? May I not go even so far as to say that the gentlest and most peace-loving of religions endorses this aspiration? This desire of Tom's is the basis on which the greatness of England is largely built, and it will not take us long to discover that Bushido does not stand on a lesser pedestal. If fighting in itself, be it offensive or defensive, is, as Quakers rightly testify, brutal and wrong, we can still say with Lessing, "We know from what failings our virtue springs."[2] "Sneaks" and "cowards" are epithets of the worst opprobrium to healthy, simple natures. Childhood begins life with these notions, and knighthood also; but, as life grows larger and its relations many-sided, the early faith seeks sanction from higher authority and more rational sources for its own justification, satisfaction, and development. If military interests had operated alone, without higher moral support, how far short of chivalry would the ideal of knighthood have fallen! In Europe, Christianity, interpreted with concessions convenient to chivalry, infused it nevertheless with spiritual data. "Religion, war, and glory were the three souls of a perfect Christian knight," says Lamartine. In Japan there were several sources of Bushido.

1 *History Philosophically Illustrated*, (3rd Ed. 1853), Vol. II, p.
2 Ruskin was one of the most gentle-hearted and peace-loving men that ever lived. Yet he believed in war with all the fervor of a worshipper of the strenuous life. "When I tell you," he says in the *Crown of Wild Olive*, "that war is the foundation of all the arts, I mean also that it is the foundation of all the high virtues and faculties of men. It is very strange to me to discover this, and very dreadful, but I saw it to be quite an undeniable fact....I found, in brief, that all great nations learned their truth of word and strength of thought in war; that they were nourished in war and wasted by peace, taught by war and deceived by peace; trained by war and betrayed by peace; in a word, that they were born in war and expired in peace."

# INAZO NITOBE
## REVERENCE FOR THE PAST AND HOPE FOR THE FUTURE

Born at the cusp of Japan's transformation from feudalism to modernization, Inazo Nitobe became his country's leading ambassador at the turn of the nineteenth century. As an educator, he influenced a generation; as an advisor, he helped usher his homeland into a new era; as an internationalist, he was Japan's face to the West, demonstrating a fascination with other cultures balanced with a deep love for his own.

Nitobe was born in 1862, the third son of a prominent Japanese family in Morioka, the castle town of Nanbu, which, at the time, was the largest of the several hundred semi-independent states. His father and grandfather were upper-level civil servants, and Nitobe was intended to assume a similar level of responsibility. During his early childhood, the caste-based feudal system was ordered to an end, and the emperor assumed supreme power in a new central government. Around that same time, seven-year-old Nitobe moved to Tokyo to become the ward and heir of his uncle, Tokitoshi Ota.

Although the age of the samurai was officially over, the feudal system faded away only over time. Nitobe always believed that its culture defined Japan, and that his country could only be understood by knowing *bushido*, the samurai's code of chivalry.

His higher education began at Sapporo Agricultural College, now Hokkaido University, which was modeled after the America land-grant colleges. Seemingly, since most of the instructors were American, Nitobe and several fellow students became Christians, perhaps influenced by the school's founding vice president, Dr. William S. Clark of Massachusetts. Going on to study at Tokyo Imperial University, Nitobe was energetic and ambitious, and at the age of only twenty-one, he told one professor that his goal was "to be a bridge across the Pacific."

He took a step toward that goal the next year, when he went to Baltimore, Maryland, to study at Johns Hopkins University, where he met Woodrow Wilson. Equally important was his introduction to Mary Elkinton, the member of a prominent Quaker family, and his joining the Quakers in 1886. The two would later marry despite the objections of both his and her families.

When he had completed his studies, Nitobe was offered a professorship at Sapporo University, on the condition that he first earn a doctorate degree. To comply, he went to Germany, where he studied at several institutions before receiving his degree from the University of Halle in 1890. Now fluent in German as well as English, Nitobe returned to the United States to marry, then he and his new wife moved to Hokkaido for his teaching position.

One of Nitobe's biographers characterizes the next six years as "a flurry of activity," including teaching, religious activities, establishing schools for working students, government consulting, and even overseeing dormitories. However, the intensity took its toll, and by 1897, he was too ill to continue working, and he resigned his post. Instead, he and Mary moved to California, where Nitobe wrote *Bushido: The Soul of Japan*. It was written in English, Nitobe said, as a response to questions from his wife and friends about Japanese ideas and customs. "I found that without understanding feudalism and bushido, the moral ideas of present Japan are a sealed volume." The book established Nitobe's reputation in the West. Just five years after its publication in 1900, it was in its tenth edition and had been translated into several languages.

*Nitobe and Mary Elkinton in Philadelphia on their wedding day in 1891.*

# Sources of Bushido

I may begin with Buddhism. It furnished a sense of calm trust in Fate, a quiet submission to the inevitable, that stoic composure in sight of danger or calamity, that disdain of life and friendliness with death. A foremost teacher of swordsmanship, when he saw his pupil master the utmost of his art, told him, "Beyond this my instruction must give way to Zen teaching." "Zen" is the Japanese equivalent for the Dhyâna, which "represents human effort to reach through meditation zones of thought beyond the range of verbal expression."[3] Its method is contemplation, and its purport, as far as I understand it, to be convinced of a principle that underlies all phenomena, and, if it can, of the Absolute itself, and thus to put oneself in harmony with this Absolute. Thus defined, the teaching was more than the dogma of a sect, and whoever attains to the perception of the Absolute raises himself above mundane things and awakes "to a new Heaven and a new Earth."

What Buddhism failed to give, Shintoism offered in abundance. Such loyalty to the sovereign, such reverence for ancestral memory, and such filial piety as are not taught by any other creed, were inculcated by the Shinto doctrines, imparting passivity to the otherwise arrogant character of the samurai. Shinto theology has no place for the dogma of "original sin." On the contrary, it believes in the innate goodness and Godlike purity of the human soul, adoring it as the adytum from which divine oracles are proclaimed. Everybody has observed that the Shinto shrines are conspicuously devoid of objects and instruments of worship, and that a plain mirror hung in the sanctuary forms the essential part of its furnishing. The presence of this article is easy to explain: it typifies the human heart, which, when perfectly placid and clear, reflects the very image of the Deity. When you stand, therefore, in front of the shrine to worship, you see your own image reflected on its shining surface, and the act of worship is tantamount to the old Delphic injunction, "Know Thyself." But self-knowledge does not imply, either in the Greek or Japanese teaching, knowledge of the

*Opposite page: The Shinto gate leading to the shrine in Miyajima, Japan.*

physical part of man, not his anatomy or his psycho-physics; knowledge was to be of a moral kind, the introspection of our moral nature. Mommsen, comparing the Greek and the Roman, says that when the former worshiped he raised his eyes to heaven, for his prayer was contemplation, while the latter veiled his head, for his was reflection. Essentially like the Roman conception of religion, our reflection brought into prominence not so much the moral as the national consciousness of the individual. Its nature-worship endeared the country to our inmost souls, while its ancestor-worship, tracing from lineage to lineage, made the Imperial family the fountainhead of the whole nation. To us the country is more than land and soil from which to mine gold or to reap grain—it is the sacred abode of the gods, the spirits of our forefathers: to us the Emperor is more than the Arch Constable of a Rechtsstaat, or even the Patron of a Culturstaat—he is the bodily representative of Heaven on earth, blending in his person its power and its mercy. If what M. Boutmy[4] says is true of English royalty—that it "is not only the image of authority, but the author and symbol of national unity," as I believe it to be, doubly and trebly may this be affirmed of royalty in Japan.

The tenets of Shintoism cover the two predominating features of the emotional life of our race—Patriotism and Loyalty. Arthur May Knapp very truly says: "In Hebrew literature it is often difficult to tell whether the writer is speaking of God or of the Commonwealth; of heaven or of Jerusalem; of the Messiah or of the nation itself."[5] A similar confusion may be noticed in the nomenclature of our national faith. I said confusion, because it will be so deemed by a logical intellect on account of its verbal ambiguity; still, being a framework of national instinct and race feelings, Shintoism never pretends to a systematic philosophy or a rational theology. This religion—or, is it not more correct to say, the race emotions which this religion expressed?—thoroughly imbued Bushido with loyalty to the sovereign and love of country. These acted more as impulses than as doctrines; for Shintoism, unlike the Medieval Christian Church, prescribed to its votaries

*The setting for a peaceful Japanese tea ceremony.*

scarcely any credenda, furnishing them at the same time with agenda of a straightforward and simple type.

As to strictly ethical doctrines, the teachings of Confucius were the most prolific source of Bushido. His enunciation of the five moral relations between master and servant (the governing and the governed), father and son, husband and wife, older and younger brother, and between friend and friend, was but a confirmation of what the race instinct had recognized before his writings were introduced from China. The calm, benignant, and worldly wise character of his politico-ethical precepts was particularly well suited to the samurai, who formed the ruling class. His aristocratic and conservative tone was well adapted to the requirements of these warrior statesmen. Next to Confucius, Mencius exercised an immense authority over Bushido. His forcible and often quite democratic theories were exceedingly taking to sympathetic natures, and they were even thought dangerous to, and subversive of, the existing social order, hence his works were for a long time under censure. Still, the words of this master mind found permanent lodgment in the heart of the samurai.

The writings of Confucius and Mencius formed the principal textbooks for youths and the highest authority in discussion among the old. A mere acquaintance with the classics of these two sages was held, however, in no high esteem. A common proverb ridicules one who has only an intellectual knowledge of Confucius, as a man ever studious but ignorant of *Analects*. A typical samurai calls a literary savant a book-smelling sot. Another compares learning to an ill-smelling vegetable that must be boiled and boiled before it is fit for use. A man who has read a little smells a little pedantic, and a man who has read much smells yet more so; both are alike unpleasant. The writer meant thereby that knowledge becomes really such only when it is assimilated in the mind of the learner and shows in his character. An intellectual specialist was considered a machine. Intellect itself was considered subordinate to ethical emotion. Man and the universe were conceived to be alike spiritual and ethical. Bushido could not accept the judgment of Huxley, that the cosmic process was unmoral.

Bushido made light of knowledge as such. It was not pursued as an end in itself, but as a means to the attainment of wisdom. Hence, he who stopped short of this end was regarded no higher than a convenient machine, which could turn out poems and maxims at bidding. Thus, knowledge was conceived as identical with its practical application in life; and this Socratic doctrine found its greatest exponent in the

Chinese philosopher, Wan Yang Ming, who never wearies of repeating, "To know and to act are one and the same."

I beg leave for a moment's digression while I am on this subject, inasmuch as some of the noblest types of bushi were strongly influenced by the teachings of this sage. Western readers will easily recognize in his writings many parallels to the New Testament. Making allowance for the terms peculiar to either teaching, the passage, "Seek ye first the kingdom of God and his righteousness; and all these things shall be added unto you," conveys a thought that may be found on almost any page of Wan Yang Ming. A Japanese disciple[6] of his says—"The lord of heaven and earth, of all living beings, dwelling in the heart of man, becomes his mind (Kokoro); hence a mind is a living thing, and is ever luminous," and again, "The spiritual light of our essential being is pure, and is not affected by the will of man. Spontaneously springing up in our mind, it shows what is right and wrong: it is then called conscience; it is even the light that proceedeth from the god of heaven." How very much do these words sound like some passages from Isaac Pennington or other philosophic mystics! I am inclined to think that the Japanese mind, as expressed in the simple tenets of the Shinto religion, was particularly open to the reception of Yang Ming's precepts. He carried his doctrine of the infallibility of conscience to extreme transcendentalism, attributing to it the faculty to perceive, not only the distinction between right and wrong, but also the nature of psychical facts and physical phenomena. He went as far as, if not farther than, Berkeley and Fichte in Idealism, denying the existence of things outside of human ken. If his system had all the logical errors charged to Solipsism, it had all the efficacy of strong conviction and its moral import in developing individuality of character and equanimity of temper cannot be gainsaid.

Thus, whatever the sources, the essential principles which Bushido imbibed from them and assimilated to itself, were few and simple. Few and simple as these were, they were sufficient to furnish a safe conduct of life even through the unsafest days of the most unsettled period of our nation's history. The wholesome, unsophisticated nature of our warrior ancestors derived ample food for their spirit from a sheaf of commonplace and fragmentary teachings, gleaned as it were on the highways and byways of ancient thought, and, stimulated by the demands of the age, formed from these gleanings anew and unique type of manhood. An acute

French savant, M. de la Mazelière, thus sums up his impressions of the sixteenth century: "Toward the middle of the sixteenth century, all is confusion in Japan, in the government, in society, in the church. But the civil wars, the manners returning to barbarism, the necessity for each to execute justice for himself, these formed men comparable to those Italians of the sixteenth century, in whom Taine praises 'the vigorous initiative, the habit of sudden resolutions and desperate undertakings, the grand capacity to do and to suffer.' In Japan as in Italy 'the rude manners of the Middle Ages made of man a superb animal, wholly militant and wholly resistant.' And this is why the sixteenth century displays in the highest degree the principal quality of the Japanese race, that great diversity which one finds there between minds (*esprits*) as well as between temperaments. While in India and even in China men seem to differ chiefly in degree of energy or intelligence, in Japan they differ by originality of character as well. Now, individuality is the sign of superior races and of civilizations already developed. If we make use of an expression dear to Nietzsche, we might say that in Asia, to speak of humanity is to speak of its plains; in Japan as in Europe, one represents it above all by its mountains."

To the pervading characteristics of the men of whom M. de la Mazelière writes, let us now address ourselves. I shall begin with Rectitude.

3 Lafcadio Hearn, *Exotics and Retrospectives*, p. 84.
4 *The English People*, p. 188.
5 *Feudal and Modern Japan*, Vol. I, p. 183.
6 Miwa Shissai.

*Zen pebble garden in Kyoto, Japan.*

# SETTING THE STAGE
## THE PREHISTORY OF SHOGUNATE JAPAN

Emperor Jimmu, the first ruler of the Land of the Luxuriant Rice Fields, claimed an impressive pedigree. One of his great-grandmothers was Ryujin, goddess of the sea. And one of his great-great-great-grandmothers was Amaterasu, goddess of the sun, who was born out of the left eye of the god of creation, Izanagi. That divine heritage could explain why Jimmu was able to live to the age of 126. In the 1860s, Japanese historians determined that they had pinned down the exact date that Jimmu founded the country: February 11, 660 BCE. Today, that date is celebrated as the holiday *kenkoku kinen no hi*, or National Foundation Day, and the emperor sitting on the Chrysanthemum Throne claims to be the descendant of Jimmu.

Japan first appeared in historical records around 300 BCE, when Chinese scribes cited a mysterious land called *Wa*. The character that the Chinese used to write Wa meant "stunted" or "dwarfed," perhaps a reference to the short-statured Jomon people who originally settled Japan. Although the Jomon were overrun by the taller Yayoi who came from China and Korea, the name stuck. By 57 BCE, shortly before Julius Caesar invaded Britain, emissaries from Wa were visiting China, and soon the scribes were giving more details of the land's geography and history. Wa eventually came to refer specifically to the kingdom of Yamato, which occupied the central and western regions of Japan.

One of the first Japanese rulers that the Chinese mentioned by name was a queen called Himiko, who reportedly ruled with magic and sorcery, bewitching her subjects. According to the Chinese, Himiko had 1,000 women as her aides but only one man, who served her meals and communicated with her subjects. She lived in a grand, heavily guarded palace surrounded by stockades. In the year 238 CE, Himiko sent her brother as an ambassador to the court of the Chinese Emperor Cao Rui; her gifts to the emperor included ten slaves and a pair of twenty-foot swathes of decorated fabric.

"You live very far across the sea, yet you have sent an emissary with tribute," Cao Rui acknowledged. "We greatly

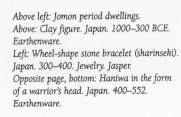

between their subjects and the kami, the Chinese notion that Himiko ruled by magic is not far-fetched.

Over the centuries that followed, the rulers of Yamato did their best to create peace and harmony between the clans. In the early seventh century, Prince Shotoku drafted one of the world's first constitutions and formalized the bureaucracy along Confucian lines, with promotions based on intellectual merit rather than mere favoritism. In the late seventh century, Empress Jito initiated a taxation system. Thirty years later, Empress Gensho organized the Japanese legal system and enacted a set of laws and codes known as the *Yoro ritsuryo*, which would remain in effect for ten more centuries, until the Meiji reforms of the 1860s.

As Yamato grew in strength, its leaders became more assertive against the patronizing attitude of their huge rival across the Western Sea. Under Prince Shotoku, the rulers of Yamato began writing the word Wa with a Chinese character that meant "harmony" or "peace" instead of "stunted." And they began referring to their country as Nihon, or the Land of the Rising Sun, as a contrast to China, which they referred to as the Land of the Setting Sun. In Chinese, the characters that the Japanese use for *Nihon* are pronounced as "jih-pen," which is how Westerners derived the English equivalent of Japan.

But despite the best efforts of the emperors and empresses to unify the land, Japan remained torn between rival clans, which often only paid lip service to the royal house while jockeying or jostling for power. Through vast periods of Japanese history, the emperor was often the pawn of one clan or another. The emperor ruled as a symbolic and spiritual leader, but political control rested in the hands of the predominant clan. This power vacuum left room for a new kind of leader: the shogun.

appreciate your loyalty and filial piety." Some historians link Himiko to the legendary Empress Jingu, the fourteenth ruler after Jimmu. Jingu, the first of nine women to rule the land, is said to have led a successful invasion of the Korean peninsula at the beginning of her reign.

At that time and for most of the centuries that followed, Yamato was a rural society, an unorganized collection of rice-farming villages dominated by feudal clans who were loosely overseen by the emperors and empresses. The chief religion, which has since become known as Shinto, revolved around the worship of *kami*, spirits that could inhabit anything on earth: people, animals, trees, oceans, or mountains. Since the early emperors of Yamato were shamanlike intercessors

*Above left: Jomon period dwellings.*
*Above: Clay figure. Japan. 1000–300 BCE. Earthenware.*
*Left: Wheel-shape stone bracelet (sharinseki). Japan. 300–400. Jewelry. Jasper.*
*Opposite page, bottom: Haniwa in the form of a warrior's head. Japan. 400–552. Earthenware.*

# THE SHOGUNATE
## GAINING CONTROL OF JAPAN

In 794 CE, six years before Charlemagne was crowned Holy Roman Emperor in Europe, Emperor Kammu of Japan was mounting a new effort to expand his borders into the lands of the Emishi, a nomadic people occupying a portion of the main Japanese island of Honshu.

For centuries, the rulers of Japan had clashed with the Emishi, who were referred to as "the eastern barbarians." In the island's mountainous woodlands, the Emishi's horseback guerilla raiders easily outmaneuvered the disciplined phalanxes of the imperial army. To crush the

Emishi, Kammu tried forcing men into the army, but that sparked a peasant revolt, and many young men disguised themselves as Buddhist priests to dodge the draft.

Nevertheless, Kammu believed that, as a "son of heaven," it was his duty to subdue the Emishi. That year, he appointed two generals to handle the task: Otomo Otomaro and Sakanoue Tamuramaro. Because this was no ordinary assignment, he bestowed on each of them a new title: *sei i tai shogun*, "great general who subdues the eastern barbarians." And thus the two men entered history as Japan's first known shoguns. *Sei i tai shogun* would remain the full title of the position throughout Japanese history, long after the Emishi were vanquished. As shogun—a word composed of two Japanese characters, *sho*, "commander," and *gun*, "military"—Tamuramaro used innovative techniques to fight the Emishi. Among other things, he ordered giant lanterns to be placed on top of the highest hills. When the Emish approached the lanterns out of curiosity, he ambushed them. Using such guerilla tactics, he penetrated deep into Emishi territory. The concept of the shogun lost momentum after Kammu's death in 806 CE, and the title was largely abandoned for more than three centuries. When it was revived, it launched an entirely new era in Japanese history.

On July 20, 1156, Emperor Toba died in the capital of Kyoto, leaving two of his sons to fight for his throne. The eldest son, Sutoku, gained the support of the Minamoto clan, which was one of the country's most powerful families. But the fourth-eldest son, Go-Shirakawa, was backed by the rival Taira clan. The dispute tore families apart. Even though the Minamoto clan leader, Tameyoshi, backed Sutoku, Tameyoshi's son Yoshitomo sided with Go-Shirakawa.

Within a week of the emperor's burial, the two factions were battling with each other in Kyoto. In a surprise nighttime attack, Go-Shirakawa's samurai warriors mounted a cavalry charge on Sutoku's palace. At first, the assault was repelled by relentless volleys of arrows. But then the attackers set fire to the palace, forcing Sutoku's samurai warriors into a hasty retreat.

The victorious Go-Shirakawa was soon enthroned as emperor. He quickly exiled his older brother Sutoku and sentenced Tameyoshi to death. In a cruel twist, the victors ordered Tameyoshi's son Yoshitomo to prove his loyalty by carrying out the death sentence. Yoshitomo refused; he could not bring himself to kill his father. Instead, an officer of the Minamoto clan, who did not want his leader to die at the hands of a Taira, ran his sword through Tameyoshi and then committed suicide.

Over the next several years, Yoshitomo brooded over his father's death. Finally, he saw a chance for revenge. In early 1160, when most members of the Taira clan had left Kyoto on a mass pilgrimage, Yoshitomo and his followers attacked the imperial palace and seized Go-Shirakawa as their hostage. But their coup was short-lived. When the Taira clan returned to Kyoto, they attacked the rebels with 3,000 mounted samurai. Yoshitomo was killed by a turncoat as he tried to escape. Most of his children were executed, but his thirteen-year-old son, Yoritomo, was allowed to live in exile, thanks to the pleadings of the matriarch of the Taira clan, who thought he resembled a son that she had lost in infancy.

Having crushed their opponents, the Taira took control of the kingdom. For the first time in history, Japan was under the control of samurai warlords, with the emperor serving as a severely weakened figurehead. In 1180, the Taira finally decided to depose Go-Shirakawa and install their own emperor: the two-year-old grandson of the clan's chieftain. In desperation, Go-Shirakawa sought help from Yoritomo, who by then had established his own heavily fortified fiefdom in Kamakura, a fishing village nearly 300 miles from Kyoto.

Emerging from exile, Yoritomo not only fought the Taira but also members of his own clan who had challenged his leadership. With an army of 25,000 men, he defeated the Taira in a series of battles and chased them out of Kyoto. The last skirmish was an intense naval battle in 1185, when a flotilla of Yoritomo's war junks sank the Taira fleet. Preferring death to capture, the grandmother of the young emperor, who was onboard one of the ships, seized him and jumped into the sea, where they both drowned.

In gratitude for Yoritomo's assistance, Go-Shirakawa named him sei i tai shogun. But by then, Yoritomo had little respect for the emperor or for his role in Japanese society. When Go-Shirakawa died in 1192, Yoritomo, as the most powerful military leader of the nation, appointed a teenage royal named Go-Toba as emperor, though in name only. While Go-Toba practiced calligraphy, painting, and poetry in the imperial palace in Kyoto, Yoritomo ruled the country from his home in Kamakura. By the age of eighteen, Go-Toba felt so irrelevant that he abdicated, allowing his two-year-old son to take the throne. Yoritomo, meanwhile, was living up to his powerful motto: "Wield power in fact, but never in name."

Yoritomo's reign as shogun set the tone for the next seven centuries of Japanese history. The emperors retained control of civil matters: appointment of bureaucrats, collection of taxes, and enactment of laws. But all military power belonged to the shoguns.

*Opposite page: Shogun touring in spring. Japan. Edo Period. Ink on paper.*

# A TIMELINE FOR SHOGUNATE JAPAN

In Japanese, the term *bakufu*, "tent office," once referred simply to the accommodations that military commanders used when they rode off into battle. But once the era of the shogun began, *bakufu* came to refer to the militaristic system of government that, in English, is usually translated as "shogunate." The shoguns held power in Japan for 800 years, an era that spanned the reign of Richard the Lionheart through the United States Civil War in the West. Below are key shougnates of that period.

## Kamakura Shogunate (1192 to 1333)

Minamoto Yoritomo, or Yoritomo of the Minamoto clan, established his stronghold in the city of Kamakura as the first bakufu in 1192. Although the emperor remained in Kyoto, the power shifted to the shogun's headquarters in Kamakura. Although Kamakura was a relatively small fishing village when Yoritomo first arrived, within the next fifty years it would grow into the fourth-largest city in the world, with more than 200,000 people.

Yoritomo set the precedent that a shogun must come from the Minamoto clan. For nearly 700 years, all of Japan's shoguns were required to prove descent from the Minamoto, although some did it with the aid of forged genealogy papers. After Yoritomo's death in 1199, his eighteen-year-old son, Yoriiye, took the title of shogun, but he was more interested in pursuing physical pleasure than in ruling the country. In 1204, Yoriiye's maternal grandfather, Tokimasa, the head of the Hojo clan, ordered his assassination and that of his younger brother. After their deaths, the Hojo family took power in Kamakura, serving as regents for the Minamoto shoguns, who were essentially their puppets. The rule of the Hojo regents lasted more than a century.

## Kemmu Restoration (1333 to 1336)

By the early fourteenth century, the Kamakura shogunate was stained by corruption and greed. In 1331, Emperor Go-Daigo launched a war to unseat the shogun in Kamakura. Although he was unsuccessful at first, his luck changed when a leading member of the Hojo clan, Ashikaga Takauji,

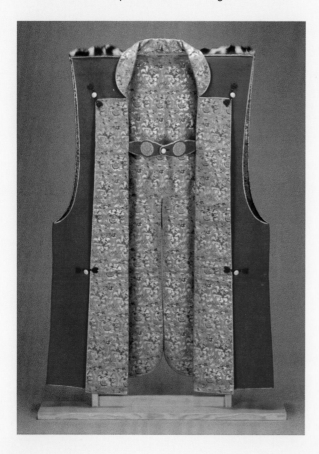

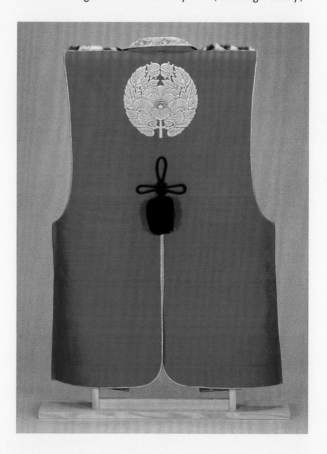

came to his aid in hopes of being named shogun. In 1333, Go-Daigo's forces set fire to Kamakura, ending the Hojo regency. The shogun retreated to his cemetery and committed suicide, together with all the members of his family and 800 of his soldiers. After the battle was over, Go-Daigo appointed his son Morinaga as shogun. But the ambitious Takauji planted false rumors that Morinaga was plotting to overthrow his father. When Morinaga was exiled to Kamakura and then later killed, Takauji declared himself to be shogun, initiating more than two centuries of reign by the Ashikaga family.

## Ashikaga Shogunate (1336 to 1573)

With Kamakura largely in ruins, Takauji established his shogunate in Kyoto, where he imprisoned Go-Daigo and installed Komyo, a son of a former emperor, in his place. Two years later, Go-Daigo disguised himself as a woman and escaped from his captivity, setting up an alternate imperial court in the southern mountains of Yoshino. The first fifty years of the Ashikaga shogunate was marked by rivalry between the northern (Kyoto) and southern (Yoshino) emperors.

Because of the division of the empire, at least in part, the Ashikaga shoguns were much weaker than their Kamakura predecessors. They increasingly relied on local lords, the *daimyo*, to enforce their will. As the decades passed, the daimyo began fighting among themselves for greater power. By 1467, their infighting broke into full-scale civil war, initiating an era known as *sengoku jidai*. The Ashikaga were incapable of quelling the violence. Instead, it took a trio of powerful daimyo—Oda Nobunaga, Toyotomi Hideyoshi, and Tokugawa Ieyasu—to reestablish order.

## Rule of the Daimyo (1573 to 1603)

Oda Nobunaga was an audacious young daimyo who had a reputation for acting foolish, but only until he was on the battlefield. By the age of twenty-five in 1559, he had united the Owari province in central Japan under his leadership. The next year, he used trickery to defeat an army nearly ten times the size of his own. Yoshimoto, a leader of

the Imawari clan, brought 25,000 troops into Owari, hoping to tame the upstart. But Nobunaga fooled him into thinking he had a much larger army, setting up a huge encampment of straw soldiers in his path. In the meantime, Nobunaga circled around the Imawari forces with 3,000 men. In a surprise attack, his forces were able to defeat the unprepared enemy and kill Yoshimoto. After that battle, many Imawari partisans came to Nobunaga's side, including the young samurai Matsudaira Motoyasu, who would later be known as Tokugawa Ieyasu.

By 1573, Nobunaga had abolished the power structure that had supported the shogun and was well on his way to uniting Japan, when a trusted general, Akechi Mitsuhide, turned against him. In 1582, Mitsuhide led his troops in a surprise attack against Nobunaga when he was protected only by his servants and bodyguards. After his defeat, Nobunaga was forced to commit suicide. Two weeks later, Mitsuhide was killed in battle against Toyotomi Hideyoshi, a foot soldier who had risen to be one of Nobunaga's top generals. In less than a decade, Hideyoshi had accomplished Nobunaga's goal of unifying Japan, and the emperor had named him regent. After Hideyoshi's death in 1598, his young son Hideyori succeeded him but was quickly replaced by Tokugawa Ieyasu.

## Tokugawa Shogunate (1603 to 1867)

When Tokugawa Ieyasu took power in 1600, he established the previously obscure town of Edo, now Tokyo, as his capital. In 1603, using forged papers to show that he had Minamoto ancestors, he received the title of shogun. During the remainder of his life, he assumed an increasing amount of power, controlling not only the military complex but also foreign policy and the feudal patronage system. His family held the shogunate until 1867, when the last Tokugawa shogun ceded his authority to Emperor Meiji.

*Above: Japanese pattern used in samurai family crests, or mon.*
*Opposite page: Campaign coat. Japan. 1700–1868. Brocade, wool, and fur with ivory buttons.*

# Rectitude or Justice

Here is the most cogent precept in the code of the samurai. Nothing is more loathsome to him than underhand dealings and crooked undertakings. The conception of Rectitude may be erroneous—it may be narrow. A well-known bushi defines it as a power of resolution—"Rectitude is the power of deciding upon a certain course of conduct in accordance with reason, without wavering—to die when it is right to die, to strike when to strike is right." Another speaks of it in the following terms: "Rectitude is the bone that gives firmness and stature. As without bones the head cannot rest on the top of the spine, nor hands move nor feet stand, so without rectitude neither talent nor learning can make of a human frame a samurai. With it the lack of accomplishments is as nothing." Mencius calls Benevolence man's mind, and Rectitude or Righteousness his path. "How lamentable," he exclaims, "is it to neglect the path and not pursue it, to lose the mind and not know to seek it again! When men's fowls and dogs are lost, they know to seek for them again, but they lose their mind and do not know to seek for it." Have we not here "as in a glass darkly" a parable propounded three hundred years later in another clime and by a greater Teacher, who called Himself the Way of Righteousness, through whom the lost could be found? But I stray from my point. Righteousness, according to Mencius, is a straight and narrow path which a man ought to take to regain the lost paradise.

Even in the latter days of feudalism, when the long continuance of peace brought leisure into the life of the warrior class, and with it dissipations of all kinds and gentle accomplishments, the epithet Gishi (a man of rectitude) was considered superior to any name that signified mastery of learning or art. The Forty-seven Faithfuls—of whom so much is made in our popular education—are known in common parlance as the Forty-seven Gishi.

In times when cunning artifice was liable to pass for military tact and downright falsehood for *ruse de guerre*, this manly virtue, frank and honest, was a jewel that shone the brightest and was most highly praised. Rectitude is a twin brother to Valor, another martial virtue. But before proceeding to speak of Valor, let me linger a little while on what I may term a derivation from Rectitude, which, at first deviating slightly from its original, became more and more removed from it, until its meaning was perverted in the popular acceptance. I speak of *Giri*, literally the Right Reason, but which came in time to mean a vague sense of duty which public opinion expected an incumbent to fulfill. In its original and unalloyed sense, it meant duty, pure and simple—hence, we speak of the Giri we owe to parents, to superiors, to inferiors, to society at large, and so forth. In these instances Giri is duty; for what else is duty than what Right Reason demands and commands us to do. Should not Right Reason be our categorical imperative?

Giri primarily meant no more than duty, and I dare say its etymology was derived from the fact that in our conduct, say to our parents, though love should be the only motive, lacking that, there must be some other authority to enforce filial piety; and they formulated this authority in Giri. Very rightly did they formulate this authority—Giri—since if love does not rush to deeds of virtue, recourse must be had to man's intellect and his reason must be quickened to convince him of the necessity of acting aright. The same is true of any other moral obligation. The instant Duty becomes onerous; Right Reason steps in to prevent our shirking it. Giri thus understood is a severe taskmaster, with a birch-rod in his hand to make sluggards perform their part. It is a secondary power in ethics; as a motive it is infinitely inferior to the Christian doctrine of love, which should be the law. I deem it a product of the conditions of an artificial society—of a society in which accident of birth and unmerited favor instituted class distinctions, in which the family was the social unit, in which seniority of age was of more account than superiority of talents, in which natural affections had often to succumb before arbitrary man-made customs. Because of this very artificiality, Giri in time degenerated into a vague sense of propriety called up to explain this and sanction that—as, for example, why a mother must, if need be, sacrifice all her other children in order to save the first-born; or why a daughter must sell her chastity to get funds to pay for the

*Above: Tsuba. Japan. Edo period.*

*Left: Actor Matsumoto Koshiro V as Kudo Toraemon Kudosuke. Toyokuni Utagawa (1786–1865). Japan. 19th century. Woodblock print.*

father's dissipation, and the like. Starting as Right Reason, Giri has, in my opinion, often stooped to casuistry. It has even degenerated into cowardly fear of censure. I might say of Giri what Scott wrote of patriotism, that "as it is the fairest, so it is often the most suspicious, mask of other feelings." Carried beyond or below Right Reason, Giri became a monstrous misnomer. It harbored under its wings every sort of sophistry and hypocrisy. It would have been easily turned into a nest of cowardice, if Bushido had not a keen and correct sense of courage, the spirit of daring and bearing.

# THE RISE OF THE SAMURAI

In 702 CE, the Japanese imperial court decided to adopt a bureaucratic structure of government that had been used in China for more than 1,000 years. The Taiho ("Great Treasure") Code established twelve ranks of officials, each divided into two subranks, with the upper rank representing the top advisors to the emperor.

The lesser officials in the lower six ranks, who conducted the mundane day-to-day affairs of the empire, were referred to as *saburapi*, "those who serve." Over the centuries, the pronunciation of the word *saburapi* evolved into *saburai* and finally into *samurai*. And "those who serve" evolved from lowly civil servants into the aristocratic leaders of the powerful clans that would come to dominate Japan.

The arming of the samurai began within several hundred years after the adoption of the Taiho Code. At that time, the emperor and his provincial lords were trying to squeeze onerous taxes from the peasantry. The tax collectors who ventured out into the countryside were sometimes attacked by angry mobs of peasants or robbed by gangs of thieves. To ensure that the revenues made it into the government's coffers, some of the saburapi were trained in martial arts and assigned to work as bodyguards for the taxmen. They did the job so well that many eventually became taxmen themselves, a lucrative position that brought them both wealth and power.

By the twelfth century, the word *saburai* had become almost interchangeable with the word *bushi*, "warrior." Already, these warriors and their clans were gaining control of the provincial governments, shoving aside or marrying into the aristocratic families who once ruled them. The samurai created their own aristocracy, headed by samurai lords known as *daimyo*, "great names," and by the mid-twelfth century, the leader of the Taira clan had established the first samurai-dominated central government, relegating the emperor to the status of figurehead. Thirty years later, the leading daimyo of the Minamoto clan earned the title of shogun, establishing that clan as the rightful successor to the shogunate and initiating a period of nearly eight centuries in which shoguns typically held more authority than the emperor.

As the samurai gained power, they were expected to be much more than warriors. Like their contemporaries, the knights of medieval Europe, they were expected to be cultured and educated and live up to a chivalric code. Ideally, the samurai were supposed to be as adept at art, poetry, music, and dance as at battling their enemies. The phrase *bun bu ryo do*, "the pen and the sword are as one," stressed the importance of writing skills, with fine calligraphy being particularly valued. It was thought that by learning the graceful use of a pen, the warriors would gain a greater appreciation for the sense of balance needed on the battlefield.

Not all samurai lived up to these ideals. Many, if not most, were semiliterates who relied on their brute strength rather than their wits. But the notion of an ideal samurai warrior took hold in the cultural imagination. During the thirteenth century, the *Tale of the Heike* romanticized the samurai in the same way that Chrétien de Troyes had idealized the legend of Sir Lancelot a few decades before. *The Tale of the Heike* is the novelized history of the rivalry between the Taira (also known as Heike) and Minamoto clans in their fight to gain control of the country. It is a tale of greed, honor, betrayal, and chivalry, involving treacherous villains and tragically noble warriors. Most of all, the book is a meditation on the impermanence of life, including the shifting fates of the samurai themselves. "The pale hue of the flowers of the teak tree," the tale asserts, "shows the truth that they who prosper must fall. The proud ones do not last long but vanish like a spring night's dream. And the mighty ones too will perish, just like dust in the wind."

The tale was prophetic. For the next 500 years, the fortunes of the samurai clans rose and fell like the waves of the ocean. When the shoguns became too proud or mighty, the daimyo rose to challenge them. And as the power of the shoguns declined, the daimyo filled the void by battling against each other, using armies of samurai to expand their territories and gain more power. During the Warring States period, from 1467 to 1567, the entire country was torn apart by disputes between the clans.

Throughout this period, the path to becoming a samurai was fluid. Thousands of peasants were brought into the army as foot soldiers, and foot soldiers who showed particular skill in battle could rise to become lesser samurai and, occasionally, full-fledged samurai.

In the 1580s, a foot soldier named Toyotomi Hideyoshi rose to become one of the most powerful daimyo the nation had ever seen, though he could not become shogun because of his peasant background and his lack of ancestors in the Minamoto clan. Instead, he was appointed to an even higher position, regent to the emperor, during one of those rare times in Japanese history when the emperor had more power than the shogun. Once Hideyoshi was in power, he blocked other peasants from following in his footsteps, so to speak. During his seven-year tenure, Hideyoshi confiscated all weapons from peasants, so that only samurai could bear swords. This put an end to peasant revolts and created a new class structure in Japan, dominated by an aristocratic class of samurai.

Within several decades, in the relative peace that followed the unification of the country after the Warring States period, the samurai gradually lost their military role and evolved into aristocratic underlings of the regional daimyo, in much the same way that the knights in Europe at that time moved away from the battlefield and into the more comfortable, effete life of country squires. The nostalgic samurai still retained reminders of their glory days, prominently displaying suits of armor and sets of swords in their homes. But the days of the samurai as pure warrior were mostly over.

*Right: White-laced armor with five lacquered plates in the Sendai style.*
*Opposite page: Shigetaka katana. Japan. Circa 1650.*

# SOCIAL STRUCTURE DURING SAMURAI TIMES

By 1192 the samurai had become the ruling class. Society under their leader, the shogun, was a feudal military dictatorship, which was strictly structured in order to maintain his authority. During the last shogunate, which lasted from 1603 to 1867, each Tokugawa leader was desperate to keep the samurai stronghold on society. As a result, life for anyone who was not a samurai was difficult.

In a society rigidly divided into classes, the samurai were the elite, with the farmers holding the next highest status. Craftsmen and traders followed, with little distinction between them, other than the fact that traders did not actually make anything but existed solely through the labors of others.

Even the samurai had a hierarchy within their own ranks. The top samurai was the shogun, and any samurai associated with him enjoyed the greatest status. The local lords, or *daimyo*, served the shogun and controlled vast amounts of land and employed samurai as guards, advisors, and their own personal armies. In large cities, including Edo (later Tokyo), samurai acted as policemen or as government officials for the shogun. Yet another group was the class of *ronin*, unattached samurai who roamed the countryside, seeking employment. Though some settled down to teach or perform, others hired out to the highest *daimyo* bidder as mercenaries.

Among the farmers, the primary reason for their relatively high status was the fact that rice was (and still is) a dietary staple for millions of Asians. Although farmers had some leverage in society, the shogun usually took measures to suppress this class as often as possible, in order to strengthen his power. As a result, farmers were confined to their land by shogunate decree, and the shogun typically took at least 20 percent of the annual rice crop for himself, with an additional percentage going to his loyal daimyo. This system often deprived the farmer of as much as half of his crop. For that reason, famine was not uncommon during shogunate times. And even during the lean times, the excessive percentages were not revised downward, and the farmers and peasants were put under even more pressure to survive. Many farmers attempted to circumvent the system

in periods of hardship by planting secret crops to supplement their meager incomes.

Below the farmers, artisans also enjoyed a respectable position in the hierarchy, for fine craftsmanship was highly prized. Masonry, carpentry, brewing, weaving, and lacquering were common endeavors, but the skill most closely associated with both shogun and samurai was, sword making. The finest swords in the world are those surviving from samurai times. Each sword could take months to form and often failed at some point in the process because of the temperamental nature of the metals involved, so that a completed sword made in this fashion was considered quite valuable and was seen as an object of fine art.

Merchants, although potentially wealthy, were ranked at the bottom of the social ladder, primarily as a result of the Confucian belief that they survived on the labors of others and did not actually produce anything of value, as the farmers and tradesmen did. Even so, some ronin resorted to merchant status to make money. Ironically, the economy was thwarted by the shogun, who prohibited wagon travel on the well-maintained roads, because of the fear that rolling armies would attack. The result of this impractical restriction was that farmers, traders, and merchants all carried their goods by horseback.

Living outside the inflexible structure of the class system was a motley group that included actors, entertainers, and priests. Though they were afforded some freedoms, these individuals did not benefit from the system's protections of life and livelihood; in effect, these people had little or no rights. Discrimination was common, especially against a class of people known as the *eta*. Despite performing a vital role in society, the eta were shunned as outcasts because they dealt with death, tanning animal hides, working as butchers, and disposing of carcasses. The Confucian society was generally vegetarian, and the Shinto held that any contact with death was taboo and necessitated ritual cleansing. Even today the discrimination persists. Lists of eta ancestry are provided to conservative families in order to prevent marriage into a lower class.

# Courage, the Spirit of Daring and Bearing

Courage was scarcely deemed worthy to be counted among virtues, unless it was exercised in the cause of Righteousness. In his *Analects* Confucius defines Courage by explaining, as is often his wont, what its negative is. "Perceiving what is right," he says, "and doing it not, argues lack of courage." Put this epigram into a positive statement, and it runs, "Courage is doing what is right." To run all kinds of hazards, to jeopardize one's self, to rush into the jaws of death—these are too often identified with Valor, and in the profession of arms such rashness of conduct— what Shakespeare calls, "valor misbegot"—is unjustly applauded; but not so in the Precepts of Knighthood. Death for a cause unworthy of dying for was called a "dog's death." "To rush into the thick of battle and to be slain in it," says a Prince of Mito, "is easy enough, and the merest churl is equal to the task; but," he continues, "it is true courage to live when it is right to live, and to die only when it is right to die," and yet the Prince had not even heard of the name of Plato, who defines courage as "the knowledge of things that a man should fear and that he should not fear." A distinction which is made in the West between moral and physical courage has long been recognized among us. What samurai youth has not heard of "Great Valor" and the "Valor of a Villain?"

Valor, Fortitude, Bravery, Fearlessness, Courage, being the qualities of soul which appeal most easily to juvenile minds, and which can be trained by exercise and example, were, so to speak, the most popular virtues, early emulated among the youth. Stories of military exploits were repeated almost before boys left their mother's breast. Does a little booby cry for any ache? The mother scolds him in this fashion: "What a coward to cry for a trifling pain! What will you do when your arm is cut off in battle? What when you are called upon to commit hara-kiri?" We all know the pathetic fortitude of a famished little boy-prince of Sendai, who in the drama is made to say to his little page, "Seest thou those tiny sparrows in the nest, how their yellow bills are opened wide, and now see! there comes their mother with worms to feed them. How eagerly and happily the little ones eat! but for a samurai, when his stomach is empty, it is a disgrace to feel hunger." Anecdotes of fortitude and bravery abound in nursery tales, though stories of this kind are not by any means the only method of early imbuing the spirit with daring and fearlessness.

Parents, with sternness sometimes verging on cruelty, set their children to tasks that called forth all the pluck that was in them. "Bears hurl their cubs down the gorge," they said. Samurai's sons were let down the steep valleys of hardship, and spurred to Sisyphus-like tasks. Occasional deprivation of food or exposure to cold was considered a highly efficacious test for inuring them to endurance. Children of tender age were sent among utter strangers with some message to deliver, were made to rise before

*Preceding pages: Cherry blossom viewing in Kyoto. Japan. 1700–1800. Six-panel folding screen. Ink and colors on gold paper.*
*Left: Antique dragon. Japan. Ivory.*
*Opposite page: The Actor Ichikawa Danjuro VII as a Samurai Warrior. Utagawa Kunisada (1786–1864). Japan. Woodblock print.*

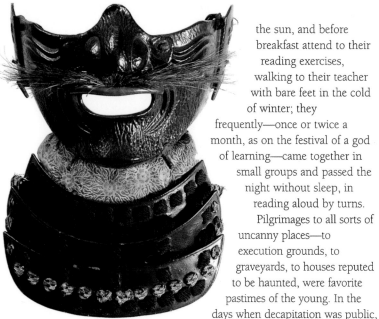

*Warrior's protective face mask, or mempo. Japan. Circa 1600s.*

the sun, and before breakfast attend to their reading exercises, walking to their teacher with bare feet in the cold of winter; they frequently—once or twice a month, as on the festival of a god of learning—came together in small groups and passed the night without sleep, in reading aloud by turns.

Pilgrimages to all sorts of uncanny places—to execution grounds, to graveyards, to houses reputed to be haunted, were favorite pastimes of the young. In the days when decapitation was public, not only were small boys sent to witness the ghastly scene, but they were made to visit alone the place in the darkness of night and there to leave a mark of their visit on the trunkless head.

Does this ultra-Spartan system[7] of "drilling the nerves" strike the modern pedagogist with horror and doubt—doubt whether the tendency would not be brutalizing, nipping in the bud the tender emotions of the heart? Let us see what other concepts Bushido had of Valor.

7 The spiritual aspect of valor is evidenced by composure—calm presence of mind. Tranquility is courage in repose. It is a statical manifestation of valor, as daring deeds are a dynamical. A truly brave man is ever serene; he is never taken by surprise; nothing ruffles the equanimity of his spirit. In the heat of battle he remains cool; in the midst of catastrophes he keeps level his mind. Earthquakes do not shake him, he laughs at storms. We admire him as truly great, who, in the menacing presence of danger or death, retains his self-possession; who, for instance, can compose a poem under impending peril or hum a strain in the face of death. Such indulgence betraying no tremor in the writing or in the voice, is taken as an infallible index of a large nature—of what we call a capacious mind (yoyu), which, far from being pressed or crowded, has always room for something more.

It passes current among us as a piece of authentic history, that as Ota Dokan, the great builder of the castle of Tokyo, was pierced through with a spear, his assassin, knowing the poetical predilection of his victim, accompanied his thrust with this couplet:

*Ah! how in moments like these*
*Our heart doth grudge the light of life;*

whereupon the expiring hero, not one whit daunted by the mortal wound in his side, added the lines:

*Had not in hours of peace,*
*It learned to lightly look on life.*

There is even a sportive element in a courageous nature. Things which are serious to ordinary people may be but play to the valiant. Hence in old warfare it was not at all rare for the parties to a conflict to exchange repartee or to begin a rhetorical contest. Combat was not solely a matter of brute force; it was, as well, an intellectual engagement.

Of such character was the battle fought on the bank of the Koromo River, late in the eleventh century. The eastern army routed, its leader, Sadato, took to flight. When the pursuing general pressed him hard and called aloud—"It is a disgrace for a warrior to show his back to the enemy," Sadato reined his horse; upon this the conquering chief shouted an impromptu verse:

*Torn into shreds is the warp of the cloth (koromo).*

Scarcely had the words escaped his lips when the defeated warrior, undismayed, completed the couplet:

*Since age has worn its threads by use.*

Yoshiie, whose bow had all the while been bent, suddenly unstrung it and turned away, leaving his prospective victim to do as he pleased. When asked the reason of his strange behavior, he replied that he could not bear to put to shame one who had kept his presence of mind while hotly pursued by his enemy.

The sorrow which overtook Antony and Octavius at the death of Brutus has been the general experience of brave

men. Kenshin, who fought for fourteen years with Shingen, when he heard of the latter's death, wept aloud at the loss of "the best of enemies." It was this same Kenshin who had set a noble example for all time, in his treatment of Shingen, whose provinces lay in a mountainous region quite away from the sea, and who had consequently depended upon the Hojo provinces of the Tokaido for salt. The Hojo prince wishing to weaken him, although not openly at war with him, had cut off from Shingen all traffic in this important article. Kenshin, hearing of his enemy's dilemma and able to obtain his salt from the coast of his own dominions, wrote Shingen that in his opinion the Hojo lord had committed a very mean act, and that although he (Kenshin) was at war with him (Shingen) he had ordered his subjects to furnish him with plenty of salt—adding, "I do not fight with salt, but with the sword," affording more than a parallel to the words of Camillus, "We Romans do not fight with gold, but with iron." Nietzsche spoke for the samurai heart when he wrote, "You are to be proud of your enemy; then, the success of your enemy is your success also." Indeed valor and honor alike required that we should own as enemies in war only such as prove worthy of being friends in peace. When valor attains this height, it becomes akin to Benevolence.

*The spiritual aspect of valor is evidenced by composure—calm presence of mind. Tranquility is courage in repose. It is a statical manifestation of valor, as daring deeds are a dynamical. A truly brave man is ever serene; he is never taken by surprise; nothing ruffles the equanimity of his spirit. In the heat of battle he remains cool; in the midst of catastrophes he keeps level his mind. Earthquakes do not shake him, he laughs at storms.*

*Above: This screen illustrates a fierce battle between the Genji and Heike armies along the Uji River Bridge. Battle on the Uji Bridge, based on a chapter in Tale of the Heike. Japan. 1615–1700. Four-panel folding screen.*

*Incense container. Japan. 1573–1615. Stoneware with underglaze iron-oxide decoration.*

# THE FOOT SOLDIER
## LEADING THE WAY INTO BATTLE

Ashikaga Toshikage, the governor of Echizen province in the late fifteenth century, was renowned for his logical thinking. He told underlings to hire people based on their skills rather than their family connections. He warned his commanders against letting superstition guide them on the battlefield. Proper planning, rather than luck or the auspiciousness of the day, was the key to success, he said. Most of all, he challenged the reliance on well-armed individual warriors rather than massive armies.

"Do not overly desire swords and daggers made by famous masters," he said, speaking of cost. "Even if you can own a sword or dagger worth 10,000 *hiki*, it can be defeated by a hundred spears each worth a hundred hiki. If you use the 10,000 hiki to buy a hundred spears and arm a hundred men with them, you can defend an entire flank."

Toshikage's words could easily be taken beyond their literal meaning. It was cheaper and perhaps even more efficient to put a hundred peasants into the field than a single pampered samurai. There was strength in numbers. Europeans at the time used massive armies of peons, like the pawns in a chess game, to do much of the dirty work for the gentrified knights. But the Japanese practiced that concept to the fullest extent possible. By the seventeenth century, the Japanese were deploying armies of more than 100,000 foot soldiers during single military actions, dwarfing any contemporary army on European battlefields.

The Japanese began using massive armies of foot soldiers under Emperor Temmu in the late seventh century. Temmu's idea was to build the bulk of his army by drafting peasants, which might have worked better if he could have figured out a way of stopping the peasants from deserting and returning to their farmlands. Over the next few hundred years, the foot soldiers were mostly mercenaries. But as demand for soldiers grew, particularly as individual clans built their own armies, the ranks included lesser samurai as well as peasants who had either been drafted into the army or had entered voluntarily, seeking more opportunities than those offered by the backbreaking work of life on the farm.

As peasants, the foot soldiers got little respect from the upper ranks of the army. Contemporary artists often depicted them as crude, almost buffoonish characters, and portraits of unshaven oafs clad in peasant garb reflect the antipathy that the nobles who led the army showed toward the lowborn grunts within their ranks. Unlike the samurai, who generally rode into battle with a pair of finely made swords and a small armory of other weapons, the foot soldiers were often armed only with a simple pike, bow, stave, or spear, such as the

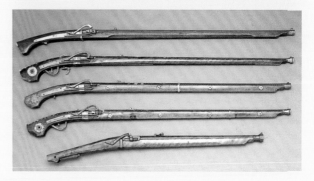

*Above: Matchlock gun (tanegashima or teppo). Japan. 1615–1868. Iron, wood, and brass.*
*Right, top: Tanegashima. Japan. Edo period.*
*Right, bottom: Five teppo. Circa 18th or early 19th century.*
*Opposite page: Night Attack on the Sanjo Palace, from the Illustrated Scrolls of the Events of Heiji Era. Heiji monogatari emaki. Detail. Japan. 13th century. Ink and color on paper.*

hundred-hiki spears that Toshikage extolled. That's if they were lucky. Many times they weren't issued any armor or weapons at all. They would rush into battle with rakes, hoes, and other farming implements and then scavenge the dead bodies of their enemies to arm themselves better. They were so poorly shod and armed that they were referred to as *ashigaru*, "light feet."

The word *ashigaru* first appears in historical writings in a firsthand account of the battle of Shijo Nawate in 1348. Eight hundred ashigaru archers launched volleys of arrows into the enemy, and though the ashigaru probably had little training in archery, the sheer number of arrows falling down from the sky onto the opposing troops helped the Sasaki clan carry the day.

Despite the fact that they often played a decisive role in battles, the ashigaru continued to be seen as coarse and crude shock troops, an image that was reinforced in 1467, when out-of-control ashigaru sacked and looted Kyoto at the outbreak of the Warring States period. As in Europe, where mounted knights were viewed as chivalrous (the word *chivalry* comes from the French *cheval*, "horse"), and peasant warriors were seen as villainous (the word *villain* comes from *villeyn*, "peasant"), in Japan, the samurai were viewed as models of restraint and honor in comparison to the unruly rabble of the ashigaru.

The image of the ashigaru began to change during the Warring States period. The leaders of the warring clans, such as Ashikaga Toshikage, began to recognize the value of the ashigaru. Some warlords started issuing light armor to their ashigaru: conical helmets of lacquered leather, breastplates formed of hardened leather strips, as well as leather shin guards and head protectors.

The introduction of firearms in the sixteenth century became a great leveler between the ashigaru and the samurai. Shooting a harquebus required much less skill than firing an arrow. For a brief time, battles became two-tiered affairs. As the ashigaru shot at each other with their harquebuses, the samurai battled using more traditional weapons. But there was no way that distinction could last. At the battle of Nagashino in 1575, harquebus-armed ashigaru working for the Oda clan, arrayed in firing lines of three shooters deep, decimated the samurai cavalry of the Takeda clan, helping the clan leader Oda Nobunaga solidify his position as Japan's leading warlord.

By the end of the Warring States period, the warlords were often deploying tens of thousands of ashigaru on the field, overwhelming their opponents with sheer numbers. Once the Warring States period had come to an end and Japan had been unified, the ashigaru were molded into a single fighting force that could be trained against foreign enemies. When Japan invaded Korea in the late sixteenth century, the invasion force included 160,000 warriors, mostly ashigaru. In comparison, when the Spanish Armada tried its invasion of England at roughly the same time, its invasion force included only 18,000 soldiers.

During the relative peace of the Edo period, the peasant soldiers outlived their usefulness. The practice of conscription came to an end. In an increasingly stratified Japan, the upper classes of samurai did not like the idea of arming peasants. Instead, lower-ranking samurai filled the positions once held by the ashigaru. And so it would remain until the Meiji era of the late nineteenth century, when the samurai system was dismantled and an increasingly warlike Japan demanded a fresh supply of troops to fight its battles.

# THE SAMURAI DIET
## MEALS OF SIMPLE PLENTY

During samurai times, a diversity of foods were available to warriors and everything was eaten mixed with the ever-present rice. The samurai diet included potatoes, radishes, cucumbers, beans, chestnuts, persimmons, nuts, tofu, yams, sour plums (especially popular with soldiers on campaign), apricots, peaches, apples, and oranges. From the sea came seven types of seaweed, as well as a variety of fish, including abalone, carp, bonito, trout, tuna, octopus, jellyfish, clams, and even whale meat. As many as fifty different types of plants, including soy and red beans, were used in cooking. Other familiar dietary ingredients included sake, soy sauce, peppers, rice vinegar, and kelp. One particular style of cooking, known as *shojin ryori*, called for large amounts of soya, sesame, or camellia oil to prepare vegetables.

Such a variety implies a largess of financial resources for the samurai, but that was not always the case. In general, the samurai class was not defined economically, and as a result, the comfort level of their lives varied widely. Samurai ran the gamut, from the very poor to the quite wealthy. Regardless, most samurai ate modestly.

An exception to this moderation occurred during the Heian period prior to the Kamakura period, when the samurai were guards for the estates of the nobility and took part in the large, elaborate banquets supplied by their masters. These feasts traditionally featured bowls of rice served with chopsticks and a bowl of soup served with salt, vinegar, and *hishio*, a fermentation of soybeans, rice, wheat, sake, and salt. A fourth plate was used for mixing the seasonings to taste for dipping. Banquet foods were classified into four general types: dried (*himono*), fresh, (*namamono*), fermented or dressed (*kubotsuki*), and desserts (*kashi*).

Dried seafood was served at these banquets, and included salted salmon, steamed and dried abalone, and dried and grilled octopus, sliced very thin. Fresh seafood, including carp, sea bream, salmon, or trout, was either sliced raw in vinegar sauce or grilled. Chinese cakes, fruits, and nuts, including pine nuts, dried chestnuts, acorns, jujube, pomegranates, peaches, apricots, persimmons, and

citrus, were the last course. Banquets usually ended with sake, the preferred drink for the samurai. Many varieties of this rice wine were developed over the centuries, Although its alcohol content was low, the samurai diet tended to enhance the alcoholic effects of the sake, and drunkenness was common in the samurai class. Such plentiful banquets changed abruptly once the Kamakura period had begun in 1192, and samurai who continued to follow the intricate dining style of the nobles of the previous era were punished severely by Minamoto Yoritomo, the first shogun.

Samurai warriors were served a ritual meal before leaving for war. Traditionally, this meal was comprised of dried chestnuts, kelp, and abalone with sake, served in three cups, because three was considered a lucky number. During military campaigns, the daily ration for soldiers was about 900 grams of husked rice, while officers usually ate sweetened, polished rice. Often, during a siege when rations were low, as was also the case in times of famine, the Buddhist-Shinto injunctions that prohibited eating meat could be lifted, allowing the hungry to catch pheasant, wild goose, quail, deer, and boar. It has also been documented that starving soldiers would kill and eat their own horses in order to survive.

The cuisine of the samurai in the Kamakura period came distinctly from peasant roots. The meals emphasized simplicity and quantity, while avoiding the refinement, ceremony, and luxury of the Heian period and shedding all Chinese influence.

*Above: Fish. Japan. 1800–1900.*
*Netsuke. Lacquered wood,*
*tortoiseshell, and rayskin.*
*Left: Bowl of uncooked rice.*
*Opposite page: Fish and waterweed.*
*Lai'an. China. 1275–1300. Hanging scroll,*
*one of a pair. Ink on paper.*

# Benevolence, the Feeling of Distress

Love, magnanimity, affection for others, sympathy, and pity were ever recognized to be supreme virtues, the highest of all the attributes of the human soul. Benevolence was deemed a princely virtue in a twofold sense; princely among the manifold attributes of a noble spirit; princely as particularly befitting a princely profession. We needed no Shakespeare to feel—though, perhaps, like the rest of the world, we needed him to express it—that mercy became a monarch better than his crown, that it was above his sceptered sway. How often both Confucius and Mencius repeat the highest requirement of a ruler of men to consist in benevolence. Confucius would say, "Let but a prince cultivate virtue, people will flock to him; with people will come to him lands; lands will bring forth for him wealth; wealth will give him the benefit of right uses. Virtue is the root, and wealth an outcome." Again, "Never has there been a case of a sovereign loving benevolence, and the people not loving righteousness," Mencius follows close at his heels and says, "Instances are on record where individuals attained to supreme power in a single state, without benevolence, but never have I heard of a whole empire falling into the hands of one who lacked this virtue." Also—"It is impossible that any one should become ruler of the people to whom they have not yielded the subjection of their hearts." Both defined this indispensable requirement in a ruler by saying, "Benevolence—Benevolence is Man."

Under the régime of feudalism, which could easily be perverted into militarism, it was to benevolence that we owed our deliverance from despotism of the worst kind. An utter surrender of "life and limb" on the part of the governed would have left nothing for the governing but self-will, and this has for its natural consequence the growth of that absolutism so often called "oriental despotism"—as though there were no despots of occidental history!

Opposite page: The Poet, Ariwara Narihira (825–880) from The Kokka. Japan. September 1910. Color lithograph.

Let it be far from me to uphold despotism of any sort; but it is a mistake to identify feudalism with it. When Frederick the Great wrote that "Kings are the first servants of the State," jurists thought rightly that a new era was reached in the development of freedom. Strangely coinciding in time, in the backwoods of northwestern Japan, Yozan of Yonézawa made exactly the same declaration, showing that feudalism was not all tyranny and oppression. A feudal prince, although unmindful of owing reciprocal obligations to his vassals, felt a higher sense of responsibility to his ancestors and to Heaven. He was a father to his subjects, whom Heaven entrusted to his care. According to the ancient Chinese Book of Poetry, "Until the house of Yin lost the hearts of the people, they could appear before Heaven." And Confucius in his Great Learning taught: "When the prince loves what the people love and hates what the people hate, then is he what is called the parent of the people." Thus are public opinion and monarchical will or democracy and absolutism merged one in the other. In a sense not usually assigned to the term, Bushido accepted and corroborated paternal government—paternal also as opposed to the less interested avuncular government (Uncle Sam's, to wit!). The difference between a despotic and a paternal government lies in this, that in the one the people obey reluctantly, while in the other they do so with "that proud submission, that dignified obedience, that subordination of heart which kept alive, even in servitude itself, the spirit of exalted freedom."[8] The old saying is not entirely false which called the king of England the "king of devils, because of his subjects' often insurrections against, and depositions of, their princes," and which made the French monarch the "king of asses, because of their infinite taxes and impositions," but which gave the title of "the king of men" to the sovereign of Spain "because of his subjects' willing obedience." But enough!

Virtue and absolute power may strike the Anglo-Saxon mind as terms which it is impossible to harmonize. Pobyedonostseff has clearly set before us the contrast in the foundations of English and other European communities;

*The koto is a horizontal, stringed, plucked instrument with a body made of paulownia wood. Its thirteen strings of waxed silk may be tuned to various scales by shifting the movable bridges on its soundboard. Koto. Japan. 1700–1850. Kiri wood, tortoiseshell, antler, silver, copper alloy, and silk.*

namely that these were organized on the basis of common interest, while that was distinguished by a strongly developed independent personality. What this Russian statesman says of the personal dependence of individuals on some social alliance and in the end of ends of the State, among the continental nations of Europe and particularly among Slavonic peoples, is doubly true of the Japanese. Hence not only is a free exercise of monarchical power not felt as heavily by us as in Europe, but it is generally moderated by parental consideration for the feelings of the people. "Absolutism," says Bismarck, "primarily demands in the ruler impartiality, honesty, devotion to duty, energy, and inward humility." If I may be allowed to make one more quotation on this subject, I will cite from the speech of the German Emperor at Coblenz, in which he spoke of "Kingship, by the grace of God, with its heavy duties, its tremendous responsibility to the Creator alone, from which no man, no minister, no parliament, can release the monarch."

We knew benevolence was a tender virtue and mother-like. If upright Rectitude and stern Justice were peculiarly masculine, Mercy had the gentleness and the persuasiveness of a feminine nature. We were warned against indulging in indiscriminate charity, without seasoning it with justice and rectitude. Masamuné expressed it well in his oft-quoted aphorism—"Rectitude carried to excess hardens into stiffness; Benevolence indulged beyond measure sinks into weakness."

Fortunately mercy was not so rare as it was beautiful, for it is universally true that "The bravest are the tenderest, the loving are the daring." "Bushi no nasaké"—the tenderness of a warrior—had a sound which appealed at once to whatever was noble in us; not that the mercy of a samurai was generically different from the mercy of any other being, but because it implied mercy where mercy was not a blind impulse, but where it recognized due regard to justice, and where mercy did not remain merely a certain state of mind, but where it was backed with

*Right: The facial features of this mask suggest it may be a mask of the Ko-omote type, used by Noh actors portraying girls on the verge of womanhood. Noh mask of a young woman. Tenka Ichi Deme. Japan. 1800–1950. Netsuke. Wood.*

*Opposite page: This mystical demon is one of several statues guarding the Suwa Shinto shrine in Nagasaki, Japan.*

power to save or kill. As economists speak of demand as being effectual or ineffectual, similarly we may call the mercy of bushi effectual, since it implied the power of acting for the good or detriment of the recipient.

Priding themselves as they did in their brute strength and privileges to turn it into account, the samurai gave full consent to what Mencius taught concerning the power of love. "Benevolence," he says, "brings under its sway whatever hinders its power, just as water subdues fire: they only doubt the power of water to quench flames who try to extinguish with a cupful a whole burning wagon-load of fagots." He also says that "the feeling of distress is the root of benevolence, therefore a benevolent man is ever mindful of those who are suffering and in distress." Thus did Mencius long anticipate Adam Smith who founds his ethical philosophy on Sympathy.

It is indeed striking how closely the code of knightly honor of one country coincides with that of others; in other words, how the much abused oriental ideas of morals find their counterparts in the noblest maxims of European literature. If the well-known lines,

*Hae tibi erunt artes—pacisque imponere morem,*
*Parcere subjectis, et debellare superbos,*

were shown a Japanese gentleman, he might readily accuse the Mantuan bard of plagiarizing from the literature of his own country.

Benevolence to the weak, the downtrodden, or the vanquished, was ever extolled as peculiarly becoming to a samurai. Lovers of Japanese art must be familiar with the representation of a priest riding backwards on a cow. The rider was once a warrior who in his day made his name a byword of terror. In that terrible battle of Sumano-ura, (1184 CE), which was one of the most decisive in our history, he overtook an enemy and in single combat had him in the clutch of his gigantic arms. Now the

etiquette of war required that on such occasions no blood should be spilt, unless the weaker party proved to be a man of rank or ability equal to that of the stronger. The grim combatant would have the name of the man under him; but he refusing to make it known, his helmet was ruthlessly torn off, when the sight of a juvenile face, fair and beardless, made the astonished knight relax his hold. Helping the youth to his feet, in paternal tones he bade the stripling go: "Off, young prince, to thy mother's side! The sword of Kumagaye shall never be tarnished by a drop of thy blood. Haste and flee o'er yon pass before thy enemies come in sight!" The young warrior refused to go and begged Kumagaye, for the honor of both, to dispatch him on the spot. Above the hoary head of the veteran gleams the cold blade, which many a time before has sundered the chords of life, but his stout heart quails; there flashes athwart his mental eye the vision of his own boy, who this self-same day marched to the sound of bugle to try his maiden arms; the strong hand of the warrior quivers; again he begs his victim to flee for his life. Finding all his entreaties vain and hearing the approaching steps of his comrades, he exclaims: "If thou art overtaken, thou mayest fall at a more ignoble hand than mine. O, thou Infinite! receive his soul!" In an instant the sword flashes in the air, and when it falls it is red with adolescent blood. When the war is ended, we find our soldier returning in triumph, but little cares he now for honor or fame; he renounces his warlike career, shaves his head, dons a priestly garb, devotes the rest of his days to holy pilgrimage, never turning his back to the West, where lies the Paradise whence salvation comes and whither the sun hastes daily for his rest.

Critics may point out flaws in this story, which is casuistically vulnerable. Let it be: all the same it shows that Tenderness, Pity, and Love were traits which adorned the most sanguinary exploits of the samurai. It was an old maxim among them that "It becometh not the fowler to slay the bird which takes refuge in his bosom." This in a large measure explains why the Red Cross movement, considered peculiarly Christian, so readily found a firm footing among us. For decades before we heard of the Geneva Convention, Bakin, our greatest novelist, had familiarized us with the medical treatment of a fallen foe. In the principality of Satsuma, noted for its martial spirit and education, the custom prevailed for young men to

*Tree on a beach in Japan.*

practice music; not the blast of trumpets or the beat of drums—"those clamorous harbingers of blood and death"—stirring us to imitate the actions of a tiger, but sad and tender melodies on the *biwa*,[9] soothing our fiery spirits, drawing our thoughts away from scent of blood and scenes of carnage. Polybius tells us of the Constitution of Arcadia, which required all youths under thirty to practice music, in order that this gentle art might alleviate the rigors of that inclement region. It is to its influence that he attributes the absence of cruelty in that part of the Arcadian mountains.

Nor was Satsuma the only place in Japan where gentleness was inculcated among the warrior class. A Prince of Shirakawa jots down his random thoughts, and among them is the following: "Though they come stealing to your bedside in the silent watches of the night, drive not away, but rather cherish these—the fragrance of flowers, the sound of distant bells, the insect humming of a frosty night." And again, "Though they may wound your feelings, these three you have only to forgive, the breeze that scatters your flowers, the cloud that hides your moon, and the man who tries to pick quarrels with you."

It was ostensibly to express, but actually to cultivate, these gentler emotions that the writing of verses was encouraged. Our poetry has therefore a strong undercurrent of pathos and tenderness. A well-known anecdote of a rustic samurai illustrates a case in point. When he was told to learn versification, and "The Warbler's Notes"[10] was given him for the subject of his first attempt, his fiery spirit rebelled and he flung at the feet of his master this uncouth production, which ran

> The brave warrior keeps apart
> The ear that might listen
> To the warbler's song.

His master, undaunted by the crude sentiment, continued to encourage the youth, until one day the music of his soul was awakened to respond to the sweet notes of the uguisu, and he wrote

> Stands the warrior, mailed and strong,
> To hear the uguisu's song,
> Warbled sweet the trees among.

We admire and enjoy the heroic incident in Körner's short life, when, as he lay wounded on the battlefield, he scribbled his famous Farewell to Life. Incidents of a similar kind were not at all unusual in our warfare. Our pithy, epigrammatic poems were particularly well suited to the improvisation of a single sentiment. Everybody of any education was either a poet or a poetaster. Not infrequently a marching soldier might be seen to halt, take his writing utensils from his belt, and compose an ode—and such papers were found afterward in the helmets or the breastplates when these were removed from their lifeless wearers.

What Christianity has done in Europe toward rousing compassion in the midst of belligerent horrors, love of music and letters has done in Japan. The cultivation of tender feelings breeds considerate regard for the sufferings of others. Modesty and complaisance, actuated by respect for others' feelings, are at the root of politeness.

8 Burke, *French Revolution*.
9 A musical instrument, resembling the guitar.
10 The *uguisu*, or warbler, sometimes called the nightingale of Japan.

*Traditional Japanese textile pattern.*

# A SMALL ISLAND OF DIVERSE LANDSCAPES

The warrior class that flourished around the turn of the first millennium had come into being in a land of environmental extremes and oddities, most obviously in its taut string of several thousand islands. The four largest islands of Japan are, from north to south, Hokkaido, Honshu (the mainland), Shikoku, and Kyushu. But even with another 3,000 smaller islands, including the most recognizable, Okinawa and Iwo Jima, Japan presents a combined landmass smaller than the state of California. As for neighbors, Korea, Russia, and China are the closest. To the west, the Sea of Japan separates the island nation from the Asian continent, while the Pacific Ocean lies on the eastern side.

Mountains with few lowlands dominate this geologically young land, where several tectonic plates have collided. The islands sit on the North American plate and the Eurasian plate, which meet in the middle of Honshu Island. Such instability gives rise to unprecedented physical phenomena. For instance, this location has produced nearly 200 volcanoes, forty of which are still active, a figure that represents 10 percent of the world's active total. From deep below the surface, as many as 1,500 earthquakes rattle the country each year, and minor tremors occur almost daily in one part or another. One of the most significant of these events to be recorded, only a half-century after the disappearance of the samurai, was the great Kanto earthquake of 1923, in which some 130,000 people died. The extensive Japanese coastline, a total of 18,486 miles, is also very susceptible to dangerous undersea quakes, which can create tsunami tidal waves of destructive proportions.

As a result of Japan's largely north-south alignment, the climate varies widely in different regions. In the south, most of the major cities, including Tokyo, enjoy a temperate to subtropical climate with four seasons, including mild winters and hot, humid summers. Early summer brings the rainy season, and typhoons hit every year during late summer. On the northern island of Hokkaido and along the coast of the Sea of Japan, the climate is colder and features heavy annual snowfall. In Okinawa in the south, on the other hand, the mean temperature of January is a warm sixty degrees Fahrenheit.

A chain of mountains divides Japan in half lengthwise, with the face on the Pacific Ocean side boasting ranges as high as 10,475 feet and the back side along the Sea of Japan having lower peaks of no more than 4,900 feet. Mount Fuji, Japan's highest peak, at 12,288 feet high, lies near Tokyo.

All of the major population centers are on the few available plains. None of these is very large, and even the Kanto Plain, which includes Tokyo, is only 5,000 square miles. Because of the lack of arable land, many areas of Japan have been reclaimed over the centuries, with dikes, dams, artificial islands, razed mountaintops, and terraced hillside rice paddies adding to the usable land. The settlement patterns of the country have also been dictated by a limited system of viable rivers, which are short, steep, swift, and all but unnavigable, except near the coastlines (though they are useful today as hydroelectric sources of power).

During the era of the samurai, considerable attention was given to the forming of administrative units within such a diverse landscape, with an effort being made to ensure that each unit would include as many different physical features as possible, but not more than its fair share. The governmental reforms of the seventh century, for example, divided the land into around sixty *kuni* or provinces, all of which encompassed coastal plains, fertile basins, and mountainous ranges. From these provinces, within a milieu of isolation and independence, the warrior class ascended.

*Above: Topographical map of the islands that compose Japan.*
*Opposite page: Japanese coastal landscape.*

# MOUNT FUJI

Within a samurai's own system of symbolism, the use of various images on weapons or clothing projected specific, personal meanings. One such image was that of Mount Fuji, which signified the impassive face of nature and the serenity of the Buddhist soul, two admirable qualities for a warrior. In ancient times, Mount Fuji figured prominently not only on the belongings of the samurai but also in the works of scholars, poets, and artists. In a much broader way, the distinctive symmetrical cone has now become the best-known symbol of Japan, as demonstrated by the huge photograph of Mount Fuji that was on display at the Japanese Pavilion during the San Francisco World's Fair of 1939.

*Rainstorm Beneath the Summit (The Black Fuji), from the series 36 Views of Mount Fuji. Circa 1760–1849. Oban Yoko-e. Woodblock print.*

The island nation of Japan is made up of the exposed tops of massive, undersea ridges jutting from the floor of the Pacific Ocean on the eastern edge of the Asian continental shelf. The country lies between, to the east, the Japan Deep, a 28,000-foot-deep north-south trench in the Pacific, and, to the west, the Sea of Japan, with depths of more than 10,000 feet. Rising from that craggy underwater world is the once-

active volcano known as Mount Fuji, on the southern end of the main island of Honshu. On a clear day, it can be seen from Tokyo, some sixty miles away.

Geographically speaking, Mount Fuji is located at the meeting point of several tectonic plates, the Eurasian plate in western Japan, the Okhotsk plate in eastern Japan, and the Philippine plate on the Izu Peninsula. Four distinct phases of development, or volcanic activity, have been identified to describe the life cycle of Mount Fuji. Originally, an andesite core was formed, which has recently been discovered buried deep inside the mountain. Over that core, several hundred thousand years ago, a basalt layer was then laid down. Approximately 100,000 years ago, an eruption created what is called Old Fuji, which was then covered some 10,000 years ago by New Fuji. The volcano's last recorded eruption occurred between December 16, 1707, and January 1, 1708, during which cinders and ash rained over the cities of Izu, Kai, Sagami, and Musashi. Though still classified as an active volcano, it is considered low risk for future eruption.

Heavily populated since the Stone Age, the area around Mount Fuji has been shrouded in myth for centuries. This beautiful peak has been revered as the ancient home of a fire god, the dwelling of Dainichi

Nyorai, the Buddha of All-Illuminating Wisdom. Although, in accordance with samurai strictures, women were not allowed to climb Mount Fuji until the Meiji era of the nineteenth century, this is nonetheless the legendary location of the ascent of an ancient Shinto goddess into heaven. The story relates that the Shinto deity Konohanasakuya-hime was as lovely as a cherry blossom. Being vain and not accepting the fact that she, like cherry blossoms, would fade, she rode a white horse to the top of Mount Fuji, where, leaving her sword behind, she rose into heaven. A shrine now stands at the supposed location of her ascension on the highest peak, Kengamine.

Early Shugendo myths claim that the first person to climb Mount Fuji was the wizard-sage En Gyoja, around 700 CE. It is more likely that the first ascents began in the twelfth or thirteenth centuries, around the time that the Chinese words for Mount Fuji were written with characters meaning "prosperity of the samurai class." Since the fifteenth century, Mount Fuji has become a popular pilgrimage destination, but today, it is also a noted mountain-climbing destination. More than 200,000 climbers a year, about a third of those foreign climbers, attempt the three- to eight-hour ascent.

As a military outpost, ancient samurai used the lower

reaches of Mount Fuji as a training camp. The shogun Minamoto Yoritomo trained his samurai in mounted archery warfare there sometime in the early Kamakura period between 1192 and 1334. But as late as 2006, the United States Marine Corps and the Japan Self-Defense Forces both operated bases near Mount Fuji.

*Above: Mount Fuji behind a field of green tea plants.*
*Opposite page: Fuji in Clear Weather, from the series 36 Views of Mount Fuji. Hokusai, Katsushika. Japan. 1760–1849. Woodblock print.*

# *Politeness*

Politeness is that courtesy and urbanity of manners which has been noticed by every foreign tourist as a marked Japanese trait. Politeness is a poor virtue, if it is actuated only by a fear of offending good taste, whereas it should be the outward manifestation of a sympathetic regard for the feelings of others. It also implies a due regard for the fitness of things, therefore due respect to social positions; for these latter express no plutocratic distinctions, but were originally distinctions for actual merit.

In its highest form, politeness almost approaches love. We may reverently say, politeness "suffereth long, and is kind; envieth not, vaunteth not itself, is not puffed up; doth not behave itself unseemly, seeketh not her own, is not easily provoked, taketh not account of evil." Is it any wonder that Professor Dean, in speaking of the six elements of Humanity, accords to Politeness an exalted position, inasmuch as it is the ripest fruit of social intercourse?

While thus extolling Politeness, far be it from me to put it in the front rank of virtues. If we analyze it, we shall find it correlated with other virtues of a higher order; for what virtue stands alone? While—or rather because—it was exalted as peculiar to the profession of arms, and as such esteemed in a degree higher than its deserts, there came into existence its counterfeits. Confucius himself has repeatedly taught that external appurtenances are as little a part of propriety as sounds are of music.

When propriety was elevated to the sine qua non of social intercourse, it was only to be expected that an elaborate system of etiquette should come into vogue to train youth in correct social behavior. How one must bow in accosting others, how he must walk and sit, were taught and learned with utmost care. Table manners grew to be a

*Opposite page: Ichikawa Danjuro and Ichikawa Monnosuke as Jagekiyo and Iwai Kumesaburo. Katsushika Hokusai. Japan. 1824. Woodblock print.*

science. Tea serving and drinking were raised to a ceremony. A man of education is, of course, expected to be master of all these. Very fitly does Mr. Veblen, in his interesting book,[11] call decorum "a product and an exponent of the leisure-class life."

I have heard slighting remarks made by Europeans upon our elaborate discipline of politeness. It has been criticized as absorbing too much of our thought and in so far a folly to observe strict obedience to it. I admit that there may be unnecessary niceties in ceremonious etiquette, but whether it partakes as much of folly as the adherence to ever-changing fashions of the West, is a question not very clear to my mind. Even fashions I do not consider solely as freaks of vanity; on the contrary, I look upon these as a ceaseless search of the human mind for the beautiful. Much less do I consider elaborate ceremony as altogether trivial; for it denotes the result of long observation as to the most appropriate method of achieving a certain result. If there is anything to do, there is certainly a best way to do it, and the best way is both the most economical and the most graceful. Mr. Spencer defines grace as the most economical manner of motion. The tea ceremony presents certain definite ways of manipulating a bowl, a spoon, a napkin, etc. To a novice it looks tedious. But one soon discovers that the way prescribed is, after all, the most saving of time and labor; in other words, the most economical use of force—hence, according to Spencer's dictum, the most graceful.

The spiritual significance of social decorum—or, I might say, to borrow from the vocabulary of the "Philosophy of Clothes," the spiritual discipline of which etiquette and ceremony are mere outward garments—is out of all proportion to what their appearance warrants us in believing. I might follow the example of Mr. Spencer and trace in our ceremonial institutions their origins and the moral motives that gave rise to them; but that is not what I shall endeavor to do in this book. It is the moral training involved in strict observance of propriety, that I wish to emphasize.

I have said that etiquette was elaborated into the finest

*Tales of Yamato, from the series Ten Designs of Old Tales. Gakutei Harunobu. Japan. 1818–1830. Woodblock engraving.*

niceties, so much so that different schools advocating different systems, came into existence. But they all united in the ultimate essential, and this was put by a great exponent of the best known school of etiquette, the Ogasawara, in the following terms: "The end of all etiquette is to so cultivate your mind that even when you are quietly seated, not the roughest ruffian can dare make onset on your person." It means, in other words, that by constant exercise in correct manners, one brings all the parts and faculties of his body into perfect order and into such harmony with itself and its environment as to express the mastery of spirit over the flesh. What

a new and deep significance the French word *biensèance*[12] comes thus to contain!

If the premise is true that gracefulness means economy of force, then it follows as a logical sequence that a constant practice of graceful deportment must bring with it a reserve and storage of force. Fine manners, therefore, mean power in repose. When the barbarian Gauls, during the sack of Rome, burst into the assembled Senate and dared pull the beards of the venerable Fathers, we think the old gentlemen were to blame, inasmuch as they lacked dignity and strength of manners. Is lofty spiritual attainment really possible through etiquette? Why not?—All roads lead to Rome!

As an example of how the simplest thing can be made into an art and then become spiritual culture, I may take *Cha-no-yu*, the tea ceremony. Tea-sipping as a fine art! Why should it not be? In the children drawing pictures on the sand, or in the savage carving on a rock, was the promise of a Raphael or a Michelangelo. How much more is the drinking of a beverage, which began with the transcendental contemplation of a Hindu anchorite, entitled to develop into a handmaid of Religion and Morality? That calmness of mind, that serenity of temper, that composure and quietness of demeanor, which are the first essentials of Cha-no-yu, are without doubt the first conditions of right thinking and right feeling.

*Models of late 16th-century Japanese warriors. 20th century. Mixed media.*

The scrupulous cleanliness of the little room, shut off from sight and sound of the madding crowd, is in itself conducive to direct one's thoughts from the world. The bare interior does not engross one's attention like the innumerable pictures and bric-a-brac of a Western parlor; the presence of *kakémono*[13] calls our attention more to grace of design than to beauty of color. The utmost refinement of taste is the object aimed at; whereas anything like display is banished with religious horror. The very fact that it was invented by a contemplative recluse, in a time when wars and the rumors of wars were incessant, is well calculated to show that this institution was more than a pastime. Before entering the quiet precincts of the tearoom, the company assembling to partake of the ceremony laid aside, together with their swords, the ferocity of the battlefield or the cares of government, there to find peace and friendship.

Cha-no-yu is more than a ceremony—it is a fine art; it is poetry, with articulate gestures for rhythm: it is a modus operandi of soul discipline. Its greatest value lies in this last phase. Not infrequently the other phases preponderated in the mind of its votaries, but that does not prove that its essence was not of a spiritual nature.

Politeness will be a great acquisition, if it does no more than impart grace to manners; but its function does not stop here. For propriety, springing as it does from motives of benevolence and modesty, and actuated by tender feelings toward the sensibilities of others, is ever a graceful expression of sympathy. Its requirement is that we should weep with those that weep and rejoice with those that rejoice. Such didactic requirement, when reduced into small everyday details of life, expresses itself in little acts scarcely noticeable, or, if noticed, is, as one missionary lady of twenty years' residence once said to me, "awfully funny." You are out in the hot glaring sun with no shade over you; a Japanese acquaintance passes by; you accost him, and instantly his hat is off—well, that is perfectly natural, but the "awfully funny" performance is, that all the while he talks with you his parasol is down and he stands in the glaring sun also. How foolish!—Yes, exactly so, provided the motive were less than this: "You are in the sun; I sympathize with you; I would willingly take you under my parasol if it were large enough, or if we were familiarly acquainted; as I cannot shade you, I will share your discomforts." Little acts of this kind, equally or more amusing, are not mere gestures or conventionalities. They are the "bodying forth" of thoughtful feelings for the comfort of others.

Another "awfully funny" custom is dictated by our canons of Politeness; but many superficial writers on Japan have dismissed it by simply attributing it to the general topsy-turvyness of the nation. Every foreigner who has observed it will confess the awkwardness he felt in making proper reply upon the occasion. In America, when you make a gift, you sing its praises to the recipient; in Japan we depreciate or slander it. The underlying idea with you is, "This is a nice gift: if it were not nice I would not dare give it to you; for it will be an insult to give you anything but what is nice." In contrast to this, our logic runs: "You are a nice person, and no gift is nice enough for you. You will not accept anything I can lay at your feet except as a token of my good will; so accept this, not for its intrinsic value, but as a token. It will be an insult to your worth to call the best gift good enough for you." Place the two ideas side by side; and we see that the ultimate idea is one and the same. Neither is "awfully funny." The American speaks of the material which makes the gift; the Japanese speaks of the spirit which prompts the gift.

It is perverse reasoning to conclude, because our sense of propriety shows itself in all the smallest ramifications of our deportment, to take the least important of them and uphold it as the type, and pass judgment upon the principle itself. Which is more important, to eat or to observe rules of propriety about eating? A Chinese sage answers, "If you take a case where the eating is all-important, and the observing the rules of propriety is of little importance, and compare them together, why merely say that the eating is of the more importance?" "Metal is heavier than feathers," but does that saying have reference to a single clasp of metal and a wagon-load of feathers? Take a piece of wood a foot thick and raise it above the pinnacle of a temple, none would call it taller than the temple. To the question, "Which is the more important, to tell the truth or to be polite?" the Japanese are said to give an answer diametrically opposite to what the American will say—but I forbear any comment until I come to speak of veracity and truthfulness.

11 *Theory of the Leisure Class*, N.Y. 1899, p. 46.
12 Etymologically well-seatedness.
13 Hanging scrolls, which may be either paintings or ideograms, used for decorative purposes.

*Top: Sake flask inlaid with mother of pearl. Japan. 19th century.*
*Bottom: Bell-shape bronze (dotaku). Japan. 100–300 BCE.*

# THE FEUDAL SYSTEM

If some brave traveler had journeyed from Europe to Japan during the Middle Ages, many things would have seemed strange and wondrous about the island nation. But at least one thing would have seemed familiar: Japan's feudal system of government. Japan's pyramidal hierarchy of *shogun*, *daimyo*, *samurai*, and *ji-samurai* (lesser samurai) closely resembled the European system of king, lords, vassals, and lesser vassals.

Before the feudal era began in the late twelfth century, Japan was dominated by a clique of ruling families united under the leadership of a relatively powerful emperor. The emperor and his Fujiwara clan were strong enough to keep a semblance of peace between the families. Most important,

the emperor exerted control over the distribution of land, which earned him the loyalty of the daimyo.

In 1180, long-standing differences between two leading clans, the Taira and the Minamoto, erupted into a bloody conflict known as the Gempei War. As the two families clashed, the power of the emperor weakened so that in order to maintain command, the emperor was forced to seek aid first from the Taira and then the Minamoto. In doing so, he exposed his own weaknesses and made enemies in both camps. From that point until the late nineteenth century, the emperor was seen as little more than a figurehead who needed support from the clans to survive, and so power shifted to the emperor's leading warlord, the shogun.

What emerged from the Gempei War was a feudal system in which the daimyo pledged fealty to the shogun, and the samurai pledged fealty to the daimyo, all in exchange for land and power. It was a system that ran on land distribution and taxes. One of the shogun's first acts after the Gempei War was to partition land among the daimyo who had fought by his side. The daimyo repartitioned the land among their leading samurai warriors, who might choose to repartition the land further among the ji-samurai, and so on down to the poorest peasants. The peasants, in turn, kept the system running by paying taxes to the ji-samurai, typically in the form of bushels of rice. A ji-samurai would pay a portion of these taxes to his samurai, who would pay taxes to the daimyo, and so on up the chain.

In theory, the emperor remained at the top of this chain. Even if he was only a figurehead, he still retained a position of wealth and status in medieval Japan, in much the same way that the emperors of modern Japan have since the end of World War II. The emperor and his family and courtiers lived in a beautiful palace in Kyoto, where they maintained a lavish lifestyle, paid for by taxes. The shogun also enjoyed a lifestyle and privileges similar to those of the emperor. Although the daimyo had lesser status, they still held vast estates dominated by towering castles, some of which were surrounded by moats, and wielded political power as members of the shogun's council.

By contrast, the samurai had varying amounts of wealth and little political power. Although they were given large portions of land, they often resided in the castles of the daimyo, thereby providing protection and overseeing everyday affairs. One of their chief duties was to ride out into the countryside to ensure that the peasants were paying their taxes properly. The peasants, who accounted for roughly 90 percent of the population, got short shrift from this arrangement. Most

*Right: Fisherman with octopus. Japan. 1700–1800. Netsuke. Wood and mother-of-pearl with horn inlaid eyes. Opposite page: Rice Planting. Ogata Gekko. Japan. 1890s–1900s. Color woodblock painting.*

were engaged in the backbreaking occupation of growing rice, while others eked out a living as fishermen, herders, or weavers. The daimyo and his surrogates squeezed the peasants for taxes, typically forcing them to give up more than two-thirds of the year's crops for the privilege of being able to remain on the land.

Periodically during the Middle Ages, the peasants would become so frustrated that they would stage revolts, often with the help of the local ji-samurai, who resented being near the bottom of the hierarchy. The laws of inheritance, which favored the firstborn son over his younger brothers, also led to violent clashes, because with each successive generation the amount of land available for the younger heirs dwindled. Brother fought against brother to gain a greater share of property.

During the Edo era, which began in 1603, the shogun maintained peace by trying to establish more equitable distribution of property and by giving the peasants slightly more freedom. Tokugawa Ieyasu gave some of his most trusted and loyal daimyos parcels of land and required them to live in Edo every other year, where they were expected to participate in public works. This gave them a stake in their land in the countryside but helped prevent them from leading uprisings because they had to be in Edo so much of the time. Each of the land-owning daimyo were also expected to donate arms and men during wartime. Through all these constraints, change in the system was minimized. Nevertheless, popular resistance to the *bakufu* feudal system began to surface in the mid-eighteenth century. The merchant class was rising, and inellectual life was flourishing. The village feudal world began to suffer economically, and the Western world gained increasing influence over the old ways. It was evident by the nineteenth century that the old samurai class system was collapsing. It was definitively ended during the Meiji period in the 1860s, when after a few battles between bakufu's defenders and its challengers, Emperor Meiji put an end to it once and for all. Its last gasp occurred in 1877 when a force of 42,000 rebels, consisting largely of samurai, was defeated.

# REVOLUTIONARY INFLUENCES FROM THE ASIAN MAINLAND

Until Commodore Perry's gunships sailed into Yokohama Harbor in 1853, Japan had a reputation in the West as being one of the world's most isolationist countries, having shut itself off from foreign influence for centuries.

There was much truth in that viewpoint. Japan's history includes long periods of isolation from the outside world, particularly when it comes to Europe and America. But intermittently, Japan's isolation was punctured by periods in which revolutionary influences entered from elsewhere. Indeed, much of what we think of as Japanese culture can be traced back to foreign roots, mostly to China.

The Chinese influence on Japan began before the country's written history. Up until roughly 300 BCE, the islands of Japan were dominated by hunters and gatherers who were probably a cross-cultural mix of peoples from Polynesia, Southeast Asia, Korea, and China. But after that, the Japanese way of life changed radically, due to new agricultural techniques that had been pioneered in northern and central China and had then migrated down the Korean peninsula. Using the Chinese method for planting rice in wet paddy fields, Japan, like China, was transformed into an agrarian society. Villages grew around the rice paddies and developed social classes of laborers and managers. As in China, where the rice-planting culture helped fuel the growth of the Xin dynasty, in Japan it formed the foundation of the kingdoms and empires that would come.

As Japan grew into nationhood, it borrowed many things from China, often via Korea: philosophy, religion, political structures, weaponry, fashions, and currency. Most of the time, these imports were so thoroughly altered that they took on uniquely Japanese characteristics, but the influence of China and Korea still ran deep.

## Buddhist Religion

According to tradition, Buddhism was officially introduced to Japan in 552 CE, when Japanese forces were intervening in a war between the Korean states of Paekche, Silla, and Koguryo. Envoys from the Japanese tribal states had undoubtedly come into contact with Buddhism during the past three or four centuries, but it was through the Japanese alliance with Paekche that the religion truly took hold. When Paekche and Koguryo lost to Silla, many Koreans from those kingdoms fled to Japan, bringing their religion with them.

Buddhist missionaries from China also helped spread the word, as did Japanese converts who traveled to China to study the religion and who then returned to their homeland to spread what they had learned. In 701, the seventeen-article *Taiho* ("Great Treasures") Code of laws written by Prince Shotoku established Buddhism as a state religion, ordaining that Buddha, Buddhist law, and the Buddhist priesthood were "three treasures ... that should be shown sincere reverence, for they are the final refuge of all living things. Few men are so bad that they cannot be taught their truth." Over the centuries, however, Japanese Buddhism took on a character of its own, infused with concepts from the existing Shinto religion, which is based on the notion that gods and spirits reside everywhere, including in inanimate objects.

## Confucian Philosophy

Along with Buddhism, the Korean refugees and Chinese missionaries also brought Confucianism. The Japanese quickly adopted Confucian ideals about the individual's responsibility to society, the value of public service, and the importance of virtuous leadership. The Taiho Code was essentially a Confucian document, which included the idea that the emperor ruled with a mandate from heaven. Japanese society incorporated much Confucian thought, although it never fully accepted the idea of the mandate from heaven, which explains how the shoguns were able to push the emperor to the side once they had taken power. The samurai had their own ideas of loyalty and honor that were melded into the Japanese version of Confucianism.

## Tang Government

In 645, Emperor Kotoku drafted the Taika Reforms, which modeled Japan's central and provisional bureaucracies after the government of the then-ruling Tang dynasty in China. Among other things, Kotoku also established a Chinese-style land distribution system, nationalizing all agricultural land and ensuring that peasant families would be able to work on roughly equal shares. The Taika Reforms set the tone for the imperial government for the next 400 years, until the shoguns replaced it with a uniquely Japanese style of warlord rule.

## Literature and Art

From the sixth century through 894, when diplomatic relations with China were temporarily severed, Japanese artists and writers did almost all of their work in the Chinese manner. Most portraits were done within China's highly stylized strictures. Many landscapes were copies of paintings of well-known landmarks in China. The rupture in formal relations between the two countries, sparked by the outbreak of a civil war in China, gave Japan a chance to develop a more indigenous style of art, architecture, and writing. It was during this era that the Japanese began to rely more on the simplified *hiragana* alphabet, whose fewer than fifty basic characters were much simpler to use than the 50,000 or so characters in the *kanji* alphabet borrowed from China. Within a century, Japanese poets and novelists were writing their works using hiragana. Nevertheless, China continued to provide literary inspiration, and Chinese books were important status symbols among the upper class. In the twelfth century, for instance, the warlord Taira Kiyomori went to great lengths to smuggle in a 1,000-volume encyclopedia the Chinese government had banned from export.

## Weapons

Steel swords were first brought to Japan by Chinese and Korean smiths who had migrated into the country in the sixth century, and for hundreds of years, they dominated the sword-making industry. The first steel swords used by samurai were nicknamed *wato*, or "Chinese swords." Although some Japanese sword makers emerged relatively early, as did Amakuni Yasutsuna in Nara in the eighth century, truly Japanese-style swords did not appear until the tenth century, after the suspension of ties with China. Centuries later, though, Chinese exports of gunpowder and cannon would help revolutionize Japanese warfare.

## Clothing

The Japanese *kimono* had its roots in the *shenyi*, "deep robe," developed in China during the Eastern Zhou dynasty, which came to an end in 256 BCE. Within several centuries, at some point in the Han dynasty, the shenyi made its way to Japan. Like the earliest versions of the shenyi, the kimono consisted of a combination of a tunic and skirt, tied at the waist with a sash known as a *pei* in China and an *obi* in Japan. Tomb murals from the late seventh century show that

Japanese clothing, shoes, and hairstyles all echoed the then-current styles in China. A few decades later, the Japanese imperial court enacted the Yoro Clothing Code, which was based on clothing restrictions that had been put into place by the Tang dynasty. Under the code, all robes were to be wrapped from left to right, as was being done in China, and that is the way that kimonos have been wrapped ever since.

## Money

Throughout much of its history, Japan was a barter society, with one of the main units of exchange being the *koku*, about five bushels of rice. By around 700 CE, however, the Japanese began using coins imported from China, such as the *kai yuan tong bao*, the round copper coin with a square cut out of the middle, the first coin to be used as Japan's official currency. Japan eventually came up with its own version of the coin, the *wado kaichin*, but it was minted only sporadically throughout the Middle Ages. A combination of barter, privately produced coins, and Chinese coins were used until 1585, when the warlord Toyotomi Hideyoshi created a series of gold and silver coins. In 1608, the shogun Tokugawa Ieyasu tried to standardize currency, using Chinese technology to produce gold, silver, and copper coins. For a long while afterward, however, Chinese coins remained the dominant currency in Japan. *Yuan*, "round thing," the Chinese word for *coin*, is the root of the Japanese word *yen*.

Despite Japan's massive borrowings from its neighbors, there is a reason that the world perceives yen, kimonos, and samurai swords as being intrinsically Japanese. Over the centuries, Japan has been gifted at taking every foreign innovation that enters its borders—including such modern imports as the transistor, automobile, cell phone, and semiconductor—and improving upon them in a way that makes them uniquely Japanese.

*Top: Circular mirror. Japan. 300–400. Bronze.*
*Middle: Hand-held lantern (toshoku bonbori). Signed "Ta." Japan. Wood, paper, and iron.*
*Bottom: Writing box with ducks and reeds. Japan. Circa 1680–1720.*
*Opposite page: Zen garden in Kyoto, Japan.*

怪鼠傳之内

冠者義高

彫竹

豊國画

# *Veracity or Truthfulness*

Without truthfulness, politeness is a farce and a show. "Propriety carried beyond right bounds," says Masamuné, "becomes a lie." An ancient poet has outdone Polonius in the advice he gives: "To thyself be faithful: if in thy heart thou strayest not from truth, without prayer of thine the Gods will keep thee whole." The apotheosis of Sincerity to which Confucius gives expression in the *Doctrine of the Mean*, attributes to it transcendental powers, almost identifying them with the Divine. "Sincerity is the end and the beginning of all things; without Sincerity there would be nothing." He then dwells with eloquence on its far-reaching and long-enduring nature, its power to produce changes without movement and by its mere presence to accomplish its purpose without effort. From the Chinese ideogram for Sincerity, which is a combination of "Word" and "Perfect," one is tempted to draw a parallel between it and the Neo-Platonic doctrine of Logos—to such height does the sage soar in his unwonted mystic flight.

Lying or equivocation was deemed equally cowardly. The bushi held that his high social position demanded a loftier standard of veracity than that of the tradesman and peasant. *Bushi no ichi-gon*—the word of a samurai or in exact German equivalent, *ein Ritterwort*—was sufficient guaranty for the truthfulness of an assertion. His word carried such weight with it that promises were generally made and fulfilled without a written pledge, which would have been deemed quite beneath his dignity. Many thrilling anecdotes were told of those who atoned by death for *ni-gon*, a double tongue.

The regard for veracity was so high that, unlike the generality of Christians who persistently violate the plain commands of the Teacher not to swear, the best of samurai looked upon an oath as derogatory to their honor. I am well aware that they did swear by different deities or upon their swords; but never has swearing degenerated into wanton form and irreverent interjection. To emphasize our words a practice of literally sealing with blood was sometimes resorted to. For the explanation of such a

practice, I need only refer my readers to Goethe's *Faust*.

A recent American writer is responsible for this statement, that if you ask an ordinary Japanese which is better, to tell a falsehood or be impolite, he will not hesitate to answer "to tell a falsehood!" Dr. Peery[14] is partly right and partly wrong; right in that an ordinary Japanese, even a samurai, may answer in the way ascribed to him, but wrong in attributing too much weight to the term he translates "falsehood." This word (in Japanese, *uso*) is employed to denote anything which is not a truth (*makoto*) or fact (*honto*). Lowell tells us that Wordsworth could not distinguish between truth and fact, and an ordinary Japanese is in this respect as good as Wordsworth. Ask a Japanese, or even an American of any refinement, to tell you whether he dislikes you or whether he is sick at his stomach, and he will not hesitate long to tell falsehoods and answer, "I like you much," or, "I am quite well, thank you." To sacrifice truth merely for the sake of politeness was regarded as an "empty form" (*kyo-rei*) and "deception by sweet words," and was never justified.

I own I am speaking now of the Bushido idea of veracity; but it may not be amiss to devote a few words to our commercial integrity, of which I have heard much complaint in foreign books and journals. A loose business morality has indeed been the worst blot on our national reputation; but before abusing it or hastily condemning the whole race for it, let us calmly study it and we shall be rewarded with consolation for the future.

Of all the great occupations of life, none was farther removed from the profession of arms than commerce. The merchant was placed lowest in the category of vocations—the knight, the tiller of the soil, the mechanic, the merchant. The samurai derived his income from land and could even indulge, if he had a mind to, in amateur farming; but the counter and abacus were abhorred. We knew the wisdom of this social arrangement. Montesquieu has made it clear that the debarring of the nobility from mercantile pursuits was an admirable social policy, in that it prevented wealth from accumulating in the hands of the powerful. The separation of power and riches kept the distribution of the latter more

*Kojima Takanori Writing a Poem on a Cherry Tree, from the series Pictures of Flowers of Japan. Ogata Gekko. 1895. Woodblock print with blind embossing.*

nearly equal. Professor Dill, the author of *Roman Society in the Last Century of the Western Empire*, has brought afresh to our mind that one cause of the decadence of the Roman Empire, was the permission given to the nobility to engage in trade, and the consequent monopoly of wealth and power by a minority of the senatorial families.

Commerce, therefore, in feudal Japan did not reach that degree of development which it would have attained under freer conditions. The obloquy attached to the calling naturally brought within its pale such as cared little for social repute. "Call one a thief and he will steal." Put a stigma on a calling and its followers adjust their morals to it, for it is natural that "the normal conscience," as Hugh Black says, "rises to the demands made on it, and easily falls to the limit of the standard expected from it." It is unnecessary to add that no business, commercial or otherwise, can be transacted without a code of morals. Our merchants of the feudal period had one among themselves, without which they could never have developed, as they did, such

fundamental mercantile institutions as the guild, the bank, the bourse, insurance, checks, bills of exchange, etc.; but in their relations with people outside their vocation, the tradesmen lived too true to the reputation of their order.

This being the case, when the country was opened to foreign trade, only the most adventurous and unscrupulous rushed to the ports, while the respectable business houses declined for some time the repeated requests of the authorities to establish branch houses. Was Bushido powerless to stay the current of commercial dishonor? Let us see.

Those who are well acquainted with our history will remember that only a few years after our treaty ports were opened to foreign trade, feudalism was abolished, and when with it the samurai's fiefs were taken and bonds issued to them in compensation, they were given liberty to invest them in mercantile transactions. Now you may ask, "Why could they not bring their much boasted veracity into their new business relations and so reform the old abuses?" Those who had eyes to see could not weep enough, those who had hearts to feel could not sympathize enough, with the fate of many a noble and honest samurai who signally and irrevocably failed in his new and unfamiliar field of trade and industry, through sheer lack of shrewdness in coping with his artful plebeian rival. When we know that eighty percent of the business houses fail in so industrial a country as America, is it any wonder that scarcely one among a hundred samurai who went into trade could succeed in his new vocation? It will be long before it will be recognized how many fortunes were wrecked in the attempt to apply Bushido ethics to business methods; but it was soon patent to every observing mind that the ways of wealth were not the ways of honor. In what respects, then, were they different?

Of the three incentives to veracity that Lecky enumerates, viz., the industrial, the political, and the philosophical, the first was altogether lacking in Bushido. As to the second, it could develop little in a political community under a feudal system. It is in its philosophical, and as Lecky says, in its highest aspect, that honesty attained elevated rank in our catalogue of virtues. With all my sincere regard for the high commercial integrity of the Anglo-Saxon race, when I ask for the ultimate ground, I am told that "Honesty is the best policy," that it pays to be honest. Is not this virtue, then, its own reward? If it is followed because it brings in more cash than falsehood, I am afraid Bushido would rather indulge in lies!

If Bushido rejects a doctrine of quid pro quo rewards, the shrewder tradesman will readily accept it. Lecky has very truly remarked that veracity owes its growth largely to commerce and manufacture; as Nietzsche puts it, "Honesty is the youngest of virtues"—in other words, it is the foster-child of industry, of modern industry. Without this mother, veracity was like a blue-blood orphan whom only the most cultivated mind could adopt and nourish. Such

minds were general among the samurai, but, for want of a more democratic and utilitarian foster-mother, the tender child failed to thrive. Industries advancing, veracity will prove an easy, nay, a profitable, virtue to practice. Just think, as late as November 1880, Bismarck sent a circular to the professional consuls of the German Empire, warning them of "a lamentable lack of reliability with regard to German shipments inter alia, apparent both as to quality and quantity." Nowadays we hear comparatively little of German carelessness and dishonesty in trade. In twenty years her merchants learned that in the end honesty pays. Already our merchants are finding that out. For the rest I recommend the reader to two recent writers for well-weighed judgment on this point.[15] It is interesting to remark in this connection that integrity and honor were the surest guaranties which even a merchant debtor could present in the form of promissory notes. It was quite a usual thing to insert such clauses as these: "In default of the repayment of the sum lent to me, I shall say nothing against being ridiculed in public;" or, "In case I fail to pay you back, you may call me a fool," and the like.

Often have I wondered whether the veracity of Bushido had any motive higher than courage. In the absence of any positive commandment against bearing false witness, lying was not condemned as sin, but simply denounced as weakness, and, as such, highly dishonorable. As a matter of fact, the idea of honesty is so intimately blended, and its Latin and its German etymology so identified with honor, that it is high time I should pause a few moments for the consideration of this feature of the Precepts of Knighthood.

14 Peery, *The Gist of Japan*, p. 86.
15 Knapp, *Feudal and Modern Japan*, Vol. I, Ch. IV. Ransome, *Japan in Transition*, Ch. VIII.

*Top: A large Kinkozan vase depicting a lady playing a koto with ladies and children beneath a wisteria. Late 19th century.*
*Bottom: Guardian dog, one of a set of two. Japan. 1200–1300. Wood.*
*Left: Long-sleeve kimono with pine, wisteria, autumn plants, and architectural elements. Japan. 1818–1850.*

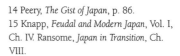

# THE CYCLE OF ZEN BUDDHISM

The central belief of Buddhism, that each individual can awaken to spiritual truth, originated in ancient India and then traveled through Korea and China, absorbing existing beliefs and practices as it spread. East Asian Mahayana Buddhism, which found its way to Japan beginning in the fifth century CE, emphasized meditation as a means of "seeing into one's own nature and becoming a Buddha."

## The Birth of Zen

Meditation to achieve an awakening came to be known as *zen*, the Japanese pronunciation of the Chinese *chan*, which itself is a version of *dhyana*, the Sanskrit word for meditation. Although anyone can attain enlightenment, the mystery of zen requires instruction by a master, who hands down wisdom to his disciple. The concepts of transmitting authority, of ancestry, and of deep knowledge meshed well with the Japanese culture of the *uji*, or clan, which was the social unit and the religious framework bridging generations of ancestors.

The Zen Buddhism that arose as a separate school of thought in China around the seventh century spawned several varieties. The practice that would eventually predominate in Japan, Rinzai Zen, saw enlightenment as a sudden awakening of consciousness, that involved not only the intense physical practice of strikes or shouts from the Zen master but also the contemplative practice of riddle solving, both of which were necessary to break through the barriers of normal thought processes.

In the early seventh century, when Prince Shotoku, himself a Buddhist, wanted to reconcile the traditional Shinto religion with Confucianism and Buddhism, he established diplomatic contact with China and sent monks there for study. Though the prince died before

many of his reforms could be enacted, those scholars did bring back a new approach that was to be well suited to the needs of the empire, particularly because of an integral master-disciple relationship. Under that thinking, the court sponsored schools, built temples and nunneries, and constructed a national cathedral. However, although influential at high levels, Buddhism was still little practiced by the population, at least not in its pure form. Several new forms of religion appeared, melding Buddhism with Japanese nature traditions, folk religions, and, significantly, with Shinto, as Shotoku had attempted a century earlier. Buddhist institutions did eventually become strong enough to threaten the empire, and when the capital was moved to Kyoto in 804, it was in large part to create a new power center. Forbidding the existing Buddhist schools to move, the government established two new Buddhist schools side by side with Shinto, thus diluting their influence, at least temporarily.

## The Ashikaga Period

Over the next four centuries, religious institutions grew wealthy and produced an elegant culture. However, that culture was subsumed in the bloody revolutions of the late twelfth century, from which emerged the era of the warrior ruler. For the 600 years that the samurai were supreme, Shinto and Buddhist institutions were free to operate, and new religious movements evolved. Warriors often combined Buddhist piety and indigenous practices while eschewing the Shinto tradition associated with the now powerless emperor.

At the time, because Japanese Buddhism was seen as having deviated from its spiritual foundations, monks traveled to China, looking for ways to revive the sect in their homeland. They brought back a form of Zen, which slowly grew as a counterbalance to the wealthy and powerful Buddhist establishment, reaching the apex of its influence during the Ashikaga period, between 1338 and 1573. Zen priests served as advisors to the court and as administrators, and the temples were centers of culture and art. Rinzai Zen was, for all practical purposes, the state religion. The official Rinzai network of hundreds of monasteries included the leading Five Mountains monasteries, centered in Kyoto and Kamakura, which brought Zen-related culture and learning to the populace. Though the monks wrote poems, painted, and designed gardens, their focus on Zen training helped to civilize the upper echelon of warrior society.

Japan was never as closed a society as some powerful interests would have liked, and outside influences continued to wash up on the islands' shores. The first Jesuit missionary arrived in 1549, following Portuguese merchants. The faith with which they proselytized came to be known as *kirishitan*. Oda Nobunaga, a strongman who wrested control of the capital in 1568, saw Christian activities as a way to lessen Buddhist influence and so encouraged them. When he was assassinated, the policies were reversed, but not before some 150,000 Japanese had converted to Catholicism. Nobunaga's successor installed a highly structured feudal order with the shogun at the top. The first shogun's edict of 1614 stated that Japan was to be called "the land of the Buddha"—Buddhism was seen as a system that supported a harmonious society and that Christianity was seen as a threat to be banned.

## The Modern Age

Other cracks in the social and religious compact also began to appear in the seventeenth century. Anti-Buddhist Confucianists joined with Shinto, which was reviving a nationalist sentiment. The climax was a revolt in the 1870s, when temples were destroyed, monks and nuns were forced into laity, and the government system of schools and temples was dismantled. Shinto was established as the state religion with the emperor as its divine head.

In spite of the continual upheavals, Zen Buddhism never faded away. Jesuit priests, the first Westerners to come into contact with Zen, introduced it to their part of the world. In the meantime, monks were sent to study in Western schools and brought back their broadened outlook, while Christian missionaries used Zen concepts and phrases to explain their own religion.

In the modern era, the ban on Christianity was lifted, Confucianism served as an ethical system for ruling regimes, and Shinto became popular with conservative Japanese who resented Western influence. Some turned to cults and folk religion, and in the years before World War II, more than 1,000 "quasi-religions" were registered.

Religious freedom came to Japan with the postwar occupation. The new civil code meant individuals were not bound by their household's religious affiliation, which further weakened the institutions of Buddhism and Shinto, but not their popular practices. In 2004, 51 percent of Japanese who claimed a faith were Shinto, 44 percent were Buddhist, 5 percent were other groups, and 1 percent were Christian. That year, the government recognized 157 schools of Buddhism, including two sects of Zen.

*Above: Amida, Lord of the Western Paradise, where Pure Land Buddhists hope to be reborn. Seated Buddha Amitabha (Japanese: Amida). Japan. 1350–1400. Hanging scroll.*
*Opposite page: Hansatsu (proprietary currency feudal lords distributed within their domains). Japan. Edo period.*

# THE SOHEI
## WARRIOR MONKS OF JAPAN

The *sohei* were Buddhist monks who, like the samurai, were warriors of feudal Japan between the tenth and sixteenth centuries. The word literally translates as "monk warriors," but other references also include the word *akuso*, which means "evil monks."

The sohei typically fought over land, spiritual appointments, and dishonorable behavior, but unpopular political appointments often gave rise to ferocious conflicts. The monks attached to a single monastery could number in the thousands and the emperor could appoint the *zasu*, or head abbott, of a temple or monastery. If the monks were displeased with an appointment, protests could escalate into lethal brawls among themselves. The first armed conflict involving monks was over such a political appointment. In 949 CE, fifty-six monks from Todaiji staged a protest at the residence of a Kyoto official, and some of

them were killed. Demonstrations of this nature by the sohei continued through the end of the tenth century.

Most conflicts, however, were instigated by sohei from differing temples who fought against rival temples in order to eliminate each other. It is thought that the first standing army of warrior monks was formed in 970 CE, following a dispute between the Enryakuji shrine on Mount Hiei and the Gion shrine of Kyoto. However, the abbot of Enryakuji, Ryogen, was known to require a twelve-year training period for monks, which included restrictions from covering their faces, from carrying weapons, and from leaving the temple at Mount Hiei. Because of this strict monastic code of conduct, it is unclear whether Ryogen used monks or mercenaries for his army.

Throughout the tenth century, Enryakuji and its army were involved in a number of armed conflicts with the Miidera temple. Both temples were of the Tendai sect of

Buddhism, and Miidera was also located at Mount Hiei, near its base. Despite their proximity and adherence to the same religious tenets, rivalry between the temples was often violent. Miidera was finally burned to the ground in 1141 by the Enryakuji monks.

Some monks, such as lords Takeda Shinga and Uesugi Kenshin, represented both their religious group and the samurai class. But in most cases, the monks were considered below the warrior class, even though they were recognized as highest among the rest of the emperor's subjects. This position in the class structure, however, did not provide a reliable income, and temples somewhat depended on political influence. Revenue from tollgates, moneylenders, and sake brewers also contributed to the income of the monks.

*Above: Square detail from wall sculpture of a cave chapel, representing the Ten Thousand Buddhas. Tang dynasty, 7th–8th century. The Longmen Grottoes, Louyang, Henan Province, China. Limestone with traces of pigment.*
*Opposite page: Temple in Kyoto, Japan.*

In a manner suggestive of their "evil monks" description, the sohei fought indiscriminately both with and against the samurai, depending on the point of the battle. For example, the samurai of the Minamoto and Taira clans utilized the sohei forces as allies in the Gempei War of the twelfth century. As a result of their participation in the conflict, Miidera and many of the temples of Nara were burned. But the monastery of Enryakuji did not participate in the conflict, probably because they received bribes of rice and silk from Taira. And because it was not directly involved, Enryakuji was not harmed and became the only sohei institution that had not been burned up until then. Following this Gempei War, the political influence of the monasteries grew mainly through peaceful means, and rebuilding became a priority. The thirteenth and fourteenth centuries were even more peaceful but still found the monks in occasional armed skirmishes over political and spiritual appointments.

Paintings of the sohei in battle dress are often difficult to distinguish from those of the samurai in battle dress. Many of them wore the o-yoroi armor of the samurai, while others preferred the do-maru, literally "torso round," of Japan's common soldiers. The do-maru was made of overlapping rows of lacquered metal or leather scales that were laced together. An armor plate would be formed with a series of these rows joined by silk cords. The do-maru wrapped around the body and was tied under the right arm. It was lighter and allowed for easier movement that the o-yoroi. A kote, or "armored sleeve," could be added for extra arm protection. A kimono typically covered the armor, and multiple kimonos could be layered. A hachimaki (headband) could be tied around the forehead, or a white cowl could be used to cover more of the head. Tabi socks and geta (wooden clogs) or waraji (straw sandals) were the traditional footwear.

The weapon usually associated with the sohei was the naginata, a long shaft with a blade attachment, which could vary in length and shape. A katana was often hung from an obi, or kimono belt, in the tachi style, which required the edge of the blade to be faced down. The belt may also have held a tanto, or dagger. Many sohei were skilled gunners

but would have more commonly used swords and daikyu (bamboo and rattan bows) with bamboo arrows. Archers fired bows from horseback, a skill that took many hours of practice to reach proficiency.

Perhaps the most powerful weapon at the monks' disposal was the sacred mikoshi. The mikoshi was a religious artifact believed to house the spirit of Sanno, the mountain king, and was carried as a portable shrine. Those who struck it were believed to be marked for death, and so the monks would carry the mikoshi with them into battle to terrify their opponents. If otherwise offended, the monks could denounce their enemies at the Kasuga shrine in Kyoto, or they could use their prayer beads to place a curse on someone.

The countryside monks of the sixteenth century, the ikko-ikki, "devoted riot," were followers of the Jodo Shinshu set of beliefs. These fundamentalist priests, along with farmers and their families, were willing to fight for their beliefs. They were opposed to samurai rule, and when they established themselves in Nagashima, Ishiyma, Honganji, and Mikawa, they pronounced that all samurai power would be demolished in their provinces. Some samurai, however, were also members of ikko-ikki and were thus divided in their loyalties.

The ikko-ikki had been a constant threat to the daimyo Oda Nobunaga for ten years or more during his attempts to unify and rule Japan. In 1571, he attacked the monks of Mount Hiei and destroyed Enryakuji, leaving an estimated 20,000 dead. Then, within just a few years, he starved the ikko-ikki into submission by blockading their fortresses and burning their garrison, killing another 20,000 people. Further fighting continued for the remaining ikko-ikki until they were forced to surrender in 1580. By the time Tokugawa Ieyasu had become shogun two decades later, the warrior monks were no longer present in Japan.

*Left: Naginata in Shira Saya. Signed "Hosakawa Masayoshi." Circa 1800. Opposite page: Bishamonten, the Guardian of the North with his Retinue. Japan. Kamakura period, late 12th–early 13th century. Ink, gold, color, and silver on silk.*

# *Honor*

The sense of honor, implying a vivid consciousness of personal dignity and worth, could not fail to characterize the samurai, born and bred to value the duties and privileges of their profession. Though the word ordinarily given nowadays as the translation of honor was not used freely, yet the idea was conveyed by such terms as *na* (name), *men-moku* (countenance), *guai-bun* (outside hearing), reminding us respectively of the biblical use of "name," of the evolution of the term "personality" from the Greek mask, and of "fame." A good name—one's reputation, the immortal part of one's self, what remains being bestial—assumed as a matter of course, any infringement upon its integrity was felt as shame, and the sense of shame (*Ren-chi-shin*) was one of the earliest to be cherished in juvenile education. "You will be laughed at," "It will disgrace you," "Are you not ashamed?" were the last appeal to correct behavior on the part of a youthful delinquent. Such a recourse to his honor touched the most sensitive spot in the child's heart, as though it had been nursed on honor while it was in its mother's womb; for most truly is honor a prenatal influence, being closely bound up with strong family consciousness. "In losing the solidarity of families," says Balzac, "society has lost the fundamental force which Montesquieu named Honor." Indeed, the sense of shame seems to me to be the earliest indication of the moral consciousness of our race. The first and worst punishment which befell humanity in consequence of tasting "the fruit of that forbidden tree" was, to my mind, not the sorrow of childbirth, nor the thorns and thistles, but the awakening of the sense of shame. Few incidents in history excel in pathos the scene of the first mother plying with heaving breast and tremulous fingers, her crude needle on the few fig leaves which her dejected husband plucked for her. This first fruit of disobedience clings to us with a tenacity that nothing else does. All the sartorial ingenuity of mankind has not yet succeeded in sewing an apron that will efficaciously hide our sense of shame. That samurai was right who refused to compromise his character by a slight humiliation in his youth; "because," he said, "dishonor is like a scar on a tree,

which time, instead of effacing, only helps to enlarge."

Mencius had taught centuries before, in almost the identical phrase, what Carlyle has latterly expressed,—namely, that "Shame is the soil of all Virtue, of good manners and good morals."

The fear of disgrace was so great that if our literature lacks such eloquence as Shakespeare puts into the mouth of Norfolk, it nevertheless hung like Damocles' sword over the head of every samurai and often assumed a morbid character. In the name of honor, deeds were perpetrated which can find no justification in the code of Bushido. At the slightest, nay, imaginary insult, the quick-tempered braggart took offense, resorted to the use of the sword, and many an unnecessary strife was raised and many an innocent life lost. The story of a well-meaning citizen who called the attention of a bushi to a flea jumping on his back, and who was forthwith cut in two, for the simple and questionable reason that inasmuch as fleas are parasites which feed on animals, it was an unpardonable insult to identify a noble warrior with a beast—I say, stories like these are too frivolous to believe. Yet, the circulation of such stories implies three things: (1) that they were invented to overawe common people; (2) that abuses were really made of the samurai's profession of honor; and (3) that a very strong sense of shame was developed among them. It is plainly unfair to take an abnormal case to cast blame upon the precepts, any more than to judge of the true teaching of Christ from the fruits of religious fanaticism and extravagance—inquisitions and hypocrisy. But, as in religious monomania there is something touchingly noble as compared with the delirium tremens of a drunkard, so in that extreme sensitiveness of the samurai about their honor do we not recognize the substratum of a genuine virtue?

The morbid excess into which the delicate code of honor was inclined to run was strongly counterbalanced by

*Opposite page: Samurai statue in Tokyo, Japan.*

*Tsuba with design of deer antler and wasp. Sukashi. Edo period. Iron.*

preaching magnanimity and patience. To take offense at slight provocation was ridiculed as "short-tempered." The popular adage said: "To bear what you think you cannot bear is really to bear." The great Iyéyasu left to posterity a few maxims, among which are the following: "The life of man is like going a long distance with a heavy load upon the shoulders. Haste not…. Reproach none, but be forever watchful of thine own shortcomings…. Forbearance is the basis of length of days." He proved in his life what he preached. A literary wit put a characteristic epigram into the mouths of three well-known personages in our history: to Nobunaga he attributed, "I will kill her, if the nightingale sings not in time;" to Hidéyoshi, "I will force her to sing for me;" and to Iyéyasu, "I will wait till she opens her lips."

Patience and long suffering were also highly commended by Mencius. In one place he writes to this effect: "Though you denude yourself and insult me, what is that to me? You cannot defile my soul by your outrage." Elsewhere he teaches that anger at a petty offense is unworthy a superior man, but indignation for a great cause is righteous wrath.

To what height of unmartial and unresisting meekness Bushido could reach in some of its votaries, may be seen in their utterances. Take, for instance, this saying of Ogawa: "When others speak all manner of evil things against thee, return not evil for evil, but rather reflect that thou wast not more faithful in the discharge of thy duties." Take another of Kumazawa: "When others blame thee, blame them not; when others are angry at thee, return

---

*"The Way is the way of Heaven and Earth; Man's place is to follow it; therefore make it the object of thy life to reverence Heaven. Heaven loves me and others with equal love; therefore with the love wherewith thou lovest thyself, love others. Make not Man thy partner but Heaven, and making Heaven thy partner do thy best. Never condemn others; but see to it that thou comest not short of thine own mark."*

---

not anger. Joy cometh only as Passion and Desire part." Still another instance I may cite from Saigo, upon whose overhanging brows "shame is ashamed to sit;" "The Way is the way of Heaven and Earth; Man's

*Katana. Signed "Bizen Kiyomitsu." Circa 1550.*

place is to follow it; therefore make it the object of thy life to reverence Heaven. Heaven loves me and others with equal love; therefore with the love wherewith thou lovest thyself, love others. Make not Man thy partner but Heaven, and making Heaven thy partner do thy best. Never condemn others; but see to it that thou comest not short of thine own mark." Some of those sayings remind us of Christian expostulations and show us how far in practical morality natural religion can approach the revealed. Not only did these sayings remain as utterances, but they were really embodied in acts.

It must be admitted that very few attained this sublime height of magnanimity, patience, and forgiveness. It was a great pity that nothing clear and general was expressed as to what constitutes honor, only a few enlightened minds being aware that it "from no condition rises," but that it lies in each acting well his part; for nothing was easier than for youths to forget in the heat of action what they had learned in Mencius in their calmer moments. Said this sage: "'Tis in every man's mind to love honor: but little doth he dream that what is truly honorable lies within himself and not anywhere else. The honor which men confer is not good honor. Those whom Châo the Great ennobles, he can make mean again." For the most part, an insult was quickly resented and repaid by death, as we shall see later, while honor—too often nothing higher than vain glory or worldly approbation—was prized as the *summum bonum* of earthly existence.

Fame, and not wealth or knowledge, was the goal toward which youths had to strive. Many a lad swore within himself as he crossed the threshold of his paternal home, that he would not recross it until he had made a name in the world; and many an ambitious mother refused to see her sons again unless they could "return home," as the expression is, "caparisoned in brocade." To shun shame or win a name, samurai boys would submit to any privations and undergo severest ordeals of bodily or mental suffering. They knew that honor won in youth grows with age. In the memorable siege of Osaka, a young son of Iyéyasu, in spite of his earnest entreaties to be put in the vanguard, was placed at the rear of the army. When the castle fell, he was so chagrined and wept so bitterly that an old councilor tried to console him with all the resources at his command. "Take comfort, Sire," said he, "at thought of the long future before you. In the many years that you may live, there will come divers occasions to distinguish yourself." The boy fixed his indignant gaze upon the man and said—"How foolishly you talk! Can ever my fourteenth year come round again?" Life itself was thought cheap if honor and fame could be attained therewith: hence, whenever a cause presented itself which was considered dearer than life, with utmost serenity and celerity was life laid down.

Of the causes in comparison with which no life was too dear to sacrifice, was the duty of loyalty, which was the keystone making feudal virtues a symmetrical arch.

Tea bowl. Japan. 16th–17th century. Stoneware pottery.

# SENGOKU JIDAI
## JAPAN'S WARRING STATES PERIOD

Throughout much of the world, the late Middle Ages was an era of great economic and political upheaval. The growth of trade guilds and the emergence of a merchant class challenged the decaying feudal system. Revolutions in faith, ranging from the Protestant Reformation of Europe to the Pure Land movement among the Buddhists of Japan, threatened the established order. In Europe, the century between 1467 and 1567 was marked by the Wars of the Roses in England, the Peasants War in Germany, and the Wars of Religion in France. In Japan, that hundred-year period was known as the *sengoku jidai*, or the Warring States period.

The sengoku jidai began with a dispute over succession in the ruling Ashikaga shogunate. For the first two decades of his rule, the shogun Ashikaga Yoshimasa had been childless, perhaps because he enjoyed the company of his male lover at least as much as that of his wife. (It was the custom at that time for samurai to take young male lovers, known as *chigo*, but Yoshimasa was particularly fond of his.)

Finally, in 1464, Yoshimasa adopted his younger brother Yoshimi with hopes of making him the heir. But within a year, Yoshimasa finally produced a son, Yoshihisa. Despite the birth, Yoshimi claimed he should be the rightful heir. Yoshimi's claims were supported by Hosokawa Katsumoto, a powerful *kanrei*, or deputy to the shogun. But Katsumoto's father-in-law, Yamana Sozen, backed the infant. By the time Yoshihisa was two, the nation was on the brink of war.

In July 1467, Katsumoto and Sozen each brought armies of around 80,000 men into Kyoto. The shogun had no taste for war. His reign had been marked by the refinement of the Japanese tea ceremony, *ikebana* flower arrangements, *Noh* dramas, and *sumi-e* ink paintings. He refused to take sides between the two armies, but he warned that whichever side struck the first blow would be viewed as rebellious.

For several months, the two armies squared off against each other until finally Katsumoto attacked the mansion of one of his father-in-law's generals. That attack launched off a full-scale war between the two forces, leading to the destruction of huge swaths of Kyoto. Over the next few days, Katsumoto took over the eastern part of the city, which is how his troops came to be known as the Eastern Army.

*Right: Yorimasa shooting at the monster Nuye. Utagawa Kuniyoshi. Circa 1845. Color woodblock print.*
*Opposite page: Samurai armor. Japan. Muromachi period. Circa 1384. Mixed media.*

Sozen controlled the other part of Kyoto with his Western Army. The court chronicles record that while Kyoto was being torn in two, the shogun spent his time reading poetry.

Over the next eleven years, in what came to be known as the Onin War, the two armies battled throughout Kyoto and its environs. The war continued even after both Katsumoto and Sozen died in 1473 of natural causes. By the time the two armies had left in 1477, Kyoto was in ruins. Shogun Yoshimasa finally anointed his natural-born son as his successor and stripped his younger brother of his courtly offices. But by then, the shogunate had been so weakened that the title of shogun was meaningless. The entire country was in a state of anarchy.

Before the Onin War, the feudal lords, the *daimyo*, had felt the obligation to keep their domains relatively peaceful in fealty to the shogun. With Kyoto riven by strife, long-simmering tensions among the daimyo bubbled over. Sons fought against fathers and younger brothers fought against elder brothers in bloody disputes over who should control the leading clans. And once the familial disputes in a clan were resolved, the clan would declare war on its neighbors in hopes of extending its territory. A dozen or so of Japan's

leading families, including the Imagawa and the Takeda, seized vast areas of land during this period, crushing their smaller rivals. The clan leaders correctly assumed that the shogun would not have the stomach to stop them from fighting with each other.

At the same time, peasant farmers in many parts of the country staged revolts against their samurai overlords, demanding more food and land. By 1486, a peasant army known as the *ikko-ikki* toppled the samurai lords of the province of Yamashiro in the first successful commoners' revolt in Japanese history. Two years later, an army of peasants and lesser samurai joined with the Buddhist monks of the Pure Land movement to take control of Kaga province. The Pure Land adherents felt that through belief in Buddha, they would be transported after death to a "pure land" of eternal bliss, and some spent their time fighting to create such a pure land on earth.

Although the peasant revolts were eventually put down, the civil strife lasted for an entire century. It was only brought to an end in the 1560s, when a young daimyo named Oda Nobunaga and two of his followers, Toyotomi Hideyoshi and Tokugawa Ieyasu, worked together to unite Japan.

# The Duty of Loyalty

Feudal morality shares other virtues in common with other systems of ethics, with other classes of people, but this virtue—homage and fealty to a superior—is its distinctive feature. I am aware that personal fidelity is a moral adhesion existing among all sorts and conditions of men,—a gang of pickpockets owe allegiance to a Fagin; but it is only in the code of chivalrous honor that loyalty assumes paramount importance.

In spite of Hegel's criticism that the fidelity of feudal vassals, being an obligation to an individual and not to a Commonwealth, is a bond established on totally unjust principles,[16] a great compatriot of his made it his boast that personal loyalty was a German virtue. Bismarck had good reason to do so, not because the *Treue* he boasts of was the monopoly of his Fatherland or of any single nation or race, but because this favored fruit of chivalry lingers latest among the people where feudalism has lasted longest. In America where "everybody is as good as anybody else," and, as the Irishman added, "better too," such exalted ideas of loyalty as we feel for our sovereign may be deemed "excellent within certain bounds," but preposterous as encouraged among us. Montesquieu complained long ago that right on one side of the Pyrenees was wrong on the other, and the recent Dreyfus trial proved the truth of his remark, save that the Pyrenees were not the sole boundary beyond which French justice finds no accord. Similarly, loyalty as we conceive it may find few admirers elsewhere, not because our conception is wrong, but because it is, I am afraid, forgotten, and also because we carry it to a degree not reached in any other country. Griffis[17] was quite right in stating that whereas in China Confucian ethics made obedience to parents the primary human duty, in Japan precedence was given to loyalty. At the risk of shocking some of my good readers, I will relate of one

*Opposite page: A 19th-century posed photograph of two samurai, each wearing a daisho and the kamishiho (hemp wings) with hakama.*

"who could endure to follow a fall'n lord" and who thus, as Shakespeare assures, "earned a place i' the story."

The story is of one of the purest characters in our history, Michizané, who, falling victim to jealousy and calumny, is exiled from the capital. Not content with this, his unrelenting enemies are now bent upon the extinction of his family. Strict search for his son—not yet grown—reveals the fact of his being secreted in a village school kept by one Genzo, a former vassal of Michizané. When orders are dispatched to the schoolmaster to deliver the head of the juvenile offender on a certain day, his first idea is to find a suitable substitute for it. He ponders over his school-list, scrutinizes with careful eyes all the boys, as they stroll into the classroom, but none among the children born of the soil bears the least resemblance to his protégé. His despair, however, is but for a moment; for, behold, a new scholar is announced—a comely boy of the same age as his master's son, escorted by a mother of noble mien.

No less conscious of the resemblance between infant lord and infant retainer, were the mother and the boy himself. In the privacy of home both had laid themselves upon the altar; the one his life—the other her heart, yet without sign to the outer world. Unwitting of what had passed between them, it is the teacher from whom comes the suggestion.

Here, then, is the scapegoat!—The rest of the narrative may be briefly told. On the day appointed, arrives the officer commissioned to identify and receive the head of the youth. Will he be deceived by the false head? The poor Genzo's hand is on the hilt of the sword, ready to strike a blow either at the man or at himself, should the examination defeat his scheme. The officer takes up the gruesome object before him, goes calmly over each feature, and in a deliberate, business-like tone, pronounces it genuine. That evening in a lonely home awaits the mother we saw in the school. Does she know the fate of her child? It is not for his return that she watches with eagerness for the opening of the wicket. Her father-in-law has been for a long time a recipient of Michizané's bounties, but since his banishment, circumstances have forced her husband to

*Onoe Kikugoro III as Nagoya in "Sato no haru meibutsu amigasa." Circa 1827. Colored woodblock print.*

follow the service of the enemy of his family's benefactor. He himself could not be untrue to his own cruel master; but his son could serve the cause of the grandsire's lord. As one acquainted with the exile's family, it was he who had been entrusted with the task of identifying the boy's head. Now the day's—yea, the life's—hard work is done, he returns home and as he crosses its threshold, he accosts his wife, saying: "Rejoice, my wife, our darling son has proved of service to his lord!"

"What an atrocious story!" I hear my readers exclaim, "Parents deliberately sacrificing their own innocent child to save the life of another man's." But this child was a conscious and willing victim: it is a story of vicarious death—as significant as, and not more revolting than, the story of Abraham's intended sacrifice of Isaac. In both cases it was obedience to the call of duty, utter submission to the command of a higher voice, whether given by a visible or an invisible angel, or heard by an outward or an inward ear; but I abstain from preaching.

The individualism of the West, which

recognizes separate interests for father and son, husband and wife, necessarily brings into strong relief the duties owed by one to the other; but Bushido held that the interest of the family and of the members thereof is intact, one and inseparable. This interest it bound up with affection—natural, instinctive, irresistible; hence, if we die for one we love with natural love (which animals themselves possess), what is that? "For if ye love them that love you, what reward have ye? Do not even the publicans the same?"

In his great history, Sanyo relates in touching language the heart struggle of Shigemori concerning his father's rebellious conduct. "If I be loyal, my father must be undone; if I obey my father, my duty to my sovereign must go amiss." Poor Shigemori! We see him afterward praying with all his soul that kind Heaven may visit him with death, that he may be released from this world where it is hard for purity and righteousness to dwell.

Many a Shigemori has his heart torn by the conflict between duty and affection. Indeed neither Shakespeare nor the Old Testament itself contains an adequate rendering of *ko*, our conception of filial piety, and yet in such conflicts Bushido never wavered in its choice of loyalty. Women, too, encouraged their offspring to sacrifice all for the king. Ever as resolute as Widow Windham and her illustrious consort, the samurai matron stood ready to give up her boys for the cause of loyalty.

Since Bushido, like Aristotle and some modern sociologists, conceived the state as antedating the individual—the latter being born into the former as part and parcel thereof—he must live and die for it or for the incumbent of its legitimate authority. Readers of *Crito* will remember the argument with which Socrates represents the laws of the city as pleading with him on the subject of his escape. Among others he makes them (the laws, or the state) say: "Since you were begotten and nurtured and educated under us, dare you once to say you are not our offspring and servant, you and your fathers before you!" These are words which do not impress us as any thing extraordinary; for the same thing has long been on the lips of Bushido, with this modification, that the laws and the state were represented with us by a personal being. Loyalty is an ethical outcome of this political theory.

I am not entirely ignorant of Mr. Spencer's view according to which political obedience—loyalty—is accredited with only a transitional function.[18] It may be so. Sufficient unto the day is the virtue thereof. We may complacently repeat it, especially as we believe that day to be a long space of time, during which, so our national anthem says, "tiny pebbles grow into mighty rocks draped with moss."

We may remember at this juncture that even among so democratic a people as the English, "the sentiment of personal fidelity to a man and his posterity which their Germanic ancestors felt for their chiefs, has," as Monsieur Boutmy recently said, "only passed more or less into their profound loyalty to the race and blood of their princes, as evidenced in their extraordinary attachment to the dynasty."

Political subordination, Mr. Spencer predicts, will give place to loyalty to the dictates of conscience. Suppose his induction is realized—will loyalty and its concomitant instinct of reverence disappear forever? We transfer our allegiance from one master to another, without being unfaithful to either; from being subjects of a ruler that wields the temporal scepter we become servants of the monarch who sits enthroned in the penetralia of our heart. A few years ago a very stupid controversy, started by the misguided disciples of Spencer, made havoc among the reading class of Japan. In their zeal to uphold the claim of the throne to undivided loyalty, they charged Christians with treasonable propensities in that they avow fidelity to their Lord and Master. They arrayed forth sophistical arguments without the wit of Sophists, and scholastic tortuosities minus the niceties of the Schoolmen. Little did they know that we can, in a sense, "serve two masters without holding to the one or despising the other," "rendering unto Caesar the things that are Caesar's and unto God the things that are God's." Did not Socrates, all the while he unflinchingly refused to concede one iota of loyalty to his daemon, obey with equal fidelity and equanimity the command of his earthly master, the State? His conscience he followed, alive; his country he served, dying. Alack the day when a state grows so powerful as to demand of its citizens the dictates of their conscience!

Bushido did not require us to make our conscience the slave of any lord or king. Thomas Mowbray was a veritable spokesman for us when he said:

*Myself I throw, dread sovereign, at thy foot.*
*My life thou shalt command, but not my*
   *shame.*

*The one my duty owes; but my fair name,*
*Despite of death, that lives upon my grave,*
*To dark dishonor's use, thou shalt not have.*

A man who sacrificed his own conscience to the capricious will or freak or fancy of a sovereign was accorded a low place in the estimate of the Precepts. Such a one was despised as *nei-shin*, a cringeling, who makes court by unscrupulous fawning, or as *chō-shin*, a favorite who steals his master's affections by means of servile compliance; these two species of subjects corresponding exactly to those which Iago describes—the one, a duteous and knee-crooking knave, doting on his own obsequious bondage, wearing out his time much like his master's ass; the other trimm'd in forms and visages of duty, keeping yet his heart attending on himself. When a subject differed from his master, the loyal path for him to pursue was to use every available means to persuade him of his error, as Kent did to King Lear. Failing in this, let the master deal with him as he wills. In cases of this kind, it was quite a usual course for the samurai to make the last appeal to the intelligence and conscience of his lord by demonstrating the sincerity of his words with the shedding of his own blood.

Life being regarded as the means whereby to serve his master, and its ideal being set upon honor, the whole education and training of a samurai were conducted accordingly.

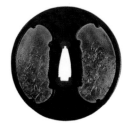

*Top: Tanto. Bizen Kiyomitsu, Circa 1550. Kiyomitsu crafted this tanto in the yori dachi style. Yori dachi–style swords proved most valuable for piercing armor.*
*Bottom: Tsuba. Edo period.*

16 *Philosophy of History* (Eng. trans. by Sibree), Pt. IV, Sec. II, Ch. I.
17 *Religions of Japan.*
18 *Principles of Ethics*, Vol. I, Pt. II, Ch. X.

# EDO
## THE SHOGUNATE CAPITAL

As one of Japan's leading warlords, Tokugawa Ieyasu was known for his daring military tactics: attacking by night, storming castles, and demolishing temples. But one of his riskiest moves was off the battlefield.

In 1590, at the request of his lord, Toyotomi Hideyoshi, who was then the most powerful *daimyo* in the land, Ieyasu gave up control of the provinces under his command and took over a string of territories, including huge swaths of marsh and wilderness, which Hideyoshi had recently seized from a rival clan. To leave his home province and move into the territory of his enemies was fraught with danger, but Ieyasu accepted the challenge. He established his new headquarters in an aging castle overlooking a tiny fishing village called Yedo, whose name translates as "gateway to the bay."

And thus began the story of the city of Edo, or Tokyo, as it has been known for the past 150 years. Within thirteen years of moving into Edo, Ieyasu had established it as the true center of political power in Japan, a position that it has maintained for more than four centuries. While the emperors continued to rule from Kyoto, Ieyasu and his successors in the Tokugawa clan turned Edo into one of the largest cities in the world.

Edo's rise to prominence began in 1598, when Hideyoshi died, touching off a power struggle between several of his underlings. In 1603, Ieyasu emerged victorious, proclaiming himself to be shogun and naming Edo as his capital, heralding the dawn of what is now known as the Edo period of Japanese history.

After two centuries of clan warfare in Japan, Ieyasu and his heirs in the Tokugawa clan took no chances at allowing rebellions to form. In the early seventeenth century, they introduced the *sankin kotai*, a system of alternate-year attendance. The system required that all 270 or so daimyo maintain residences in Edo for themselves and their extended families and that they would remain in those residences for a fixed number of months every other year, ensuring that the shogun could keep his eye on them. Whenever they left Edo to visit their home provinces, they had to leave behind their families, who could be held hostage if the daimyo stepped out of line.

This sankin kotai system led to the creation of numerous villas for the wealthy daimyo and their retainers in Edo. The swamps surrounding Edo were drained, hills were leveled, and forests were cut down in order to

provide room for the daimyo and all of their samurai. This concentration of wealth drew, from throughout the countryside, farmers, craftsmen, merchants, artists, performers, and prostitutes who hoped to sell their wares or services to the nobility. By the 1650s, Edo was a vast complex of villas, palaces, and temples, surrounded by a sea of lower-class tenements. Roughly half the people lived in long row houses made of wood and paper, along narrow alleyways that had sewage running in trenches down the middle. The lowest class consisted of the shopkeepers, considered to be of less value than farmers or artisans because they did not produce anything. They typically lived in small rooms above or adjoining their shops, with an entire family living in a single-room apartment of only one hundred square feet, where the kitchen consisted of a stove in the entryway and the beds were sheets of matted straw, or *tatami*, rolled out on the floor.

The construction materials of wooden walls, paper doorways, and straw matting made Edo a tinderbox. In 1657, the Great Meireki Fire ravaged the city, destroying as much as 70 percent of the *Edo* and killing more than 100,000 people. Though the city had a fire department, the *hikeshi*,

*Left: Helmet with the hollyhock-leaf crest of Tokugawa and dragonflies. Mixed media.*
*Above: Inro depicting the courtesan Morokoshi of Echizen-ya writing a letter. Hosada Eishi. Japan. Polished lacquers and inlaid gold foil on a lacquer ground.*
*Opposite page: Hero of a Monogatari. Ariwara no Narimira. 17th–19th century. Black and white photo of woodblock print.*

207

organized just two decades before, it was too small and poorly equipped to cope with the blaze.

The fire transformed the city. The narrow alleyways, some of which had been as little as three feet wide, were broadened to create better firebreaks, which had the side benefit of giving the residents more space to move around. The survivors of the fire were given generous government funds to rebuild their homes, which typically gave them nicer residences than they had previously had. Most important, when the city was rebuilt, it was organized into self-sufficient neighborhoods called *cho*. Each cho had its own shops, temples, shrines, and fire and police departments, along with a watchtower to keep an eye out for flames. The governing councils of the cho, known as *chokai*, oversaw municipal planning and religious festivals. Although Japan remained a military dictatorship under the command of the all-powerful shogun, the cho in Edo and other large cities allowed commoners a smattering of democracy, giving them a say in their day-to-day affairs.

By the mid-eighteenth century, Edo had as many as a million people, making it the biggest city in the world outside of China. The city was divided into a number of distinctive neighborhoods. Tsujiki, the theater district, was home to playhouses for *kabuki*, Noh, and *rakugo*, where individual performers would kneel before the audience to tell comic monologues. Kiyobashi, one of the largest commercial districts, was divided into different cho for artisans of varying crafts: silversmiths, blacksmiths, gunsmiths, stonemasons, tatami weavers, bucket makers, and so on. Asakusa was home to some of the city's largest temples, as well as, incongruously, the headquarters of many of the *yakuza*, the Mafia-like gangs dominated by the roaming, masterless samurai known as *ronin*. Odenmacho, "horse-messenger neighborhood," was one of the chief centers of the shogun's postal system. And then there was Yoshiwara, the "floating world of pleasure," home to as many as 3,000 prostitutes at its peak.

Edo was no utopia. As with any big city, there were problems with crime, corruption, filth, and poverty. But the Edo period is nevertheless looked upon as a golden

era for Japan, when the country was largely at peace and the arts flourished. Although the samurai still wore their swords when walking through the streets, many of them spent their spare time with their ink brushes, composing haiku poems or painting minimalist landscapes. Books of poetry, history, theology, and fiction were printed, illustrated with woodcut prints called *ukiyo-e* (a term that is much more nuanced than the commonly translated "pictures of the floating world," suggesting, more correctly, images of the transient, temporal, impure world of all human activity). Tailors crafted elegant clothing with multicolored layers of silk and brocade. Fine works of art were created using stone, porcelain, and lacquer. A new era was being ushered in, with the centuries-old *bakufu* feudal code beginning to crumble, modernity arriving with the redistribution of land, and economic influences of the Western world coming to the island empire that had protected itself for so long from change.

The Edo era came to an end in 1868, when Emperor Meiji forced the resignation of the last Tokugawa shogun

Top left: *The Teahouse at Edo. Kunishand. Circa 1827. Woodblock print.*
Above: *Takigawa from the Tea-House. Ogi. Color woodblock print.*

and renamed the city Tokyo, "eastern capital" (as opposed to Saikyo, "western capital," which was Meiji's name for the old imperial capital of Kyoto). Even now, the Japanese still think wistfully about the spirit of old Edo as they walk through the temple grounds and narrow alleys of Asakusa, which was flattened by bombers in World War II but has been rebuilt as a reminder of the days of the samurai.

# THE SHOGUNATE INVASION OF KOREA

It was before dawn on a cool spring morning of 1592 when an amphibious army of more than 6,000 samurai and their soldiers launched an assault on the Korean port of Pusan. Thus began Japan's first true attempt at military expansion abroad—an attempt to put the rest of northern Asia under the control of the samurai. But instead of resulting in a samurai empire, it would usher in an era of isolationism for Japan.

Japanese warlord Toyotomi Hideyoshi began laying the groundwork for the invasion not long after the emperor appointed him *kampaku* (regent), the primary military leader of Japan. For the first time in more than a century, the warring states of Japan were largely united under a single commander. Now Hideyoshi looked abroad for other challenges. In 1590, the year that Hideyoshi had crushed the stronghold of his last remaining rival in Japan, he received a team of ambassadors from Korea, which was trying to reestablish long-dormant diplomatic ties. Hideyoshi had been waiting for this day and had already sent several envoys to Korea's King Seonjo, while simultaneously commissioning spy ships to chart the Korean coast for a possible invasion route. When the ambassadors arrived in Kyoto, Hideyoshi treated them in a purposely insulting manner. After a frugal meal of rice and low-quality sake, Hideyoshi asked the ambassadors

*Arrival of the Southern Barbarians. Anonymous. 17th Century. Six-panel screen with ink, color, gold pigment, and gold leaf on paper.*

After a one-day battle, Pusan fell, thousands of its residents slaughtered. The nearby fortresses of Tadaejin and Dongnae also fell quickly. The Japanese could have possibly emerged victorious if it had not been for the foresight of Korean admiral Yi Sun-sin, who had been worried about the threat of Japanese invasion for more than a year. Using a technique that the Koreans had decades earlier employed against Japanese pirates, Yi had converted several of his vessels into *kobukson*, "turtle ships." On each of these, a thick wooden roof, resembling a turtle's shell, was erected over the main deck. The roof was thick enough to protect against fusillades of arrows from enemy ships, and it was studded with sharp iron spikes to discourage the enemy from boarding. To aid in firing against the enemy, rows of narrow portholes on the ship allowed the use of archers, who were reinforced with cannon—eleven on each side of the ship. Throughout the coming months, Sun-sin established supremacy at sea, successfully preventing Hideyoshi from supplying his invasion force with necessary reinforcements and provisions.

Sun-sin's success at sea helped the Koreans bide their time as they waited for help from China. In January 1593, the Chinese sent nearly 100,000 soldiers into Korea, where they checked the Japanese advance and, with the help of the remnants of the Korean army, pushed them back to Pusan. For the next four years, Korea and Japan formed an uneasy truce. In 1597, war once again erupted after an exchange of insulting messages between Hideyoshi and the Chinese emperor. Nearly 80,000 Japanese troops streamed out of Pusan, aiming to bring Korea under their control. Despite a number of initial successes, however, they were largely confined to Pusan's Gyeongsang province, hemmed in by Korean and Chinese troops. Sun-sin once again defeated the Japanese navy, and the war came to an end in the fall of 1598, when Hideyoshi, on his deathbed in Kyoto, ordered his army to return to Japan.

Historians estimate that Hideyoshi's Korean invasion resulted in as many as one million civilian and military casualties during the war. The defeat, after seven years in battle with nothing but death and debt to show for it, left bitter feelings in Japan. Many warlords turned against Hideyoshi's Toyotomi clan, preferring instead the leadership of his vassal Tokugawa Ieyasu, who had opposed the war from its inception and had kept his troops out. Months after the war's end, Ieyasu staged a coup against Hideyoshi's five-year-old son and heir, Hideyori. Within two years, he had established himself as the dominant warlord, and in 1603, he was appointed shogun. Ieyasu and his successors never again engaged in foreign war, bringing war-torn Japan more than two centuries of peaceful isolationism.

to carry a letter back to Seonjo announcing his intention to attack China using Korea as his main staging area.

The tone of Hideyoshi's letter was deliberately provocative. In addition, as Hideyoshi knew, the idea of using Korea as a beachhead was thoroughly unrealistic. Since 1392, Korea had prospered as a vassal state of the Chinese, and there was no reason to expect that relationship to suddenly change. Without a doubt, Hideyoshi wanted the Koreans to refuse his request, which is exactly what happened. But the Koreans were totally unprepared for battle. After enjoying nearly two centuries of peace, they lacked a large army and had few modern weapons, such as cannon or harquebuses.

# The Education and Training of a Samurai

The first point to observe in knightly pedagogies was to build up character, leaving in the shade the subtler faculties of prudence, intelligence, and dialectics. We have seen the important part aesthetic accomplishments played in his education. Indispensable as they were to a man of culture, they were accessories rather than essentials of samurai training. Intellectual superiority was, of course, esteemed; but the word *Chi*, which was employed to denote intellectuality, meant wisdom in the first instance and placed knowledge only in a very subordinate place. The tripod that supported the framework of Bushido was said to be *Chi*, *Jin*, *Yu*, respectively Wisdom, Benevolence, and Courage. A samurai was essentially a man of action. Science was without the pale of his activity. He took advantage of it in so far as it concerned his profession of arms. Religion and theology were relegated to the priests; he concerned himself with them in so far as they helped to nourish courage. Like an English poet the samurai believed "'tis not the creed that saves the man; but it is the man that justifies the creed." Philosophy and literature formed the chief part of his intellectual training; but even in the pursuit of these, it was not objective truth that he strove after—literature was pursued mainly as a pastime, and philosophy as a practical aid in the formation of character, if not for the exposition of some military or political problem.

From what has been said, it will not be surprising to note that the curriculum of studies, according to the pedagogics of Bushido, consisted mainly of the following, fencing, archery, jiujutsu[19] or *yawara*, horsemanship, the use of the spear, tactics, calligraphy, ethics, literature, and history. Of these, jiujutsu and

*Right: Iron tsuba. Sukashi. Moon-and-sun design. Edo period.*
*Opposite page: Nakamura Kansuke Tadatoki, one of the forty-seven ronin. Utagawa Kuniyoshi (1797–1861). Japan. Edo period, 1847. Woodblock print (nishiki-e); ink and color on paper.*

calligraphy may require a few words of explanation. Great stress was laid on good writing, probably because our logograms, partaking as they do of the nature of pictures, possess artistic value, and also because chirography was accepted as indicative of one's personal character. Jiujutsu may be briefly defined as an application of anatomical knowledge to the purpose of offense or defense. It differs from wrestling, in that it does not depend upon muscular strength. It differs from other forms of attack in that it uses no weapon. Its feat consists in clutching or striking such part of the enemy's body as will make him numb and incapable of resistance. Its object is not to kill, but to incapacitate one for action for the time being.

A subject of study which one would expect to find in military education and which is rather conspicuous by its absence in the Bushido course of instruction, is mathematics. This, however, can be readily explained in part by the fact that feudal warfare was not carried on with scientific precision. Not only that, but the whole training of the samurai was unfavorable to fostering numerical notions.

Chivalry is uneconomical; it boasts of penury. It says with Ventidius that "ambition, the soldier's virtue, rather makes choice of loss, than gain which darkens him." Don Quixote takes more pride in his rusty spear and skin-and-bone horse than in gold and lands, and a samurai is in hearty sympathy with his exaggerated confrère of La Mancha. He disdains money itself—the art of making or hoarding it. It is to him veritably filthy lucre. The hackneyed expression to describe the decadence of an age is "that the civilians loved money and the soldiers feared death." Niggardliness of gold and of life excites as much disapprobation as their lavish use is panegyrized. "Less than all things," says a current precept, "men must grudge money: it is by riches that wisdom is hindered." Hence children

*Tsuba. Kano Natsuo. 19th century. Iron.*

*The accessories needed to make Japanese tea, or matcha.*

were brought up with utter disregard of economy. It was considered bad taste to speak of it, and ignorance of the value of different coins was a token of good breeding. Knowledge of numbers was indispensable in the mustering of forces as well, as in the distribution of benefices and fiefs; but the counting of money was left to meaner hands. In many feudatories, public finance was administered by a lower kind of samurai or by priests. Every thinking bushi knew well enough that money formed the sinews of war; but he did not think of raising the appreciation of money to a virtue. It is true that thrift was enjoined by Bushido, but not for economical reasons so much as for the exercise of abstinence. Luxury was thought the greatest menace to manhood, and severest simplicity was required of the warrior class, sumptuary laws being enforced in many of the clans.

We read that in ancient Rome the farmers of revenue and other financial agents were gradually raised to the rank of knights, the State thereby showing its appreciation of their service and of the importance of money itself. How closely this was connected with the luxury and avarice of the Romans may be imagined. Not so with the Precepts of Knighthood. These persisted in systematically regarding finance as something low—low as compared with moral and intellectual vocations.

Money and the love of it being thus diligently ignored, Bushido itself could long remain free from a thousand and one evils of which money is the root. This is sufficient reason for the fact that our public men have long been free from corruption; but, alas, how fast plutocracy is making its way in our time and generation!

The mental discipline which would nowadays be chiefly aided by the study of mathematics, was supplied by literary exegesis and deontological discussions. Very few abstract subjects troubled the mind of the young, the chief aim of their education being, as I have said, decision of character. People whose minds were simply stored with information found no great admirers. Of the three services of studies that Bacon gives—for delight, ornament, and ability—Bushido had decided preference for the last, where their use was "in judgment and the disposition of business." Whether it was for the disposition of public business or for the exercise of

> *Money and the love of it being thus diligently ignored, Bushido itself could long remain free from a thousand and one evils of which money is the root.*

self-control, it was with a practical end in view that education was conducted. "Learning without thought," said Confucius, "is labor lost: thought without learning is perilous."

When character and not intelligence, when the soul and not the head, is chosen by a teacher for the material to work upon and to develop, his vocation partakes of a sacred character. "It is the parent who has borne me: it is the teacher who makes me man." With this idea, therefore, the esteem in which one's preceptor was held was very high. A man to evoke such confidence and respect from the young, must necessarily be endowed with superior personality, without lacking erudition. He was a father to the fatherless, and an adviser to the erring. "Thy father and thy mother"—so runs our maxim— "are like heaven and earth; thy teacher and thy lord are like the sun and moon."

The present system of paying for every sort of service was not in vogue among the adherents of Bushido. It believed in a service which can be rendered only without money and without price. Spiritual service, be it of priest or teacher, was not to be repaid in gold or silver, not because it was valueless but because it was invaluable. Here the nonarithmetical honor instinct of Bushido taught a truer lesson than modern Political Economy; for wages and salaries can be paid only for services whose results are definite, tangible, and measurable, whereas the best service done in education—namely, in soul development (and this includes the services of a pastor), is not definite, tangible, or measurable. Being immeasurable, money, the ostensible measure of value, is of inadequate use. Usage sanctioned that pupils brought to their teachers money or goods at different seasons of the year; but these were not payments but offerings, which indeed were welcome to the recipients as they were usually men of stern calibre, boasting of honorable penury, too dignified to work with their hands and too proud to beg. They were grave personifications of high spirits undaunted by adversity. They were an embodiment of what was considered as an end of all learning, and were thus a living example of that discipline of disciplines, self-control, which was universally required of samurai.

19 The same word as that misspelled *jiu-jitsu* in common English parlance. It is the gentle art. It "uses no weapon." (W.E.G.)

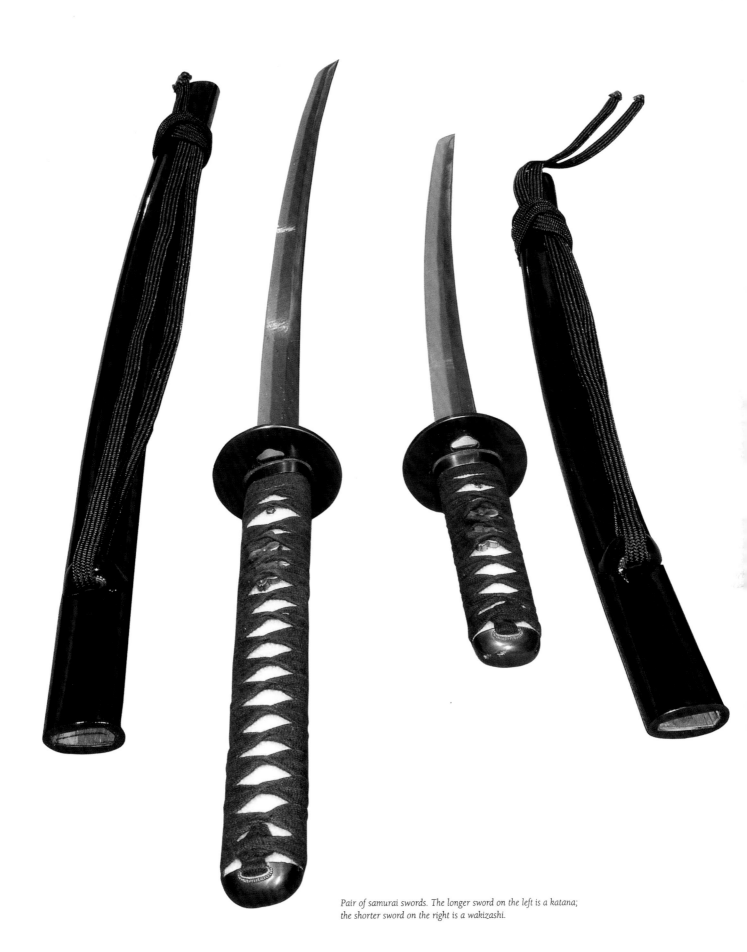

*Pair of samurai swords. The longer sword on the left is a katana; the shorter sword on the right is a wakizashi.*

# RYU
## SCHOOLS FOR SONS OF THE SAMURAI

Originally, the Japanese word *ryu* referred to the flowing current of a body of water. But by the Middle Ages, the word was used for schools where youths above the age of thirteen were brought into the flow of education. There were ryu for such things as calligraphy, painting, flower arranging, and, in the case of would-be samurai, the martial arts.

Throughout Japan, ryu were established for training the sons of the *bushi* to be samurai. Most of the ryu were taught by retired samurai, too old or too injured to return to the battlefield, but lithe enough to pass their techniques on to

their apprentices. The most common schools at that time were the *otome ryu*, which conveyed an aura of secrecy. A teacher would set himself up in a particular *han*, or district, and train all the district's samurai. Usually, his pay would be in the form of bushels of rice from the han's tax revenues.

But there were exceptions to that rule. Some ryu were set up to train warriors and offer protection for a particular village. For example, the Maniwa Nen ryu was founded in 1591 to serve and protect the small village of Maniwa, near what is now Narita International Airport. The style of sword fighting taught by the school is not quite as polished or elegant as the classical tradition of fighting, but the students have proved themselves in tournaments against rival schools. The school remains active today, with students trained in the use of *fukuro shinai*, or mock swords made of bamboo.

Other ryu were established to train guards for temples and religious shrines. The Kashima Shin ryu, for instance, was established in the sixteenth century to train the guardians of a Shinto shrine to Takemikazuchi Mikoto, a warlike deity whose spirit lived within swords. The school's regimen included training by the *sensei*, or teachers, in the use of the *katana* sword, the staves known as *jo* and *bo*, and the scythelike *kama* and in the art of *jujutsu*, or hand-to-hand combat. The *soke*, or headmaster, was paid from taxes the shrine collected on farmlands that were under its control.

The oldest samurai ryu still in existence is the Tenshin Shoden Katori Shinto ryu founded in the fifteenth century in the village of Iizasa, now part of the city of Takomachi. The ryu was founded by Iizasa Ienao, a highly respected spearman and swordsman, who served the *daimyo* of the Chiba clan. In the 1440s, when Ienao was in his fifties, the Chiba family fell into disfavor, the daimyo was deposed, and Ienao's property was confiscated.

Ienao retired to the temple of Katori, one of the three holiest Shinto sanctuaries in Japan, dedicated to Futsunushi Kami, another deity that dwells within swords. According to legend, Ienao spent 1,000 days at the shrine, practicing martial arts day and night, until Futsunushi came to him in a dream and gave him previously unknown secret strategies. Equipped with that god-given advice, which was later written in a book called *Mokuroku heiho shinsho*, Ienao returned to his village of Iizasa. With the financial backing of local samurai, he opened a ryu that taught twelve basic subjects, including the use of the *naginata* (spear) and *yari* (long pike), as well as techniques for *ninjutsu* (spying), *senjutsu* (strategy), and *chikujojutsu* (fortifications). The ryu is still in Iizasa today, and in 1960, it became the first school of martial arts to be named an "intangible cultural asset" by the Japanese government.

Although many have survived to this day, samurai-era ryu, collectively known as *koryu*, "old schools," no longer command the prestige they once held. Their image and sense of purpose were severely diminished after Emperor Meiji dislodged the samurai system in 1868. Meiji's prohibitions against the use of the samurai sword robbed the schools of much of their usefulness. And the decline of the power of the samurai system meant that there was no reason for municipalities to continue to support the ryu with tax revenues. The soke and sensei extracted fees from their

*Daisho kake helmet.*

students and supplemented that income with part-time jobs. Even today, koryu teachers find it hard to make a living without outside employment.

Starting in the early twentieth century, new ryu were founded in Japan to teach youths some modernized martial arts skills. In 1925, the army created the Toyama ryu to teach soldiers how to use a modified version of the katana on the battlefield. In 1938, a father-and-son team launched the Shotokan ryu to teach their personal style of karate. The lessons taught from these ryu flow side by side with the lessons of the koryu of ancient times.

*Opposite page: Karate dojo with wooden frames and paper walls.*

# Self-Control

The discipline of fortitude on the one hand, inculcating endurance without a groan, and the teaching of politeness on the other, requiring us not to mar the pleasure or serenity of another by manifestations of our own sorrow or pain, combined to engender a stoical turn of mind, and eventually to confirm it into a national trait of apparent stoicism. I say apparent stoicism, because I do not believe that true stoicism can ever become the characteristic of a whole nation, and also because some of our national manners and customs may seem to a foreign observer hard-hearted. Yet we are really as susceptible to tender emotion as any race under the sky.

I am inclined to think that in one sense we have to feel more than others—yes, doubly more—since the very attempt to restrain natural promptings entails suffering. Imagine boys—and girls, too—brought up not to resort to the shedding of a tear or the uttering of a groan for the relief of their feelings,—and there is a physiological problem whether such effort steels their nerves or makes them more sensitive.

It was considered unmanly for a samurai to betray his emotions on his face. "He shows no sign of joy or anger," was a phrase used in describing a strong character. The most natural affections were kept under control. A father could embrace his son only at the expense of his dignity; a husband would not kiss his wife—no, not in the presence of other people, whatever he might do in private! There may be some truth in the remark of a witty youth when he said, "American husbands kiss their wives in public and beat them in private; Japanese husbands beat theirs in public and kiss them in private."

Calmness of behavior, composure of mind, should not be disturbed by passion of any kind. I remember when, during the late war with China, a regiment left a certain town, a large concourse of people flocked to the station to bid farewell to the general and his army. On this occasion an American resident resorted to the place, expecting to witness loud demonstrations, as the nation itself was highly

*Opposite page: Statue of a Japanese warrior. Ivory.*

excited and there were fathers, mothers, and sweethearts of the soldiers in the crowd. The American was strangely disappointed; for as the whistle blew and the train began to move, the hats of thousands of people were silently taken off and their heads bowed in reverential farewell; no waving of handkerchiefs, no word uttered, but deep silence in which only an attentive ear could catch a few broken sobs. In domestic life, too, I know of a father who spent whole nights listening to the breathing of a sick child, standing behind the door that he might not be caught in such an act of parental weakness! I know of a mother who, in her last moments, refrained from sending for her son, that he might not be disturbed in his studies. Our history and everyday life are replete with examples of heroic matrons who can well bear comparison with some of the most touching pages of Plutarch. Among our peasantry an Ian Maclaren would be sure to find many a Marget Howe.

It is the same discipline of self-restraint which is accountable for the absence of more frequent revivals in the Christian churches of Japan. When a man or woman feels his or her soul stirred, the first instinct is to quietly suppress any indication of it. In rare instances is the tongue set free by an irresistible spirit, when we have eloquence of sincerity and fervor. It is putting a premium upon a breach of the third commandment to encourage speaking lightly of spiritual experience. It is truly jarring to Japanese ears to hear the most sacred words, the most secret heart experiences, thrown out in promiscuous audiences. "Dost thou feel the soil of thy soul stirred with tender thoughts? It is time for seeds to sprout. Disturb it not with speech; but let it work alone in quietness and secrecy," writes a young samurai in his diary.

To give in so many articulate words one's inmost thoughts and feelings—notably the religious—is taken among us as an unmistakable sign that they are neither very profound nor very sincere. "Only a pomegranate is he"—so runs a popular saying—"who, when he gapes his mouth, displays the contents of his heart."

It is not altogether perverseness of oriental minds that the instant our emotions are moved we try to guard our

*Moronao, the villain of Chushingura (the kabuki play telling the heroic story of the forty-seven ronin, or masterless samurai, who sacrificed their lives to avenge their fallen leader). Utagawa Kunisada. 1852. Color woodblock print.*

lips in order to hide them. Speech is very often with us, as the Frenchman defined it, "the art of concealing thought."

Call upon a Japanese friend in time of deepest affliction and he will invariably receive you laughing, with red eyes or moist cheeks. At first you may think him hysterical. Press him for explanation and you will get a few broken commonplaces—"Human life has sorrow;" "They who meet must part;" "He that is born must die;" "It is foolish to count the years of a child that is gone, but a woman's heart will indulge in follies;" and the like. So the noble words of a noble Hohenzollern—"Lerne zu leiden ohne Klagen"— had found many responsive minds among us, long before they were uttered.

Indeed, the Japanese have recourse to risibility whenever the frailties of human nature are put to severest test. I think we possess a better reason than Democritus himself for our Abderian tendency; for laughter with us oftenest veils an effort to regain balance of temper, when disturbed by any untoward circumstance. It is a counterpoise of sorrow or rage.

The suppression of feelings being thus steadily insisted upon, they find their safety-valve in poetical aphorism. A poet of the tenth century writes, "In Japan and China as well, humanity, when moved by sorrow, tells its bitter grief in verse." A mother who tries to console her broken heart by fancying her departed child absent on his wonted chase after the dragonfly hums,

> How far today in chase, I wonder,
> Has gone my hunter of the dragonfly!

I refrain from quoting other examples, for I know I could do only scant justice to the pearly gems of our literature, were I to render into a foreign tongue the thoughts which were wrung drop by drop from bleeding hearts and threaded into beads of rarest value. I hope I have in a measure shown that inner working of our minds which often presents an appearance of callousness or of a hysterical mixture of laughter and dejection, and whose sanity is sometimes called in question.

It has also been suggested that our endurance of pain and indifference to death are due to less sensitive nerves. This is plausible as far as it goes. The next question is—Why are our nerves less tightly strung? It may be our climate is not so stimulating as the American. It may be our monarchical form of government does not excite us as much as the Republic does the Frenchman. It may be that we do not read *Sartor Resartus* as zealously as the Englishman. Personally, I believe it was our very excitability and sensitiveness which made it a necessity to recognize and enforce constant self-repression; but whatever may be the explanation, without taking into account long years of discipline in self-control, none can be correct.

Discipline in self-control can easily go too far. It can well repress the genial current of the soul. It can force pliant natures into distortions and monstrosities. It can beget bigotry, breed hypocrisy, or hebetate affections. Be a virtue never so noble, it has its counterpart and counterfeit. We must recognize in each virtue its own positive excellence and follow its positive ideal, and the ideal of self-restraint is to keep our mind level—as our expression is—or, to borrow a Greek term, attain the state of euthymia, which Democritus called the highest good.

The acme of self-control is reached and best illustrated in the first of the two institutions which we shall now bring to view; namely, the institutions of suicide and redress.
to borrow a Greek term, attain the state of euthymia, which Democritus called the highest good.

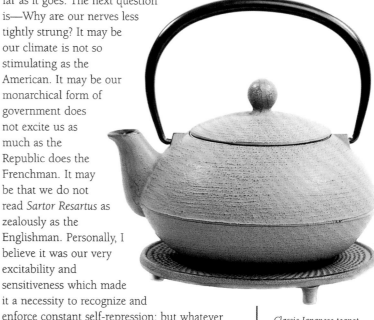

*Classic Japanese teapot.*

> *How far today in chase, I wonder, Has gone my hunter of the dragonfly!*

# THE DEATH-DEALING EDGE
## THE DEVELOPMENT OF THE SWORD BLADE

From the earliest days of Japan, the sword was looked upon with great veneration. Warriors composed poems about their swords. Worshippers left swords as sacrifices at temples or erected shrines to particularly noteworthy swords. Shinto priests told of how, near the beginning of time, the Thunder God sent his sword to pacify the Land of the Reed Plains, which would later become Japan. The blood spatters on his exalted sword then gave birth to eight powerful deities with such names as Root-Splitter and Rock-Splitter.

Despite the supernatural powers ascribed to swords, they were produced with human sweat, toil, and muscle. The forging of a single samurai blade was a multipart process that could take days or weeks to complete. But the finished product was worth the wait. Samurai swords are believed by many experts to be the finest swords ever produced—so fine that the early Japanese could hardly be blamed for thinking there was something supernatural about their origins.

To create a fine *katana*, the prototypical samurai long sword, the forging process began with a chunk of high-grade iron, which was heated and hammered into a flat bar. The bar was cooled in water and oil and broken into smaller bars, which were then reassembled and forged once more into a single bar after removing any impurities from the metal. The charcoal fires sucked the oxygen out of the iron and added enough carbon to transform the iron into high-grade steel. The longer the steel spent in the flames, the harder it got, although it also became more brittle.

Among master sword makers, this process was repeated up to fifteen times or more to fashion the *hadagane*, the outer layer of the blade. The repeated folding, hammering, and welding created a distinctive texture in the metal known as a *jihada, jigane,* or *hamon*. Because each artisan or school of sword makers had its own style of hammering and folding, an expert can often tell by studying the jihada where a sword was manufactured, when it was made, and even who the smith was.

When the outer layer was nearly complete, the *shingane*, the core of the blade, was prepared. As with the hadagane, the shingane was repeatedly heated, hammered, folded, and welded. But it was not folded as many times as the outer layer and, as a result, spent less time in the charcoal-fueled blaze. Its lower carbon content made the shingane softer and less brittle than the hadagane.

Once the shingane was ready, the hadagane was heated and shaped into a long enveloping curl, into which the shingane was inserted. The two were then heated and hammered into a *sunobe*, a single rectangular bar that tapers into a diagonal point at the tip. Embedding the shingane within the hadagane was one of the most distinctive elements of Japanese sword making. By melding the two, the smith created a blade that had combined a powerful razor-sharp cutting edge with a soft but resilient inner core to withstand the rigors of battle.

Then the sword maker reheated the sunobe to hammer it into shape. The tip of the sword was shaped into a curved point called the *kissaki*. From the back edge (*mune*) of the sword to the cutting edge (*fukura*), a number of ridges and slopes were hammered into the metal. First came the *iori*, or ridgeline, which ran parallel to the mune almost to the tip of the sword. Then there was the *shinogiji*, a flat plateau between the *iori* and a second ridgeline called the *shinogi*. From the *shinogi* came an area known as the *hiraji*, which sloped into the fukura.

Putting all of these details into the sunobe was a laborious process. The sword maker worked on the sunobe section by section, repeatedly heating, hammering, and cooling the metal. A great deal of skill was required to keep the hot metal from losing its shape.

Once the artisan was satisfied with the sunobe, he gave it a relatively rough filing and then prepared it for the final heat treatment, coating the sword with a thick mixture of clay (sometimes including such materials as charcoal or powdered grinding stone). The clay coating was purposely uneven; the

sword smith coated the sunobe far more thickly on its back and sides than on the cutting edge. This technique, known as heat differential, ensured that after the sword was heated, it would cool more rapidly along the blade, which would harden it and begin the process of bending the sword into a curve. A curved sword was preferred to a straight sword because it was easier to pull out of the sheath.

At last came the *yaki-ire*, the final heating. The early smiths recommended that the swords be heated until they were glowing like "the color of the moon about to set out on its journey across the heavens on a June or July evening." The yaki-ire often took place in the dead of night, so that no outside lighting could interfere as the sword smith stared into the fire to see if the sword was turning the appropriate color. The process generally took place in either February or August. Sword makers believed that the temperature for the water for cooling the sword was best in those two months; even if swords were made in other months, they were often inscribed as having been forged in February or August.

All of these seemingly imprecise measurements—the temperature of the water in August, the hue of the waning summer's moon, the color of the sword in the flame—were handed down with as much precision as possible from each master craftsman to his apprentices, so the method of making a sword could be repeated and perfected from generation to generation. The work of the artisans, inspired by the old Shinto legends and imbued with mystic-sounding rituals, lifted the samurai sword from being a mere weapon and, in the minds of many of its bearers, gave it a touch of the divine.

*Opposite page: Naginata blade showing maker's inscription. Hosakawa Masayoshi. Circa 1800.*
*Right: Tachi and ito-maki tachi koshirae, crafted by swordsmith Kagemitsu in 1325.*
*Below: Detail of tachi blade.*

# ANATOMY OF A SWORD

*Tsuka (hilt).* For hundreds of years, the *tsuka,* the handle of a samurai sword, was adorned with artistic embellishments representing the natural beauty of Japan or the character of the swordsman. The *tsuka* was traditionally made of either iron or hardwood, such as the Japanese magnolia, but more recently have been made of polymers or twisted leather.

*Same (shagreen).* Since the Heian era, which began in 794 CE, tsuka have been covered with *same,* the skin of stingrays or sharks. In the intervening centuries, shagreen became a favored material for sword grips throughout the world, reaching Europe by the seventeenth century. Unlike other materials, these skins did not shrink or fall apart when wet, and their rough surface provided a good grip for sweaty hands. Although the shagreen on samurai swords came in many different colors, it had to be white for the swords used at the shogun's palace in Edo.

*Ito (braid).* The *ito,* the braids of silk or cotton that are used to wrap a sword's handle, came in a wide variety of colors, including white, brown, blue, gray, and black. They were wrapped in a crisscross pattern that created a chain of diamond shapes.

*Menuki (ornaments). Menuki,* the ornaments that are wrapped into the ito to help with the grip of the sword, guided the hand to its proper place. The menuki, which could be seen through the diamond-shaped gaps in the ito wrapping, came in a variety of designs of animals, trees, flowers, or leaves. The menuki were typically affixed into place after the second or third fold of the ito wrapping.

*Mekugi (peg).* The *mekugi,* a small bamboo peg, held the hilt to the sword. Carving a mekugi could be a painstaking process, since it had to be shaped to fit through a *mekugi ana,* or peg hole, which could vary from sword to sword. Bamboo was the preferred material, since it is as strong as some metals but flexible enough to absorb the pressure when the sword hits an object.

*Kashira (pommel).* The *kashira,* like most other metal parts of the samurai sword, was often decorated with detailed artistic etchings of nature. But it was not mere decoration. Some moves, for instance, required a swordsman to use the kashira to hit an opponent in the solar plexus (known as the *tsuka ate,* "hilt strike") or directly between the eyes (known as the *ganmen ate,* "strike to the face").

*Tsuba (guard).* The *tsuba,* a plate of metal at the lower end of the tsuka, was designed to protect the swordsman's hand from touching the blade as well as to give him better control over his weapon. In the beginning, the tsuba was a circle of leather rimmed by wood or iron, but it eventually evolved into an iron plate, which allowed for range of artistic experimentation.

By the early Muromachi period, which began in 1392, tsuba making became a profession unto itself. Tsuba makers etched prayers or mottoes into the metal or created images known as *sukashi.* Some sukashi were geometric patterns, while others showed reverse silhouettes of fish, butterflies, birds, flowers, trees, blossoms, or sheaves of grain. Over the centuries, the sukashi became more refined, and some tsuba makers began using brass inlays or positive silhouettes for their designs. Similarly, instead of using

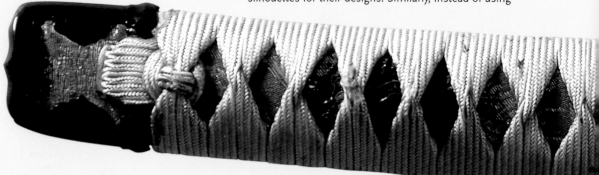

*Above: Handachi mounts. Bizen Kiyomitsu. Circa 1550.*
*Opposite page: Shigetaka. Circa 1650.*

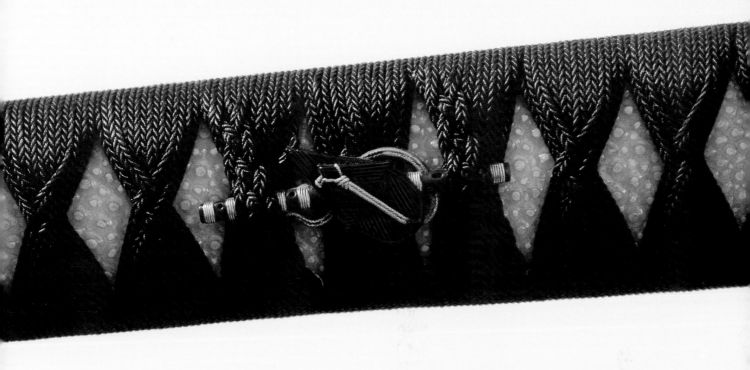

utilitarian round or rectangular shapes for the tsuba, the smiths introduced a wide variety of contours, including the crosslike *tate ito gata* and the *kiku gata*, which is meant to resemble a chrysanthemum.

During the Edo period, the tsuba became more decorative, forged out of such metals as brass or copper or out of such alloys as *shaduko* (copper and gold, producing a purplish black color), *shibuichi* (copper and silver, producing brown), and *sentoku* (copper, lead, and zinc, producing gray). In some rare instances, tsuba were made of pure gold or pure silver. Many of these metals were too light for use in battle but added an aesthetic element to swords intended for ceremonies or displays. Not all tsuba are works of art. During the Edo period, only plain, unadorned tsuba could be brought into the shogun's palace. Nevertheless, the artistry shown in these designs transformed tsuba into treasured heirlooms.

*Seppa (spacers). Seppa* were flat metal ovals that fit on each side of the tsuka. Like washers, their function was to allow the adjustments in tightness of the tsuka to all other parts.

*Fuchi (handle collar).* The *fuchi*, the metal collar at the lower end of the tsuba, was often adorned with images of rice stalks, sycamore leaves, dragons, and other symbols. There was typically at least one seppa between the fuchi and the tsuba.

*Habaki (blade collar).* The *habaki* was the metal collar on the top of the blade. There was typically at least one seppa between the habaki and the tsuba.

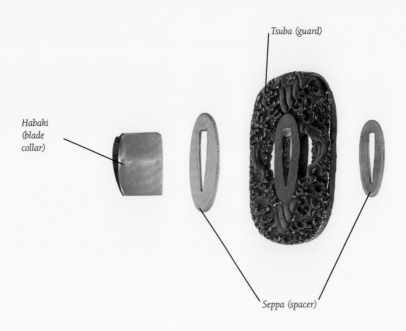

Tsuba (guard)

Habaki
(blade
collar)

Seppa (spacer)

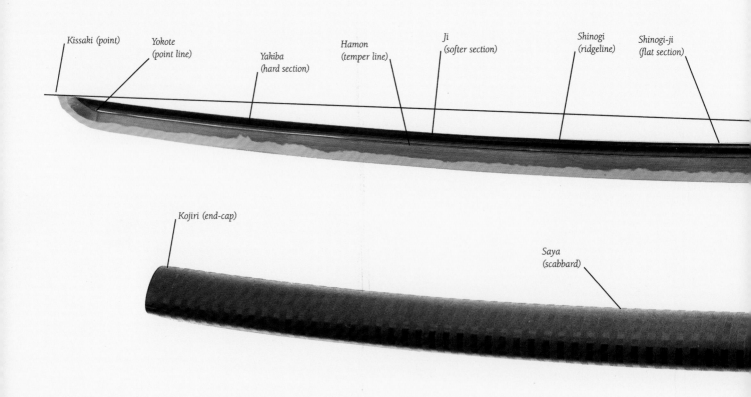

Kissaki (point)

Yokote
(point line)

Yakiba
(hard section)

Hamon
(temper line)

Ji
(softer section)

Shinogi
(ridgeline)

Shinogi-ji
(flat section)

Kojiri (end-cap)

Saya
(scabbard)

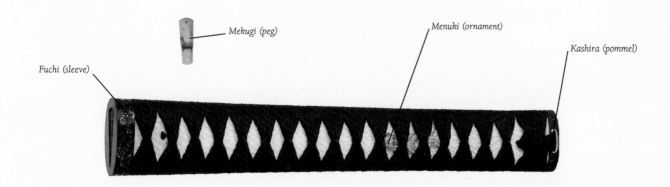

*Mekugi (peg)*

*Menuki (ornament)*

*Kashira (pommel)*

*Fuchi (sleeve)*

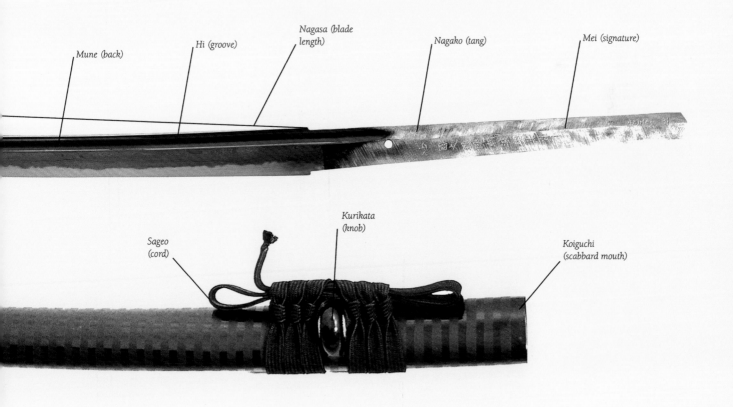

*Mune (back)*

*Hi (groove)*

*Nagasa (blade length)*

*Nagako (tang)*

*Mei (signature)*

*Sageo (cord)*

*Kurikata (knob)*

*Koiguchi (scabbard mouth)*

# The Institutions of Suicide and Redress

Of these two institutions (the former known as *hara-kiri* and the latter as *kataki-uchi*), many foreign writers have treated more or less fully.

To begin with suicide, let me state that I confine my observations only to *seppuku* or *kappuku*, popularly known as hara-kiri—which means self-immolation by disembowelment. "Ripping the abdomen? How absurd!"—so cry those to whom the name is new. Absurdly odd as it may sound at first to foreign ears, it cannot be so very foreign to students of Shakespeare, who puts these words in Brutus's mouth—"Thy (Caesar's) spirit walks abroad and turns our swords into our proper entrails." Listen to a modern English poet, who in his *Light of Asia*, speaks of a sword piercing the bowels of a queen—none blames him for bad English or breach of modesty. Or, to take still another example, look at Guercino's painting of Cato's death, in the Palazzo Rossa in Genoa. Whoever has read the swan-song which Addison makes Cato sing will not jeer at the sword half-buried in his abdomen. In our minds this mode of death is associated with instances of noblest deeds and of most touching pathos, so that nothing repugnant, much less ludicrous, mars our conception of it. So wonderful is the transforming power of virtue, of greatness, of tenderness, that the vilest form of death assumes a sublimity and becomes a symbol of new life, or else—the sign which Constantine beheld would not conquer the world!

Not for extraneous associations only does seppuku lose in our mind any taint of absurdity; for the choice of this particular part of the body to operate upon was based on an old anatomical belief as to the seat of the soul and of the affections. When Moses wrote of Joseph's "bowels yearning upon his brother," or David prayed the Lord not to forget his bowels, or when Isaiah, Jeremiah, and other inspired men of old spoke of the "sounding" or the "troubling" of bowels, they all and each endorsed the belief prevalent among the Japanese that in the abdomen was enshrined the soul. The Semites habitually spoke of the liver and kidneys

*Opposie page: Minamoto Yorimasa Stting on a Chair in Formal Court Dress, from "Famous Generals of Japan." Yoshitora. Japan. Circa 1858. Color woodblock print.*

and surrounding fat as the seat of emotion and of life. The term *hara* was more comprehensive than the Greek *phren* or *thumos*, and the Japanese and Hellenese alike thought the spirit of man to dwell somewhere in that region. Such a notion is by no means confined to the peoples of antiquity. The French, in spite of the theory propounded by one of their most distinguished philosophers, Descartes, that the soul is located in the pineal gland, still insist in using the term *ventre* in a sense, which, if anatomically too vague, is nevertheless physiologically significant. Similarly, *entrailles* stands in their language for affection and compassion. Nor is such belief mere superstition, being more scientific than the general idea of making the heart the center of the feelings. Without asking a friar, the Japanese knew better than Romeo "in what vile part of this anatomy one's name did lodge." Modern neurologists speak of the abdominal and pelvic brains, denoting thereby sympathetic nerve centers in those parts which are strongly affected by any psychical action. This view of mental physiology once admitted, the syllogism of seppuku is easy to construct. "I will open the seat of my soul and show you how it fares with it. See for yourself whether it is polluted or clean."

I do not wish to be understood as asserting religious or even moral justification of suicide, but the high estimate placed upon honor was ample excuse with many for taking one's own life. How many acquiesced in the sentiment expressed by Garth,

> When honor's lost, 'tis a relief to die;
> Death's but a sure retreat from infamy,

and have smilingly surrendered their souls to oblivion! Death when honor was involved was accepted in Bushido as a key to the solution of many complex problems, so that to an ambitious samurai a natural departure from life seemed a rather tame affair and a consummation not devoutly to be wished for. I dare say that many good Christians, if only they are honest enough, will confess the fascination of, if not positive admiration for, the sublime composure with which Cato, Brutus, Petronius, and a host

*Heiji Uprising of 1159. Japanese School. 1568–1615. Ink on paper.*

seppuku was not a mere suicidal process. It was an institution, legal and ceremonial. An invention of the middle ages, it was a process by which warriors could expiate their crimes, apologize for errors, escape from disgrace, redeem their friends, or prove their sincerity. When enforced as a legal punishment, it was practiced with due ceremony. It was a refinement of self-destruction, and none could perform it without the utmost coolness of temper and composure of demeanor, and for these reasons it was particularly befitting the profession of bushi.

Antiquarian curiosity, if nothing else, would tempt me to give here a description of this obsolete ceremonial; but seeing that such a description was made by a far abler writer, whose book is not much read nowadays, I am tempted to make a somewhat lengthy quotation. Mitford, in his *Tales of Old Japan*, after giving a translation of a treatise on seppuku from a rare Japanese manuscript, goes on to describe an instance of such an execution of which he was an eyewitness:

We (seven foreign representatives) were invited to follow the Japanese witness into the *hondo* or main hall of the temple, where the ceremony was to be performed. It was an imposing scene. A large hall with a high roof supported by dark pillars of wood. From the ceiling hung a profusion of those huge gilt lamps and ornaments peculiar to Buddhist temples. In front of the high altar, where the floor, covered with beautiful white mats, is raised some three or four inches from the ground, was laid a rug of scarlet felt. Tall candles placed at regular intervals gave out a dim mysterious light, just sufficient to let all the proceedings be seen. The seven Japanese took their places on the left of the raised floor, the seven foreigners on the right. No other person was present.

After the interval of a few minutes of anxious suspense, Taki Zenzaburo, a stalwart man thirty-two years of age, with a noble air, walked into the hall attired in his dress of ceremony, with the peculiar hempen-cloth wings which are worn on great occasions. He was accompanied by a *kaishaku* and three officers, who wore the *jimbaori* or war surcoat with gold tissue facings. The word *kaishaku*, it should be observed, is one to which our word executioner is no equivalent term. The office is that of a gentleman: in many cases it is performed by a kinsman or friend of the condemned, and the relation between them is rather that of principal and second than that of victim and executioner. In this instance the

of other ancient worthies terminated their own earthly existence. Is it too bold to hint that the death of the first of the philosophers was partly suicidal? When we are told so minutely by his pupils how their master willingly submitted to the mandate of the state—which he knew was morally mistaken—in spite of the possibilities of escape, and how he took up the cup of hemlock in his own hand, even offering libation from its deadly contents, do we not discern in his whole proceeding and demeanor, an act of self-immolation? No physical compulsion here, as in ordinary cases of execution. True the verdict of the judges was compulsory: it said, "Thou shalt die—and that by thy own hand." If suicide meant no more than dying by one's own hand, Socrates was a clear case of suicide. But nobody would charge him with the crime; Plato, who was averse to it, would not call his master a suicide.

Now my readers will understand that

kaishaku was a pupil of Taki Zenzaburo, and was selected by friends of the latter from among their own number for his skill in swordsmanship.

With the kaishaku on his left hand, Taki Zenzaburo advanced slowly toward the Japanese witnesses, and the two bowed before them, then drawing near to the foreigners they saluted us in the same way, perhaps even with more deference; in each case the salutation was ceremoniously returned. Slowly and with great dignity the condemned man mounted on to the raised floor, prostrated himself before the high altar twice, and seated[20] himself on the felt carpet with his back to the high altar, the kaishaku crouching on his left-hand side. One of the three attendant officers then came forward, bearing a stand of the kind used in the temple for offerings, on which, wrapped in paper, lay the *wakizashi*, the short sword or dirk of the Japanese, nine inches and a half in length, with a point and an edge as sharp as a razor's. This he handed, prostrating himself, to the condemned man, who received it reverently, raising it to his head with both hands, and placed it in front of himself.

After another profound obeisance, Taki Zenzaburo, in a voice which betrayed just so much emotion and hesitation as might be expected from a man who is making a painful confession, but with no sign of either in his face or manner, spoke as follows: "I, and I alone, unwarrantably gave the order to fire on the foreigners at Kobe, and again as they tried to escape. For this crime I disembowel myself, and I beg you who are present to do me the honor of witnessing the act."

Bowing once more, the speaker allowed his upper garments to slip down to his girdle, and remained naked to the waist. Carefully, according to custom, he tucked his sleeves under his knees to prevent himself from falling backward; for a noble Japanese gentleman should die falling forwards. Deliberately, with a steady hand he took the dirk that lay before him; he looked at it wistfully, almost affectionately; for a moment he seemed to collect his thoughts for the last time, and then stabbing himself deeply below the waist in the left-hand side, he drew the dirk slowly across to his right side, and turning it in the wound, gave a slight cut upwards. During this sickeningly painful operation he never moved a muscle of his face. When he drew out the dirk, he leaned forward and stretched out his neck; an expression of pain for the first time crossed his face, but he uttered no sound. At that moment the kaishaku, who, still crouching by his side, had been keenly watching his every movement, sprang to his feet, poised his sword for a second in the air; there was a flash, a heavy, ugly thud, a crashing fall; with one blow the head had been severed from the body.

A dead silence followed, broken only by the hideous noise of the blood throbbing out of the inert head before us, which but a moment before had been a brave and chivalrous man. It was horrible.

The kaishaku made a low bow, wiped his sword with a piece of paper which he had ready for the purpose, and retired from the raised floor; and the stained dirk was solemnly borne away, a bloody proof of the execution.

The two representatives of the Mikado then left their places, and crossing over to where the foreign witnesses sat, called to us to witness that the sentence of death upon Taki Zenzaburo had been faithfully carried out. The ceremony being at an end, we left the temple.

I might multiply any number of descriptions of seppuku from literature or from the relation of eyewitnesses; but one more instance will suffice.

Two brothers, Sakon and Naiki, respectively twenty-four and seventeen years of age, made an effort to kill Iyéyasu in order to avenge their father's wrongs; but before they could enter the camp they were made prisoners. The old general admired the pluck of the youths who dared an attempt on his life and ordered that they should be allowed to die an honorable death. Their little brother Hachimaro, a mere infant of eight summers, was condemned to a similar fate, as the sentence was pronounced on all the male members of the family, and the three were taken to a monastery where it was to be executed. A physician who was present on the occasion has left us a diary from which the following scene is translated.

When they were all seated in a row for final despatch, Sakon turned to the youngest and said—"Go thou first, for I wish to be sure that

*Left: Wakizashi.*
*Top: Dragonfly and flower tsuba. Edo period. Soft metal.*
*Above: Tsuba with design of monkey reaching for moon. Edo period.*

231

Top: Palanquin. Japan.
Mixed media.
Above: Writing case decorated
with a cockerel, writing case
with a bamboo design and a
kobako attributed to Ogata
Korin (1658–1716), and a
message box by the Kajikawa
family. 16th–18th century.
lacquered gold and silver.

thou doest it aright." Upon the little one's replying that, as he had never seen seppuku performed, he would like to see his brothers do it and then he could follow them, the older brothers smiled between their tears: "Well said, little fellow! So canst thou well boast of being our father's child." When they had placed him between them, Sakon thrust the dagger into the left side of his own abdomen and asked—"Look, brother! Dost understand now? Only, don't push the dagger too far, lest thou fall back. Lean forward, rather, and keep thy knees well composed." Naiki did likewise and said to the boy—"Keep thy eyes open or else thou mayst look like a dying woman. If thy dagger feels anything within and thy strength fails, take courage and double thy effort to cut across." The child looked from one to the other, and when both had expired, he calmly half denuded himself and followed the example set him on either hand.

The glorification of seppuku offered, naturally enough, no small temptation to its unwarranted committal. For causes entirely incompatible with reason, or for reasons entirely undeserving of death, hot-headed youths rushed into it as insects fly into fire; mixed and dubious motives drove more samurai to this deed than nuns into convent gates. Life was cheap—cheap as reckoned by the popular standard of honor. The saddest feature was that honor, which was always in the *agio*, so to speak, was not always solid gold, but alloyed with baser metals. No one circle in the *Inferno* will boast of greater density of Japanese population than the seventh, to which Dante consigns all victims of self-destruction!

And yet, for a true samurai to hasten death or to court it was alike cowardice. A typical fighter, when he lost battle after battle and was pursued from plain to hill and from bush to cavern, found himself hungry and alone in the dark hollow of a tree, his sword blunt with use, his bow broken and arrows exhausted—did not the noblest of the Romans fall upon his own sword in Philippi under like circumstances?—deemed it cowardly to die, but with a fortitude approaching a Christian martyr's, cheered himself with an impromptu verse:

*Come! evermore come,*
*Ye dread sorrows and pains!*
*And heap on my burden'd back;*
*That I not one test may lack*
*Of what strength in me remains!*

This, then, was the Bushido teaching—Bear and face all calamities and adversities with patience and a pure conscience; for as Mencius[21] taught, "When Heaven is about to confer a great office on anyone, it first exercises his mind with suffering and his sinews and bones with toil; it exposes his body to hunger and subjects him to extreme poverty; and it confounds his undertakings. In all these ways it stimulates his mind, hardens his nature, and supplies his incompetencies." True honor lies in fulfilling Heaven's decree and no death incurred in so doing is ignominious, whereas death to avoid what Heaven has in store is cowardly indeed! In that quaint book of Sir Thomas Browne's, *Religio Medici*, there is an exact English equivalent for what is repeatedly taught in our Precepts. Let me quote it: "It is a brave act of valor to contemn death, but where life is more terrible than death, it is then the truest valor to dare to live." A renowned priest of the seventeenth century satirically observed—"Talk as he may, a samurai who ne'er has died is apt in decisive moments to flee or hide." Again—Him who once has died in the bottom of his breast, no spears of Sanada nor all the arrows of Tametomo can pierce. How near we come to the portals of the temple whose Builder taught "he that loseth his life for my sake shall find it!" These are but a few of the numerous examples which tend to confirm the moral identity of the human species, notwithstanding an attempt so assiduously made to render the distinction between Christian and Pagan as great as possible.

We have thus seen that the Bushido institution of suicide was neither so irrational nor barbarous as its abuse strikes us at first sight. We will now see whether its sister institution of Redress—or call it Revenge, if you will—has its mitigating features. I hope I can dispose of this question in a few words, since a similar institution, or call it custom, if that suits you better, has at some time prevailed among all peoples and has not yet become entirely obsolete, as attested by the continuance of duelling and lynching. Why, has not an American captain recently challenged Esterhazy, that the wrongs of Dreyfus be avenged? Among a savage tribe which has no marriage, adultery is not a sin, and only the jealousy of a lover protects a woman from abuse:

so in a time which has no criminal court, murder is not a crime, and only the vigilant vengeance of the victim's people preserves social order. "What is the most beautiful thing on earth?" said Osiris to Horus. The reply was, "To avenge a parent's wrongs,"—to which a Japanese would have added "and a master's."

In revenge there is something which satisfies one's sense of justice. The avenger reasons: "My good father did not deserve death. He who killed him did great evil. My father, if he were alive, would not tolerate a deed like this: Heaven itself hates wrongdoing. It is the will of my father; it is the will of Heaven that the evil-doer ceases from his work. He must perish by my hand; because he shed my father's blood, I, who am his flesh and blood, must shed the murderer's. The same Heaven shall not shelter him and me." The ratiocination is simple and childish (though we know Hamlet did not reason much more deeply), nevertheless it shows an innate sense of exact balance and equal justice "An eye for an eye, a tooth for a tooth." Our sense of revenge is as exact as our mathematical faculty, and until both terms of the equation are satisfied, we cannot get over the sense of something left undone.

In Judaism, which believed in a jealous God, or in Greek mythology, which provided a Nemesis, vengeance may be left to superhuman agencies; but common sense furnished Bushido with the institution of redress as a kind of ethical court of equity, where people could take cases not to be judged in accordance with ordinary law. The master of the forty-seven Ronins was condemned to death; he had no court of higher instance to appeal to; his faithful retainers addressed themselves to vengeance, the only Supreme Court existing; they in their turn were condemned by common law, but the popular instinct passed a different judgment and hence their memory is still kept as green and fragrant as are their graves at Sengakuji to this day.

Though Lao-tse taught to recompense injury with kindness, the voice of Confucius was very much louder, which counselled that injury must be recompensed with justice; and yet revenge was justified only when it was undertaken in behalf of our superiors and benefactors. One's own wrongs, including injuries done to wife and children, were to be borne and forgiven. A samurai could therefore fully sympathize with Hannibal's oath to avenge his country's wrongs, but he scorns James Hamilton for wearing in his girdle a handful of earth from his wife's grave, as an eternal incentive to avenge her wrongs on the Regent Murray.

Both of these institutions of suicide and redress lost their *raison d'être* at the promulgation of the criminal code. No more do we hear of romantic adventures of a fair maiden as she tracks in disguise the murderer of her parent. No more can we witness tragedies of family vendetta enacted. The knight errantry of Miyamoto Musashi is now a tale of the past. The well-ordered police spies out the criminal for the injured party and the law metes out justice. The whole state and society will see that wrong is righted. The sense of justice satisfied, there is no need of *kataki-uchi*. If this had meant that "hunger of the heart which feeds upon the hope of glutting that hunger with the life blood of the victim," as a New England divine has described it, a few paragraphs in the Criminal Code would not so entirely have made an end of it.

As to seppuku, though it too has no existence *de jure*, we still hear of it from time to time, and shall continue to hear, I am afraid, as long as the past is remembered. Many painless and time-saving methods of self-immolation will come in vogue, as its votaries are increasing with fearful rapidity throughout the world; but Professor Morselli will have to concede to seppuku an aristocratic position among them. He maintains that "when suicide is accomplished by very painful means or at the cost of prolonged agony, in ninety-nine cases out of a hundred, it may be assigned as the act of a mind disordered by fanaticism, by madness, or by morbid excitement."[22] But a normal seppuku does not savor of fanaticism, or madness or excitement, utmost *sang froid* being necessary to its successful accomplishment. Of the two kinds into which Dr. Strahan[23] divides suicide, the Rational or Quasi, and the Irrational or True, seppuku is the best example of the former type.

From these bloody institutions, as well as from the general tenor of Bushido, it is easy to infer that the sword played an important part in social discipline and life. The saying passed as an axiom which called the sword the soul of the samurai.

20 Seated himself—that is, in the Japanese fashion, his knees and toes touching the ground and his body resting on his heels. In this position, which is one of respect, he remained until his death.

21 I use Dr. Legge's translation verbatim.

22 Morselli, *Suicide*, p. 314.

23 *Suicide and Insanity*.

*Tessen, a wooden fan adapted as a weapon to be used in unconventional situations. Carved from kokutan.*

# SEPPUKU
## THE HONORABLE SUICIDE

The first historical reference to *seppuku*, or "honorable suicide," was recorded in 1180 and described the samurai Minamoto Yorimasa, who took refuge in a Buddhist temple and then killed himself after losing one of the first battles of the Gempei War. Seppuku was instituted to allow the samurai to have a respectable death to restore and protect his name as a warrior, rather than live a life of shame because of defeat or disgrace. The samurai lived by the *bushi* code of conduct, which espoused an honorable life as its primary goal; the concept of an honorable death was not viewed as a separate act, or component, of the samurai's life goal, but rather as an integral and obvious priority. This point is illustrated in the book *Hagakure*, by seventeenth-century samurai Yamamoto Tsunetomo, who explains that "the way of the samurai is found in death."

Seppuku ensured a quick release for the spirit, which lived in the belly. Several types of seppuku were practiced, depending on the method and intention. The most common form was *hara-kiri*, "belly-cutting," in which a short sword (*wakizashi*) or dagger (*tanto*) was deeply stabbed below the waist on the left-hand side and drawn across to the right-hand side of the abdomen. It was completed with a sharp upward cut at the end. This method was typically used when a *kaishaku*, the second, was present to cut off the head of the samurai at the point of utmost pain. Importantly, an expert kaishaku

was not to completely sever the head but would leave it attached by a strip of skin across the throat. When the kaishaku was not present, the *jumonji-giri*, "cross-shaped cut" method of seppuku was usually employed. This involved the same cut used in hara-kiri, with the addition of a second, more painful vertical cut across the belly. This method required the samurai to quietly endure a death achieved more slowly through the eventual loss of blood. (*Hara-kiri* is the common, vulgar word form of *seppuku* and is a term that would not have been used by the samurai.)

Seppuku was often performed following a loss in battle, which allowed the samurai to avoid the shame of torture at the hands of the enemy. The victor in a battle would sometimes demonstrate grace in forcing the defeated samurai to commit suicide, which allowed the defeated to retain his honor in death. It was also used as an honorable punishment for serious crimes (for which commoners would be executed straightaway, because they did not belong to the samurai class). Once the seppuku sentence was given, the samurai criminal would then typically be given a timeframe within which seppuku must be committed. If the deed were not completed within the specified period, an execution would then take place, and dishonor would shame both the criminal and his family.

Other reasons for committing seppuku were to show both disagreement with and an ultimate loyalty to a *daimyo*. Followers of a fallen general or lord would commit *junshi*, which literally means "following in death," often next to the body of their leader, or immediately upon learning of his death. This expression of grief and affection was denounced during the Edo period as an

unacceptable way for a samurai's retainers, or his men, to fulfill their responsibilities to the heirs of their lord. Another case, battlefield seppuku, typically happened hurriedly to avoid capture and involved whatever means necessary to bring about death. There are several legendary seppuku incidents. Especially notable examples include that of a samurai falling off a horse onto his own sword and that of Nitta Yoshisada, who is said to have cut off his own head. A frequently occurring example, expiatory suicide, *sokotsu-shi*, literally "the very act itself

*Short sword, one of a set of two. Osafune Tadamitsu. 1479. Japan. Steel blade (wakizashi) and black lacquer scabbard with gold mounted tsuba and fittings.*

wiping the slate clean," was used to bring honor back to a warrior and his family following a personal failure in judgment or in battle, which would be considered a dishonorable act. The least common reason for seppuku was *kanshi,* "death of understanding," or suicide through remonstration. This was used as a severe, dramatic type of protest when all other forms of persuasion failed. Oda Nobunaga, the young *daimyo* of Hirate Nakatsukasa Kiyohide, changed his ways when Kiyohide commited suicide to make the youthful and irreverent warrior take his administrative responsibilities seriously.

The preferred method of seppuku was a ritualistic ceremony that involved precise etiquette, preparation, and witnesses. The ceremony could take place in a home, but a Buddhist temple or garden was ideal. Shinto temples could not be used, because death would defile the temple. Witnesses, the kaishaku, and attendants would be present at the ceremony. The white *kamishimo* outer garment was worn by the participant, and he would sit in the *seiza* position with his knees and toes touching the ground, with his body resting on his heels. An attendant would then place a *sanbo,* the unlacquered wooden table, in front of the participant. A sake cup, paper, writing utensils, and the *kozuka,* or disemboweling blade, would be included on the table. There may have also been a small meal provided, depending on the preference of the participant and whether the seppuku was a matter of personal choice or a capital punishment sentence. The kozuka was typically the samurai's own wakizashi or tanto. The handle of the weapon was often wrapped in several sheets of paper in order to provide a secure grip.

The samurai would drink from the sake cup and then write a death poem. He would then slip his arms out of his garment to uncover the upper body to the waist. The sleeves of the garment would be tucked under his knees to prevent his body from falling backward or slumping to the side. He would then stab himself, and the kaishaku would administer one blow to the neck. The kaishaku's duty as assistant was to prevent the samurai from making a mistake that would disgrace his dead body. A friend or other trusted samurai was usually enlisted to be the kaishaku. A skilled swordsman was necessary so that the head could be cut with one precise blow.

Writing a death poem was a traditional means of expression when time allowed. In 1582, Akechi Mitsutoshi, in an astounding demonstration, committed seppuku and used a brush stained with his own blood to write his death

*A samurai's wife preparing to commit seppuku, or ritual suicide, after the death of her husband. Utagawa Kuniyoshi. 1848.*

poem on a door. But Minamoto Yorimasa, in the first recorded instance of seppuku, wrote his death poem on the back of his war fan. Such an accomplishment, with the enemy storming his temple refuge, provided a great example of grace and honor.

Samurai women also engaged in a form of ritual suicide called *jigai,* "self injury." Jigai typically involved cutting the jugular vein with a tanto or the similar *kaiken.* Women would prepare for jigai by tying their ankles together so that the body would be found in a dignified manner following the convulsions of death. Jigai, like seppuku, would be committed to avoid the dishonor of capture and rape by an enemy army. Many women committed jigai to follow their husbands in death and also to protest dishonorable actions by their husbands. Seppuku was forbidden by decrees in both 1603 and 1663, but because the practice continued, it was again officially abolished in 1868 at the beginning of the Meiji restoration.

圭芥者天類

左兵衛佐源頼朝

# The Sword, the Soul of the Samurai

Bushido made the sword the emblem of power and prowess. When Mahomet proclaimed that "the sword is the key of Heaven and of Hell," he only echoed a Japanese sentiment. Very early the samurai boy learned to wield it. It was a momentous occasion for him when at the age of five he was appareled in the paraphernalia of samurai costume, placed upon a *go-board*,[24] and initiated into the rights of the military profession by having thrust into his girdle a real sword, instead of the toy dirk with which he had been playing. After this first ceremony of *adoptio per arma*, he was no more to be seen outside his father's gates without this badge of his status, even if it was usually substituted for everyday wear by a gilded wooden dirk. Not many years pass before he wears constantly the genuine steel, though blunt, and then the sham arms are thrown aside and with enjoyment keener than his newly acquired blades, he marches out to try their edge on wood and stone. When he reaches man's estate at the age of fifteen, being given independence of action, he can now pride himself upon the possession of arms sharp enough for any work. The very possession of the dangerous instrument imparts to him a feeling and an air of self-respect and responsibility. "He beareth not his sword in vain." What he carries in his belt is a symbol of what he carries in his mind and heart—loyalty and honor. The two swords, the longer and the shorter— called respectively *daito* and *shoto* or *katana* and *wakizashi*—never leave his side. When at home, they grace the most conspicuous place in study or parlor; by night they guard his pillow within easy reach of his hand. Constant companions, they are beloved, and proper names of endearment given them. Being venerated, they are well-nigh worshiped. The Father of History has recorded as a curious piece of information that the Scythians sacrificed to an iron scimitar. Many a temple and many a family in Japan hoards a sword as an object of adoration. Even the commonest dirk has due respect paid to it. Any insult to it is tantamount to personal affront. Woe to him who carelessly steps over a weapon lying on the floor!

So precious an object cannot long escape the notice and the skill of artists nor the vanity of its owner, especially in times of peace, when it is worn with no more use than a crosier by a bishop or a scepter by a king. Sharkskin and finest silk for hilt, silver and gold for guard, lacquer of varied hues for scabbard, robbed the deadliest weapon of half its terror; but these appurtenances are playthings compared with the blade itself.

The swordsmith was not a mere artisan but an inspired artist and his workshop a sanctuary. Daily he commenced his craft with prayer and purification, or, as the phrase was, "he committed his soul and spirit into the forging and tempering of the steel." Every swing of the sledge, every plunge into water, every friction on the grindstone was a religious act of no slight import. Was it the spirit of the master or of his tutelary god that cast a formidable spell over our sword? Perfect as a work of art, setting at defiance its Toledo and Damascus rivals, there is more than art could impart. Its cold blade, collecting on its surface the moment it is drawn the vapors of the atmosphere; its immaculate texture, flashing light of bluish hue; its matchless edge, upon which histories and possibilities hang; the curve of its back, uniting exquisite grace with utmost strength—all these thrill us with mixed feelings of power and beauty, of awe and terror. Harmless were its mission, if it only remained a thing of beauty and joy! But, ever within reach of the hand, it presented no small temptation for abuse. Too often did the blade flash forth from its peaceful sheath.

> *Every swing of the sledge, every plunge into water, every friction on the grindstone, was a religious act of no slight import.*

*Opposite page: Samurai Combat. Japan. 19th century. Color woodblock print.*

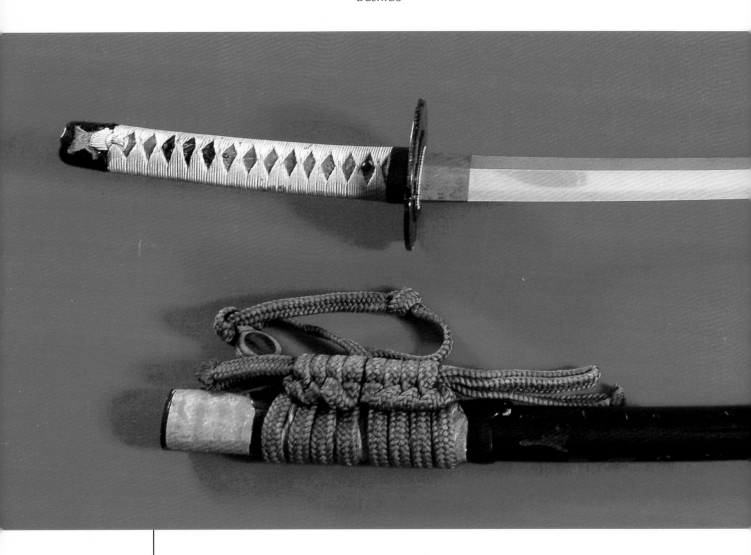

*Japanese sword. Bizen Kiyomitsu. Circa 1550.*

The abuse sometimes went so far as to try the acquired steel on some harmless creature's neck.

The question that concerns us most is, however—Did Bushido justify the promiscuous use of the weapon? The answer is unequivocally, no! As it laid great stress on its proper use, so did it denounce and abhor its misuse. A dastard or a braggart was he who brandished his weapon on undeserved occasions. A self-possessed man knows the right time to use it, and such times come but rarely. Let us listen to the late Count Katsu, who passed through one of the most turbulent times of our history, when assassinations, suicides, and other sanguinary practices were the order of the day. Endowed as he once was with almost dictatorial powers, repeatedly marked out as an object for assassination, he never tarnished his sword with blood. In relating some of his reminiscences to a friend he says, in a quaint, plebeian way peculiar to him: "I have a great dislike for killing people and so I haven't killed one single man. I have released those whose heads should have been chopped off. A friend said to me one day, 'You don't kill enough. Don't you eat pepper and eggplants?' Well, some people are no better! But you see that fellow was slain himself. My escape may be due to my dislike of killing. I had the hilt of my sword so tightly fastened to the scabbard that it was hard to draw the blade. I made up my mind that though they cut me, I will not cut. Yes, yes! some people are truly like fleas and mosquitoes and they bite—but what does their biting amount to? It itches a little, that's all; it won't endanger life." These are the words of one whose Bushido training was tried in the fiery furnace of adversity and triumph. The popular apothegm—"To be beaten is to conquer," meaning true conquest consists in not opposing a riotous foe; and "The best won victory is that obtained without shedding of blood," and others of similar import—will show that after all the ultimate ideal of knighthood was peace.

It was a great pity that this high ideal was left

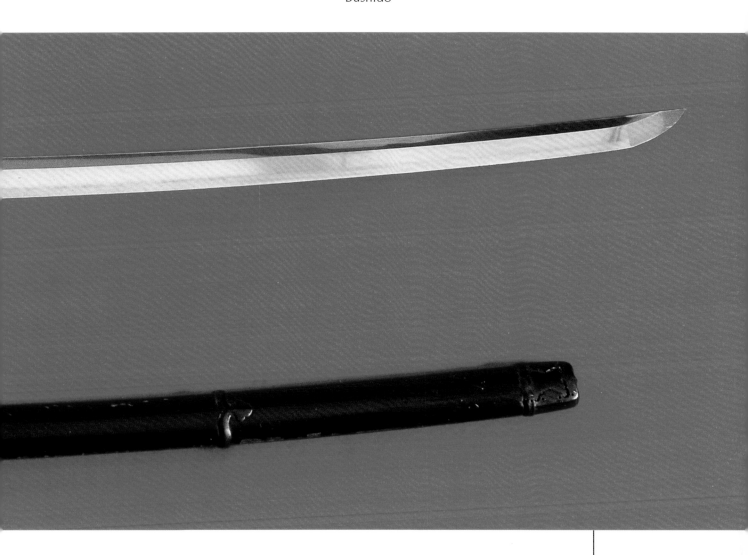

exclusively to priests and moralists to preach, while the samurai went on practicing and extolling martial traits. In this they went so far as to tinge the ideals of womanhood with Amazonian character. Here we may profitably devote a few paragraphs to the subject of the training and position of woman.

24 The game of go is sometimes called Japanese checkers, but is much more intricate than the English game. The go board contains 361 squares and is supposed to represent a battlefield—the object of the game being to occupy as much space as possible.

"To be beaten is to conquer," meaning true conquest consists in not opposing a riotous foe; and "The best won victory is that obtained without shedding of blood," and others of similar import— will show that after all the ultimate ideal of knighthood was peace.

# KATANA, WAKIZASHI, AND TANTO
## THE THREE TYPES OF SWORDS

Although Japanese warriors have wielded many different types of swords throughout history, the *katana*—a curved sword typically about forty-two inches long—is the blade that has become most linked with the samurai. The katana was believed to embody the warrior's soul.

The katana first gained popularity during the early Muromachi era, from 1394 to 1466. The manufacture of the katana represented the epitome of medieval Japanese workmanship. Master sword smiths heated and folded the steel of the blade more than 200 times before it was deemed suitable for use. Artisans working with gold, leather, shagreen, and silken cords crafted the hilt, scabbard, and related embellishments.

Lighter and easier to wield than the European swords of its day, the katana's value went beyond its effectiveness on the battlefield. It was one of the samurai's most prized possessions: the most visible symbol of his status as a warrior. Some samurai valued their katana so highly that they gave them names and treated them as if they were living companion beings.

From the moment he was born, a samurai was expected to learn how to use a katana. When a boy was born into a samurai family, he would go through a special ceremony in which he received his first sword, called the *mamori-gatana*. This was a miniaturized katana, carried in a special charm pouch called the *mamori*, which was also used to carry images of the gods. The mamori-gatana, which was worn until the age of five, was meant to bring luck and protection to the wearer. Wives of samurai were also given mamori-gatana on their wedding nights.

At the age of thirteen, boys became samurai in a ceremony called *genpuku*, during which they were given adult names to replace their childhood nicknames and were presented with their first real swords and armor. Besides a full-sized katana, they were usually given a shorter sword known as the *wakizashi*, "side companion." Together, the katana and the wakizashi formed a set called a *daisho*, which translates as "big and small."

When the word *wakizashi* was first used in the fourteenth century , it referred to any sword worn to the side of a warrior's primary sword. Later, the word was used to denote a specific class of relatively small swords—typically with blades of twelve to twenty-four inches—that were used as companion swords to the katana.

The wakizashi served a dual purpose: it could be used as a backup weapon if the katana was damaged or it could be used in close quarters on the battlefield when the katana's length could be a disadvantage. Master swordsmen sometimes wielded a katana and a wakizashi simultaneously, one in each hand—a formidable sight on the battlefield. Miyamoto Musashi, a samurai in the early seventeenth century, was said to be particularly adept with that ambidextrous skill.

Because of its smaller size, the wakizashi could be used at all times. When entering a building, for instance, a samurai would typically give his katana to a servant, who would place it on a special rack known as the *katana-kake*. But he would continue to wear his wakizashi, which was viewed as a less threatening weapon. Samurai wore their wakizashi during all their waking hours. And when they slept, they kept the

*Although this tachi blade is unsigned, it is attributed to Kunitoshi of the Rai school of Yamashiro province.*

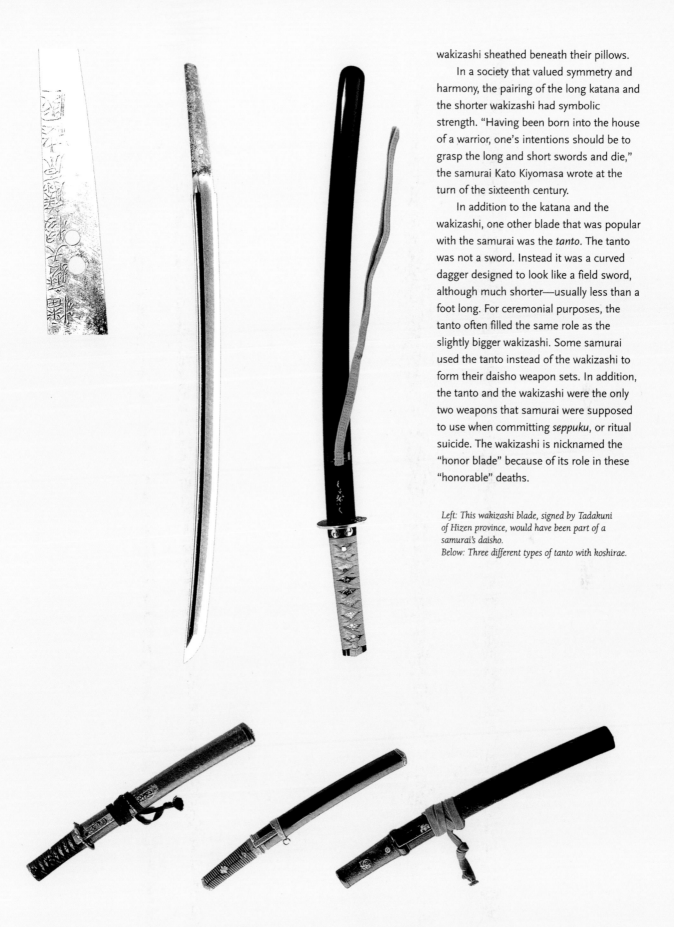

wakizashi sheathed beneath their pillows.

In a society that valued symmetry and harmony, the pairing of the long katana and the shorter wakizashi had symbolic strength. "Having been born into the house of a warrior, one's intentions should be to grasp the long and short swords and die," the samurai Kato Kiyomasa wrote at the turn of the sixteenth century.

In addition to the katana and the wakizashi, one other blade that was popular with the samurai was the *tanto*. The tanto was not a sword. Instead it was a curved dagger designed to look like a field sword, although much shorter—usually less than a foot long. For ceremonial purposes, the tanto often filled the same role as the slightly bigger wakizashi. Some samurai used the tanto instead of the wakizashi to form their daisho weapon sets. In addition, the tanto and the wakizashi were the only two weapons that samurai were supposed to use when committing *seppuku*, or ritual suicide. The wakizashi is nicknamed the "honor blade" because of its role in these "honorable" deaths.

*Left: This wakizashi blade, signed by Tadakuni of Hizen province, would have been part of a samurai's daisho.*
*Below: Three different types of tanto with koshirae.*

# THE SAMURAI ARSENAL

"The sword is the soul of the samurai," says the *Bushido*. But the samurai did not limit themselves to just one weapon. Knives, pikes, spears, bows, muskets, and cannon were also part of the samurai's arsenal.

*Naginata (long stave)*. Though similar in length to the halberd, the long wooden pole of the *naginata* ended not with an axe but with a three-foot curved blade. Acknowledged as a superior weapon for thrusting cuts, it was primarily used to force mounted samurai off their steeds. In fact, it was because of the naginata that samurai started wearing shin guards as part of their armor. Although fighting was mostly a male profession, the naginata was often used by female samurai when they participated in battle. In 1201, Lady Hangaku wielded a naginata as she led 3,000 warriors against an army besieging her castle. Women were still using the naginata in the last samurai battles of 1868, and even today, women in martial arts classes in Japan are trained in the use of naginata.

*Yari (spear)*. By the fifteenth century, the *yari* began displacing the naginata as the weapon of choice in mass combat. In battles where thousands of warriors charged at each other on foot or horseback, the yari was often more effective than the samurai's sword, which was best used in one-on-one duels. The yari was used to great effect by seven warriors at the battle of Shizugatake in 1583. After the battle, they became known as the *shichihon-yari*, or Seven Spears, a phrase that later came to be used as an affectionate term for other groups of samurai who showed prowess on the field.

*Bo/Jo (staff)*. The *bo*, a six-foot-long staff of wood or bamboo, has been used as a weapon in Asia since before the beginning of recorded history. But its popularity in Japan dates to the early seventeenth century, after the shogun banned any non-samurai from using swords, guns, or other sophisticated weapons. Deprived of their swords, peasants used the bo or its shorter cousin, the *jo*, which is around four feet long.

*Daikyu (longbow)*. As early as the third century, Chinese writers referred to Japanese as "the people of the longbow," meaning the *daikyu* was in use in Japan long before the creation of the samurai sword. Made of bamboo glued to softwood and bound by rattan or leather, the longbow stood as tall as eight feet, much taller than the warrior who used it. Its strings were made of long strands of hemp or sinew. Because of its great size, the daikyu required extraordinary strength, which put a limit on the number of people who could effectively use it. Nevertheless, it remained an important combat weapon even after the introduction of firearms. Its advantage was speed. Even the best musketeer took at least fifteen seconds when loading a harquebus, and poorly trained shooters could take up to a minute, so using the bow was much faster. Archers continued to play an important role in warfare well into the eighteenth century. Protected by mobile bamboo walls known as *tedate*, the archers typically stood at the left flank of the army and would typically begin the battle with a volley of arrows, while musketeers would continue the action from the right flank.

*Hankyu (short bow)*. The *hankyu*, "half-sized bow," was made in the same shape as the daikyu, but as its name implies, it was roughly half as big. It was typically used for fighting in close quarters.

*O-yumi/Tappa-yumi (crossbows)*. Japanese crossbows came in two basic sizes. The *o-yumi*, as long as twelve feet, was similar to the tension catapult in Europe, capable of lobbing huge arrows at the enemy. The *tappa-yumi*, designed to be fired from the shoulder, was much lighter and thus more portable.

*Opposite page: Three posed samurai with a variety of weapons including a naginata, a su-yari, and a bow.*
*Below: The gun on top is of customary length, while the one pictured underneath is a wall gun. Tanegashima. Edo period.*

*Teppo (harquebus).* The harquebus, a matchlock gun, was inadvertently introduced to the Japanese after a well-armed Portuguese trading ship wrecked on the island of Tanegashima in 1543. After the warlords who controlled Tanegashima spotted the weapon, they demanded more. Recognizing a new market for weapons, Portuguese and Dutch traders began peddling the harquebus throughout Japan. Within a decade, however, the market for foreign guns dried up, because the Japanese had succeeded in copying the design and producing their own *teppo* on a massive scale. By the end of the sixteenth century, there were more firearms in Japan than in any European nation. Moreover, the Japanese had improved on the weapons, standardizing the bores in the barrels so that bullets could also be mass-produced. Although many samurai used the harquebus, there was still widespread grumbling. Traditionalists complained that mechanized warfare detracted from the glory and honor of manual combat. Perhaps more important, they worried what the harquebus could do to their own status. It was easier to train peasants to use a gun than a sword, which made it easier for warlords to field hundreds of thousands of troops into battle. In the crush of such numbers, the individual deeds of a samurai could go unnoticed.

*Kunikuzushi (cannon).* By the 1570s, Portuguese traders had introduced the cannon to the Japanese arsenal. The most popular was a breech-loading cannon nicknamed *kunikuzushi,* "destroyer of provinces," after a villainous character in a *kabuki* play. The kunikuzushi required more than eight pounds of gunpowder to fire a ten-ounce lead cannonball and smaller shot. By the early seventeenth century, the Japanese had begun making cannon capable of firing eighteen-pound balls.

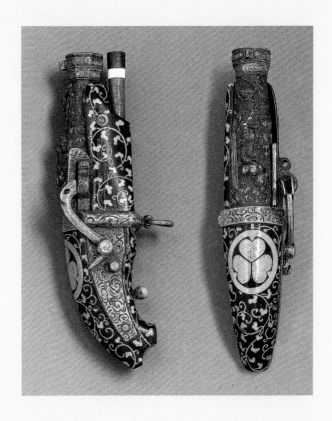

*Above: This rare miniature teppo is signed "Hara Matsuda" and is intricately carved with monkeys on the barrel. Note the hollyhock leaf motif, or mon, associated with the Tokugawa shogunate, on the grip.*
*Below: The carvings on this naginata include the manji-mon, or swastika crest, an ancient Buddhist symbol.*
*Opposite page: A variety of yajiri, or arrowheads, of many shapes, sizes, and materials. While some seem to have been made for practical purposes, the larger yajiri pictured here were probably used for votive offerings.*

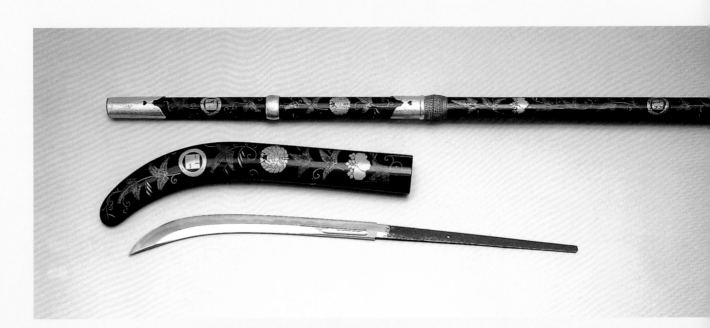

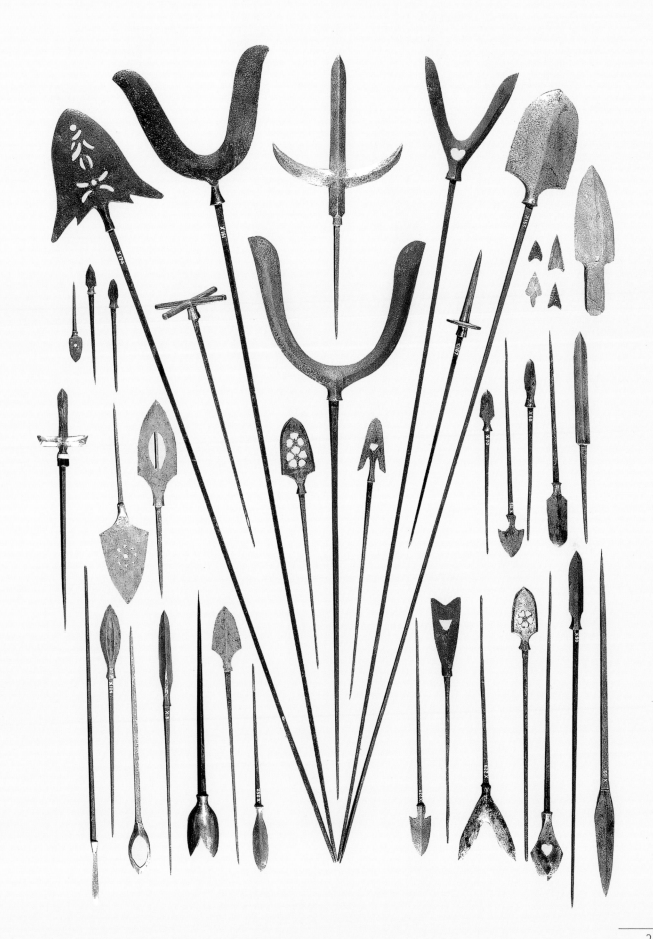

# HISTORY OF THE BOW

The story of the bow is a complicated one, dating back well before written history begins. Bow technology evolved in different ways in different parts of the world, including Europe and the Middle East, with styles, techniques, and uses as diverse as the civilizations themselves. However, archery and the bow itself remain major components of Asian cultural identity: in Korea, the archery tradition still produces world champion bowmen; in China, skill with the composite bow was a requirement for officers in the imperial army until early in the twentieth century; and in Japan, the traditional style of archery, called *kyudo*, remains a recreational and spiritual activity in Japanese society today.

Going back millennia, the Chinese are credited with much of the development of archery technology, decidedly because of their acumen with the apparatus and process, but also possibly because they maintained some of the world's best records of their military and weaponry. The Mongolian nomads and the Chinese were often engaged in territorial struggles, and military technology, particularly regarding bows, was observed and borrowed across enemy lines. Chinese and Mongolian bows were similar to each other. The style of Chinese bows that were used in the Qing dynasty was based on the heavy Manchu war bow. Though that traditional Chinese bow is no longer made anywhere in the world, the design was very close to that of the bow still made in Mongolia today.

The typical bow throughout Chinese history was the composite bow, used in China from at least the Warring States period, which began in the fifth century BCE and ended with the unification of China by the Qin dynasty. This appearance coincided approximately with the adoption of horses as draft (chariot) or riding animals. The benefits of a composite bow were all related to energy: how much can it store? How well does that energy transfer to the arrow? How easily can it be manipulated by the archer? This type of bow scored favorably in all of these categories. In its construction, the composite bow used a wooden core, which had multiple layers of horn and sinew attached to it with glues. This horn and sinew stored more energy than wood alone, so the energy delivered to the arrow was greater and allowed the bow to be shorter and lighter. Some Mongolian composite bows have been shown to withstand a draw weight of nearly 160 pounds.

Almost all composite bows were also recurve bows. This means that when the bow was viewed in profile, the ends of the bow curved away from the archer. The recurve design allowed the bow to store more energy than a straight bow, allowing for more draw weight in the early draw, thus maintaining more energy for the final stages of the draw, when it really counted. It would be possible to make a bow of wood that looks like a composite bow, but it could not store the energy and would break at full draw.

The main advantage of the composite bows over a self bow (made from one piece of wood) was its combination of smaller size with higher power. It was more suitable for use from horseback, and also from a chariot. However, there were drawbacks. Construction required more time and a greater variety of materials, and the animal glue was not durable enough to last for long periods of time.

The materials used came from the everyday life of the Chinese people. The horn was most commonly that of water buffalo, although goat and sheep horn were also used. The wood for the core was selected for two traits: its weight, because light woods were more practical for wielding and transporting; and the nature of its surface, because the wood also had to be able to adhere to glue. These requirements made bamboo, plentiful in China, an obvious candidate for the core wood. The sinews came from the legs of deer and other domesticated animals, which were widely available in agrarian Chinese life. Hide glue or gelatin made from fish bladders were used to attach layers of sinew to the back of the bow. It was also used to attach the horn and sinews to the wooden core.

The Japanese long bow, known as a *yumi*, shared many characteristics with that of the Chinese bow, but the yumi soon surpassed its Chinese counterpart in design and efficiency. This bow was also a recurve bow, like its Chinese counterpart, but it was asymmetrical. When viewed from profile, there was significantly more bow above the arm than below it. The arrow was typically notched around a foot below the center of the bow. This

*Opposite page: Traditional archery competition using the Japanese yumi (bow) and ya (arrows). Chikanobu Toyohara (1838–1912). Japan. Woodblock print.*

design increased string tension as well as the balance of the device. The asymmetrical design was beneficial to the Japanese, who were small in size. A warrior could easily move the bow from one side to the other while firing from horseback, or while in a defensive kneeling position.

As was the case with the Japanese samurai sword, the construction of the yumi was a careful and reverential process. The wood of choice was usually mulberry, which was reinforced by bamboo and toughened by fire. The layers were bound tightly together by thread and the securing points were covered in smooth lacquer. The entire instrument was then coated many times over with a shiny, polished lacquer that protected the wood from the tensions of drawing and the effects of weather. On the whole, the traditional yumi has held the honor of being the most efficient, durable, and accurate bow ever created.

The string of a yumi, called the *tsuru*, was traditionally made of braided hemp. Strings were not replaced until they broke. The break was a result of the flexing of the bow away from the direction of the archer, but the increased flexibility was considered essential to the development of the individual yumi. The point on the string where the arrow rested was reinforced with hemp and glue, which helped prevent the eroding effects of repeated friction from the fingers, and helped to stabilize the arrow on the string.

The yumi is considered the greatest achievement in traditional bow technology, and the Japanese practitioners of kyudo respect it accordingly. The construction, manipulation, and care of the yumi rival that of a samurai sword. Indeed, it is believed that the spirit of the person who made the yumi is a part of the weapon itself. It is seen as disrespectful to step over a yumi that lies on the ground or to touch another person's yumi without permission.

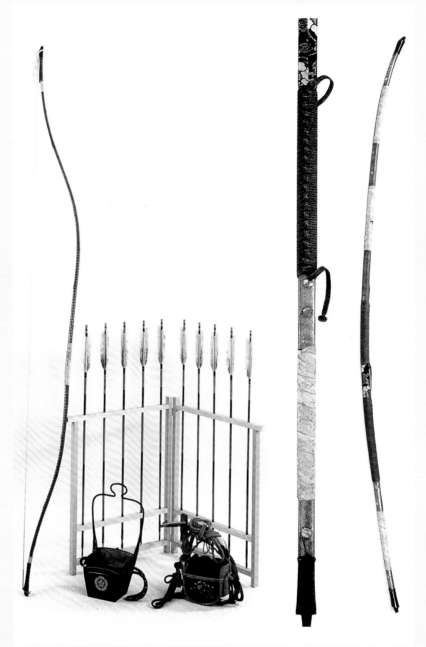

*The bow shown here in detail was officially registered as an Important Art Object by the Japanese government in 1940.*

The bow was an essential technological development in Asian life. Whether used as a weapon for battle or hunting, as a hobby for competitions or personal development, or as a meditative and spiritual tool, it has had a long and storied relationship with the people of Asia.

*Opposite page: Samurai Warrior. Signed "Miyao." Circa 1890. Bronze.*

# The Training and Position of Woman

The female half of our species has sometimes been called the paragon of paradoxes, because the intuitive working of its mind is beyond the comprehension of men's "arithmetical understanding." The Chinese ideogram denoting "the mysterious," "the unknowable," consists of two parts, one meaning "young" and the other "woman," because the physical charms and delicate thoughts of the fair sex are above the coarse mental caliber of our sex to explain.

In the Bushido ideal of woman, however, there is little mystery and only a seeming paradox. I have said that it was Amazonian, but that is only half the truth. Ideographically the Chinese represent wife by a woman holding a broom—certainly not to brandish it offensively or defensively against her conjugal ally, neither for witchcraft, but for the more harmless uses for which the besom was first invented—the idea involved being thus not less homely than the etymological derivation of the English wife (weaver) and daughter (*duhitar*, milkmaid). Without confining the sphere of woman's activity to *Küche, Kirche, Kinder*, as the present German Kaiser is said to do, the Bushido ideal of womanhood was preeminently domestic. These seeming contradictions—domesticity and Amazonian traits—are not inconsistent with the Precepts of Knighthood, as we shall see.

Bushido being a teaching primarily intended for the masculine sex, the virtues it prized in woman were naturally far from being distinctly feminine. Winckelmann remarks that "the supreme beauty of Greek art is rather male than female," and Lecky adds that it was true in the moral conception of the Greeks as in their art. Bushido similarly praised those women most "who emancipated themselves from the frailty of their sex and displayed a heroic fortitude worthy of the strongest and the bravest of

*Opposite page: Figures in an Interior. A Courtesan Looking at Her Shinzo Who Is Reading a Love Letter. Suzuki Harunobu (1725–1770). Chuban Tate-e.*

men."[25] Young girls therefore, were trained to repress their feelings, to indurate their nerves, to manipulate weapons—especially the long-handled sword called *nagi-nata*—so as to be able to hold their own against unexpected odds. Yet the primary motive for exercises of this martial character was not for use in the field; it was twofold—personal and domestic. Woman owning no suzerain of her own, formed her own bodyguard. With her weapon she guarded her personal sanctity with as much zeal as her husband did his master's. The domestic utility of her warlike training was in the education of her sons, as we shall see later.

Fencing and similar exercises, if rarely of practical use, were a wholesome counterbalance to the otherwise sedentary habits of woman. But these exercises were not followed only for hygienic purposes. They could be turned into use in times of need. Girls, when they reached womanhood, were presented with dirks (*kai-ken*, pocket poniards), which might be directed to the bosom of their assailants, or, if advisable, to their own. The latter was very often the case: and yet I will not judge them severely. Even the Christian conscience with its horror of self-immolation, will not be harsh with them, seeing Pelagia and Domnina, two suicides, were canonized for their purity and piety. When a Japanese Virginia saw her chastity menaced, she did not wait for her father's dagger. Her own weapon lay always in her bosom. It was a disgrace to her not to know the proper way in which she had to perpetrate self-destruction. For example, little as she was taught in anatomy, she must know the exact spot to cut in her throat: she must know how to tie her lower limbs together with a belt so that, whatever the agonies of death might be, her corpse be found in utmost modesty with the limbs properly composed. Is not a caution like this worthy of the Christian Perpetua or the Vestal Cornelia? I would not put such an abrupt interrogation, were it not for a misconception, based on our bathing customs and other trifles, that chastity is unknown among us.[26] On the contrary, chastity was a preeminent virtue of the samurai woman, held above life itself. A young woman, taken prisoner, seeing herself in danger of violence at the hands of the rough soldiery, says she will obey their pleasure, provided she be first allowed to write a line to her sisters, whom war has dispersed in every direction. When the epistle is finished, off she runs to the nearest well and saves her honor by drowning. The letter she leaves behind ends with these verses—

*For fear lest clouds may dim her light,*
*Should she but graze this nether sphere,*
*The young moon poised above the height*
*Doth hastily betake to flight.*

It would be unfair to give my readers an idea that masculinity alone was our highest ideal for woman. Far from it! Accomplishments and the gentler graces of life were required of them. Music, dancing, and literature were not neglected.

*Cherry blossom-viewing. Japan. 1600–1700. Six-panel folding screen. Ink, colors, and gold on paper. The terrain of this folding screen suggests that the artist was depicting Mount Yoshino in southern Nara prefecture, which is known for the spectacular beauty of its cherry blossoms.*

Some of the finest verses in our literature were expressions of feminine sentiments; in fact, women played an important role in the history of Japanese belles-lettres. Dancing was taught (I am speaking of samurai girls and not of geisha) only to smooth the angularity of their movements. Music was to regale the weary hours of their fathers and husbands; hence it was not for the technique, the art as such, that music was learned; for the ultimate object was purification of heart, since it was said that no harmony of sound is attainable without the player's heart being in harmony with herself. Here again we see the same idea prevailing which we notice in the training of youths—that accomplishments were ever kept subservient to moral worth. Just enough of music and dancing to add grace and brightness to life, but never to foster vanity and extravagance. I sympathize with the Persian prince, who, when taken into a ballroom in London and asked to take part in the merriment, bluntly remarked that in his country they provided a particular set of girls to do that kind of business for them.

The accomplishments of our women were not acquired

for show or social ascendency. They were a home diversion; and if they shone in social parties, it was as the attributes of a hostess—in other words, as a part of the household contrivance for hospitality. Domesticity guided their education. It may be said that the accomplishments of the women of Old Japan, be they martial or pacific in character, were mainly intended for the home; and, however far they might roam, they never lost sight of the hearth as the center. It was to maintain its honor and integrity that they slaved, drudged, and gave up their lives. Night and day, in tones at once firm and tender, brave and plaintive, they sang to their little nests. As daughter, woman sacrificed herself for her father, as wife for her husband, and as mother for her son. Thus from earliest youth she was taught to deny herself. Her life was not one of independence, but of dependent service. Man's helpmeet, if her presence is helpful she stays on the stage with him: if it hinders his work, she retires behind the curtain. Not infrequently does it happen that a youth becomes enamored of a maiden who returns his love with equal ardor, but, when she realizes his interest in her makes him forgetful of his duties, disfigures her person that her attractions may cease. Adzuma, the ideal wife in the minds of samurai girls, finds herself loved by a man who, in order to win her affection, conspires against her husband. Upon pretense of joining in the guilty plot, she manages in the dark to take her husband's place, and the sword of the lover assassin descends upon her own devoted head.

The following epistle written by the wife of a young *daimio*, before taking her own life, needs no comment:

Oft have I heard that no accident or chance ever mars the march of events here below, and that all moves in accordance with a plan. To take shelter under a common bough or a drink of the same river, is alike ordained from ages prior to our birth. Since we were joined in ties of eternal wedlock, now two short years ago, my heart hath followed thee, even as its shadow followeth an object, inseparably bound heart to heart, loving and being loved.

Learning but recently, however, that the coming battle is to be the last of thy labor and life, take the farewell greeting of thy loving partner. I have heard that Kowu, the mighty warrior of ancient China, lost a battle, loth to part with his favorite Gu. Yoshinaka, too, brave as he was, brought disaster to his cause, too weak to bid prompt farewell to his wife. Why should I, to whom earth no longer offers hope or joy—why should I detain thee or thy thoughts by living? Why should I not, rather, await thee on the road which all mortal kind must sometime tread? Never, prithee, never forget the many benefits which our good master Hideyori hath heaped upon thee. The gratitude we owe him is as deep as the sea and as high as the hills.

Woman's surrender of herself to the good of her husband, home, and family was as willing and honorable as the man's self-surrender to the good of his lord and country. Self-renunciation, without which no life-enigma can be solved, was the keynote of the loyalty of man as well as of the domesticity of woman. She was no more the slave of man than was her husband of his liege-lord, and the part she played was recognized as *naijo*, "the inner help." In the ascending scale of service stood woman, who annihilated herself for man, that he might annihilate himself for the master, that he in turn might obey Heaven. I know the weakness of this teaching and that the superiority of Christianity is nowhere more manifest than here, in that it requires of each and every living soul direct responsibility to its Creator. Nevertheless, as far as the doctrine of service—the serving of a cause higher than one's own self, even at the sacrifice of one's individuality; I say the doctrine of service, which is the greatest that Christ preached and is the sacred keynote of his mission—as far as that is concerned, Bushido is based on eternal truth.

My readers will not accuse me of undue prejudice in favor of slavish surrender of volition. I accept in a large measure the view advanced with breadth of learning and defended with profundity of thought by Hegel, that history is the unfolding and realization of freedom. The point I wish to make is that the whole teaching of Bushido was so thoroughly imbued with the spirit of self-sacrifice, that it was required not only of woman but of man. Hence, until the influence of its Precepts is entirely done away with, our society will not realize the view rashly expressed by an American exponent of woman's rights, who exclaimed, "May all the daughters of Japan rise in revolt against ancient customs!" Can such a revolt succeed? Will it improve the female status? Will the rights they gain by such a summary process repay the loss of that sweetness of disposition, that gentleness of manner, which are their present heritage? Was not the loss of domesticity on the part of Roman matrons followed by moral corruption too gross to mention? Can the American reformer assure us that a revolt of our daughters is the true course for their historical development to take? These are grave questions. Changes must and will come without revolts! In the meantime let us see whether the status of the fair sex under the Bushido regimen was really so bad as to justify a revolt.

We hear much of the outward respect European knights paid to "God and the ladies," the incongruity of the two terms making Gibbon blush; we are also told by Hallam that the morality of chivalry was coarse, that gallantry implied illicit love. The effect of chivalry on the weaker vessel was food for reflection on the part of philosophers, M. Guizot contending that feudalism and chivalry wrought wholesome influences, while Mr. Spencer tells us that in a militant society (and what is feudal society if not militant?) the position of woman is necessarily low, improving only as

*Two Beauties under a Blossoming Cherry Tree. Tesai Hokuba. Japan. 1615–1868. Ink and color on silk.*

*This figure represents an unknown Shinto goddess. Statues like these were not meant to be seen, and were kept hidden as part of a shrine. Female Shinto spirit. Japan. 1100–1200. Wood with traces of pigment.*

society becomes more industrial. Now is M. Guizot's theory true of Japan, or is Mr. Spencer's? In reply I might aver that both are right. The military class in Japan was restricted to the samurai, comprising nearly two million souls. Above them were the military nobles, the daimio, and the court nobles, the *kugé*—these higher, sybaritical nobles being fighters only in name. Below them were masses of the common people—mechanics, tradesmen, and peasants—whose life was devoted to arts of peace. Thus what Herbert Spencer gives as the characteristics of a militant type of society may be said to have been exclusively confined to the samurai class, while those of the industrial type were applicable to the classes above and below it. This is well illustrated by the position of woman; for in no class did she experience less freedom than among the samurai. Strange to say, the lower the social class—as, for instance, among small artisans—the more equal was the position of husband and wife. Among the higher nobility, too, the difference in the relations of the sexes was less marked, chiefly because there were few occasions to bring the differences of sex into prominence, the leisurely nobleman having become literally effeminate. Thus Spencer's dictum was fully exemplified in Old Japan. As to Guizot's, those who read his presentation of a feudal community will remember that he had the higher nobility especially under consideration, so that his generalization applies to the daimio and the kugé.

I shall be guilty of gross injustice to historical truth if my words give one a very low opinion of the status of woman under Bushido. I do not hesitate to state that she was not treated as man's equal; but until we learn to discriminate between difference and inequalities, there will always be misunderstandings upon this subject.

When we think in how few respects men are equal among themselves, e.g., before law courts or voting polls, it seems idle to trouble ourselves with a discussion on the equality of sexes. When the American Declaration of Independence said that all men were created equal, it had no reference to their mental or physical gifts: it simply repeated what Ulpian long ago announced, that before the law all men are equal. Legal rights were in this case the measure of their equality. Were the law the only scale by which to measure the position of woman in a community, it would be as easy to tell where she stands as to give her *avoirdupois* in pounds and ounces. But the question is: Is there a correct standard in comparing the relative social position of the sexes? Is it right, is it enough, to compare woman's status to man's as the value of silver is compared with that of gold, and give the ratio numerically? Such a method of calculation excludes from consideration the most important kind of value which a human being possesses, namely, the intrinsic. In view of the manifold variety of requisites for making each sex fulfill its earthly mission, the standard to be adopted in measuring its relative position must be of a composite character; or, to borrow from economic language, it must be a multiple standard. Bushido had a standard of its own and it was binomial. It tried to gauge the value of woman on the battlefield and by the hearth. There she counted for very little; here for all. The treatment accorded her corresponded to this double measurement—as a social-political unit not much, while as wife and mother she received highest respect and deepest affection. Why among so military a nation as the Romans, were their matrons so highly venerated? Was it not because they were *matrona*, mothers? Not as fighters or lawgivers, but as their mothers did men bow before them. So with us. While fathers and husbands were absent in field or camp, the government of the household was left entirely in the hands of mothers and wives. The education of the young, even their defense, was entrusted to them. The warlike exercises of women, of which I have spoken, were primarily to enable them intelligently to direct and follow the education of their children.

I have noticed a rather superficial notion prevailing among half-informed foreigners, that because the common Japanese expression for one's wife is "my rustic wife" and the like, she is despised and held in little esteem. When it is told that such phrases as "my foolish father," "my swinish son," "my awkward self," etc., are in current use, is not the answer clear enough?

To me it seems that our idea of marital union goes in some ways further than the so-called Christian. "Man and woman shall be one flesh." The individualism of the Anglo-Saxon cannot let go of the idea that husband and wife are two persons; hence when they disagree, their separate rights are recognized, and when they agree, they exhaust their vocabulary in all sorts of silly pet-names and nonsensical blandishments. It sounds highly irrational to our ears, when a husband or wife speaks to a third party of his other half—better or worse—as being lovely, bright, kind, and what not. Is it good taste to speak of one's self as "my bright self," "my lovely disposition," and so forth? We think praising one's own wife or one's own husband is praising a part of one's own self, and self-praise is regarded, to say the least, as bad taste among us—and I hope, among Christian nations too! I have diverged at some length because the polite debasement of one's consort was a usage most in vogue among the samurai.

The Teutonic races beginning their tribal life with a superstitious awe of the fair sex (though this is really wearing off in Germany!), and the Americans beginning their social life under the painful consciousness of the numerical insufficiency of women[27] (who, now increasing, are, I am afraid, fast losing the prestige their colonial mothers enjoyed), the respect man pays to woman has in Western civilization become the chief standard of morality. But in the martial ethics of Bushido, the main watershed dividing the good and the bad was sought elsewhere. It was located along the line of duty which bound man to his own divine soul and then to other souls, in the five relations I have mentioned in the early part of this paper. Of these we have brought to our reader's notice loyalty, the relation between one man as vassal and another as lord. Upon the rest, I have only dwelt incidentally as occasion presented itself; because they were not peculiar to Bushido. Being founded on natural affections, they could but be common to all mankind, though in some particulars they may have been accentuated by conditions which its teachings induced. In this connection, there comes before me the peculiar strength and tenderness of friendship between man and man, which often added to the bond of brotherhood a romantic attachment doubtless intensified by the separation of the sexes in youth, a separation which denied to affection the natural channel open to it in Western chivalry or in the free intercourse of Anglo-Saxon lands. I might fill pages with Japanese versions of the story of Damon and Pythias or Achilles and Patroclos, or tell in Bushido parlance of ties as sympathetic as those which bound David and Jonathan.

25 Lecky, *History of European Morals II*, p. 383.
26 For a very sensible explanation of nudity and bathing see Finck's *Lotos Time in Japan*, pp. 286-297.
27 I refer to those days when girls were imported from England and given in marriage for so many pounds of tobacco, etc.

*Above: Design used for samurai family crests, or mon.*
*Left: A Standing Courtesan in a Black Kimono Scattered with White Flowerheads Holding a Wad of Paper. Utagawa Kunisada. Color, gofun, and gold on silk.*

# FEMME FATALE
## THE SAMURAI WOMAN

With a certain degree of petulance, some academics quibble that the term *samurai* refers specifically and exclusively to the male warrior. But most modern scholars of Japanese history would disagree, and go on to speak admiringly of the few samurai women who blazed through the battlefields beside their sons, husbands, brothers, and fathers.

In the early days of feudal Japan, with her husband frequently engaged in war abroad, the samurai wife took on a great deal of responsibility at home. It was up to her to manage the household and oversee food crops, along with the financial dealings that those two things entailed; she supervised the servants; she ensured that her children were well educated, especially in the ideals of loyalty, courage, and physical skill; and she was allowed to inherit and handle her own property. And throughout all, she was expected to exhibit an inner strength and unwavering self-control. Beyond these obligations she was required to be capable of protecting her home or village from enemies, with force if necessary. To that end, that she had been properly trained as a young girl to use two weapons: the *naginata*, the long wooden shaft that ended in a curved sword that she had probably brought with her into the marriage; and the *kaiken*, the short dagger that she always kept on her person.

Invested with the same set of *bushi*, or warrior, skills as those of her male relatives, she naturally took to the battlefield and council rooms with the same ferocious loyalty to clan and ruler that they did. Some of these women wielded their power in more subtle ways. Hojo Masako, the wife of Minamoto Yoritomo, who became the first shogun in 1192, rose to power after her husband's death. Masako became a Buddhist nun instead of committing suicide according to custom. From the nunnery, she maneuvered the Hojo clan into a position of controlling power over her own son and then a succession of Minamoto puppet shoguns.

Another samurai woman who took advantage of her circumstances was Hino Tomiko, who ruled in the place of her husband, Ashikaga Yoshimasa, when he lost interest in shogunate politics of the late fifteenth century. In a similar way, the bushi wife Nene often simply overruled the decisions of her husband, Toyotomi Hideyoshi.

The most impressive of the samurai women, though, were those whose stories emerged from the killing grounds themselves. Hangaku Gozen (the term *gozen* being a title of honor instead of a surname) commanded an army of 3,000

warriors when she assisted her brother and nephew in a rebellion against the Minamoto shogun in 1201. Holding off the shogunate army of 10,000 for a while, Hangaku, sometimes known as Itagaki, was finally wounded and captured. Curiously, she survived to marry one of her former enemies, as opposed to finding a way to take her own life in the expected act of *jigai*, the severing of the jugular vein in the samurai woman's equivalent of *seppuku*.

That very act of traditional suicide motivated the wife of Mimura Kotoku during the Warring States period between 1467 and 1568. When her husband's castle was attacked and many of his samurai killed, she was stunned by the number of women and children who then took their own lives according to the custom. Throwing on armor and leading a band of nearly a hundred soldiers, she stormed from the castle, slicing her way through the enemy with her naginata.

In 1868, at the end of the samurai era, in one of the confrontations that brought about its demise, Nakano Takeko fought among the significantly outnumbered Aizu clan against the imperial forces who were trying to eradicate the shogunate and the samurai class altogether. From a group of twenty women fighting at the front, she cut a path through the enemy line with her skillful use of the naginata, unstoppable until she took a bullet in the chest. So that she wouldn't be disgraced by being captured by the enemy, her sister decapitated her, as they had apparently agreed upon beforehand, and her head was returned to her home with honor.

By far best documented samurai woman was Tomoe Gozen, who fought under Minamoto Yoshinaka, either as his wife or perhaps as an officer, during the Gempei War of the late twelfth century. Renowned for her beauty, fierce fighting spirit, skill with the sword and bow, and mastery of the war horse, Tomoe Gozen reportedly was sent out on the battlefield as Yoshinaka's first captain. Stories of her final days are conflicting; some report that she died on the battlefield side by side with her love Yoshinaka, and others that she was last seen riding into the sunset with his severed head, to protect him from disgrace at the hands of the enemy. Or perhaps she became a nun.

*Tomoe Gozen. Edo period about 1840 (Tenpo 11). Japan. Utagawa Kuniyoshi, Japanese, 1797–1861. Woodblock print (mishiki-e). Ink and color on paper. Photograph © 2008 Museum of Fine Arts, Boston.*

御前に

山本兵衛小伜一安太夫の

兼遠を仮親として義

也国の戦ひ平家の勇士

有国を討神武以来離

本舞有の大力あり

# WOMEN IN SHOGUNATE JAPAN

The female samurai of early feudal Japan, in her stance as a peer when it came to waging war, represented the exception to the rule for the majority of women of the times. Generally, a woman had one specific role, that of caretaker—of husband, home, farm, finances, children, and elderly parents. Yet in spite of that seeming lopsidedness, women of the first millennium of the modern period enjoyed relative equality in terms of rights of marriage, education, and property. As centuries passed, and the times grew more peaceful and more men reclaimed and asserted their dominance at home, social conventions changed, so that by the era of the Tokugawa shogunate, the rules of proper conduct for women had grown more formal and inflexible than at any other point in Japanese history.

The less turbulent times notwithstanding, the origin of this adjustment in social mores lay in no small part with the rising authority of Buddhist and Confucian teachings, which promoted ideals for women that in no way included carrying weapons, much less fighting in wars. Eventually, the rights that women had previously enjoyed began to be taken away, to a point of utter subjugation, and by the sixteenth century, the guidelines of the Three Obediences codified their existence. According to those tenets, a woman had no hope of independence throughout life: when she was young, she obeyed her father; when she was married, she obeyed her husband; when she was widowed, she obeyed her son.

Ironically, one way for a woman to escape the confines of shogun society was through religion. In earlier times, women had functioned as Shinto shamans and had been revered for their judgment regarding difficult social issues. With the newer religion, Buddhist nuns held the same power as Buddhist monks. A samurai widow, her only other option being suicide, was expected to become a Buddhist nun, and many did. Among those women who used their influence as Buddhist nuns, the most famous was Hojo Masako. When her husband, the shogun Minamoto Yoritomo, died in 1199, she assumed control of the shogunate, installing her own family, the Hojo clan, in a regency status over her son Yoriie. For generations, the Hojo remained the power behind the Minamoto shoguns, and for that reason, she was fondly referred to as Mother Shogun. But such an example points to an exception to the rule.

The plight of the powerless woman of modest birth in the provinces was reflected in the thousands of women who were sequestered in the inner courts of the shogun's palace. The women in this closed society paid close attention to rank among themselves. Some of their positions included the seven elders, who ran the palace with an iron rod; nuns who performed official duties; ladies in charge of hand water and tobacco; those who specialized in ritual music and ritual events; and at the very bottom, the "honorable pups" or

"honorable dogs," who ran errands and lived on scraps and leftovers. Rarely, some movement between ranks might conceivably be possible for these tragic figures, but the one line that could never be crossed was the distinction between a woman of noble birth, who was allowed to enter the presence of the shogun, and one of ignoble birth, who throughout her entire career would never see him, unless by some chance he should take notice of her attractiveness and select her for the night.

On the other hand, concubines, who were seen exclusively by the shogun, could be of either noble or common birth, so long as they were beautiful. And because concubines retired at the age of thirty, a fresh set of recruits was constantly needed. Conditions were claustrophobic, for each of the concubines had several maids in attendance and several shaven-headed nuns acting as guards to her quarters. But, in general, life in the palace was elegant and leisurely. A considerable amount of time was spent preparing for the shogun's three daily visits, in the morning, afternoon, and evening. With her maids helping her, the young woman's first task was to shave her eyebrows and blacken her teeth with a dye of sumac-leaf gall, sake, and iron, for unpainted teeth were considered ugly. Next came applying thick white makeup, outlining her eyes in black, rouging her cheeks, and pasting a red safflower dye on her lips. Then her long hair was oiled, combed out, and twisted into a knot.

Because there were no other men allowed in the inner palace, protecting the shogun was left to the women, and thus, every woman had a *naginata* of her own and had been trained from an early age in hand-to-hand combat. So great was the reputation of the women of the inner palace that no shogun was ever attacked inside it. That daunting task of keeping the shogun alive extended even to the most intimate circumstances. After a concubine was requested, she was stripped and searched to make sure there were no weapons or notes on her body or in her hair. Once the girl and the shogun were in bed, there would be two ladies-in-waiting lying wide awake in the room, one on each side, with two more listening behind screens not far way, to ensure that the girl did not make any improper requests.

If this was oppressive for the concubine, it had to be for the shogun as well. Perhaps for that reason, early shoguns spent a lot of time in the informal, unregulated bath, where there was just one lower-class girl to scrub his back. This loose environment produced numerous offspring, known as the "children of the bath." Eventually, the elders intervened and required the shogun to bathe in the men's palace.

*Preceding pages: Tea Time in Japan. Circa 1900. Colored photograph.*
*Left: A Beauty in Snow. Isoda Koryusai (circa 1764–1788). Hanging scroll. Ink and color on silk.*
*Opposite page: Standing Courtesan. Japan. 1688–1704. Hanging scroll. Ink and color on paper.*

# The Influence of Bushido

We have brought into view only a few of the more prominent peaks which rise above the range of knightly virtues, in themselves so much more elevated than the general level of our national life. As the sun in its rising first tips the highest peaks with russet hue, and then gradually casts its rays on the valley below, so the ethical system which first enlightened the military order drew in course of time followers from amongst the masses. Democracy raises up a natural prince for its leader, and aristocracy infuses a princely spirit among the people. Virtues are no less contagious than vices. "There needs but one wise man in a company, and all are wise, so rapid is the contagion," says Emerson. No social class or caste can resist the diffusive power of moral influence.

Prate as we may of the triumphant march of Anglo-Saxon liberty, rarely has it received impetus from the masses. Was it not rather the work of the squires and gentlemen? Very truly does M. Taine say, "These three syllables, as used across the channel, summarize the history of English society." Democracy may make self-confident retorts to such a statement and fling back the question— "When Adam delved and Eve span, where then was the gentleman?" All the more pity that a gentleman was not present in Eden! The first parents missed him sorely and paid a high price for his absence. Had he been there, not only would the garden have been more tastefully dressed, but they would have learned without painful experience that disobedience to Jehovah was disloyalty and dishonor, treason and rebellion.

What Japan was she owed to the samurai. They were not only the flower of the nation but its root as well. All the gracious gifts of Heaven flowed through them. Though they kept themselves socially aloof from the populace, they set a moral standard for them and guided them by their example. I admit Bushido had its esoteric and exoteric teachings; these were eudemonistic, looking after the welfare and happiness of the commonalty, while those were aretaic, emphasizing the practice of virtues for their own sake.

In the most chivalrous days of Europe, knights formed numerically but a small fraction of the population, but, as Emerson says—"In English literature half the drama and all the novels, from Sir Philip Sidney to Sir Walter Scott, paint this figure (gentleman)." Write in place of Sidney and Scott, Chikamatsu and Bakin, and you have in a nutshell the main features of the literary history of Japan.

The innumerable avenues of popular amusement and instruction—the theaters, the storyteller's booths, the preacher's dais, the musical recitations, the novels—have taken for their chief theme the stories of the samurai. The peasants round the open fire in their huts never tire of repeating the achievements of Yoshitsuné and his faithful retainer Benkei, or of the two brave Soga brothers; the dusky urchins listen with gaping mouths until the last stick burns out and the fire dies in its embers, still leaving their hearts aglow with the tale that is told. The clerks and the shopboys, after their day's work is over and the *amado*[28] of the store are closed, gather together to relate the story of Nobunaga and Hidéyoshi far into the night, until slumber overtakes their weary eyes and transports them from the drudgery of the counter to the exploits of the field. The very babe just beginning to toddle is taught to lisp the adventures of Momotaro, the daring conqueror of ogreland. Even girls are so imbued with the love of knightly deeds and virtues that, like Desdemona, they would seriously incline to devour with greedy ear the romance of the samurai.

The samurai grew to be the beau ideal of the whole race. "As among flowers the cherry is queen, so among men the samurai is lord," so sang the populace. Debarred from commercial pursuits, the military class itself did not aid commerce; but there was no channel of human activity, no avenue of thought, which did not receive in some measure an impetus from Bushido. Intellectual and moral Japan was directly or indirectly the work of Knighthood.

Mr. Mallock, in his exceedingly suggestive book,

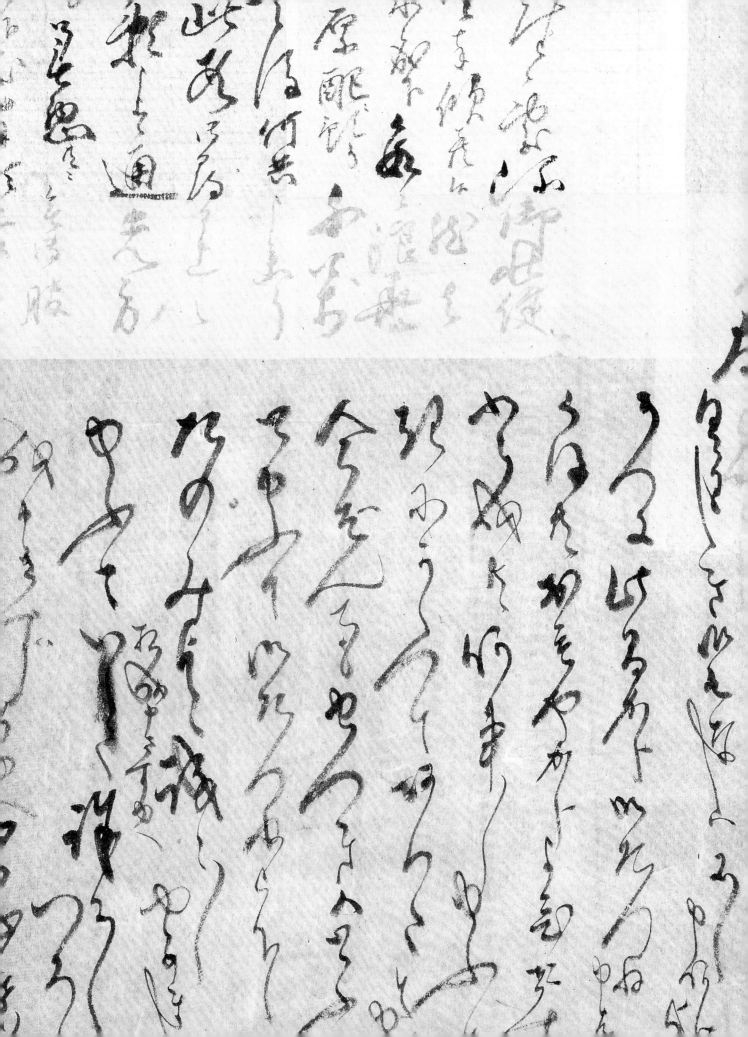

Depiction of Spiritual and Material Worlds. 15th century. Pen and ink and gold leaf on panel.

Above and opposite page, bottom: Jutte, carried as a defensive weapon. Circa 1800–1900. Iron.

*Aristocracy and Evolution*, has eloquently told us that "social evolution, in so far as it is other than biological, may be defined as the unintended result of the intentions of great men;" further, that historical progress is produced by a struggle "not among the community generally, to live, but a struggle amongst a small section of the community to lead, to direct, to employ, the majority in the best way." Whatever may be said about the soundness of his argument, these statements are amply verified in the part played by bushi in the social progress, as far as it went, of our Empire.

How the spirit of Bushido permeated all social classes is also shown in the development of a certain order of men, known as *otoko-daté*, the natural leaders of democracy. Staunch fellows were they, every inch of them strong with the strength of massive manhood. At once the spokesmen and the guardians of popular rights, they had each a following of hundreds and thousands of souls who proffered in the same fashion that samurai did to daimio, the willing service of "limb and life, of body, chattels, and earthly honor." Backed by a vast multitude of rash and impetuous working men, those born

"bosses" formed a formidable check to the rampancy of the two-sworded order.

In manifold ways has Bushido filtered down from the social class where it originated, and acted as leaven among the masses, furnishing a moral standard for the whole people. The Precepts of Knighthood, begun at first as the glory of the elite, became in time an aspiration and inspiration to the nation at large; and though the populace could not attain the moral height of those loftier souls, yet Yamato Damashii, the Soul of Japan, ultimately came to express the *Volksgeist* of the Island Realm. If religion is no more than "Morality touched by emotion," as Matthew Arnold defines it, few ethical systems are better entitled to the rank of religion than Bushido. Motoori has put the mute utterance of the nation into words when he sings:

> Isles of blest Japan!
>   Should your Yamato spirit
> Strangers seek to scan,
>   Say—scenting morn's sunlit air,
>   Blows the cherry wild and fair!

Yes, the *sakura*[29] has for ages been the favorite of our people and the emblem of our character. Mark particularly the terms of definition which the poet uses, the words the wild cherry flower scenting the morning sun.

The Yamato spirit is not a tame, tender plant, but a wild—in the sense of natural—growth; it is indigenous to the soil; its accidental qualities it may share with the flowers of other lands, but in its essence it remains the original, spontaneous outgrowth of our clime. But its nativity is not its sole claim to our affection. The refinement and grace of its beauty appeal to our aesthetic sense as no other flower can. We cannot share the admiration of the Europeans for their roses, which lack the simplicity of our flower. Then, too, the thorns that are hidden beneath the sweetness of the rose, the tenacity with which she clings to life, as though loath or afraid to die rather than drop untimely, preferring to rot on her stem; her showy colors and heavy odors—all these are traits so unlike our flower, which carries no dagger or poison under its beauty, which is ever ready to depart life at the call of nature, whose colors are never gorgeous, and whose light fragrance never palls. Beauty of color and of form is limited in its showing; it is a fixed quality of existence, whereas fragrance is volatile, ethereal as the breathing of life. So in all religious ceremonies frankincense and myrrh play a prominent part. There is something spiritual in redolence. When the delicious perfume of the sakura quickens the morning air, as the sun in its course rises to illumine first the isles of the Far East, few sensations are more serenely exhilarating than to inhale, as it were, the very breath of beauteous day.

When the Creator himself is pictured as making new resolutions in his heart upon smelling a sweet savor (Gen. VIII, 21), is it any wonder that the sweet-smelling season of the cherry blossom should call forth the whole nation from their little habitations? Blame them not, if for a time their limbs forget their toil and moil and their hearts their pangs and sorrows. Their brief pleasure ended, they return to their daily tasks with new strength and new resolutions. Thus in ways more than one is the sakura the flower of the nation.

Is, then, this flower, so sweet and evanescent, blown whithersoever the wind listeth, and, shedding a puff of perfume, ready to vanish forever, is this flower the type of the Yamato spirit? Is the Soul of Japan so frailly mortal?

28 Outside shutters.
29 *Cerasus pseudo-cerasus*, Lindley.

*Ducks. A pair of two-panel screens. Anonymous. 18th century.*

# THE GEISHA CLASS
## MASTERS OF THE ARTS

Pronounced "gay-sha" and translated as "artist," the word *geisha* has been misunderstood by the Western world for as long as there has been contact with Japan. Rooted in the Tokugawa era of isolationism, the geisha became a master of arts in a time when wives were not permitted outside the home and a woman was needed to provide entertainment. For these women, intense training in artistic and social skills traditionally began as early as the preteen years. The following steps mark advancement in the life of a woman of this class.

*Shikomi.* As a very young girl, the *shikomi* does chores around the house to earn her keep before becoming an apprentice herself.

*Misedashi.* At about age fifteen, a shikomi finds an *oneesan*, a mentor with whom she undergoes the *misedashi* ceremony that binds them together as sisters. The new apprentice begins her training to become a geisha.

*Maiko.* As an apprentice, a *maiko* spends several years learning the arts, and she attends parties to observe the proper forms of entertaining and to begin making contacts.

*Erikae.* The *erikae*, the "turning of the collar," ceremony marks the transition from maiko to geisha.

*Geisha.* Until she retires, a geisha lives in the district where she works. If she finds a *danna*, or patron, she may move out of the house into her own apartment.

*Hiki-iwai.* The *hiki-iwai* retirement ceremony indicates she no longer entertains and may discontinue her studies. She can also become the head of her own house or a teahouse, or she may leave the geisha life entirely.

Training to be a geisha was a long process and a young woman typically spent about six years studying the art of music, dance, calligraphy, language and conversation, hostessing, and the tea ceremony. During training, she lived in the *okiya*, which is something like a boarding house for geisha and maiko. The okiya was a big part of her life, because the women in the okiya were her geisha family, and the *okaasan* was her new mother and managed her career.

A maiko lived by certain rules that applied only to her level of apprenticeship. Her dress, hair, and demeanor were flashier. She wore wooden clogs, the *okobo*, instead of sandals, her kimono was brighter and longer, and her hair arranged a bit higher—all to make her showier and to compensate for her lack of complete training. A maiko went to practice her skills at a *kaburenjo* school, which may have included a theater where public geisha performances were held. Besides the arts mentioned earlier, a maiko also learned grace and etiquette. Walking on her tall clogs in a floor-length kimono without tripping was an art form in itself.

Each maiko was paired to an oneesan, "older sister," who was a full geisha and served as a mentor. In the misedashi pairing ceremony, the maiko took a new geisha name that was derived from her oneesan's name. A maiko spent several years learning from her oneesan the practical lessons that the classroom couldn't teach her. She attended parties where she would melt into the background like a wallflower and observe keenly everything the oneesan did, for this is where she also learned the social hierarchy by discerning which guest to greet first and how low to bow for each. This was not her only duty, however. Attending these parties was the way that the oneesan introduced the maiko to the outside world; important relationships with customers and teahouses made during this time would carry over into her geisha career.

Contrary to our modern-day perceptions, the first geisha were actually men who banged drums, sang, and told amusing stories. However, by the mid-seventeenth century, women had taken control of the profession and soon enjoyed a total monopoly. One explanation for the change suggests that a group of women lured business away from prostitutes by hiring themselves out to sing and dance at parties, while another theory relates the story of one unsuccessful prostitute who turned to entertaining as a geisha to survive and thus became a hit. Here, perhaps, another popular myth also needs to be dispelled. Geisha were not prostitutes. The confusion lies in the fact that, during the Allied Occupation of Japan following World War II, prostitutes posing in geisha-style apparel catered to the enlisted men. These "gee-sha girls" evoked the image of what a geisha was supposed to be to the Western world. But subtle costume differences actually distinguished the two groups. A true geisha wore various stylized hairdos through a series of wigs (after years of rigorously manipulating her own hair, it begins to thin and fall out). And the geisha's *obi* was fastened in a complex arrangement behind her, while a prostitute's was tied in front, for ease of access. If both geisha and prostitutes attended a party, one look at a woman's hairstyle, kimono, and makeup would instantly indicate which she was.

Regardless of how the female geisha came about, they did pose a threat to the prostitutes. Because geisha were not connected to the brothels, those owners and managers received no money from the geisha's wages. As a way of undermining the geisha's popularity and getting the focus back on registered prostitutes, the government set stringent regulations on the geisha concerning their style of dress, how and where they could entertain, and the hours they could work. Moreover, to make sure sex was left up to the prostitutes, geisha could not be hired singly. But the plan backfired, and the restrictions only fueled the success of the geisha by making them even more desirable.

A geisha, as a living piece of art, is often compared to a walking china doll, and her makeup, hair, and manner are all calculated. The geisha is meant to be the embodiment of a man's perfect woman, and men do pay large sums to have a geisha cater to them. Today, the cost to have a geisha at a party ranges from $200 to $300 per person for every two hours that she attends the event. Geisha are exclusive hostesses but are not independent contractors. When a geisha is needed to host a party, she is hired through one of two ways: calls are made to the okaasan of an okiya or to a teahouse where geisha entertain. The central office for geisha affairs, which controls all bookings, is then contacted by the okaasan or teahouse mistress, who then charges the client for services. Registration with the central office is required for every geisha, in order to work in her district. A certain percentage of what a geisha earns goes toward maintaining the okiya and supporting the people living there who are not working geisha, including apprentices, retirees, and housemaids.

As in the past, getting ready for work involves hours of preparation for the modern geisha, for her distinctive appearance is part of her allure. A geisha kimono, unlike a regular kimono, exposes her neckline, which in Japanese culture is considered the most sensual part of a woman.

The kimono, very intricate and very expensive, is quite difficult to put on correctly; in fact, it is almost impossible for a woman to get into one by herself, with its multiple layers and yards of exquisite fabric that must be tucked and folded into place.

All geisha are single, and one who desires marriage must retire. Personal relationships do occur, however, and a formal institution was developed to account for this. Should a geisha want or need the support of a patron, she finds a danna, a man with the means to support an expensive geisha lifestyle and education. He and the geisha do not need to be in love, but the intimate nature of the relationship is considered a bonus for the danna. These relationships are rare, very carefully chosen, and intended to be long-term in nature. A ceremony similar to a marriage ceremony is performed, and when the geisha and danna decide to part, another ceremony is performed to make their "divorce" official.

By the late 1970s, the official number of registered geisha had dropped dramatically to around 1,500. Today, estimates put that number under 1,000. Few are drawn to the rigorous, structured lifestyle of the geisha for very long, with most retiring early to pursue other careers.

*Above: Three Women Preparing a Meal. 19th century. Woodblock. Opposite page: Sake cup depicting a landscape with boats and a bridge under Mount Fuji. Japan. 19th century. Lacquers and inlay of gold foil on lacquer ground.*

# Is Bushido Still Alive?

Or has Western civilization, in its march through the land, already wiped out every trace of its ancient discipline?

It was a sad thing if a nation's soul could die so fast. That was a poor soul that could succumb so easily to extraneous influences.

The aggregate of psychological elements which constitute a national character is as tenacious as the "irreducible elements of species, of the fins of fish, of the beak of the bird, of the tooth of the carnivorous animal." In his recent book, full of shallow asseverations and brilliant generalizations, M. LeBon[30] says, "The discoveries due to the intelligence are the common patrimony of humanity; qualities or defects of character constitute the exclusive patrimony of each people: they are the firm rock which the waters must wash day by day for centuries, before they can wear away even its external asperities." These are strong words and would be highly worth pondering over, provided there were qualities and defects of character which constitute the exclusive patrimony of each people. Schematizing theories of this sort had been advanced long before LeBon began to write his book, and they were exploded long ago by Theodor Waitz and Hugh Murray. In studying the various virtues instilled by Bushido, we have drawn upon European sources for comparison and illustrations, and we have seen that no one quality of character was its exclusive patrimony. It is true the aggregate of moral qualities presents a quite unique aspect. It is this aggregate which Emerson names a "compound result into which every great force enters as an ingredient." But, instead of making it, as LeBon does, an exclusive patrimony of a race or people, the Concord philosopher calls it "an element which unites the most forcible persons of every country; makes them intelligible and agreeable to each other; and is somewhat so precise that it is at once felt if an individual lack the Masonic sign."

The character which Bushido stamped on our nation and on the samurai in particular, cannot be said to form "an irreducible element of species," but nevertheless as to

*The Japanese referred to the Portuguese citizens as "nanban," or southern barbarians, because they would sail to Japan from the south. Arrival of a Portuguese ship. Japan. 1575–1615. Six-panel folding screen, one of a pair. Ink, colors, and gold on paper.*

the vitality which it retains there is no doubt. Were Bushido a mere physical force, the momentum it has gained in the last seven hundred years could not stop so abruptly. Were it transmitted only by heredity, its influence must be immensely widespread. Just think, as M. Cheysson, a French economist, has calculated, that supposing there be three generations in a century, "each of us would have in his veins the blood of at least twenty millions of the people living in the year 1000 A.D." The merest peasant that grubs the soil, "bowed by the weight of centuries," has in his veins the blood of ages, and is thus a brother to us as much as "to the ox."

An unconscious and irresistible power, Bushido has been moving the nation and individuals. It was an honest confession of the race when Yoshida Shoin, one of the most brilliant pioneers of Modern Japan, wrote on the eve of his execution the following stanza—

*Full well I knew this course must end in death;*
*It was Yamato spirit urged me on*
*To dare whate'er betide.*

Unformulated, Bushido was and still is the animating spirit, the motor force of our country.

Mr. Ransome says that "there are three distinct Japans in existence side by side today, the old, which has not wholly died out; the new, hardly yet born except in spirit; and the transition, passing now through its most critical throes." While this is very true in most respects, and particularly as regards tangible and concrete institutions, the statement, as applied to fundamental ethical notions, requires some modification; for Bushido, the maker and product of Old Japan, is still the guiding principle of the transition and will prove the formative force of the new era.

The great statesmen who steered the ship of our state through the hurricane of the Restoration and the whirlpool of national rejuvenation, were men who knew no other moral teaching than the Precepts of Knighthood. Some writers[31] have lately tried to prove that the Christian missionaries contributed an appreciable quota to the making of New Japan. I would fain render honor to whom honor is due: but this honor can hardly be accorded to the good missionaries. More fitting it will be to their profession to stick to the scriptural injunction of preferring one another in honor, than

*An ivory netsuke of a rat. Kaigyokusai Masatsugu of Osaka. Circa 1800s.*

to advance a claim in which they have no proofs to back them. For myself, I believe that Christian missionaries are doing great things for Japan—in the domain of education, and especially of moral education—only, the mysterious though not the less certain working of the Spirit is still hidden in divine secrecy. Whatever they do is still of indirect effect. No, as yet Christian missions have effected but little visible in molding the character of New Japan. No, it was Bushido, pure and simple, that urged us on for weal or woe. Open the biographies of the makers of Modern Japan—of Sakuma, of Saigo, of Okubo, of Kido, not to mention the reminiscences of living men such as Ito, Okuma, Itagaki, etc.—and you will find that it was under the impetus of samuraihood that they thought and wrought. When Mr. Henry Norman declared, after his study and observation of the Far East,[32] that only the respect in which Japan differed from other oriental despotisms lay in "the ruling influence among her people of the strictest, loftiest, and the most punctilious codes of honor that man has ever devised," he touched the main spring which has made New Japan what she is and which will make her what she is destined to be.

The transformation of Japan is a fact patent to the whole world. In a work of such magnitude various motives naturally entered; but if one were to name the principal, one would not hesitate to name Bushido. When we opened the whole country to foreign trade, when we introduced the latest improvements in every department of life, when we began to study Western politics and sciences, our guiding motive was not the development of our physical resources and the increase of wealth; much less was it a blind imitation of Western customs.

A close observer of oriental institutions and peoples has written:

We are told every day how Europe has influenced Japan, and forget that the change in those islands was entirely self-generated, that Europeans did not teach Japan, but that Japan of herself chose to learn from Europe methods of organization, civil and military, which have so far proved successful. She imported European mechanical science, as the Turks years before imported European artillery. That is not exactly influence," continues Mr. Townsend, "unless, indeed, England is influenced by purchasing tea of China. Where is the European apostle," asks our author, "or philosopher or statesman or agitator who has re-made Japan?[33]

Mr. Townsend has well perceived that the spring of action which brought about the changes in Japan lay entirely within our own selves; and if he had only probed into our psychology, his keen powers of observation would easily have convinced him that that spring was no other than Bushido. The sense of honor which cannot bear being looked down upon as an inferior power—that was the strongest of motives. Pecuniary or industrial considerations were awakened later in the process of transformation.

The influence of Bushido is still so palpable that he who runs may read. A glimpse into Japanese life will make it manifest. Read Hearn, the most eloquent and truthful interpreter of the Japanese mind, and you see the working of that mind to be an example of the working of Bushido. The universal politeness of the people, which is the legacy of knightly ways, is too well known to be repeated anew. The physical endurance, fortitude, and bravery that "the little Jap" possesses, were sufficiently proved in the Sino-Japanese war.[34] "Is there any nation more loyal and patriotic?" is a question asked by many; and for the proud answer, "There is not," we must thank the Precepts of Knighthood.

On the other hand, it is fair to recognize that for the very faults and defects of our character, Bushido is largely responsible. Our lack of abstruse philosophy—while some of our young men have already gained international reputation in scientific researches, not one has achieved anything in philosophical lines—is traceable to the neglect of metaphysical training under Bushido's regimen of education. Our sense of honor is responsible for our exaggerated sensitiveness and touchiness; and if there is the conceit in us with which some foreigners charge us, that, too, is a pathological outcome of honor.

Have you seen in your tour of Japan many a young man with unkempt hair, dressed in shabbiest garb, carrying in his hand a large cane or a book, stalking about the streets with an air of utter indifference to mundane things? He is the *shosei* (student), to whom the earth is too small and the Heavens are not high enough. He has his own theories of the universe and of life. He dwells in castles of air and feeds on ethereal words of wisdom. In his eyes beams the fire of ambition; his mind is athirst for knowledge. Penury is only a stimulus to drive him onward; worldly goods are in his sight shackles to his character. He is the repository of loyalty and patriotism. He is the self-imposed guardian of national honor. With all his virtues and his faults, he is the last fragment of Bushido.

Deep-rooted and powerful as is still the effect of Bushido, I have said that it is an unconscious and mute influence. The heart of the people responds, without knowing the reason why, to any appeal made to what it has inherited, and hence the same moral idea expressed in a newly translated term and in an old Bushido term, has a vastly different degree of efficacy. A backsliding Christian, whom no pastoral persuasion could help from downward tendency, was reverted from his course by an appeal made to his loyalty, the fidelity he once swore to his Master. The word "Loyalty" revived all the noble sentiments that were permitted to grow lukewarm. A band of unruly youths engaged in a long continued "students' strike" in a college, on account of their dissatisfaction with a certain teacher, disbanded at two simple questions put by the Director—"Is your professor a blameless character? If so, you ought to respect him and keep him in the school. Is he weak? If so, it is not manly to push a falling man." The scientific incapacity of the professor, which was the beginning of the trouble, dwindled into insignificance in comparison with the moral issues hinted at. By arousing the sentiments nurtured by Bushido, moral renovation of great magnitude can be accomplished.

One cause of the failure of mission work is that most of the missionaries are grossly ignorant of our history—"What do we care for heathen records?" some say—and consequently estrange their religion from the habits of thought we and our forefathers have been accustomed to for centuries past. Mocking a nation's history!—as though the career of any people—even of the lowest African savages possessing no record—were not a page in the general history of mankind, written by the hand of God Himself. The very lost races are a palimpsest to be deciphered by a seeing eye. To a philosophic and pious mind, the races themselves are marks of Divine chirography clearly traced in black and white as on their skin; and if this simile holds good, the yellow race forms a precious page inscribed in hieroglyphics of gold! Ignoring the past career of a people, missionaries claim that Christianity is a new religion, whereas, to my mind, it is an "old, old story," which, if presented in intelligible words—

that is to say, if expressed in the vocabulary familiar in the moral development of a people—will find easy lodgment in their hearts, irrespective of race or nationality. Christianity in its American or English form—with more of Anglo-Saxon freaks and fancies than grace and purity of its Founder—is a poor scion to graft on Bushido stock. Should the propagator of the new faith uproot the entire stock, root, and branches, and plant the seeds of the Gospel on the ravaged soil? Such a heroic process may be possible—in Hawaii, where, it is alleged, the church militant had complete success in amassing spoils of wealth itself, and in annihilating the aboriginal race: such a process is most decidedly impossible in Japan—nay, it is a process which Jesus himself would never have employed in founding his kingdom on earth.

It behooves us to take more to heart the following words of a saintly man, devout Christian and profound scholar:

Men have divided the world into heathen and Christian, without considering how much good may have been hidden in the one, or how much evil may have been mingled with the other. They have compared the best part of themselves with the worst of their neighbors, the ideal of Christianity with the corruption of Greece or the East. They have not aimed at impartiality, but have been contented to accumulate all that could be said in praise of their own, and in dispraise of other forms of religion.[35]

But, whatever may be the error committed by individuals, there is little doubt that the fundamental principle of the religion they profess is a power which we must take into account in reckoning the future of Bushido, whose days seem to be already numbered. Ominous signs are in the air that betoken its future. Not only signs, but redoubtable forces are at work to threaten it.

30 *The Psychology of Peoples*, p. 33.
31 Speer, *Missions and Politics in Asia*, Lecture IV, pp. 189–192; Dennis: *Christian Missions and Social Progress*, Vol. 1, p. 32, Vol. II, p. 70, etc.
32 *The Far East*, p. 375.
33 Meredith Townsend, *Asia and Europe*, N.Y., 1900, 28.
34 Among other works on the subject, read Eastlake and Yamada on *Heroic Japan*, and Diosy on *The New Far East*.
35 Jowett, *Sermons on Faith and Doctrine*, II.

*Above: Inro decorated with a carp in a waterfall. Lacquer. Left: A 315 circular buckler or target, decorated with a shield charged with three bugle-horns surmounted by a foliated helmet, all surrounded with a band of flowing scrolls, in gold on a black ground. Wood and gesso. 16th century.*

273

# THE LAST SHOGUN

When Tokugawa Yoshinobu became shogun of Japan on January 10, 1867, shoguns had been ruling Japan for the past 675 years, including 257 years under the Tokugawa clan. But in recent decades, the Tokugawa shogunate had been showing its age. The past several shoguns had been afflicted with indolence, incompetence, and ineptitude. Their failings had raised the vocal ire of the imperial family, which until then had remained silent for centuries as the shoguns held sway.

The elders of the Tokugawa clan were counting on young Yoshinobu to change all that. At the age of twenty-nine, he was youthful, charismatic, and well educated. If anyone could help reform the aging shogunate, he could. Instead, within eleven months of taking power, Yoshinobu would step down, spelling an end to the shogunate and the legendary rule of the samurai forever.

Yoshinobu was born on October 28, 1837, as the seventh son of Tokugawa Nariaki, the *daimyo*. During the Tokugawa shogunate, only three families—known as the Three Houses, or *gosanke*—were eligible to become shogun. Nariaki headed the lowliest of the gosanke, ruling Hitachi from the castle town of Mito. Although Mito was less than sixty miles from Edo (Tokyo), it was a provincial backwater. One of Nariaki's greatest accomplishments was founding a garden that drew visitors from outside the province to view its blossoms. But in early 1853, after American warships forced the shogunate to open trade negotiations, Nariaki became politically active, publishing a tract titled "Japan, Reject the Westerners," proclaiming that war would be preferable to the concessions granted by shogun Tokugawa Iesada, who was mentally unstable.

By that time, Nariaki had stepped back from running the day-to-day operations of his family, letting the adolescent Yoshinobu take charge. Like most upper-class samurai, Yoshinobu had received a broad education in literature, the martial arts, and public policy. Nariaki hoped his experience as a clan leader would entitle him to become shogun after the death of Iesada, who had no heirs.

When Iesada died in 1858, Nariaki and other supporters named Yoshinobu as a potential successor. But Ii Naosuke, an architect of the American trade deal, successfully promoted his twelve-year-old son, Iemochi, as shogun instead. In the political purge that followed, Yoshinobu and the others who supported him were briefly placed under house arrest, and Yoshinobu was temporarily forced to give up his leadership position in the family.

Iemochi's rule as shogun, with his father governing behind the scenes, was plagued with mismanagement, unrest, and unhappiness with the trade deals with the United States and other foreign nations. After Naosuke was assassinated in 1860, Iemochi increasingly relied on Yoshinobu to help him quash rioting in Kyoto and rebellion in Choshu. Yoshinobu even helped Iemochi patch up relations with Emperor Komei, who had been a fierce critic of the trade deals. In 1863, Komei arranged for Iemochi to marry one of his daughters. But Iemochi did not have much time to enjoy married bliss. On July 20, 1866, he died, three days after turning twenty. The official cause was heart failure brought on by beriberi. But in an age that was plagued by assassinations and poisonings, there is reason to be suspicious of Iemochi's relatively early demise, like the untimely deaths of several of his predecessors.

After Iemochi's death, Yoshinobu was chosen as the fifteenth shogun of the Tokugawa clan. Despite his father's distaste for foreigners, Yoshinobu thought there was much Japan could learn from the diplomats in the country. He invited the entire diplomatic corps to meet with him in Osaka, where he peppered them with questions about their governments, taxation systems, economies, and bureaucracies. In particular, he asked European diplomats how their countries had been able to make the transition from feudalism into the Industrial Age.

In January 1867, the month he took office, Yoshinobu started reshaping the military after the European model, with French uniforms and weapons purchased from the

United States. He revamped the tax system, regularized the salaries of government employees, and started preparations for land reforms. When one of his aides returned from a study trip to Holland, Yoshinobu commissioned him to draft plans for a modern form of government, complete with checks and balances among the administrative branch, the courts, and a two-house parliament.

As Yoshinobu launched into his reforms, however, changes were afoot in the emperor's palace in Kyoto. Emperor Komei died on January 30, 1867, succeeded by his fourteen-year-old son, Mitsuhito. Some samurai in the imperial court, led by the heads of the Satsuma, Choshu, and Tosa clans, had long disliked the Tokugawa. They saw this as their chance to end the shogunate once and for all. They convinced the new emperor that Yoshinobu's reforms were designed to undermine the power of the imperial family, and they warned against the spread of foreign influences. Using the slogan *sonno joi* ("Revere the emperor, expel the barbarians"), they rallied commoners into demonstrations against Yoshinobu and then petitioned the emperor to ask him to step down as shogun.

In November, a chastened Yoshinobu abdicated in return for being offered the post of chairing a governing council of the *daimyo* families. But the Satsuma and Choshu continued to maneuver against him. They told their troops that they had obtained an arrest warrant from Emperor Mitsuhito, which was later shown to be a forgery, and ordered them into battle against Yoshinobu. "With the help of his gang of bandits, [Yoshinobu] ... has plunged the populace into an abyss," the supposed warrant said. "His all-encompassing evil threatens

to overturn the Land of the Gods.... If we fail to strike down this traitor, what excuse can we give to the spirit of the late emperor...? Implement the wishes of our heart by slaughtering the traitorous subject Yoshinobu."

As their troops moved on Yoshinobu, the Satsuma and Choshu got the emperor to strip him of his titles and take away his lands. Although Yoshinobu's forces easily outnumbered those of his enemies, he had no stomach for a fight. He felt that a civil war would be destructive, especially at a time when foreign nations were laying designs on Japan. So after several battles, he sent a trusted retainer to the emperor, offering to give up the leadership of the Tokugawa clan and turn over the castle at Edo to the imperial family.

"I shamefully confess that the current unsatisfactory conditions are due to my own failings and incompetence," he wrote the emperor. "With foreign contacts growing each day, the foundations of the state will shatter unless the government is directed by one central authority. But...if the entire people support the empire, it will be able to maintain its rank and dignity among the countries on earth."

After his abdication, Yoshinobu moved to the Tokugawa clan's lands in Shizuoka, where Tokugawa Ieyasu, the first Tokugawa shogun, had retired two and a half centuries before. With their clan displaced from power, many Tokugawa ended up unemployed and destitute. They blamed their losses on Yoshinobu's surrender, which in their minds was something a samurai should never do. Because some of these out-of-work samurai even talked of killing Yoshinobu in revenge, the former shogun lived for years in hermitlike isolation, anticipating the threat of assassination.

During the years of Yoshinobu's self-imposed exile, Emperor Mitsuhito embarked on many of the changes that the shogun had proposed, including a modernized army, a parliamentary system of government, taxation and land reforms, and a European-style education system. He called his reign *Meiji jidai*, or "the era of reform," and he is now known as the Emperor Meiji.

In the meantime, Yoshinobu devoted himself to such traditional pursuits as painting, archery, and hunting, as well as more modern hobbies such as photography and cycling. In 1902, the emperor finally recognized that he was not a threat and gave him the title of *koshaku* (prince), the highest title he could bestow. Eleven years later, on January 22, 1913, Japan's last shogun died.

*Left: Shogun Rulers. 19th century. Woodblock print.*
*Opposite page: The House of the Shogun. 18th century. Ink on silk.*

# The Future of Bushido

Few historical comparisons can be more judiciously made than between the Chivalry of Europe and the Bushido of Japan, and, if history repeats itself, it certainly will do with the fate of the latter what it did with that of the former. The particular and local causes for the decay of chivalry which St. Palaye gives, have, of course, little application to Japanese conditions; but the larger and more general causes that helped to undermine knighthood and chivalry in and after the Middle Ages are as surely working for the decline of Bushido.

One remarkable difference between the experience of Europe and of Japan is, that whereas in Europe, when chivalry was weaned from feudalism and was adopted by the Church, it obtained a fresh lease of life, in Japan no religion was large enough to nourish it; hence, when the mother institution, feudalism, was gone, Bushido, left an orphan, had to shift for itself. The present elaborate military organization might take it under its patronage, but we know that modern warfare can afford little room for its continuous growth. Shintoism, which fostered it in its infancy, is itself superannuated. The hoary sages of ancient China are being supplanted by the intellectual parvenu of the type of Bentham and Mill. Moral theories of a comfortable kind, flattering to the Chauvinistic tendencies of the time, and therefore thought well-adapted to the need of this day, have been invented and propounded; but as yet we hear only their shrill voices echoing through the columns of yellow journalism.

Principalities and powers are arrayed against the Precepts of Knighthood. Already, as Veblen says, "the decay of the ceremonial code—or, as it is otherwise called, the vulgarization of life—among the industrial classes proper, has become one of the chief enormities of latter-day civilization in the eyes of all persons of delicate sensibilities." The irresistible tide of triumphant democracy, which can tolerate no form or shape of trust—and Bushido was a trust organized by those who monopolized reserve capital of intellect and culture, fixing the grades and value of moral qualities—is alone powerful enough to engulf the remnant of Bushido. The

*A group of armored samurai with a variety of weapons. 19th century.*

present societary forces are antagonistic to petty class spirit, and chivalry is, as Freeman severely criticizes, a class spirit. Modern society, if it pretends to any unity, cannot admit "purely personal obligations devised in the interests of an exclusive class."[36] Add to this the progress of popular instruction, of industrial arts and habits, of wealth and city-life—then we can easily see that neither the keenest cuts of samurai's sword nor the sharpest shafts shot from Bushido's boldest bows can aught avail. The state built upon the rock of Honor and fortified by the same—shall we call it the Ehrenstaat or, after the manner of Carlyle, the Heroarchy?—is fast falling into the hands of quibbling lawyers and gibbering politicians armed with logic-chopping engines of war. The words which a great thinker used in speaking of Theresa and Antigone may aptly be repeated of the samurai, that "the medium in which their ardent deeds took shape is forever gone."

Alas for knightly virtues! alas for samurai pride! Morality ushered into the world with the sound of bugles and drums, is destined to fade away as "the captains and the kings depart."

If history can teach us anything, the state built on martial virtues—be it a city like Sparta or an Empire like Rome—can never make on earth a "continuing city." Universal and natural as is the fighting instinct in man, fruitful as it has proved to be of noble sentiments and manly virtues, it does

*Above: Lion Dance Shishi-mai Mask. Japan. Wood, lacquer, cloth, and cord.*
*Right: Shinagawa: Departure of a Daimyo, in later editions called Sunrise, No. 2 from the series 53 Stations of the Tokaido (Tokaido gojusan tsugi no uchi), published by Hoeido, 1833. Hiroshige, Ando or Utagawa (1797–1858). Oban size, yoko-e horizontal format, color woodblock print.*

not comprehend the whole man. Beneath the instinct to fight there lurks a diviner instinct to love. We have seen that Shintoism, Mencius, and Wan Yang Ming have all clearly taught it; but Bushido and all other militant schools of ethics, engrossed, doubtless, with questions of immediate practical need, too often forgot duly to emphasize this fact. Life has grown larger in these latter times. Callings nobler and broader than a warrior's claim our attention today. With an enlarged view of life, with the growth of democracy, with better knowledge of other peoples and nations, the Confucian idea of benevolence—dare I also add the Buddhist idea of pity?—will expand into the Christian conception of love. Men have become more than subjects, having grown to the estate of citizens: nay, they are more than citizens, being men. Though war clouds hang heavy upon our horizon, we will believe that the wings of the angel of peace can disperse them. The history of the world confirms the prophecy the "the meek shall inherit the earth." A nation that sells its birthright of peace, and backslides from the front rank of industrialism into the file of filibusterism, makes a poor bargain indeed!

When the conditions of society are so changed that they have become not only adverse but hostile to Bushido, it is time for it to prepare for an honorable burial. It is just as difficult to point out when chivalry dies, as to determine the exact time of its inception. Dr. Miller says that chivalry was formally abolished in the year 1559, when Henry II of France was slain in a tournament. With us, the edict formally abolishing feudalism in 1870

was the signal to toll the knell of Bushido. The edict, issued two years later, prohibiting the wearing of swords, rang out the old, "the unbought grace of life, the cheap defense of nations, the nurse of manly sentiment and heroic enterprise," it rang in the new age of "sophisters, economists, and calculators."

It has been said that Japan won her late war with China by means of Murata guns and Krupp cannon; it has been said the victory was the work of a modern school system; but these are less than half-truths. Does ever a piano, be it of the choicest workmanship of Ehrbar or Steinway, burst forth into the Rhapsodies of Liszt or the Sonatas of Beethoven, without a master's hand? Or, if guns win battles, why did not Louis Napoleon beat the Prussians with his Mitrailleuse, or the Spaniards with their Mausers the Filipinos, whose arms were no better than the old-fashioned Remingtons? Needless to repeat what has grown a trite saying—that it is the spirit that quickeneth, without which the best of implements profiteth but little. The most improved guns and cannon do not shoot of their own accord; the most modern educational system does not make a coward a hero. No! What won the battles on the Yalu, in Corea and Manchuria, was the ghosts of our fathers, guiding our hands and beating in our hearts. They are not dead, those ghosts, the spirits of our warlike ancestors. To those who have eyes to see, they are clearly visible. Scratch a Japanese of the most advanced ideas, and he will show a samurai. The great inheritance of honor, of valor, and of all martial virtues is, as Professor Cramb very fitly expresses it, "but ours on trust, the fief inalienable of the dead and of the generation to come," and the summons of the present is to guard this heritage, nor to bate one jot of the ancient spirit; the summons of the future will be so to widen its scope as to apply it in all walks and relations of life.

It has been predicted—and predictions have been corroborated by the events of the last half century—that the moral system of Feudal Japan, like its castles and its armories, will crumble into dust, and new ethics rise phoenix-like to lead New Japan in her path of progress. Desirable and probable as the fulfillment of such a prophecy is, we must not forget that a phoenix rises only from its own ashes, and that it is not a bird of passage, neither does it fly on pinions borrowed from other birds. "The Kingdom of God is within you." It does not come rolling down the mountains, however lofty; it does not come sailing across the seas, however broad. "God has granted," says the Koran, "to every people a prophet in its own tongue." The seeds of the Kingdom, as vouched for and apprehended by the Japanese mind, blossomed in Bushido. Now its days are closing—sad to say, before its full fruition—and we turn in every direction for other sources of sweetness and light, of strength and comfort, but among them there is as yet nothing found to take its place. The profit-and-loss philosophy of utilitarians and materialists finds favor among logic-choppers with half a soul. The only other ethical system which is powerful enough to cope with utilitarianism and materialism is Christianity, in comparison with which Bushido, it must be confessed, is like "a dimly burning wick" which the Messiah was proclaimed not to quench but to fan into a flame. Like His Hebrew precursors, the prophets—notably Isaiah, Jeremiah, Amos, and Habakkuk—Bushido laid particular stress on the moral conduct of rulers and public men and of nations, whereas the ethics of Christ, which deal almost solely with individuals and His personal followers, will find more and more practical application as individualism, in its capacity of a moral factor, grows in potency. The domineering, self-assertive, so-called master-morality of Nietzsche, itself akin in some respects to Bushido, is, if I am not greatly mistaken, a passing phase or temporary reaction against what he terms, by morbid distortion, the humble, self-denying slave-morality of the Nazarene.

Christianity and materialism (including utilitarianism) —or will the future reduce them to still more archaic forms of Hebraism and Hellenism?—will divide the world between them. Lesser systems of morals will ally themselves on either side for their preservation. On which side will Bushido enlist? Having no set dogma or formula to defend, it can afford to disappear as an entity; like the cherry blossom, it is willing to die at the first gust of the morning breeze. But a total extinction will never be its lot. Who can say that stoicism is dead? It is dead as a system; but it is alive as a virtue: its energy and vitality are still felt through many channels of life—in the philosophy of Western nations, in the jurisprudence of all the civilized world. Nay, wherever man struggles to raise himself above himself, wherever his spirit masters his flesh by his own exertions, there we see the immortal discipline of Zeno at work.

Bushido as an independent code of ethics may vanish, but its power will not perish from the earth; its schools of martial prowess or civic honor may be demolished, but its light and its glory will long survive their ruins. Like its symbolic flower, after it is blown to the four winds, it will still bless mankind with the perfume with which it will enrich life. Ages after, when its customaries shall have been buried and its very name forgotten, its odors will come floating in the air as from a far-off unseen hill, "the wayside gaze beyond;" then in the beautiful language of the Quaker poet,

*The traveler owns the grateful sense*
*Of sweetness near he knows not whence,*
*And, pausing, takes with forehead bare*
*The benediction of the air.*

36 *Norman Conquest*, Vol. V, p. 482.

*The Great Wisdom Sutra (Daihannya-kyo). Japan. 1177. Calligraphy. Handscroll fragment; ink on paper.*

*Sixty-two-ribbed Suji helmet. Mixed media.*

# GRAPHIC SYMBOLS ON SAMURAI ACCOUTREMENTS

For centuries, the samurai sword has been more than a weapon. It has been an expression of the warrior's personal philosophy or artistic inclinations. In the early Middle Ages, swords were inscribed with Sanskrit quotes from Buddhist scriptures and marked by distinctive, individualized grooves. As Japan emerged from its Warring States period and entered the relative calm of the Edo era, the swords, hilts, sheaths, guards, pommels, and other accoutrements were marked with a number of highly personalized symbols and motifs. Below are just a few of the more common thematic elements.

*Cherry blossoms and autumn leaves.* Intricately rendered depictions of flowering trees and leafy branches seem jarringly at odds with the death-dealing nature of the samurai sword. But the blossoms and leaves are not mere decorations. They are an expression of the samurai's fatalism. Once the cherry blossoms bloom, it is only a matter of days before they wilt and fall to the ground. The same is true of leaves that turn color in fall. Cherry blossoms and autumn leaves (particularly maple leaves) are used repeatedly in Japanese art and literature as symbols of the shortness of life. A verse in the poetry anthology *Man'yoshu* in the early eighth century CE likened death to being "gone like a golden leaf in autumn."

*Crashing waves.* Ocean waves are yet another symbol of life's impermanence. They are a powerful force when they rise from the sea, but then they crash into nothingness, their foamy crests dissipate, and other waves rise to take their places. A Japanese literary critic in the early tenth century said that poets should be "startled into thinking about the shortness of life by seeing the dew on the grass or the froth on the water."

*Plum blossoms.* Like the cherry blossom, the plum blossom is an expression of the transience of life. But its symbolism

does not stop there. The plum is the first tree to blossom as winter comes to a close, which makes it a symbol of strength and resilience. Although imminent death looms in the background, the plum blossom's symbolism has more to do with victory over adversity.

*Bamboo.* Because bamboo stalks can remain firm against the wind without breaking, they are a symbol of strength and fortitude.

*Pine trees.* The evergreen nature of the pine tree makes it a symbol of steadfastness and, in particular, the reliability of true friendship. The bamboo, pine, and plum blossom motifs are often grouped into a trio called the *shochikubai*, literally "pine-bamboo-plum," symbolizing the unity of all their qualities.

*Tigers.* The tiger represents the *yang* (masculine side) of the Buddhist concept of duality. As such, it symbolizes courage, invincibility, might, power, and ferocity. It also has the power of the wind. On Japanese swords, particularly on the *tsuba*, or sword guard, the tiger is sometimes depicted as entering a grove of bamboo stalks—a visual representation of a balance between force and stolidity, the power of the wind tempered by the strength of character that can withstand the wind's fury.

*Dragons.* The Japanese dragon is a wingless, snakelike beast with short legs and three-clawed feet. Antlers spring from its bearded, camel-like head. It is a water creature, associated with the sea and clouds, and unlike European dragons, it spits out water instead of breathing fire. Instead of being a fearsome creature, it represents goodness, kindness, power, and freedom. The dragon is the *yin* (feminine side) to the tiger's *yang*, and the two often appear on the same sword, although not necessarily side by side. The tension between the two is the symbolic meaning behind the title of the 2000 Chinese

sword-fighting epic *Crouching Tiger, Hidden Dragon*, referring to the yin and yang qualities of the two warriors.

*Bats.* As a symbol of good luck, the bat is one of many motifs used on the sword, particularly in the *menuki*, the hilt ornaments that help guide the hand into the correct position. The seemingly intuitive way in which bats can fly through the dark was an inspiration for samurai, who strived to wield their swords with equally intuitive powers. (This was, of course, in an age before people realized that intuition had nothing to do with a bat's flight.)

*Full moons.* In Buddhist thought, the full moon represents the mind, perfect truth, and the knowledge of the dharma. Its glow represents the luminescence that can shine from a truly enlightened mind. Fujiwara Michinaga, who ruled over Japan as regent from 995 to 1017, saw something different:

> *A full moon makes me feel*
> *Like the world is truly mine.*
> *Like the moon, I glow*
> *Unhidden by clouds.*

*Crescent moons.* A crescent moon, sometimes referred to as a "bow moon" because of its similarity to a samurai bow, is believed to have protective powers. The crescent appears in the family crests of at least eight prominent samurai families and, together with stylized deer antlers, it was one of the most common crests used on the helmets of soldiers in battle.

*Cranes.* The elegant crane, said to live 1,000 years, represents serenity and long life. In ancient myths, the crane was responsible for carrying good-hearted sages to heaven. His white feathers represent purity, and the red plumage around the head symbolizes vitality.

*Turtles.* Like the crane, the turtle represents longevity. But in the turtle's case, it is 10,000 years of life instead of a mere millennium.

*Butterflies.* The butterfly was one of the first symbols used by the upper class in Japan, because of its peaceful elegance.

*Dragonflies.* According to legend, Japan's first emperor, Jimmu, once ascended a tall mountain and looked down upon Honshu, the main island of the archipelago. From his vantage point, the island looked like an enormous dragonfly tripping across the water. Since then, Honshu has often been referred to as Akistushima (Dragonfly Island), and the dragonfly has been adopted as a national symbol. (In another version of the tale, Emperor Yuriyaku bestowed the

name on Honshu to honor a dragonfly that had devoured the horsefly that had bitten the emperor's arm.) Dragonflies represent good harvests, strength, and victory in battle, which is why a number of samurai families incorporated the image of the dragonfly into their crests.

*Octopus.* The octopus represents the lover, with many arms to hold a cherished one. On Japanese swords, octopuses often appear in very suggestive poses. But the octopus also represents intelligence, skillful evasion, and spirituality.

*Koi.* In Japan, koi are highly revered. Because they are undaunted as they swim upstream to mate, they symbolize overcoming difficulties, battling against the flow, and striving for a higher purpose. And because they do not immediately flop around when pulled out of the water, they represent bravery and acceptance of fate.

*Mount Fuji.* Japan's most recognizable mountain represents the quiet stolidity of nature, as well as the serenity of Buddhism.

*Lotus.* In Buddhism, the lotus represents the enlightened person, rising up from the mud to unfold unblemished in the light of the sun.

*Chrysanthemum.* The chrysanthemum was brought from China to Japan in the early eighth century, at a time when the Japanese upper class craved Chinese imports. To the Japanese, the flower's petals represented the rays of the rising sun, and the orderly opening of the petals represented perfection. Eventually, the imperial family adopted the sixteen-petal variety of chrysanthemum as its official seal. Although white chrysanthemums are associated with death, red flowers signify health, healing, strength, courage, dignity, and happiness. The chrysanthemum also carries the message of fatalism, however. The falling of the flower's petals, one by one, represents old habits and beliefs being cast aside as a person moves from birth to death.

*Above, top to bottom: Iron tsuba with dragonfly and crab inlay. Edo period; iron tsuba with dragon and clouds carving and inlay. Edo period; iron tsuba with cherry blossom cutout. Edo period.*
*Opposite page: Gun with cherry blossom motif. Bajou-Zutsu. Edo period.*

# FUTURE SAMURAI
## THE LEGENDARY WARRIOR INFILTRATES POPULAR CULTURE

Throughout Japanese history, the tales of the samurai and their shoguns have been told in many forms: poetry, fiction, song, *kabuki*. But in the past century, since the invention of film, stories of the samurai have crossed international boundaries, creating a new appreciation for the ways of old Japan.

The first movie to feature samurai was produced before the last samurai died. That film, a silent version of *Chushingura*, or *The Forty-Seven Ronin*, originally a well-known kabuki play, was shot in stages between 1908 and 1912. The movie told the true story of how forty-seven *ronin* (free-roving samurai) avenged the death of their master in 1702 and then committed suicide. At that time, there were still a number of former samurai living in Japan, including the last shogun, Tokugawa Yoshinobu, who had relinquished his title in 1867 and lived until 1913. In fact, anyone in the movie audience above the age of fifty-five would have been born into an era in which Japan was dominated by samurai and *daimyo* under the shogun, so a movie about ronin would have had a relevance that later generations could only imagine.

By the 1920s, samurai movies were a popular film genre, typically centering on lone warriors struggling between duty to society (*giri*) and duty to oneself (*ninjo*). Most of the movies during that time of cultural upheaval, as the last vestiges of feudalism were dying, were openly skeptical about the traditional concept of giri. After centuries of Japan's being divided into a harsh caste system, with the samurai class on top and the vast majority of people on the lower rungs, the filmmakers of newly

*A movie poster advertising the 1941 film The 47 Ronin by Shochiku Kinema Kenkyu-jo.*

democratic Japan took the opportunity to criticize the ancient moral code or poke fun at the caste system. For instance, in the 1937 movie *Hitobada kannon* (*Temple of the Goddess Hitobada*), a common thief outwits a samurai, and in the 1932 movie *Koukushi muso* (*Peerless Patriot*) a relatively lowborn swordsman successfully impersonates and then bests an aristocratic samurai.

One popular film, *Zanjin zamba ken* (*Man-Slashing, Horse-Piercing Sword*), produced in 1930, shows a young samurai joining a peasant rebellion against the oppression of the local overlord, who was, among other things, responsible for the death of the samurai's father. Historically, there were a number of low-level samurai and ronin who took part in peasant rebellions. But by glorifying the samurai's action, the filmmaker was implicitly telling his audience to question the authority of those above them and rebel against any injustices.

Filmmaker Itami Mansuko took up the same message in his 1936 film *Kakita Akanishi*, in which a group of midlevel samurai defeat the lordly retainers who are manipulating a clueless *daimyo*. Film critic Donald Ritchie, in his book *A Hundred Years of Japanese Film*, notes that the director's son maintains that the film, released on the eve of Japan's invasion of China, was intended to be an allegory: the evil retainers were meant to represent the clique of militarists who surrounded the easily swayed Emperor Hirohito.

As Japan went to war, the government cracked down on the film industry's subtle attempts at criticism. The government pressured filmmakers to make *kokusaka-eiga*, the national policy films. The ideals espoused by the samurai, particularly duty to the emperor and death before dishonor, meshed perfectly with the government's propaganda goals.

The 1940 epic *Kawanakajima gassen* (*Battle of Kawanakajima*) extolled the bravery of soldiers during a samurai battle in 1561, in which more than 60 percent of the warriors on each side were wounded or killed, and many leaders on the losing side committed *seppuku*. A kokusaka-eiga version of *Chushingura*, released at about the time of the Pearl Harbor attack in 1941, stressed the nobility of making the ultimate sacrifice to honor.

After the war ended, the U.S. military government occupying Japan recognized the potentially powerful propaganda messages that samurai films could carry. The military banned any film that showed revenge as a central theme, portrayed feudal loyalty as desirable, or depicted suicide as honorable.

A movie poster for the 1950 Japanese film Scandal. Shochiku Company, Limited.

As Japan struggled to pull itself out of the rubble of the war, a new generation of filmmakers produced samurai stories that were rife with ambiguity. After seeing their homes bombed and their friends and relatives die in battle, they questioned the value of blind loyalty to ancient creeds. The leader of this movement was Akira Kurosawa, a descendant of samurai and the son of the principal of a military-run school. *Shichinin no samurai* (*Seven Samurai*), 1954, is set in a small village ravaged by bandits. When the aristocratic samurai in their district refuse the villagers' request for help, the villagers turn to seven low-ranking ronin who provide aid, at the cost of four of their lives. *Yojimbo* (*The Bodyguard*), 1961, tells the story of a ronin who agrees to work for two rival crime bosses in a small town. It was through these films that many non-Japanese received their first taste of samurai culture.

When samurai-themed films reached America, the samurai-as-antihero idea helped create the cowboy-as-antihero theme in 1960s Hollywood. In *The Magnificent*

*Seven*, a 1960 remake of *Seven Samurai* set in the Wild West, actors Yul Brynner and Steve McQueen play lowlife ronin-type gunslingers out to save a town. Similarly, the 1964 Clint Eastwood vehicle *A Fistful of Dollars* was a Western version of *Yojimbo*.

Among other film genres, gangster epics have also been influenced by the samurai tales. The character and plot of *Yojimbo* were later transported into Prohibition-era Texas for the 1996 Bruce Willis gangster film *Last Man Standing*. Films like *Ronin*, with Robert De Niro, and *Ghost Dog: The Way of the Samurai*, starring Forest Whitaker, drew parallels between sword-wielding ronin and gun-wielding American assassins.

The samurai epic has even been taken into outer space, most notably in *Star Wars*. Darth Vader's costume was largely based on the mask, armor, and flowing cape of the samurai. The 1980 TV miniseries *Shogun* faithfully tells of Tokugawa Ieyasu's rise to power. The 2003 movie *The Last Samurai*, starring Tom Cruise as an American cavalry officer in Japan, less faithfully tells the story of the 1877 samurai rebellion against the Meiji emperor. In recent years, the samurai have made the transition from film to comic books and video games. Samurai have been featured in many computer games, ranging from fighting games such as *Samurai Showdown* and *Seven Samurai 20XX*, to strategic games such as *Ultima Online: Samurai Empire* to *Shogun: Total War*, which incorporates the military philosophy of Sun Tzu's *Art of War*. American comic book artists, inspired by the Japanese *manga* genre, have recounted samurai tales ranging from Frank Miller's DC Comics series *Ronin* in the 1980s, to Dark Horse's 2001 publication of *Lone Wolf and Cub 2100*, a futuristic retelling of the 1970s manga series *Kozure Okami*, which tells how one of the shogun's former executioners and his son become hired killers after being betrayed by other samurai and nobles.

# The Sword &
the Mind

## Yagyu Munenori

# CONTENTS

*Preceding pages: The Tale of Musashibo Benkei. Tosa, Mitsuhiro. fl.c. 1430–45.*
*Ink, pigment, silver, and gold on paper.*

*Opposite: A Soldier in Full Armour. Japanese School. 19th century.*
*Woodblock print.*

# The Life-Taking Sword

## Preface

From antiquity it has been said, "Weapons are an inauspicious instrument, abhorred by the Way of Heaven, and to be used only when unavoidable. That is the Way of Heaven." How is this so? Bows and arrows, long swords, *naginata*—such are the weapons of the warrior, such are the instruments of ill fortune and inauspiciousness. Inasmuch as the Way of Heaven is the life-giving Way, then taking up arms to kill is truly unpropitious. To go against the Way of Heaven, verily, is abhorrent. Be that as it may, it is said too that taking up arms to kill when unavoidable, is also the Way of Heaven. Why must this be so? Flowers blossom and greenery flourishes in the spring breeze, yet when the autumn frost comes, leaves fall and trees whither. Such is the decree of the Way of Heaven. There is a season to strike down what has come to fullness. People, too, will

*Opposite: Hideyoshi (1536–98) Blowing a Conch Shell, from 100 Phases of the Moon. Tsukioka Yoshitoshi (1839–92). Color lithograph.*
*Above: A Japanese Tattooed Man. Anonymous. Hand colored print. Circa 1880.*

take an opportunity to do evil, and when that evil has come to fullness, it must be struck down. This is why it is said the use of weapons can also be the Way of Heaven. Because of the evil of one man, thousands may suffer. But by killing the evil of one man, thousands may live. Does all this not show certainly that the sword that kills is the sword that gives life?

In the use of weapons, there is a science. Should one kill without knowledge of this science, he will undoubtedly be killed himself. Given thoughtful consideration, in regard to the art of war, the martial art of two swords in combat, one man against another, has but one loser and one winner. This is extraordinarily small martial art. In the winning or losing, the gains and losses are insignificant. Great martial art is when one individual's winning is a victory for the whole land, and one individual's losing is a loss for the whole land. The individual is the commander; the land, the multitude of military forces. The multitude of military forces is the commander's hands and feet. Making the multitude of forces work well is to make the commander's hands and feet work well. If the multitude of forces does not work, the commander's hands and feet do not work.

As are the hands and feet working well to win, achieving the great function of the great potential, when one faces off with two swords, so too, it must be said, is the commander's martial art in winning a battle by strategizing and deploying the multitude of forces.

Moreover, it goes without saying that two battle formations rise up against each other and go out on the battlefield to determine victory or defeat, whereas one who is the commander stages tightly in his chest two battle formations rising up, and in his mind leads his great army into battle. This is martial art of the mind.

Not forgetting disturbance in times of peace is martial art. Grasping the exploits of the government, understanding when chaos will break out, and pacifying the potentially chaotic situation—this too is an art of war. When a country is already at peace, mental preparation in preserving the security of the country and selecting leaders and officials for lands near and far is also an art of war. When leaders, officials, and representatives pursue personal interests, causing the common people to suffer, this naturally pushes a nation to the brink of destruction. Observing the situation closely and calculating to prevent the nation from being destroyed by self-interested leaders, officials, and representatives, is like watching the martial arts of a combatant to see if he is "hiding a *shuriken* in his hand," that is, to anticipate his movements. Should one not observe with utmost assiduity? This is what makes martial art a thing of great potential.

Furthermore, there are sycophants surrounding rulers who act righteously in the presence of superiors and yet look down on their subordinates. Unless their palms are greased, these people speak and act as if good be evil, so the guileless suffer and the guilty, on the other hand, exult. To see this moment before it occurs is more important than noticing an opponent's shuriken.

The country is the ruler's country; the people are the ruler's people. Those who serve near the ruler are his subjects, just as those are too who serve from afar. And how far apart is their distance? They are like the hands and the feet in service to the ruler. Are the feet, however far away, so unlike the hands? If they both feel pain and itch the same, which is closer, which is farther away? If those close to the ruler deceive those far away and cause the guileless to suffer, even a spotless ruler will be resented.

Those close to a ruler number no more than five or ten. Those far away are many. When many people resent the ruler, they should speak their minds. When those close to the ruler have sought their own interests from the start, instead of attending thoughtfully, and serve so as to cause people to resent the ruler, one must speak one's mind to the ruler.

However, this is not the fault of the ruler, but of those who serve close to the ruler. It is essential that such a situation be keenly anticipated, and those far away from the ruler as well not be excluded from his largesse. Being able to perceive such an emergent situation is also a martial art.

In one's personal relationships as well, one must have the heart and mind of martial art when acting in emergent situations, even when there are no inconsistencies. Being able to perceive an emergent situation, even in a group, is an art of war. If one does not perceive an emergent situation, one may remain too long among company with whom one should not, bring offense without reason, say things without seeing other's state of mind, thereby get into a quarrel, even lose one's life—all depending on whether one can or cannot perceive an emergent situation.

Even the proper placement of objects in a room, each in its right place, is grasping the potential of a situation, requiring the mindfulness of martial art. Truly, facts may vary but the principle remains the same. Managing the affairs of a country is no different?

*Right: Yagyu Munenori's grave. Diane Skoss, 1997. Photograph.*

To assume that the art of war is only about killing people is uncouth. It is not about killing people; it is about killing evil. It is a stratagem to give life to a myriad of people by killing the evil of one man. What is recorded in these three scrolls is a book that must stay in the house, within the family. This is not to say, however, that the Way is a secret. The book is kept secret to transmit knowledge. Not transmitting the knowledge would be the same as not writing it down. Consider this well, my descendants!

# YAGYU MUNENORI
# MAN OF SWORD AND STATE

Born in sixteenth-century Japan, Yagyu Munenori founded the Edo branch of Yagyu shinkage ryu (New Shadow Style), one of two sword fighting styles followed by the Tokugawa Shogunate, a feudal regime of the Edo period of Japan. The youngest of five sons of the Yagyu clan leader Yagyu Muneyoshi, Munenori learned his essential techniques from his father. At that time in Japan, it was unusual for a youngest son to be trained in this way. However Munenori's older brothers were not eligible for such training since one had been injured in battle, one killed, and two trained as priests. That left Munenori to follow in his father's footsteps, and he did it well, eventually serving three shoguns, earning the high rank of daimyo, and exerting perhaps more political power than any other swordsman in history.

Munenori's first major accomplishment was to serve the future shogun Tokugawa Ieyasu by leading his warrior followers against the rival camp headed by Ishida Mitsunari. Munenori's men won, and Ieyasu went on to become shogun, at which point Munenori's fortunes took a leap forward. He became Ieyasu's official swordmaster and his shinkage ryu school was soon considered the ultimate standard for swordsmanship. He went on to teach Ieyasu's son Hidetata the craft, and was later an advisor of the third shogun Iemitsu.

In the course of his career, Munenori's swordsmanship teachings began to absorb the great man's battlefield experience and his study of zen Buddhism. The shinkage ryu school evolved as more than a way of mastering one's opponent in armed conflict; it was a way of embracing deeper meaning in life and acheiving a high level of self-realization.

Munenori recorded his teachings in writing, and in 1632, he completed his *Heiho Kaden Sho*, the complete treatise on swordsmanship now known to English-speaking readers as *The Sword and the Mind*.

Some fictional accounts of Munenori's life maintain that his relations were strained with his sons, Yagyu Jubei Mitsuyoshi and Yagyu Munefuyu (who also became accomplished and well-known swordsmen). There is no factual basis for this, however. Legends are long as well about Munenori's alleged rivalry with his contemporary, the great samurai swordsman Miyamoto Musashi, toward whom Munenori is said to have a powerful antipathy. It is even said that in an effort to eliminate the competing swordsman (and author of *The Book of Five Rings*), Munenori resorted to sneak attacks and dealings with unsavory characters. If this is the case, he was unsuccessful. The more likely scenario is that, like all larger-than-life, powerful leaders, Munenori draws out the imagination to such an extent that historical fact is, after nearly four hundred years, now merged with fiction—at least on the popular culture front.

Munenori is a legendary swordsman, and thus many fantastical tales of accomplishment and fictional allegories have been attached to his name over the years. One particular legend is the tale of Munenori's ability to detect impending danger. In an ancient tale, Munenori's assistant attempted to sneak behind him while Munenori meditated in his garden, but Munenori sensed the impending attack and leapt to his feet. Upon realizing that it was merely his assistant who had approached him, Munenori was troubled by his misjudgment. He later learned that his assistant had admitted to "thinking" of attacking him, and realized that he had achieved a new level of sensory perception, as he was able to detect his assistant's mental desire to attack.

One fact about Yagyu Munenori is immutable: his timeless text defining shinkage ryu swordsmanship and its relationship to social life, philosophy, and politics, is as relevant today as it was in 1632. Still in print in Japanese and many other languages, the treatise has been translated multiple times into English. Munenori's *Heiho Kaden Sho* translates in English to *Book of the Family Transmission of Swordsmanship*, and is broken into three sections: "The Shoe-Offering Bridge," "The Life-Taking Sword," and "The Life-Giving Sword." In their profound simplicity and penetrating wisdom, these teachings of the powerful man of both sword and state are applicable eternally to the central issues of engagement in all walks of life.

# 大學
# The Great Learning

It is said that *The Great Learning* is the gate to the beginning of one's studies. When arriving at a house, first one enters through the gate. The gate is a sign that one has arrived at the house. Passing through the gate, one enters the house and meets the master. Learning is the gate that leads to the Way. Learning is the gate, not the house. Do not look at the gate and think it is the house. The house is what lies within, reached by passing though the gate. Do not think that because learning is the gate, reading books will lead to the Way. Books are the gate which leads to the Way. No matter how much one has learned or how many Chinese characters one knows, there are people who enter the Way of darkness. Even if one faces the pages of the book and reads well as if one can interpret the commentary of the ancients, if the principles be dark, one cannot make the Way one's own. Be that as it may, reaching the Way

without learning is also hard. And yet it is difficult to say that one has made clear the Way because one studies hard and speaks well. There are those, too, who obtain the Way naturally who have never studied.

In *The Great Learning* is written of "expanding knowledge and rectifying things." Expanding knowledge, meaning comprehensively, is to know, at least as much as the next man, the principles of all things, expanding knowledge until there is no unknown. Rectifying things is to know things comprehensively, knowing comprehensively the principle of all things until there is nothing that is unknown and nothing that cannot be done. Once no thing is unknown, there is no thing to be done. Without knowing the principle, one can realize nothing.

In all things there is uncertainty because of not knowing. Things cling to one's mind because of doubting. Once the principle has been made clear, nothing clings to one's mind. This is called expanding knowledge and rectifying things. Once there is nothing clinging to one's mind, all things become easy to do. That is why the learning of all the arts is for the purpose of clearing one's mind.

The beginner's mind does not know anything, so there are no questions in the mind. Once one has begun to study, there are things on one's mind. These things become an obstruction, and everything becomes difficult to do. If one can clear one's heart and mind of one's studies, and practice too disappears, then when one performs the various techniques, regardless of what one has learned, the techniques become easy to do and do not deviate from the teaching. When performing these things, one can forget the self and accomplish the teachings. Through this one should understand the Way of martial arts.

The kernel of expanding knowledge is learning the various techniques of the sword, the postures, the look of the eyes, and to master all the teachings and practice them. And when one has mastered the teachings, and when all that one has learned disappears from the mind, when the heart/mind itself disappears, this then is

*Dragon armor helmet. Edo period.*

the spirit of rectifying things. When one has mastered the diverse teachings and accomplished the discipline of training, the hands, feet, and body may move but the heart/mind will remain at rest. One will have become detached from one's learning but not disengaged from it, and will have the freedom to perform all manner of techniques. When this comes to pass, whither one's own heart/mind? One will not know. Neither will demons nor tempters from the Way be able to enter into it. For the purpose of reaching this state one has learned. Once one has learned this, learning itself disappears.

This is the essential enlightenment of all the martial arts. To forget learning, to abandon the mind that clings, to lose oneself completely, are the ultimate desiderata of the Way. This level is entering through learning and arriving at No-Learning.

# 気と志
# Ki and Will

The heart/mind that looks inward and focuses intently is called Will. Inwardly manifested is Will, outwardly manifested is called Ki. By way of example, Will can be said to be master of the house and Ki the servant. Inwardly manifested Will exploits Ki. If Ki overruns the mark, one stumbles. Ki should be restrained by Will so as not to be hurried. In martial arts terms, strengthening *shita no tsukuri*, creating a lower centeredness, is called Will; a face-to-face bout to kill or be killed is called Ki. One's shita no tsukuri is tightened, and Ki is not to be rushed or driven. Controlling Ki by means of one's Will, and remaining calm so Will is not wrenched by Ki, is of the essence.

# 表裏
# Appearance and Reality

Appearance and reality are the foundation of the martial arts. Manipulating appearance and reality is a stratagem, the use of falsehood to gain the truth. Appearance and reality can entrap one's opponent when used expediently, even if he

sees through the ruse. When one's manipulation of appearance and reality entrap an opponent, yours is the victory by letting him fall into the trap. If an opponent does not fall into your trap, yet another one can be devised. Thereby your opponent is taken in, even if he does not fall for your first trap. In Buddhism this is called *hōben*, expedient means. Even when the truth is hidden on the inside and deceit is practiced on the outside, and in the end one is led to the path of truth, then all deception becomes the truth. In the religion of the gods of heaven and earth, this is called "the mystery of the gods." The mystery is kept secret to arouse people's faith. When people have faith, there is divine merit. In the way of the warrior, this is called military strategy. Even though strategy is deceit, when deceit is used to win without harming others, deceit becomes truth in the end. This is called putting things in order by doing the opposite.

# 草を打ちて蛇を驚かす
# Beating the Grass to Scare Up Snakes

There is a Zen saying, "Beat the grass to scare up snakes." Frightening one's opponent with a little scare is a tactic like beating the grass to scare up snakes that lie within. Doing the unexpected as a maneuver to scare one's opponent is a deception, an appearance hiding the reality. This is an art of war. The opponent's mind is distracted by being startled, and his skill lapses. Even the gesture of raising one's fan or raising one's hand can distract an opponent. Even flinging aside the sword one carries is an art of war. If one attains mastery of No-Sword, one never lacks a sword. Your opponent's sword is your sword. This is the working of the Incipient Moment.

*Netsuke. Ryoo (a character in Bugaku dance). Japan. Circa 1800–1900.*

*A miniature lacquer palanquin. Japan. Meiji Period, late 19th century.*

*Military leader's fan. Japan. 1615–1868. Bronze.*

# THE SHOE-OFFERING BRIDGE
# THE THREE LEARNINGS

*Itto Ryodan: Splitting the opponent in two with a single stroke.*

A master of *shinkage ryu* swordsmanship, Yagyu Munenori popularized the style through his writings and teachings. "The Shoe-Offering Bridge" refers to a fable from the Chinese Han dynasty. When an old man lost his shoe under a bridge, a young man named Chang Liang retrieved it and realized the man was the legendary recluse Huang-shih Kung. Impressed and appreciative of the young man's help, Huang-shih Kung taught him the wealth of information he had on the art of war, which Liang later used to help the emperor found the Han dynasty.

"The Three Learnings", the first section of Munenori's "Shoe-Offering Bridge" chapter, refers to the three elements necessary to become a master of shinkage ryu swordsmanship: posture, arms and legs, and the sword. The initial postures are shown in the series of manuevers here.

*Zentei Setsutetsu: Cutting through nails, severing steel.*

*Hankai Hanko: Turning halfway, facing halfway.*

*Usen Saten: Wheeling right, turning left.*

*Chotan Ichimi: Long and short are one.*

# THE SWORD IN JAPANESE HISTORY

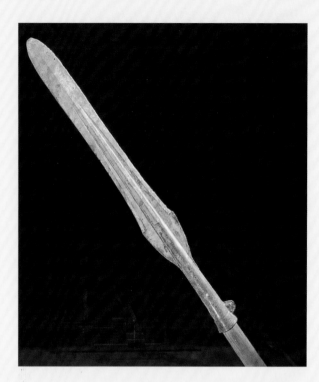

Though the emperor's original sacred sword is thought to have disappeared in the Gempei War of the twelfth century CE, even today a royal sword is maintained but is kept hidden from public view, as are the other two treasures. The emperor's double-edge straight sword, his *tsurugi*, is invested with symbolism regarding power and its consequences. Or, to look at it in philosophical terms, this type of sword embodies the concept of *yin yang*, the idea of positive and negative qualities in the same proportion. That is, the blade edge equally faces the emperor as well as his people. With the edge that faces out, the emperor rules others through strength, but he also knows that, if he does not rule wisely, the edge that faces inward may pass judgment on him later.

For the samurai, though, the sword was not only his main weapon of everyday life, but it also, to his way of

For the Japanese themselves, it is not an exaggeration to say that their country is a land "forged by the sword." And because the sword, the *nihonto*, plays such a large part in their mythology and folklore, it is only fitting that its long history begin with the legend that follows. Around 100 BCE, Sasa no wo no Mikoto, nephew of the sun goddess Amaterasu, slew the eight-headed dragon, and in its tail found a sword. This sword was to become one of the emperor's three sacred treasures from the gods, the other two being a mirror and a jewel. Together, the three articles represented, valor, wisdom, and benevolence, respectively.

*Above left: Lance point. Yayoi Period. 200 BCE–100 CE. Japan. Bronze.*

*Above: Handachi Mounts. Japan. Circa 1550.*

thinking, stood for his very soul, as he used it to defend himself, his family, and his country. In many cases, the samurai who distinguished himself in battle received an exceptional sword, made by a well-known and highly regarded master, and this could become an heirloom to be passed down through generations as a reflection of the family's honor and history.

## The Samurai's Arsenal

Because the sword was connected to the samurai's heritage, the warrior would do anything to preserve his weapon. Such mottoes as the following were often engraved on the warrior's swords: "There is nothing between heaven and earth that man need fear who carries at his side this magnificent blade. One's fate is in the hands of heaven, but a skillful fighter does not meet with death. In the last days, one's sword becomes the wealth of one's posterity." As a sign of honor, the samurai carried the two-sword set known as the *daisho*, one long and one short, and was a member of the only class allowed to do so. The earliest swords were straight, but later the curved blade was developed. Other than that, few changes were made in the sword for more than a millennium, with only the dimensions of the sword varying according to individual needs and tastes. Regardless of subtle variation, certain characteristics of a *nihonto* (sword) are considered to be strongly desirable. It's said that a sword should:

-Be sharp,
-Resist bending,
-Not break (absorb shock),
-Be appealing to the eye, and
-Be relatively light and easy to wield.

Generally, blades were well over two feet in length, as in the *tachi* of the earliest times, or were slightly shorter, as in the *katana*, while the shorter blades were less than two feet in length, as in the *wakizashi*, or closer to one foot, as in the *tanto*, the more daggerlike sword. The long blade was the samurai's most important weapon, the shorter one a secondary. Traditionally, the sword's single-edged curved blade allowed it to be drawn quickly. The tachi was designed to be carried slung from the warrior's left hip, dangling in its scabbard, while the katana, the wakizashi, and the tanto

were worn thrust through the warrior's belt on the left side of his body, with the cutting edge turned up.

The longest sword, the tachi, was worn with its cutting edge down, to facilitate horseback riding. This piece, favored during the Gempei War, functioned as the warrior's primary weapon until the Sengoku era of the sixteenth century, after which it became more of a ceremonial object for display at court or other occasions of high protocol. With the development of the katana, which replaced the tachi in popularity, that "shorter long sword" became the main component of the daisho, because its less cumbersome length was preferred for close-quarter fighting. As indicated, the wakizashi, the second half of the daisho, was used as a backup on the battlefield or for self-defense indoors and was also the instrument with which the act of ritual suicide would be carried out, if need be. The katana was not generally worn

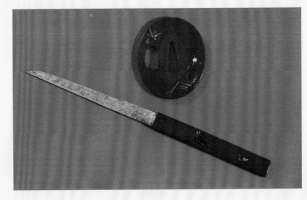

*Kozuka and tsuba. Circa 1700.*

inside the house but was left in a reserved place at the front door as a form of correct etiquette; however, the wakizashi never left the warrior's side, for his sense of security and his protection in any event that might arise.

For more than 1,000 years, sword makers, *kaji*, devoted their best work to the making of this superb item. On a practical level, the samurai demanded that his sword possess the sharpest edge possible, because he knew that a dull sword would tend to break during battle, a situation that could quickly alter the balance between life and death. Although there is no disputing the extraordinary effectiveness of the Japanese sword as a weapon (and many

believed its effectiveness far surpassed that of the weapons of other nations), on a higher level, it was also regarded as the emblem of the warrior's virtue, courage, and strength, guarding both his and his ancestor's names from any unworthy deeds.

## The Making of the Sword

For centuries, the manufacture of the Japanese sword maintained an exceptional degree of quality. In a process founded on the five traditional elements of the universe, the blade contained the purity and self-restraint of clay, metal, and wood and the energy and zest of the fire and water that forged it. With the addition of a sixth element, the artisan, the sword arose from the combination and the quality of these variables, making each piece as unique as the smith himself. The sword maker, who ranked socially among the highest in the artisan class (along with the metalworker, who made the sword fittings), was held in high regard. In fact, even samurai, nobles, and emperors were known to undertake the forging of a sword blade for the sake of the esteem associated with it. For example, the Emperor Go-toba in the twelfth century declared the making of swords to be an occupation worthy of princes, and a few of the blades that he created are still preserved in Japan. Another class of citizen, the priest, the monk, or the lay priest, also commonly aspired to the role of sword maker, for the procedure could be viewed in the light of a religious ceremony.

At the beginning of this multistep procedure, the sword smith sought to ensure his success by cleansing himself and his work area of evil spirits and then invoking the help of deities. Such rites lent a kind of sacredness to the making of the sword, as it became an object with a personality of its own, with a "soul." For this reason, the sword, even today, is handled with great respect and reverence.

The steel used in making a Japanese sword contains many elements yet rusts very easily. In Europe, coal was used to smelt sword steel, but the temperature used was, of necessity, so high that unwanted impurities found their way into the metal. In Japan, because no coal was available, charcoal was used at a lower temperature, which didn't cause impurities to melt as much and reduced the carbon content of the blade. From the smelted ore, the smith heated and pounded a billet of steel into the desired shape for the sword. Often, several grades of steel were hammered together to form the blade. A smith employed specially trained hammerers to do part of this welding process under his watchful eye. The folding and the heating and the pounding with heavy hammers forged the blade tightly and eliminated all impurities, which produced a strong but flexible blade that would not break under strain, and had a hard edge that would be sharpened later by the polisher. Folding the metal numerous times during the forging process produced more than a half-million layers and created the beautiful wood-grain effect on the surface. The blade was then tempered, with an exacting combination of heated metal and the right degree of coolness of the water. A smith would not let a tempered blade go out of his forge if it had flaws or imperfections and would only send it to the polisher after he had determined it to be of the highest quality.

When sharpened and finished by the polisher, the tempered edge took on a milky white or frosted appearance in various patterns. With the same skill and expertise as the smith, the polisher used a series of nine grades of polishing stones to achieve the final shape and texture of the metal, taking as much as two months to polish one blade properly. With its blade having taken on a milky white or frosted appearance, the bare sword was then housed in a wooden scabbard fitted with a handle and a hand guard.

At the beginning of the sixteenth century, it became increasingly popular for the sword smith to engrave his name on the *tang* of the sword (the end of the blade that is later encased in the hilt). He was not required to sign every one he made, nor did he do it for any reason except pride in his work. The signature might be accompanied by other information such as a date, a place of residence, or a motto. Soon the lesser-known smiths realized that, if a popular artisan's name were affixed to a blade, it would increase its value. The forgeries that occurred can cause confusion and problems for modern-day collectors, who must study authenticated examples and the characteristics of each sword smith's work to determine whether the signature is genuine. Another problem with signatures arises because the sword was often shortened at the hilt end, where the name might have originally been. Such swords were sometimes shortened because of personal preference, but also national law sometimes required the length of a sword to be shorter.

Though smiths flourished in most parts of Japan, swords were made in one of the five main schools or styles,

*Above: Monsini koshirae.*

the *gokaden*, which were named after the provinces where they originated: Yamashiro, Yamato, Bizen, Soshu, and Mino. The styles differed only in minor distinguishing characteristics, such as a wider blade, a more-tempered edge, or more curvature. Many famous smiths, and thousands of outstanding but lesser-known smiths illuminate the history of Japan. Since that history was dominated by warring factions—families, peasantry, monks, lords, and emperors—the sword maker always found himself in great demand.

## TIMELINE

### The Yayoi, Yamato, and Asuka Eras (200s to 600s CE)

The history of the Japanese sword can be traced to the end of the Yayoi era, when Queen Himiko, in the year 239 CE, took control of the thirty-four territories called Yamataikoku, which fell to the kingdom of the Yamato Chotei in less than a century. Recent excavations of ancient gravesites from this period show that the swords of this time were made of bronze.

In the year 607, the Crown Prince Shotokutaishi sent Ono no Imoko as an ambassador to Kure, an area in southern China that was known to produce the highest-quality blades at the time. Interestingly, the majority of ancient swords in Japan were originally either Chinese or Korean, that is, until smiths emigrated from those countries to Japan, and the local smiths adapted the foreign methods to forge their own style.

Before the year 650, most swords were of the straight, flat style, with no ridgeline, but the exact reason and time that blades began to be forged with a curve is not recorded. The late sword smith Kobayashi Yasuhiro observed that a sword will tend to develop a curve naturally as a result of

the cooling of different steels at different rates during the hardening-quenching process (differential hardening) required to make a cutting edge. Curved blades may have been created accidentally this way, at which time it is likely that smiths discovered that a curved edge cuts more efficiently than a straight edge.

### The Nara Era (710 to 793 CE)

The period saw three sword styles, now known as the *jo-koto* classification: *hira zukuri* (no ridgeline), *kiriha zukuri* (ridgeline very close to the edge), and *kissakimoroha zukuri* (doubled-edge with ridgeline). During this time, before the Heian era, diplomatic communications between China and Japan were severed, and the wars that spread internally throughout Japan fostered a constant demand for these styles of sword.

*Tachi. Kirimon-Ashikaga family. Circa 1500.*

## The Heian Era (794 to 1185 CE)

The straight sword continued to lose popularity, and the demand for the

*Wild Boar Iron Tsuba. Edo Late. 1800s.*

*shinogi zukuri* (ridgeline close to the top of the blade) became stronger. This style is still being produced today. The high quality of these swords, now known by their *koto*, "old sword," classification, began to attract the attention of China and other

countries. In 1167, Kiyomori, the leader of the Taira (Heike) clan, became essentially the ruler of Japan. Although this was the first time a samurai had come into power, the political structure did not change from that set by previous nobles. Sometime later, after five years of hard fighting, the Heike clan was finally defeated and ruined by their rivals, the Minamoto clan, in Dannoura in March 1185. Young Emperor Antoku, died at the age of eight, along with the Taira family, and his sacred sword (one of the three great treasures of Japan, bestowed upon the emperor by the gods) was lost in the sea.

## The Kamakura Era (1185 to 1337)

In 1192, Minamoto Yoritomo became the first shogun and formed his *bakufu* government in Kamakura. Yoritomo's political system, run by samurai for the samurai class,

resulted in the gathering of a large group of sword smiths to support his military. Some of the more notable smiths included Masamune, Sadamune, Yukimitsu, Shintogo, Kunihiro, and Kunimitsu, all of whom produced excellent blades. However, because of civil wars and the Mongolian invasions of 1274 and 1281, many of these fine blades were destroyed. Also because of the Mongols, the very design of Japanese blades changed dramatically, as clamshell-shape edges on longer swords evolved for advantage against the Mongols' thick leather armor. Battlefield tactics changed as well, emerging from the traditional one-on-one style of combat to coordinated group battles.

## The Muromachi Era (1338 to 1573)

During this period of many wars, fighting methods had changed largely as a result of the experience gained during the Mongolian invasions. In addition to a strong focus on the use of cavalry (something the Mongols were famous for), close-range infantry fighting also increased in popularity, with the long tachi gradually being replaced by the katana, which could be drawn more rapidly.

In 1441, with the assassination of the sixth-generation shogun, Ashikaga Yoshinori, the bakufu lost power and civil wars broke out. Because the last one hundred years of the Muromachi era involved the largest number of wars in Japanese history, the period came to be known as the *sengoku jidai*, the civil war era. During this time, power could be snatched through revolt, and position and rank could be gained by lower-ranking officials when higher-ranking officials were killed in battle.

In 1573, not long after guns had been introduced to Japan, the Takeda clan fought the allied forces of Oda Nobunaga and Tokugawa Ieyasu at the battle of Nagashino. Takeda's cavalry of 15,000 well-trained and highly motivated

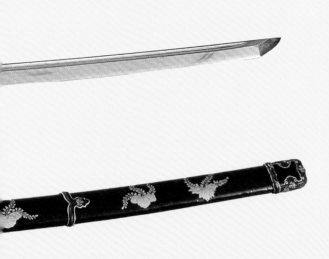

until 1764, when they would come to be known by the *shinshinto*, "new-new sword," classification. During that time frame, the Tokugawa government established by Ieyasu would go on to last through fifteen generations and span a period of 265 years. In the early years of the Tokugawa shogunate, when Ieyasu killed Hideyori and set fire to his castle, many fine swords were destroyed. Some of the blades were retempered by the sword smith Yasutsugu, but the rest were lost forever. The surviving blades were kept by the Tokugawa family in Owari.

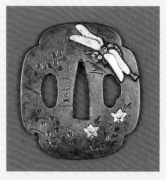

*Dragonfly and flower soft metal tsuba. Edo period. 1800s.*

Just decades later, following the revolt of Christians and peasants in the village of Shimabara, Japan began to isolate itself from the influence of other countries, and a ban was placed on importing and exporting goods to and from Japan. Not long afterward, a massive fire in Edo consumed most of the city and the main structure of the castle there, and with it, some thirty crates, each containing thirty swords. Of the thirty crates, twenty-five were totally destroyed. The third generation of Yasutsugu smiths effectively retempered several famous swords from the remaining lot. In yet another fire, this one in 1816, the Toshogu shrine in Nikko, where Ieyasu was buried, caught fire and burned down. Fortunately, even though many fine blades were damaged by that fire, the shrine's symbolic sword, *sukezane*, remained unharmed.

In 1853, after Commodore Perry landed in Tokyo Bay, civil war broke out between the shogunate and the supporters of the emperor (the Satsuma, Chosu, and Tosa clans), and within a decade or so, the ruling lord, Tokugawa Yoshinobu, had resigned control of the government, the act that ended the era of shogun rule.

men is now believed to have been Japan's strongest in history, but the Tokugawa and Oda clans had a combined force of 35,000 troops with 3,000 matchlock guns. In that battle, Takeda's army lost 12,000 men to firearms alone. As a result, military strategists projected that the firearm, not the sword, would be the most important tactical element in future military campaigns.

## The Azuchi-Momoyama Era (1574 to 1602)

Oda Nobunaga was almost successful in controlling all of Japan but was assassinated by one of his retainers, Akechi Mitsuhide, who was then defeated in battle by one of Nobunaga's generals, Toyotomi Hideyoshi. Eventually, Hideyoshi was able to unify Japan, but only until his death in 1598. Only a few years later, that distinction would fall to Tokugawa Ieyasu, who fought and defeated the Toyotomi clan in the battle of Sekigahara. Seizing a significant portion of land and resources, Ieyasu then seized power and assumed control of Japan.

The swords that were being produced by the end of this period would come to be known by the *shinto*, "new sword," classification.

## The Edo Era (1603 to 1867)

The shinto classification of swords would prevail for almost two centuries,

*Kashira with oxalis flower family mon. Edo period. 1800s.*

## The Meiji Era (1868 to 1911)

With the Emperor Meiji restored to power, the new government required all samurai to cut off their topknots and conform to the standards of modern society. The wearing of swords was discouraged and, within a few years, completely banned in public. The year 1877 saw the last civil war break out in Japan, when Saigo Takamori, a samurai of the Satsuma clan, led 30,000 men in an unsuccessful campaign against the new government. Takamori, after being shot in the thigh and stomach, is believed to have committed the ritual suicide of olden days.

Three generations of emperors ruled during this period, but after this time, it was established that the ruler was not, in fact, a descendant of a god, but rather was born of human lineage. Correspondingly, the country became more democratic and began to look to America for matters regarding political policy. Nonetheless, as recently as World War II officers still carried swords, in keeping with the samurai spirit, although many important specimens were lost or destroyed when major Japanese cities were burned down in American air raids. The swords that were produced during this period and even into the present would come to be classified as *gendaito*, a term used to represent the modern examples that were built in the time-honored, handmade fashion.

## The Modern Era (Since 1945)

Since before World War II, the imperial army and navy required its high-ranking officers to wear *gunto*, tachi-length swords made specifically for military use, with possession closely managed by the government. These weapons had to be provided in such large quantities for the war that the quality suffered. Such swords, which may have stamps, serial numbers, stainless-steel blades, and fake temper lines or may have even been machine-made, are not looked on as true Japanese swords. Additionally, these swords should be examined carefully, as many of them are hazardous to use. However, some gunto were produced by sword smiths, using traditional methods, and these are often of a grade high enough to be considered authentic specimens. Nobuhisa and Yoshichika were smiths who created fine examples during this time, and Miyairi Shohei in particular became what is known as a National Living Treasure.

After World War II, sword makers changed their focus and began creating swords that were works of art, rather than being fully practical. While beautiful, these swords often do not cut well, lack sufficient sharpness, and in some cases are too highly tempered (causing the edge to become brittle and dangerous to the user and to spectators at demonstrations). After the war, Japanese law restricted smiths to forging a maximum of two long swords or three wakizashi a month, causing *gendaito* to become expensive collector's items. When forged at high temperatures for quicker, higher production rates, the iron of the blade melts too easily, and the sword edge becomes fragile and cracks easily. The older koto-type swords are more historically valuable because of their proven ability in battle and, except for those that have been worn thin from numerous polishings, are thus much more expensive for the connoisseur. As a caveat here, it perhaps should be mentioned that every generation of sword makers has had its share of both high- and low-quality production. Shinto, shinshinto, and gendaito all were made during peaceful times, so some of them were crafted primarily as objects of beauty and, though aesthetically appealing, often lacked the requisite characteristics. Such is the case even today, when some smiths take pride in their skill and traditions, while many have strayed from the basic objective of creating a sword that is beautiful, strong, and sharp, but doesn't bend or break.

The oldest of the Japanese swords, which can still be viewed in museums around the world, usually have a history of being passed down through generations of high-ranking generals and honorable warriors. But thousands of excellent vords were destroyed by wars and natural disasters, mostly inflicted by humans.

However, those who appreciate the art and craft of the sword, and its place in Japanese history, have protected enough fine blades that the tradition of the kaji lives to this day.

*Hachiwari (Helmet Splitter) Circa 1700.*

# THE SHOE-OFFERING BRIDGE
## THE NINE ITEMS

*Hissho: Sure victory.*

While the first section of Munenori's "The Shoe-Offering Bridge" outlines the foundational elements of *shinkage ryu* swordsmanship, the second section builds upon those basic moves with nine additional ones that can be characterized as furthering the swordsman's strategy. "The Nine Items" includes maneuvers that draw from other schools of swordsmanship and prepare the swordsman to respond to his opponent, as backup in case the initial strike goes awry, or for leading one's opponent into a move that will put him at a disadvantage, allowing for the final definitive strike.

Together, "The Three Elements" and "The Nine Items" make up the core maneuvers of *The Sword and the Mind*. A third portion of "The Shoe-Offering Bridge" is included in many translations. This portion, usually known as The Goblin's Selection, includes eight attack moves not illustrated here. The following demonstration illustrates the remainder of the core moves from *The Sword and the Mind*, "The Nine Items."

*The mind is to be held in a state of Waiting, the body in a state of Attacking. This is because if the mind is in Attack it will rush precipitously; keeping the mind restrained and in repose, one's body is used in attack to force your opponent's hand first.*

Gyakufu: Cross wind.

Jutachi: Cross-shaped sword.

Kaboku: Softening.

Attacking is to assault single-mindedly, striking fiercely from the moment one faces off with one's opponent, striving to strike the first blow. This feeling of attack is the same whether it is in the mind of the opponent or in one's own mind. Waiting is not to attack hastily, but to wait for one's opponent to make the first move.

*Ozume: Large-scale parrying.*

*Shokei: Shortcut.*

*Yaegaki: Eightfold or double fence.*

*Kozume: Delicate parrying.*

*Murakumo: Rising cloud.*

機前

# The Incipient Moment

The Incipient Moment (*kizen*) is anticipating your opponent's move before he has seized the opportunity. By Ki (機) is meant Ki (気), the energy that is reserved in the chest. This Ki (機) equals Ki (気). To observe keenly your opponent's energy, and to act corresponding to the presence of this energy is called the Incipient Moment. This operation is a feature of Zen, in which it is called Zen-ki, the Zen interrelationship. Ki is the energy hidden within that is not manifested. It is like a hidden drop-bolt in a door. Observing keenly the imperceptible workings concealed within, and acting upon that, is called the art of war of the Incipient Moment.

懸待

# Attacking and Waiting

Attacking is to assault single-mindedly, striking fiercely from the moment one faces off with one's opponent, striving to strike the first blow. This feeling of attack is the same whether it is in the mind of the opponent or in one's own mind. Waiting is not to attack hastily, but to wait for one's opponent to make the first move. One should understand that waiting is exercising extreme vigilance. Attacking and Waiting are two distinct acts. The principles of Attacking and Waiting apply to both the body and the sword. The body, attacking, charges the opponent, the sword, waiting, holds back; the body and limbs lure the opponent into taking the initiative, and victory is had in forcing the opponent's hand. In so doing, the body and limbs are attacking, the sword is waiting; the body and limbs attacking is for the purpose of forcing the opponent's move first.

*Opposite page: Asahina, from the series 3 designs of breaking gates. 1827. Gakutei Harunobu fl. 1818–30. Woodblock engraving.*

*Tsuba. Edo period.*

心と身とに懸待

# The Mental and Physical in Attacking and Waiting

The mind is to be held in a state of Waiting, the body in a state of Attacking. This is because if the mind is in Attack it will rush precipitously; keeping the mind restrained and in repose, one's body is used in attack to force your opponent's hand first. If one's mind is in Attack, defeat will be yours for trying to kill your opponent straightaway. In other cases, it can be understood that the mind is to be in Attack and the body in Waiting. The reason for this is by causing the mind to work resolutely, placing the mind in Attack and the sword in Waiting, the mind forces a man's hand. The body can be understood to mean nothing less than the hand that holds the sword. So it is said that the mind is in Attack and the body in Waiting. Although there are two meanings, they are ultimately the same. In any event, victory is yours by forcing your opponent's hand.

*Katana. Second generation Shigataka. Circa 1650.*

# 敵懸の時、我立相ふ習
# Lessons for Facing an Opponent When Attacking

These are the three points for focusing the eyes:
- The Two Stars (the opponent's two clinched fists holding his sword)
- The Peaks and Valleys (the opponent's bending and extending his arms)
- The Distant Mountains, during engagement (the chest and shoulders)

The details of these points for focusing the eyes are to be transmitted orally.

These are the two points for the sword and for body posture:
- The Rhythm of Near and Far (avoiding opponent's direct attack)
- The Position of the Body, and the Sandalwood State of Mind (avoiding simultaneous engagement of two swords)

These are five points for the body and the sword, each to be learned by dueling (difficult to express in writing):
- Making fists into a shield
- Making the body one
- Taking opponent's fist on your shoulder
- Keeping the rear leg extended
- Keeping the same stance and guard as opponent's, whatever it may be

Now, the proper state of mind for each of these five points before facing off with an opponent is to concentrate on preparing your mind—centering your mind so as to ascertain your opponent's moves—and to fix your mind resolutely. It is essential to keep the mind unwavering once engaged. Suddenly facing off an opponent without mental preparation, one cannot perform the lessons learned or anything at all.

# 敵待の時、立あふ習
# Lessons for Facing an Opponent When Waiting

As for these three points—The Two Stars, Peaks and Valleys, and Distant Mountains—never take your eyes off the three foci when an opponent is unyieldingly in his Waiting. These three points of focus, however, are used for both Attacking and Waiting. They are indispensable. When assaulting an opponent, focus your eyes on the Peak; when engaged blade to blade, focus your eyes on the Distant Mountains. Always keep an eye on the Two Stars.

# 三ケ心持
# Mental Preparation for the Three Ploys

The three ploys are, namely, three ways of seeing: striking, point-in-line, and learned attack. When it is difficult to calculate how your opponent will move, one

*Crows in snow. Six-panel folding screen. Japan. Circa 1700–1800.*

should use these three ploys to intuit his intentions. For an opponent who is set steadfastly in Waiting, use these three ploys for the three ways of seeing, maneuvering artfully, and thereby gaining victory by forcing your opponent's hand.

## 色に就き色に随ふ
# Applying Oneself to Change of Mind
### Adapting to Change of Mind

The core of these words is that when one communicates various changes of mind to an opponent who is in Waiting, his changes of mind then become manifested. Adapting to these changes of mind, one wins.

## 二目遣
# Using Both Eyes

For an opponent in Waiting, one should use artifice of various sorts to see what he will do; pretending to look but not looking, pretending not to look but looking, ever vigilant, never resting one's gaze on one place, with roving eyes, look about flittingly. There is a line of a poem that says, "By stealing a look, the dragonfly dodges the butcherbird." Seeing a butcherbird in a stolen glance, the dragonfly escapes in flight. A butcherbird (*hakurō*) is a shrike. Watching an opponent's moves with stolen glances, one must work vigilantly. In Sarugaku Nō drama, there is a term, *futatsu me tsukai*, referring to using the eyes in a stealthy manner. This means to look once and then to look again from the corner of the eye. This means not resting the gaze on any one place.

*Portrait of Tokugawa Ieyasu (1543–1616), Japanese School. 17th century.*

# THE TOKUGAWA SHOGUNATE
# THE POWERFUL HOUSE THAT MUNENORI SERVED

Yagyu Munenori, author of *The Sword and the Mind*, was born into an age of upheaval in Japan. It was the Warring States period, when armies of rival clans roamed the countryside, attacking each other at will. By the time of Munenori's birth in 1571, however, power was beginning to coalesce into the hands of a triumvirate of samurai warlords: Oda Nobunaga, Toyotomi Hideyoshi, and Tokugawa Ieyasu, the man whom Munenori would eventually serve and who was destined to found Japan's most powerful and longest-lasting shogun dynasty.

Tokugawa Ieyasu was born on January 31, 1543, in Okazaki castle in Mikawa province, a feudal fief roughly a third of the way from Kyoto to modern Tokyo. When Ieyasu was about five years old, the Oda clan invaded Mikawa, and his father, Hirotada, asked the neighboring Imagawa clan for help. The Imagawa agreed, but only if Hirotada would deliver his young son as a hostage. When the head of the Oda clan, Nobuhide, heard of this, he dispatched a detachment of warriors to capture the young boy as he was being transported to the Imagawa. Nobuhide threatened to kill the boy unless Hirotada renounced all ties with the Imagawa clan. But Hirotada refused, saying that Ieyasu's death would only serve to show the Imagawa how serious he was about the alliance. Instead of killing the boy, Nobuhide kept him as a hostage, and so Ieyasu spent several years in the Oda capital in Nagoya, in close proximity to Nobuhide's son Nobunaga.

In 1551, Oda Nobuhide died in a plague. The Imagawa clan, sensing that the seventeen-year-old Nobunaga was not prepared to take the reins, quickly besieged Nagoya castle. They dropped their siege only after Nobunaga agreed to surrender eight-year-old Ieyasu as a hostage. Since Hirotada had died two years before, and because Ieyasu was now the rightful heir to his clan's holdings in Mikawa, the Imagawa thought it would be advantageous to keep him under their control, raising him to be a loyal samurai.

When Ieyasu came of age at thirteen, the Imagawa chieftain gave the boy his niece as a wife, in the hopes of further cementing his ties to the clan. Ieyasu was allowed to return to Mikaw, under the condition that he would lead his

*Yori suit of armor by Myochin Nagamichi. Circa 1600.*

army into battle against the Oda clan. Two years later, Ieyasu led a siege of Terabe castle but was driven off when Oda Nobunaga sent reinforcements.

In 1560, the Imagawa invaded Oda territory with an army of

311

*Osaka castle at sakura (cherry blossom) time.*

gave up his dream of becoming the most powerful daimyo, and he knew he would have to be patient. "The strong, virile ones in life understand the meaning of patience," he later wrote. "Patience means restraining your inclinations. . . . I am not as strong as I could be, but I have long known and practiced patience. And if my descendants wish to be like me, they must study patience too."

Some years later, Hideyoshi had just captured eight provinces from the Hojo clan, including large swamps and wilderness, which he offered to give Ieyasu in return for the five provinces under his command. Despite the unevenness of the trade, Ieyasu accepted the offer, transferring his soldiers to a rundown castle overseeing the sleepy fishing village of Edo in an obscure corner of Japan's eastern coast. It turned out to be a brilliant move. By keeping his distance from Hideyoshi, he was able to turn Edo (now Tokyo) into a powerful military stronghold. In 1598, Hideyoshi died, leaving his lands to his five-year-old son, Hideyori. Before he died, he appointed a Council of Five Elders, including Ieyasu, to act as regents. But the transition created a power vacuum, a situation that Ieyasu was quick to exploit by leading an army to Fushimi and seizing Hideyori's residence in Osaka castle, touching off a civil war.

roughly 25,000 soldiers, a staggering force that easily outnumbered the Oda army. With high hopes of crushing Nobunaga, seventeen-year-old Ieyasu and his contingent of samurai from Mikawa captured a fort at the border and occupied it as the rest of the Imagawa army moved on. But Nobunaga had other plans. At the front of the invaders' forces, he threw up a dummy army of straw men fitted with spare helmets, and in the meantime, he led his troops behind enemy lines to attack from the rear. In a surprise assault, Nobunaga's men stormed the enemy camp, killing the Imagawa *daimyo* and establishing Nobunaga as the leading warlord in the region. Within months, Ieyasu had joined Nobunaga's side, and the two warriors formed a quick friendship, later being joined by Toyotomi Hideyoshi, one of Nobunaga's sandal bearers, who would go on to become one of his top generals.

Over the next several years, Ieyasu strengthened his control over Mikawa province, battling the Imagawa and quashing a rebellion of warrior monks. In 1567, he changed his name to Tokugawa Ieyasu, claiming to belong to the Tokugawa warrior clan, which had ties to the emperor's Fujiwara clan, as well as to the Minamoto clan, the family of Japan's shoguns. Because no proof exists that he had any Tokugawa ancestors, there is suspicion that he simply forged his genealogy. His claims of Minamoto ancestry would be helpful when he pushed to become shogun.

After gaining control of Mikawa, Ieyasu began expanding his territories while continuing to assist Nobunaga in his drive to unify Japan under his command. In 1582, Ieyasu lost his chief patron when Oda Nobunaga was assassinated. In the struggle for power that followed, Toyotomi Hideyoshi, Nobunaga's onetime sandal bearer, became the single most powerful daimyo in Japan and strove to assert the same kind of control that Nobunaga had had. After a short-lived rebellion, Ieyasu agreed to accept Hideyoshi's leadership. But he never

*Tanegashima powder flask, ball dispenser, musket box. Circa 1700.*

Two years later, on October 21, 1600, Ieyasu and the other regents squared off against each other on the plains of Sekigahara, near Japan's central mountain range. It was the biggest battle in Japanese history, with 89,000 soldiers in Ieyasu's so-called Eastern Army facing 82,000 soldiers in the elders' so-called Western Army. Despite his advantage in numbers, Ieyasu knew he could not defeat the Western Army without help, so he convinced some enemy generals to defect, with the offer of land and riches. With their help, he defeated the Western Army and established himself as the unequaled power in Japan. Within three years, he was named shogun, establishing the Tokugawa rule, which would hold power until 1868.

## 打にうたれよ、うたれて勝つ心持
# Hit and Be Hit— Winning by Being Hit

To kill a man with one slash of the sword is easy. To not let oneself be killed by the sword is difficult. Even though a man with intentions to kill slashes at you, keep him at a sword's length, remain composed, and then let him strike you. Even if an opponent strikes thinking he will score a hit, he will not be able to strike as long as one keeps one's distance. The sword that does not reach its target is a dead sword. Finessing his shortcoming, you strike the winning blow. Your opponent's vain attempt to make the first move allows you to take him with your first strike. Once sword blades have been engaged, do not let your opponent raise his hands. Once the fight is under way, if one wavers over what to do next, one will surely be cut down by the opponent's next strike. At this point, laxity equals defeat. Because one's mind lingers on the strike just made, one's opponent scores a blow, and one's initiative comes to naught. Do not let the mind dwell on a strike just made, wondering whether it has hit or missed the mark. Strike again and again—two or three, even four or five times—not letting the opponent even raise his head. The moment of victory is determined by a single blow of the sword.

## 三拍子
# Three Tempos

One tempo is the simultaneous striking of two blades; another is moving in and striking from beneath when your opponent's sword is raised; yet another is crossing over your opponent's lowered sword and striking. The tempo of striking simultaneously is bad, the tempo of striking separately is good. When the tempo is simultaneous, one's opponent's use of the sword becomes easier, but unwieldy when the tempo is different. One should strike so as to make the opponent's sword unwieldy. Whether striking from above or below, one should strike with No-Tempo. All tempos that can be followed are bad.

## 大拍子小拍子、小拍子大拍子
# Long vs. Short Tempo—Short vs. Long Tempo

When an opponent uses his sword taking a long tempo stance, one should wield one's sword using a short tempo. If your opponent uses a short tempo, you should take a long tempo. This too must be understood in terms of using one's own tempo of swordsmanship that does not match your opponent's. If he adopts your tempo, his sword becomes more facile. For example, a skillful singer will sing seamlessly over the beat in such a way that an unskilled drummer will not be able to keep time. Similarly, as putting together a skillful singer with a poor drummer, or a skillful drummer with a poor singer, making it hard to sing or drum, manipulating an opponent's tempo is called long-against-short-tempo and short-against-long-tempo. When an unskillful singer is borne away on a long tempo, a skillful drummer may try to beat lightly with a short tempo, but cannot. Similarly, when a skillful singer sings lightly an unskillful drummer will be unable to keep up the tempo. A skillful birdcatcher shows the bird his pole, jostling it to make it sway, and thereby slickly spears his prey. Taken in by the swaying tempo of the pole, the bird flutters and flaps its wings, but unable to take flight, is impaled. A tempo different from your opponent's should be maintained. If your tempo differs from your opponent's, you can step in without his closing the gap. Mindfulness of this kind should be contemplated deeply.

*Sumotori or wrestlers. Felice Beato (1830–1904). Circa 1870–80. Hand-colored albumen print.*

# THE SINGING NIHONTO
# THE SAMURAI'S SWORDS

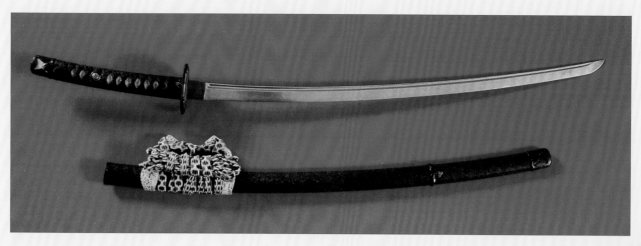

*Handachi mounted tachi. Circa 1830.*

A Japanese sword, often called a *nihonto,* is made in many varying lengths and sizes, depending on its purpose, and is categorized according to its utility, style, and origin in battle and martial art. Two of the most common types of nihonto are the *katana* and the *tachi.*

The katana, a curved, single-edge sword measuring nearly a hundred centimeters in length, became a popular battle weapon for samurai when it originated in the fifteenth century, effectively superseding the older and similarly constructed tachi. Somewhat longer and slightly more curved than the katana, the tachi was worn attached to the Japanese *obi,* or sash belt, with the edge facing down, and was favored by warriors on horseback. However, over the fifteenth and sixteenth centuries, with more warriors on foot, these samurai faced an increasing need for weapons conducive to battle in tight quarters. As a result, many tachi were cut down to the length of the katana, to make them more useful for close-range fighting. But eventually, the katana completely replaced the tachi in military use, and the tachi became only a ceremonial sword.

Often, the katana was paired with a sword known as a *wakizashi,* a much shorter weapon worn on the belt during battle. Together, the two pieces were called the samurai's *daisho* and, whether worn in battle or in ceremony, represented the honor and social standing of the samurai. While the longer sword was traditionally used for defeating

*Katana. Second generation Shigataka. Circa 1650*

an opponent in battle, the wakizashi was reserved for decapitating a fallen opponent and also for *seppuku*, the samurai tradition of ritual suicide. Because Japanese swords were measured in a specific unit, the *shaku*, which equals approximately thirty centimeters, any blade longer than two shaku was known as a *daito*. Both the tachi and the katana fit into this category of swords. The wakizashi, also known as a *shoto*, was typically between only one an⌟ two *shaku*, shorter than a katana but still a sword.

The katana was also characterized by its *tsuba*, a round or square guard on the end of the sword grip, which allowed control of the arm and protection of the hand for the swordsman. In the early fifteenth century, tsuba were designed for utility rather than decoration and were made of strong metals. Later, during the Edo period, tsuba became ornamental and were fashioned from less practical materials such as wood, silver, and gold, and could be highly ornate.

As is the case with so many aspects of Japanese culture, the term for swords, *nihonto*, originated in ancient China, with the appearance of the poem "Song of Nihonto," by the poet Ouyang Xiu of the Song dynasty. However, the word became more common in Japan during the late Tokugawa shogunate; because of the influx of imported Western swords, the term *nihonto* was adopted by the Japanese as an expression of nationalism and resistance to Western culture.

Swords disappeared rapidly from Japanese culture following the arrival of Matthew Perry in 1853 and the resulting connection with the rest of the world. By the Meiji Restoration sword smiths were out of work; the Heitorei edict of 1876 put an end to the public carrying of both swords and guns. Around the beginning of the twentieth century, swords began to be produced again, but primarily in mass using less sophisticated techniques. A rare few imperial artisans, including Gassan Sadakazu and Gassan Sadakatzu, maintained the old traditions. All nihonto were banned during the American occupation following World War II and many were destroyed. Only the intervention of General Douglas MacArthur, after a personal petition by Dr. Junji Honma, saved the majority of the historic swords that exist today.

*Handachi mounted tachi. Circa 1830.*

*The katana is carried by the side, blade-edge up. One hand grips the scabbard before drawing the sword.*

*Grasping the sheath near the top with the left hand, the blade is pulled from the sheath with the right hand.*

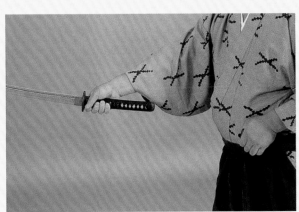

*The right hand brings the sword blade, fully removed from the sheath, forward in a single motion.*

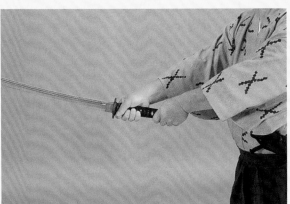

*The bottom hand grips the handle under the forward hand for a full grip. The sword is ready to engage the target.*

*Top: The wakazashi, short sword, carried with the longer katana in a daisho, represented the proud identity of the Japanese samurai.*

*Sword handle showing Kashira. Circa 1700.*

*Kozuka handle. Circa 1700.*

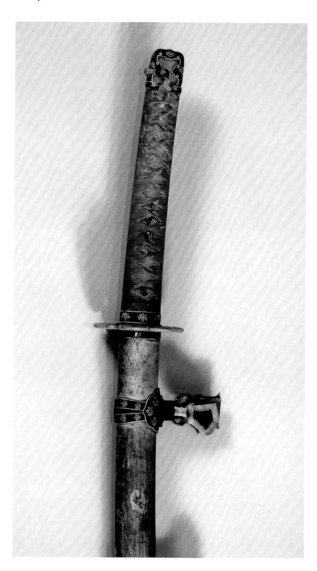

*Kirimon, Ashikaga family. Tachi period. Circa 1500.*

## 章歌の心付
# Observing the Tempo

One cannot keep time in song or dance without knowing the tempo. In the art of war as well, one must understand tempo. One must perceive keenly how an opponent handles his sword, know in which way he will wield it, and be able to see into his mind, with the same mental faculties of one who understands the tempo of song and dance. If the opponent's moves and comportment are well understood, one is free to develop one's own gambits.

## 六ケ条
# Six Techniques

1. Counterblow
2. Three inches between the blades
3. The quick, stealthy approach
4. Watching the elbows in *jōdan* position
5. Wheeling swords, keep a discerning eye on left and right
6. Maintaining the three-foot perimeter

Unless acquired through oral transmission by studying with a teacher, these six techniques cannot be learned. They cannot be communicated comprehensively in writing. When one uses these techniques to strike various opening gestures and pretexts to deceive one's opponent, and yet he remains unfazed and refuses to make advances, having assumed an unyielding Waiting position, and when one then closes in stealthily within the three-foot perimeter, he will be unable to contain himself and launches into Attack, you force his hand, letting him strike, and then deliver the coup de grâce. In any event, if one's opponent does not strike, you cannot defeat him.

Even if one's opponent does strike at you, if you are well aware of the out-of-reach perimeter, you will not be struck suddenly again. Having finished practicing this step, one can move close to the opponent without fear, make him strike out, and then defeat him. This is the attitude of preempting the initiative.

## 四ケ条
# Four Techniques

1. The Great Deception and the Initial Attack must be transmitted orally.
2. Vigilance, in both Attacking and Waiting, must be transmitted orally.
3. The forearm's length perimeter of a small sword
4. During engagement, Attacking and Waiting: the body in Attack, the sword in Waiting

Each of these four techniques is to be learned in practice with a teacher, and to be transmitted orally.

*Kirimon, Ashikaga family. Tachi period. Circa 1500.*

# THE THREE SWORDSMEN
# HIDETSUNA, MUNEYOSHI, AND MUNENORI

Kamiizumi Hidetsuna, more commonly known as Kamiizumi Ise no Kami Nobutsuna, received his martial arts training at an early age at Kamiizumi castle, where his father was the commander. Early in his career, Hidetsuna took part in defending Minowa castle from a siege by a neighboring warlord, Takeda Shingen. After a protracted battle, Shingen found that Hidetsuna held the only territory left. Shingen was so impressed by Hidetsuna's feat that he asked to have Hidetsuna change his name to Nobutsuna, which would link Hidetsuna to the Takeda clan.

Hidetsuna accepted the change but did not want the responsibilities and requested permission to go on a warrior pilgrimage, a *musha shugyo*. During his pilgrimage, an incident occurred that helped place Nobutsuna into the history books. When he learned that a bandit was holding a young child hostage in a house, Nobutsuna shaved his head to impersonate one of the priests who were allowed inside to provide food. While the bandit turned his attention to the rice balls given to him, Nobutsuna killed him and saved the child. (A scene in the movie *Seven Samurai* depicts this rescue.) Nobutsuna's skill became legendary after this.

Shortly thereafter, a duel with another famous swordsman, Yagyu Muneyoshi, was arranged. Muneyoshi did not have nearly the status as Nobutsuna, so Hikita Bungoro, Nobutsuna's nephew, was sent to fight Muneyoshi instead. Because this was an exhibition of style and not a real fight, bamboo swords, or *fukuro shinai*, were used, and this event records the first known use of the bamboo swords now used in *kendo* fighting. When Bungoro succeeded in striking an astonished Muneyoshi several times, Muneyoshi asked to become Nobutsuna's student.

Yagyu Sekishusai Muneyoshi was considered one of the most famous swordsmen in Japanese history. Indeed, his fame pulled the Yagyu family out of the obscurity of minor nobility to become the official instructors of swordsmanship of the Tokugawa shoguns. Muneyoshi had fought for the first time at the age of sixteen. Although his clan was defeated, he had already begun to make a name for himself, and it was this fame that eventually led to the contest between himself and the nephew of Nobutsuna. After two years of training as a student of Nobutsuna, Muneyoshi

became his mentor's successor and, after Nobutsuna's death, founded the *Yagyu shinkage ryu* style of fighting.

With the success of his school came an invitation to the court of Tokugawa Ieyasu in Kyoto in 1594. Here Muneyoshi and his son, Munenori, put on an impressive exhibition of swordsmanship. Afterward, Ieyasu invited Muneyoshi to become his sword instructor. Muneyoshi declined, excusing himself because of his impending retirement, and instead offered the services of his son. By the time Muneyoshi died

*Statue outside Tenryu-ji temple in Arashiyama in Kyoto.*

twelve years later, in 1606, Ieyasu had become shogun, and Munenori had become his official sword master.

Soon after this prestigious appointment, Munenori incorporated Zen Buddhism into his fighting style, emphasizing mental attitude over technique. His guide for this system, which employed the Zen empty-mind theory, was called *heiho kaden sho,* and it was during this time, after adding a Zen element to his technique, that accounts record his having slain seven attackers while defending his shogun.

Munenori's prominence and influence continue to modern times. In a more prosaic example of his notoriety, the 1980 television miniseries *Shogun* featured a character based on Munenori. However, that portrayal was highly fictionalized, and exaggerated character flaws prominent in the show do not appear to coincide with real life.

風水の音をきく

# Hear the Sound of Wind and Water

Whatever the case may be, this is a Way founded on deception. The experience of victory is nothing more than attacking with various pretexts, shifting from one tactic to the next, and forcing your opponent's hand. Before engagement, be aware that the adversary is in Attack, and never let your heedfulness slacken. *Shita no tsukuri*, a downward centeredness, is indispensable. If you do not consider your opponent in Attack, your usual techniques will be futile when you are set upon precipitately and furiously the moment the fight begins.

Once one is engaged, it is essential to put the mind, body, and feet in Attack, and the hands in Waiting. Take in everything before your eyes. This is the lesson of grasping what is before you. If one does not observe with uttermost calm, all the lessons of the sword will be useless.

"Hearing the sound of wind and water" means to be calm and silent above and to stay intensely alert underneath. The wind has no voice; it makes a sound when it hits something. When it blows above, it is silent. When it blows below, touching tree, bamboo, and all creation, its sound is boisterous and frenzied.

Water too has no voice when it falls from above. Touching things when it comes down, it makes a rushing sound. Taking these figures as examples, the saying means being calm and silent above while staying intensely alert underneath. These are instances of having utmost calm and stirless quiet on the surface, while keeping resolutely alert on the inside.

It is bad when the body, hands, and feet are rushed. Attacking and Waiting should be applied one on the inside and one on the outside. It is bad to be fixed on one over the other. One should contemplate the mutually changing *yin* and *yang*. Movement is yang, stillness is yin. Yin and yang move within and without; when yang moves within, be still without in yin. When yin is within, yang is manifested without.

This holds for the martial arts as well: activating the Ki within, moving resolutely, while without one remains stirless and quiet. This is in accordance to the precepts of nature. What is more, when furiously in Attack on the exterior, if one is calm within while in Attack without, so that the inner mind is not seized by the outside, the exterior will not be in disarray. If one moves both exterior and interior, at once there will be disarray. Attacking and Waiting, moving and stirless, should interchange with exterior and interior. Waterfowl float on the surface of the water, placid above while paddling below. In the same way,

*Roben Waterfall at Ohyama in Sagami Province. From the series* A Tour of Waterfalls in Various Provinces. Pilgrims Bathing at the Bottom of the Waterfall. *Katsushika Hokusai (1760–1849). Oban Tate-e. Catalogue No. 1709c.*

if one keeps the inner mind vigilant and accumulates results from this practice, inner mind and outside dissolve, inside and outside become one, without the least impediment. To reach this level is the ultimate achievement.

病気

# Sickness

To think with a one-track mind of winning is a sickness. To think with a one-track mind of martial arts is a sickness. To think with a one-track mind of displaying what one has learned is a sickness, as is thinking only of Attacking or only of Waiting. To think obsessively about getting rid of sickness is also a sickness. To fixate the mind on any single thing is considered a sickness. All these various sicknesses exist in the mind, therefore, one must temper the mind to be rid of them.

*Opposite page: Ono Waterfall, The Kiso Highway. From the series* A Journey to the Waterfalls of All the Provinces. *Katsushika Hokusai (1760–1849). Oban Tate-e. Catalogue No. 1710c.*

*The Mist Spraying Waterfall at Nikko. From the series One Hundred Views of Famous Places in the Provinces. Hiroshige II (1826–1869).*

## 病をさるに初重

# Understanding the Beginning Level of Eliminating Sickness

Go beyond thought to enter No-Thought, go beyond attachment to enter Non-Attachment. The crux of this is that thinking to eliminate sickness is itself thought. The desire to eradicate sickness is immersed in thought. What we call sickness is, in fact, obsessive thinking. Thinking to eradicate sickness is a thought. However, one can use thought to eliminate thought. Eliminating thought, one is void of thought. In such a way, one arrives at No-Thought by going through thought. If one can eliminate the sickness of remaining thought with thought, after that both the thought of eliminating and the thoughts to be eliminated will vanish. This is called using a wedge to remove a wedge. When a wedge is stuck, drive another wedge into it and the first wedge will loosen and come out. Once the stuck wedge is removed, the wedge driven in afterward will not remain either. When sickness is gone, the thought of removing sickness also does not remain afterward. Thus, this is called using thought to arrive at No-Thought. The thought of getting rid of sickness is being attached to sickness, but in using that attachment to remove sickness, the attachment will not remain. Thus, this is called using attachment to arrive at Non-Attachment.

## 病をさるに後重

# Understanding the Advanced Level of Eliminating Sickness

In the advanced level, eliminating sickness is having no mind at all to think of eliminating sickness. To think of eliminating is itself sickness. To resign to sickness, while mingling in the midst of sickness, is to eliminate sickness. Thinking of eliminating sickness exists in the mind where sickness is not eliminated. Therefore, sickness is not eliminated at all, and whatever one does or thinks is done with attachment, so there is no special merit in it. In what way should this be understood? The answer is: these two levels, beginning and advanced, are set up for this purpose. Having accumulated results from cultivating the beginner's mind, one's attachments are left behind, without one's thinking to eliminate them. By sickness is meant attachment. Attachment is deeply despised in Buddhism. A monk who has left attachment behind can mingle in the dust of the mundane world without being of the world. Whatever he does, he does freely, stopping whenever the time is right. An expert practitioner of the arts cannot be called a *meijin*, a master, unless he is free from attachment to his various skills. Dust and dirt cling to an uncut gemstone, but a cut and polished gemstone will remain unscathed even if it falls into the mud. Polish the gem of your mind by discipline and cultivation so it remains unscathed, resign to sickness, discard the mind, whatever you do, do freely.

*Opposite page: Rokuban hidara-Gempei. Utagawa Kunisada (1786–1864). Circa 1825. Colored woodblock print.*

# THE TSUBA
# THE PALETTE OF THE SWORD

The *katana* and other styles of Japanese swords were historically characterized by the *tsuba*, a round or square guard on the end of the sword grip. Modern Japanese swords fashioned for ceremonial purposes still feature the tsuba, usually with intricate artwork and engraving.

The tsuba allowed control of the arm and protection of the hand for the swordsman. In a duel, the swordsman used the tsuba to push off from his opponent; the two swordsmen would lock their swords together and then push away to resume a fighting stance and regain balance. The *tsubazeriai,* a standoff before an important sword fight, literally translates as "clash with tsuba," but the word has transitioned into usage in modern Japanese language as an expression that means "preparing" for something.

In the early age of the samurai, tsuba were designed for straightforward utility and were made of strong metals, but later, during the Edo period, tsuba became ornamental and were fashioned from less practical materials such as wood and gold. In contrast to earlier examples, modern tsuba are even more heavily decorated and are made from such materials as silver, brass, gold, copper, and iron, and they often feature an inlay above the design to create the effect of depth. It is also common for a Japanese swordsman with samurai roots to design a tsuba with a family crest, so that it might be passed down through generations.

Guards made with softer metals were often formed into the same shapes as iron tsuba but were much thinner and featured raised rims to offer rigidity. One type, the *kagamishi* tsuba, was cast from bronze and typically presented geometric figures and organic motifs. In this way, the metals and designs used are often compared to those of mirrors of the same period. More commonly, the decoration of tsuba ranged from dragons to family crests, with nearly everything in between. Many schools and families developed their own styles, and during certain periods, military requirements affected the designs and carvings allowed. The shape of the tsuba could also vary widely, though many were traditionally made in either rounded or squared shapes. A *kobushi,* or fist-shaped tsuba, was also a popular form. Inlay coverings, known as *zogan,* were common on ancient tsuba.

The *gomoku-zogan,* "mixed inlay," was one in which brass wiring was wound haphazardly over the design.

The *hira-zogan* was an inlay polished to lie flush with the surface of the tsuba design.

The *numome-zogan* was a design in which the iron surface of the tsuba was covered with hatched etchings or cuts and then covered with a wire or foil inlay.

A *sumi-zogan,* "ink inlay," was chiseled into the tsuba with slanted edges to create depth. The result would resemble an ink painting beneath the surface of the tsuba.

Artisans also used many methods of carving to decorate tsuba:

*Katakiribori* was a method in which an artisan chiseled the iron or metal in imitation of a painter's brushstrokes, creating uneven lines in both width and depth.

*Kebori,* "hair chiseling," was a method in which the artist used strokes uniform in both depth and size.

*Guribori* involved welding layers of copper with *shaduko* (an alloy of mostly copper with some gold) to give the tsuba the impression of carved lacquer.

*Sukidashibori,* literally "relief carving," was a method in which the artist carved a shallow design and then cut away the ground of the tsuba to leave a raised design.

*Takabori iroe* used the same method of raised design as sukidashibori, but with a metal different from that of the main body of metal of the tsuba. An inlay was then created of additional metals.

*Above: Tosho tsuba. Momoyama period. Circa 1600s. Iron.*
*Opposite page: Detail of tsuba on tachi. Kirimon, Ashifaga family. Circa 1500.*

*Top left: Iron tsuba with Sukashi cuts. Signed by Masahiro at age 62. Late Edo period. 1800s.*

*Top right: Iron tsuba with brass inlaid hawk feathers and flower. Edo period. 1700s.*

*Above left: Iron tsuba with Sukashi war fan & brass flower inlay. Edo period. 1800s.*

*Above right: Iron tsuba with brass Hhawk feathers & flower inlayed brass. Late 1500s.*

*Left: Tsuba. Edo period. 1600–1870.*

*Opposite page, top left: Iron tsuba hammered with Christian cross. Sukashi. Edo period. 1600s.*

*Opposite page, top right: Iron tsuba with carved waves. Edo period. Choshu school. 1800s.*

*Opposite page, middle left: Iron tsuba with dragonfly carved & inlayed. Edo period. 1800s.*

*Opposite page, middle right: Iron tsuba, signed by sword maker Yashutomo. Edo period. 1800s.*

*Opposite page, bottom left: Iron tsuba with Sukashi dragonfly. Edo period. 1800s.*

*Opposite page, bottom right: Iron tsuba with carved and inlayed dragon in clouds and matching fuchi. Edo period. 1800s.*

*Sword pommel, early Japanese, 6th century. Bronze with gilt.*

平常心是れ道
# The Normal Mind

A monk asked Kotoku, the Old Virtuous One, "What is the Way?" Kotoku replied saying, "The normal mind is the Way." This story contains a principle that connects all the arts. When asked to explain what the Way is, the Old Virtuous One said that the normal mind is the Way. Truly, this is the ultimate. This is the level in which sicknesses of the mind are all eliminated and one has achieved a normal mind, free from sickness while mingling with sickness. Applying this to the worldly affairs, when one is shooting a bow and being mindful of shooting a bow, the aim of the bow will be erratic and uncontrolled. When wielding a sword, if one is being mindful of wielding a sword, the sword point will be unmanageable. When writing with a brush, if one is being mindful of writing with a brush, one's brush will be ungainly. Even when one is playing the *koto*, if one is mindful of playing, the melody will go off-key.

When an archer forgets his mindfulness of shooting and shoots the bow with a normal mind, unconscious of what he is doing, the bow will be unwavering. When wielding a sword or riding a horse, one does not "wield a sword" or "ride a horse." Just as one does not "write" or "play the koto." When everything is done with a normal mind, with no intention of accomplishing anything, then everything goes smoothly and effortlessly.

Whatever Way you choose to follow, if you think, "This is it!" or fixate on it, then this is not the Way. A person who has nothing in his chest—he is on the Way. When one has nothing in one's chest, everything becomes simple and achievable, whatever one does. It is like a mirror that reflects every form clearly because it is clear and formless. Inside the heart of one on the Way is like a mirror: because it is void and clear, it has No-Mind and can accomplish anything. This is the normal mind. One who can accomplish anything with his normal mind is called a *meijin*.

In whatever one does, if one holds onto the intention of doing it correctly and focuses single-mindedly, one will flounder. Doing something well once, one thinks "well done," and then does it once more, but poorly. Or, doing something well twice, and once poorly, one rejoices in doing well two out of three times, then once again does poorly, leaving nothing settled. This is because one does it with the thought of doing well. When one is oblivious to accruing skills, and has accumulated experience, thoughts of wanting to make swift progress will fall away neatly. Then, in everything one does, without realizing it, one has reached No-Thought and No-Mind. Like the movements of a wooden puppet, one will have No-Self and one's body, hands, and feet will act on their on accord, without giving them thought. Ten times out of ten one will not stumble. Even at this moment, if the mind is engaged, however slightly, one will blunder. When one has No-Mind one succeeds every time. No-Mind does not mean a total lack of mind. It is simply the Normal Mind.

木人花鳥に対するが如し
# Like a Man of Wood Watching Flowers and Birds

In the words of Layman Pang, "Like a man of wood watching flowers and birds," the heart and mind are not moved even though his eyes are on flowers and birds. This is quite rational because a wooden man has no heart and mind to be moved. How is it that a person with a heart and mind becomes like a wooden man? The wooden man is a trope. A person with a heart and mind has nothing in common with wood. As a human being, one cannot be like bamboo and wood. In seeing flowers, one does not see them by creating anew a heart/mind that sees flowers.

It can be said, rather, that one sees with the Normal Mind, with No-Mind. When shooting a bow, one does not shoot by creating anew the percipience of shooting a bow. Rather, one shoots with the Normal Mind. The Normal Mind is said to be No-Mind. If one changes the Normal Mind, one doesn't create a new one; one's form will also change so as to move you inside and outside. If one does everything with a modulating mind, nothing will be as it should be. Even if it be only a single word spoken, people will praise it insofar as it is said in a modulating manner. What is called the Unmoving Mind of the Buddhas is truly recognized as praiseworthy.

The two sections above are to be used in acquiring a mind that can eliminate the sickness of the martial arts.

# 中峯知尚云く、放心心を具せよ
# Freeing the Mind

Master Zhongfeng Mingben said, "One must possess a mind that frees the mind." There are two levels, beginning and advanced, attached to these words. When one frees the mind, it travels until it has come to a stop, therefore the first level of practice teaches to not let the mind stop, but to make it return steadily. When one strikes a blow with his sword, the mind lingers where the blow was struck; this teaching is to make the mind return soundly to oneself.

The advanced level is to let the mind go free, to go wherever it will. Let go of the mind so that it will not be dilatory even when it is set free. To make an instrument of the mind that frees the mind means that one will not be free so long as one possesses a mind-freeing mind that continues to get caught in a net and pulled back to oneself. The mind that is not dilatory even when it is set free is called the mind-freeing mind. If one makes an instrument of this mind-freeing mind, freedom is engaged. Being caught in a net is not freedom. Even dogs and cats are best raised unleashed. Tying up a dog or cat is no way to raise them.

People who read Confucian texts obsess over the word "deference," thinking it superlative, and spending their whole life on respect, turn their minds into something like a leashed cat. Neither is Buddhism without the word "deference." The scriptures relate of one being *isshin buran*, single-minded and undisturbed. This corresponds to the word "deference." It means placing the mind on one thing and not letting it fly off in other directions. Of course there are places where "We deferentially call on the Buddha…" is recited, and "being deferential" is facing an image of the Buddha in a single-minded, respectful obeisance. These examples all have meanings in accord with the word deference.

However, these are *hōben*, expedients, at any rate, for subduing a mind disturbed. A well-controlled mind does not use expedients to placate it.

When one's mouth invokes the Great Sage Fudo, the posture correct and palms pressed together, contemplate the image of Acalanātha in your heart and mind. At this time, the three forms—physical, oral, mental—are made equal, and one is single-minded and undisturbed. This is called "the three mysteries in equilibrium." In other words, this is in accord with the word "respect." Respect is indispensable to the virtue of *honshin*, Original Mind, yet this state of mind lasts only as long as one practices the ritual. When one releases one's hands in prayer and stops chanting the Buddha's name, the image of Buddha in the mind also disappears, and the mind returns to its former disturbed state. This is not a mind pacified wholly.

A person who has been able to pacify the mind once does not purify the physical, oral, and mental forms; he can mingle in the dust of the world unstained. Though he is active all day, he is unmoved, like the moon, unchanging in its mutability, moving in myriad ripples upon the water, remains unmoved in its true form. Such is the state of one who has attained the highest level of Buddhist Law. Here I have recorded the instructions received from a Zen monk.

*A Fine Framed Roironuri Panel in Gold and Black Hiramakie Depicting a Boy Running to Catch Two Dragonflies Flying Above a Veranda. Japan. Meiji period.*

*Face mask (mempo). Circa 1600.*

*Netsuke. Masanao (IV or V). Japan. Circa 1900–1950. Wood.*

*Guardians (pair).*
*Hanging scroll.*
*Japan. 1500–1573.*

# BUDDHISM AND THE SWORDSMAN
# THE INTEGRATION OF RELIGION AND COMBAT

Although Buddhism projects the image of being a religion of peace, its history in Japan has been intertwined with warfare. In the Middle Ages, small armies of Buddhist priests and monks became warriors, typically fighting on behalf of peasants' rights, and many samurai, disenchanted with the battlefield, also became Buddhist monks. But for the typical samurai, there was no distinction, even in the heat of battle, between his work as a warrior and his adherence to Zen Buddhism. Zen, after all, had many important applications in warfare, particularly in helping the warrior maintain his focus and not to fear death.

The person most responsible for bringing Zen to the samurai was a Buddhist monk named Dogen Zenji, who was born in the year 1200. After receiving a basic education in Buddhist teachings at the Hiyei monastery, Dogen Zenji crossed the sea for China, where he spent four years at the foot of a Zen master. When he came home around 1227, he did his best to live in quiet meditation, writing poems about the transitory nature of life, the eternal peace of nirvana, the beauties of nature, and the distracting vanities of the world. "To study the Way is to study the self," Dogen Zenji taught. "To study the self is to forget the self. To forget the self is to be enlightened by everything in the universe."

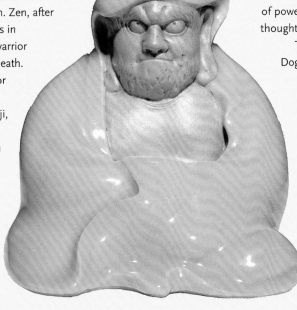

*A koryo-style celadon figure of Daruma Sozan. Meiji period.*

As Dogen Zenji's writings spread, scholars and aristocrats came from throughout Japan to talk to him. The more popular he became, the more he craved solitude, eventually retreating into a remote monastery that an admiring warlord had constructed for him. Nevertheless, twenty years later, when Hojo Tokiyori, the shogun's regent, asked him to come to Kamakura, he complied.

At that time, most of Japan's affairs were officially managed by the shogun in his samurai stronghold in Kamakura, but in practice, the true power in Kamakura was exercised behind the scenes, by the shogun's regents. Hojo Tokiyori was a skilled regent who devoted much of his time to settling land disputes between his vassals and establishing a stronger court system. But beginning with the year and a half that Dogen Zenji resided in the seat of power Kamakura, Tokiyori turned his thoughts to religion.

Through his conversations with Dogen Zenji, Tokiyori became so thoroughly captivated by Zen that he began ordering the construction of Zen temples, much to the consternation of the adherents of the two dominant Buddhist sects, Tendai and Shingon, who referred to Zen practitioners as "devils." Tokiyori was not swayed by their objections. In 1256, he abdicated his office and became a Zen monk, although he continued to hold his powers as regent. It was under Tokiyori's regime that samurai began to be associated with Zen. A popular saying during the Kamakura period divided the Buddhist sects according to caste: Tendai was for the emperor, Shingon was for the nobility, Pure Land (a populist utopian faith) was for the peasants, and Zen was for the samurai, who found practical applications for its emphasis on a fully focused mind and its view on the impermanent nature of life.

For Dogen Zenji and his followers, the key to understanding life came through a form of individual meditation known as *zazen*, literally "sitting Zen," or meditating cross-legged in a Buddha-like pose, with one hand outstretched, its palm facing up to receive wisdom. To calm his mind, the practitioner directed his focus on breathing or on the energy center located below the navel. In the Soto form of Zen adopted by the samurai, the goal was to achieve *shikantaza*, "trancelike sitting," a state in which the meditators are totally alert to their surroundings and yet are free of thoughts, without focusing on any particular object or occurrence.

With enough practice, it was not necessary for the samurai to remain seated to achieve the state of zazen. Once a person achieves enlightenment, "there is no gap between. . .zazen and everyday life," wrote Dogen Zenji. Essentially, zazen simply consists of concentration and focus, important qualities on the battlefield, or any situations where it is impossible to squat into the lotus position. Suzuki Shosan, a samurai who became a monk after fighting in some of the major battles of the late sixteenth century, wrote that "all the arts, including the art of war, are produced with the energy from meditation. The art of war cannot develop in an unfocused mind. . . .This energy of meditation is everything." He warned that most warriors only have this state of mind when they are performing their duties. As soon as they put down their swords, they relax their attention. But a true practitioner of Zen, he said, always uses the energy of meditation, never relaxing it. "That's why he is never defeated."

Another thing that attracted the samurai to Zen was its emphasis on impermanence, or *mujo*. In Buddhism, impermanence is one of the three characteristics of existence (the other two being dissatisfaction and separation from the soul). Existence is a cycle of constant birth, death, and rebirth. Nothing is permanent; everything is fated to die. In Japanese, this belief is expressed in the phrase *setsuna shometsu*, "everything dies as soon as it is born."

Belief in impermanence is a key element of samurai philosophy, since it prepares the warrior for death on the battlefield. For this reason, samurai decorated their swords and armor with pictures of such things as fruit

*Chest protector and hip guards. Japan. 1800–1868. Textile, metal, and leather.*

blossoms, snowflakes, and ocean waves. Fruit blossoms bloom, die, and disintegrate within a matter of weeks; snowflakes melt at the touch of heat and evaporate; ocean waves crest, crash, and disappear. All are symbols of the impermanence and the relative shortness of life and of the ever-present possibility of death.

Takeda Shingen, a samurai renowned for his cavalry tactics, put it this way: "Zen has no secrets other than seriously thinking about life and death." Shingen memorably quoted a Zen saying about impermanence when he faced death on the battlefield. As he was lying prone, with an enemy swordsman about to chop off his head, he was asked if he had any last words. "A snowflake on a red-hot furnace," Shingen replied, but it ended up not being his day to die. As he parried the enemy's sword with his ironclad war fan, two of his aides ran up and killed his attacker. Such calmness and acceptance reflect important concepts for warriors on the battlefield; once it is understood that life is impermanent, it becomes easier to think about death; the more death is thought about, the less it is feared; and the less death is feared, the more easily it can be avoided.

Suzuki Shosan, the samurai who became a monk, told his students to "set everything aside and study only death. Study death all the time, freeing yourself from it, so when it finally comes, you won't be disconcerted." Shosan wrote that, by constantly studying death *(shi ni narau)*, practitioners could receive "death energy," the heart-pounding, adrenaline-filled energy that comes when facing the possibility of imminent demise. "I adopt the mind of a person who's about to have his throat cut, just as if somebody's about to slash my own throat. . . ," he wrote. "At first I thought it was harmful, but later I understood that this was the perfect cure for any disease." To live each day as if it were your last can provide the sense of freedom that comes from knowing you have nothing left to lose.

*Opposite page: Himeji castle.*

# The Life-Giving Sword

## 百様の構
## One Hundred Stances

"Even if there are a hundred kinds of stances and positions, victory is won with one only." The epitome of this thought is the *shuji shuriken*—what might one's opponent be "concealing in the palm of his hand"?—and how is one to observe and anticipate his actions?

Even if teachings and lessons of a hundred or a thousand kinds of stances and techniques are acquired, including learning a hundred skills, the shuji shuriken alone is the look of the eyes. Even if the opponent knows a hundred stances, and oneself knows a hundred, the decisive point is the shuji shuriken of the eyes. Because this is secretly transmitted, it is not written in its true Chinese characters, but in characters borrowed for their sound.

## 有無の拍子

## The Rhythm of Existence and Nonexistence and the Existence of Both What Is and What Is Not

These teachings of Existence and Nonexistence refer to shuji shuriken, the knowledge of aptitude and potentiality. When revealed, they are existent; when concealed, they are nonexistent. These revealing and concealing "existence and nonexistence" are called shuji shuriken, the knowledge of aptitude and potentiality. They are in the hand that clasps the sword.

In Buddhism, the doctrine of existence and nonexistence are communicated, and used here as a correlative. The masses see the existent, but not the nonexistent. With shuji shuriken, knowledge of aptitude and potentiality, one can see both the existent and nonexistent—both the existent and nonexistent exist. When there is existence, strike the existent; when there is nonexistence, strike the nonexistent. Also, strike the nonexistent without waiting for its existence; strike the existent without waiting for its nonexistence. Therefore it is said that both existence and nonexistence exist.

In a commentary on Laozi's classic it is said "ever existent, ever nonexistent." Existence is ever present; nonexistence is ever present. When concealed, existence becomes nonexistence; when revealed, nonexistence becomes existence.

For example, when a waterfowl floats on the water, it is existence. When it dives under the water, it is nonexistence. Therefore, even when one thinks something exists, when concealed, it is nonexistence; even when one thinks something is nonexistent, when revealed, it exists. Existence and nonexistence, then, are simply concealing and revealing, essentially one and the same. Thus both existence and nonexistence are ever present.

In Buddhism, these are called fundamental existence and fundamental nonexistence. When a person dies, the existent is concealed; when a person is born the nonexistent is revealed—in substance, ever present. In reality, the same.

It is said that existence and nonexistence are in the hand that clasps the sword. This is a secret transmission. It is called shuji shuriken, the knowledge of aptitude and potentiality. When one's hand is hidden, what is present is concealed. When one's hand is palm side up, what is not present is revealed. Be that as it may, these words are difficult to understand without transmission via face-to-face communication.

When there is existence, one should see it and strike it; when there is nonexistence, one should see it and strike it. That is why it is said "both existence and the nonexistence exist." The thing called existence is, by any other name, nonexistence. The thing called nonexistence is, by any other name, existence. Existence and nonexistence are not two.

# The Sword & the Mind

If one misapprehends the existence and nonexistence of these shuriken, knowledge of aptitude and potentiality, victory will not be yours, even though one exhausts one hundred techniques. All manner of martial art is perfected in this one step.

*Preceding pages: Incident at Kawakanajima, in which Shingen deflects Kenshin's blow with his iron war fan.*
*Below: Hideyoshi, adorned in kabuto (sun rays), directs the battle.*

# THE ART AND SCIENCE OF SWORD MAKING

The ancient Japanese art and science of making a *katana* blade is one of extreme precision, skill, and patience. The blade of a samurai sword is not just a solid formation of metal; it is actually tens of thousands of layers of steel folded again and again to achieve the proper thickness.

Ancient Japanese smiths used *tamahagane*, a pure steel, to make blades, and today, swords made from tamahagane are considered some of the strongest in the world. At the start of the process, smelters spend days shoveling tons of iron-rich sand and charcoal into a *tatara*, or clay furnace, as much as twenty-five tons to make one single batch of tamahagane. The charcoal, because of its high-carbon content, allows the tatara to reach up to 2,500 degrees Fahrenheit.

The traditional smelting method takes three full days and three full nights. During the procedure, it is important that smelters keep the tamahagane from reaching a molten state. The amount of carbon in the steel must vary across the sword to produce a range of hardness and softness throughout the blade. Makers of the katana use both high-carbon and low-carbon tamahagane. The high-carbon metal is extremely rigid and allows the sword to have a razor-sharp edge but is also brittle and easy to break, while the tough low-carbon metal offers shock absorption. On the third night of the smelting procedure, the tatara masters break open the furnace and expose the tamahagane to the air, allowing pieces of the newly formed steel to break apart, and be examined to determine levels of carbon.

The tatara masters then choose the best pieces of

*Sword making was a high art in ancient Japan, passed down from generation to generation. Traditional sword makers, although they are few, continue these practices into modern times.*

*The smith heats and hammers the steel.*

*The polisher sharpens the edge of the forged blade.*

*A decorative menuki, also used to help the swordsman position his hand, is attached to the grip.*

*A wooden scabbard is created and may be decorated with leather, stones, or fine metals.*

tamahagane to send to a sword smith, who begins the process of removing impurities and forming the blade. The smith heats and hammers the steel, folding it over many times to combine the iron and carbon.

After eliminating every trace of slag from the blade, the smith reheats the high-carbon steel and shapes it into a long, horseshoe-shaped channel, after which he hammers the low-carbon steel and shapes it to fit snugly inside the channel. The two metals are forged together so that the hard steel forms the outer shell and blade, soon to have a razor-sharp edge, while the soft shell serves as the shock-absorbing core. These two elements together make one of the most durable weapons in the world.

Once the steel has been formed for the blade, the sword is covered with a mixture of clay and powdered charcoal, a mixture that insulates the blade and gives it the unique, wavy design known as the *hamon.* The katana is then placed back into the furnace and heated up to 1,500 degrees Fahrenheit, enough to soften the blade for curving. Having been heated to the smith's preference, the katana is quickly pulled from the fire and plunged into a large trough of

water. The rapid cooling of the blade during quenching affects the high- and low-carbon portions of the blade differently; the low-carbon steel contracts more quickly and freely than the high-carbon steel, causing the blade to bend.

Once the katana has been fully forged, bent, and cooled, the katana is sent to a polisher, who focuses on the sword's sharp edge. It can take nearly two weeks for the polisher to perfect the blade, rubbing it with "water stones," valuable pieces often passed through generations.

When the katana blade has been perfected by the polisher, metalworkers form the *tsuba,* the guard of the sword. The tsuba is fashioned from iron or other strong metals and is usually decorated with symbolic designs that have evolved throughout history. The tsuba has always been revered as one of the most important distinguishing qualities of the katana. In a final step, a wooden scabbard, or handle, is created, artfully covered with a combination of various decorative leathers, stones, and fine metals. In the end, nearly fifteen different masters of the trade, and often close to six months of time, have been invested in creating a single fine quality katana.

*Sake bottle, from Oribe. Japan. Ceramic.*

*Sake bottle. Japanese school. 17th century. Kyoto earthenware with overglaze enamels.*

*Battle flag. Japan. 1615–1800. Silk, paper, and gold foil.*

## 水月
# The Moon on the Water and Its Reflection

Between one's opponent and oneself, there is a certain distance at which one is outside the reach of the opponent's sword. This distance is maintained from which to deploy martial arts. To approach an opponent by stepping into this space or stealing into it is called "the moon on the water," like unto the moon's reflection cleaving the water. One should face off with an opponent only after having established a stage for the Moon on the Water in one's mind before the start of the bout. This distance must be transmitted orally.

## 神妙剣
# The Halcyon Sword

## 座の心懸身に取り足にとる
### Mindfulness of the Position Kept in the Body and Legs

The Halcyon Sword is of supreme importance. One has in oneself a place for wearing it; as for "oneself," the character for sword (*ken*) in Halcyon Sword is written and understood as "sword." Whether at the ready on the right or on the left, so long as the sword does not stray from the Halcyon Sword position, there is a point in using the character ken. As for one's opponent, the character ken for sword should be written and understood as the character ken for "see." Having seen clearly the position of the Halycon Swords so as to tear into one's opponent, the seeing is crucial. Thus there is import in the character ken for "seeing."

## 神・妙二字の釈
# Explanation of the Characters Used for "Halcyon"

*Shin* (spirit) is within, *myō* (wonder) is revealed without. Thus the word *shinmyō*, a supernatural wonder. By way of example, because shin resides within a tree, flowers blossom, wafting their scent, greenery effloresces, branches and leaves flourish; this is called myō, a wonder. Break down a tree, and still one will not see with the eyes anything like this thing called shin, but without it there would be no outward manifestation of flowers and greenery. For the shin of a person, too, there is nothing like shin inside a split-open body for the eye to see. However, because shin exists within, one is able to accomplish all manner of works.

When shin is situated in the place of the Halcyon Sword, wonders of all kinds are revealed in the hands and feet, and flowers are made to bloom in battle. Shin is the master of the mind. Shin resides within, using the heart and mind without. What is more, the heart and mind make service of Ki, the will. Making service of Ki, the mind works on the outside for the sake of shin. The heart and mind, if it tarries in one place, will function inadequately. For this reason, it is crucial that the heart and mind do not linger in one place. For example, the master of a house stays at home and sends a servant out on an errand. If the servant tarries on his mission and does not return, he will be unavailable for service. Likewise, if the heart and mind tarry over things and do not return to their original state, one's capability in the martial arts will slacken. This is why not letting the heart and mind tarry in one place applies to all things, not only the martial arts. Shin and heart/mind, these are two understandings.

## 歩みの事
# Pace

- Eliminating sickness: Three Points; Sickness in the Opponent
- Fixing the Gaze: Keeping Rhythm: to be transmitted orally
- Movement

In one's pace, be neither too fast nor too slow. Walking as one usually walks, stride smoothly in a casual manner. Go neither too far nor not far enough. Take the median. One goes too quickly because one is scared or upset. One goes too slowly because one is a coward and fears one's enemy. Be in a state of equipoise.

Wave a fan in front of a person's eyes and he will usually blink. This is normal—blinking does not mean that one is upset. But if something is swept before the eyes a number of times to startle, but without causing blinking at all, then one is upset. The mind that resists being made to blink by holding itself in check is more upset than when blinking. What is called the Immovable Mind equals what is normal. When something comes toward the eyes, the eyes will blink. This is the state of not being upset. First and foremost is simply not to forfeit the normal mind. To think, "I will not move!" is to have already done so. Moving itself is an unmovable principle. A turning waterwheel is normal, a stopped one something other than normal; blinking eyes are normal, the unblinking a mind in motion. It is good to stride smoothly in a normal manner, in an unchanging normal mind. At this stage, neither one's appearance nor one's mind is upset.

## 一理
## 向構の時の心懸　鑓の時の心持　無刀の用心

# The First Principle
## Mental Attitude in a Bout
## Attitude When Facing a Spear
## Precautions for No-Sword

What is called "the First Principle" is a cipher, a secret word in martial arts. For the most part in martial arts, it is to be free in whatever one does. What one does under pressure—that is the primary concern. Bear this in mind, watch carefully, and do not let oneself be caught unawares—these taken together are called the First Principle. The caution one takes in facing off an opponent with swords when one is barely outside his reach, or when

a spear comes within a forearm's length is called the First Principle. This is the caution exercised when, backed against a wall, one cannot retreat from an oncoming attack. It should be understood as exercising caution toward the gravest, most perilous of situations. When one has no sword, the forearm's length perimeter will become quite impossible if the eyes are locked on one spot, the mind lingers on one place, or one becomes negligent. Keeping things of this sort in mind is called the First Principle, and its secrecy is to be maintained.

## 敵身方両一尺　相寸、無刀の用心

# One Forearm's Length on Either Side
## When Swords Are Equal Length, Take No-Sword Precautions

Weapons of both combatants are to be kept a forearm's length from the body. Within a forearm's perimeter, one can sidestep and elude the opponent's blade. Entering this space is dangerous.

## 是極一刀

# This Is Supreme / First Sword

"This is supreme" signifies what is preeminent. "First Sword" does not signify the sword. It is a cipher for seeing the Incipient Moment in one's opponent. The all-important First Sword means that seeing an opponent's moves is the supreme First Sword; apprehending the opponent's Incipient Moment as the First Sword, apprehend the sword that strikes, following the opponent's movement, as the second sword. One is to make this fundamental, and use it in various ways. These are the *shuriken*, the Moon on the Water, the Halcyon Sword, and Sickness. These four, plus working of hands and feet make five, all told. These are learned as Five Contemplations, One Look. Seeing the shuriken, is One Look. The remaining four are kept in the mind, therefore they are called the Contemplations. Perceiving with the eye is called seeing, perceiving with the mind is called contemplating. This signifies meditation. These are called not the Four Contemplations and One Look, but rather the Five Contemplations, because five contemplations is the comprehensive term—one of which, the shuriken, is called the One Look. Shuriken, Moon on the Water, Halcyon Sword, Sickness, and Body-Hands-Feet—these are five items. Four of these are perceived in the mind, whereas one, the shuriken, is perceived with the naked eye, and is therefore called One Look.

## 水月、神妙剣、病気、身手足、此四の分別

# Differentiating Moon on the Water, Halcyon Sword, Sickness, and Body-Hands-Feet

Moon on the Water is choosing the location for a bout. Halcyon Sword is choosing a location on the body. Body-Hands-Feet is watching what one's opponent does, and one's own movement. Eliminating Sickness is for the purpose of seeing the shuriken. Therefore, the cardinal point is whether or not one can see the shuriken. The other four are generalities. Eliminating Sickness is for the purpose of seeing the shuriken. If sickness is not eliminated, one will be taken by it, resulting in a misreading. When one misreads the facts, one loses. Sickness means sickness of the mind. Sickness of the mind is when the mind lingers here and there. One must not let the mind tarry on the place where one has struck a blow of the sword. This is forsaking the mind without renouncing it.

## 敵のかまへ

# Opponent's Stance

When one's opponent takes a stance, confronting you with the tip of his blade, strike as he raises his sword. When one thinks to strike an opponent, let him strike at you. So long as the opponent strikes at you, he is as good as struck.

## 水月の場をとれ

# Take the Moon on the Water Position

Take the position of Moon on the Water, and from there focus on your state of mind. When one tries to take up a place, and one's opponent has already taken his place first, then make that place your own. So long as the perimeter does not change, even if the opponent advances five feet, or you advance five feet, the distance between the two of you remains the same. If someone has taken up a certain place, it is best to let him keep

*Maple Leaves and the Tekona Shrine and Bridge at Mama, from the series One Hundred Views of Famous Places in Edo. Ando Hiroshige (1797–1858). Japan.*

it. Getting over-involved in taking a place is bad. Maintain a resilience of the body.

## 足ぶみ

# Footwork

Footwork and body alignment should be such that the position of the Halcyon Sword is not let go. This frame of mind should be remembered all along, even before squaring off.

# BISHAMON
# THE GOD OF WARRIORS

Because Buddhism's founder, a warrior-prince named Gautama, eschewed warfare and preached nonviolence after gaining enlightenment, the religion is often thought of as pacifist in nature. "Do not kill" was the first of the five prohibitions in Buddhism, and killing was one of the ten major sins.

Yet from its beginnings, as with all major religions, an undercurrent of violence ran beneath the message of peace. In Japan, the violent nature of Buddhism is expressed through Bishamon, the armor-clad, spear-wielding god of war, who was the patron deity of the samurai. The concept of Bishamon, like most elements of Buddhism, has roots reaching directly back to India, where he was known as Vaishravana, one of the four kings ordained by heaven to rule the four directions, with Vaishravana being the guardian of the north.

When Prince Gautama was born, Vaishravana became his follower. And once Gautama had become a Buddha after gaining enlightenment, Vaishravana served as his messenger and protector, teaching him and his followers chants to ward off wild *yaksha*, the demonic ogres who haunted the wilderness, attacking and eating human trespassers. Through performing such valuable services, Vaishravana eventually attained the stage of *sotapanna*, meaning he would only have to be reincarnated seven more times before enlightenment. As with most of the demigods in Buddhism, when Vaishravana died, another Vaishravana was anointed to take his place, a process that was meant to continue for eternity.

As Buddhism migrated north through China and Korea to Japan, Vaishravana's name and image both began to change. In China, he was known as Píshamen Tian; in

*Bishamon was the patron deity of the samurai.*
*A Fine Large Wood Statue of Bishamon, Guardian of the North. Japan. 18th Century.*

Korea, he was Damun Cheonwang; and in Japan, he was formally referred to as Bishamonten (the Japanese suffix *ten*, like the Chinese *tian*, means "holy" or "heavenly"). In addition to his name, Vaishravana's nature evolved as well.

Within a few decades after Buddhism had been officially introduced to Japan, in 552 CE, roughly a thousand years after the religion was founded by Gautama, the imperial family had converted to Buddhism, and a cult dedicated to Bishamon had begun. But by the time Vaishravana had reached Japan, he was no longer a mere man, seven steps short of enlightenment; instead, he was a *kami*, which translates variously as a spirit or a god. Rather than using chants to stop evildoers, he took on a more militaristic function. In his right hand, the blue-skinned, full-bearded Bishamon held a weapon, typically a halberd or spear, signifying his skills in battle. In his left hand, he held a miniature pagoda, representing a treasure house, because he would share his riches with those who proved themselves worthy. As indicated, Bishamon was rapidly incorporated into the Japanese royal family. He was one of several gods who were said to be the grandparents or great-grandparents of the legendary Emperor Jimmu, the founder of the imperial line. More important, he was deemed to be a member of the *shichi fukujin*, the Seven Gods of Good Fortune.

In the year 597 CE, Prince Shotoku, the author of Japan's first constitution, became a leading proponent of the Bishamon cult. He invoked Bishamon's warlike powers as he battled the enemies of his kingdom—that is, followers of Shinto and other traditional religions who did not like to have Buddhism forced down their throats. When the wars were over, Shotoku built a temple to

*Tsuba with cut-out dragon. Kinai of Echizen. Japan. 18th century. Iron.*

innovative tactics, such as his practice of constantly trading wounded troops on the front lines with fresh replacements from the rear. He was so adept at battle that many of his followers believed that he was a reincarnation of Bishamon. The Dragon of Echigo, some called him, while others referred to him as Kenshin the War God. His best-known saying, when one of his enemies was trying to blockade food supplies, was suitably warlike: "Wars are won with swords and spears, not rice and salt."

But it would be a mistake to think that Bishamon was merely a god of war or that all of his followers were bloodthirsty. Bishamon was also a distributor of wealth, a protector of the righteous, a vanquisher of demons, a destroyer of plagues and pestilences, and a healer of disease. His Sanskrit-based name translates as "one who hears everything in the kingdom," the implication being that he was completely versed in the Buddha's teachings because of his fine listening skills. A Japanese ode to Bishamon ends with the words "in the present world he confers wisdom and fortune." And that is probably how many pacifist Buddhists would prefer to think of him.

Bishamon on Mount Shigi, northwest of the holy city of Nara. A statue of a tiger guarded the sacred temple as a reminder to believers that Bishamon would appear on Mount Shigi every twelve years, on the hour of the tiger on the day of the tiger in the year of the tiger.

Around the year 800 CE, Japan's first shogun, Sakanoue Tamuramaro, prayed to Bishamon for victory against a cruel warlord named Akuuro, who was living in Kamakura. After Tamuramaro won his battle, he built a shrine with 108 statues of Bishamon, who, besides being a patron of warriors, was said to be a punisher of evildoers. More than 200 years later, Minamoto Yoriyoshi, the next man to hold the title of shogun, also became a devotee, praying for his victories at the same temple that Tamuramaro had built. According to one legend, borrowed from an earlier Chinese tale, Bishamon descended to earth in a dark cloud in order to chase away some of Yoriyoshi's enemies. After Yoriyoshi emerged victorious, his military stronghold in Kamakura became the true center of power in Japan, and the samurai who joined his army also joined him in worshipping Bishamon and other gods of war. Some samurai even had images of Bishamon embossed into their sword blades.

Perhaps one of the most devoted followers of Bishamon was Uesugi Kenshin, a *daimyo*, or lord, who ruled Echigo province in the mid-sixteenth century, toward the latter end of the Warring States period. Claiming Bishamon and the Shinto war god Hachiman as his inspirations, Kenshin became renowned for his martial arts skills and his

*Battle of Hogen in 1156. Japan. 1568–1615. Ink on paper.*

神妙剣見る事、三段の分別

# Seeing the Halcyon Sword: Differentiating Three Levels

Seeing with the mind is fundamental. It is because one sees from the mind that the eyes also see. Therefore seeing with the eyes is secondary to seeing with the mind. Next after that is seeing with the body-feet-hands. Not letting one's body-feet-hands miss the opponent's Halcyon Sword is called seeing with body-feet-hands. Seeing with the mind is for the benefit of seeing with the eyes. Seeing with the eyes is aiming the feet and hands at the position of the opponent's Halcyon Sword.

心は水の中の月に似たり、形は鏡の上の影の如し

# Mind Is Like the Moon on the Water, Body Is Like a Reflection in a Mirror

The sense for applying these phrases to the martial arts is this: an image of the moon lodges in the water, an image of the body lodges in a mirror. The reflection of things in a person's heart and mind is like the moon reflecting on the water, reflecting at once, without pause. The position of the Halcyon Sword is like unto water, the heart and mind like unto the moon. The heart and mind should be reflected in the position of the Halcyon Sword. Where the heart and mind go, the body goes. The body follows the heart and mind.

A mirror is like unto the Halcyon Sword in the sense that these phrases apply to moving one's body like a reflection toward the position of the Halcyon Sword. The principle of this is not to release the hands and feet from the position of the Halcyon Sword.

The reflecting of the moon on the water is an immediate occurrence. It casts its reflection on the water from high, high up in the sky as soon as the clouds disperse. The moon's reflection is not something that descends gradually from the sky. It is reflected at once, in the blink of an eye. This is a trope for the way things reflect in a person's heart and mind, as immediately as the moon reflects on the water.

In Buddhist scripture it is said that the immediacy of the mind is like the moon reflected on the water or an image reflected in a mirror. This does not mean that the moon reflected on the water appears to be there, but is not—if one tries scooping it from the water. But rather that from high up in the sky the moon casts a reflection instantaneously. Just as a form in front of a mirror is reflected immediately. This is a trope for immediacy. Such is the way a person's mind reflects on things. The mind may travel as far away as China in the blink of an eye. Just as one thinks to be dozing off, one's dreams travel more than a thousand miles away to one's native village. The Buddha explained this sort of reflection of the mind as being like the moon on the water or an image in a mirror. These phrases, similarly, apply to the "Moon on the Water" in martial arts. Like the moon reflecting on the water, one should cast one's mind on an appropriate place. As the mind goes, so goes the body. Thus, as soon as a bout is under way, one should locate one's body in the appropriate place as an image is reflected in a mirror. If one's mind does not go before, prepared in advance, the body will not go. The location is "Moon on the Water"; the body is the "Halcyon Sword." In either event, the meaning of locating the body-feet-hands is the same.

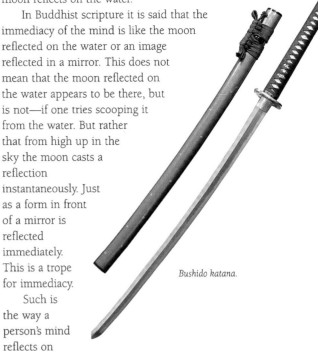

*Bushido katana.*

急々にかかる事

# Quick Attack

A quick attack is extraordinarily bad. Keeping one's *shita no tsukuri*—mental preparation—keen, attack quickly only after having taken everything in once the bout has begun. It is crucial not to get excited.

# THE EVOLUTION OF JAPANESE ARMOR

*Detail of dark blue samurai armor.*

In the earliest days of Japanese warfare, samurai fought protected by breastplates made of leather strips sewn onto cloth, and by metal helmets. Both can be found in burial mounds dating back to before 400 BCE. Over the centuries, the armor evolved into colorful, elaborate suits of lamellar, or plates of lacquered leather, iron, and steel tied together with cords. This not only protected the warrior but served to announce his clan, rank, and lineage. The armor became a potent symbol of the glories of Japanese chivalry and is even today displayed in the homes of the wealthy and influential.

Lamellar armor was common throughout many areas of the ancient world, such as Sparta, Scythia, and Assyria, but the oldest lamellar uniforms ever found were in a tomb in China, dating back to the fifth century BCE. The Chinese used plates of iron or strips of buffalo hide to make their armor, to which they then applied thick coats of lacquer to strengthen the hide

and protect the iron from rust. Finally, the plates were stitched together with cords of leather or silk. By the late eighth century CE, this style of armor had made it to Japan, where it was sometimes referred to as *karakawa*, "Chinese leather."

The Japanese quickly turned lamellar into their own creation. Each family of samurai had its own armor makers, known as *gusokushi*, who personalized the armor. They ensured that it fit appropriately and also added distinctive embellishments, such as family mons, geometric designs, and images from nature such as cherry blossoms or seaweed.

The trick was to ensure that the armor was heavy enough to ward off attacks, but light enough to allow swift movement. Key pieces of samurai armor included:

*Kabuto (helmet).* The helmet typically came in two pieces: the *hachi*, to protect the top of the head, and the *shikoro*, to protect the neck. Often, there was also a distinctive ornament depicting the family's crest or a symbol of particular importance to the wearer.

*Hachi (helmet dome).* The *hachi* was originally a simple bowl-shaped helmet of metal strips welded together, which could be used with or without a shikoro. Eventually, the helmet evolved into a wide variety of shapes, including *shiinomigata* (acorn-shaped), *momogata* (peach-shaped), and *sujikabuto* (veined). By the fifteenth century, the helmet was bolstered by an array of long metal strips *(hoshikabuto)* that radiated out from an opening in the top called the *tehen.* The tehen began as a hole that samurai could pass their topknots through, but in later years it was used as a base for ornaments.

*Shikoro (neck shield).* The *shikoro* was an array of lamellar plates suspended from the helmet to protect the back and sides of the neck. In the beginning, the plates hung straight down from the helmet, but by the fifteenth century, the shikoro curved outward, which provided the warrior with more freedom of movement.

*Maedate, wakidate, or ushirodate (front, side, or rear crests).* Samurai decorated their helmets with crests, which could identify them during the confusion of the battlefield. Many warriors used their *mon* (family emblem) as a crest; others used symbols that reflected their religious leanings or other interests. Deer antlers, crescent moons, wings, and buffalo horns were among the more popular motifs.

*Mempo (face mask).* Samurai used leather or metal masks to cover the jaws, cheeks, nose, and chin, or sometimes the

Samurai helmet with a half-face mask. Japan. 1615–1650. Iron, leather, laminated paper, lacquer, and textile.

entire face. These mempo were often highly decorative, with the mouths shaped into scowls or grimaces. Some were etched with mustaches and beards, while others resembled Buddhist demons.

*Do (cuirass).* The *do* was typically a C-shaped piece of lamellar armor that wrapped around the torso, protecting the stomach, chest, and back (although some only protected the front). It was open at the right side, allowing the samurai to slide into it and then close it with cords beneath his right arm.

*Odoshi (lacing).* The *odoshi,* lacing made up of cords of silk or leather, held the armored plates together. It was also used as a means of identifying warriors on the battlefield, because different armies and different ranks within each army wore different colors of odoshi. For instance, the *Tale of the Heike,* written in 1371, recounts how one leading general laced his armor with green silk, while his deputy used flame-red lacing.

*32-plate suji-bashi. Dated Tebun 9th year (1532). Inlaid with silver tendrils and a dragon on the peak.*

*Blue-laced armor with an uichidashi do and 56-plate helmet. 1851.*

*Suit of armor (Yori). Saotome Iyetada. Japan. Circa 1600.*

*Sode (shoulder guards). Sode* were generally made of seven strips of lamellar, forming vertical sleeves for the shoulders and upper arms. One of the earliest forms of shoulder guards, the *hiro sode,* "broad sleeves," was narrower at the top than bottom, but eventually armorers developed *tsubo sode,* "jar sleeves," which were broader at the top, making a better fit for the contours of the upper arm. During the Warring States period, the sode were hinged to allow for better movement.

*Kote (armored sleeves).* In the early days, samurai typically only wore armor on their left arm, leaving their right arm bare. This the armor helped samurai archers keep the flowing sleeves of their robes from interfering with their arrows as they drew their bows. By the late twelfth century, samurai began wearing *kote* on both arms, made of the same material and using the same patterns as the *suneate* and *haidate,* protecting the legs.

*Kusazuri (armored skirting).* Similar to the leather skirting of Roman warriors, the kusazuri were long lamellar strips that protected the waist and upper thighs.

*Haidate (thigh guards).* Thigh guards were added in the late thirteenth century or early fourteenth century. Relatively few samurai wore them, because they impeded movement on the ground. On horseback, haidate were an invaluable protection against the swords, pikes, and lances of enemy foot soldiers trying to harass the cavalry. Most haidate were made with small rectangular or slightly rounded metal plates tied together with lacing.

*Tateage (knee guards).* Starting in the twelfth century, samurai used *tateage* made of plate metal or solidly lacquered leather to protect their knees. Eventually, most tateage were made of *kikko,* fabric interwoven with metallic plates, typically oblongs or hexagons, similar to the brigandine used by European knights.

*Suneate (shin guards).* Suneate consisted of vertical lamellar plates connected by hinges or chain mail. Originally, they were three simple plates that fit on the legs, but those were constricting, so by the Warring States period of the sixteenth century, they were splinted to provide movement.

*Opposite page: Fine Edo period armor.*

*A large Satsuma vase. Japan. 1868–1912.*

## 心をかへす事
# Making the Mind Return

The nuance of this phrase is: if, having struck a blow of the sword, one thinks "I have scored a blow," the mind that thinks "I have scored a blow" stops then and there. Because the mind does not return from the blow just struck, one's mind goes blank and the opponent's "second sword" scores a blow. The initiative one has taken is lost, and one is defeated by the opponent's counterblow.

Making the mind return means after having struck a blow do not leave the mind there, but rather after striking, pull the mind back to observe one's opponent's temperament. Once struck, the opponent's temperament changes. Having been struck, he will take umbrage and become angry. When angered, an opponent becomes vicious. If one is lax here, one will be struck.

It is best to regard one's opponent who has been struck as an angry boar. If one is aware of having struck a blow, the mind dwells on it and one becomes careless. Be awake to the fact that the opponent's energy will flow when he is struck. Also, the opponent will become cautious quickly about the place he was struck, so if one tries to strike again with the same intentions, one will miss. When one strikes and misses, the opponent seizes the opportunity to strike.

Making the mind return means not to let it linger at the point where one has struck and to pull it back to oneself. The idea is to make the mind return so as to observe the opponent's temperament. Or, not letting the mind return, but wielding multiple blows where one has dealt a direct hit, striking without letting up, not allowing the opponent to even turn his head, this is also the ultimate state of mind. This is known as "having a space no wider than a hair's breadth." The point is to keep striking without the slightest opening, a hair's breadth, between strokes.

In a Zen *mondo*, question and answer session, known as the "Battlefield of the Law," the space between a question and an answer is not even a hair's breadth. Should one dally, one will be bested by one's opponent. Who wins and who loses will be made clear. This is what is meant by

*Earthenware vase. Japan. Late 19th century.*

leaving no space, not so much as a hair's breadth. This is the quickness of sword strokes one after another.

## 一法と云ふ心持　空の心持　捧心の心持
# Understanding Total Elimination, the Void, Presenting the Mind

The meaning of total elimination is the eliminating of a number of things all at once. A number of things means sickness of many kinds; sickness means sickness of the mind. All these sicknesses in the mind are to be disposed of en masse. The many kinds of sickness are recorded elsewhere in this book. In general terms, sickness is the mind that is dilatory. In Buddhism this is called attachment, and is strictly renounced. If the mind is attached to one place and dallies there, one will miss what one should see, and suffer staggering defeat. The mind that dallies is a sickness. By total elimination is meant eradicating all these sicknesses en masse. Eliminate sickness all at once so as not to ignore "the only one."

"The only one," now, is called the Void. The Void is a cipher, a hidden word that must be transmitted secretly. By the Void is meant the mind of one's opponent. Mind is without form or substance, therefore it is Void. Seeing "the Void, the only one," means to see the mind of one's opponent. Buddhism enlightens one to the emptiness of mind. Although there are those who preach that mind is emptiness, it is said that the enlightened man is rare.

As regards "presenting the mind," the opponent's mind is presented in the hands that grasp the sword. The clinched fists that grasp the sword are to be struck even before he makes a move. "Total elimination" is for the purpose of seeing the incipient moment, just before he makes a move. This is known as eliminating a hundred sicknesses all at once, and not failing to see the Void.

The opponent's mind is in his hands; it is presented in his hands. Striking them when not moving is called "striking the Void." The Void does not move; having no form, it has no movement. Striking the Void means striking quickly before any movement. This thing called Void is the fundamental truth of Buddhism.

In the concept of Void, there is a distinction between false void and true void, false meaning counterfeit and true meaning actual. The false void is an analogy for nothingness, true void being emptiness, namely emptiness of mind. Although the mind is like emptiness, being without form, the One Mind is master of the body, performing manifold actions that are all in the mind. The movement and workings of the mind are the mind's doing. When the mind is not active, it is void; when the void is active, it is mind. When emptiness moves, it becomes mind and works in the hands and feet. As one is to hit quickly the clenched fists holding the sword before they move, it is called "striking the void."

Even though it is called "presenting the mind," the mind cannot be seen with the human eye. It is called void because it cannot be seen, and it is called void because it does not move. Although the mind is presented in the hands that grasp the sword, it cannot be seen with the eye. One is to strike quickly when the mind is presented to the hands but has yet to move. One may say this emptiness of the mind is nothing because it cannot be seen, but when the emptiness of mind moves, many things can happen. It grasps in the hands and treads in the feet, working all manner of wonders—this is the movement and working of emptiness of mind.

Comprehending this mind by reading books is difficult; obtaining this way by listening to sermons is also difficult. People who write and people who preach write and preach only as in the religious writings and sermons of the past. Those who have realized the Original Mind are rare. All human beings' works and wonders are workings of the mind, and this mind is also in the heavens and the earth. This is called the mind of heaven and earth. When this mind moves, there is thunder and lightning, wind and rain, unseasonable clouds form, snow and hail blasts and sleet falls in midsummer, sending calamities and suffering on humanity. Therefore, in matters of heaven and earth, Void is the master; in matters of the body, it is master of the body. When dancing, it is master of the dance; when performing Noh it is master of Noh. When using martial arts, it is master of martial arts; when shooting a gun, it is master of the gun. When shooting a bow, it is master of the bow; when riding a horse, it is master of the horse. If there is deviance in the master, one cannot ride a horse, hit a target with a bow, or have true aim with a gun.

When the mind has obtained its proper standing and position in the body, and is situated where it should be, one is free in all Ways. Each man thinks he has opened his mind and is able to apply it usefully, but the man who has rightfully found it is rare. Proof of their lack of enlightenment will be manifested in the body, visible to all who are able to discern.

When enlightened, all that one does, all one's physical actions, will be straight and right. If he is not straight and right, he cannot very well be called enlightened. The straight and true mind is called the Original Mind, or the Mind of the Way. The twisted, defiled mind is called the mind of delusion, or the human mind. Praiseworthy is he who is enlightened to his own Original Mind, and whose actions are in concert with that Original Mind.

I do not speak these words like this with my own understanding. Although I speak like this, it is difficult to be straight and true in mind, and to act in concert with a mind straight and true. Nonetheless, I record it because it is the Way. Be that as it may, in martial arts, techniques cannot be realized so long as the mind is straight and true, and the body, hands, and feet are not in concert. Everyday behavior may not be in conformity with the Way, but this attainment of the Way is the sine qua non of the Way of martial arts. Even though all one's actions do not deviate from this mind, and one conforms to this mind in learning and the arts, it is not possible to apply to other areas. When all is comprehended and all has become possible, one is called a virtuoso. Those who master one skill or one art are called master of their particular path, but this cannot be called virtuosity.

*Inro decorated with Nio. Japan. 1615–1868. Lacquer.*

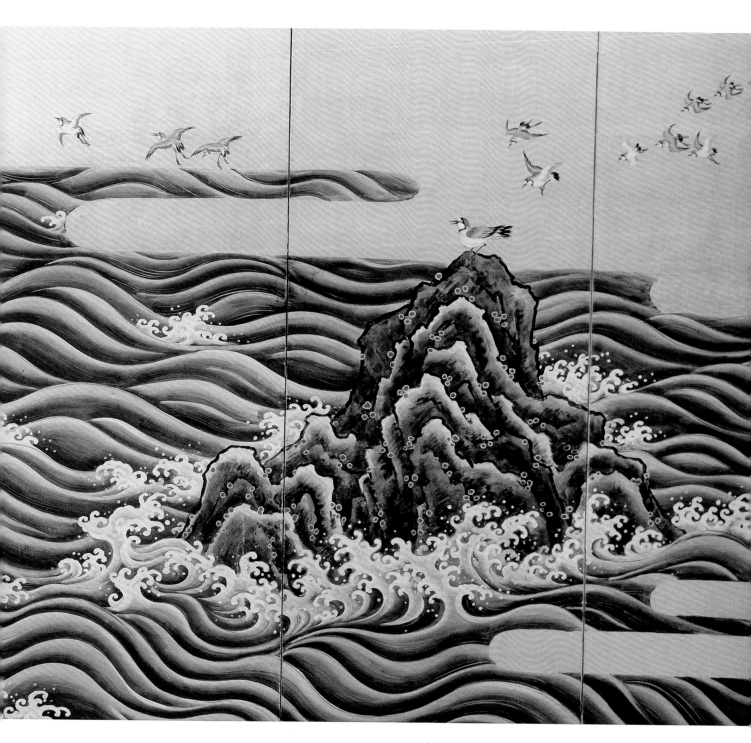

*A six-leaf screen in Sumi. Color on Gold Ground Painted with Breaking Waves Around Rocks. Japan. 19th century.*

# 心に本心、妄心とて二つあり
# True Mind and False Mind

*It is the mind itself*
*that is the mind*
*bewildering the mind.*
*Do not loose the mind,*
*O mind,*
*to the mind!*

These lines of poetry are from *Saru Uta*, "Song of Leaving." This poem expresses the true (constant) and the false (perturbed). There are two minds, the Original Mind and the false mind.

*It is the mind itself.* This mind is the deluded mind, which is bad because it is false and misleads the Original Mind.
*That is the mind.* This, too, is the false mind.
*Bewildering the mind.* The Original Mind that is misled by the false mind.
*Do not loose the mind.* The Original Mind.
*O mind.* The Original Mind, addressed directly, not to leave the mind to the false mind.
*To the mind!* The false mind.

Obtain the Original Mind, and act in concert with it, and all will be straight and true. If this Original Mind is twisted and defiled by the shadow of the false mind that overclouds it, all actions become twisted and defiled. The Original Mind and the false mind are not like black and white, which when placed side by side are clearly separate. The Original Mind is the original face one has before one's mother and father were born; having no form, it is not born and does not die. It is form that is given at birth by one's parents, and not the mind, being formless and without substance. It is present at birth, provided in the body.

Zen is acknowledged as a teaching that disseminates this mind. There is also something that has a semblance to Zen in which many people say similar things that are not the true path, so even followers of Zen are not identical. As regards the false mind, it is excitable and private. Its excitable nature, if one were to describe it, is in the blood. Blood flows and rises, changing the color of the face, and anger is expressed. Also, when people hate what one loves, one becomes angry and begrudging. But when others hate what one hates in the same way, one is delighted and turns wrong into right. When people are given money, they are delighted to receive it; their faces beam with smiles, and blood flow produces a glow. Then they take what is wrong and make it right.

These are all minds that spring up in the body from blood force in the flesh, corresponding to the moment. These are called the false mind. When this false mind develops, the Original Mind is overshadowed, becoming a false mind so only bad things materialize. Therefore, he who understands the Way is venerated because he dissolves the false mind by means of the Original Mind. For he who is not of the Way, the Original Mind is hidden and the false mind flourishes. Therefore, he acts unlawfully and his name is besmirched. Although this poem mentioned has no special distinction, it clearly distinguishes between the false (wrong) and the true (right). Everything the false mind does is wrong. If the false mind develops, one will lose at martial arts, miss the mark with bow and gun, and be unable to ride a horse. One's performance of Noh and one's dancing will be unpleasant to watch and unpleasant to hear, and what one says will be misspoken. Everything will go awry.

When in conformity with the Original Mind, all one's actions will be good. If one hatches a falsehood, but then denies it, that is the false mind acting, so its falsehood will soon become exposed. If one's heart and mind are true, people who listen will eventually recognize it, without the need for explanation. The Original Mind needs no explanation.

The false mind is a sickness of the mind. Eliminating this false mind is eliminating sickness. Eliminating this sickness, the mind is disease-free. This healthy mind is called the Original Mind. If one achieves the Original Mind, one will be a *meijin* of the martial arts. Without exception, all things conform to this principle.

*Haniwa warrior. Japan. Late 6th century. Red earthenware.*

354

# ZEN NON-THINKING
# TRUE MIND, FALSE MIND

In *The Sword and the Mind*, Yagyu Munenori warns warriors to beware of how the False Mind can distort the True Mind, which in turn will distort everything that the warrior does. But what is the False Mind? What is the True Mind? And what kind of impact can the False Mind have on a person, whether a warrior or not?

The idea of a True Mind in opposition to a False Mind is a core concept of Buddhism, which has been echoed (although not entirely replicated) in Sigmund Freud's teachings regarding the ego and the id. Under Buddhist teachings, the True Mind is the eternal mind, the so-called Buddha Mind, the mind that exists within everyone and everything and in which everything exists.

The *Surangama sutra,* which is thought to have been written during the eighth century CE in China and then subsequently refined and popularized in Japan, discusses the True Mind in the following way: "People erroneously think the mind is inside the body. They don't know that the physical body and the outside mountains, rivers, heavens, and wide earth are all objects in the bright True Mind." Metaphysically, then, to be in touch with the True Mind is to be in touch with the entirety of creation.

On a practical level, the True Mind means being totally aware of your surroundings, down to the smallest detail, and seeing things as they are and not as you fear or hope they might be. The True Mind is instinctual and looks at things objectively, without allowing subjective thought to interfere. It thus has some resemblance to Freud's concept of the unconscious ego, which starts out as the mind we are equipped with in the womb. In Freud's version, the unconscious ego never stays pure for long; it is continuously altered by experience. To the Buddhists, the True Mind is always present, naked and pure.

The False Mind, on the other hand, is the mind that is totally shaped by experience, emotions, and desires, in the manner of the Freudian id. The False Mind, sometimes called the Mind of Illusion, is dominated by thoughts of hunger, thirst, greed, lust, anger, love, sadness, and joy. In the *Surangama sutra,* Buddha warns that such worldly attachments and contaminations can cause one's perception to become unreliable, "causing them to wander about ignorantly and out of control."

*Yoro Waterfall, Mino Province, from the series A Journey to the Waterfalls of all the Provinces. Katsushika Hokusai. (1760–1849). Japan.*

Equally important, the False Mind cannot stop thinking, for it is constantly making calculations and judgments regarding its surroundings. But the True Mind is one with the True Mind of creation, so no thought is needed. The reason that Munenori stresses the difference between the False Mind and the True Mind is because of its applications on the battlefield. A warrior consumed by anger, distracted by hunger, or obsessed with tactical calculations will not be at his best performance. A warrior who can clear his mind and be totally aware of his surroundings, responding to them without thinking, can perform more optimally.

# THE ZEN FACTOR IN ARCHERY

Although *kyudo* may be rooted in violent activities such as hunting and warfare, masterful execution requires a state of mind that is anything but violent. Modern-day practitioners liken it more to meditation than martial arts. Kyudo is more of a spiritual journey than a sporting event.

One of the first western books to discuss the spirituality of shooting was *Zen in the Art of Archery* by Eugen Herrigel. Thanks to this book, the popularity of kyudo exploded. In it, Herrigel explains, "the archer ceases to be conscious of himself as the one who is engaged in hitting the bull's-eye which confronts him. This state of the unconscious is realized only when, completely empty and rid of the self, he becomes one with the perfecting of his technical skill, though there is in it something of a quite different order which cannot be attained by any progressive study of the art."

*A traditional Japanese garden.*

This connection between kydo and Zen is considered controversial by some, with shrugged shoulders by others. Nevertheless, many kyudo practitioners today do either find the connection helpful to their practice, or feel it parallels the "no-mindedness" needed to succeed. By reaching a state of no-mindedness, the ego is thought to dissolve and meld with the bow and the target. If performed properly, thoughts, feelings, worries, and distractions are released, allowing for a calm and assured shoot.

But one should not be romanced into thinking that a calm and meditative mind was the only intended goal of kyudo. Kyudo was developed as a martial art. It was intended to help the archer shoot to kill, be it in war or in the hunt. However, meditative elements are at play no matter the scenario. By breathing regularly and expanding the mind and body as one, the archer remains calm in the face of pressure.

## 無刀之巻
# No Sword

No Sword does not necessarily mean that one must take the opponent's sword. Neither does it mean taking his sword with a flourish to make a name for one's self. No Sword is not getting killed when one has no sword. It is not the original intention to go about seizing a sword for display.

It is not an attempt to seize relentlessly what one is being prevented from grasping. No Sword is also not taking the sword when one's opponent tries to prevent it from being seized. He who is determined not to have his sword taken, forgets what he is against, and tries only to prevent having his sword seized, rendering him unable to cut down his opponent. Not getting oneself killed is a victory. Making it an art to take someone's sword is not the principle. It is the practice of preventing oneself from being cut down when having no sword of one's own.

What is called No Sword is not the art of taking another's sword. It is for the purpose of using freely all tools. When one is without a sword, if one can just take another's sword and make it one's own, then what in one's hand will not be useful? Even if one has only a fan, one can triumph over an opponent's sword. This is what should be uppermost in one's mind about No Sword.

When having no sword, one is walking along with a bamboo cane, and someone draws a long sword and attacks, one should be able to take his sword by wielding one's bamboo cane. Even if one does not take his sword, one wins by keeping him at bay and not being cut down. Think of this frame of mind as the original intention of No Sword.

No Sword is not for the purpose of the taking of the sword of one's opponent; neither is it for cutting down people. When the opponent is set tenaciously on killing, then that is when his sword should be taken. Taking the sword is not the original aim to begin with. It is for the sake of obtaining understanding of the boundaries. Knowing the perimeter between two combatants that will keep one out of striking range of the opponent's sword.

When one knows the striking range perimeter, one fears not the opponent's sword. When one's body is open to his strike, judge the workings of the open perimeter. With No Sword, one cannot take the opponent's sword so long as it is out of striking range. To take the sword, it must be within striking range. When one is open to be killed, that is the time to take it.

No Sword is letting others hold onto their swords, while one uses one's own hands as instruments in combat against them. A sword's reach is long, the reach of the hands short. One must move in close to an opponent, within killing range, to achieve this. One must distinguish the interaction of an opponent's sword against one's hands. In such a case, the opponent's sword goes beyond one's body, and one then positions oneself under his sword hilt, devising a way to control his sword. In these circumstances, do not be confined to one style. His sword will not be taken, in any event, unless one moves in closely.

No Sword is the preeminent secret of this school. Physical stances, sword positions, taking a stand, distance, movement, artifice, thrusting, attacking, appearance, and reality: each of these comes from the design of No Sword. Therefore, it is the most important perspective.

大機大用

# The Great Potential and the Great Function

Everything has form and function. Where there is form there is function. For example, a bow is form, whereas drawing, shooting, and hitting the target are functions of the bow. A lamp is form, light is its function. Water is form, moisture is function. An apricot tree is form, fragrance and color are its function. A sword is form, cutting and thrusting are functions.

Therefore, Potential is form, whereas what manifests outwardly from it in various workings are form. Because an apricot tree has form, flowers blossom from its form, producing color and fragrance. In the same way fragrance is produced, function dwells within Potential and works without—thrusting, attacking,· manipulating appearance and reality, using Attacking and Waiting, and various ploys, working on the outside because Potential is ready within. This is called Function.

"Great" is a word of praise, as in *Daimyōjin*, Great Saint; *Daigongen*, Great Incarnation; and *Daibōsatsu*, Great Bodhisattva, an expression of acclaim. Because Great Function exists, Great Potential appears. When Zen monks make their bodies work freely and at will, in accord with truth and corresponding to principle in all they say and do, this is called Great Spiritual Power and the Great Function of the Great Potential. What is called supernatural powers and supernatural occurrences are not marvels created by gods or demons come down from the sky; these terms mean working freely and at will in whatever one does. All the numerous sword positions, manipulating appearance and reality, ploys, wielding weapons, leaping up and leaping down, snatching a blade, kicking someone down, all manner of works are called Great Function when one attains freedom outside the teachings. If Potential is not always possessed within, Function will not appear.

Even when one is seated indoors, first look up, and then to the right and to the left, to take notice of anything that might unexpectedly fall from above. When one is sitting by a door or screen, regard whether or not it might collapse. Or, when in attendance near high-ranking nobles, be alert to the possibility of something untoward happening. Do not let down your guard even when going in and out of a door, but remain always vigilant. These are all examples of Potential.

When exceptional effects arise instantly of their own accord because the Potential is always within, this is called Great Function.

When this Potential is not full-fledged, Function is not manifested. Potential matures and Great Function develops when mindfulness is accrued and skills are accumulated in all paths. When Potential hardens and solidifies, there is no Function. Maturing, it spreads throughout the body, so that Function develops everywhere, in hands, feet, eyes, and ears.

He who practices martial arts using only what he has learned, will be unable to lift a hand against a man of Great Potential and Great Function.

Another thing to have is called the stare. Glared at once by someone with the Great Potential, one will be transfixed by the stare, stand there and forget to draw one's sword. If one hesitates for even the time it takes to blink an eye, defeat will come swiftly. When glared at by a cat, a mouse will fall from the beam. Seized by the look in the cat's eye, the mouse forgets its own feet to run with, and falls. He who encounters a man of Great Potential is like a mouse meeting a cat.

There is a Zen saying, "When the Great Function is manifested, it has no rules." By manifested, is meant the Great Function of a man of Great Potential appears before one's eyes. This man is not the least concerned with learning or rules. Rules are practice, codes, and edicts. In all paths, there are practice, codes, and edicts, but

*This Kanji signifies strength, power, force, energy, might, ability, vigor, and capability.*

*A pair of gold fundame kobako. Japan. Late 19th century.*

# SHINTO RELIGION INTERFACES WITH BUDDHISM

*The gates from Heian shrine, one of the largest temples in Kyoto, Japan.*

The two primary religions in Japan today are Shinto and Buddhism. Most Japanese do not believe in one or the other but take parts of each as guides in their daily lives, a process of duality known as syncretism. For example, a person who might have had a Shinto wedding might prefer a Buddhist funeral; Buddhism offers a view of the afterlife, but within the Shinto system of beliefs, anything dealing with death is defiled, and there is little mention and no details of an afterlife.

The Shinto religion is an ancient methodology that has been handed down from generation to generation, through stories and everyday practices. Unlike almost all other theologies, Shinto has no real founder, no written texts or scriptures, and no actual religious laws to follow, for Shintoists generally follow Confucian codes of conduct.

The term *Shinto,* for the primitive mix of nature worship, fertility cults, hero worship, shamanism, and divination techniques, comes from the Chinese phrase *shin tao,* "way of the gods." The Shinto creation story recalls the lives of deities, the *kami.* Two in particular, Izanagi no Mikoto and Izanami no Mikoto, gave birth to the Japanese islands. One of their daughters, Amaterasu Omikami, the sun goddess, was the ancestor of the imperial family and is regarded as the chief deity.

The kami of the Shinto religion bear little or no resemblance to anything in any monotheistic religion. Shinto lacks principle religious concepts of the wrath of God, omnipotence, omnipresence, or even sin. Most kami are revered ancestors, such as famous warriors, and all but the last of the emperors. Some are connected to physical objects, including unusual natural landscapes such as groupings of trees or splendid waterfalls.

Four main ideals are associated with Shinto practices. *Tradition and the family* as a concept focuses on the family as the main vehicle for preserving traditions, with major celebrations centered around birth and marriage. The *love of nature* deifies anything natural; since contact with nature is a way of being close to the gods, natural objects are worshipped as sacred spirits. A third ideal is *physical cleanliness,* and to that end, Shintoists take frequent baths and wash their hands and rinse their mouths before entering a shrine. Lastly, attending kami-related *honor festivals and dedication ceremonies* is an important principle for Shintoists. Events like these are intended for the entertainment of the kami, as well as of the participants and observers, as in the case of the original *sumo* wrestling tournaments.

No regularly scheduled services are set up in a Shinto shrine. Adherents visit the shrine at their own leisure, some on the first and fifteenth of the month and on festival days or rites of passage, while others stop at a shrine daily. Shinto shrines are the homes of the kami and so are located in the naturally beautiful places that are regarded as sacred. Within the inner sanctuary of a shrine, a carefully wrapped object of some sort, usually a mirror or wooden image, is used to represent the residing kami. Only the chief priest is allowed to enter into this inner sanctum. A gateway marks the entrance to the shrine grounds. Anything beyond the gateway is sacred, and in order to pass through, visitors to the shrine must first ritually cleanse themselves by washing their hands and rinsing their mouths in the basin provided for that purpose. Outside the shrine, *origami,* literally "folding paper," is often found hanging from nearby tree branches. (Origami is never cut, out of respect for the tree; the fantastic paper figures are made entirely from folding one piece of paper.)

Various rites of passage are followed in Shinto. The equivalent of a baptism is performed between one and three months after birth, on the newborn's first visit to the shrine. A few years later, for boys aged five and for girls aged three and seven, another special celebration, on November 15, offers an opportunity to give thanks to the kami for both protection and for continued healthy growth. Each January 15 is Adults Day, a commemorative day for those who have attained their twentieth birthdays.

*Red Japanese Shinto shrine just outside Tokyo, Japan.*

After the arrival of Buddhism in 552 CE, Shinto began to wane, and eventually, around the eighth century, Shinto and Buddhism evolved into a mutual coexistence, with Buddhist temples being built on sites of Shinto shrines and people beginning to worship the deities of both. Shinto kami were soon elevated to the status of Buddhist *deva,* or gods, and by the late eighth century, Buddhist statues had begun to appear in Shinto shrines, and the kami had begun to receive *bodhisattva* names reserved for enlightened beings. But in some more extreme cases, Buddhist priests had even gained control of Shinto shrines. Among the common folk, though, a typical traditional family home would now have had two shrines, one Shinto and one Buddhist.

As might be expected with the intermingling of beliefs, an anti-Buddhist movement in the late fifteenth century sought to perpetuate a purer form of Shinto, called Ise or Watari Shinto after the city of Ise where it began. However, the various forms continued to be practiced until after World War II, when Shinto lost its official religion status, and shrine membership and contributions, which had been mandatory under governmental rule, became voluntary. Though a secular atmosphere prevails in Japan today, streets are commonly festooned with Shinto, Buddhist, and Christian decorations on festival days.

the one who has attained the highest level can let go of them lightly, acting as a free agent. Acting freely and independently, outside the rules, he is called a man of Great Potential and Great Function.

This Ki (Potential) means being resolute inwardly and being able to foresee all things. Therefore, when that Ki, ever focused, hardens or solidifies, then one is over-involved in Ki and thus not free. This is because Ki is not yet ripe. Through accumulated efforts, Ki ripens and spreads throughout the body, working freely. This is called the Great Function.

|  |  |
|---|---|
| | Supernatural Power |
| | Supernatural Transformation |
| Heart/Mind – Potential – | Great Function – [continues] |
| | A Thousand Hands |
| | Ten Thousand Hands |
| | |
| | Respond to Potential (of opponent) |
| Great Function – | Following Transformation |
| | All Events |
| | All Things |

Ki, Potential (機), is in other words Ki, energy (気), according to its place. Heart/Mind is the interior, whereas Ki, energy, is the entrance. Ki, Potential, is like a drop-bolt in a door. Heart/Mind is master of the whole body, to be understood as that which is situated in the interior. Ki, energy, is at the doorway, working outside for the master, the Heart/Mind.

Dividing the heart/mind into good and bad is through Ki, Potential, as it goes out from Ki to good and to bad. Ki (energy) that keeps guard at the doorway is called Ki (Potential). When someone opens a door and goes outside, whether to do good or do evil, or even work supernatural wonders, depends on the thoughts in his mind before opening the door.

That is why this Potential is so important. When working, this Potential develops outside and the Great Function presents itself. In any case, if it is understood as Ki (energy), that will not be wrong. The name changes depending on the situation.

Nonetheless, one may speak of the interior and the doorway, but there is nothing established as interior and doorway in the body. Interior and doorway are used analogously. When a person speaks, for instance, the beginning of his speech may be called the doorway, and the end of their speech may be called the interior. In these words the place of interior and doorway is not determined.

心は万境に随つて転ず、転処実に能く幽なり

# The Turning Mind

In the words of a hymn by the Venerable Manorhita, "Turning, turning, the mind follows ten thousand facets and infinite are its axes." This verse is a secret of Zen meditation, cited here because this idea is crucial to martial arts. Those who do not practice Zen meditation will find it particularly difficult to comprehend.

In the martial arts, the "ten thousand facets" means the numerous actions of one's opponent; and the mind turns to each one of them. When one's opponent brandishes his sword, for example, one's mind turns to his sword. If he circles to the right, one's mind turns to the right; if he circles to the left, one's mind turns to the left. This is called "turning and following ten thousand facets."

"Infinite are its axes"—this is the crux of martial arts. When the mind leaves no trace behind like the white waves trailing a moving boat, disappearing in its wake and turning ahead, not lingering in the least, this is how to understand "infinite are its axes."

Being "infinite" means to be indiscernible; the mind is undeterred, not stopping at any one place. If the mind lingers here and there, stopping in one place, one will lose in martial arts. Lingering at the turning point, one will be annihilated.

The mind, having neither shape nor form, is indiscernible to the eye. But when it clings and stays in one place, the mind is seen such as it is. It is like undyed silk: dye it red, it turns red; dye it purple, it turns purple. A man's mind, too, dyed by things is rendered visible. If the mind becomes infatuated with boys and young men, eventually this will become visible to others. When thoughts are within, their colors are visible without.

Watching an opponent's moves closely, if one lets the mind linger over them, one will be defeated in martial arts. The verse mentioned here is cited to express "Do not let the mind stop." The last two lines of the verse have been omitted and are not recorded here. In Zen meditation, the whole verse should be known; in martial arts, the first two lines are enough.

*Reishi fungus. Ryokuzan. Japan. 1870–1930. Elephant ivory.*

# 兵法の、仏法にかなひ、禅に通する事多し
# Martial Arts, Buddhist Dharma, and Zen

Many things in martial arts are in accordance with Buddhist law and correspond to Zen. Among them, especially, are the aversion to attachment and the aversion to lingering over things. This is the most important point. Not to linger is considered essential.

The courtesan Eguchi responded to a poem by the Buddhist monk Saigyō with her own poem:

> To one who has rejected the world,
> Who asks for a room in the inn,
> I say only: do not let your mind dwell
> On this temporary lodging

In martial arts, are these last lines of the verse not to be treasured? No matter what kind of secret transmission one receives or what moves one uses, if the mind dwells on the move, one will suffer defeat in martial arts. It is essential to practice not letting the mind dwell on any one place, on the moves of one's opponent, on one's own skills, or on cutting and thrusting.

# 是非巳に去り了つて、薦取せよ
# Right and Wrong

The monk Longqi said to the people, "The pillar of Propriety does not see the pillar. The pillar of Impropriety does not see the pillar. Eliminate propriety and impropriety altogether, and discriminate what lies between."

This story is to be applied to all disciplines. A certain wise man related this story, and since it applies to the marital arts, it is recorded here. By the pillar of Propriety and the pillar of Impropriety is meant that the difference between right and wrong, good and evil, is erected firmly in the heart just as Propriety and Impropriety stand as two pillars. Simply keeping what is right in the mind will suddenly turn vexing, and all the more so if it is something wrong. That is why the saying goes "One does not see the pillar." This indicates that one should not look at the pillars of Propriety and Impropriety, right and wrong. These distinctions of propriety/impropriety and good/bad are a sickness of the mind. So long as this sickness does not leave the mind, nothing will turn out well. Therefore, it is said: discriminate what lies between Propriety and Impropriety, by having eliminated Propriety and Impropriety altogether. Once having cut off Propriety/Impropriety, one must commingle with them, and advance from out of the midst of Propriety/Impropriety to the uttermost level. Even for one who is practiced and proficient in Buddhist Dharma, the crucial eye that is cutting off Propriety/Impropriety is truly difficult to possess.

# 法尚応捨、何況非法
# Repudiating the Truth

"Even the Law should be abandoned—to say nothing of the false Law!" The gist of this quotation is that the "Law" means the correct teaching of truth; even the correct teaching should not stay in the mind once enlightenment is attained. Thus it is said, "Even the truth should be repudiated." After becoming enlightened to the true teaching, if one keeps in his chest, it will sully the heart—how much more so will the false Law. The truth should be repudiated—not to mention the false—this should not remain in the heart.

Once all true precepts have been observed, do not let them remain in the heart. Cut them off without restraint, emptying the heart, and performing one's actions with the ordinary, everyday mind. Unless one reaches this level, one can hardly be called a *meijin* of the martial arts.

Because martial art is our family enterprise, I speak to it here. But these teachings are not restricted to the martial arts alone. All the Ways are like this. When martial arts are used, unless one eliminates the mind of martial arts, it is a sickness. In shooting a bow, if one does eliminate the mind of shooting a bow, it is a sickness of archery.

If only one can wield a sword and shoot a bow with the normal mind, archery will become effortless and swordsmanship free and unrestrained. Undaunted by anything, the normal mind will be good for all things. If the normal mind is lost, one's voice will tremble no matter what one tries to say. If the normal mind is lost, one's hand will tremble when trying to write in front of others. The normal mind leaves nothing in the heart, but lightly casts off all traces, so that the heart is emptied. This is the normal mind. People who read the Confucian classics do not understand the principle of emptying the mind, and fall to thinking only about "deference." Deference is not the highest achievement; it is the first few steps of a discipline.

# THE EDO PERIOD
# THE FLOURISHING OF URBANIZATION AND THE ARTS

The Edo period of Japanese history, also referred to as the Tokugawa period, lasted from 1603, when the first shogunate was officially established by Tokugawa Ieyasu, to 1868, when the fifteenth and last shogun, Tokugawa Yoshinobu, resigned to make way for the restoration of the imperial rule of the Meiji. But the Edo period also marked the beginning of the early modern era of Japanese history. With the consolidation of the country under the Tokugawa followed by centuries of peaceful stability, a trend in urbanization resulted, as seen in the cities of Osaka, Kyoto, and Edo. Along with a relatively wealthier populace and a more leisurely lifestyle, such urban centers fostered a blossoming of the arts. The arts, however, served as only a temporary respite from the rigidly structured society of the times.

The control of the shogunate extended to religious orders, the court, the nobility, and even the emperor. The Tokugawa, in particular, ensured the cooperation of the emperor by rebuilding palaces and granting new lands to imperial families. Or marriages were dispensed for familial alliances, as with the binding tie of 1619, when Shogun Ieyasu's granddaughter was made an imperial consort. To the masses, the imperial family was seen as having political power, but in reality, it was the shogun who wielded real power.

The early Edo era coincided with the end of the Nanban trade period, when extensive worldwide commerce with Europe and the Americas spread. Ieyasu, with a certain ambivalence, encouraged foreign trade, but

*Phoenix, eight-panel folding screen, Edo period, Japan 1835 (Tenpo 6). Ink, colour cut gold-leaf and sprinkled gold on paper.*
*Photograph © 2008 Museum of Fine Arts, Boston.*

he was suspicious of outsiders and sought to restrict exposure to outside influences, to the point of prohibiting the construction of ocean going ships. To govern other areas of life, a code of laws was established that encompassed private conduct, marriage, dress, and types of weapons and numbers of troops allowed; required feudal lords to reside in Edo every other year to curtail insubordination; banned Christianity; restricted castles to one per domain; and stipulated that *bakufu*, or shogun, regulations were the national law.

The population during the Edo period was divided into four distinct classes, with little or no social mixing. At the top was the samurai class, due to their proximity to the shogun, who was actually a samurai who had been elevated to the apex of his class. This elite group represented approximately five percent of the population. Members of the samurai class followed ancient traditions, which resulted in a renewed interest in Japanese history and in cultivation of the philosophies of Confucian scholar-administrators. The development of the concept of *bushido,* "way of the warrior," grew out of this. Next down the pyramid were the peasants or farmers. Being more than eighty percent of the population, they were heavily taxed by the shogun, to keep them from prospering too much to become a threat, which is a common trait of the feudal system. After the farmers came the craftsmen, who were valuable individuals whose expertise was prized by the samurai, but not quite enough to elevate them above the level of a rice farmer. The most successful craftsmen were the sword smiths, who produced the fabled *katana,* or samurai sword. At the bottom of the class system were the merchants. Because they didn't actually produce

*Parasol Maker. Japan. 1600–1868. Ivory.*

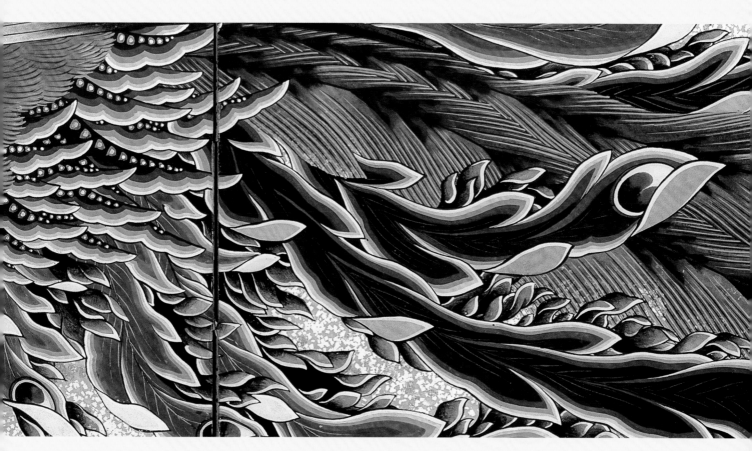

anything, they were relegated to the lowest class, in part because of the Confucian ideology regarding the relationship between productivity and value.

Outside of the class system resided two other groups: the

Man's kimono. Japan. 1600–1868. Silk.

*eta,* who primarily dealt with death in the form of butchering animals, tanning hides, and undertaking, and the *hinin,* who were the town guards, street cleaners, and executioners. Since both groups broke Buddhist taboos against eating meat and being in contact with death of any sort, these groups were viewed as unclean. And even their names branded them. *Eta* means "filthy," and *hinin* means "nonhuman." Any hinin could be killed for no reason at all with no consequences for the murder, except for perhaps a modest fine.

With the rule of the Tokugawa in the Edo period came ever-lessening military hostilities and economic prosperity. Merchants became wealthy as commercial houses in Osaka and Edo became more prominent. Because the wealth of the samurai and the *daimyo,* or lord, was measured in rice, these two groups became even more dependent on the merchants to convert their wealth into money in order to participate in the economic boom.

As a result of a corresponding population boom, by

1700, Edo had grown to nearly one million citizens, more by far than London or Paris at that time, while Osaka and Kyoto had grown to nearly half a million people each. Though merchants now had wealth, they still had no better status and no more power than before. Nonetheless, by 1761, Japan saw the combined capital wealth of more than 200 commercial houses surpass that of several of the *daimyo* estates. Along with these constraints in class, only in the Yoshihara district or other licensed entertainment quarters could such merchants mingle with samurai, who, as opposed to the tradesmen, had higher status and power but no great wealth.

With this prosperity and population growth came another special way of life, the *chonindo,* "way of the townspeople," which was a distinct culture found in cities such as Osaka, Kyoto, and Edo. While this subculture encouraged the bushido qualities of diligence, honesty, honor, loyalty, and frugality, it also blended Shinto, neo-Confucian, and Buddhist beliefs. Surprisingly, the arts flourished under this system, with advances being made in mathematics, cartography, engineering, and medicine, and quality of workmanship being particularly prized. Within this flowering of the middle classes, which became known as *ukiyo,* "floating world," talent in poetry and painting were highly esteemed, as was the entertainment skill of the *geisha* class and the dancers and singers of *kabuki* theater. The floating world formed a refuge from the hierarchical society of the Edo era. For such artists, it afforded a freedom of association and expression previously unknown amid the tightly restrained and defined classical traditions.

The most famous social and artistic creation of this period was *ukiyo-e,* distinctive woodblock prints, the oldest of which date back to the late seventeenth century. The founder of this technique was Edo artist Hishikawa Moronobu (1618 to 1694), who came from a family of textile producers and designers. Though the ukiyo-e style developed in an isolated island nation over a period of several hundred years, the impact of these prints, especially the polychrome examples of the late eighteenth century, was to become strikingly apparent in European art of the nineteenth century. Early ukiyoe prints played an influential role in the works of Edgar Degas and Vincent van Gogh, and the French artists Manet and Monet copied the color schemes in what they termed *japonisme.* But for the Japanese, many of the symbols in the ukiyo-e prints were evident only to the trained eye. Even so, the beauty and grace of this unique art form has a universal appeal.

*Opposite page: The Cheerful Type from the series Twelve Modern-Day Beauties. Keisai Eisen (1790–1848). Japan. 1822.*

# TANEGASHIMA
# THE MATCHLOCK GUN

*In firing position, the right hand presses the stock of the tanegashima (matchlock) against the cheek, as opposed to the shoulder.*

The Japanese matchlock gun was introduced in 1543 at Tanegashima Island, Japan. The popular story is that Portuguese traders from a Chinese merchant or pirate ship had several of the arquebuses, or matchlock muskets. Matchlocks are prepared for firing by loading the powder charge into the muzzle; then tamping a lead ball on top of the

powder with a ramrod. At that point a small amount of priming powder is poured into the pan on the side of the breech end and its cover is closed. A lighted cord or match is inserted into the hammer or cock that is then pulled back into cocked position. The cord is woven cotton soaked in a nitrate solution and dried, making a slow-burning fuse. (In Europe it is called a slow match.) This cord smolders with a hot coal at the end near the pan. The primer pan cover is opened just prior to releasing the hammer. When the trigger is pulled, it releases the underspring tension, and the hot end contacts the primer powder. To make sure that the hot end of the cord is glowing, the shooter has to blow on it. Various sizes of ammunition were made as round cast lead balls; they were measured in weight rather than diameter, ranging from one monme (8.5mm.) to one hundred monme (48mm).

Tanegashima was the first name used to refer to the Japanese version of the original musket brought by the Portuguese. The governor of Tanegashima, Hyobunosoke Tokitaka, bought two guns and practiced shooting them. A year later the Portuguese returned with a gun maker who trained Tokitaka's sword makers in the art of gun barrel making, called tanegashima tsutsu. The major changes in design were that the butt end or stock was made short for cheek shooting rather than shoulder shooting, and the hammer fell forward toward the muzzle as opposed to falling to the rear toward the breech as did the original arquebus of European design. For cheek shooting, the grip was a pistol grip shape and was held against the right cheek when fired.

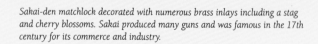

*Sakai-den matchlock decorated with numerous brass inlays including a stag and cherry blossoms. Sakai produced many guns and was famous in the 17th century for its commerce and industry.*

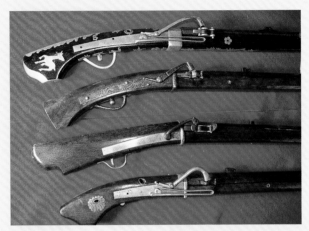

From top: circa 1800 Sakai Tsutsu; circa 1800 Kuitomo Tetsupou; Satsuma Tsutsu with small lock in the style of the earliest guns; circa 1650 Bajoututu, longer than the pistol matchlock and meant to be fired from horseback.

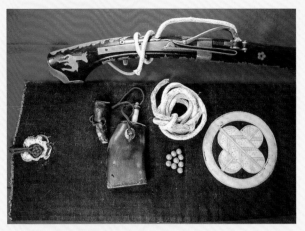

Sakai matchlock with matchcord, powder flask, lead balls, and carrying case with Taka No Ha mon decoration. Many Sakai guns were inscribed "Live in Sakai," followed by a family name and the name of the gunsmith.

The gun was quickly favored as a hunting weapon, but soon it was recognized as a powerful weapon for warfare. Gun-making spread to Sakai, a harbor town in Izumi Province. The Ashikaga shogun had a factory that produced thousands. Every warlord in the country soon realized that the matchlock gun, or *teppo*, was a wonderful killing weapon, and gun manufacturing went into full swing in other areas of Japan. (The matchlock gun later went by the name *hinawa*, which is used today.)

The tanegashima or teppo was primarily manufactured in Sakai, Kunitomo, and Satsuma; others were made in Hizen, Bizen, Tosa, Choushu, Awa, Kishu, Hino, Mino, Seki, Yunezawa, and Sendai. Each had its own characteristics unique to place or school of manufacture, such as stock shapes and decoration and types of locks, although all were the same in their operation. Oak was the usual wood of choice for stocks. Brass springs and fittings were used on some and iron fittings on others. The brass leaf springs were affixed onto the outside of the lock plate while a steel coil spring was located inside under the plate on others.

Woodworkers, metal smiths, and barrel makers contributed to the finished product with great pride. The barrels were made by wrapping hot strips of steel around a rod that was then hammer forged. The bore was polished smooth. Most barrels were finished in an octagon shape,

and lengths ranged from two feet to more than three feet, and most were signed by the maker. Some guns were adorned with brass and copper decorations on the stock. Family *mon*, usually in silver, were inlaid on the barrel as well as pictorial inlays of animals, dragons, and flowers. The long production time and the excellent workmanship made the teppo far superior to what was made in Europe. Its successful use in battle as well as the methods utilized by Nobunaga were not applied in Europe until decades later.

The Japanese used the matchlock design for more than 300 years. The flintlock mechanism was never used as it was in Europe and North America. The percussion or cap lock was only adopted in Japan in the late nineteenth century, and many matchlocks were converted to percussion fire. At first there was some resistance from various samurai because they felt guns were not befitting a samurai. That soon changed, and the gun became a required weapon to train with, and it was added to the samurai curriculum.

Nobunaga was successful in battle at Nagashino in 1575 because of the effectiveness of his 3,000 or more matchlock guns. Iyeyasu Tokulawa later used matchlock guns at Sekigahara in 1600 where opposing forces were defeated. That historic battle led the way for the unification of Japan under one commander (Shogun) in 1603: Iyeyasu Tokugawa himself.

# The Book of Five Rings

Miyamoto Musashi

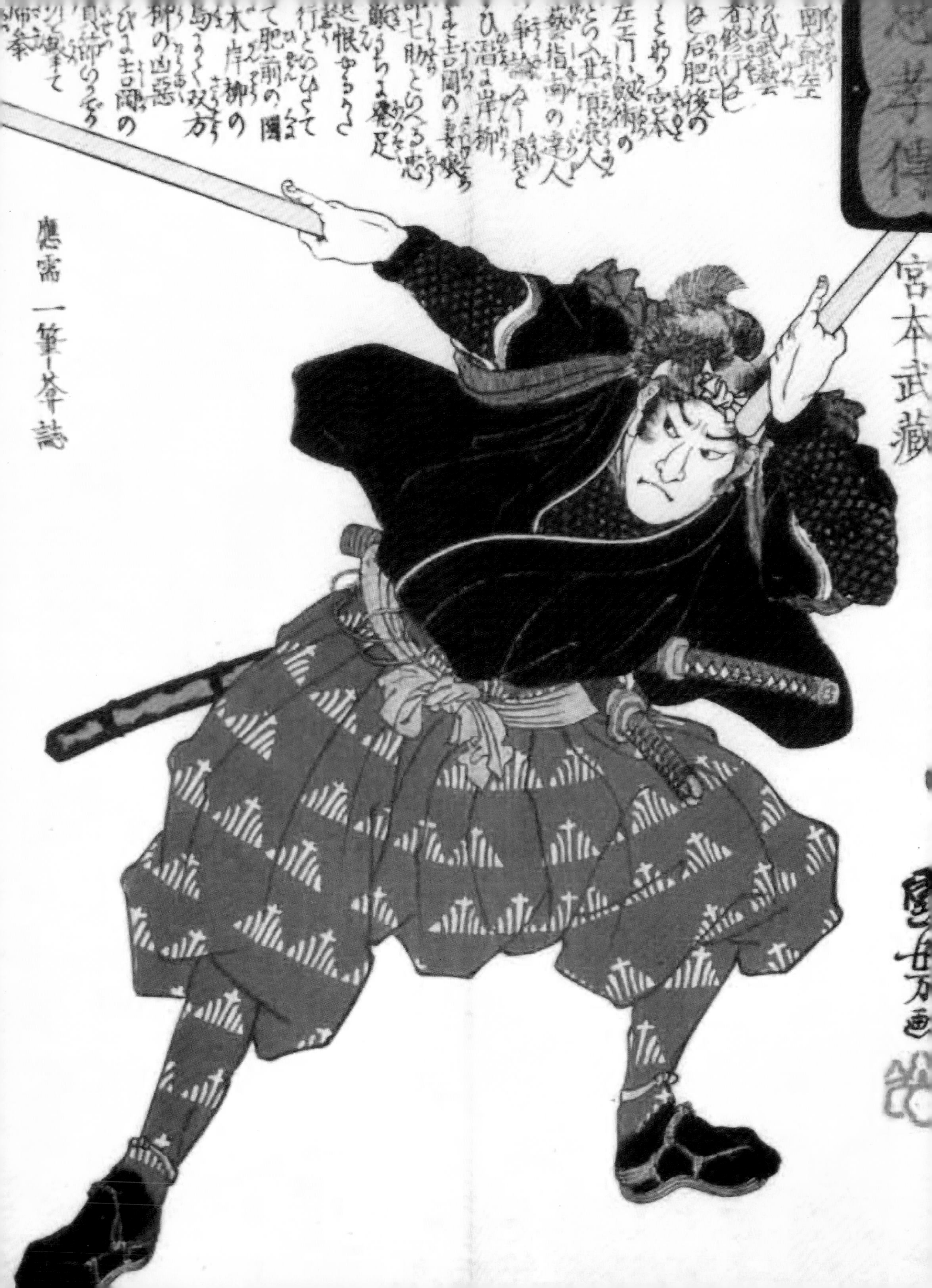
宮本武蔵
應需 一筆菴誌

# CONTENTS

Preceding page: Sakura namiki zu (A Grove of Cherry Trees). Hiroshige Ando
(1791–1858). Circa 1868–1926. Woodcut print.
Opposite: Musashi Miyamoto with Two Bokken (wooden sticks). Japan. Scroll.

# MIYAMOTO MUSASHI

Most widely known because of two popular texts, his own *Gorin no sho* (*The Book of Five Rings*) and Yoshikawa Eiji's novel *Musashi*, Miyamoto Musashi was a legendary Japanese swordsman, writer, and artist who heavily influenced the Western perception of the Japanese mind. Born as Shinmen Takezo in the Harima province of Japan sometime before 1600, Musashi was famous for his spectacular duelling record and his mastery of many schools of swordsmanship.

As a young man, he purportedly defeated most of the skilled martial artists of his province before moving to Kyoto in the early seventeenth century. Musashi is thought to have won more than sixty duels without suffering defeat, including a renowned battle with the master of the Yoshioka school, Yoshioka Seijuro, who chronicles these conflicts in the biography *Musashi*.

Musashi goes down in history as one of the most skilled swordsmen of his century, admired for his spectacular use of two swords at once and his mastery of martial art using a simple bamboo sword. He is thought to have served at Osaka castle for a period of several years around 1615, though much information about Musashi's life between 1600 and 1640 is recognized as a mixture of fact and fiction. He took up art later in life, and is revered as an accomplished painter, particularly for his landscapes and self-portraits.

Musashi's *The Book of Five Rings,* one of the most highly regarded works ever written on swordsmanship, advocates his two-sword styles of fighting using both *katana* and *wakizashi*, respectively, the long and short single-edge swords. He finished his book around 1645, the same year he died. The text, which focuses on *kenjutsu* and other martial arts, is now cited with *The Art of War* and Munenori's *The Sword and the Mind* as one of the world's most important written influences on military strategy, philosophy, and competitive thinking.

*Miyamoto Musashi, self-portrait. Miyamoto Musashi (1584–1645). Japan. Circa 1640.*

# Prologue

Having spent many years cultivating the Way of martial arts called *Niten Ichi-ryū*, the School of Two Heavens, I now will attempt to put it into writing for the first time, during these early days of the tenth month of the twentieth year of Kan-ei (1643). I have climbed Mount Iwato in the land of Higo, Kyushu. I bow to Heaven, make obeisance to Kannon, and turn toward the Buddha. I am Shinmen Musashi no Kami, Fujiwara no Genshin, a warrior born in Harima province, now sixty years of age.

From my young years of long ago, I have set my heart and mind on the Way of martial arts. At thirteen, I had my first duel. At that time I struck down a formidable martial artist called Arima Kihei of the *Shintō-ryū*, New Hitting-the-Mark School. At sixteen I defeated a martial artist called Akiyama of Tajima province. When I was twenty-one, I went to Kyoto, the capital, and met martial artists from all over the country, engaging in numerous duels, but never once failing to attain victory.

After that I traveled from province to province, encountering martial artists of various schools. I never lost a match even though I dueled more than sixty times.

*Ichikawa Danjuro VII Overpowering an Officer of the Law. Japan. Circa 1830–44. Woodblock print with blind embossing.*

This all took place between the ages of thirteen and twenty-eight or twenty-nine.

Passed the age of thirty, I looked back on the footprints of my past. My victories lay not in having mastered martial arts. Perhaps it was because I was innately skilled in the Way and had not departed from the laws of Heaven, or maybe it was in the deficiencies of the other schools of martial arts. From then on I practiced from morning to night to attain still deeper principles, and came naturally to a realization of the Way of martial arts. I was then about fifty.

Having no Way to investigate since then, I passed the time. For me there was no teacher in anything; I put my stock in the principles of the martial arts, learning the Way of all arts and skills. Writing this book now, I do not use the old precepts of Buddhist Dharma, Confucius, or Taoism, neither the old stories from war chronicles nor books on military tactics. To reveal my mind about Niten Ichi-Ryū and it's true meaning, I take up my brush and begin to write, with the Way of Heaven and Kannon as mirrors, on the night of the tenth day of the tenth month, at the hour of the tiger, 4:30 am.

# *Chi no maki*

## *The Earth Scroll*

Martial arts are the Way of the warrior. Above all, commanders should practice these arts, and soldiers too must know this Way. There is no warrior in the world today able to discern clearly the Way of martial arts.

First, the Way is revealed diversely: the Way of saving people by Buddhist Dharma, the Way of Confucius to perfect one's learning, a doctor's Way of healing diseases, a poet's teaching of the Way of poetry. Others are practitioners of the Way of tea or archery, and all manner of arts and skills. Each practicing the Way he prefers, developing a propensity for one or the other. But rare is the man who is fond of the Way of martial arts.

First and foremost, the Way of the warrior is *bunbu*—the pen and the sword, both literary arts and culture, and the martial arts—and he should have a penchant for both Ways. Even though he may be untalented, every warrior should strive to employ his martial arts, each according to his abilities.

For the most part, it is thought that the warrior concerns himself only with being prepared to die. The Way of death is not restricted to warriors only. Monks, women, peasants and those below them have a sense of duty and shame, and resign themselves to death. In this there is no distinction. The Way of martial arts practiced by warriors is based on besting others in all things. Whether by winning a single duel or defeating a throng in battle, one tries to build a name for one's master and oneself, and establish oneself in the world. This is possible by the virtue of martial arts.

One should be aware that some people in the world might think that even once the Way of martial arts is learned, it will not be of service when the moment of truth comes. In this respect, practicing them so as to be of service at any time, and teaching them so as to be of service in all things—this is the true Way of martial arts.

## 兵法の道といふ事
# Heiho no michi

### ON THE WAY OF MARTIAL ARTS

From China to Japan, practitioners of this Way have been called masters of the Way of martial arts. It must be that warriors learn this Way.

There are those who make a living who are called martial artists these days, but this is nothing but swordsmanship.

*Model of a 16th-century Japanese warrior. Japan. 20th century.*

In recent years, priests of Kashima and Kantori shrines in Hitachi province have established such schools based on transmission from the gods, traveling from province to province and instructing people. But this is a recent affair.

Within the Ten Skills, *jūnō*, and Seven Arts, *shichigei*, of ancient times, so-called "benefits," *rikata*, or "profitable measures," have been included as an art. However, what is called benefits cannot be restricted to swordsmanship alone. Even swordsmanship itself is difficult to comprehend by the benefit of winning with sword fighting alone. Of course this will not lead to accomplishing martial arts.

Looking at the world, one sees that all the arts are made into things to sell; one thinks of oneself as something to sell, and devises ways to make all tools into things to sell. Between the flower and the fruit, the fruits of one's labor seem less than the flower of frippery.

The Way of martial arts is especially fraught with colorful displays of technique, clambering over who has the best *dojo*, and profit seeking—among both those who teach the Way and those who study it. As has been said, "half–cooked martial arts are a source of great affliction."

For those who live and have their being in the world, there are four Ways: warrior, farmer, artisan, and merchant. First is the Way of the farmer. Equipping himself with various farming tools, the farmer watches spring and autumn come and go, tending unceasingly to the change of the seasons. This is the Way of the farmer.

Second is the Way of the merchant. The sake maker obtains the various tools of his trade and makes a living from profit according to the quality of his sake, good or bad. In whatever business he labors, the merchant makes a living according to his place, from profit earned. This is the Way of the merchant.

Third is the Way of the gentleman warrior. The warrior creates various weapons and must understand the uses of each one. Without a mastery of weapons and a comprehension of the merits of each one, the warrior shows a lack of accomplishment.

Fourth is the Way of the artisan. The Way of the carpenter entails skillfully crafting tools of all sorts, knowing how to use each one skillfully, making proper measurements with carpenter's square and ruler according to plans, and making a living by performing his work well. These are the four Ways of the samurai, farmer, artisan, and merchant.

Now the Way of carpentry will be used as an analogy for describing martial arts. There are houses of nobility, houses of warriors, houses of the four branches of Fujiwara; houses collapse, houses continue. There are schools and styles and "houses" of tradition. House is an analogue of the Way of the carpenter. The word for carpenter is written with Chinese characters meaning "great skill," and since the Way of martial arts also depends on great skill, carpentry is discussed in comparison with martial arts.

Should one wish to learn martial arts, ponder over this book. Let the teacher be the needle, let the disciple be the thread. Constant practice is required.

兵法の道、大工に喩へたる事

# Heiho no michi, daiku ni tatoetaru

## COMPARING THE WAY OF MARTIAL ARTS TO CARPENTRY

The master warrior, like the master carpenter, must discern the codes of the country and know the codes of the provinces and the codes for building his own house; this is the Way of the master carpenter. The master of carpentry knows the measurements and plans of halls, pagodas, temples, and the design of palaces and pavilions. He employs people to build houses. The master carpenter and the master warrior are the same in this regard.

In choosing wood to build a house, wood that is straight, free from knots, and of good appearance can be used as front pillars; wood that has some knots, but is straight and strong can be used for rear pillars. Wood that is somewhat weak but has no knots and a fine appearance can be used variously in thresholds, lintels, doors, and screens. A house of wood that is knotted and crooked but still strong—if how the wood is used is carefully considered—will stand a long time. Even timber that is knotted, crooked, and weak can be used for scaffolding, and later for firewood.

When the master carpenter employs workers, he knows their level of ability and assigns tasks accordingly; flooring; doors and screens; thresholds, lintels, and ceilings, and so on. The unskilled are made to lay floor joists, even less skilled to carve wedges. When the master carpenter employs workers according to skills assessment, the work progresses smoothly. Seeing that work progresses efficiently and smoothly, exercising judgment in all things, understanding what is important, discerning levels of morale, boosting confidence, understanding limitations—these are the concerns of the master carpenter. The principle of martial arts is likewise.

*Tea Bowl with Mt. Fuji. Japanese school. 19th century. Stoneware with black glaze.*

*Netsuke depicting a child hiding a theatrical mask behind his back. Japan. Late 19th century. Wood and ivory.*

*Netsuke depicting two rabbits. Japan. 1800–1850. Elephant ivory with inlaid horn eyes.*

# 兵法の道、士卒たる者の事
# Heiho no michi, shisotsu taru mono

## THE WAY OF MARTIAL ARTS AND THE SOLDIER

The soldier, just like the carpenter, sharpens his own tools, makes various implements, and keeps them in his tool kit. Following instructions from the master carpenter, they carve pillars and beams with adzes, level floors and shelves with planes, and even make fretwork and carvings. He sees to correct measurements and to detailed, skillful work. This is the code of carpenters. When one has learned all the elements and skills of the carpenter's trade, ultimately one can become a master carpenter.

It is crucial that the carpenter be accustomed to keeping his tools sharp and polished. With these tools the carpenter's craft is mastering the making of such things as shelves, tables, lamp stands, chopping boards, and lids for pots. Being a soldier is like this. Consider this well.

A carpenter's knowledge must include keeping his work straight, fitting joints together, using a plane well, avoiding abrasion and warping. This is essential. Anyone wishing to know the Way of martial arts should keep in mind all the things written here and reflect deeply on them.

*The Sadaijin in ceremonial costume. Japan. 15th century. Polychrome wood.*

# 此一流、二刀と名付くる事
# Kono heiho no sho, go-kan ni shitatsuru

## THE FIVE-SCROLL STRUCTURE OF THIS BOOK

This book is divided into five paths of martial arts, each section explaining their virtues; it is written in five scrolls, namely Earth, Water, Fire, Wind, and Void.

First, the Earth Scroll is the framework of the Way of martial arts, a study of my school. The true Way of martial arts is difficult to realize through swordsmanship alone. From great things small things are known, and through the shallows the depths are reached. A straight path delineates the surface of the earth: for this reason the first scroll is named the Earth Scroll.

Second is the Water Scroll. Make the mind like water, the base, the model. Water takes the shape of the vessel—square or round—that contains it, becoming a drop, becoming an ocean. Water has the color and clarity of lapis lazuli depths. Since water has clarity and purity, details of my school are written down in this scroll.

When one can apprehend correctly the principles of mastering swordsmanship, when one can defeat a single opponent unstintingly, then one can defeat everyone in the world. The heart and mind of defeating one man is the same as when against a thousand or ten thousand opponents.

The martial art of commanders is to make the great from the small, like constructing a great image of the Buddha from a one-foot scale model. The details of this matter are impossible to describe. Grasping myriad things from one thing is a virtue of martial arts. Affairs of my school are recorded in this Water Scroll.

Third is the Fire Scroll. In this scroll are recorded aspects of fighting. Fire may be large or small, and has a terrible force, so matters of fighting are recorded here. The way of doing battle is the same whether it is the fighting between two men or the battle of ten thousand men against ten thousand. One should perceive things reflectively, attending mindfully to the large and intentionally to the small.

The large is easy to see, the small difficult. Specifically, it is impossible to change instantly the fighting skills of a multitude of people; whereas one man's mind changes quickly, so the small things are difficult to gauge. This has to be reflected upon carefully. Matters described in the Fire Scroll can happen so quickly, it is essential in the martial arts to practice day after day to become habituated, regarding them as commonplace so the mind does not change. Therefore, aspects of fighting in battles are recorded in this Fire Scroll.

Fourth is the Wind Scroll. Calling this scroll the Wind Scroll is not because my own school is described here, but rather the various other schools of martial arts in the

*Opposite: Miyamoto Musashi Getting His Fortune Told. Utagawa Kuniyoshi. 1797–1861. Japan. 19th century. Woodblock print.*

# THE BOOK OF FIVE RINGS
## A PRIMER

*A classical Japanese interior with paper sliding doors, wooden floor, and teapot reflects the Buddhist detachment from material things.*

More than two millennia before Miyamoto Musashi wrote *The Book of Five Rings*, mystics in India developed the belief that the universe was composed of five basic elements: earth (*prithivi*), water (*jala*), fire (*tejas*), air (*vayu*), and the void (*akasa*). This idea of five elements eventually travelled to the West, where it was absorbed by early Greek philosophers, although *void*, which the Greeks had formerly made a central component of their universe, was downplayed; soon the concept of only four elements was being spread throughout Europe. Even today in the West, the signs of the zodiac are divided among the four elements.

In Asia, however, the five elements were fully adopted by Buddhism and transported to Japan by way of China and Korea. By the time Musashi wrote his book, it was commonly accepted by Japanese Buddhists that the five elements not only permeated the entire visible world, but that they could also be used to codify such invisible traits as philosophy and personality. Musashi drew on this concept as he wrote *The Book of Five Rings*, applying the five individual components to swordsmanship and strategy.

*Earth (chi)* In Hinduism and Buddhism, earth is an element that is associated with stability, gravity, confidence, and certainty, in other words, the state of being well-grounded.

For Musashi, the first step toward achieving *chi* was to be fully aware of one's surroundings, from the smallest thing to the largest and from the shallowest to the deepest. Being fully aware of one's environment also entailed paying attention to the timing and rhythm of changes in one's environment, not only things that are happening and near at hand, but also things that will happen in the near future and things that are already happening in the present.

Once a person is fully grounded, he or she should be able to recognize what tools, techniques, or strategies are appropriate for a particular time or place. As a martial arts teacher, of course, Musashi concentrated on weaponry, and his book included a list of common sense rules for how and when warriors should use their weapons. Because of the wide swing of the halberd and the long-distance range of the spear, these two weapons, he wrote, were generally appropriate only on the battlefield and were not helpful in close-quarter fighting. For similar reasons, Musashi wrote that the short sword, the *wakizashi*, was best for fighting in close quarters and enclosed spaces. Although those seem like elementary points, Musashi's real theme was that there are appropriate and inappropriate uses for any weapon, and it was incumbent upon a confident, well-informed warrior to know what they were.

*Water (sui)* The element of water is associated with adaptability, flexibility, and suppleness. Water can be still, be a trickle, be a roaring river, and sometimes be a storm-

*The hot springs and shrine at the volcanic peninsula of Sakurajima, Kyushu, Japan.*

tossed ocean. It adapts to its surroundings, and yet it always remains the same element, which gives it a sense of stability and tranquility even when it is in motion. Notably, in the traditional order of the elements, which rise from the element of the lowest power (earth) to the highest (the void), water comes directly after earth, as if to say that one must be well-grounded before learning to be flexible. When applying the element of water to martial arts, Musashi stressed the importance of fluidity of motion. In one of his sword moves, the "flowing water cut," the arm and sword flow out like a stream from the body, which remains a still pool. While the other moves he cited do not specifically mention water, he does emphasize fluidity and adaptability in motion. Just as water conforms itself to the shape of the receptacle that holds it, so a warrior should conform his stance to that of his enemy.

*Fire (ka)* Associated with force, movement, drive, and intensity, the element of fire, as Musashi pointed out, is intense whether it is a tiny flame or a blazing inferno. Fire can also be unpredictable, changing direction within a moment, and with that in mind, Musashi recommended a bit of unpredictability on the battlefield, as in tricking the enemy into attacks or chasing them into traps. Do the opposite of what the enemy anticipates, he wrote; if they think they will be attacked "like the sea," attack them "like a mountain" instead.

*The element of water is associated with adaptability, flexibility, and suppleness.*

*Wind (fu)* Wind represents freedom and the ability to move, grow, and expand without constraints. Internally, it means being open-minded or carefree. In Musashi's "Wind" chapter, which he also calls the "Tradition" chapter, he outlined rival teachings and long-standing methods regarding sword fighting. But that is not because he found *wind* to be synonymous with *tradition.* Instead, he promoted the understanding of other fighting schools, free of whatever flaws and constraints they possess. He repeatedly described how he disliked dogma. The only way to win, he said, is to be true to your own spirit rather than a particular dogma.

*Void (ku)* In both Hinduism and Buddhism, the void, which can also be translated as "sky" or "heavens," is the unseen essence that infuses all things, which is why it is the highest of all the elements. In a person, the element represents spirit, thought, creativity, and the ability to be spontaneous. Because the void is unseen, it cannot be taught; instead, it has to be experienced. And that explains why Musashi's chapter on the void is the shortest chapter in his book. He

felt he could not truly explain to students what the void is. In fact, he could only tell them what it is not. He reverted to ancient Chinese Buddhist concepts, such as *wu chi* (the infinite) and *tai chi* (the uncarved block), to explain the void. In essence, achieving the void means the ability to act appropriately without thinking, to let your actions spring from the natural rhythm that surrounds you. Knowledge of the void, Musashi wrote, is the foundation and true spirit of the way of the warrior.

*Plate used underneath an incense burner bearing names of the makers and workshop seals. Japanese School. Meiji period, late 19th century. Metal. Names right to left: uchimono (casting) Kurokawa Eishou, choukou (sculpting, carving, engraving) Kamijou Ikki, zougan (inlaid work) Kashima Ippu.*

*Hachiwari (helmet splitter). Japan. Circa 1700.*

world. By the word *wind* is meant *style* as in "old style" and "new style," styles of houses, and so on. So here is written explicitly about the various other schools of martial art, hence the Wind Scroll. Unless one understands others well, one cannot understand oneself.

Among those who labor on the Way and in all walks of life are men of heterodoxy. Even if one strives to do right on one's path, one may stray and not be on the true path even if one thinks otherwise. If one does not pursue the true path to the end, a little heterodoxy in the mind at the beginning later will turn into something largely divergent. Reflect well on this.

Quite naturally, other's martial arts are thought to be nothing but swordsmanship. The virtues and practices of my martial arts however are a different matter entirely. To make known the martial arts of the world, I record matters of other schools in this Wind Scroll.

Fifth is the Void Scroll. The reason for calling this scroll the Void Scroll is because at the very mention of the word *void* one can no longer speak of what is innermost depths and what is entrance gate. Once principles are attained, principles are let go. One has freedom in the martial arts naturally, and naturally achieves wonders. Knowing the rhythm when the time comes, one strikes naturally and one hits the mark naturally. All this is the Way of the Void. In this Void Scroll are recorded matters of entering naturally the true Way.

*Top: Handachi (sword with sheath). Japan. Circa 1550.*
*Below: Kirimon-Ashifaga family. Japan. Circa 1500.*

此一流、二刀と名付くる事

# Kono ichi-ryu, nito to natsukuru

## NAMING THIS SCHOOL NI TŌ, TWO SWORDS

As for two swords, it is the duty of all warriors, both commanders and soldiers, to wear two swords directly at his side. In olden times these were called *tachi* and *katana*, the great sword and the sword. Nowadays they are called katana and *wakizashi*, the sword and the short sword. There is no need to describe in detail the carrying of two swords. In our era, the Way of the warrior is to wear two swords at his side, whether he knows anything about them or not. To transmit the advantages of two swords, this school is called *Nitō Ichi-ryū*, the School of Two Swords.

The spear, the *naginata*, and so on are considered additional weapons among the tools of the warrior.

Beginners in the Way of this school should pursue the path and its practices wielding both swords, tachi in one hand, katana in the other. No tool should be left untouched when one's life is in the balance. No one should be willing to die with his swords untested at his side. Holding something in either hand, however, one cannot manipulate it freely to the left and right. The purpose is to make one accustomed to wielding the long sword with one hand. The spear, naginata, and other large weapons do not apply, but the long sword and short sword are both weapons that can be held in one hand.

# FUCHI-KASHIRA
# TWOFOLD ARTISTRY ON THE HILT OF THE SWORD

There is a saying that "the sword is only as good as its hilt," because a poor hilt can alter the swing of the finest blade. On a samurai sword, the hilt is only as good as its *fuchi* and *kashira*, the ring and cap that help hold the hilt of the sword in place.

The *fuchi*, "border" or "edge," is a wide metal ring at the base of the hilt (*tsuka*), adjacent to the blade. The *kashira*, "head," is a pommel made of metal or horn that encircles the opposite end of the tsuka. The tsuka is made of two carved pieces of wood that are glued together, wrapped in shagreen, and then wrapped again with silk or cotton cords. The fuchi and kashira, like the shagreen and the cords, help bind the wooden halves of the hilt together.

In one style of binding during the samurai era, the cords of the sword were wrapped around the kashira, but more commonly the cords were wrapped around the tsuka and threaded through holes drilled into the kashira, then tied tightly together.

During close combat, when a long blade might become unwieldy, the kashira at the butt end of the sword had an offensive purpose. In a move known as the *tsuka ate*, "hilt strike," the swordsman would jam his kashira into his opponent's solar plexus. In a move known as the *ganmen ate*, "strike to the face," the swordsman would thrust the kashira between the opponent's eyes.

Today the fuchi and kashira are more valued for their decorative qualities. Like many pieces of sword hardware, these items have offered a palette for artisans over the last several hundred years. Considering the nature of the sword, relatively few scenes of war were depicted. Instead, these pieces of battle equipment bear peaceful images of roses, chrysanthemums, sycamore leaves, plum blossoms, rice stalks, beetles, butterflies, and Buddhas. Except for the occasional image of a dragon or a samurai warrior, nothing indicates that the fuchi and kashira were parts of a death-dealing weapon. The images were generally made of solid steel, although some fancier swords were embellished with decorations of gold or other precious metals.

The fuchi and kashira came in a number of different shapes and sizes. Seventeenth-century sword smith Nishigaki Kanjiro and his descendants, one of the most

*Iron fuchi-kashira with dragonfly (tonbo) motif and gold highlights. Edo period. Circa 1750.*

*Soft metal fuchi-kashira with gold dragon decoration. Circa 1800.*

renowned families for making sword accoutrements, crafted their fuchi to resemble the necks of jars and their kashira in the shape of bulls' nose rings. In contrast, rival sword maker Shimizu Jingo and his clan made fuchi that looked like miniature drums.

Because so many craftsmen made matching sets of fuchi and kashira, today the two are viewed as a pair and referred to by the collective name *fuchi-kashira*. A well-preserved antique set, especially if the pieces match, is considered a highly sought-after collectible.

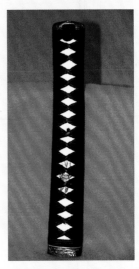

*Tsuka showing dragonfly fuchi-kashira in place.*

*Musashi on the back of a whale. Utagawa Kuniyoshi*
*(1798–1861). Japan. 19th century.*

*Tsuba decorated with fans. Japan. Circa 19th century. Copper with enamel.*

spaces, the short sword in circumscribed ones. In the beginning, this is the basic intention of the Way.

In this School of Two Swords, one can win whether with a long or short sword. That is why the length of the long sword is not established. The Way of this school is having the heart and mind to achieve victory by any means. Wielding two swords is better than one long sword when one man is fighting a throng of people or when one is sequestered or confined to a small space. There is no need to record in minute detail matters of this kind. Myriad things must be understood from one point. When one has attained the Way of martial arts there will be nothing one cannot see in all one's doings. Reflect deeply on this.

# 兵法二つの字の利を知る事
# Heiho futatsu no ji no ri o shiru

## UNDERSTANDING THE CONVENTIONS OF THE WORDS *MARTIAL ARTS*

In this particular Way, one who mastered the long sword has come to be called in our world *heihōsha*, a martial artist. Practitioners on the path of the warrior arts are known by the weapons they use: one who masters the bow is called an archer, one who masters the gun is called a marksman, one who masters the *yari*, or spear, is called a *yari-tsukai*, one who masters naginata is called a *naginata-tsukai*. By the same token, one who masters the long sword would be called a longswordsman, and one who masters the short sword a shortswordsman. Such weapons as bow, gun, yari, and naginata are tools of the warrior and hence, all belong to the Way of martial arts. There is a reason, however, for restricting reference to martial arts to longswordsmanship. Both governing the world and governing the self are accomplished by the virtue and dignity of the long sword. Therefore, the long sword is the foundation of martial arts.

With the power of long sword in one's possession, a single man can defeat ten men. When one man can defeat ten men, one hundred men can defeat a thousand, and a thousand men can defeat ten thousand. In this School of Two Swords, one man is considered the same as ten thousand; all the Ways of the warrior are called martial arts.

Of the various Ways such as Confucian, Buddhist, tea, etiquette, dance, and so on, none of these is the Way of the warrior. Even if one is not on any of these paths, if the Way is known widely, there is nothing in which they are not

The bad thing about wielding a long sword in each hand is that, first it is no good on horseback, and no good for quick pursuits, no good on boggy ground, muddy fields, rocky plains, steep roads, or in crowds.

If one wields a bow or a spear or other weapons in the left hand, these are all weapons manageable with one hand, but in wielding a long sword it too must be used with one hand; using two hands to wield one long sword is not the true Way. If it is difficult to strike down a man using one hand, then strike using two hands. No time or effort is needed. First, the purpose is to grow accustomed to wielding a long sword in one hand, because for Two Swords, learning to wield a long sword with one hand is the Way.

For anyone holding a long sword in one hand for the first time, it is heavy and difficult to swing. But everything is like that when first taken up: a bow is hard to draw, naginata is hard to swing. In any case, becoming accustomed to using each weapon, one becomes stronger at drawing the bow, one becomes better at swinging the long sword. Obtaining the power of the Way, one uses weapons easily.

The Way of the long sword is not in how quickly one can wield the sword, as is recorded in the second section, the Water Scroll. The long sword is to be wielded in open encountered. Whichever the case may be, as human beings, it is essential for each person to polish his own respective path.

# 兵法に武具の利を知るといふ事
# Heiho ni bugu no ri o shiru

## KNOWING THE EFFECTIVENESS OF WEAPONS IN MARTIAL ARTS

In categorizing the effectiveness of the warrior's tools—whichever tool it may be—there is an occasion and time to use them. The wakizashi, or short sword, is most effective in close quarters in which the enemy can be closely engaged. The long sword can be used effectively in any situation. The naginata is inferior to the spear on the battlefield. The spear takes the lead and the naginata the rear. Used at the same level of training, the spear provides slightly more strength.

Both the spear and the naginata have their uses, but neither is effective in tight spaces. Neither are they suited to taking prisoners, but rather are to be used on the field of combat. They are essential weapons for the battleground. However, if one learns to use them indoors, paying attention to little things and losing sight of the true Way, they will not be helpful in real encounters.

The bow is useful on the battlefield, in making advances and retreats. It can be shot quickly in rapid succession from among the spearmen and other ranks, and is especially suited for battle on open ground. For laying siege to a castle and for distances of more than forty yards, however, the bow is inadequate. In today's world the bow certainly and other martial arts as well are more the flower of show than the fruit of effects. Such art and skill are of no use in real combat.

From inside castle walls, no weapon is better than a gun. It has many advantages even on open ground, before engagement has begun. But once the battle commences, it becomes inadequate.

One of the virtues of the bow is that the flight of arrows can be seen with the eye. The gun's inadequacy is that the path of gunshot cannot be seen. This requires careful consideration.

As regards horses, they must be strong, built for endurance, and not be capricious. So too the tools of the warrior: as a horse walks imposingly, the long and short swords cut imposingly. The spear and naginata pierce imposingly. The bow and the gun must be sturdy and sure. No special preference should be given to any particular weapon. Too much is the same as not enough. Not

imitating anyone else, one should have weapons suited to oneself and that one uses easily. Commanders and soldiers alike should not have strong preferences. One must think out these things thoroughly.

# 兵法の拍子の事
# Heiho no byōshi

## TIMING IN MARTIAL ARTS

In all things there is an element of timing, but timing in martial arts in particular is difficult to master without practice. Timing is demonstrated in the world in such things as dance in the Way of Noh and in the music of Gagaku. This timing is good when they are in rhythm. In the Way of martial arts, there is timing and harmony in the shooting of a bow, the firing of a gun, and even riding a horse. In the various arts and skills of the warrior, timing cannot be overlooked.

There is even timing in emptiness.

There is timing in the life of a warrior, too, in rising in the world and in declining, in harmony and in discord. Similarly, there is timing in the Way of the merchant, in amassing fortune and losing it. In all paths of life there is a rising and a falling in timing. The timing of flourishing and the timing of declining must be keenly distinguished. Timing in martial arts is various. First know right timing and understand wrong timing, and discern appropriate timing from among the large and small and between slow and fast timing. Knowing the timing of things spatial and

*Okimono of people playing go. Sei. Japan. 19th century. Ivory.*

the timing of the reversal of things is the specialty of martial arts. Martial arts cannot be certain without knowledge of the timing of the reversal of things.

Victory in battle is gained by knowing the timing of one's opponents, and by using timing that the opponent does not expect, creating the timing of emptiness from the timing of wisdom. Above all, aspects of timing are recorded in all five scrolls of this book. Reflect on the things written here and practice them tirelessly.

By practicing and carrying out morning and night the above-mentioned Niten Ichi-ryū Way of martial arts, one's heart and mind will open up naturally. Transmitting it to the world as martial arts of both the one and the many, I record it here for the first time in these five scrolls: Earth, Water, Fire, Wind, and Void.

These are the rules for anyone wishing to learn my martial arts.

1. Do not deviate from the true Way.
2. Practice and nurture the Way of martial arts.
3. Become acquainted with the arts.
4. Know the Way of professions.
5. Discern the advantages and disadvantages in everything.
6. Cultivate the power of discernment of truth in all things.
7. Perceive what cannot be seen with the eye.
8. Attend to even the smallest detail.
9. Do nothing that is useless.

For the most part, the Way of martial arts is to be practiced bearing these principles in mind. In this Way in particular, unless one can perceive the straight and true in the wide field of vision, one cannot master martial arts. Once this principle has been learned, one will not be defeated when up against twenty or thirty men.

More than anything, one must maintain an energetic study of martial arts, and labor earnestly and forthrightly, thereby making victory possible with one's hands and with one's eyes. Also when one can use one's whole body at will through training, then one can gain victory with one's body. With further cultivation of the heart and mind one can defeat the enemy with one's mind. Having reached this point, how can one then be defeated by others?

Moreover, martial arts on a collective level is also winning at keeping talented subordinates, employing many people, demonstrating correct personal comportment, governing the country, caring for the people, and maintaining order. Understanding how not to be bested by others, improving oneself, making a name for oneself—in whichever path one pursues—these are all part of martial arts.

Dictated by Shinmen Musashi to Teruo Mangonojō on the twelfth day of the fifth month, the second year of

*Hokusai Manga. Katsushika Hokusai (1760–1849). Japan. 19th century. Ink on paper.*

# THE MON
## PERSONAL IDENTIFICATION, CLAN PRIDE

The symbols of the Japanese *mon* (which can translated to either "badge" or "crest")were first associated with the military in the twelfth century, when mon were used on battle banners by Yoritomo, the builder of the Kamakura Shogunate. Stylized symbols of flowers and birds had for many generations been associated with privileged families, and used to identify their personal effects. And in feudal times before 1200, royalty (*kuge*), lords (*daimyo*), and warriors (*samurai*) were allowed to wear mon. But otherwise, until the interaction with the West during the Meiji era, Japan knew nothing of organized decoration for military or other service.

Unlike western heraldry, which depends on intricately colored internal design, the mon is identified only by its simple black form. It may occasionally have been colored to contrast on clothing, stand out on a *daimyo*'s ship, or be painted in gold on a warrior's armor, but the universality of the plain black form persists even today.

Initially, powerful clans considered samurai equal to the family name and eligible to use its mon. This became common by the mid-Muromachi period (1337–1573). During the following hundred years, several books were published that listed names and mon of warriors. In the age of battles (1450–1600), it became increasingly necessary in battle to identify individual soldiers (*ashigaru*) with the commanders' mon. When families fought against each other, mon were modified to avoid confusion. The three most notable mon are associated with shoguns and emperors: the paulownia (*kiri*) used by Ashikaga Hideyoshi, the hollyhock (*aoi*) used by Tokugawa Ieyasu, and the chrysanthemum (*kiku*) used by Hirohito. The imperial court often granted the use of its mon to warriors for their distinguished service.

*A military officer's family mon depicting a knotted goose.*

By the Edo period (1603–1867), mon became increasingly popular on sword furniture (*koshirai*). Some sword guards (*tsuba*) were patterned on or inlaid with mon. Mon continued to be worn by *saimyo*. Visiting diamyo to the shogun's castle were required to wear mon, as were persons employed by the shogun. Merchants also wore mon to distinguish their service; these became company symbols later in the Genroku period (1688–1703).

*Kyu-Gunto* swords (1875–1886) wielded by Japanese soldiers often featured a small family mon (*kamon*) disk soldered or pinned to the pommel (*kashira* or *kabutogane*).

*Iron tsuba with crossed hawk feather (taka no ha) family mon. Japan. 18th century.*

Since there was no law or legal enforcement, more and more common people (*heimin*) soon boasted adopted mon for personal use. Kabuki actors began wearing mon on their clothing, and handed their mon down through their families. Even farmers had them. By 1750, books of mon designs were available to aid in selection of mon for formal kimono. After the Meiji restoration (1868), when western clothing became fashionable, the mon was still worn on formal occasions on black robes, a tradition that persists to modern times.

The adoption of mon in contemporary times has spread to personal, family, corporate, school, and club applications, in and outside Japan.

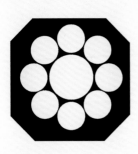

Martial arts schools commonly adopt a mon as a trademark symbol. The criteria that Japanese use today to adopt mon for personal use include associations with nature, remembrance of a family member, respect for a notable person in history, or just decorative fancy.

Mon can be seen today on both historical and modern mass-produced armor and sword hardware such as *koshirae, tsuba, fuchi-kashira,*

and *saya*, where the mon has been applied for purely decorative use. However, on an old and original piece, a mon could potentially signify that the item belonged to a particular family or person, and was placed there to identify the owner. If that is the case, a legend may lie behind the mon's deceptively simple form.

Japanese terms for types of mon:

| | |
|---|---|
| Kamon | Family mon |
| Jomon | Established crest. Main or official crest. Formal mon. |
| Hanmom | Another word for established crest |
| Shomon | Genuine crest |
| Omote mon | Front crest |
| Buko no mon | Martial merit for battle |
| Kaemon | Other crests used by the family |
| Fukumon | Supplementary crest |
| Betsumon | Separate crest |
| Hikaemon | Reserve crest |
| Uramon | Rear crest |

*Family mon opposite page counterclockwise from top: well frame, paulownia, imperial chrysanthemum, hollyhock. This page clockwise from top: dragonfly, crossed hawk feather, rabbit, cherry blossom, nine stars, crane.*

*Helmet with star-sword constellation and taka mo ha (hawk feather) mon in gold paint.*

# KYUDO
# THE ART OF JAPANESE ARCHERY

Translating literally to "the way of the bow," *kyudo* encompasses the ancient Japanese tradition of archery as a martial art and ceremonial practice. Many people think of Kyudo as Zen archery or meditation archery, because the sacred form is a highly mental and spiritual art concentrated on the archer's lifelong search for truth. Many consider kyudo to be the purest form of martial art, incorporating physical, spiritual, mental, and moral development into the tradition.

The ultimate achievements of a devotion to kyudo are *Shin*, *Zen*, and *Bi*. To achieve Shin, or "truth," a master archer perfects the practice of holding, drawing, and shooting with a bow. His or her developed mastery guides the archer's progress toward recognizing reality in its pure form. With the guidance of the bow, the archer is believed to develop a sound moral conscience, achieving Zen. The process of finding both truth and Zen leads to beauty, or Bi. The archer's emotional and mental maturity give the performance of archery an aesthetic and esoteric quality, combining skill and spirituality to produce art.

The practice of kyudo is meticulous and precise, involving many steps that an archer must practice for decades to perfect. The first four steps include:

*Ashibumi.* the positioning of the feet
*Dozukuri.* the formation of the body
*Yugamae.* readying the bow
*Uchiokoshi.* raising the bow.

These steps are performed with precision and concentration. Once the archer raises the bow, he performs:

*Kai.* the full draw
*Hanare.* the release of the arrow
*Zanshin.* remaining in position and mentally following through with the shot before returning to a state of pure concentration.

While Western archery also requires particular steps and techniques, the goal is quite different from that of Japanese archery. Japanese bows date to as early as the fourth century BCE, when increased contact between Japan and China is thought to have had a great influence on Japanese archery. Western bows are typically designed for the purpose of aim and accuracy in hitting a target, but Japanese bows are cut from bamboo, a difficult material from which to build a bow.

The art of constructing a bow, or *yumi*, requires tremendous skill and strength. Drawing the yumi requires a strong arm and steady concentration. Archers of the kyudo tradition do not focus on hitting their targets as their main objective. While marksmanship is important, most followers of kyudo adhere to the philosophy of *seisha seichu*, which translates to "correct shooting is correct hitting." In other words, the process is more important than the result of hitting a target.

The ancient teachings of kyudo were guided by the Confucian idea that practicing archery daily for several decades could lead a person to find and understand his or her true self. The martial art form has grown under the influence of hundreds of years of Shinto and Zen Buddhist religions as well as the evolving needs of warriors over centuries of battle. In ancient Japan, court nobles practiced archery as a form of ceremonial martial art, while the Japanese warrior class emphasized archery as an actual warfare technique, referred to as *kyujutsu*.

In the sixteenth century, firearms were introduced to Japan by shipwrecked Portuguese soldiers who landed on an island off of Kyushu. When firearms were incorporated into the Japanese military, the use of the bow in battle grew obsolete. Warriors continued, however, to train with the bow as they considered it an important part of physical and mental refinement. A kyudo instructor named Honda Toshizane created a hybrid style of kyudo that combined warrior-style archery with the ceremonial archery practiced by the royal court nobles of Japan. His style became known as the Honda *ryu*, and was favored by the public.

There are nearly half a million archers still practicing kyudo today. *Dojos* exist around the world, teaching varying styles and techniques. In 1953, the All Nippon Kyudo Federation formed a committee to streamline the practice of kyudo and harmonize the form. The committee's purpose was to examine the profound elements of the martial art practiced in each school and establish a style that incorporated each of the best techniques. The result was *The Kyudo Manual*, or *kyudo kyohon*, a four-volume series explaining the principles and techniques of kyudo. The manual is used today as a resource for the most widely accepted practices of Zen archery in Japan and within most kyudo federations around the world.

*Arrowheads. Japan. Circa 1650.*

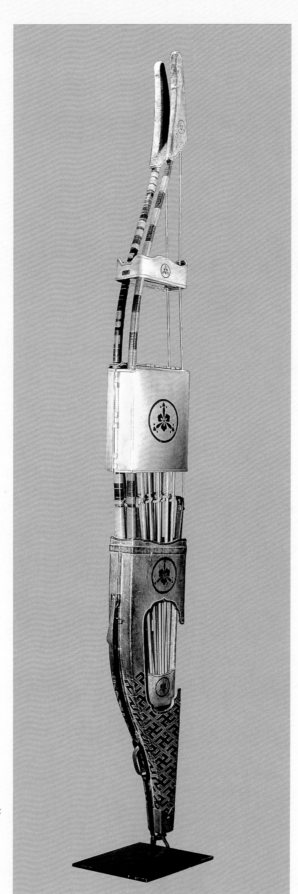

*Yumidai (archery set). Late 18th or early 19th century. Features mon of the Fuji family. Bamboo, metal, and gilded leather. More than 8 feet high.*

# THE YUMI
## THE JAPANESE LONG BOW

The techniques of Japanese bow making, or *yumi* making, have remained relatively unchanged for nearly five centuries. Unlike many Western bows used for hunting, the yumi is tall and thin and often spans more than six feet in length. Traditional yumis are constructed of bamboo, leather, and wood.

The shape of the yumi is perhaps its most important aspect. The grip is located slightly off the center toward the lower tip of the bow. The upper and lower portions of the bow have differing curves, giving the bow an asymmetrical shape. There are several theories about the asymmetrical design of the yumi. Some believe that the differing curves were designed especially for archers on horseback, the shorter arcs allowing the archer to swap the bow from one side of the horse to the other with ease. The curves also provide a wrist positioning that enabled the archer to use maximum force. Other theories explain the asymmetrical curvature as a result of lacking technology in laminating techniques. Yet, the yumi is still made in the same asymmetrical shape today, even when fashioned from synthetic fibers using advanced laminating techniques.

The string or *tsuru* of a yumi was traditionally made of hemp, but many modern bows use Kevlar and other synthetic materials, which last longer than natural fibers. For the health of the yumi, archers typically do not replace the string until it is broken, because the flexing of the bow against the string is healthy for the shape and maintenance of the bamboo.

Perhaps the most interesting aspect of the yumi is its role in the life of a devoted kyudo student. The yumi is looked upon as sacred and is respected accordingly. A yumi is thought to hold within it the spirit of its maker, and many archers believe that the yumi holds intrinsic teaching powers. Most kyudo students treat the yumi with extreme care, shielding it from excessive heat or weather and carrying it upright. A student never steps over a yumi that is lying on the ground, because it would be considered disrespectful to both the bow and its owner. Archers refrain from touching the yumi of other archers without permission, as the action can be viewed as comparable to touching another's spouse in an inappropriate way.

There are three basic types of yumi in use today: a standard bamboo bow, a lacquered bamboo bow, and a synthetic bow. Most students of kyudo prefer the traditional bamboo yumi, because its structure and creation has not changed much over the last five centuries. However, often novice archers are encouraged to begin training with a synthetic bow, which requires less care to maintain. Synthetic bows made from carbon fiber or fiberglass-coated wood are more durable, less expensive, and easier to find. A modern lacquered yumi is handmade these days by only a few bow makers, and can cost several thousand dollars or more. Lacquered yumi are mostly used in ceremonies by advanced archers, because they are less practical for students of kyudo and general archery practice.

Yumi can be made to have different pull strengths and come in a wide array of sizes and lengths. Many beginners start with a bow with a pull of around twenty-two pounds. The average highly experienced female archer uses a yumi with a pull of around thirty-five pounds, whereas a highly experienced male typically uses a bow with a pull strength of forty to forty-five pounds.

The curves and shape of a yumi are greatly affected by its string. A yumi that is flat when unstrung is usually left unstrung when unused. A yumi of this shape is sometimes referred to as "tired." On the other hand, a yumi that remains curved when unstrung has typically been left strung for long periods of time in an effort to conserve the shape or "tame" the bow.

Because of the delicacy of such materials as bamboo and natural fibers, a yumi that is not cared for is often useless after a short time. However, yumi that receive good care and conditioning can last through generations.

# Sui no maki

2

## The Water Scroll

The heart of Niten Ichi-ryū martial arts is based on water, and as one who practices the leading-edge method, I call this the Water Scroll, in which is recorded the long sword modus operandi of this school. A detailed description of this Way as I understand it in my heart, however, is not possible. Even if the words are unconnected, the principle should be understood intuitively. Each and every word written in this book should be pondered. Thinking loosely about it, one will encounter many things that do not conform to the Way.

The principles of martial arts, although written down in terms of one-on-one combat, must be understood as a battle between an army of multitudes on each side, and seen on a large scale.

In this Way in particular, if one misconstrues the path even slightly, one will stray from the course and fall into a bad state of affairs.

Just reading this book will not lead one to the Way of martial arts. Think of this book as being written for oneself; do not think only of reading or learning or imitating, but take the principles as if discovered within one's heart and mind, make them a part of oneself, and work on them continually.

## 兵法心持の事
# Heiho kokoromochi

### FRAME OF MIND IN MARTIAL ARTS

In the Way of the martial arts, one's frame of mind should be no different from one's normal mind. In both everyday life and in martial arts do not change it in the least. Make the mind open and direct, neither too tense nor too lax, centering it so as not to let it waver, letting it relax calmly, weigh this instant in the mind carefully, never letting the relaxation stop.

Even when one is tranquil, the mind is not tranquil; even when one is rushed, the mind is not rushed at all. The mind is not tugged by the body; the body is not tugged by the mind. Heed the mind, not the body. Do not let the mind tend toward either too little or too much. Even if weak

*Two Men Washing a Horse in a Waterfall. From the series The Yoshitsune Horse Washing Waterfalls at Yoshino in Izumi Province. Katsushika Hokusai (1760–1849). Oban Tate-E.*

*Opposite: The Syllable Wo: Hayami Sōzaemon Fujiwara no Mitsutaka, from the series Biographies of the Faithful Samurai. Utagawa Yoshitora (1836–1887). Japan. 1866. Ink and color on paper.*

*The Battle of Kurikaradani. Utagawa Kuniyoshi. (1797–1861).*
*Japan. 1845. Ink and color on paper.*

minded on the outside, be strong minded on the inside, and do not let one's mind be discerned by others.

Those small in stature must know the mind of the large; the large in stature must know the mind of the small. Large or small, one must keep the mind straight and free from prejudice. With the inner mind uncluttered and open, one must place one's wisdom on a high level. It is crucial to polish intently one's mind and one's wisdom. Polish one's wisdom, discern between the just and unjust, know what is good and what is bad, experience the various Ways of the arts and skills, and once one cannot be deceived by people of the world, then in one's mind is realized the wisdom of the art of war.

Wisdom of the art of war is unlike any other thing. On the battlefield, even when under extreme duress, one must have mastered the principles of the art of war and one must have attained a mind that does not move.

*Kake (sword stand).*

# 兵法の身なりの事
# Heiho no mi nari

## THE BODY IN MARTIAL ARTS

In using the body, keep the head erect, tilting the face neither downward, upward, nor sideward. The eyes do not move. Do not wrinkle the forehead but furrow the brows. Keeping the eyes steady, try not to blink, and narrow the eyes slightly. The expression on the face is calm, the nose straight, chin slightly forward. The back of the neck is straight, with strength focused in the nape. From the shoulders down, feel the whole body as one, shoulders lowered, spine straight, and buttocks not protruding. Concentrate energy from the knees down to the tips of the toes. Tighten the abdomen so the waist does not bend. Wedge the scabbard of the wakizashi against the waist so the belt does not loosen. This is the teaching called "tightening the wedge."

In all things of the martial arts, it is essential to make one's everyday physical stance the stance used in martial arts, and make the stance used in martial arts the same as one's everyday stance. Reflect well on this.

*Matchlock pistol. Japan. 1615–1868. Iron, wood, lacquer, gold, and silver.*

# 兵法の目付といふ事
# Heiho no metsuke

## THE GAZE IN MARTIAL ARTS

The gaze should range large and wide. The gaze is twofold: observing, *kan*, and seeing, *ken*. The eyes that observe should be stronger, the eyes that see weaker. It is most important in martial arts to see the faraway closely and the close from faraway. To know the opponent's sword and yet not to look at it in the least is crucial in martial arts. This takes practice. The gaze is the same in both large-scale and small-scale martial arts.

It is necessary to see out of the corner of both eyes without moving the eyeballs. This is difficult to master right away when one is in a hurry. Remember what is written here; always be aware of the gaze, discipline oneself so whatever happens the gaze does not change.

# 太刀の特様の事
# Tachi no mochiyo

## HOLDING THE LONG SWORD

When wielding the long sword, one's thumb and forefinger float lightly in their grip, whereas the middle finger is neither too tight nor too slack, and the fourth and little fingers grip tightly. It is bad to have slackness in the hand.

Take up the sword with the thought that it is for killing the enemy. Even when cutting down an opponent, one should not change the grip of the sword, and one's grip should not falter. When one strikes an opponent's sword, checks it, parries, or pins, change the feeling in just the thumb and forefinger; in any event, one should grip the sword with the thought to kill.

One's grip when testing the blade or when striking in combat should be the same: gripping the sword to cut a man down. As a rule, to fix on one thing or to settle on one thing is unacceptable in both the long sword and the hand. Fixing on something is the hand of death, flexibility the hand of life. This must be well understood.

*Dragon armor. Japan.*

# MENUKI
## THE SWORD'S SECRETLY USEFUL EMBELLISHMENT

*Set composed of Kozuka, Kogai, and menuki in shakdo wood with nanako granulation, engraved with peony flowers, symbol of spring for Taoists, Mitkoronomo.*

*Menuki,* the tiny metal sculptures that helped a warrior's hand find the proper grip on the hilt of his sword, may be the fanciest artworks designed never to be seen. The menuki formed a bestiary in miniature: richly detailed figurines of gold, silver, copper, or bronze, typically depicting animals in motion, such as prowling tigers, flying storks, galloping horses, charging boars, swinging monkeys, or writhing dragons. Some menuki depicted stationary objects, such as arrangements of flowers or the snow-topped peak of Mount Fuji, while others showed humans, ranging from battling samurai or ninja to fishermen grappling with their catch.

Despite the detail, craftsmanship, and fine metals that have gone into the menuki, throughout most of their history they have been largely or wholly invisible beneath the silken cords that bind the hilt of the sword. Depending on how the sword is wrapped, the menuki may only be felt, rather than seen. And to an untrained hand, they feel like mere bumps beneath the cords.

On the earliest samurai swords, there were no menuki. Instead, there were *motagi,* a pair of ornamental caps, one on each side of the hilt, designed to cover the *mekugi,* a pair of pins that screwed into each other to hold the hilt to the tang of the sword. Eventually, the mekugi evolved into a single pin of hard bamboo, and the motagi disappeared and were replaced by a pair of menuki, again, one on each side of the sword, located near the heads of the mekugi.

Menuki were positioned in specific locations on top of the *make,* the swath of shagreen that covered the hilt. The traditional method, particularly when the sword was carried with its edge up, was to place the menuki slightly toward the saber on the *omote* (front) side of the hilt but toward the pommel on the *ura* (back) side. On the other hand, when the sword was carried with its edge down, the menuki were placed in the opposite positions on each side, as *gyaku-menuki* (reverse menuki).

Once the menuki were in position, they were held in place by the silken cords that were wrapped tightly around the hilt. Depending on how thickly the cords were wrapped, it was often impossible to see anything but a thin sliver, if that, of the menuki lying beneath. The menuki were nearly invisible when the warrior used the *katate-maki* (battle wrap) method of wrapping the sword, but they were a bit more visible under the *hineri-maki* wrap, which left diamond-shape windows beneath the cords.

Whether the menuki were seen or unseen, the swordsman could feel them beneath the cords. They helped him find the proper position for his palms when gripping the hilt. And they helped him maintain his grip while wielding the sword. In the heat of battle, it was a bit easier to hold onto a bumpy hilt than a smooth one.

These days, it takes a true swordsman to appreciate the utilitarian value of the menuki. More often than not, they are thought of as mere decorations, rather than useful guides for the positioning of the hand. Like so many accessories for the samurai sword, they are valued as collectibles and are seen in display cases nearly as often as on the hilt.

# 足づかいの事
# Ashizukai

### FOOTWORK

In footwork, step firmly on the heel, letting the toes float slightly. Whether one's footwork is wide or narrow, slow or fast, it should be as one normally walks. The three kinds of steps known as flying steps, floating steps, and unyielding steps are no good. Of extreme importance in this Way is the step known as yin-yang. The *yin-yang* step refers to not moving one foot only. When striking, when pulling back, when parrying, one moves right-left, right-left with the yin-yang step. One is not to step with one foot only. Regard this carefully.

# 五方の構えの事
# Goho no kamae

### FIVE STANCES

The five stances are Upper Position, Middle Position, Lower Position, Right Side, and Left Side. Stances, *kamae*, may be divided into these five kinds, but each of them is for cutting a man down. Besides these five there are no other stances. Whatever stance one takes, do not think of it as taking a stance, think of it as killing. Whether one's stance is large or small depends on the situation; take the most advantageous one. Upper, Lower, and Middle Positions are basal, Right Side and Left Side are practicable. The Right Side and Left Side are for confining situations when there is no space above or to one side. Which stance to use—Right or Left—is decided depending on circumstances. The important thing of this Way is to understand that the ultimate stance is the Middle Position. The Middle Position is the essence of all stances. Look at this as martial arts on a large scale: the Middle Position is the seat of the commander, and following the commander are the other four stances. Consider this well.

*Late Edo period matchlocks. Signed "Koshu Kunimoto Tamba."*

*Decorative architectural features such as this became quite popular on village shrines after the construction of the ornate Nikko Toshogu shrine in the early 17th century.*

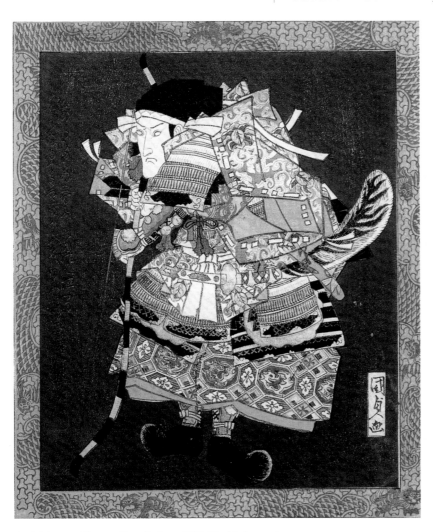

*Bando Mitsugoro. Utagawa Kunisada. Japan. 1820. Woodblock engraving.*

*Village rice planters, vulnerable to attack by bandits, were dependent on the protection of local samurai.*

# 太刀の道といふ事
# Tachi no michi

## THE WAY OF THE LONG SWORD

Knowing the Way of the long sword means that even when handling with two fingers the sword one usually carries, one understands how to wield it and can flash it freely. If one tries to swing the long sword quickly, one goes against the Way of the long sword, and cannot swing it freely. To be handled well, the long sword is to be wielded calmly. If one tries to swing it too quickly, as one would a fan or a short sword, one departs from the Way of the long sword and so it is hard to handle. This is called "short sword chopping" and cannot be used for cutting down a man with a long sword. When one cuts downward with a long sword, raise it upwards in a way that is easy to do. When one swings the long sword sideways, bring it back sideways in a way that is easy to do. Extend the elbows as wide as possible and swing forcefully—this is the Way of the long sword.

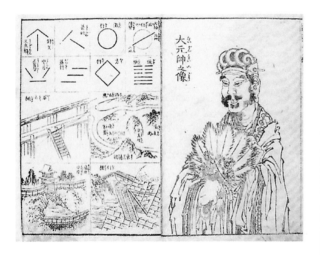

*Statue of Daigensai. Katsushika Hokusai (1760–1849). Japan. Edo Period, 19th century. Woodblock print, ink on paper.*

# 五つの表の次第
# Itsutsu no omote no shidai

## FIVE BASIC APPROACHES

The first approach, for which the stance is Middle Position, is to confront the opponent with the tip of one's sword pointed in his face. When moving into the opponent, and he attacks with a long sword, check him by glancing his sword to the right. When the opponent attacks again, return his sword point upwards, keeping one's sword in its downward position, then when he hits once more, one can strike his hands from below. This is the first basic form.

These five basic approaches are difficult to understand by what is written here alone. These five basic approaches must be practiced with the long sword in hand. Through these five swordplay forms, one will understand my Way of the long sword, and whatever the techniques deployed by one's opponent, they too will be made clear. This is the teaching: there are no stances other than the five stances in the Two Sword school of the long sword. Train and practice diligently.

*Knowing the Way of the long sword means that even when handling with two fingers the sword one usually carries, one understands how to wield it and can flash it freely. If one tries to swing the long sword quickly, one goes against the Way of the long sword, and cannot swing it freely.*

The second approach, for which the stance is Upper Position, is to strike the opponent just as he is about to strike. If one's sword misses the opponent, keep the sword where it is, then when the opponent strikes again, hit him from below with an upward motion. The same is true for striking him again. In this approach are diverse frames of mind and various rhythms. If through these approaches one trains and practices in this school, one will know fully the five forms of the long sword and be able to win whatever the circumstances. Practice it.

The third approach, for which the stance is Lower Position, is to strike the opponent's hands from below, with

*Minamoto no Muneyuki Ason, from the series "100 Poems by 100 Poets Explained by a Nurse." Katsushika Hokusai (1760–1849). Japan. Circa 1835. Woodblock print.*

a feeling of pulling back, at the same time he tries to strike. As the opponent's hands are struck, he will strike again; as the opponent tries to knock down one's sword, keep that position, then after he has struck, cut across both his arms. The aim is to cut down the opponent all at once from the Lower Position the instant he attacks. On one's path of the long sword, the stance in Lower Position will be frequently encountered, both in the early stages and in the later as well. Practice and train with the long sword in hand.

The fourth approach is to hit the opponent's hands from below as he strikes. When one's sword strikes upward from below and the opponent tries to knock it down, fend off the path of his sword as it comes, aiming for his hands and cutting crossways and upward toward one's shoulder. This is the Way to wield a long sword. This also is the way to win by fending off the path of the opponent's sword when he tries to strike again. Study this well.

The fifth approach, for which the sword is held

horizontally in the Right Side stance, is to swing the sword crossways from below to the Upper Position, then to cut straight from above. This too is important knowledge for the Way of the long sword. If one can use a sword according to this form, then one can wield freely a heavy long sword.

The details of these five basic approaches are not to be written down. To master the Way of the long sword of my school, to learn its basic rhythms, to be able to discriminate opponent's techniques of the sword, one must first take these five basic approaches and make them a part of one's everyday practice, always polishing one's skills. Even while fighting an opponent, one polishes one's use of the long sword, discerning the mind of the opponent, testing various rhythms, and winning under any circumstances. All this requires thoughtful deliberation.

# WARRIOR'S DAY OFF
## A SAMURAI IN CASUAL DRESS

When the samurai was on the battlefield, he looked like a killing machine in armor. Off the field was another matter. More often than not, the samurai was swathed in luxurious silk robes and trousers that were so baggy they looked like skirts. The generic term for these clothes was *kimono*, "wearing item," referring to a broad array of clothing in its original sense, but the word *kimono* is now mainly used to denote a particular kind of full-length robe. In the days of the samurai, a kimono ensemble might include an under-robe, a half-robe, trousers, an open shirt, a vest, or an overcoat.

During the Heian period, from 794 to 1185 CE, after wrapping himself in a loincloth, a samurai would don the *kosode*, a kimono-shaped, ankle-length undergarment of white silk. The kosode was designed with relatively narrow sleeves, which would fit neatly inside the broader arms of the robes worn over it. After the end of the Heian period, the kosode evolved into outerwear, but it is still distinguished by its narrow sleeves. Taking the kosode's place as the chief undergarment was a two-piece white slip known as the *juban*.

Besides the kosode, the samurai had a large number of choices, as indicated by the following list.

*Hitoe.* An unlined robe typically meant for summer wear. During the Heian period, these robes were generally colored white, red, or blue-green, although in later periods reddish orange and pale green became popular. Toward the end of the Edo period, which spanned from 1603 to 1868, some hitoe were decorated with scenes depicting autumn or winter, a reminder of cool weather during the summer heat.

*Noshi.* A long, voluminous coat with a pocketlike fold along the lower back, called the *hakoe*. During winter, the samurai wore the *noshi* with a lining underneath; in summer, there was no lining.

*Okatabira.* A medium-sized robe that essentially filled the role of a T-shirt, worn under the hitoe or noshi. The *okatabira* kept its wearers warm in winter and protected the other clothing from perspiration in summer. In fact, it is also known as the *asetori no katabira*, "sweat-collecting garment." Perhaps to disguise the sweat stains, the okatabira was a dark reddish orange in summertime but a bright white in winter.

*Karaginu.* The long robe that the aristocrats originally wore for hunting. Like many robes, the *karaginu* had wide sleeves that draped well below the arms, but it was also equipped with cords that allowed them to be tied at the wrist, which was much more practical when handling a bow and arrow. The front of the karaginu was typically pulled above the *obi* (sash) and bunched up around the belly, perhaps a throwback to the way it had been worn by horseback hunters, and the back could either be similarly bunched up or left free to fall to the ankles. By the late twelfth century, it had evolved into formal wear, although it could not be worn in the shogun's court except for informal functions.

*Yukata.* A relatively narrow cotton kimono that was originally a bathrobe, which is the literal translation of *yukata*. Even today, the yukata is often worn after bathing, whether at home or at a spa. But over the centuries, it has become acceptable to wear yukata outside. These days, yukata are mostly worn by women, but they are also standard wear for *sumo* wrestlers, who are expected to wear them year-round.

*Hitatare.* A loose shirt that looks somewhat like a waist-length kimono. During the Heian period, *hitatare* were simple hemp and linen garments mostly worn by peasants. The sleeves were relatively short and narrow, so as not to interfere with manual labor. In winter, the peasants also wore them at night over their kosodes to keep warm. By the late twelfth century, the hitatare had caught on among the upper classes, who broadened the sleeves to make them more impressive and began making them out of silk in addition to older materials.

*Kataginu.* A long open vest or sleeveless jacket, which was often quilted to provide warmth. The *kataginu* was typically worn in an ensemble that included the outerwear kosode and hakama. During the Edo period, the kataginu evolved to include wide, creased wings jutting out from the shoulders.

*Dobuku.* An open-fronted jacket made of sturdy fabric, with a tie around the upper chest to pull it closed. It started as the garb of street vendors, but by the end of the sixteenth century, it had been adopted by the aristocracy.

*Picture Book of Plays for Saruwaka. Anonymous. 18th century. Catalogue No. 1689c. Illustrations in ink on paper.*

*Hakama.* Broad, flowing trousers, which were typically part of a matched ensemble. The *hakama* were often paired with specific pieces of clothing in formal or informal suits. In such pairings, the hakama and the upper garment would typically be cut from the same fabric and sewn in the same style. Specific ensembles included the *hitatare sugata*, in which the hakama and hitatare are paired together, and the *kataginu kamishimo*, a pairing with the kataginu.

*Nagabakama.* The very long and very wide pants that trailed on the ground behind the feet. During the Edo period, high-ranking samurai at formal events, such as an audience with the shogun, were sometimes asked to wear *nagabakama*. The samurai had to take great care to avoid tripping over the trouser legs, which easily got entangled underfoot. During an age of court intrigue, the benefit of the nagabakama is that it kept the wearer from being engaged in too much mischief.

*Geta.* Wooden sandals built on a pair of platforms to keep the wearer above the ground.

*Waraji.* Rope sandals.

*Zori.* Flat sandals made of rice straw, lacquered wood, leather, or other materials.

*Tabi.* Split-toed socks.

*Tate eboshi.* A two-foot high conical hat, typically worn in formal settings.

*Kasa.* A large straw hat or, in another variation curious-looking to Western eyes, something akin to a wicker basket to cover the entire head. Such a hat was no doubt useful for someone who did not want to be recognized, although alternatively a cloth cap or hood could be worn.

In general, most samurai leisure clothes were gaudy, with bright neon colors and flamboyant floral designs, geometric patterns, images of bamboo shoots, storks, dragons, or other flora and fauna. However, as if to remind passersby that he was really a warrior, the samurai wore an important accessory when going out in public: his *daisho*, or "big and small" set of swords. The samurai would thrust the two weapons through his obi and keep them on display as a symbol of his social status.

# 有構無構の教への事
# Uko muko no oshie

## THE STANCE-WITHOUT-A-STANCE TEACHING

Having a stance without a stance means there is no fixed form for taking up a long sword. Be that as it may, there are five ways of holding the sword to be encountered. How the sword is held depends both on one's relationship with the opponent, and on the place, as well as on the circumstances; whichever way the sword is held, it is to be held to cut down easily one's opponent.

Depending on the situation, the Upper Position, if one feels like lowering it slightly, can become the Middle Position; the Middle Position can be raised slightly, depending on the merits of doing so, to become the Upper Position. At times the Lower Position as well can be raised slightly to become the Middle Position. Both the Left Side and Right Side Positions also can be thrust slightly toward the center, depending on one's standing, to become either Middle or Lower Positions.

Along these lines, the principle is to assume a position that is a stance without a stance. In any event, foremost when taking up the sword is the intention to kill the enemy. Even when one parries, strikes, checks, engages, or obstructs an opponent's attacking blade, all these feats must be understood as opportunities to cut down the opponent. If one thinks to parry, thinks to strike, thinks to check, thinks to engage or obstruct, then one is rendered incapable of cutting down the opponent. It is crucial to regard everything as an opportunity to kill. Consider this well.

In the large-scale martial arts, arraying the troops for battle is also a stance. Every step is an opportunity to win a battle. Fixed formations are bad. This must be managed exhaustively.

# 敵を打つに、一拍子の打の事
# Teki o utsu ni, hitotsu byoshi no uchi

## STRIKING THE ENEMY WITH ONE WELL-TIMED BLOW

In the timing of striking an opponent is such a thing as the one well-timed blow. When one closes within striking distance with an opponent, strike directly as quickly as possible, without moving one's body or attaching one's mind to any single thing, before the opponent has made up his mind. The timing of making a blow before one's opponent thinks to pull back, parry, or strike is called the one well-timed blow. Having mastered this timing, one must practice making the intervening stroke quickly.

# 二のこしの拍子の事
# Ni no koshi no hyoshi

## THE TIMING OF THE SECOND DIAPHRAGM

The timing of the Second Diaphragm is when one moves in to strike and the opponent quickly retreats or blocks; one feints a blow and then strikes the opponent just as he tenses up and begins to relax. This is the timing of the Second Diaphragm. It is very difficult to master this stroke just by reading this book. It is something that will come together suddenly after one has received the teaching.

# 無念無想の打といふ事
# Munen muso no uchi

## NO DESIGN, NO CONCEPTION

When one's opponent is going to strike and one also decides to strike, one's body is prepared to hit and one's mind is prepared to hit; the hands strike naturally from the Void, with speed and strength. This is called the No Design, No Conception Strke, and is the most important stroke. This stroke is encountered frequently. Learn it well and practice it.

# 流水の打といふ事
# Ryusui no uchi

## THE FLOWING WATER STROKE

The Flowing Water Stroke is used when contesting on equal par with an opponent, when he tries to retreat quickly, break quickly, or parry quickly, make oneself large in body and mind, swing one's sword from behind slowly like still water, striking expansively and strongly. Once this stroke has been learned, one can certainly strike well. It is essential to discern the opponent's grade.

# 緑のあたりといふ事
# En no atari

## THE STROKE OF FORTUNE

When one lashes out at an opponent with one's sword, and he tries to check it or thrust it aside, strike his head, strike his hands, and strike his legs all with one stroke. Striking anywhere one can with one sweep of the sword is called the Stroke of Fortune. This stroke must be practiced thoroughly; it is always encountered. Through frequent combat, it will be understood.

# 石火のあたりといふ事
# Sekka no atari

## THE FLASHING STROKE

The Flashing Stroke is when one's sword and the opponent's sword clash together and one strikes as strongly as possible without raising one's sword in the least. One must strike quickly, concentrating strength in the three areas of the legs, torso, and hands. Without continued practiced, this stroke is difficult to achieve. Train well, and it will be a powerful blow.

# 紅葉の打といふ事
# Momiji no uchi

## THE AUTUMN LEAVES STROKE

The Autumn Leaves Stroke is knocking down the sword of the opponent and taking control of it. When the opponent takes a stance with his sword before one's eyes and tries to strike, hit, or parry one's sword, hit it hard with the No Design, No Conception, or even with the Flashing Stroke. When one then strikes with the blade point pressing downward, sticking closely to one's opponent, his sword will always drop. If this stroke is practiced rigorously, one can easily knock down the opponent's sword. Practice continually, without ceasing.

# 太刀に代はる身といふ事
# Tachi ni kawaru mi

## THE BODY IN PLACE OF THE SWORD

The Body in Place of the Sword can also be called the Sword in Place of the Body. For the most part, when striking an opponent, one does not attack with body and sword at the same time. According to the circumstances of striking an opponent, assume the posture of attacking with one's body, and then strike with the sword without a body posture. Even if one strikes with the sword, and the body is motionless, usually the body strikes first, followed by a blow of the sword. Study well this stroke and practice it conscientiously.

*Wild Geese and Reeds. Miyamoto Musashi (1584–1645). Japan. 17th century. Ink on paper.*

## 打つと当るといふ事
# Utsu to ataru

### STRIKING AND HITTING

Striking and hitting are two different things. The spirit of striking, whichever stroke one chooses, is to strike resolutely and precisely. The spirit of hitting is like ramming into someone. Even if one were to hit an opponent strongly in such a way that he dies instantly, this is a hit. Hitting means making a hit as intended. This must be contemplated thoroughly. Hitting an opponent's hands or legs means first to hit, so as to strike hard after making a hit. Hitting is in the spirit of "making contact." Mastering this, one will understand that it is an exceptional thing. Work on this well.

## 秋猿の身といふ事
# Shuko no mi

### THE BODY OF THE SHORT-ARMED MONKEY

The Body of the Short-Armed Monkey means not advancing the arms. It is closing in on an opponent quickly, before he strikes, and not extending one's arms at all when moving in closely. If one thinks to reach out with the arms, the body will invariably shrink back, so one must move in on the opponent quickly with the entire body. When one is within arm's length, it is easy to close in with the body. This requires careful study.

## 漆膠の身といふ事
# Shitsuko no mi

### THE ADHESIVE BODY

The Adhesive Body is moving in and sticking closely to one's opponent like lacquer and glue, and not separating. Moving in closely on the opponent, one makes the head, body, and legs adhere tightly. Usually people advance with their heads and legs quickly, but the body lags behind. Stick tightly to the opponent's body, so there is no space between the two. Think carefully on this.

*Opposite: Miyamoto Musashi killing a giant nue. Utagawa Kuniyoshi (1797–1861). Japan. 19th century.*

## たけくらべといふ事
# Takekurabe

### COMPARING HEIGHTS

Comparing Heights is moving in alongside the opponent and, in whatever situation one may be, extending fully one's legs, diaphragm, and neck, so as not to let the body shrink back; move in face to face with the opponent as if to compare heights and show oneself the taller of the two. The essential thing is extending one's stature and moving in powerfully.

## ねばりをかくるといふ事
# Nebari o kakuru

### STICKINESS

When two blades strike together at the same time, and the opponent catches one's blow, move in closely with one's sword sticking to the opponent's sword without separating. Stickiness means the two swords are not easily drawn apart; one must close in without being too forceful. When sticking to the opponent's sword as if glued together, one may move in as quietly as one wants. Stickiness and entanglement are not the same things. Stickiness is strong; entanglement is weak. Discern the difference between these two.

## 身のあたりといふ事
# Mi no atari

### THE BODY BLOW

The Body Blow is stepping up to the opponent's side and hitting him with one's body. Turning one's face a little to the side, and thrusting forward one's left shoulder, hit the opponent in the chest. In making the hit, concentrate one's strength in the body; with a burst of energy, jettison oneself into the opponent's chest. Once one has learned this way of closing in on the opponent, one will be strong enough to knock a man ten or twenty feet. It is possible to hit an opponent so hard he nearly dies. Train and practice rigorously.

# THE TANTO
## A PERSONAL SWORD FOR DAILY LIFE

When the word *tanto* was first introduced into the Japanese language during the early Middle Ages, it was written with a pair of characters that translated as "short sword." These days, *tanto* translates better as "dagger," because it refers to a weapon of less than a foot in length.

The first known tanto appeared during the middle of the Heian period, which ran from 794 to 1185 CE. The word *heian* translates as "safety" or "tranquility" in Japanese, and as the name implies, this was a relatively peaceful era in Japan. With the imperial family concentrating more on literature and the arts than military affairs, there was little incentive to produce high-quality weapons. The first tanto were merely crude blades lacking the artistic qualities later associated with Japanese swords.

It was during the war-torn Kamakura era, between 1185 and 1333, that the tanto came into its own. The Kamakura era saw the rise of the shogun, the growth of feudalism, a Mongol invasion, and a civil war, which for a period of time resulted in two lines of emperors governing separately in the north and in the south. With that as a backdrop, a group of master sword makers known as the "immutable smiths" emerged to perfect the *tachi*, a sword that averaged about thirty inches (seventy-eight centimeters), and its shorter companion, the tanto. It was during the thirteenth century that a sword smith named Toshiro Yoshimitsu emerged to perfect the tanto. Even now, 800 years later, he is acknowledged as the best tanto maker of all time and one of the top three sword makers.

*Tanto. Bizen Kiyomitsu Yori Dachi style for Armor Piercing.*

*Three Aikichi Tanto (swords) of the Meiji period. Japan. Late 19th century.*

Yoshimitsu crafted tanto of between eight and twelve inches (twenty to thirty centimeters), roughly the length they are today. He used the *hira-zukuri* style, meaning that the sides have no ridge line and the surface is nearly flat, with gently sloping file marks, as opposed to the *shinogi-zukuri* style of ridges, plateaus, and slopes used on the *katana*.

By the sixteenth century, when the tachi had been largely replaced by the better-crafted katana, a short sword called the *wakizashi* had been introduced, that rivaled the tanto but never replaced it. Instead, the tanto was often viewed as being interchangeable with the wakizashi, with its length of between twelve and twenty-four inches (thirty and sixty centimeters). Like the wakizashi, the tanto could be joined with the katana in a *daisho*, a pairing of large and small blades. And together with the wakizashi, the tanto was the only weapon that a samurai could use to properly commit *seppuku*, or ritual suicide.

During the Muromachi period, from 1338 to 1573, Japan was in a state of near constant warfare. The weapons that were created for soldiers on the front lines were designed for maximum bloodshed rather than aesthetics.

When the Edo era dawned in the early seventeenth century, peace came to Japan. Sword smiths continued to make tanto, but many were made for display instead of violent usage. Women sometimes carried small tanto, or *kaiken,* in order to protect themselves, and criminals sometimes carried tanto concealed in fans. But not until the wave of militarism in the days prior to World War II did the tanto regain its popularity, as members of the imperial court proudly wore the tanto while preparing their nation for war.

## 三つの受けの事
# Mitsu no uke

### THREE WAYS TO PARRY

There are three ways to parry a blow. When closing in on an opponent, so as to parry the blow of his sword, make as if to stab him in the eye, then dash his sword to the right, thereby parrying his blow. Second is the thrusting parry: thrust the opponent's sword toward his right eye with the idea of slashing his throat, parrying his blow with a stabbing thrust. Third is when the opponent attacks and one closes in with a shorter sword; without concern for the parrying sword, one closes in as if to hit the opponent in the face with one's left hand. These are the three ways to parry. In any case, clench one's left hand into a fist and make as to punch one's opponent in the face. Thorough training and practice is required.

## おもてをさすといふ事
# Omote o sasu

### STABBING THE FACE

Stabbing the face is used when blade to blade with an opponent; it is essential to remain intent on stabbing the opponent in the face with one's sword tip in between each other's sword blows. If one remains intent on stabbing the opponent in the face, he will dodge with both his face and his body. When he does so, one can take advantage of various opportunities to best him. Ponder this deeply. During a battle, if the opponent tries to shrink back, victory over him is already assured. Never forget the maneuver of Stabbing the Face. Cultivate its advantages in the course of practicing martial arts.

## 心をさすといふ事
# Mune o sasu

### STABBING THE HEART

Stabbing the Heart is for fighting in spaces in which one is obstructed from above or to the sides and unable to slash with the sword one stabs the opponent. To deflect the opponent's sword of attack, align the ridge of one's blade directly toward the opponent, drawing it back and not letting the sword point vacillate, thrust it into his chest. When one is fatigued or unable to cut with the sword this tactic is especially useful. Learn it well.

## 喝咄といふ事
# Katsutotsu

### CRY AND SHOUT

Crying out and shouting are used whenever one attacks in an attempt to take down an opponent and the opponent strikes back; raise one's sword from below as if to stab him, and make a riposte. In any event, cry out with an upward thrust of the sword and shout with a counterblow of the sword, crying out and shouting by turns as one strikes. This timing is encountered frequently in dueling. The way to Cry and Shout is to raise the blade point, aiming to stab the opponent, then to strike all at once simultaneously as the sword is raised. This timing must be practiced hard and studied well.

*Bushido tanto.*

*The Actor Bando Tokuke as Takahastu Yajuro, a Samurai. Utagawa Kunisada (1786–1864). Japan. Circa 19th century. Woodblock print.*

# はりうけといふ事
# Hariuke

## THE CHOPPING PARRY

The Chopping Parry is used when two swords clash and it is difficult to break the rhythm of the blows; make a chopping move to the opponent's sword as he strikes, chopping then striking. Chopping does not mean jabbing and hitting hard or blocking his blow. Respond to the opponent's strike by chopping at his sword, then quickly delivering a blow. Taking the lead by chopping and being the first to strike are essential. When the rhythm of the Chopping Parry is precise, however hard the opponent strikes, as long as one has the least intention to hit, the tip of one's sword will not fall. This must be realized by practice and examined thoroughly.

# 多敵の位の事
# Tateki no kurai

## ONE AGAINST MANY

One Against Many is when a single person takes on a throng of people. Unsheathing both one's katana and wakizashi, hold them wide apart left and right, extending them horizontally. Even if the enemy attacks from all four sides, the sense is to chase them into one direction. Perceiving which opponent attacks first, which next, deal with them forthwith, as each advances; surveying the scene, note the positions from which the enemy attacks, and swing both swords at the same time left and right, free from each other. It is bad to wait. Quickly assume the stance with both swords ready at the side, and slash powerfully into the opponent as he comes forth; overcoming him, turn immediately to the next, and cut him down as he advances. The important thing is to drive the opponents into a line like a school of fish, and when they appear to congregate and break rank, slash powerfully then, without a moment's delay, into the fray. The only way to do it is drive them around from the front when they form a group. Similarly, it will be hard to make progress by trying to strike them down as one waits for them to advance. One wins by understanding the rhythms of the opponents' attack and knowing where is the weak spot in their ranks. If one assembled a large band of competitors now and then and learned the way of maneuvering and driving the group without giving them room to move, one could easily manage a single opponent, or ten or twenty opponents, with confidence. This must be practiced and studied well.

# 打合いの利の事
# Uchiai no ri

## ADVANTAGE IN COMBAT

Advantage in Combat refers to cultivating the principles of martial arts to accomplish victory with the long sword. This is not recorded summarily in words. One learns the way of victory through practicing well. All this is in the long sword that reveals the true path of martial arts. This is transmitted orally.

## 一つの打といふ事
# Hitotsu no uchi

### ONE STROKE

With an understanding of One Stroke, one can gain certain victory. One cannot appreciate this, however, without adequate study of martial arts. Through training and practice, one will be able to conduct martial arts single-mindedly, and be able to attain victory as one desires. Study well.

*Japanese garden in Kamakura, Japan. A warrior might retire to such a garden to calm his mind and develop what would ultimately be in combat a right-thinking strategy.*

## 直通の位といふ事
# Chokutsu no kurai

### STATE OF DIRECT COMMUNICATION

The essence of Direct Communication is transmitted when one receives the true Way of Nitō Ichi-ryū, the School of Two Swords. Practicing well is essential to disciplining one's body in martial arts. Transmitted orally.

# Epilogue

The above is an outline of the art of swordsmanship in my school, Niten Ichi-ryū, which I have recorded in this scroll. To learn how to take up the long sword and attain victory over others, one must first understand the Five Positions using the Five Basic Approaches, then learn how to wield a long sword so one's entire body moves freely, listening to the mind and understanding the rhythm of the Way, commanding the sword with one's self. When the body and feet work together in harmony with one's wishes, one can defeat one man, one can defeat two men, and come to know the good and the bad in martial arts. Training and practicing what is contained in this book, one item at a time, fighting with opponents, one will attain gradually the principles of the Way of martial arts. Always bearing this in mind, but without haste, develop one's expertise dueling whenever the occasion arises, taking on any and all opponents, and understand their minds.

A path of a thousand miles is walked one step at a time. Be patient, and understand that the practice of the Way of martial arts is a samurai's duty; today resolve to best the self of yesterday; tomorrow resolve to best a man of lesser skill; and later resolve to best those of greater skill. Practice and train according to this book, and steel the mind so it does not get sidetracked. For example, no matter how many opponents one defeats, if it goes against the teachings it cannot be the true Way. When this principle is born in mind, one should be able to understand how to beat even dozens of men by oneself. Once this becomes possible, one should attain the Way of victory for one against many or one against one through knowledge of the art of swordsmanship. It is said, one thousand days of practice for hard discipline (*tan*), ten thousand days of practice for refinement (*ren*). This must be studied assiduously.

The twelfth day of the fifth month, the second year of Shōhō (1645)

Teruo Magonojo                   Shinmen Musashi

# SAMURAI CODE
# THE WARRIOR'S BELIEF SYSTEM

*Opposite page and above: Suit of armor (yori). Saotome Iyetada. Circa 1600.*

Since the beginning of Japan's recorded history, warriors were idealized as paragons of virtue and honor. Although their deeds were often gruesomely bloody by modern standards, the best of the samurai tried to adhere to Buddhist and Shinto religious principles, the writings of the ancient Chinese philosophies of Kongfuzi (Confucius) and Meng Ke (Mencius), and the high-minded *kyuba no michi*, "way of the bow and the horse," that is, the way of the mounted archer, which was a largely unwritten code of chivalrous conduct.

Not until the early seventeenth century, when the age of the warring samurai was largely over, did the authorities start to codify the warriors' precepts, although early traces of kyuba no michi can be found in the writings of medieval samurai. At the heart of the code were the seven virtues of rectitude, courage, benevolence, respect, honesty, honor, and loyalty, a list that had many similarities to the seven virtues that governed the actions of Europe's medieval knights (restraint, valor, generosity, diligence, patience, kindness, and humility), which in turn were adopted from earlier Greek and Roman sources. Perhaps some day, scholars will find that they both derive from a common source.

*Part of a narrative handscroll (emaki) that told the story of Sugawara Michizane (845–903 CE) and the founding of the Tenjin shrine. In the Shinto religion, after death persons of superior talent were worshipped as kami, or supernatural beings. Michizane, a scholar, poet, and calligrapher, was deified and given the title "holy god" (tenjin), and a shrine dedicated to him was founded in Kyoto's Kitano district. Thus he came to be known as Kitano Tenjin. Legends of Kitano Tenjin (Kitano Tenjin engi). Japan. 1200–1300. Hanging scroll, ink and colors on paper.*

*Rectitude (gi).* First on the list of samurai virtues was the quality of being just, that is, expressing moral correctness through upholding a worthy cause and personal conduct. Nitobe Inazo, a Japanese academic born in 1862, six years before the end of the samurai era, quoted an unnamed samurai as comparing *gi* to the skeleton on which the entire body depends: "As without bones the head cannot rest on top of the spine, nor hands move, nor feet stand, so without rectitude neither talent nor learning can make of a human frame a samurai." In fact, "backbone" would be a fitting translation for the virtue of gi.

*Courage (yu).* To be effective, all warriors had to be fearless in battle. From their earliest youth, the sons of samurai were trained to be unafraid. They were made to spend nights in graveyards or were taken to witness beheadings at execution grounds, because showing fear or revulsion was simply unacceptable. But the virtue of *yu* does not include bravery that is foolhardy or driven by ego. "To rush into the thick of battle and be slain in it is easy enough," wrote a prince from the province of Mito. "The merest churl is equal to the task." Unless such a death occurred for a virtuous reason, it was a "dog's death." Yu entailed the courage to live when it

was the right time to live and to die only when it was the right time to die.

*Benevolence (jin).* Confucius and Mencius, the two guiding lights of samurai philosophy, emphasized the importance of benevolence, not only for its own sake, but also because of the effect it creates in others. "There has never been a case where a leader loves benevolence and his followers do not love virtue," Confucius asserted. Mencius noted that benevolence "brings under its sway whatever hinders its power, just as water quenches fire." A third authority, Hojo Shigetoki, a high-ranking officer in the shogun's government in the early thirteenth century, specified another reason for showing benevolence: karma.

"Those who treat other people roughly in this existence will be treated roughly by them in the next, since karma lasts forever in everything," Shigetoki wrote to his son in 1256, after he retired to a monastery. "Those who want to get rid of bad karma in this existence should treat others well, even people who are not kind to them." Shigetoki's letter, which has since come to be known as "The Message of Master Gokurakuji," represents one of the earliest expositions of kyuba no michi.

*Respect (rei).* Samurai were taught to show respect to all around them. That was especially true when dealing with their peers, but they were also expected to show at least some form of politeness to the lowliest in society. "To be a samurai is to be polite at all times," emphasized the samurai general Hojo Nagauji in the early sixteenth century. Nagauji, the *daimyo,* or lord, who governed Odawara castle and its environs, tried to practice what he preached. The respect that he showed to his subordinates helped attract more samurai to his service. But he also paid attention to the needs of the common worker. For instance, he cut farmers' taxes from one-half to two-fifths of the harvest. After serving as *daimyo* for many years, he retired to a monastery, where he penned his *Twenty-One Precepts.* He stressed that to be in alignment with the will of the gods, it was necessary to "respect those above you honestly and with all your heart and to have empathy with those below you."

*Honesty (makoto).* Confucius, in his *Doctrine of the Mean,* stressed the importance of honesty and sincerity. "Sincerity is the end and the beginning of all things. Without sincerity, there would be nothing," he wrote. The samurai hewed to honesty to such an extent that the phrase *bushi no ichi-gon,* "the word of a samurai," became synonymous with telling the truth.

The daimyo Kuroda Nagamasa, in a letter to his son written in 1622, instructed that "it is essential that [a leader] knows the way of truth." Because Nagamasa linked honesty to justice, for him, the "way of truth" entailed scrutinizing every matter to make sure that it was done rightfully, recognizing what was good and what was evil, rewarding the good and punishing the evil. A leader's actions, he said, should be "clear as the bright sun in the bright sky, and he should think everything over deeply in his mind to make sure there are no mistakes." Furthermore, Nagamasa, one of the few Christian samurai in the service of the shogun Tokugawa Ieyasu, took pains to encourage honesty among his retainers. To that end, he set aside one night each month as a "meeting without anger," in which he would invite his top associates to freely discuss their concerns, under the condition that nobody (including himself) would get angry and nobody would gossip about the discussion at a later point.

*Honor (meiyo).* The concept of honor has been deeply embedded in Japanese society. To do something that is dishonorable, or something humiliating, is to lose face, which is inexcusable. Nitobe Inazo told of a samurai who said he refused to compromise his character by a slight humiliation in his youth, "because dishonor is like a scar on a tree which time, instead of effacing, only helps enlarge." In battle, dishonor included shirking duties or running away from danger. The concept of "death before dishonor" was deeply ingrained within the samurai mindset. In 1383, the daimyo Shiba Yoshimasa wrote that, in battle, the warrior should think not only of his own reputation, but also of the effect that a dishonorable act would have on his possible descendants. "He should not scandalize his name forever by holding his life too dear," Yoshimasa wrote in the *Chikubasho,* a set of precepts for young men in his clan.

*Loyalty (chugi).* One of the overriding principles of kyuba no michi was that a samurai owed unquestioning loyalty to his master, which, in most cases, meant the daimyo of his clan. In *The Message of Master Gokurakuji,* Hojo Shigetoki stressed that loyalty to one's master should trump all other concerns. "One who serves as an official or in the master's court should not think of a hundred people or a thousand people, but should consider only the authority of the master. He should not draw the line at his own life or anything else he values."

Torii Mototada, a retainer of the daimyo Tokugawa Ieyasu, provided a supreme example of samurai loyalty. In August 1600, Mototada learned that Ieyasu's deadly enemy, Toyotomi Hideyoshi, was leading an army of 40,000 warriors toward Mototada's castle, destroying everything in its path. Mototada, whose garrison was vastly outnumbered, could have easily escaped. Instead, he stayed to fight, explaining in a letter to his son that his family had served the Tokugawa clan for generations and would not stop now. "I am resolved to make a stand inside our castle and die a quick death," he wrote, in a letter that would become part of the samurai canon. "It would not be very difficult to break through their lines and escape... . But that is not the true meaning of being a warrior, and it would be hard to describe as loyalty. Instead, I will face the forces of the entire country here, and...die a resplendent death." For ten days, Mototada fended off Hideyoshi's army. With his castle on fire, Mototada ordered his small group of followers to charge against Hideyoshi in wave after wave, until they were nearly all dead. With the enemy closing in, Mototada committed *seppuku* rather than be captured. His loyalty bought time for Ieyasu to rally his troops and ultimately prevail against Hideyoshi.

> *"Sincerity is the end and the beginning of all things. Without sincerity, there would be nothing."*

# Ka no maki

## The Fire Scroll

The power of fire being an analogy for combat in the martial arts of Nitō Ichi-ryū, School of Two Swords, things relating to the victory and defeat of combat are considered as the book of fire, and so are written down here.

First and foremost, people of the world, one and all, think narrowly about advantage in martial arts, thinking only of nonessentials. Using their fingertips, some know the advantage of three or four inches of the wrist. Some understand how to win using a fan with a movement of the forearm. Or, using a bamboo sword or other instrument, they learn the slight advantage of speed, practicing their hand and feet movements, focusing on taking advantage of a little more speed.

In my martial arts, I have learned through numerous contests, putting my life on the line, the principles of living and dying, studying the Way of the sword, learning the strengths and weaknesses of the opponents' sword strikes, discerning the uses of the sword's blade and ridge, and practicing how to cut down opponents. No thought was paid to the small and the weak. Especially when wearing full armor (*roku gu*), one pays no heed to small things.

Moreover, my Way of martial arts is knowing with certitude the path to victory in life-threatening combat whether it be one against five or ten men. What then is the difference between the reasoning of one person overcoming ten people and a thousand people overcoming ten thousand? This has to be studied well.

Be that as it may, there is no way to assemble a thousand or ten thousand people for usual practice to learn this martial art. Even when taking up the sword alone, measure the knowledge and strategy of each and every opponent, know their moves, their strengths and weaknesses; armed with the wisdom and power of martial

arts, learn to beat ten thousand, and one will become a master of the Way.

Who in this world can attain the correct Way of my school of martial arts? Always committed to perfecting the Way, training and polishing one's skills night and day, one gains, upon mastery, freedom to act at will, spontaneously attains miraculous strength, and comes to possess extraordinary powers of discernment. This is the character for cultivating martial arts as a warrior.

## 場の次第といふ事
# Ba no shidai
### SENSE OF PLACE

It is important to determine the right place to stand in positioning oneself. Take up a stance with the sun at one's back. If the situation does not allow this, then strive to keep the sun to one's right. As for indoors as well, keep the light behind oneself or to one's right. So as to keep the place behind oneself unobstructed, see that the space to one's left is wide open, and take a stance that closes the space to one's right. As for night as well, if the opponent can be seen, keep the fires behind oneself and the lights to one's right, taking a stance with an understanding of the above. To look down upon the opponent, be aware of taking a stance from a slightly higher place. In a room, the *kamiza*, the seat of honor, is regarded as a high place.

In any event, when it comes to the clash of swords, strive to chase the opponents around to one's left; it is crucial to keep obstacles to the rear of the opponent, and then however possible chase them into an obstacle. When opponents are pressed against an obstacle, do not let them consider the situation, but charge in fiercely so they cannot look around. Indoors, chase the opponents against

*Suit of armor (yori). Saotome Iyetada. Circa 1600.*

thresholds, lintels, doors, screens, verandas, pillars or into other obstacles, again not letting them observe the situation. In any case, chase the opponent into places where footing is bad or where there are obstacles on either side. Take advantage of the details of the setting to establish dominance over the situation. Study this thoroughly and practice diligently.

# 三つの先といふ事
# Mitsu no sen

## THREE WAYS TO FORESTALL THE ENEMY

There are three ways to forestall the enemy. One is to take the initiative and attack the opponent first; this is called *ken no sen*, setting up the opponent. Another is forestall the opponent as he attacks; this is called *tai no sen*, waiting for the opponent's initiative. One more is to take the lead when swords clash together simultaneously; this is called *tai tai no sen*, mutual engagement. These are the three ways. At the beginning of any confrontation, there is no other way of taking initiative but these three. Since one can attain victory quickly by taking the initiative, it is the number one concern in martial arts.

In taking the lead, various things are involved. But which of the three to take depends on first sizing up the situation, perceiving the opponent's intentions, and using the wisdom of one's martial arts to win. So they cannot be written down in full detail.

First is *ken no sen*: when one decides to attack, remain quiet and then attack suddenly and quickly, preempting the opponent. One can take the lead through strong and quick movements on the outside while leaving breathing room on the inside. Or one can galvanize intensely one's spirit, moving the feet a little faster than normal, and attacking violently all at once, the moment one closes in with the opponent. One can also win by letting go of the mind, concentrating intently only on crushing the opponent at the same game from beginning to end. These are all *ken no sen*.

Second is *tai no sen*: when the opponent attacks, one remains unfazed but feigns weakness. As he approaches, leap aside with a powerful thrust, seeming to fly away; then, when one sees the opponent relax, immediately dash in aggressively and overcome him. This is one way. Alternatively, when the opponent attacks, and one also moves in even more forcefully, as soon as one catches a break in the opponent's timing, victory is in one's hands then and there. This is the principle of *tai no sen*, waiting for the opponent's attack.

Third is *tai tai no sen*, taking the lead in a state of mutual engagement. When an opponent attacks quickly, one attacks him calmly and strongly; as the opponent approaches, concentrate unflinchingly on one's posture, and when the opponent appears to relax, defeat him forcefully at once. Similarly, when an opponent attacks quietly, one quickens one's attack a little, gliding with one's body; when the opponent draws near, follow his intentions, and striking soundly, trounce him. This is *tai tai no sen*.

These things are hard to write about in detail; they must be implemented by following the instructions outlined here. These three ways of taking the lead depend on the circumstances and on understanding advantages. Even though this does not mean one is always first to attack, by the same token, one would want to take the lead by forestalling the opponent, pulling him around. In

*Dragon ceiling painting at Kenninji Temple, a historic Zen Buddhist temple near Gion in Kyoto. Founded in 1202, it is the first Zen temple in Japan.*

any event, taking the initiative is attaining sure victory through the power of knowledge of martial arts. Thorough training and practice are required.

# 枕をおさゆるといふ事
# Makura o osayuru

### HOLDING DOWN THE PILLOW

Holding Down the Pillow is keeping the opponent from raising his head. In the way of victory in martial arts, it is bad to be led about by others. One wants to lead about the opponent, however one wishes. The opponent likewise will also be thinking the same thing, just as one is aiming to do so, but without perceiving what the other is doing, taking the lead is impossible. In martial arts there is stopping an opponent's blows, checking his thrusts, and wresting free of his grasp. Holding Down the Pillow means that when one has attained the true Way of my martial arts and is engaged with the opponent, one perceives whatever moves the opponent intends to make—before he makes the move. When he is about to strike, nip it in the bud, before he has a chance to strike, not letting him follow through. This is Holding Down the Pillow.

For example, when the opponent starts to attack, attack him from the get-go; when he starts to jump, jump in and stop him; when he starts to slash, slash him before he can make a cut. Through all these means one can hold back the opponent. When the opponent makes a move, allow him to perform useless actions and suppress his useful actions. It is essential in martial arts not to let the opponent act. This also means that repeated moves to hold him at bay will result in failure. First, while carrying out one's skills in accordance with the Way of martial arts in all things, circumvent the opponent's initial move at its very inception, rendering all his plans useless. One who can commandeer an opponent at will in this fashion is a master of martial arts. This comes from practice and training. Holding Down the Pillow must be studied well.

# 渡を越すといふ事
# To o kosu

### CROSSING A FORD

Crossing a Ford means, for example, crossing the sea at places called straits, also places to cross a sea as wide as forty or fifty *ri* are called fords. In crossing the human world as well, there will be many places in the course of a lifetime that could be called Crossing a Ford. On the seaways, knowing where the fords are, knowing the soundness of the boat, the weather, navigating alone, without so much as launching an escort, one responds to the situation of the moment, at times catching a crosswind, at times running before the wind, knowing that even if the wind direction shifts one could row two or three ri to harbor, piloting the boat and crossing the ford. Having this understanding, one must be able to cross dangerous fords in passing through the world of men as well. Crossing a Ford is also crucial in martial arts, in the midst of battle. Discerning the opponent's capability and aware of one's own mastery, cross the ford via the principles of martial arts, as a good pilot crosses over seaways. Having crossed the ford successfully moreover, one can find peace of mind. To Cross a Ford is to make the opponent's weakness apparent, and to put one's self a step ahead of the opponent; then one can generally achieve swift victory. Crossing a Ford is important in both large-scale and one-on-one combat of martial arts. Examine this carefully.

# 景気を知るといふ事
# Keiki o shiru

### KNOWING THE TIMES

In large-scale martial arts, Knowing the Times refers to discerning the opponents' disposition—prosperity or decline—and knowing the intentions of their troops, keenly observing the state of affairs according to their circumstances, determining how to maneuver one's troops to taste a sure victory via the principles of martial arts, and fighting from a position of foreknowledge. In one-on-one martial arts as well, one must identify the opponent's

*Flag of Japan. Parchment.*

*Hibachi were mainly used to generate warmth, but could be used for heating water or cooking. Brazier (hibachi) formed from a tree trunk. Japan. 1869. Wood and iron.*

*Stacked pebbles and bamboo leaf: natural strength and balance, essential in every aspect of the martial arts.*

*The armies of Uesugi Kenshin and Takeda Shingen at a
16th-century encounter at Kawanakajima.*

# SAMURAI BATTLES
## THE MAJOR CONFRONTATIONS

The history of medieval Japan is pockmarked by wars and battles between rival samurai clans. Following are some of the major battles that defined the samurai era.

### Battle of Kyoto, Hogen Rebellion, July 11, 1156

After Emperor Toba died in June 1156, two of his sons vied for the throne: Sutoko, backed by the Minamoto clan, and Go-Shirakawa, backed by the rival Taira. On July 10, the two clans squared off against each other in Kyoto. On July 11, under cover of darkness, 600 Taira samurai attacked Sutoku's palace on horseback and burned it down. Although

*Onodera junai Hidetomo shading his eyes. Utagawa Kuniyoshi (1797–1861). Japan. 19th century.*

Go-Shirakawa won the throne, the battle revealed his weaknesses; he would be nowhere without help from the samurai. Within a few years, he had become little more than a puppet of the Taira. For the next 700 years, samurai warlords, and not the emperor, held the true power in Japan.

### Battle of Uji, Gempei War, June 23, 1180

In March 1180, a second dispute over imperial accession touched off the five-year Gempei War between the Taira and Minamoto clans. When the Taira army rode out of Kyoto to crush the Minamoto rebels, the Minamoto fled, crossing the Uji River and tearing the planks of the wooden bridge behind them to prevent the Taira from following. But the Taira forded the river, defeating the Minamoto on the opposite shore. Minamoto Yorimasa, commander of the Minamoto forces, committed *seppuku* at the end of the battle. This was the first known case of a Japanese general's killing himself rather than surrendering, setting a precedent that would be followed through World War II.

### Battle of Dannoura, Gempei War, April 25, 1185

The Gempei War ended when a fleet of Minamoto warships off the southern tip of Honshu met a Taira fleet carrying six-year-old Emperor Antoku. Archers on each side launched volleys against their enemies until the Taira surrounded and boarded the Minamoto ships. As the two forces engaged in hand-to-hand combat, the Minamoto archers kept firing, targeting the oarsmen of the Taira ships. As the ocean's tide shifted, the Taira lost control of their ships and the Minamoto emerged victorious. Many Taira jumped into the sea, preferring suicide to surrender. Among the victims was the boy emperor, who was dragged beneath the waves by his grandmother. After the battle, Shogun Minamoto Yoritomo took charge of the government. His stronghold in Kamakura would be the power center of Japan for nearly 150 years.

### Battles of Hakata Bay, Mongol Invasion, November 20, 1274, and August 15, 1281

In 1274, the Mongol emperor Kublai Khan attacked Japan when it refused to pay tribute to him. After conquering

*Battle at Awazuhara, from The Tale of the Heike, one of a pair. Ujigawa Awazuhara Gassen. Japan. 1600–1700. Ink, colors, and gold on paper.*

Tsushima Island and Iki, the Mongol fleet landed at Hakata Bay, where it staged an amphibious assault armed with catapults, explosives, and arrows. But an overwhelming number of samurai forced them back to their ships, inflicting heavy casualties. When a storm rose that night, the ships set sail, fearing they would be dashed to bits on the Japanese shores. Most of the ships were lost in the storm; the survivors returned to their base in Korea.

On June 21, 1281, the Mongols returned with roughly tens of thousands of warriors. This time, the samurai were better prepared, with fortifications along the beachhead. They met the invaders using Mongol-style phalanxes. And they engaged in guerilla tactics, with small teams of samurai boarding the enemy ships at night, killing as many Mongols as possible and then escaping under cover of darkness. The Mongols soon retreated to Tsushima, waiting for expected reinforcements. In mid-August, they set sail to attack again, but a huge typhoon arose, sinking most of the fleet and drowning almost all of the warriors. The Japanese called that typhoon a *kamikaze*, "divine wind." The suicidal kamikaze pilots of World War II saw themselves as a similarly divine wind, protecting Japan from attack.

## Burning of Kyoto, Onin War, Summer of 1467

In July 1467, a pair of relatively minor samurai clans began fighting each other in Kyoto, in a dispute known as the Onin War. By September, much of Kyoto had been burned and most civilians had fled the city. Because the shogun did not intervene, other clans soon decided they could fight each other without being punished. Thus began Japan's Warring States period, in which clans throughout the country jockeyed for power.

## Battle of Uedahara, Warring States, February 14, 1548

This was the first battle in Japan in which soldiers used firearms, which were transported to Asia by Portuguese traders. Murakami Yoshikiyo, a retainer for the Uesugi clan, won the battle with the help of fifty harquebuses. But it would take a long time for firearms to catch on, because they took time to load and were mostly useless in the rain.

## Battle of Okehazama, Warring States, June 1560

In the spring of 1560, the Imagawa clan invaded the territory of the Oda clan with 40,000 warriors. (There were actually only 25,000 warrios, but the Imagawa inflated their numbers in hopes of driving the much smaller Oda into submission.) Despite being heavily outnumbered, Oda Nobunaga, the twenty-six-year-old leader of the clan, decided to stop Imagawa. First, Nobunaga set up a huge encampment of straw soldiers in the invaders' path. On the eve of the Imagawa attack, the warriors celebrated their imminent victory by getting drunk. In the meantime, Nobunaga circled around the army with 3,000 men. In a surprise attack, he crushed the invaders. This was a pivotal battle in Japanese history, beginning Nobunaga's campaign to unify all the clans of Japan under a single leader. Tokugawa Ieyasu, who had been an Imagawa retainer, joined Nobunaga's side after the battle. Forty years later, he would unify Japan under the Tokugawa shogunate, which held power for more than 250 years.

*The First Man Across the Uji River, from The Tale of Heike. Ujigawa Awazuhara Gassen. Japan. 1650–1700. Ink, color, and gold leaf on paper.*

## Battle of Nagashino, June 28, 1575

Although Japanese soldiers had been using firearms for nearly thirty years, they never demonstrated their full potential until 1575. In mid-June, the famed cavalry leader Takeda Katsuyori besieged Nagashino castle. Oda Nobunaga and Tokugawa Ieyasu brought 38,000 soldiers to relieve the siege, more than twice as many as Kaysuyori's force of 15,000. Still, the reinforcements took no chances. Nobunaga built a series of wooden stockades near a stream that divided the two sides. On the opposite side was a steep bank, which was perfect for one of Katsuyori's cavalry charges. Nobunaga stationed more than 1,000 harquebusiers in the stockades, with canopies to protect them from rain.

The stockades did not dissuade Katsuyori from attacking. With rain pouring down, he figured the guns would not fire. He charged at the position, ordering his cavalry down the

hill and across the river. Once the Takeda horses were midstream, the harquebusiers opened fire. As soon as one volley of shots was fired, the gunmen were replaced from the rear, so that the first group could reload. Under constant gunfire, the cavalry was decimated. The battle marks a major turning point away from feudal warfare and toward modern warfare.

## Battle of Sekigahara, October 21, 1600

In the early summer of 1600, Ishida Mitsunari and several other clan leaders met at Sawayama castle and declared war on Tokugawa Ieyasu, who was on a path to becoming absolute ruler. Over the next couple of months, the rebels took over one Tokugawa-owned castle after another and then marched on Sekigahara, in Mino province. With help from his son and other clan leaders, Ieyasu quickly put together a fighting force of nearly 89,000 men,

slightly higher than the 82,000 under Mitsunari's command. When he arrived at Sekigahara, he realized that even that number would not be enough to overcome Mitsunari's heavily fortified positions. To secure help, Ieyasu secretly contacted enemy clan leaders, promising them land if they would join him. Kobayama Hideaki, who commanded the rebel defenses on Mount Matsuo, could not make up his mind what to do. Frustrated, Ieyasu ordered his harquebusiers to start shooting at him. That did the trick. Hideaki turned to attack his own rebel center, as did other would-be traitors who were on the fence, and the uprising soon dissolved.

There would be a handful of later battles, most notably the siege of Osaka in 1615, but the battle of Sekigahara was essentially the last conflict of the samurai era. When Ieyasu became shogun, he brought an era of dictatorial peace to Japan. On the other hand, he created enemies who, powerless to fight him, licked their wounds for 200 years. After the battle of Sekigahara, Ieyasu had destroyed and demeaned a number of clan leaders who had not been

helpful in the fight, including the leaders of the Mori, Shimazu, and Chosokabe clans. Their descendants never forgot their disgrace. In the 1860s, the leaders of these clans worked to bring down the Tokugawa shogunate, which paved the way for the Meiji restoration and the end of shoguns and samurai.

*The graves of the legendary forty-seven ronin at Sengaku. a Soto Zen Buddhist temple.*

*Hachiwari (helmet splitter). Circa 1700.*

school, observe his character of the enemy, discern people's strong and weak points, strategize against opponent's expectations, know his highs and lows, the timing of intervals, and make the first move. If one's power of discernment is strong, the state of affairs of everything will be apparent always. Able to perform freely in the martial arts, one will see into the minds of opponents and find many ways to victory. This must be cultivated intensively.

# 剣をふむといふ事
# Ken o fumu

### TREADING DOWN THE SWORD

Treading Down the Sword is a matter for use exclusively in martial arts. First, in large-scale martial arts, when opponents come at one attacking with bows and gun, doing whatever they can do, once they discharge their weapons and go about reloading, it is hard for one to rush their ranks when stringing a bow or loading a gun. One must attack quickly while the enemy is releasing its volley.

If one attacks quickly, it is hard for the enemy to use a bow or shoot a gun. However the enemy attacks, one can gain victory by taking in everything naturally and treading down whatever the enemy does. In one-on-one combat as well, if one strikes after the opponent's slashing attack, resulting in a clashing exchange of blows, one's headway is impeded. The opponent's attacking sword is met with a sense of trampling it underfoot, as one overpowers him from the outset, not allowing him to strike the second blow.

Treading is something done not only with the feet. One must tread with the body, tread with the mind, and of course tread with the sword, so the opponent cannot attack a second time. This means, in other words, to forfend, to forestall, in all things. It is not charging the opponent to overcome him all at once, but following up immediately. This must be studied carefully.

# 崩を知るといふ事
# Kuzure o shiru

### KNOWING COLLAPSE

Collapse is something that happens to all things. Houses collapse, people collapse, enemies collapse—they collapse by being out of step with the times. In large-scale martial arts, it is essential to understand the timing of the opponent's collapse and to pursue him without missing a beat. If one misses the timing of his collapse, there is a chance he will regain his footing. In one-on-one martial arts one can see an adversary's timing fail during combat and begin to fall apart. If such an opportunity is lost, the enemy will recoup and all will come to naught. It is important to keep after him relentlessly when he falters, to prevent him from regaining his position. Keeping after him must be immediate and powerful; the attack must be thoroughgoing so he cannot rebound. The thoroughgoing attack must be examined carefully. If the attack is not thoroughgoing, there is a tendency to drag. This requires exceptional thinking.

# 敵になるといふ事
# Teki ni naru

### BECOMING THE ENEMY

Becoming the Enemy is putting oneself in the opponent's place and thinking from his perspective. People in the world think someone like a burglar holed up in a house is a powerful enemy. From the burglar's position, however, the whole world is against him; he is hopelessly trapped. The one holed up inside is the pheasant; the one who goes in to take him down is the hawk. Consider this well.

In large-scale martial arts also, opponents are regarded as powerful and to be handled cautiously. But if one has good men, knows well the principles of martial arts, and understands how to triumph over the enemy, there is no need to worry. In one-on-one martial arts as well, think from the enemy's position. Meeting a master of martial arts who has a strong grasp of principles and practice, one thinks one will surely lose. Think deeply on these things.

*Episode from the story of the Soga brothers (soga monogatari), one of a pair. Japan. 1615–1868. Six-panel folding screen.*

# 四手をはなすといふ事
# Yotsude o hanasu

## RELEASING FOUR HANDS

Releasing Four Hands is used when both one and one's opponent are engaged in the same manner, resulting in a deadlock, and fighting has come to a standstill. When one thinks a deadlock is about to occur, change one's mind immediately and win by taking a different track. In large-scale martial arts as well, if there is a deadlock and things come to a standstill, there will be a loss in men. It is crucial to change one's approach quickly and win with a tactic the enemy doesn't expect. In one-on-one combat too, when a deadlock seems imminent it is important to change one's course immediately, discern the opponent's condition, and determine how to win by taking advantage of various different tactics.

# 陰をうごかすといふ事
# Kage o ugokasu

## MAKING SHADOWS MOVE

Making Shadows Move is used when one cannot perceive the enemy's mind. In large-scale martial arts, when one cannot determine the enemy's condition, pretend to attack powerfully to see what moves they will make. Then it is easy to defeat them by taking into account various tactics for each move. In one-on-one combat as well, when an opponent wields his sword behind or to his side, when he is suddenly about to hit, his sword reveals his intentions. Once his intentions become apparent, claim the advantage right away and stake a sure victory. If one hesitates, one's timing will be off.

# 影をおさゆるといふ事
# Kage o osayuru

## HOLDING DOWN SHADOWS

Holding Down Shadows is used when one can perceive the enemy's intention to attack. In large-scale martial arts, this is suppressing the enemy's move right at the point they are about to act. If one shows strongly one's advantage over the opponent, they will change their minds, held back by this strong attitude. By changing one's mind too, and by emptying it, one can take the initiative and claim victory. In one-on-one martial arts as well, check the enemy's strong impulse with one's advantageous timing, then seek victory in that halting moment, taking the initiative. Work on this extensively.

## 移らかすといふ事
# Utsurakasu

### CONTAGION

Contagion is in all things. Such things as sleep can be contagious, and such things as yawning can be contagious. Even time can be a contagion. In large-scale martial arts, when the enemy is uneasy and shows an inclination to rush, one should carry on as though unconcerned, exhibiting complete calm and composure. The enemy will then be taken in by one's display and become more relaxed. When one thinks this feeling has spread throughout the enemy, empty one's mind and attack quickly and powerfully, thereby gaining the winning hand. In one-on-one martial arts as well, it is important to be relaxed in body and mind, to seize the enemy's moment of repose, and attack quickly and strongly, taking the

initiative to win. There is also something similar to this, called "intoxication." One intoxicating state is boredom, another is nervousness, and yet another is weak-spiritedness. This must be assayed thoroughly.

## むかつかするといふ事
# Mukatsuka suru

### TO UNSETTLE

Unsettling things happen everywhere. One cause is danger. Another is unreasonable demand. A third is surprise. Examine this well. In large-scale martial arts, unsettling things are essential. It is necessary to attack fiercely and forcefully where enemies do not expect it. While the enemy's mind is unsettled, use this advantageously to take the lead and win. In one-on-one martial arts as well, one is to appear relaxed at first, then attack suddenly and powerfully. As the enemy's mind begins to sway it is critical to follow his movement, and not letting him catch his breath, claim the advantage and determine victory straightaway. This must be worked out diligently.

## おびやかすといふ事
# Obiyakasu

### TO FRIGHTEN

Fright is in all things. There is fright in the unexpected. In large-scale martial arts, frightening the enemy is not just something before one's eyes. One can frighten with such things as sounds, by making the small appear large, and one can frighten by making a move from the side unexpectedly. These are all ways to frighten someone. If one can take advantage of the enemy's fright, one can claim victory. In single combat as well, one can frighten with the body, one can frighten with the sword, one can frighten with the voice. It is important to catch the enemy unawares, using his fright to one's advantage, and defeat him right away. Thorough investigation is required.

*Daikoku. Japan. Late 19th or early 20th century. Wood.*

## まぶるゝといふ事
# Mabururu

### STICKINESS

Stickiness is used when one is engaged closely with the opponent in a mutual exchange of force, and one sees that things are not going one's way, then one sticks tightly to the opponent straightaway. It is important to use this sticking together to one's advantage to claim victory. In both large-scale and small-scale martial arts, when one has squared off with and opponent and swords are engaged but it is not clear who will win, stick close to the opponent directly, as if inseparable, meanwhile one claims the advantage, sees the victory, and wins powerfully. This is essential. Study it well.

## かどにさはるといふ事
# Kado in sawaru

### CRAMPING THE CORNERS

Cramping the Corners means that when pushing against anything that is strong, it is not easy to move it all at once. In large-scale martial arts, observe the enemy's number, and cramp the corner where they have charged ahead, and gain the upper hand. When the corner falls, all the others will feel the fall. As the corner is falling, it is crucial for one to be aware of each corner's breaking out and know when to overthrow them. In one-on-one martial arts as well, when one hurts the corner of the enemy's body, the entire body gradually weakens to the point of collapse, and it is easy to overcome him. Thorough investigation is required to discern how to win.

## うろめかすといふ事
# Uromekasu

### DEMORALIZING THE ENEMY

Demoralizing the enemy is keeping him from having presence of mind. This can be used in large-scale martial arts, gauging the mind of the enemy on the battlefield and using one's

knowledge of military strategy, one can lead their thoughts here and there, confusing them with this or that, slow or fast, and catch the timing for demoralizing the enemy, determining clearly how to win. In one-on-one martial arts also, one executes various moves corresponding to the moment, feigning a hit or a thrust, making the opponent think one is closing in, demoralizing the opponent, and thereby winning as one wills. This is the essence of fighting. Study it diligently.

---

*In large-scale martial arts, unsettling things are essential. It is necessary to attack fiercely and forcefully where enemies do not expect it. While the enemy's mind is unsettled, use this advantageously to take the lead and win.*

---

## 三つの声といふ事
# Mitsu no koe

### THREE SHOUTS

Three Shouts are divided into initial, middle, and final shouts. The important thing is to shout out according to time and place. A shout, because it expresses force, is used in such situations as fires or storms; the voice shows energy and power. In large-scale martial arts, shouting at the start of battle should be as loud as possible, during the battle low-pitched and deep, and after winning the battle loud and strong. These are the three shouts. In one-on-one martial arts, feint a blow and shout to make the opponent move, and then strike with the sword after crying out. Also, shouting after cutting down the enemy is a cry of victory. These are known as *sen go no koe*, before and after shouts. Never flourish the sword and shout at the same time. When shouting during a battle, shout in a low voice to keep one's timing. Consider this well.

*Han dachi mounted tachi. Circa 1830.*

# THE INRO AS STATUS SYMBOL
## HOW THE SAMURAI CARRIED PERSONAL ITEMS

For the past couple of centuries, the coat pocket and the pants pocket have been so commonplace that it's easy to forget what life was like before they were invented. But for thousands of years, people lacked the luxury of having pockets into which they could stuff their coins or other small belongings. This was particularly true in Japan, where the graceful asymmetry of the *kimono* did not allow for such a utilitarian impingement as a pocket.

For the Japanese, the solution came through the *sagemono*, small containers that dangled from the belt and held coins, pens, medicines, and other necessities. Some sagemono were little more than unadorned leather pouches or miniature woven baskets. But others, especially the ones known as *inro*, were so finely crafted that they are now sought after as collectors' items.

The use of sagemono began in the earliest days of Japanese history. The oldest surviving Japanese book, the *Kojiki*, written in the early seventh century CE, mentions a particular sagemono known as the *hiuchi-bukuro*, a simple leather pouch that carried flints for starting fires. Prince Yamato-Take, one of the heroes of the *Kojiki*, pulled a flint out of his pouch to start the fire that helped him escape from a trap laid by his enemies. Another use for these leather pouches arose with the introduction of coins in the fourteenth century, when the Japanese began wearing them to carry their money. Over the next several centuries, these evolved into *kinchaku*, drawstring pouches that were elaborately decorated with embroidered silk or rich brocade. In fact, kinchaku remain popular today, used to carry everything

*Chinese men on bridge (reverse side). Toju. Japan. 1800-1900. Lacquered wood with gold dust, mother-of-pearl, and coral bead.*

from cell phones to *bento* box lunches. As the years went by, other sagemono were developed for specialized purposes, such as carrying tobacco and pipes or writing brushes and ink.

But perhaps the best-known sagemono is the inro, which began as a simple dual-chamber box designed to carry an inkpad and an *inkan*, a personal seal, still in use today to sign official documents. The inro was originally designed to remain in the home, where it was placed in an alcove near the door, along with the *yakuro* medicine box. But by the sixteenth century, samurai began to wear them in public, strapped to their belts. The inkan, after all, was a powerful symbol of social status, and only a person in the samurai class or above held such a device.

Because of its power as a status symbol, the inro was showier than most other sagemono. Instead of being crafted out of leather, they were made from such materials as ivory, bone, boxwood, or lacquerware. As time went on, the inro grew larger, with separate compartments for such items as medicinal powders or snuff. The compartments, a series of tiny boxes, were secured by a silken cord, which connected them with the *ojime*, an elaborately carved sliding bead that kept the inro shut. The inro was fastened to the belt of its owner with a dual cord held in place by a toggle called the *netsuke*, "attaching base." The netsuke, typically between one and three inches long, was made of such exotic materials as boar tusk, hippopotamus teeth, walrus tusk, whalebone, tiger teeth, palm nuts, petrified wood, or

*Portable writing set decorated with images of European figures, ships, and Mount Fuji. Japan. 19th century. Elephant ivory with copper alloy bead.*

*netsuke,* were hollowed out to reveal carvings inside. Others, the *karakuri netsuke,* were constructed with mechanical moving parts or hidden surprises. Still others, the *kagamibuta netsuke,* had polished metal lids that could double as pocket mirrors.

Once Western clothing began to replace the kimono in the nineteenth century, the practical value of the inro declined.

Pockets eventually replaced the inro, in the same way that they had replaced the belt pouches once worn in

*Inro with Ebisu and Daikoku (two of the Seven Gods of Good Fortune). Japan. 19th century. Lacquered wood, mother of pearl, antler, and enamel.*

even the beak of the helmeted hornbill, as well as the more prosaic coral, bamboo, agate, porcelain, or lacquerware.

Starting in the seventeenth century, Japanese artisans began decorating the inro, ojime, and netsuke with images of such diverse subjects as octopuses, warriors, turtles, frogs, priests, fruit, dragons, beans, chestnuts, lyres, *Noh* masks, or the animals of the zodiac. The netsuke in particular became a showcase of craftsmanship. Some, the *anabori*

Europe. Today, even though the typical Japanese keeps his or her ink and ink pads in a small, unobtrusive container that can easily be slipped into a pocket, craftsmen still continue to create inro, ojime, and netsuke for purely artistic purposes. Moreover, a well-crafted, well-preserved antique netsuke can fetch as much as $10,000 at auction—not bad for a toggle.

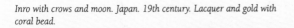

*Inro with crows and moon. Japan. 19th century. Lacquer and gold with coral bead.*

*Netsuke in the form of a reclining crane, used as a toggle on an elegant inro. Japan. 19th century. Lacquered wood with gold and cinnabar.*

433

# まぎる々といふ事
# Mazaruru

## MINGLING

Mingling in the case of large-scale combat is when troops are engaged and the enemy is strong, that is the time to attack one point of the formation as if mingling with them; when the enemy appears to collapse, leave them and attack another strong point. In general, the attack is in a winding pattern. This is also important in small-scale martial arts, when fighting one-against-many. When one has beaten enemies in one quarter, and driven them back in another, next strike yet another, grasping the enemy's timing, weaving left and right, weighing the enemy's condition and attacking forthwith. When one has taken in the enemy's strength, and is going to slash through, seize tightly the winning advantage without holding back. In one-on-one combat as well, use this frame of mind when moving in on a powerful opponent. Mingling, then is stepping in without any reservation, and mixing in. Understand this clearly.

# ひしぐといふ事
# Hishigu

## CRUSHING

Crushing is seeing the opponent as weak while one's self becomes stronger—a crushing frame of mind is important. In large-scale martial arts, one looks through the enemy small in number, or even large in number; when they appear confused and weak, beat them down with an overbearing, superior force. If one's crushing is weak, they may recover. Understand the feeling of keeping them in the palm of one's hand when crushing them. In one-on-one martial arts as well, if the enemy is less skillful, or when his timing is off, or he begins to retreat, do not let him catch his breath. It is important to squash him all at once without letting him look away. It is imperative not to let him recoup at all. Study this well.

*Palace and horse race at Kamo shrine. Japan. 1615–1650. Six-panel folding screen.*

# 山海の変わりといふ事
# San kai no kawari

### MOUNTAIN-SEA CHANGING

Mountain-Sea refers to the repetition of the same thing over and over when fighting an opponent, which is a bad thing. The same thing inevitably may have to be repeated, but should not happen a third time. When one is making a move on an opponent and is unsuccessful the first time, there is nothing to gain in using the same approach again. Attack quickly with a different maneuver. If that too fails, try again with yet another. The Way of martial arts, therefore, is being aware to act as the sea when the enemy is like a mountain, and as a mountain when the enemy is like the sea. Thorough contemplation is required.

# 底を抜くといふ事
# Soko o nuku

### PROBING THE DEPTHS

Probing the Depths is used when fighting an opponent and one appears to have the upper hand by advantage of the Way, if the enemy has steeled his heart, outwardly defeated but still inwardly unvanquished. In such a case, one must quickly change one's way of thinking and demoralize the enemy, making him feel defeated from the depths of his being. Probing the Depths can be done with the sword, with the body, or with the mind. It cannot be considered in one way alone. Once the enemy has reached the depths of collapse, one no longer need be concerned with him. But otherwise one remains concerned. So long as the enemy stays spirited, he is far from collapsing. In both small and large-scale martial arts, Probing the Depths must be a part of rigorous training and practice.

*Kabuki actors dressed like samurai. Japan. Circa 1880.*
*Hand-colored photograph.*

## 新に成るといふ事
# Arata ni naru

### STARTING AFRESH

Starting Afresh is applied when one is fighting with the enemy and one is feeling entangled and not making headway. Throw away those feelings and think of beginning everything afresh. Adapting to the timing, one will determine how to win. Whenever one feels deadlocked with the enemy, change one's mind immediately and one can win with a special advantage. This is Starting Afresh. In large-scale martial arts, it is critical to know how to Start Afresh. Through mastery of the Way, one will be able to see it easily. Reflect deeply on this.

## 鼠頭牛首といふ事
# Soto goshu

### RAT'S HEAD, OX'S NECK: SMALL AND LARGE

When one is fighting with the enemy and there is entanglement and mutual over-involvement in small things, think of the Small and Large of martial arts, of shifting suddenly one's mind from minutia to a larger frame. Shifting the Large and Small is one strategy of martial arts. Understanding Small and Large is critical for the warriors, even in his everyday mind. In both large- and small-scale martial arts, this frame of mind is essential. This matter must be given due consideration.

## 将卒を知るといふ事
# Sho sotsu o shiru

### A COMMANDER KNOWS THE TROOPS

A Commander Knows the Troops is always applied in combat after one has attained self-mastery. Once the wisdom of martial arts is attained in carrying out this strategy, one will want to think of one's enemies as one's own troops, understanding that one can have them follow orders and be able to move them about freely at one's bidding. One becomes the commander; the opponents become the troops. This must be worked out carefully.

*Ebisu, one of Japan's Seven Gods of Good Fortune. Japan. Early 19th century. Wood with remnants of color.*

## 束をはなすといふ事
# Tsuka o hanasu

### RELEASING THE HILT

Releasing the Hilt has various meanings. One meaning is winning without a sword. Another is not winning with a sword. Because there are various senses, each one cannot be recorded. Diligent training and practice are required.

## 岩尾の身といふ事
# Iwao no mi

### THE BODY OF A ROCK WALL

The Body of a Rock Wall is when one has attained the Way of martial arts and suddenly becomes like a rock wall, one cannot be touched by anything, one cannot be moved by anything. This is transmitted orally.

# THE RONIN
# THE SAMURAI WHO ANSWERED TO NO SHOGUN

The Japanese word *ronin* translates loosely to a man who is floating in the waves. During the early eras of Japanese history, the word was used to describe runaway serfs, but during the feudal era, the word came to describe the samurai who, for one reason or another, had left the service of his lord and master and now found himself adrift in the Japanese countryside.

Ronin first emerged during the Warring States period, from 1467 to 1573. This was a time of major upheaval in Japan, as the heads of feudal clans clashed with one another. Some clan leaders, or *daimyo*, were killed, others

were displaced, and still others remained in power but lost some of their lands or status. Many of the samurai who served these defeated daimyo remained loyal, even to the point of committing *seppuku*, or ritual suicide, after a lord was killed, as required by the samurai code.

But other samurai simply chose to ignore the *bushido* code. If their daimyo had been killed or disgraced, they might leave their ancestral lands and wander out into the countryside. They might then be joined by other samurai who had been just as carelessly tossed aside when their masters no longer needed them. Some of these floating samurai formed gangs of bandits, but more often they became freelance warriors, willing to serve any daimyo who offered them reasonable pay and status. The longer the wars continued, the more samurai were displaced, constantly moving from one daimyo to another. Todo Takatora, one of the most famous ronin, worked under six different daimyo before he latched onto Tokugawa Ieyasu, a powerful shogun whose actions would forever alter the ronin way of life.

When Ieyasu emerged victorious from the battle of Sekigahara in 1600, war-ravaged Japan was finally united under a single leader, which meant that the daimyo no longer needed vast armies of samurai. It is estimated that as many as half a million samurai were stripped of their status when Ieyasu consolidated power in Edo (modern Tokyo). In 1615, as many as 100,000 of these ronin fled to Osaka, joining a rebellion by Toyotomi Hideyori, who claimed that he was the rightful shogun. After a long siege, Ieyasu defeated Hideyori (who committed *seppuku*) and slaughtered thousands of ronin as they fled the battlefield.

Over the next thirty years, as peace came to Japan, the Edo government pared down the army, putting thousands of samurai out of work. The samurai were given two choices: either move to their daimyo's palace and serve as faithful retainers or become peasants. But some chose a third path: they became ronin. Between 1650 and 1652, a number of ronin bands rebelled, but the uprisings were not successful, and the rebel leadership was brutally repressed. After

*Portrait of a Ronin, from Seichin Gushi Shozo. Utagawa Kuniyoshi (1798–1861). Japan. 19th century. Woodblock print.*

*Ronin Attacking the Kiras Gate, scene from Act XI of Chushingura or The Loyal League: A Japanese Romance. Utagawa Kuniyoshi (1798–1861). Japan. 19th century. Woodblock print.*

*The Chushingura, Act II, when the ronin attack Moronao's castle. Utagawa Kuniyoshi (1798–1861). Japan. Circa 1854. Color woodblock print.*

martial arts instructor Yui Shosetsu led an unsuccessful rebellion, all of his close relatives were crucified, even after he had committed seppuku. On the other hand, the government, hoping to keep the peace, paved the way for many of the ronin to reenter society as bureaucrats, policemen, artists, writers, teachers, and bodyguards. Between the 1650s and a short period of rebellion at the dawn of the Meiji era in the 1860s, the ronin were generally at peace, with one major and memorable exception.

In 1701, the ronin Naganori Asano was serving as a guard in the palace of Shogun Tokugawa Tsuyanoshi when a visitor arrived from Kyoto: Yoshinaka Kira, a high-ranking kinsman of the emperor. Kira did not like Asano, thinking that a ronin from the countryside was not worthy of the shogun's court. Kira constantly insulted and berated Asano, who bore it silently until the day that Kira tripped on the stairs, losing his sandal. Kira claimed that it was Asano's fault that he had tripped, and he demanded that Asano pick up the sandal and put it back on his foot. In Japanese society, the idea of picking up someone else's footwear or touching someone else's foot is repugnant. Asano pulled out his sword and struck Kira, who was saved from death by his retainers. Since drawing a sword in the shogun's palace was a crime punishable by death, Tsuyanoshi, even though he knew Asano had been provoked, had no choice but to order his faithful retainer Asano to commit seppuku.

Asano had forty-seven ronin retainers. After he committed seppuku, they lost their jobs in the palace. Although they wanted to avenge their master's death, they knew it would be impossible to fight through the guards in the palace to get to Kira, who was expecting them to attack. Instead, they dispersed throughout the countryside. They became beggars and public drunkards, suffering the insults of friends and neighbors as they silently put into place their plan to lull Kira into a false sense of security. Finally, after more than a year had passed, the forty-seven ronin traveled to Kira's hometown of Ryogoku, stormed his palace, killed his small crew of guards, and cornered him in his rice storehouse. They offered him the chance to commit seppuku, but he begged for mercy. Disgusted, they chopped off his head and carried it to Asano's grave. With their mission accomplished, they said prayers to Asano's spirit and then committed mass suicide, to reunite with their master and to atone for acting disloyally to their shogun.

The story of Asano and his followers has since been retold in countless books, as well as in the kabuki play *Chushingura* and in several films, notably the 1941 film *The 47 Ronin* by Kenji Mizoguchi, which was intended to revive the ronin spirit among soldiers and sailors heading off to World War II. Even today, people throughout Japan still visit the graveyard where Asano and his ronin are laid to rest. The ronin are seen as heroes who willingly suffered abuse to prove their honor and loyalty, although some might question whether they took matters a bit too far.

# Epilogue

The above written record is solely what has been ever on my mind about Niten Ichi-ryū swordsmanship, as it has been spoken. Now writing down for the first time these principles, I have some misgivings about the order, and cannot describe them fully. Be that as it may, for one who wishes to learn the Way, they can serve as guideposts on the path. Since my youth I have labored on the path of martial arts, training my hands and body for mastery of swordsmanship, accumulating all manner of experiences. Scrutinizing other schools, I see that some pay lip service, some exhibit fine handwork; and well they may appear to the eyes of others, yet there is not a kernel of truth among them. Of course they think in doing these things they are training their bodies and cultivating their minds, but they are all a blight on the Way of martial arts, and their bad influence endures forever. The true Way of martial arts in the world is corrupted, causing the art of war to be abandoned. The true path of swordsmanship is fighting the enemy and winning, and nothing other than this. He who attains the wisdom of my martial arts and who practices it correctly will achieve victory beyond questioning.

The twelfth day of the fifth month, the second year of Shōhō (1645)

Teruo Magonojo        Shinmen Musashi

*Shojiro with a sword. Natori Shunsen. Japan. 1924. Color woodblock print.*

# TAMESHIGIRI
## TEST-CUTTING A SWORD BLADE

The practice of test cutting a new sword blade, *tameshigiri,* has a long history. During the Sengoku era (the Warring States period between 1467 and 1568), the practice arose of using human corpses for test cutting. Because the Sengoku-era battles often resulted in high casualties, many bodies were available for tameshigiri. Anyouji Kaganokami, considered the founder of this testing, was the first to use dead bodies as targets, with records indicating that he began practicing on corpses around the year 1504.

Tani Daizen was a famous test cutter who also utilized this method with corpses from 1550 to 1580. Though he was first a retainer to Saito Dosan in the Mino province, he later became a retainer to Oda Nobunaga. In the battle of Honganji at Osaka, Daizen distinguished himself by single-handedly killing five of the enemy's top retainers, and afterward, he received a certificate of appreciation from Nobunaga, commending his bravery and recognizing his great value as a warrior. During the conquest of the Mouri clan in 1580, he fought in Toyotomi Hideyoshi's army in the attack on Miki castle, the battle in which he died, at the age of fifty. His tameshigiri techniques were handed down to his son, Yasutomo, who in turn taught them to his own disciples.

Yasutomo also served Hideyoshi in many battles, including the battle of Shizugatake in 1583 against Shibata Katsuie, the battle of Komaki-Nagakude in 1584 against the allied armies of Tokugawa Ieyasu and Oda Nobuo, the conquest of the

*Sensei Toshishiro Obata stands in front of a makiwara, or target, which is made from the top, or omote, covering of a tatami mat. The target is rolled into a long cylinder and soaked in water before cutting.*

Shimazu clan in 1587, and various campaigns in Korea. He grew famous for his many military exploits, and Hideyoshi honored him with the title *dewanokami,* after which he was known as Tani Dewanokami. Because of his extensive experience, he also became known as a master of tameshigiri. One of his most famous disciples was Nakagawa Saheita, who wrote many *hidensho* (secret manuals) and in turn also had many disciples of his own.

After the battle of Sekigahara in 1600, Yasutomo became a retainer to Tokugawa Ieyasu, with an annual stipend of 16,000 *koku.* In the Osaka summer campaign of 1615, the Toyotomi clan was destroyed, and Tokugawa gained control of all of Japan, both in name and in reality. In his later years, before he died in 1627 at the age of sixty-five, Yasutomo became the shogun's *courtyotogishu,* an old veteran who shares war stories with the shogun.

In 1637, after Christian peasants had revolted against the local governor in the Shimabara rebellion, peace reigned over the land during the entirety of the Tokugawa era, from 1603 to 1867. In the Sengoku era, a samurai had proved his fighting skills and the quality of his sword in battle, but when the quiet years of the Tokugawa era came, samurai no longer had the opportunity to test their swords in combat. Some resorted to practicing *tsujigiri,* in which a new blade is tested on casual passersby, but the government strongly prohibited this, and after laws were passed to severely punished anyone who committed this act, instances became less common.

*Obata performs an inazumi, or lightning cut. The first cut is made with a kiriage, or rising cut, and the second is a horizontal yokokiri cut on the already cut piece, before it falls away.*

*Here Obata is in the process of cutting using nitoken right kesa, in which two swords are used to cut the target diagonally.*

## Shitoka: The Professional Sword Tester

During this time professional swordmen known as *shitoka* appeared. They tested swords owned by the Tokugawa family and those of many *daimyo* (feudal lords). In Edo and other large cities, shitoka often used the corpses of criminals for test cutting. Nakagawa Saheita's disciple Yamano Kaemon Nagahisa became a shitoka for the Tokugawa government with Saheita's recommendation, and after his death, his son Yamano Kanjuro Hisahide took his place. Some of Yamano Kanjuro Hisahide's disciples became shitoka for the government, such as Ugai Jurozaemon, Matsumoto Chodayu, and Yamada Asaemon, among others. Because they had been chosen to work for the Tokugawa government, each of these shitoka became famous, and still existing today are swords that have their *tameshimei* (the sword tester's name) inscribed on the tang.

During the early days of government-endorsed shitoka, the swordsmen performed both testing and the execution of criminals, because at that time, these jobs were not clearly defined or even particularly distinguished from one another. *Ikido tameshi,* or tameshigiri performed on live criminals was common. For tameshigiri on corpses, decapitated bodies were piled on top of one another and then attacked by the shitoka to see how many bodies the sword could slice through in one stroke. Yamano Kanjuro cut through seven bodies with the sword *Kanifusa*, while Matsumoto Chodayu

*Two cuts are performed concurrently: a left kiriage rising cut and a right kesa downward cut.*

*The swordsman prepares to cut two targets nitoken (two swords) by raising the swords to the jodan kamae upper position.*

*The execution of a left and a right kesa results in cutting both targets in a downward motion at the same time.*

successfully cut through six bodies with the sword *Yasutsuna*. Many shitoka could cut through four bodies successfully.

After the Edo government was established, criminals were sentenced according to preceding records of punishment, and judging and sentencing therefore took extra time because of the tedious process of checking old documentation. During the reign of the eighth-generation Tokugawa shogun, Yoshimune, the *osadamegaki hyakkajyo* provisions for sentencing criminals were created to expedite the sentencing process. The osadamegaki applied to ordinary citizens but not to samurai or monks. It was during this time that the governmental jobs of shitoka and executioner were separated and treated as distinct occupations. The shitoka at this time were Yamano Hisatoyo and Matsumoto Chodayu, whose replacements were Kuramochi Yasuzaemon and the second Yamada Asaemon. After Kuramochi died, the Yamada family held the position of governmental shitoka exclusively.

Born in 1657, Asaemon became the Yamada family's first-generation honorary shitoka. For eight generations, the Yamada family worked as shitoka for the Tokugawa government, each succeeding head of the family inheriting the name Asaemon. They continued working in this position until April 1870, the third year of the Meiji restoration, when testing swords on criminal bodies became forbidden, but they still functioned as substitute executioners until 1882, when new laws were passed forbidding decapitation.

There were two main public execution grounds for felons in Edo, one in Suzugamori and the other in Kozukappara. At the time, the only bodies used for test cutting were the

decapitated bodies of men who had been sentenced to *shizai*, the death penalty for felons. When someone was sentenced to *geshunin*, or death by decapitation for unintentional manslaughter, the body was not test-cut but was instead returned to the family. It is important to note that punishments given to felons during the Edo era were very severe. Often entire estates would be confiscated by the government, and anyone convicted of murder was sentenced to shizai. For the most part, felons were executed by beheading, and their decapitated bodies were then used for test cutting. However, the bodies of samurai, monks, women, and children were not used for test cutting.

Asaemon's job was to test swords on the bodies of recently executed criminals. After testing a sword, he would then report its performance, that is, whether it cut well or not, to the government. The official name of the executioner was *uchiyaku-doushin*, or, more commonly, *kubikiri-yakunin*, and he operated under the *machi-bugyo* (city magistrate). Though some experienced executioners were skilled enough to behead convicts with one hand, novice executioners were required to practice on *tatami* mats. If an executioner failed to behead the convict on the first swing, he would be sprayed with blood, and the convict would struggle and cry out if still alive. If the executioner failed to behead the convict with the third swing, he would use the blade to slit the convict's throat. As one might expect, executioners sometimes were not willing to do their jobs. In these situations, Yamada Asaemon was requested to act as a substitute for the executioner. After decapitating a criminal, he would test swords on the body and hence was nicknamed Kubikiri Aseamon ("Beheading Asaemon").

The Yamada family's part-time job was executing criminals under the order of the Tokugawa government, but their main occupation was shitoka. Throughout their eight generations as official shitoka, they tested not only government swords but also swords belonging to many daimyo and private owners as well. Many records have survived of shito tameshigiri performed for famous sword smiths, and these have been a great contribution to sword society. However, since it was the duty of the samurai to distinguish themselves in battle, the execution of criminals and the practice of tameshigiri on bodies was not highly regarded in terms of the samurai code. Therefore, even though Asaemon worked for the Tokugawa government, his status remained that of a *ronin*, the masterless samurai. The fact that human bodies were used in tameshigiri's history cannot be avoided. Though in modern times it would be considered inhumane or barbaric to test-cut the corpses of executed criminals, people in feudal Japan believed that criminals deserved punishment and that the act would serve as a warning that would help prevent crime. There were actually only a few shitoka who tested swords on human bodies; normally a samurai would perform shizan tameshigiri on bamboo or *makiwara* (the straw bundles used as archery targets) to test his technique. It is important to understand the difference between shizan and shito, and it is of great importance that modern tameshigiri never be performed on animals or humans, whether living or dead.

Some literature on tameshigiri explains how it is to be performed on human beings. The sources for this literature are the *tameshigiri hidensho,* which were written by shitoka during the Edo era. Since these hidensho were written specifically for students who were learning to become the type of shitoka who test-cuts the bodies of criminals, these manuals were kept secret. If these teachings and their diagrams were to be published today, they would be shocking to say the least. In *shinkendo,* the modern practice of the long sword, the type of tameshigiri used is shizan, which involves the cutting of straw mats and bamboo as the best materials for evaluating a swordsman's cutting technique.

## Shito: Testing the Strength of the Sword

In addition to improving the sharpness of their swords, smiths worked constantly to improve the strength of their handiwork. Many methods were used to test the strength of a sword blade. For example, the flat of the blade would be hit against the surface of water, the back would be struck against an iron pole, or metal balls would be dropped onto the blade. Straw, bamboo, and hard materials such as wood, deer antlers, coins, metal, and *kabuto* helmets were used for test cutting. Swords were tested to determine how much stress they could handle, sometimes until they broke.

*Obata is shown about to cut a double thickness makiwara target using two swords.*

*The cut is executed by using left kesa with the two swords in a parallel downward motion.*

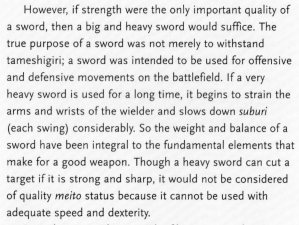

*Obata addresses the target in preparation for a nitoken cut with both swords lowered to his side.*

*Two right kesa with nitoken cuts are made on a downward sweep of the swords simultaneously.*

However, if strength were the only important quality of a sword, then a big and heavy sword would suffice. The true purpose of a sword was not merely to withstand tameshigiri; a sword was intended to be used for offensive and defensive movements on the battlefield. If a very heavy sword is used for a long time, it begins to strain the arms and wrists of the wielder and slows down *suburi* (each swing) considerably. So the weight and balance of a sword have been integral to the fundamental elements that make for a good weapon. Though a heavy sword can cut a target if it is strong and sharp, it would not be considered of quality *meito* status because it cannot be used with adequate speed and dexterity.

A smith can test the strength of his own swords using tameshigiri or a combination of other methods. But because of possible bias, he might consider a mediocre sword to be qualified as *meito* because it meets his standards of performance, which may or may not be objective. This is why separate fields of sword appraisal developed in Japan. In order for a sword to be considered meito, a third party who is especially knowledgeable about swords, such as a shitoka or a master swordsman, must vouch for it.

In March 1852, a *shitokai* competition was held by the Matsushiro clan of Nagano prefecture. Present at the shitokai were ten *metsukeyaku* (examiners), two *togishi* (sword polishers), an *agekai* (surgeon, in case of injuries), and seven skilled samurai, all of whom tested the swords of

twelve smiths to determine whose sword was the strongest. They used various methods and materials, such as dry straw, bamboo wrapped in straw, *kotetsu* (old metal), deer antlers, hats filled with iron sand, alloys of brass and iron and of silver and copper, and even a metal kabuto. If a sword survived test cutting on these materials, then the flat and back were struck until they broke. No sword in the shitokai was able to cut through the kabuto, but the sword that performed beyond all others was forged by Yamaura Saneo, who was recognized for this achievement. Saneo's brother was Minamoto Kiyomaro, one of the most famous smiths during the Edo era. Kiyomaro's swords not only possessed great strength and cutting power but also were some of the most beautiful Japanese swords ever created.

Only the aesthetic qualities of a sword can be determined by looking at it. Even with today's technology, one cannot determine how well a sword will perform without actually using it. In any era, shito must be performed in order to assess the true strength of a sword.

## Kabutowari: Helmet splitting

The most prominent test in shito tameshigiri was *kabutowari*, helmet splitting. However, there are not many records of successful kabutowari, and in fact, there were very few attempts even made. Although important cultural assets and artifacts with historical value were never used for kabutowari, there was some apprehension surrounding the

*A kiriage is a lower to upper diagonal cut made at an approximate 35-degree angle to the target.*

*Obata makes a second kiriage cut on the same target within a split-second of his initial cut.*

test because of the risk of damaging valuable kabuto and swords, as well as the fact that the actual test was very dangerous for the shitoka performing it.

The low success rate of this particular test also made it risky for both the owner of the sword and the smith who created it. If the kabuto was not split and the sword was damaged, then the smith was dishonored and the owner would be disappointed and would end up with a damaged sword. Yet even if the sword suffered no damage and the kabuto were not split, then the test cutter would be considered at fault for having poor technique, and he would be dishonored. Traditionally, a swordsman would only perform kabutowari once in his career.

The literal translation of *kabutowari* is "helmet break," so the purpose of kabutowari was to break the helmet, not to cut through it. If the goal were to cut through the helmet, then this practice would be called *kabutogiri*, "helmet cutting," and no such tameshigiri

*On February 14, 1994, swordmaster Toshishiro Obata performed kabutowari, or helmet-splitting, on a Momoyama period (16th century) forged metal helmet, or kabuto, leaving a record-breaking gash of 13 centimeters.*

exists. When the forged steel of the sword struck the forged steel of the helmet with full power, the sword would rebound from the helmet as a result of the velocity and power of the swing, regardless of whether the helmet broke or not. The test cutter would feel a strong shock from the sword's impact on the kabuto. Therefore, the shitoka had to have excellent balance to avoid falling backward, and he also needed a good *tenouchi* (grip) to prevent the sword from flying out of his hands and possibly striking him. A *hamaguriba*, the convex-beveled, shell-shaped sword, was best suited for kabutowari because the edge was thick and would resist breaking.

Since there were no visual means of documenting these tests, such as today's film, kabutowari was always performed in the presence of the sword's owner as well as several examiners who would keep an accurate record of the results. It was said that usually a surgeon would be present during kabutowari, just in case the sword broke and pieces of it injured the tester or the observers. Historically, kabutowari was practiced as the result of a power struggle between sword smiths and kabuto makers. The helmet-splitting test was essentially a contest between the two crafts to determine which one produced the strongest implements. Since instances of kabutowari were carefully documented during the transition between the Edo and Meiji eras, the test results can be proved and have prevented any false legends from arising.

*Battle scenes from Tale of the Heike. Japan. 1650–1700. Six-panel folding screen.*

# Fu no maki

## The Wind Scroll

In martial arts it is important to know the Ways of other schools, so I have written about the various other schools of martial arts here in this Wind Scroll. Without knowledge of the Ways of other schools, one cannot understand clearly the Way of my school. Scrutinizing others' martial arts, I see those who use large long swords, *ookinaru tachi*, and focus on feats of strength. Some schools are devoted to martial arts using a shorter long sword, *kodachi*, or "little long sword." There are also schools that devise a large number of techniques and moves with the long sword, that transmit the Way by formal, *omote*, and secret, *oku*, teachings.

Inside this scroll I reveal clearly that none of these schools is the true Way, showing the good and the bad, the right and the wrong. The principles on my school are completely different from theirs. Other schools turn their martial art into a trade, using flowery presentations and showy techniques to make a livelihood. Can this be called the true Way? Or is swordsmanship alone, viewed as martial arts in a narrow sense by the public, the true Way? Learning to handle a long sword and training the hands and body to determine victory—is this the true Way? Neither is the true Way. In this book I have revealed one by one the deficiencies of other schools. Reflect deeply on these things to understand the advantages of Niten Ichi-ryū.

## 他流に大きなる太刀を持つ事
## Taryu ni ookinaru tachi o motsu

### EXTRA-LONG SWORDS IN OTHER SCHOOLS

There are other schools that have a fondness for extra-long swords. From the point of view of my martial art, I see them as weak schools. The reason being, these other schools know not the principle of defeating the enemy by any means; their preference for the extra-long sword is by virtue of its length; from a distance they think they can beat the enemy. The popular maxim, *issun te masari*, even an inch gives one the upper hand, is nothing more than a judgment by people who are ignorant of martial arts. To try to win from a distance, therefore, by sword length instead of by an understanding of the principles of martial arts is because of a weakness of spirit. That is why I see this as weak martial art.

When one is engaged closely with an opponent and deadlock ensues, the longer one's sword the harder it is to strike; it cannot be swung around freely, and becomes a millstone. Then one becomes more inferior than a man wielding a small *wakizashi*. He who is fond of the extra-long sword is not without his reasons, but it is reasonable only to him. Seen from the true Way of the world, he lacks reason. When using a shorter long sword over an extra-long sword, must one not necessarily lose?

When the space is such that one is constricted above and below and to the sides, or one is in a position in which only the wakizashi is used, a preference for an extra-long sword in these circumstances is an affront to martial arts and in bad faith. Also, some people of lesser strength cannot handle an extra-long sword. From days of yore it has been said that the great and small go together, so there is no reason to dislike the extra-long sword; rather the thing to be disliked is excessive attachment to it. In large-scale martial arts, an extra-long sword is a large battalion, a shorter long sword a small battalion. Can a small battalion not confront a large battalion? There are many examples of a small battalion defeating a large battalion. In my school there is a loathing of such prejudicial thinking. Consider this well.

*The Sea off Satta in Suruga Province, from the series Thirty-Six Views of Mt. Fuji. Ando Hiroshige (1797–1858). Japan. 19th century.*

# PIRACY AND NAVIES
# WAR ON THE WATERS

The waters surrounding the island of Japan made fighting on ships possible for the pirates and the navies of Japan, as well as that of its neighboring countries, particularly China and Korea. Naval warfare's importance in the history of Japan was demostrated early when the invading Mongol fleet was destroyed by hurricanes on two different occasions. The Japanese called the destructive hurricanes, which saved them from invasion in 1274 and again in 1281, *kamikaze,* "divine winds."

The sea battle of Dannoura, between the Taira and Minamoto families, was also pivotal in the history of Japan. The flow of the tide in the narrow straits of Shimonoseki, where the battle took place, initially gave the advantage to the Taira ships, which carried not only the eight-year-old Emperor Antoku but also the mirror, the sword, and the jewel that symbolized his kingship. The samurai from both families fought from ship to ship using long-range archery and fire and then with daggers and swords as the ships moved closer together. When the tide changed, the Minamoto ships took the advantage. Once the Taira were certain they were defeated, the young emperor's grandmother plunged into the water with him in her arms to prevent his capture by the Minamoto, and many of the Taira jumped into the ocean to follow her to her watery grave. In this way, the Minamoto became the ruling clan of Japan.

Although the original Chinese sailboats known as *junks* had been used in these waters as early as 770 BCE, the ships used in naval warfare varied in shape, size, and design, with one clear standout among the early examples. The Japanese navy, which included many samurai and was by Toyotomi Hideyoshi, attacked Korea in 1592 and again in 1597, resulting in the capture of the cities of Pyongyang and Hanseong (later Seoul). In response, Korean Admiral Yi Sun-sin ordered the construction of the world's first ironclad ships, known as *kobukson,* "turtle ships." Reinforcements from China's Ming navy partnered with Sun-sin and the turtle ships to cut the Japanese line and force Hideyoshi to retreat. The exact design of the turtle ship is not known, but besides its reputation as being covered with iron plates, it was known to be armed with gun ports and with cannon that could shoot in every direction.

A variety of weapons were used in conflicts between ships, against ships from land, and from ships to land. But Japanese pirates dealt with Chinese military science in the form of explosive weapons. Because warships were made of wood, fire was an effective tactic, which led to the use of firebombs in naval warfare. The Mori family produced a small version of the thunderclap bomb, which acted as a hand grenade, and was know as the *horokubiya,* literally "cooking pot fire arrows." The name was used to distinguish them from the *bo hiya,* shafted fire arrows shot from bows. Two halves of the bomb were filled with gunpowder and sometimes lead shot or iron fragments, and a fuse was attached. A short rope was used to help with throwing, or a net was attached to a pole, which could be used to hurl them toward a ship.

Japanese pirates harassed Korea from 1356. In response, Korea requested firearms from China via a special envoy to the imperial court. By 1377, Chinese models of handguns and bombards (stone-hurling cannon) were being systematically manufactured in Korea. Wooden arrows fitted with metal heads and fins were fired from some of these weapons. The firearms that the Koreans received permission to make were the prototypes of artillery used effectively against the invading Japanese in 1592 by Admiral Yi Sun-sin of the Korean navy.

Japanese pirates were the first to use the Portuguese harquebuses. Until the ninth century, many of the pirates in the Far East used Japan as a base, even though they were from Korea, China, and even Portugal. The threat of Japanese pirates was so intense that it prompted Ming general Qi Jiguang to develop a special curved sword, the *Wodao,* to fight them.

Cheng I Sao, a female Chinese pirate, took over her husband's Red Flag pirate fleet in 1807 after he drowned. She later married her late husband's commander, Chang Pao, and together they led ruthless attacks, meting out severe punishment, typically in the form of beheading. The Chinese government finally offered her a retirement package to gain peace in the region, and she became proprietor of a gambling house, where she died in 1844 at the age of sixty.

*Yoshitsune, with Benkei and Other Retainers in their Ship Beset by the Ghosts of Taira. Utagawa Kuniyoshi (1798–1861). Japan. 1853. Woodblock print.*

## 他流において強みの太刀といふ事

# Taryu ni oite tsuyomi no tachi

### THE STRONG SWORD IN OTHER SCHOOLS

When it comes to long swords, there should be no strong sword or weak sword. A sword swung with the aim to swing powerfully is a rough sword, and one cannot win with a rough sword alone. Moreover, a strong sword used to cut a man down with an unreasonably strong slash will not succeed. Even if one were to test one's blade, an intentionally powerful slash is not good.

No one would think to strike strongly or to strike weakly when facing an enemy in mortal combat. When thinking only of cutting down a man, there is no feeling of strength, no feeling of weakness, only the thought of killing the enemy. Striking the opponent's sword strongly, delivering a concentrated powerful blow with one's sword will go wrong, being overspent. Striking another's sword with a powerful blow, one's own sword will be broken. Thus, the strong sword does not exist.

In large-scale martial arts as well, when one has strong forces and hopes to attain a strong victory in battle, the enemy too, as a matter of course, has assembled strong men and aims to fight fiercely. In either case, they are the same. Victory in all things is impossible without correct principles. In my school, not the smallest thought is given to things illogical; the point is to attain victory any way one can by means of the wisdom of martial arts. Work diligently on this.

## 他流に短き太刀を用ゐる事

# Taryu ni tanki tachi o mochiiru

### USING SHORTER LONG SWORDS IN OTHER SCHOOLS

Using only the shorter long sword to win is not the true Way. From ancient days, swords were divided into *tachi* and *katana*, and called long and short swords. A strong man can wield easily even a large long sword, so there is no case for unreasonably preferring a shorter

*Samurai. Pat Nicolle (1907-1995). Japan. 20th century. Gouache on paper.*

# NINJA IN THE SHADOWS
## THE SPECIAL FORCES OF SPIES AND ASSASSINS

In medieval Japan, the samurai held as exalted a position as the knights of Europe. They were seen as paragons of honor, virtue, and nobility, hewing to the strictures of the lofty *bushido* code, and a breach of honor was a crime worthy of the intensely painful suicide known as *seppuku*.

But the samurai were not the only warriors in Japan. Lurking in the shadows was an army of spies, saboteurs, assassins, and guerillas, using tactics that would have offended the sensibilities of the high-minded samurai. They were referred to as *shinobi no mono*, "stealthy people." With the language changes of the past fifty years, the Japanese characters that make up the words *shinobi* and *mono* have been more commonly read with an alternate pronunciation: *ninja*.

Although spies have been used in Japan throughout its known history, ninja did not emerge as trained fighters until the mid-fourteenth century, when the nation was split between two rival emperors vying for the throne. Taking advantage of this civil war, the mountainous province of Iga briefly gained its independence from the central government, aided by a loose-knit coalition of warrior priests, rebellious peasants, and rogue samurai, or *ronin*. In its battle for independence, Iga used guerilla tactics against the imperial army, including *ninjutsu*, that is, the Japanese art of stealth.

*Taiheki*, a history written in the late fourteenth century, tells of how during a night of rain and wind, a team of highly skilled ninja (or perhaps only one, since the Japanese wording does not distinguish between singular and plural) crept up to the fortress of Hachiman-yama and burned it down, starting with its relatively unprotected temple. Another account relates how a samurai cut down a ninja (or team of ninja) that had infiltrated his castle.

From the relatively brief references in the *Taiheki*, it is hard to tell whether these attackers came from Iga, but by the fifteenth century, Iga and its neighboring province, Koga, were known as the two centers for ninjutsu. At that time, ninja were sometimes referred to as *Iga-mono*, or Iga people.

Jiraiya, legendary ninja and title character of Japanese folktale Jiraiya Goketsu Monogatari. Eight Hundred Heroes of Our Country's Suikoden. Utagawa Kuniyoshi. (1798–1861). Japan. 19th century.

Ninja were a counterculture to the upper-class samurai. They lived in humble peasant villages, offering protection from any thieves or attackers. The ninja master, or *jonin*, "upper ninja," typically lived in the center of the village, surrounded by the homes of his subordinates, who were prepared to protect him in case of attack. In the secretive world of the ninja, the jonin's identity was often concealed from all but his closest followers. Immediately below the jonin were the *chunin*, "middle ninja," who managed the daily activities of the clan, trained the *genin*, "lower ninja," in the skills of the trade, and oversaw their assignments. The chunin would also conduct negotiations with outsiders who wanted to hire the genin to do their dirty work.

Most ninja were born into the profession, and from an early age, they were taught the art of stealth. They were taught methods of concealment, such as how to hide in scantily furnished rooms or leafless trees. They were taught the skills of breaking and entering (*toiri no jutsu*), such as using portable ladders to scale walls and specially designed crowbars to pry open doors. They were such good acrobats that the legend spread that they could soar through the air like arrows or spring to the roof of a building with a single bound.

Ninja were also trained to be masters of disguise. Sometimes, they disguised themselves as traveling entertainers, including *hokashi* (tumblers, magicians, monkey handlers) and *sarugakushi* (actors, singers, dancers), offering public performances as they assessed their enemy's territory. Other times they traveled as *komuso* (flute-playing priests with baskets on their heads), *yamabushi* (mountain ascetics), *shukke* (Buddhist priests), or *shonin* (merchants), all of whom were often seen wandering the countryside, engaging in small talk with strangers about current events. Or sometimes they went out as mere peasants, too lowly to be noticed by the samurai they were spying on. These disguises were collectively referred to as the *shihode*, "seven ways of going," although

*A traditional Japanese temple tucked into the trees of the countryside exemplifies the hidden out-of-the-way environment where a ninja band might hide. Unlike the high-profile samurai associated with powerful lords, the ninja maintained a low profile among the peasantry until ready to spring into action.*

there were other disguises that the ninja used as well. It is a myth that ninja dressed only in tight black costumes when they were on the attack. Some dressed as warriors, others as peasants. And even those who dressed in the stereotypical *shinobi shozoku,* "stealthy clothing," did not always wear black; dark grays and blues were also favored colors.

Once they had zeroed in on their victims, ninja could be ruthless. Without hesitation, they would stab an opponent in the back, slip poison into their host's food, or kill an assassination target lying asleep in bed. But a ninja knew his limitations. When facing unbeatable odds, he would try to escape so he could live to fight again, instead of making a brave but suicidal last stand in the manner of the samurai. If he were to be captured, he would not usually commit *seppuku,* although he might be executed in an equally gruesome fashion.

This is not to say that the ninja had no scruples. They were fiercely loyal and strictly adhered to their own definitions of honor and duty. But because of the ninja's lower-class backgrounds and the unseemly methods they used, most samurai thought of them as being lower than the lowest class. They called them *hinin,* "nonhumans." On the other hand, some professional jealousy may have been involved. Some tales say that at least a few samurai moonlighted as ninja, engaging in activities by night that they would never want to be seen doing in the light of day.

It was during the Warring States period, from the 1460s through 1581, that ninja truly made their mark on society. At that time, feudal clans throughout Japan were fighting each other to gain power and extend their territories. Iga and Koga were torn apart by dozens of clans vying for turf. By allying themselves with victorious clans, a number of ninja were able to gain land and power, and some ninja built their own castles, began samurai-like clans, and dressed in full samurai attire.

The ninja's hold on Iga came to an end in 1581 when they rebelled for the second time against Oda Nobunaga, the feudal lord who was then on his way to reuniting the warring states. This time Nobunga burned most of the province to the ground. The surviving ninja spread throughout the land. Many were hired by feudal lords for their martial skills. In 1582, one of Nobunaga's top lieutenants, Tokugawa Ieyasu, hired a team of 200 ninja from Iga as his bodyguard, and then six years later, he hired 110 ninja from Koga. After the emperor named him shogun in 1603, these ninja formed the core of his secret police, or *oniwaban,* "guards of the gardens," although their true duty was to serve as spies in Japan's far-flung provinces. With Japan at relative peace, however, there was little need for spies. Some ninja joined the police, others entered the *yakuza* organized crime group, and still others simply rejoined common society, but they were never again a powerful military force.

sword. This is because spears and halberds are also used for their length. Those fond of the shorter long sword think they can jump in and stab the enemy, cutting in between the gaps of his flourishing sword. This is misguided and bad.

What is more, aiming for the gaps, one loses everything, becoming entangled with the enemy, which is undesirable. Similarly, trying to use a shorter long sword to break into the enemy's defense and lay siege upon them will not work in the midst of large forces. Some may think that by taking up the shorter long sword alone against many enemies one will be able to slash through, jump about freely, and spin around, but these are all defensive sword moves, and one will become entangled with the enemy. This is not the Way of certainty.

On the other hand, one could assume a strong and direct position, chase the enemy around, make him jump aside, devising moves to disorient him—this is the Way with the single purpose of achieving absolute victory. This same principle applies to large-scale martial arts. Under equal circumstances, one could move large forces against the enemy, attack suddenly, and wipe them out on the spot. This mind is central to the art of war.

The martial arts that people of the world usually practice are parrying, checking, evading, and slipping through. Their hearts and minds then become habituated to these skills, such that the enemy controls and exploits them. The Way of martial arts is straight and true; it is critical to know how to drive the enemy and to subdue them. Think on this carefully.

# 他流に太刀かず多き事
# Taryu ni tachi kazu ooki

## NUMEROUS SWORD SKILLS IN OTHER SCHOOLS

Other schools teach many methods of using the long sword, turning the Way into something to sell, and no doubt to ingratiate themselves with beginners over the numerous sword skills to know. This is loathsome to martial arts. The reason being it is wrong to think that there are numerous ways to cut a man down. There are no different ways in the world to cut a man down. Whether one is knowledgeable, whether a woman or a child, the ways to strike or cut are not many. If there are differences, they are stabbing and slashing, but no others. Anyway, when it comes to the martial art of killing the enemy, there is no reason so many methods should be used.

Even so, depending on the place and circumstances, use of one's long sword may be constricted by the surroundings, above or to the sides, but there are still five sword positions, the five directions. Any additions to this— such as cutting a man down by twisting the hands, bending the body, jumping out—are not the true Way. To cut a man down, twisting, bending, and jumping are not ways to cut. These are useless. In my martial arts, it is critical that both the mind and the body are straight, attaining victory by causing the enemy to twist and bend, causing the enemy's heart and mind to twist and turn. Study this carefully.

# 他流に太刀の構を用ゐる事
# Taryu ni tachi no kamae o mochiiru

## SWORD STANCES IN OTHER SCHOOLS

Placing importance on the position of the sword alone is wrong. Taking up a sword stance in the world usually means there are no enemies. The reason being, establishing standard forms as the precedents of old or rules of today does not lead to the Way of victory. Devising means to put the opponent in bad situations is key. In all things, assuming a stance is making use of the immoveable. Making a stand in a castle or in a battalion is to be strong and unmoved, even when under attack. This is the usual meaning.

On the path to victory in martial arts, one must be set on taking the lead in all things. The attitude for taking a stance is one of waiting for a chance to take the initiative. Work on this diligently. Who wins in martial arts is determined by ruffling the opponent's stance, catching him unawares, throwing him into confusion, or vexing him, or terrifying him, taking advantage of his mistiming when flustered to claim one's victory. Taking a stance that is one of defense, therefore, is loathed. That is why there is in my school of martial arts the so-called stance without a stance.

In large-scale martial arts as well, the important thing in fighting is to ascertain the number of troops, grasp the situation on the battlefield, understand the status of one's troops, gain from their strong points, embolden them, and then get under way. Being attacked first by someone is completely different from being the one doing the attacking. Learning to wield a sword well, catching and parrying well, is like using one's spear and halberd to build a rampart. In striking an opponent, on the other hand, one could pull up a wooden stake and wield it as a spear or halberd. This requires thorough examination.

## 他流に目付といふ事
# Taryu ni metsuke

### THE GAZE IN OTHER SCHOOLS

The type of gaze used depends on the school. In some schools the eyes are fixed on the opponent's sword; in some the eyes are fixed on the opponent's hand; and in some schools on the face; in some on the feet, and so forth. When the eyes are fixed like this on a particular spot it can be disorienting. Then it becomes what is called a sickness in martial arts. By way of example, in the game of *kemari*, someone who kicks a ball may not keep his eyes on the ball, but he can perform skilled and difficult kicks, because being an accomplished player, he doesn't have to look closely. In the skills of jugglers also, intimate in the knowledge of their arts, they can balance a door on their nose and juggle swords, all this without fixing their gaze. Well versed in their craft, they see things naturally.

In martial arts as well, as one becomes familiar with each man he fights, learns the content of his mind, and becomes practiced in the Way of martial arts, one then can judge the speed and distance of a sword. For the most part, the gaze in martial arts is fixed on a person's heart and mind. As for matters of large-scale martial arts, the eyes are focused on the condition of the enemy troops. Of two ways of using the eyes, perceiving and seeing, perceiving is stronger. Perceiving the impulses of the enemy's heart and mind, observing the circumstances, getting a wide view, taking in the conditions for battle, perceiving the strengths and weaknesses of the moment, one can see clearly how to win.

In both large- and small-scale martial arts, the eyes are not lost on small details. As already mentioned, a narrow focus on detail misses the larger view, leading to confusion and letting a sure victory out of one's sight. Study this principle well, training and practicing diligently.

## 他流に足つかひ有る事
# Taryu ni ashitsukai

### FOOTWORK IN OTHER SCHOOLS

There are various methods of footwork, such as the floating step, the jumping step, the springing step, the treading step, the crow step, and other quick steps. From the point of view of my martial arts, all these seem unsatisfactory and without footing. The floating step I dislike because in the course of battle one's step necessarily tends toward unsteadiness, so it is important to tread as soundly and surely as possible. Also, the jumping step I dislike because in

*Samurai in complete armor. Felice Beato (1834–1907). Japan. 1860s. Photograph.*

jumping up one becomes absorbed in the jumping. Since there is no need to keep jumping, a jumping step is bad. Again, the springing step is unsatisfactory because in springing up one misses the next move. The treading step, a waiting stance, is especially disliked. In addition, there are the crow step and various other quick steps.

Sometimes one may engage the enemy on swampy or boggy ground, or in mountains and rivers, or on rocky fields, or on narrow roads; depending on the place, there are circumstances in which one cannot jump or step quickly. In my martial arts, the footwork does not change; it is the same as walking down a road as usual. Follow the opponent's timing, adapting one's body to the situation whether hurried or calm; one must control one's step, striding without laxity or excess.

In large-scale martial arts as well, footwork is critical. The reason being, if one attacks wildly without knowledge of the opponent's intent, one's timing will be off and winning difficult. Or, advancing too slowly, one does notice the opponent's disorientation; victory will be lost and making a quick favorable outcome will be impossible. It is important to claim victory by noticing when the opponent unravels and not let him relax at all. Train and practice assiduously.

# KUSARIGAMA
## THE DEADLY SICKLE AND CHAIN

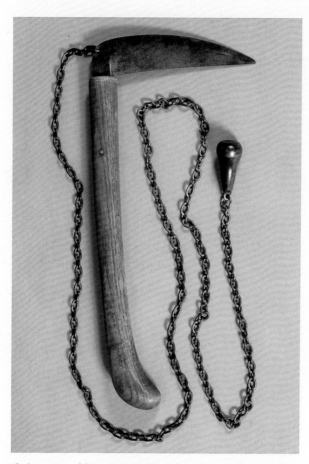

*The kusarigama of the araki school style consists of a chain attached to the back of a blade with a forged heavy iron plummet.*

The origin of the *kusarigama,* the traditional sickle-and-chain weapon, is unclear. However, farmers in ancient Japan used the *kama,* a tool similar to a scythe, as a grain-cutting implement when they harvested rice for food and grass for horses. It is thought to date back to the seventh century CE, when a weighted chain *(konpi)* was added to a blade, thus modifying it for use in warfare. But according to documentation, it had certainly been adopted as a weapon by several martial arts schools that flourished during the Edo period a millennium later.

Different schools have their own versions of kusarigama. Some attach the chain to the back of the blade, and others

attach the chain to the base of the handle. The chain and heavily weighted ball at the end are well-forged iron, while the blade is hand-forged and sharpened on one or both sides of the cutting edge. The physical features influence the use and techniques of the respective schools, since some blades curve and others are straight.

The method of its use, the *kusarigama-jutsu,* involves swinging the weighted chain in a large circle overhead and then releasing the chain in a whipping motion forward, an action that could entangle an opponent's sword or spear and could easily immobilize his arms or legs as well. Then the wielder could strike with the blade, held in the opposite hand, or with the heavily weighted end of the chain, causing injury or even death to the opponent while allowing himself to remain safely outside the range of his opponent's weapons.

*A right guard position with the kusarigama is shown here. Both the handle and chain are gripped in this position.*

Many historical accounts of battles featured kusarigama prominently. For example, the seventeenth-century kusarigama teacher Yamada Shinryukan had developed a reputation for killing excellent swordsmen because of his proficiency with this unusual weapon. When he was lured by the swordsman Araki Mataemon into a bamboo grove, where the chain could be of no use, Mataemon then used his sword to kill the master technician of the kusarigama. On another occasion, Miyamoto Musashi encountered the famous chain-wielder and skilled swordsman Sishido

Baiken. Musashi, himself perhaps the greatest swordsman of all time and thus too wily to be caught within the range of the kusarigama, threw a knife from a distance to injure Baiken and then moved in to perform the killing blow with his sword.

Thus an ordinary scythe passed from farm to military usage. Perhaps foot soldiers cleared paths with it and of necessity began to use it in close-quarter combat. But then again, perhaps the legend is true that Nen Ami Jion, having received a vision of a divinity holding the kama in one hand and a metal weight in the other, then created the unique kusarigama. However it came to be, this ancient weapon still lives in martial arts schools today.

*The weighted chain also can be used to strike an opponent or entangle a sword or other weapon while maintaining the ready position with the sickle.*

# 他の兵法に早きを用ゐる事
# Taryu ni hayaki o mochiiru

## SPEED IN OTHER SCHOOLS

In martial arts, speed is not the true Way. One's speed is a matter of how fast or slow one is in all things, depending on whether one's timing is on or off. Mastering a Way, one's performance never appears fast. Some people, for example, can run forty or fifty *li*; but this does not mean they run from morning to night. If one is not proficient in the Way, he may run all day but not make any progress. In the Way of dance, when a poor singer accompanies a skilled singer, the tempo will lag, making them rush. When the Noh piece "Old Pine" is played on the drums, it is a quiet song, but, again, an unskilled player will slow it down or speed it up. "Takasago" on the other hand, has a brisk tempo, but it is not to be performed too fast.

"He who hurries, stumbles," as the saying goes; and he will not be on time. Of course, being too slow is bad, too. A skilled person's performance appears relaxed but never misses a beat. He who is disciplined in all things never appears rushed. Principles of the Way can be known from these examples. In martial arts, speed is especially bad. The reason being, it is hard to move one's body and feet quickly in say a marsh or a bog, again depending on the place. Killing quickly with a long sword, all the more so, is impossible. If one tries to cut quickly, a fan or a short sword won't do; no cut at all will be possible. Consider this well. In large-scale martial arts as well, a hurried, rushed frame of mind is bad. Having a sense of Holding Down the Pillow, one cannot be even a little slow. Moreover, when someone rushes wildly about, it is important to do the opposite, and remain calm, not letting him pull one in. Work on this well, training and practicing diligently.

# 他流に奥表という事
# Taryu ni oku omote

## FORMAL AND SECRET TEACHINGS IN OTHER SCHOOLS

In matters of martial arts, is it possible to say what are formal teachings and what are secret teachings? In the arts there are sometimes entrance gates to enter into the realm of sub rosa principles by so-called secret transmission and ultimate realization, but in man-to-man combat there is no

*Father and Son Members of the Forty-Seven Ronin from Chushingura, the Treasury of Loyal Retainers: The People Involved in the Night Attack. Utagawa Kunisada (1786–1865). Japan. Circa 1845–1860. Color woodblock print.*

such thing as fighting with formal principles or killing with secret principles. In the teaching of the Way of my martial arts, beginners have to learn techniques that are easy to acquire, first teaching them principles that are easy to understand. For principles that are hard to understand, I assess the capability of each student, following up with the teaching of deeper principles gradually. Be that as it may, for the most part I foster an understanding of things through principles relating to actual combat with the enemy; there is no such thing as an entrance gate to enter the realm of sub rosa principles.

In the world as well, if one goes into the depths of the mountains, and decides to go yet deeper, one instead will emerge at the gate. For every path, there are secret teachings to be gained and formal teachings to be learned. For learning principles of martial arts, what should be concealed? And what should be revealed? Accordingly, in the transmission of my Way, I have distaste for written pledges or tallies of penalties. Observing student's intellectual aptitude, teaching them the straight path, eliminating the ill effects of the "five ways" or "six ways" of martial arts, so that they enter naturally into the true Way of the warrior, liberating their minds from doubt—this is the Way I teach martial arts. Train and practice this diligently.

*Flower Garland Sutra. Japan. 1240. Ink on paper.*

# Epilogue

In the above nine sections I have recorded the outlines of the martial arts of other schools, collected here in this Wind Scroll. Although it is important to describe in detail each school, from the entrance gate to the hidden teachings, I intentionally have not written the names of schools or their secrets. The reason being, the views of each school, the rationale of each path, are interpreted variously, according to the person, depending on his heart and mind. Even in the same school there are some small differences of opinion. For posterity's sake, I have not written the name of which school is described.

I have divided the gist of other schools into nine categories. From the viewpoint of what is right in the world, from the viewpoint of right-thinking people, a preference for the long sword or the short sword, partiality toward strength or weakness, coarseness or fineness, are all paths of prejudice. Even if I do not point out the entrance gate and secret teachings of other schools, everyone will recognize them. In my school, there is neither entrance gate nor secret teaching of the long sword; there is no hidden meaning in sword stances. There is only the understanding of its virtues in one's heart and mind. This is the essence of martial arts.

Twelfth day of the fifth month, the second year of Shōhō (1645)

Teruo Magonojo      Shinmen Musashi

*Pot depicting dragons and clouds. Issai. Japan. Late 19th or early 20th century. Unglazed earthenware.*

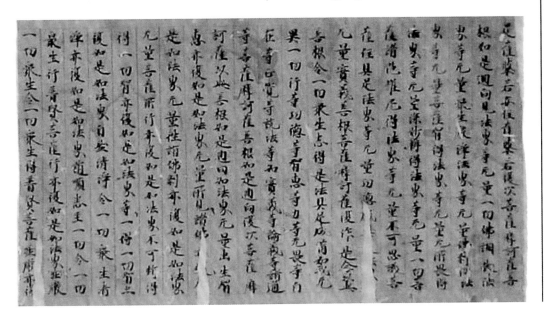

*Sake bottle. Japan. Late 19th century. Glazed ceramic with brown iron oxide underglaze and calligraphy.*

# Ku no maki

## The Scroll of the Void

*Japanese hieroglyph on textile material.*

The Way of martial arts of Nitō Ichi-ryū, the School of Two Swords, is recorded in the Scroll of the Void. The meaning of Void is the realm where nothing exists, or nothing can be known. It is emptiness. Void of course is nothingness. Knowing the nonexistent from knowing the existent—that is Void. Mistakenly looking at things, people of the world think things they don't understand are Void. This is not the real Void. This is all delusion.

In the Way of martial arts as well, in practicing the Way of the warrior, not knowing the code of warriors is not Void; being lost in various things, one may call having nowhere to turn Void, but this is not the true meaning of Void. Warriors learn the Way of martial arts with certainty and discipline themselves in other techniques of the arts. The Way that is practiced by warriors has not the least darkness. With an uncluttered heart and mind, ever vigilant day by day, hour by hour, polishing both the heart/mind (*shin*) and will (*i*), sharpening both the eye of perception (*kan*) and the eye of sight (*ken*), know that the true Void is where there is no cloudiness, and the sky is cleared of confusion.

Until one has realized the real Way, whether in Buddhist dharma or laws of the world, one may think only one's own path is sure and good, but from the viewpoint of the straight way of the mind, when taken together with precepts of the world, one has departed from the true Way, pulled by personal prejudices of the mind and different ways of seeing.

Know well this principle, and taking what is straight as the foundation, taking the real mind as the Way, spreading the practice of martial arts in the world, grasping it correctly, clearly, and fully, taking the Void as the Way, one will see the Way as the Void. In the Void there is good, but it is without evil. Wisdom exists. Reason exists. The Way exists. The mind is Void.

Twelfth day of the fifth month, the second year of Shōhō (1645)

Teruo Magonojo                    Shinmen Musashi

*Opposite page: Japanese Samurai, including Yoritomo, founder of the Bakafu Code. Dan Escott (1928–1987) Japan. 20th century.*

*Chinese calligraphy brushes in green ceramic container, such as might be used for producing elegant calligraphy on an important scroll.*

# THE MEIJI PERIOD
## THE END OF SHOGUNATE GOVERNMENT

*A clerk. Felice Beato (1834–1907). Japan. Circa 1868. Hand-tinted albumen print.*

On November 3, 1852, Nakayama Yoshiko, a mistress of Emperor Komei of Japan, gave birth to a son, Sachinomiya, who would grow to become one of the most pivotal leaders in Japanese history. By the time he was fifteen, Sachinomiya, who was then known as Emperor Mutsuhito but is now known as the Emperor Meiji, would put an end to the seven-century rule of samurai and shogun, dragging Japan into the modern era.

When Sachinomiya was born, Japan was a feudal agrarian nation, ruled by a military dictatorship. Society was arranged into a rigid caste structure, with the samurai on top, enjoying lavish lifestyles supported by the taxes of the lower classes. Sachinomiya's father, the emperor, was a mere figurehead. The true ruler was the shogun, Tokugawa Ieyoshi, scion of a family that had held autocratic power since 1600, and the center of power was the shogun's palace in Edo (now known as Tokyo), not the emperor's palace in Kyoto.

The erosion of the shogunate began on July 8, 1853, just eight months after Sachinomiya was born, when Commodore Matthew Perry sailed a squadron of U.S. warships into Uraga Harbor, just south of Edo. For more than 200 years, Japan had isolated itself from nearly all other nations through a policy called *sakoku*, "country in chains." The shoguns considered foreign thoughts to be dangerous. Only two nations, China and the Netherlands, were allowed to trade with Japan, and their merchants were restricted to the confines of Nagasaki. Ships that tried to land at other ports were fired upon or otherwise chased away under serious threat.

But when Perry showed up, his squadron was so well armed that the authorities allowed him to come ashore, where he demanded that Japan open itself to trade with the United States. Before he went back to his ship, he notified the authorities he would return in a few months with even more warships to get an answer. Shogun Ieyoshi was completely unnerved by Perry's demands, and within days of the visit, he became seriously ill. In less than three weeks, he was dead (whether by illness or poison is a matter of debate), and his son Tokugawa Iesada took over. But Iesada was a mentally unstable man who was easily cowed into signing disadvantageous treaties with the Americans as well as the English, Dutch, and Russians who came after them. The chains of sakoku had broken, and the power of the shoguns was weakening.

The opening of trade did three things. First, it exposed the Japanese people to the world that lay beyond their shores, making them aware of possibilities they had never contemplated before. Second, the ease with which a handful of foreigners made the shogun bend to their will showed

*A sake seller. Felice Beato (1834–1907). Japan. Circa 1868. Hand-tinted albumen print.*

*Japanese women dressing. Felice Beato (1834–1907). Circa 1870–1880. Japan. Hand-tinted albumen print.*

emperor. After the throne passed to Komei's fourteen-year-old son, Mutsuhito (formerly Sachinomiya), some of the leading members of his court, many of whom had long-standing grudges against the Tokugawa clan, felt it was time to quash the shogunate. And since Mutsuhito was still only an adolescent boy, these elders were able to convince him that they were acting in the country's best interests.

After bolstering public sentiment in favor of Emperor Mutsuhito, the counselors petitioned the current shogun, Tokugawa Yoshinobu, to give up his title, which he had inherited only a year before. In return, the counselors pledged, Yoshinobu would be named to head a new national governing council, composed of all the leading samurai. Yoshinobu, a thirty-year-old who had high hopes of modernizing the nation, agreed. On November 30, 1867, he stepped down from his post, and for the first time since 1192, there was no shogun in Japan.

But that was only the beginning of the revolution against samurai rule. Within two months of Yoshinobu's abdication as shogun, the imperial court withdrew its offer to have him head the governing council. Instead, he was stripped of all his titles and lands, provoking a short-lived civil war between his supporters and the imperial army, which crushed the rebels in 1869. A subsequent wave of assassinations and minor samurai rebellions did not come to an end until 1881. Since he had accepted the emperor's rule, Yoshinobu was under constant fear of assassination by former samurai who thought he had capitulated too quickly.

In the meantime, Emperor Mutsuhito stripped the samurai of their lands, prohibited them from collecting taxes for their personal use (the government paid them stipends instead), and barred them from carrying their long swords on the streets, which had been one of the most visible symbols of their status. Mutsuhito seized the shogun's castle in Edo and took it for his own residence, renaming the city Tokyo, "eastern capital," to distinguish it from Kyoto, "western capital."

Undoubtedly with the help or at the instigation of his counselors, Mutsuhito proclaimed that his reign would be known as the Meiji Jidai, or the Age of Enlightened Rule. His first historically significant act came in April 7, 1868, when he introduced the Five-Charter Oath, a general statement of "progressive" principles, which promised to:

how weak the shogunate truly was. Rivals of the Tokugawa clan began to dream of the day when the shogun would no longer exist. Finally, the treaties created a deep rift between Emperor Komei and the shogunate. Iesada had not only negotiated with the Americans without even consulting the emperor, but he had also gone so far as to sign his name as "the supreme ruler of Japan," which was technically the emperor's position.

Soon after the treaties were signed, Komei began to openly criticize the shoguns for giving the foreigners too much power. It had been centuries since an emperor had so openly challenged the shogunate, and the common people loved it. During the years between Perry's arrival and Komei's death in 1867, there was a perceptible shift of public opinion away from the shogun and toward the

- Establish deliberative assemblies throughout the country, so that all matters would be subject to public discussion.
- Involve all classes, high and low (not just samurai), in the conduct of state affairs.
- Revoke all class restrictions on employment, so that the common people as well as bureaucrats and military officials could pursue whatever calling they wanted. "If only one of the millions of people in this country is unable to find his place in society, it will be entirely our fault," the young emperor wrote in a public letter that was issued.
- Replace the "evil customs of the past" with the "just laws of nature." Although those phrases are vague, they are in direct contrast to the samurai mantra that the customs of the past were glorious. The "just laws" that dated back before samurai times stressed obedience to the divinely appointed emperor, who counted several gods among his ancestors.
- Conduct an international search for ways of strengthening the imperial rule.

The architects of the Five-Charter Oath were no democrats; they were clan leaders whose ideal government dated to the ancient days before the shoguns, when the emperors allowed an oligarchy of counselors to rule the land. Mutsuhito's counselors wanted to play a similar role in modern society. And despite the subsequent drafting of a constitution, the formation of a parliament, and the development of an institution of public redress, Japan remained largely under the control of a tight-knit oligarchy through the end of World War II.

On the other hand, the reforms that Mutsuhito instituted, whether they came from him or his counselors, did pull Japan out of its nearly medieval feudalism and into the industrial age. Under the last item on the Five-Charter Oath, Mutsuhito dispatched teams of academics and politicians to Europe and to the United States, to study foreign ways and bring back whatever seemed useful. Based on the findings of those academics, Japan modeled its education system and its criminal and civil code largely after the French and German models. Its army was patterned on the Prussian model, and its navy on the British model.

The Japanese economy was revolutionized as well, aided by the rapid growth of the *zaibatsu*, corporations that combined the old samurai-style clannishness with Western-style business techniques. For instance, the Mitsubishi Shipping Company was founded in 1870, Mitsui Bank was launched in 1876, and Sumitomo, which had been a pharmaceutical and mining firm for two centuries, expanded into banking, warehousing, and telecommunications in the late nineteenth century. All of those names continue to dominate the Japanese economy today.

By the early twentieth century, Japan was emerging as a world power, capable of besting the world's biggest empire, czarist Russia, in a war in the northern Pacific. By then, Emperor Mutsuhito had made amends with the last shogun, Tokugawa Yoshinobu, pulling him out of self-imposed internal exile to become a prominent figure of the new regime. The two men died within sixteen months of each other, the emperor in July 1912 and the shogun in November 1913, closing the final page of the age of the samurai.

*Door pull, used on door panels that served as dividers between rooms and as outside walls. Japan. 19th century. Metal.*

*Ceramic head rest. Japan. Late 19th or early 20th century. Glazed stoneware with brown iron oxide underglaze decoration.*

*Fishing tool for spearing eels. Hadegi-mura, Kumenan-cho, Okayama. Meiji period, early 20th century. Metal, fabric.*

*This vessel, called itto masu, holds a capacity of one to, or 4.8 gallons of grain. Japan. 19th century. Wood and iron.*

# Hagakure

## Yamamoto Tsunetomo

川東琳画

# CONTENTS

*Preceding pages: Night Attack on the Sanjo Palace, from Illustrated Scrolls of the Events of the Heiji Era. Japan. 13th century. Ink and color on paper. Opposite page: Hagiya Isaburo. Japan. Ink and color on paper.*

# YAMAMOTO TSUNETOMO

Born in 1659, Yamamoto Tsunetomo served as a samurai for thirty years under his lord, Nabeshima Mitsushige, in the Saga domain in Hizen province. Though he is legendary for his most famous text, *Hagakure*, little is known about the later years of his life, aside from the philosophies espoused in his vast and now influential writings.

In 1700, Tsunetomo's lord, Nabeshima, died, leaving him without a master. In Japanese tradition, it was common for samurai to follow the practice of *junshi,* commiting suicide to follow one's lord in death. Because Nabeshima looked down on the practice of junshi, Tsunetomo chose to retreat to the mountains, giving up his devotion to the clan and becoming a reclusive Buddhist monk. It was there in the secluded woods of the mountains that Tsunetomo, now known as Yamamoto Jocho, began his work on the record of his lord's teachings and doings. He titled this work *Hagakure*, which translates loosely to *In the Shadow of Leaves* or *Hidden Behind the Leaves*.

Tsunetomo narrated his beliefs about *bushido,* "the way of the samurai," to his fellow samurai and friend Tsuramoto Tashiro. He believed that understanding and accepting death allowed one to live a life that transcended the struggles of survival, thereby achieving a higher grace and purity. He also criticized many of the ways of the *ronin,* the lordless samurai, and proposed his own controversial beliefs about the bushido code.

Tsunetomo's philosophy revolved around living in the present moment. He believed that all action should be not only honorable but immediate. He disapproved of the premeditated, long-term campaign of vengeance staged by the forty-seven ronin, that took place during his lifetime and is now glorified in samurai history.

While he was living, Tsunetomo's *Hagukare* never gained a wide following, but by the first part of the twentieth century, it had become one of the most famous texts directly from the samurai era on the subject of bushido and the art of Japanese chivalry.

> *"There is surely nothing other than the single purpose of the present moment. A man's whole life is a succession of moment after moment. If one fully understands the present moment, there will be nothing else to do, and nothing else to pursue."*
> *—Hagakure*

*Opposite page: Moss garden at the Sanzen-in in Kyoto.*
*Above: Yamamoto Tsunetomo.*
*Right: Sodegarami (sleeve entangler). A polearm consisting of a wooden pole with iron hooks attached on the end and iron barbs attached part way down the pole. Used to control wrongdoers by catching onto their clothing. Circa 1700.*

# From the First Chapter 1

Although it stands to reason that a samurai should be mindful of the Way of the Samurai, it would seem that we are all negligent. Consequently, if someone were to ask, "What is the true meaning of the Way of the Samurai?" the person who would be able to answer promptly is rare. This is because it has not been established in one's mind beforehand. From this, one's unmindfulness of the Way can be known.

Negligence is an extreme thing. The Way of the Samurai is found in death. When it comes to either/or, there is only the quick choice of death. It is not particularly difficult. Be determined and advance. To say that dying without reaching one's aim is to die a dog's death is the frivolous way of sophisticates. When pressed with the choice of life or death, it is not necessary to gain one's aim.

We all want to live. And in large part we make our logic according to what we like. But not having attained our aim and continuing to live is cowardice. This is a thin dangerous line. To die without gaining one's aim is a dog's death and fanaticism. But there is no shame in this. This is the substance of the Way of the Samurai. If by setting one's heart right every morning and evening, one is able to live as though his body were already dead, he gains freedom in the Way. His whole life will be without blame, and he will succeed in his calling.

A man is a good retainer to the extent that he earnestly places importance in his master. This is the highest sort of retainer. If one is born into a prominent family that goes back for generations, it is sufficient to deeply consider the matter of obligation to one's ancestors, to lay down one's body and mind, and to earnestly esteem one's master. It is further good fortune if, more than this, one has wisdom and talent and can use them appropriately. But even a person who is good for nothing and exceedingly clumsy will be a reliable retainer if only he has the determination to think earnestly of his master. Having only wisdom and talent is the lowest tier of usefulness.

*Night Attack on the Sanjo Palace, from Illustrated Scrolls of the Events of the Heiji Era. Japan. 13th century. Ink and color on paper.*

According to their nature, there are both people who have quick intelligence, and those who must withdraw and take time to think things over. Looking into this thoroughly, if one thinks selflessly and adheres to the four vows of the Nabeshima samurai, surprising wisdom will occur regardless of the high or low points of one's nature.

People think that they can clear up profound matters if they consider them deeply, but they exercise perverse thoughts and come to no good because they do their reflecting with only self-interest at the center.

It is difficult for a fool's habits to change to selflessness. In confronting a matter, however, if at first you leave it alone, fix the four vows in your heart, exclude self-interest, and make an effort, you will not go far from your mark.

Because we do most things relying only on our own sagacity, we become self-interested and turn our backs on reason, and things do not turn out well. As seen by other people this is sordid, weak, narrow and inefficient. When one is not capable of true intelligence, it is good to consult with someone of good sense. An advisor will fulfill the Way when he makes a decision by selfless and frank intelligence because he is not personally involved. This way of doing things will certainly be seen by others as being strongly rooted. It is, for example, like a large tree with many roots. One man's intelligence is like a tree that has been simply stuck in the ground.

We learn about the sayings and deeds of the men of old in order to entrust ourselves to their wisdom and prevent

selfishness. When we throw off our own biases, follow the sayings of the ancients, and confer with other people, matters should go well and without mishap. Lord Katsushige borrowed from the wisdom of Lord Naoshige. This is mentioned in the *Ohanashikikigaki*. We should be grateful for his concern.

Moreover, there was a certain man who engaged a number of his younger brothers as retainers, and whenever he visited Edo or the Kamigata area, he would have them accompany him. As he consulted with them every day on both private and public matters, it is said that he was without mishap.

Sagara Kyuma was completely at one with his master and served him as though his own body were already dead. He was one man in a thousand.

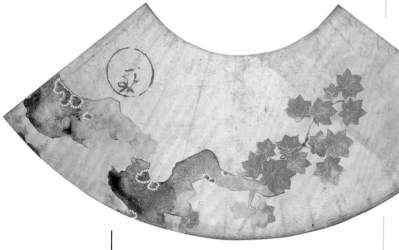

Once there was an important meeting at Master Sakyo's Mizugae Villa, and it was commanded that Kyuma was to commit *seppuku*. At that time in Osaki there was a teahouse on the third floor of the suburban residence of Master Taku Nut. Kyuma rented this, and gathering together all the good-for-nothings in Saga, he put on a puppet show, operating one of the puppets himself, carousing and drinking all day and night. Thus, overlooking Master Sakyo's villa, he carried on and caused a great disturbance. In instigating this disaster, he gallantly thought only of his master and was resolved to committing suicide.

Being a retainer is nothing other than being a supporter of one's lord, entrusting matters of good and evil to him, and renouncing self-interest. If there are but two or three men of this type, the fief will be secure.

If one looks at the world when affairs are going smoothly, there are many who go about putting in their appearance, being useful by their wisdom, discrimination, and artfulness. However, if the lord should retire or go into seclusion, there are many who will quickly turn their backs on him and ingratiate themselves to the man of the day. Such a thing is unpleasant even to think about. Men of high position, low position, deep wisdom, and artfulness all feel that they are the ones who are working righteously, but when it comes to the point of throwing away one's life for his lord, all get weak in the knees. This is rather disgraceful. The fact that a useless person often becomes a matchless warrior at such times is because he has already given up his life and has become one with his lord. At the time of Mitsushige's death there was an example of this. His one resolved attendant was I alone. The others followed in my wake. Always the pretentious, self-asserting notables turn their backs on the man just as his eyes are closing in death.

Loyalty is said to be important in the pledge between lord and retainer. Though it may seem unobtainable, it is right before your eyes. If you once set yourself to it, you will become a superb retainer at that very moment.

To give a person one's opinion and correct his faults is an important thing. It is compassionate and comes first in matters of service. But the way of doing this is extremely difficult. To discover the good and bad points of a person is an easy thing, and to give an opinion concerning them is easy, too. For the most part, people think that they are being kind by saying the things that others find distasteful or difficult to say. But if it is not received well, they think that there is nothing more to be done. This is completely worthless. It is the same as bringing shame to a person by slandering him. It is nothing more than getting it off one's chest.

To give a person an opinion one must first judge well whether that person is of the disposition to receive it or not. One must become close with him and make sure that he continually trusts one's word. Approaching subjects that are dear to him, seek the best way to speak and to be well understood. Judge the occasion, and determine whether it is better by letter or at the time of leave-taking. Praise his good points and use every device to encourage him, perhaps by talking about one's own faults without touching on his, but so that they will occur to him. Have him receive this in the way that a man would drink water when his throat is dry, and it will be an opinion that will correct faults.

*This is extremely difficult. If a person's fault is a habit of some years prior, by and large it won't be remedied. I have had this experience myself. To be intimate with all one's comrades, correcting each other's faults, and being of one mind to be of use to the master is the great compassion of a retainer. By bringing shame to a person, how could one expect to make him a better man?*

It is bad taste to yawn in front of people. When one unexpectedly has to yawn, if he rubs his forehead in an upward direction, the sensation will stop. If that does not work, he can lick his lips while keeping his mouth closed, or simply hide it with his hand or his sleeve in such a way that no one will know what he is doing. It is the same with sneezing. One will appear foolish. There are other things besides these about which a person should use care and training.

When a certain person was saying that present matters of economy should be detailed, someone replied that this is not good at all.

It is a fact that ash will not live where the water is too clear. But if there is duckweed or something, the fish will hide under its shadow and thrive. Thus, the lower classes will live in tranquillity if certain matters are a bit overlooked or left unheard. This fact should be understood with regard to people's conduct.

Once when Lord Mitsushige was a little boy and was supposed to recite from a copybook for the priest Kaion, he called the other children and acolytes and said, "Please come here and listen. It's difficult to read if there are hardly any people listening." The priest was impressed and said to the acolytes, "That's the spirit in which to do everything."

Every morning one should first do reverence to his master and parents and then to his patron deities and guardian Buddhas. If he will only make his master first in importance, his parents will rejoice, and the gods and Buddhas will give their assent. For a warrior there is nothing other than thinking of his master. If one creates this resolution within himself, he will always be mindful of the master's person and will not depart from him even for a moment.

Moreover, a woman should consider her husband first, just as he considers his master first. According to a certain person, a number of years ago Matsuguma Kyoan told this story:

In the practice of medicine there is a differentiation of treatment according to the *Yin* and *Yang* of men and women. There is also a difference in pulse. In the last fifty years, however, men's pulses have become the same as women's. Noticing this, in the treatment of eye disease I applied women's treatment to men and found it suitable. When I observed the application of men's

treatment to men, there was no result. Thus I knew that men's spirit had weakened and that they had become the same as women, and the end of the world had come. Since I witnessed this with certainty, I kept it a secret.

When looking at the men of today with this in mind, those who could be thought to have a woman's pulse are many indeed, and those who seem like real men few. Because of this, if one were to make a little effort, he would be able to take the upper hand quite easily. That there are few men who are able to cut well in beheadings is further proof that men's courage has waned. And when one comes to speak of *kaishaku*, it has become an age of men who are prudent and clever at making excuses. Forty or fifty years ago, when such things as *matanuki* were considered manly, a man wouldn't show an unscarred thigh to his fellows, so he would pierce it himself.

All of man's work is a bloody business. That fact, today, is considered foolish, affairs are finished cleverly with words alone, and jobs that require effort are avoided. I would like young men to have some understanding of this.

The priest Tannen used to say, "People come to no understanding because priests teach only the doctrine of 'No Mind.' What is called 'No Mind' is a mind that is pure and lacks complication. This is interesting."

*Sake flask. Japan. 19th century. Dried calabash gourd, metal, and fibers.*

*Frat bowl with chrysanthemum and water design. Japan. 19th century. Ceramic.*

*Toshoku bonbori (hand-held lantern). Japan. 19th century. Lacquered wood, paper, and iron.*

Lord Sanenori said, "In the midst of a single breath, where perversity cannot be held, is the Way." If so, then the Way is one. But there is no one who can understand this clarity at first. Purity is something that cannot be attained except by piling effort upon effort.

There is nothing that we should be quite so grateful for as the last line of the poem that goes, "When your own heart asks." It can probably be thought of in the same way as the *Nembutsu*, and previously it was on the lips of many people. Recently, people who are called "clever" adorn themselves with superficial wisdom and only deceive others. For this reason they are inferior to dull-witted folk. A dull-witted person is direct. If one looks deeply into his heart with the above phrase, there will be no hidden places. It is a good examiner. One should be of the mind that meeting this examiner he will not be embarrassed.

The word *gen* means "illusion" or "apparition." In India, a man who uses conjury is called a *genjutsushi* ["a master of illusion technique"]. Everything in this world is but a marionette show. Thus we use the word *gen*.

To hate injustice and stand on righteousness is a difficult thing. Furthermore, to think that being righteous is the best one can do and to do one's utmost to be righteous will, on the contrary, bring many mistakes. The Way is in a higher place than righteousness. This is very difficult to discover, but it is the highest wisdom. When seen from this standpoint, things like righteousness are rather shallow. If one does not understand this on his own, it cannot be known. There is a method of getting to this Way, however, even if one cannot discover it by himself. This is found in consultation with others. Even a person who has not attained this Way sees others from the side. It is like the saying from the game of go: "He who sees from the side has eight eyes." The saying "Thought by thought we see our own mistakes" also means that the highest Way is in discussion with others. Listening to the old stories and reading books are for the purpose of sloughing off one's own discrimination and attaching oneself to that of the ancients.

A certain swordsman in his declining years said the following:

*In one's life, there are levels in the pursuit of study. In the lowest level, a person studies but nothing comes of it, and he feels that both he and others are unskillful. At this point he is worthless. In the middle level he is still useless but is aware of his own insufficiencies and can also see the insufficiencies of others. In a higher level he has pride concerning his own ability, rejoices in praise from others, and laments the lack of ability in his fellows. This man has worth. In the highest level a man has the look of knowing nothing. These are the levels in general. But there is one transcending level, and this is the most excellent of all. This person is aware of the endlessness of entering deeply into a certain Way and never thinks of himself as having finished. He truly knows his own insufficiencies and never in his whole life thinks that he has succeeded. He has no thoughts of pride but with self-abasement knows the Way to the end. It is said that Master Yagyu once*

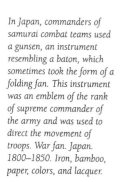

*In Japan, commanders of samurai combat teams used a gunsen, an instrument resembling a baton, which sometimes took the form of a folding fan. This instrument was an emblem of the rank of supreme commander of the army and was used to direct the movement of troops. War fan. Japan. 1800–1850. Iron, bamboo, paper, colors, and lacquer.*

remarked, *"I do not know the way to defeat others, but the way to defeat myself."*

Throughout your life advance daily, becoming more skillful than yesterday, more skillful than today. This is never-ending.

Among the maxims on Lord Naoshige's wall there was this one: "Matters of great concern should be treated lightly." Master Ittei commented, "Matters of small concern should be treated seriously." Among one's affairs there should not be more than two or three matters of what one could call great concern. If these are deliberated upon during ordinary times, they can be understood. Thinking about things previously and then handling them lightly when the time comes is what this is all about. To face an event anew and solve it lightly is difficult if you are not resolved beforehand, and there will always be uncertainty in hitting your mark. However, if the foundation is laid previously, you can think of the saying "Matters of great concern should be treated lightly" as your own basis for action.

A certain person spent several years of service in Osaka and then returned home. When he made his appearance at the local bureau, everyone was put out and he was made a laughingstock because he spoke in the Kamigata dialect. Seen in this light, when one spends a long time in Edo or the Kamigata area, he had better use his native dialect even more than usual.

When in a more sophisticated area it is natural that one's disposition be affected by different styles. But it is vulgar and foolish to look down upon the ways of one's own district as being boorish, or to be even a bit open to the persuasion of the other place's ways and to think about giving up one's own. That one's own district is unsophisticated and unpolished is a great treasure. Imitating another style is simply a sham.

A certain man said to the priest Shungaku, "The Lotus Sutra Sect's character is not good because it's so fearsome." Shungaku replied, "It is by reason of its fearsome character that it is the Lotus Sutra Sect. If its character were not so, it would be a different sect altogether." This is reasonable.

At the time when there was a council concerning the promotion of a certain man, the council members were at the point of deciding that promotion was useless because of the fact that the man had previously been involved in a drunken brawl. But someone said, "If we were to cast aside every man who had made a mistake once, useful men could probably not come by. A man who makes a mistake once will be considerably more prudent and useful because of his repentance. I feel that he should be promoted."

Someone else then asked, "Will you guarantee him?" The man replied, "Of course I will."

The others asked, "By what will you guarantee him?"

And he replied, "I can guarantee him by the fact that he is a man who has erred once. A man who has never once erred is dangerous." This said, the man was promoted.

At the time of a deliberation concerning criminals, Nakano Kazuma proposed making the punishment one degree lighter than what would be appropriate. This is a treasury of wisdom that only he was the possessor of. At that time, though there were several men in attendance, if it had not been for Kazuma alone, no one would have opened his mouth. For this reason he is called Master Commencement and Master Twenty-five Days. A certain person was brought to shame because he did not take revenge. The way of revenge lies in simply forcing one's way into a place and being cut down. There is no shame in this. By thinking that you must complete the job you will run out of time. By considering things like how many men the enemy has, time piles up; in the end you will give up. No matter if the enemy has thousands of men, there is fulfillment in simply standing them off and being determined to cut them all down, starting from one end. You will finish the greater part of it.

Concerning the night assault of Lord Asano's ronin, the fact that they did not commit seppuku at the Sengakuji was an error, for there was a long delay between the time their lord was struck down and the time when they struck down the enemy. If Lord Kira had died of illness within that period, it would have been extremely regrettable. Because the men of the Kamigata area have a very clever sort of wisdom, they do well at praiseworthy acts but cannot do things indiscriminately, as was done in the Nagasaki fight.

Although all things are not to be judged in this manner, I mention it in the investigation of the Way of the Samurai. When the time comes, there is no moment for reasoning. And if you have not done your inquiring beforehand, there is most often shame. Reading books and listening to people's talk are for the purpose of prior resolution.

Above all, the Way of the Samurai should be in being aware that you do not know what is going to happen next, and in querying every item day and night. Victory and defeat are matters of the temporary force of circumstances. The way of avoiding shame is different. It is simply in death. Even if it seems certain that you will lose, retaliate.

*Palanquin of the Date family with arabesque design. Japan. Mid-19th century. Maki-e lacquer.*

# THE ROLE OF THE SAMURAI
# DURING THE EDO PERIOD

*Hagakure* was written during Japan's Edo period, which lasted from 1603 to 1868. This peaceful period in Japan's history began when Tokugawa Ieyasu became shogun in 1603, following his success at the battle of Sekigahara a few years earlier. Edo (later Tokyo) became the center of Ieyasu's government, which he ruled until his death in 1616. During his thirteen-year reign, Ieyasu promoted foreign trade and redistributed lands among the *daimyo,* or feudal lords, favoring those who had shown their loyalty to him before the battle of Sekigahara. After his capture of Osaka castle in

1615, which marked the destruction of his last remaining rivals, the Toyotomi clan, the peace that followed allowed samurai warriors to pursue interests beyond the martial arts, but it also eroded the power, influence, and necessity of the warrior class.

The Japanese government, which established a supreme court in Edo, became increasingly more centralized, as power was removed from the daimyo and transferred to the shogun. The daimyo, who previously may not have come in contact with the shogunate except through individual

government. Relatedly, as the daimyo's financial resources diminished, samurai found it necessary to pursue other means of support through writing, teaching, politics, and agriculture.

The Edo period saw the systematic removal of the English, Spanish, Portuguese, and Dutch presence from Japan, which eventually closed itself off to foreign trade, banned foreign books, and prohibited citizens from leaving the country. These factors eliminated some of the educational opportunities samurai might have experienced through travel and thus contact with other cultures. However, during the isolation, Japan experienced an increase in the number of books that were printed and read, newspapers that were developed, plays and dances that were performed, and genre paintings that recorded the events of daily life.

The arrival of United States warships commanded by Commodore Matthew C. Perry eventually resulted in a treaty and a modification of Japan's isolationist view, which effectively prepared the country for the changes that would take place during the Meiji restoration.

*Opposite page: Summer, Iris At Yatsuhashi In Mikawa Province, from the series Flowers of the Four Seasons with Historical Associations. Ando Hiroshige (1797–1858). Japan. 19th century.*
*Left: Suit of armor. Japan. 1615–1868. Lacquered iron plates, leather, textile, and cord.*
*Below: The Last Stand of the Kusanoki Clan, the Battle of Shijo Nawate, 1348. Utagawa Kuniyoshi (1798–1861). Japan. Circa 1851. Woodblock print.*

allegiances or battles, were now forced to interact. Confiscation of lands owned by daimyo increased the property of the government, while the buying and selling of land became prohibited, and special permission had to be obtained to build, change, or remodel castles. In spite of the prevailing peace, peasants revolted from time to time against heavy taxation.

The daimyo was required to spend every other year in Edo, and his wife and oldest son were held hostage there to ensure his peaceful return from his rural home. With his increased presence in Edo, the daimyo required a city mansion as a second home, a necessity that was expensive enough not only to reduce the resources he could have used to plot against the shogun, but also lessened his ability to pay the samurai in his service. And large contingents of these armed warriors would have been essential for escorting the daimyo to and from Edo.

To protect their daimyo and prepare for the threat of future conflicts, the samurai would have maintained their skills in riding, archery, marksmanship, and fencing. But without a distinct military purpose that required constant attention, samurai became focused on education in the arts, including poetry, calligraphy, philosophy, architecture, and

*Below: The Brocade Bridge In Snow, from the series One Hundred Views of Famous Places in the Provinces. Hiroshige II (1826–1869). Japan. 19th century.*

Neither wisdom nor technique has a place in this. A real man does not think of victory or defeat. He plunges recklessly toward an irrational death. By doing this, you will awaken from your dreams.

There are two things that will blemish a retainer, and these are riches and honor. If one but remains in strained circumstances, he will not be marred.

Once there was a certain man who was very clever, but it was his character to always see the negative points of his jobs. In such a way, one will be useless. If one does not get it into his head from the very beginning that the world is full of unseemly situations, for the most part his demeanor will be poor and he will not be believed by others. And if one is not believed by others, no matter how good a person he may be, he will not have the essence of a good person. This can also be considered as a blemish.

There was a man who said, "Such and such a person has a violent disposition, but this is what I said right to his face...." This was an unbecoming

thing to say, and it was said simply because he wanted to be known as a rough fellow. It was rather low, and it can be seen that he was still rather immature. It is because a samurai has correct manners that he is admired. Speaking of other people in this way is no different from an exchange between low-class spearmen. It is vulgar.

It is not good to settle into a set of opinions. It is a mistake to put forth effort and obtain some understanding and then stop at that. At first putting forth great effort to be sure that you have grasped the basics, then practicing so that they may come to fruition is something that will never stop for your whole lifetime. Do not rely on following the degree of understanding that you have discovered, but simply think, "This is not enough."

One should search throughout his whole life how best to follow the Way. And he should study, setting his mind to work without putting things off. Within this is the Way.

These are from the recorded sayings of Yamamoto Jin'emon:

If you can understand one affair, you will understand eight.

An affected laugh shows lack of self-respect in a man and lewdness in a woman.

Whether speaking formally or informally, one should look his listener in the eye. A polite greeting is done at the beginning and finished. Speaking with downcast eyes is carelessness.

It is carelessness to go about with one's hands inside the slits in the sides of his *hakama*.

After reading books and the like, it is best to burn them or throw them away. It is said that reading books is the work of the Imperial Court, but the work of the House of Nakano is found in military valor, grasping the staff of oak.

A samurai with no group and no horse is not a samurai at all.

A *kusemono* is a man to rely upon.

It is said that one should rise at four in the morning, bathe and arrange his hair daily, eat when the sun comes up, and retire when it becomes dark.

A samurai will use a toothpick even though he has not eaten. Inside the skin of a dog, outside the hide of a tiger.

How should a person respond when he is asked, "As a human being, what is essential in terms of purpose and discipline?" First, let us say, "It is to become of the mind that is right now pure and lacking complications." People in general all seem to be dejected. When one has a pure and uncomplicated mind, his expression will be lively. When one is attending to matters, there is one

thing that comes forth from his heart. That is, in terms of one's lord, loyalty; in terms of one's parents, filial piety; in martial affairs, bravery; and apart from that, something that can be used by all the world.

This is very difficult to discover. Once discovered, it is again difficult to keep in constant effect. There is nothing outside the thought of the immediate moment.

Every morning, the samurai of fifty or sixty years ago would bathe, shave their foreheads, put lotion in their hair, cut their fingernails and toenails, rubbing them with pumice and then with wood sorrel, and without fail pay attention to their personal appearance. It goes without saying that their armor in general was kept free from rust, that it was dusted, shined, and arranged.

Although it seems that taking special care of one's appearance is similar to showiness, it is nothing akin to elegance. Even if you are aware that you may be struck down today and are firmly resolved to an inevitable death, if you are slain with an unseemly appearance, you will show your lack of previous resolve, will be despised by your enemy, and will appear unclean. For this reason it is said that both old and young should take care of their appearance.

Although you say that this is troublesome and time-consuming, a samurai's work is in such things. It is neither busy-work nor time-consuming. In constantly hardening one's resolution to die in battle, deliberately becoming as one already dead, and working at one's job and dealing with military affairs, there should be no shame. But when the time comes, a person will be shamed if he is not conscious of these things even in his dreams, and rather passes his days in self-interest and self-indulgence. And if he thinks that this is not shameful, and feels that nothing else matters as long as he is comfortable, then his dissipated and discourteous actions will be repeatedly regrettable.

The person without previous resolution to inevitable death makes certain that his death will be in bad form. But if one is resolved to death beforehand, in what way can he be despicable? One should be especially diligent in this concern.

Furthermore, during the last thirty years customs have changed; now when young samurai jeer together, if there is not just talk about money matters, loss and gain, secrets, clothing styles, or matters of sex, there is no reason to gather together at all. Customs are going to pieces. One can say that formerly when a man reached the age of twenty or thirty, he did not carry despicable things in his heart, and thus neither did such words

appear. If an elder unwittingly said something of that sort, he thought of it as a sort of injury. This new custom probably appears because people attach importance to being beautiful before society and to household finances. What things a person should be able to accomplish if he had no haughtiness concerning his place in society!

It is a wretched thing that the young men of today are so contriving and so proud of their material possessions. Men with contriving hearts are lacking in duty. Lacking in duty, they will have no self-respect. According to Master Ittei, even a poor penman will become substantial in the art of calligraphy if he studies by imitating a good model and puts forth effort. A retainer should be able to become substantial too, if he takes a good retainer as his model.

Today, however, there are no models of good retainers. In light of this, it would be good to make a model and to learn from that. To do this, one should look at many people and choose from each person his best point only. For example, one person for politeness, one for bravery, one for the proper way of speaking, one for correct conduct and one for steadiness of mind. Thus will the model be made.

An apprentice will not be up to his teacher's good points in the world of the arts either but will receive and imitate only his bad ones. This is worthless. There are people who are good at manners but have no uprightness. In imitating someone like this, one is likely to ignore the politeness and imitate only the lack of uprightness. If one perceives a person's good points, he will have a model teacher for anything.

When delivering something like an important letter or other written materials, grasp it firmly in your hand as you go and do not release it once, but hand it over directly to the recipient.

A retainer is a man who remains consistently undistracted twenty-four hours a day, whether he is in the presence of his master or in public. If one is careless during his rest period, the public will see him as being only careless.

Regardless of class, a person who does something beyond his social standing will at some point commit mean or cowardly acts. In the lower classes there are even people who will run away. One should be careful with menials and the like.

*Top left and right: Two musicians. Japan. Ivory. Above: Three masks. Japan. Ivory.*

# ART OF THE SAMURAI

The samurai influence on Japanese culture extends to artistic forms not related to warfare, particularly painting and theater. During the Edo period, idealist painting became a way to depart from various traditions and was embraced by members of the discontented samurai class. This *nanga,* or southern, school of painting was practiced by professional painters as well as by physicians, monks, scholars, and merchants. Angular brushwork and dramatic geographical features were characteristic of this style, as was the case in the majority of Japanese schools. A well-known example of nanga painting is *High Winds and Banking Geese* by samurai Uragami Gyokudo (1745 to 1820). Gyokudo served the Ikeda family until 1794, when he resigned because of his wife's death and began to practice nanga painting.

Another type of art, *ukiyo-e,* which uses woodblocks to create paintings and prints, became popular through depictions of *kabuki* actors. Kabuki, which means to "outstep the bounds of common sense," was founded by a woman called Izumo Okuni, who danced in a dry riverbed before an audience when she first arrived in Edo. The simple kabuki dance performances that she initiated evolved into more complex reenactments of the lives of noblemen and samurai, particularly famous battles.

The love stories, tragedies, and other dramas in the repertoire of kabuki theater were popular with townspeople, while the traditional, highly stylized *Noh* theater appealed to the upper social classes. In contrast to the subdued, religiously themed Noh plays, kabuki integrated music, dance, brilliantly colored costumes, extreme makeup, masks, lighting effects, changing scenery, props (such as real swords), dramatic incidents, and illusions via the use of trapdoors and other special effects. Actors often used a bridgelike aisle, the *hana michi,* to extend the stage into the audience. Although samurai were commonly portrayed in kabuki plays, as in the *Forty-Seven Ronin,* the social mores of the time would have initially prohibited the upper-class samurai from attending.

The lewd, bawdy humor of kabuki was a concern to the government, which placed restrictions on both the theater and its actors. For instance, early kabuki plays enlisted both male and female participants, but in 1629, the shogunate banned women from acting. As a result, *onnagata,* female impersonators, became increasingly important to the theater and increasingly popular with the masses. Though images of individuals of the samurai age are limited, portraits of famous actors playing samurai, their facial expressions accentuated with the bold lines of *kumadori* makeup, are an integral component of Japanese art, especially in examples of ukiyo-e.

Publishers of ukiyo-e commissioned artists and released their work in the form of playbills and posters. Another common form was the series, which might involve one actor or scenes from a play and would be released in installments for mass-market appeal.

One artist, Sharaku, who is thought to have been an actor of the Noh theater, famously painted kabuki actors in a twisted, grotesque manner. Sharaku's publisher dropped him after ten months, presumably because his depictions insulted the popular kabuki actors.

*Opposite page: From the series Famous Actors Past and Present. Utagawa Kunisada (1786–1865). Utagawa Yoshitora. Active 1850–1880. Japan. Circa 1860–1865.*
*Top: From the series Famous Actors Past and Present. Utagawa Kunisada (1786–1865). Utagawa Yoshitora. Active 1850–1880. Japan. Circa 1860–1865.*
*Left: Memorial Portrait of Ando Hiroshige. Utagawa Kunisada (1786–1865). Japan. 19th century. Woodblock print.*

# From the Second Chapter

It is said that much sake, self-pride, and luxury are to be avoided by a samurai. There is no cause for anxiety when you are unhappy, but when you become a little elated, these three things become dangerous. Look at the human condition. It is unseemly for a person to become prideful and extravagant when things are going well. Therefore, it is better to have some unhappiness while one is still young, for if a person does not experience some bitterness, his disposition will not settle down. A person who becomes fatigued when unhappy is useless. Meeting with people should be a matter of quickly grasping their temperament and reacting appropriately to this person and that. Especially with an extremely argumentative person, after yielding considerably, one should argue him down with superior logic, but without sounding harsh, and in a fashion that will allow no resentment to be left afterward. This is a function of both the heart and words. This was an opinion given by a priest concerning personal encounters.

Dreams are truthful manifestations. When I occasionally have dreams of dying in battle or committing *seppuku*, if I brace myself with courage, my frame of mind within the dream gradually changes.

This concerns the dream I had on the night of the twenty-seventh day of the fifth month.

If one were to say in a word what the condition of being a samurai is, its basis lies first in seriously devoting one's body and soul to his master. And if one is asked what to do beyond this, it would be to fit oneself inwardly with intelligence, humanity, and courage. The combining of these three virtues may seem unobtainable to the ordinary person, but it is easy. Intelligence is nothing more than discussing things with others. Limitless wisdom comes from this. Humanity is something done for the sake of others, simply comparing oneself with them and putting them in the fore. Courage is gritting one's teeth; it is simply doing that and pushing ahead, paying no attention to the circumstances. Anything that seems above these three is not necessary to be known.

As for outward aspects, there is personal appearance, one's way of speaking, and calligraphy. And as all of these are daily matters, they improve by constant practice. Basically, one should perceive their nature to be one of quiet strength. If one has accomplished all these things, then he should have knowledge of our area's history and customs. After that he may study the various arts as recreation. If you think it over, being a retainer is simple. And these days, if you observe people who are even a bit useful, you will see that they have accomplished these three outward aspects.

A certain priest said that if one thoughtlessly crosses a river of unknown depths and shallows, he will die in its currents without ever reaching the other side or finishing his business. This is the same as when one is indiscriminately eager in being a retainer without understanding the customs of the times or the likes and dislikes of the master and, as a result, is of no use and brings ruin upon himself. To try to enter the good graces of the master is unbecoming. One should consider first stepping back and getting some understanding of the depths and shallows and then work without doing anything the master dislikes.

If you attach a number of bags of cloves to your body, you will not be affected by inclemency or colds. Some years ago Nakano Kazuma returned to this province as a messenger by horse in the dead of winter, and though he was an old man, he was not the least bit in pain. It is said that that was because of his having used cloves. Furthermore, drinking a decoction of the feces from a dappled horse is the way to stop bleeding from an injury received by falling off a horse.

A faultless person is one who withdraws from affairs. This must be done with strength.

There is surely nothing other than the single purpose of the present moment. A man's whole life is a succession

*Samurai Chosyu of the clan, during the Boshin War period. Felice Beato. Japan. 1860s. Hand-colored albumen silver print.*

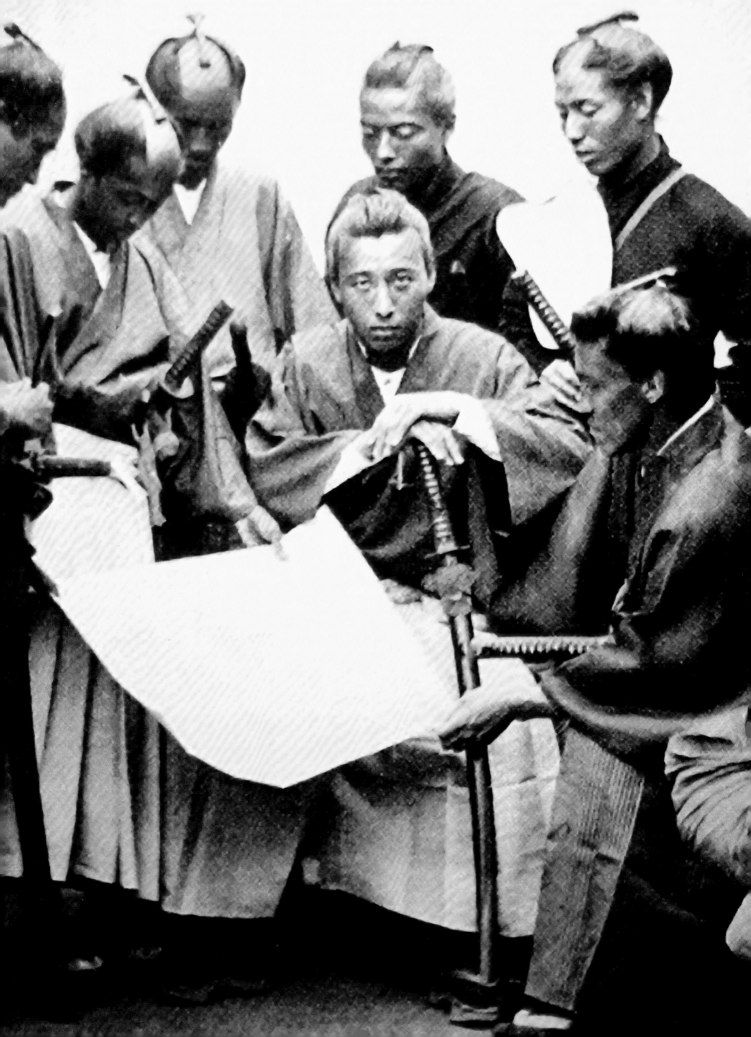

*Zenibako (money box). Japan. 18th or 19th century. Wood and cast iron.*

of moment after moment. If one fully understands the present moment, there will be nothing else to do, and nothing else to pursue. Live being true to the single purpose of the moment.

Everyone lets the present moment slip by, and then looks for it as though he thought it were somewhere else. No one seems to have noticed this fact. But grasping this firmly, one must pile experience upon experience. And once one has come to this understanding he will be a different person from that point on, though he may not always bear it in mind.

When one understands this settling into single-mindedness well, his affairs will thin out. Loyalty is also contained within this single-mindedness.

It is said that what is called "the spirit of an ape" is something to which one cannot return. That this spirit gradually dissipates is due to the world's coming to an end. In the same way, a single year does not have just spring or summer. A single day, too, is the same.

For this reason, although one would like to change today's world back to the spirit of one hundred years or more ago, it cannot be done. Thus it is important to make the best out of every generation. This is the mistake of people who are attached to past generations. They have no understanding of this point.

On the other hand, people who only know the disposition of the present day and dislike the ways of the past are too lax.

Be true to the thought of the moment and avoid distraction. Other than continuing to exert yourself, enter into nothing else, but go to the extent of living single thought by single thought.

The brave men of old times were for the most part rowdies. As they were of the disposition to be out running amuck,

*Right: Aizu. Katsushika Hokusai (1760–1849). Japan. 19th century. Ink on paper.*

their vitality was strong and they were brave. When I had doubts about this and asked, Tsunetomo said, "It is understandable that since their vitality was strong they were generally rough and went about running amuck. These days rowdiness is nonexistent because man's vitality has weakened. Vitality has fallen behind, but man's character has improved. Valor is yet a different thing. Although men have become gentle these days because of the lack of vitality, this does not mean that they are inferior in being crazy to die. That has nothing to do with vitality."

Concerning the military tactics of Lord Naoshige, Ushida Shoemon said that it was characteristic of his retainers to face a situation with no previous knowledge of what was to happen, and for him to freely bring everything to a finish by a single word. When he was at the point of passing from this world, he said nothing, even when his chief retainers came to see him.

Once Lord Ieyasu gained nothing in a battle, but in a later judgment it was said, "Ieyasu is a general of great courage. Of his retainers who died in battle, not one of them died with his back turned. They all died facing the enemy lines." Since a warrior's daily frame of mind is manifested even after death, it is something that can bring shame to him.

As Yasuda Ukyo said about offering up the last wine cup, only the end of things is important. One's whole life should be like this. When guests are leaving, the mood of being reluctant to say farewell is essential. If this mood is lacking, one will appear bored and the day and evening's conversation will disappear. In all dealings with people it is essential to have a fresh approach. One should constantly give the impression that he is doing something exceptional. It is said that this is possible with but a little understanding.

Our bodies are given life from the midst of nothingness. Existing where there is nothing is the meaning of the phrase "Form is emptiness." That all things are provided for by nothingness is the meaning of the phrase "Emptiness is form." One should not think that these are two separate things.

Uesugi Kenshin said, "I never knew about winning from beginning to end, but only about not being behind in a situation." This is interesting. A retainer will be dumbfounded if he is behind in a situation. In each and every instance one's function or responsiveness will not be shallow if he is not behind.

One should be wary of talking on end about such subjects as learning, morality, or folklore in front of elders or people of rank. It is disagreeable to listen to.

In the Kamigata area they have a sort of tiered lunch box they use for a single day when flower viewing. Upon returning, they throw them away, trampling them underfoot. As might be expected, this is one of my recollections of the capital [Kyoto]. The end is important in all things.

While walking along the road together, Tsunetomo said, "Is not man like a well-operated puppet? It is a piece of dexterous workmanship that he can run, jump, leap, and even talk, though there are no strings attached. Will we not be guests at next year's Ben Festival? This world is vanity indeed. People always forget this."

It was once said to one of the young lords that "right now" is "at that time," and "at that time" is "right now." One will miss the occasion if he thinks that these two are different. For example, if one were called before the master to explain something right away, he would most likely be perplexed. This is proof that he understands the two to be different. If, however, a person makes "right now" and "at that time" one, though he will never be an advisor to the master, still he is a retainer, and in order to be able to say something clearly, whether it be in front of the master, the elders or even the shogun at Edo Castle, it should be practiced beforehand in the corner of one's bedroom.

All things are like this. Accordingly, one should inquire into things carefully. It is the same for martial training as for official business. When one attempts to concentrate things in this manner, won't daily negligence and today's lack of resolve be understood?

Even though one has made some blunder in governmental work, it can probably be excused by pleading clumsiness or inexperience. But what kind of excuse may be given for the failure of the men who were involved in this recent unexpected event? Master Jin'emon always used to say, "It is enough if a warrior is simply a stalwart," and this is just such a case. If one felt that such a failure were a mortification, it would be the least he could do to cut open his stomach, rather than live on in shame with a burning in his breast and the feeling that he had no place to go, and, as his luck as a warrior had run out, he was no longer able to function quickly and had been given a bad name. But if one regretted losing his life and reasoned that he should live because such a death would be useless, then for the next five, ten, or twenty years of his life, he would be pointed at from behind and covered with shame. After his death his corpse would be smeared with disgrace, his guiltless descendants would receive his dishonor for having been born in his line, his ancestors' name would be dragged down, and all the members of his family would be blemished. Such circumstances are truly regrettable.

If one has no earnest daily intention, does not consider what it is to be a warrior even in his dreams, and lives through the day idly, he can be said to be worthy of punishment.

Presumably it can be said that a man who has been cut down was lacking in ability and had run out of luck as a warrior. The man who cut him down, compelled by unavoidable circumstances and feeling that there was nothing else to be done, also put his life on the line, and thus there should be no evidence of cowardice. Being short-tempered is inappropriate, but it cannot be said that two men who face each other are cowards. In this recent event, however, the men who lived and covered themselves with shame were not true warriors.

One should every day think over and make an effort to implant in his mind the saying, "At that time is right now." It is said that it is strange indeed that anyone is able to pass through life by one means or another in negligence. Thus, the Way of the Samurai is, morning after morning, the practice of death, considering whether it will be here or be there, imagining the most sightly way of dying, and putting one's mind firmly in death. Although this may be a most difficult thing, if one will do it, it can be done. There is nothing that one should suppose cannot be done.

Moreover, the influence of words is important in military affairs. It would have been

*Netsuke depicting a peasant resting with a heavy burden. Ryugyoku. Japan. Late 19th century. Wood with ivory inlays.*

*Aritaware serving platter with crane and tortoise motif in medallion form. Japan. 19th century. Porcelain with blue cobalt underglaze.*

*Netsuke depicting a sleeping shÿjÿ. Masakazu. Japan. Mid-19th century. Boxwood.*

best for stopping the man in this recent event, too. When the situation is too much, one may either cut the man down, or, if the man is escaping, yell something like, "Don't run! Only cowards run!" and thus, according to what the situation demands, achieve one's goals by the influence of words. There was a certain man who was said to be good at judging men's dispositions and formerly had everyone's attention, and he was able to handle such cases. This is proof that "right now" is no different from "when the time comes." The position of *yokoza no yari* is another example of this. It is something that should be made one's aim beforehand.

The things to be deeply considered beforehand are many. If there is someone who has killed a man in the lord's mansion and has managed to escape, as one does not know whether he may still be swinging his sword and advancing toward the room next to the lord's, he should cut the man down. Indeed, one may be blamed later in an investigation as a confederate of the killer, or as someone who had a grudge against him. But at that time one should think only of cutting the man down and not anticipate later blame.

Even if one's head were to be suddenly cut off, he should be able to do one more action with certainty. The last moments of Nitta Yoshisada are proof of this. Had his spirit been weak, he would have fallen the moment his head was severed.

Recently, there is the example of Ono Doken. These actions occurred because of simple determination. With martial valor, if one becomes like a revengeful ghost and shows great determination, though his head is cut off, he should not die.

Whether people are of high or low birth, rich or poor, old or young, enlightened or confused, they are all alike in that they will one day die. It is not that we don't know that we are going to die, but we grasp at straws. While knowing that we will die someday, we think that all the others will die before us and that we will be the last to go. Death seems a long way off.

Is this not shallow thinking? It is worthless and is only a joke within a dream. It will not do to think in such a way and be negligent. Insofar as death is always at one's door, one should make sufficient effort and act quickly.

It is good to carry some powdered rouge in one's sleeve. It may happen that when one is sobering up or waking from sleep, his complexion may be poor. At such a time it is good to take out and apply some powdered rouge.

There are times when a person gets carried away and talks on without thinking much. But this can be seen by observers when one's mind is flippant and lacking truth. After such an occasion it is best to come face to face with the truth and express it. The truth will then be arrived at in one's own heart too. Even when greeting someone lightly, one should consider the circumstances and after deliberation speak in a way that will not injure the man's feelings.

Furthermore, if there is a person who is criticizing the Way of the Samurai or one's own province, one should speak with him severely, without the least bit of ceremony. One must be resolved in advance.

Although a person who excels in an art regards others as competitors, last year Hyodo Sachu gave up the title of Master of Renga to Yamaguchi Shochin. A praiseworthy act.

The priest Tannen used to hang up wind-bells but said, "It's not because I like the sound. I hang them in order to know the wind conditions in the event of fire, for that is the only worry in having a large temple." When the wind blew, he himself walked about at night. Throughout his whole life the fire in his brazier was never out, and he always put a paper lantern and lighter by his pillow. He said, "People are flustered during an emergency, and there is no one to quickly strike a light."

If one makes a distinction between public places and one's sleeping quarters, or between being on the battlefield and on the tatami, when the

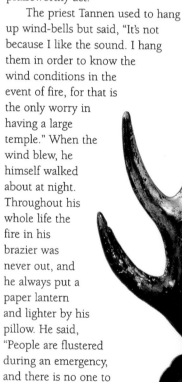

moment comes there will not be time for making amends. There is only the matter of constant awareness. If it were not for men who demonstrate valor on the tatami, one could not find them on the battlefield either.

Bravery and cowardice are not things that can be conjectured in times of peace. They are in different categories.

Though it may be said that the gods dislike impurity, if one thinks a bit, he will see that he has not been negligent in his daily worship. Thus, one's previous faithfulness has been exactly for the sake of praying for good fortune in such times as when one is barbed in blood and climbing over the dead. At such a time, if it is a god that turns back when one is defiled, then one should know clearly that praying is ineffective and should worship regardless of defilement.

In times of great trouble or disaster, one word will suffice. At times of happiness, too, one word will be enough. And when meeting or talking with others, one word will do. One should think well and then speak. This is clear and firm, and one should learn it with no doubts. It is a matter of putting forth one's whole effort and having the correct attitude previously. This is very difficult to explain but is something that everyone should work on in his heart. If a person has not learned this in his heart, it is not likely that he will understand it.

Human life is truly a short affair. It is better to live doing the things that you like. It is foolish to live within this dream of a world seeing unpleasantness and doing only things that you do not like.

But it is important never to tell this to young people as it is something that would be harmful if incorrectly understood.

Personally, I like to sleep. And I intend to appropriately confine myself more and more to my living quarters and pass my life away sleeping.

I had a dream on the night of the twenty-eighth day of the twelfth month in the third year of Shotoku. The content of the dream changed gradually to the extent that I strengthened my will. The condition of a person is revealed by his dreams. It would be good to make companions of your dreams and to put forth effort.

Shame and repentance are like upsetting a pot of water. When a certain friend of mine listened to the way that a man who had stolen his sword ornament confessed, he felt compassion. If one will rectify his mistakes, their traces will soon disappear.

According to what the Buddhist priest Kaion said, a person becomes more and more prideful if he gains a little understanding because he thinks he knows his own limits and weak points. However, it is a difficult thing to truly know one's own limits and weak points.

At a glance, every individual's own measure of dignity is manifested just as it is. There is dignity in personal appearance. There is dignity in a calm aspect. There is dignity in a paucity of words. There is dignity in flawlessness of manners. There is dignity in solemn behavior. And there is dignity in deep insight and a clear perspective.

These are all reflected on the surface. But in the end, their foundation is simplicity of thought and tautness of spirit.

Covetousness, anger and foolishness are things to sort out well. When bad things happen in the world, if you look at them comparatively, they are not unrelated to these three things. Looking comparatively at the good things, you will see that they are not excluded from wisdom, humanity, and bravery.

This is according to what Nakano Kazuma Toshiaki said. There are people who feel that using old utensils for the Tea Ceremony is coarse, and that it is better to use new, clean utensils. There are also people who are wont to use old materials because of their lack of gaudiness. Both are mistaken. Old utensils, although they are things that are used by the humble, are also used by the higher classes because of their value. Their value is revered.

A retainer is just like this. A person rises from the humble to the higher classes because he has value. At the same time, to feel that a person of no family cannot do the same work as one of

*Container (kaioke) for shell-matching game (Kai-Awase). Japan. 19th century. Lacquered wood.*

*Left: Sixty-two-ribbed Suji helmet. Japan. Mixed media.*

*Below: Pagoda and mountains near Mount Aso. Situated in the middle of Kyushu island, the area is nicknamed Hi n o Kuni, or "fire country," after the volcanoes responsible for its birth. Aso, although no longer active, is considered the largest volcano in the world, with a crater that measures more than 75 miles in circumference. Many other volcanoes in the area remain active, and the farmland in this part of Japan is some of its most fertile.*

higher family, or that a man who has heretofore been only a foot soldier should not be allowed to become a leader, is entirely wrong thinking. As for a person who has risen from the humble, his value should be prized and especially respected, even more than that of a person who was born into his class.

My father Jin'emon said that when he was young he was taken from time to time to the entrance of the Chinese settlement in order to be exposed to the atmosphere of the city and to become used to people. From the time he was five years old he was sent as family representative to various people's homes, and in order to make him strong he was made to put on a warrior's straw sandals and visit the temples of his ancestors from the time he was seven.

It is said that one will not be able to do great works if he does not behave with some reserve toward his master, the chief retainers, and elders. What is done casually and freely will not work out well. It is a matter of attitude.

It is unfitting that one be ignorant of the history and origins of his clan and its retainers. But there are times when extensive knowledge becomes a hindrance. One should use discretion. Knowing the circumstances can be an obstruction in everyday affairs, too. One should use discretion.

It is written that the priest Shungaku said, "In just refusing to retreat from something one gains the strength of two men." This is interesting. Something that is not done at that time and at that place will remain unfinished for a lifetime. At a time when it is difficult to complete matters with the strength of a single man, one will bring it to a conclusion with the strength of two. If one thinks about it later, he will be negligent all his life.

"Stamp quickly and pass through a wall of iron" is another interesting phrase. To quickly break in and stamp through directly is the first step of celerity. In connection with this, Hideyoshi can be thought of as the only man who has grasped solidly the chance of a lifetime since the creation of Japan.

People who talk on and on about matters of little importance probably have some complaint in the back of their mind. But in order to be ambiguous and to hide this they repeat what they are saying over and over. To hear something like this causes doubt to arise in one's breast.

One should be careful and not say things that are likely to cause trouble at the time. When some difficulty arises in this world, people get excited, and before one knows it the matter is on everyone's lips. This is useless. If worse comes to worse, you may become the subject of gossip, or at least you will have made enemies by saying something unnecessary and will have created ill will. It is said that at such a time it is better to stay at home and think of poetry. To talk about other people's affairs is a great mistake. To praise them, too, is unfitting. In any event, it is best to know your own ability well, to put forth effort in your endeavors, and to be discreet in speech.

The heart of a virtuous person has settled down, and he does not rush about at things. A person of little merit is not at peace but walks about making trouble and is in conflict with all.

It is a good viewpoint to see the world as a dream. When you have something like a nightmare, you will wake up and tell yourself that it was only a dream. It is said that the world we live in is not a bit different from this.

People with intelligence will use it to fashion things both true and false and will try to push through whatever they want with their clever reasoning. This is injury from intelligence. Nothing you do will have effect if you do not use truth.

In affairs like lawsuits or even in arguments, by losing quickly one will lose in fine fashion. It is like *sumo* [wrestling]. If one thinks only of winning, a sordid victory will be worse than a defeat. For the most part, it becomes a squalid defeat.

Feeling deeply the difference between oneself and others, bearing ill will and falling out with people—these things come from a heart that lacks compassion. If one wraps up everything with a heart of compassion, there will be no coming into conflict with people.

A person who knows but a little will put on an air of knowledge. This is a matter of inexperience. When someone knows something well, it will not be seen in his manner. This person is genteel.

When going someplace for a talk or something similar, it is best to let the person know ahead of time, and then go. To go without knowing whether the other party is busy, or when he has some particular anxiety, is awkward. There is nothing that surpasses not going where you have not been invited. Good friends are rare. Even if someone is invited somewhere, he should use understanding. It is difficult to feel deeply the sensitivities of people other than those who go out only rarely. Fiascos at pleasure gatherings are numerous.

However, you should not be brusque toward a person who has come to visit, even if you are busy.

It is bad to carry even a good thing too far. Even concerning things such as Buddhism, Buddhist sermons, and moral lessons, talking too much will bring harm.

The late Jin'emon said that it is better not to bring up daughters. They are a blemish to the family name and a shame to the parents. The eldest daughter is special, but it is better to disregard the others.

The priest Keiho related that Lord Aki once said that martial valor is a matter of becoming a fanatic. I thought that this was surprisingly in accord with my own resolve and thereafter became more and more extreme in my fanaticism.

The late Nakano Kazuma said that the original purpose of the Tea Ceremony is to cleanse the six senses. For the eyes there are the hanging scroll and flower arrangement. For the nose there is the incense. For the ears there is the sound of the hot water. For the mouth there is the taste of the tea. And for the hands and feet there is the correctness of term. When the five senses have thus been cleansed, the mind will of itself be purified. The Tea Ceremony will cleanse the mind when the mind is clogged up. I do not depart from the heart of the Tea Ceremony for twenty-four hours a day, yet this is absolutely not a matter of tasteful living. Moreover, the tea utensils are something that should be in accord with one's social position.

In the poem, "Under the deep snows in the last village / Last night numerous branches of plum blossomed," the opulence of the phrase "numerous branches" was changed to "a single branch." It is said that this "single branch" contains true tranquillity.

*Jomon figurine. Japan. Earthenware.*

*Decorative beam-end in the form of a kirin. Japan. 19th century. Wood.*

# SUPERIOR SAMURAI

Long before there were shogunates in Japan, there were warring clans, and from these would arise the mighty warriors known as samurai. The samurai were first assembled by Emperor Jemmu in the ninth century CE, when they were hardly more than barbarian fighters. But by the twelfth century, they had become an educated and cultured class and had begun to lay the groundwork for what would later be known as their *bushido* code. By the sixteenth century, they had become all-powerful in the Japanese military aristocracy, second only to their masters. Some of the most famous samurai are from the Sengoku period forward, leading up through the end of the Edo period, when the Meiji restoration banned the existence of the celebrated breed of warrior. Below are listed some of the most celebrated samurai warriors.

## Toyotomi Hideyoshi

Though he is sometimes referred to as "the unifier of Japan," many believe that Toyotomi Hideyoshi shares that distinction with two other samurai commanders, Tokugawa Ieyasu and Oda Nobunaga. In the somewhat common turncoat way of war, all three of these leaders would become less than friends over the course of time. Hideyoshi's story is one of a peasant boy rising to become one of the most successful and influential leaders of the Sengoku period. He entered battle at an early age, having been hired on by Oda Nobunga when both were still young, and he secured a victory for his leader at Inabayama in 1573. Hideyoshi, along with Ieyasu and Nobunga, was instrumental in the defeat of the Takeda clan, which would eventually result in the elevation of the Tokugawa as masters of Japan. In his elder, sickly years, having completed construction of Osaka castle, Hideyoshi launched two campaigns against Korea in pursuit of the goal of his late master, Nobunaga, to conquer western lands. However, Hideyoshi didn't anticipate the strength of the Korean forces, and when he died in 1598, the campaigns were abandoned.

## Tokugawa Ieyasu

Another battle-seasoned leader, Tokugawa Ieyasu, rose from relative obscurity to become one of the top field generals of the Sengoku wars and the first shogun of the powerful Tokugawa clan. He, along with Oda Nobunaga and Toyotomi Hideyoshi, is also one of the "three unifiers of Japan." Ieyasu's forces, often as strong as 30,000 warriors, fought alongside but independent of Nobunaga's forces against Takeda armies. His greatest victory occurred at Sekigahara in the year 1600, when he and other forces brought the once-dominant Takeda clan to its knees, making Ieyasu and his Tokugawa clan the strongest in Japan. In 1603, he was named shogun by the emperor. His final major battle came in 1615, when he defeated Hideyori, the heir to Toyotomi Hideyoshi, at Osaka castle. When he forced Hideyori to commit suicide and then killed his enemy's infant son, he essentially destroyed the Toyotomi and procured full control of Japan for his clan.

## Oda Nobunaga

Along with Ieyasu and Hideyoshi, Oda Nobunaga represents one of the so-called unifiers of Japan. Nobunaga, a legendary samurai of the Sengoku period, was a fearless leader and is credited with bringing an end to the long, powerful Takeda regime. During his reign as shogun, though, he made the mistake of bringing a talented general (with a long-standing grudge), Akechi Mitsuhide, into his close circles, a decision that would lead to his death. In June 1582, fresh from his conquest of the Takeda, he made his way to Edo (later Tokyo) with a small force to assist Hideyoshi in capturing Takamatsu castle. But his former confidante Mitsushide lay in wait for him at Hanno temple in Kyoto, where Nobunaga died, probably when forced to commit *sepukku*.

*Above: Helmet with side flaps bearing gilded family crest, and half-mask with lacquered iron face plate and throat guard. Suit of armor. Japan. 1615–1868. Lacquered iron plates, leather, textile, and cord.*

## Yagyu Munenori

One of the most famous Japanese samurai of all time, Yagyu Munenori is known for both his highly skilled swordsmanship and his time-honored writings. Munenori was born into a pedigree of martial arts greatness; his father was a master in his own time and taught his son the art of sword training known as *shinkage ryu*. The gifted samurai rose to greatness during the height of the Edo period as top swordsman for the Tokugawa shogunate in the early seventeenth century. Munenori achieved official sword master status at the age of fifty-two and would serve under the reign of three different Tokugawa shoguns, also becoming inspector general over all warlords and samurai warriors during that regime. Munenori's life work, captured in *The Sword and the Mind*, is hailed as one of the most definitive books on swordsmanship and military strategy ever written.

## Miyamoto Musashi

Perhaps the fiercest and most dominating Japanese warrior in the history of the samurai, and a well-respected painter, Miyamoto Musashi produced the classic writings that would become *The Book of Five Rings (Go rin no shohoo)*, one of the most highly regarded books on combat and strategy in history. Written in Musashi's later years, the book captures the insight and knowledge that Musashi gained through many years of combat. The details of his early life are contradictory. It is thought that he was born

*Above: Gusoku similiar to what daimyo Oda Nobunaga wore. He played a key role in initiating the policy of uniting the feuding clans under one shogun and was the most powerful daimyo of his time.*
*Right: Close-up of Nobunaga helmet and mask.*

around 1584 in Harima province during Japan's Warring States period, and that his father was an expert swordsman, but that he was actually raised by his uncle, a Buddhist priest. Skilled in many areas of martial arts, Musashi killed his first samurai at the age of thirteen, wielding a six-foot-long wooden pole to beat to death his better-armed opponent. Musashi spent much of his early life traveling about Japan as a *ronin* warrior, seeking out other samurai for combat, fighting sixty duels without suffering a defeat, and often using unorthodox weapons such as wooden swords, poles, and even two swords at once to bring down his adversaries.

## Tomoe Gozen

Female samurai are rare in the history of Japan, and Tomoe Gozen tops the list as the most famous. Reported to be very beautiful in appearance, she was an accomplished swordswoman, archer, and rider. Tomoe fought during the time of the Heike Wars (1180 to 1185) and was either the wife or mistress of a famous general, Kiso Yoshinaka. Her best-known, though perhaps apocryphal, encounter was at the battle of Awazu, where she was last seen riding off with the head of a samurai held high in her hand. Yoshinaka's forces were defeated in that battle, and according to one legend, Tomoe retired shortly afterward, having become a nun in a Buddhist convent.

## Uesugi Kenshin

Perhaps the most notorious rivalry of the samurai era, certainly during the Sengoku period, was that between Uesugi Kenshin, "the dragon of Echigo," and Takeda Shingen, "the tiger of Kai." Kenshin was celebrated as a superb battlefield commander and is most noted for taking on Shingen's rival forces in the well-known battles of

*Above: Armor similar to that of Takeda Shingen, one of the greatest samurai commanders.*
*Above right: Kabuto (helmet). Kashu Ju Munetaka. Unkai School. Japan. Circa 1700.*

Kawanakajima. Their fourth and largest battle was in 1561, an encounter that divides many scholars over who was victorious. Kenshin did outlive Shingen, though he is said to have cried upon hearing of the death of his old rival. Kenshin is one of the few commanders to outperform Oda Nobunaga in battle, a feat that occurred in 1577 when he successfully repelled Nobunaga's forces at Tedorigawa. He would die before ever having a chance to meet the renowned commander in battle again.

## Takeda Shingen

Noted samurai Takeda Shingen was the eldest son of Takeda Nobutora, the exceedingly aggressive warlord who established the powerful Takeda shogunate during the Sengoku period. Shingen was largely responsible for defending and expanding the realm, reaching the pinnacle of his power in the 1570s. One of his most bitter rivals was Uesugi Kenshin, warlord of the Echigo province, and the two are believed to have engaged in a spectacular one-to-one fight in which Kenshin attacked with his sword and Shingen parried with his iron war fan. As strong as his clan was,

however, Shingen was not able to defeat two of the most powerful samarai of the era, Oda Nobunaga and Tokugawa Ieyasu, and because of his significant losses to those forces, the Takeda never recovered. Shingen's death, purportedly, came at the hands of a sniper while he was laying siege to Noda castle in Mikawa in 1573. Several decades later, when Ieyasu had brought Japan under Tokugawa control, the new shogun, in a tribute to his former adversary, adopted the governmental and military tactics that Shingen had employed so successfully in an earlier time.

## Hojo Soun

Also known as Ise Shinkuro, Hojo Soun was a samurai commander during the early part of the Sengoku period. Some consider him to be the first great military leader of the period, and he is also believed to have been highly skilled as an administrator and problem solver. He is best known for conquering lands for his adopted clan, the Hojo, including the taking of the shogun capital of Kamakura in 1512 and then Arai castle several years later. The addition of Hojo to his name was done to cement his relationship to the clan that he had helped come to power. Unlike many samurai, Hojo Soun lived a long life, dying at the age of eighty-eight.

*Left: Close-up of Shingen helmet and mask.*
*Above: Kabuto (helmet). Circa 1600.*

# From the Third Chapter

Lord Naoshige once said, "There is nothing felt quite so deeply as *giri*. There are times when someone like a cousin dies and it is not a matter of shedding tears. But we may hear of someone who lived fifty or a hundred years ago, of whom we know nothing and who has no family ties with us whatsoever, and yet from a sense of *giri* shed tears."

When Lord Naoshige was passing by a place called Chiriku, someone said to him, "In this place there lives a man who is over ninety years old. Since this man is so fortunate, why don't you stop and see him?" Naoshige heard this and said, "How could anyone be more pitiful than this man? How many of his children and grandchildren do you suppose he has seen fall before his very eyes? Where is the good fortune in that?"

It seems that he did not stop to see the man.

When Lord Naoshige was speaking to his grandson, Lord Motoshige, he said, "No matter whether one be of high or low rank, a family line is something that will decline when its time has come. If one tries to keep it from going to ruin at that time, it will have an unsightly finish. If one thinks that the time has come, it is best to let it go down with good grace. Doing so, he may even cause it to be maintained."

It is said that Motoshige's younger brother heard this from him.

*Left: Mirror, Tumuli period. Japan. 5th century. Bronze.*

*Opposite page: Samurai with raised sword. Felice Beato (1825–1908). Japan. Circa 1860. Albumen print.*

# JAPANESE CALLIGRAPHY
## A FINE ART

The classical written Chinese that was introduced to Japan during the fourth century was the first vehicle for written communication in Japan. The educated classes exclusively used *kanji*, the Chinese characters, until adaptations were made and *kanbun*, a hybrid of Chinese-Japanese characters and language, was developed.

*Shodo* calligraphy, which women at court used as a pastime and as a vehicle for recording poetry, was introduced to Japan from China during the Heian period, between 784 and 1185 CE. This era produced the world's first novel, *The Tale of Genji*. In this work, written by Lady Murasaki Shikibu, life in the Heian court is reflected through the life of Prince Genji. The next style of calligraphy, *wayou*, the first uniquely Japanese version, was developed by Ono no Toufuu, Fijiwara

no Sukemasa, and Fujiwara no Yukinari, who are known as the *Sanseki*, or the Three Traces.

*Hiragana* and *katakana*, two phonetic Japanese syllabaries, distinguish Japanese calligraphy from Chinese calligraphy. While hiragana is used to indicate the tense and gender of a kanji word, katakana is more specifically used for words borrowed from other languages.

As calligraphy became an increasingly integral part of Japanese culture, the personal *suzuribako*, the writing box, was an important identifier of the status of its owner. Writing boxes that have been preserved from the Edo period and before reflect a variety of craftsmanship levels and are considered to be works of art. They were made of tin or wood and were typically lacquered, and the materials used to adorn

the boxes included shell, silver, lead, copper, and mother-of-pearl. Along with the outside of the box, the inside of the lid and the trays for the tools were also often decorated. Intricate designs included poetry, religious symbols, and landscapes. The writing box would have contained an inkstone, an ink stick, a water dropper, two types of brushes, and a paperweight often figured as an accoutrement. Before beginning to write, the calligrapher would slowly grind the *sumi*, the solid block of soot or charcoal mixed with glue, onto a *suzuri* (inkstone) and mix it with water from the *suiteki* (dropper), which was often a decorative item itself and was usually made of copper. With a brush, the ink was applied to the distinctive *washi*, paper made for this purpose from the kozo, mitsumata, and gampi trees.

Calligraphy was considered one of the fine arts and was often employed to display poetry as part of a painting, as well as for governmental documents and everyday communications. The various types of calligraphy were named to explain their primary purpose:

*Sousho:* Cursive script with a preponderance of near-vertical lines ("grass writing"), which is considered aesthetically pleasing but is perhaps the hardest to read.
*Tensho:* The name seal, usually red, that is recognized as an official substitute for a signature.
*Reisho:* The clerical script of official documents.
*Kaisho:* Square script found in everyday writing and in magazines and newspapers, which is easily read because of its bold strokes.
*Gyousho:* Running or semicursive script, a simpler, softer version of kaisho used in an informal, abbreviated manner.

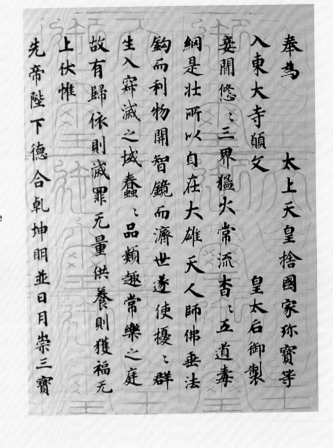

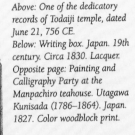

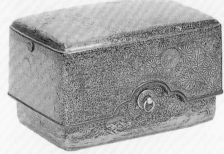

*Above: One of the dedicatory records of Todaiji temple, dated June 21, 756 CE.*
*Below: Writing box. Japan. 19th century. Circa 1830. Lacquer.*
*Opposite page: Painting and Calligraphy Party at the Manpachiro teahouse. Utagawa Kunisada (1786–1864). Japan. 1827. Color woodblock print.*

# From the Fourth Chapter

When Nabeshima Tadanao was fifteen years old, a manservant in the kitchen committed some rude act and a foot soldier was about to beat him, but in the end the servant cut the soldier down. The clan elders deemed the death sentence appropriate, saying that the man had in the first place erred in matters concerning the ranks of men, and that he had also shed the blood of his opponent. Tadanao heard this and said, "Which is worse, to err in matters concerning the ranks of men or to stray from the Way of the Samurai?"

The elders were unable to answer. Then Tadanao said, "I have read that when the crime itself is unclear, the punishment should be light. Put him in confinement for a while." Once, when Lord Katsushige was hunting at Shiroishi, he shot a large boar. Everyone came running up to see it and said, "Well, well. You have brought down an uncommonly large one!" Suddenly the boar got up and dashed into their midst. All of them fled in confusion, but Nabeshima Matabet drew his sword and finished it off. At that point Lord Katsushige covered his face with his sleeve and said, "It sure is dusty." This was presumably because he did not want to see the spectacle of his flustered men.

When Lord Katsushige was young, he was instructed by his father, Lord Naoshige, "For practice in cutting, execute some men who have been condemned to death."

Thus, in the place that is now within the western gate, ten men were lined up, and Katsushige continued to decapitate one after another until he had executed nine of them. When he came to the tenth, he saw that the man was young and healthy and said, "I'm tired of cutting now. I'll spare this man's life." And the man's life was saved.

Lord Katsushige always used to say that there are four kinds of retainers. They are the "quick, then lagging," the "lagging, then quick," the "continually quick," and the "continually lagging."

The "continually quick" are men who when given orders will undertake their execution quickly and settle the matter well. Fukuchi Kichizaemon and the like resemble this type.

The "lagging, then quick" are men who, though lacking in understanding when given orders, prepare quickly and bring the matter to a conclusion. I suppose that Nakano Kazuma and men similar are like this.

The "quick, then lagging" are men who when given orders seem to be going to settle things but in their preparation take time and procrastinate. There are many people like this.

Other than these, one could say that the rest are "continually lagging."

御寶筋

願主

泉屋帝兵衛

元和六庚申歳生吉日

Left: A Japanese man converted to Christianity. Japan. 17th century. Oil on panel.
Opposite page: Scenes of Urban Life under the Bakufu. Tosa School. Japan. 1800. Color woodblock print.

505

# From the Fifth Chapter

*Hagakure*, as it has traveled through the centuries, is understandably a bit worn. The original document no longer exists. The fifth chapter has disappeared and now belongs to the ages.

*Iron sukashi tsuba, maple leaf design. Japan. 19th century.*

# ZEN BUDDHISM, CONFUCIANISM, AND BUSHIDO CODE IN HAGAKURE

Peppering the pages of Tsunetomo's reflective writings are references to a certain Master Ittei and to an individual known as Tannen. From his writings, it's clear that these two figures, the former a leading scholar of Confucianism and the latter a noted Zen Buddhist priest, held positions of influence on the author of the *Hagakure,* though to what extent isn't known for certain. However, it might be safe to speculate that the teachings of these two religious fathers were uppermost in Yamamoto Tsunetomo's mind when he left the patronage of his feudal lord to become a Buddhist priest and to live in relative seclusion for the next twenty years. The dissimilar, though probably not completely divergent, viewpoints of these two religious worthies might be thought to symbolize the conflicted mind of an aging samurai who was out of sync with his times.

Much has been made of the biographical details of Tsunetomo's case: his entry into the service of Nabeshima Mitsushige in 1668 at the age of nine; his faultless devotion to his lord, but his personal disappointment in having no war, not even one battle, to wage in the recently won era of peace; his contempt for what he saw as the softness of the new breed of samurai, whose swords were now mostly ceremonial; his recognition that the samurai class had entered a phase of both political and spiritual decline; and his utter frustration in being prohibited, by way of a new law and the express wish of Mitsushige, from committing the ritual suicide that had formerly been expected of a samurai upon the death of his lord. Perhaps there's little wonder, then, that Tsunetomo, having been brought up as a samurai but thwarted at every turn, retreated to a nearby monastery. However, when approached by a young samurai scribe, the elderly warrior priest was convinced to provide an oral history of his times, and in doing so, he was able, at least in part, to reconcile the bushido code of his younger, secular life with the tenets of Zen Buddhism and Confucianism, to produce what would become *Hagakure,* the often-quoted "bible" from the mind of perhaps "the last true samurai." Though Tsunetomo does give a memorably vivid sense of the glory days of the samurai, his work doesn't project a deep or cohesive philosophy. But within his disconnected recollections of stories from generations past are, nonetheless, the elegantly terse directives that were to stand as authoritative for more future generations than he probably could have ever imagined.

Tsunetomo arrived at his guidelines from a three-part perspective. He assimilated certain aspects of Confucianism, particularly its emphasis on reverence toward the elderly and benevolence toward the young, morality, loyalty, and the filial piety that extended to all personal relationships, all of which practiced together would lead to humaneness and social harmony. Building from that, he broadened the Confucian idea of ritual, a term implying politeness and correct etiquette, to encompass the Zen Buddhist concept of mindfulness of the smallest details of everyday life as a way of gaining insight and wisdom. He maintained strict samurai precept, that living is simply a matter of being prepared to die at any moment, the prospect of which was made more palatable and attainable by the recommended steps toward purity of heart, mind, and action.

*Above and below left: Two-sided inro, decorated with the figures of the Buddha, Confucius, and Lao Tzu. Serizawa Ryumin and Kajikawa Hogetsu. Japan. 19th century. Gold lacquer..*
*Opposite page, left: Departure from Kashima. Japan. 14th century. Ink and color on silk.*
*Opposite page, right: Bodhisattva Samantabhadra, one of a set of three. Japan. 1333–1573. Ink and color on silk.*

To these ends, he urged the morning recitation of four vows:

*Never to be outdone in the Way of the Samurai.*
*To be of good use to the master.*
*To be filial to my parents.*
*To manifest great compassion, and to act for the sake of Man.*

The first and second vows arose specifically from the bushido code of honor, and the third and fourth vows from his religious beliefs. He further elaborates on this:

*If one dedicates these four vows to the gods and Buddhas every morning, he will have the strength of two men and will never slip backward. One must edge forward like the inchworm, bit by bit. The gods and Buddhas, too, first started with a vow.*

He makes another connection between Buddhists and *bushi*, when he advises the monk to pursue the courage of the warrior and the warrior to pursue the compassion of the monk, adding that what he had learned about the way of the samurai had undoubtedly assisted him on the path to spiritual enlightenment.

At the very end of *Hagakure* lies a telling passage:

*Although it is unfitting for someone like me to say this, in dying it is my hope not to become a Buddha. Rather, my will is permeated with the resolution to help manage the affairs of the province, though I be reborn as a Nabeshima samurai seven times.*

With only two more years on earth, Tsunetomo finally voices his profound personal ambitions.

# From the Sixth Chapter

When Lord Takanobu was at the battle of Bungo, a messenger came from the enemy camp bearing sake and food. Takanobu wanted to partake of this quickly, but the men at his side stopped him, saying, "Presents from the enemy are likely to be poisoned. This is not something that a general should eat."

Takanobu heard them out and then said, "Even if it is poisoned, how much of an effect would that have on things? Call the messenger here!" He then broke open the barrel right in front of the messenger, drank three large cups of sake, offered the messenger one too, gave him a reply, and sent him back to his camp. Takagi Akifusa turned against the Ryuzoji clan, appealed to Maeda Iyo no kami Iesada, and was sheltered by him. Akifusa was a warrior of matchless valor and was an accomplished and agile swordsman. His retainers were Ingazaemon and Fudozaemon, stalwarts in no way inferior, and they left Akifusa's side neither day nor night. Thus it happened that a request was sent from Lord Takanobu to Iesada to kill Akifusa. At one point, when Akifusa was seated on the veranda having Ingazaemon wash his feet, Iesada came running up behind him and struck off his head. Before his head fell, Akifusa drew out his short sword and turned to strike, but cut off Ingazaemon's head. The two heads fell into the washbasin together. Akifusa's head then rose into the midst of those present. This was the sort of magic technique that he consistently had.

The priest Tannen used to say in his daily talks that a monk cannot fulfill the Buddhist Way if he does not manifest compassion without and persistently store up courage within. And if a warrior does not manifest courage on the outside and hold enough compassion within his heart to burst his chest, he cannot become a retainer. Therefore, the monk pursues courage with the warrior as his model, and the warrior pursues the compassion of the monk.

I traveled about for many years and met men of wisdom but never found the means to the pursuit of knowledge. Therefore, whenever I heard of a man of courage in one place or another, I would go and look for him regardless of

*Opposite page: Kabuki Actor. Utagawa Kunisada (1786–1864). Japan. Circa 1859. Woodblock on paper.*

*Above: Sliding doors depicting a thunder god. Suzuki Kiitsu (1796–1858). Japan. Late Edo period.*

the hardships on the way. I have learned clearly that these stories of the Way of the Samurai have been an aid on the road to Buddhism. Now a warrior with his armor will rush into the enemy camp, making that armor his strength. Do you suppose that a monk with a single rosary can dash into the midst of spears and long swords, armed with only meekness and compassion? If he does not have great courage, he will do no dashing at all. As proof of this, the priest offering the incense at a great Buddhist memorial service may tremble, and this is because he has no courage.

Things like kicking a man back from the dead, or pulling all living creatures out of hell, are all matters of courage. Nevertheless, monks of recent times all entertain false ideas and desire to become laudably gentle; there are none who complete the Way. Furthermore, among warriors there are some cowards who advance Buddhism. These are regrettable matters. It is a great mistake for a young samurai to learn about Buddhism. The reason is that he will see things in two ways. A person who does not set himself in just one direction will be of no value at all. It is fine for retired old men to learn about Buddhism as a diversion, but if a warrior makes loyalty and filial piety one load, and courage and compassion another, and carries these twenty-four hours a day until his shoulders wear out, he will be a samurai.

In one's morning and evening worship, and as one goes about his day, he had best recite the name of his master. It is not a bit different from the Buddha's names and holy words. Furthermore, one should be in harmony with his family gods. These are matters of the strength of one's fate. Compassion is like a mother who nurtures one's fate. Examples of the ruin of merciless warriors who were brave alone are conspicuous in both past and present.

There was a certain point in the conversation when a retainer of Lord Nabeshima Naohiro said, "There are no men here upon whom the master can truly rely. Although I am consistently useless, I am the only one who would throw away his life for you."

It is said that Lord Naohiro got outrageously angry, saying, "Among our retainers there is not a one who holds his life in regret! You are talking arrogance!" and he was at the point of striking him when the man was pulled away by others who were there.

Once when Master Tanesada, the founder of the China family, was coming by sea to the island of Shikoku, a strong wind began blowing, and the boat was damaged. The boat was saved from sinking by abalone, gathering together and covering over the damaged sections. From that time on none of the China family or any of its retainers ate abalone. If one of them mistakenly ate one, it is said that his body was covered with boils in the shape of abalone.

At the fall of the castle at Arima, on the twenty-eighth day in the vicinity of the inmost citadel, Mitsuse Gender sat down on a levee between the fields. When Nakano

Shintohi passed by and asked the reason for this, Mitsuse replied, "I have abdominal pains and can't go a step farther. I have sent the members of my group ahead, so please take command." This situation was reported by the overseer, pronounced to be a case of cowardice, and Mitsuse was ordered to commit seppuku.

Long ago, abdominal pains were called "cowardice grass." This is because they come suddenly and render a person immobile.

At the time of Lord Nabeshima Naohiro's death, Lord Mitsushige forbade Naohiro's retainers the practice of tsuifuku. His messenger went to Naohiro's mansion and made the declaration, but those who received this news could in no way agree to it. From their midst Ishimaru Uneme (later called Seizaemon) spoke from the lowest seat, "It is improper for me as a younger person to speak out, but I think that what Lord Katsushige has said is reasonable. As a person who received the master's care when I was young, I had whole-heartedly decided on tsuifuku. But hearing Lord Katsushige's dictum and being convinced of his reasoning, no matter what the others may do, I am giving up the idea of tsuifuku and will serve the master's successor." Hearing this, the others all followed suit.

Once Lord Masaie was playing shogi with Lord Hideyoshi and there were a number of daimyo watching. When it came time to withdraw, although Lord Masaie could stand, his feet were numb and he could not walk. He made his withdrawal crawling away, causing everyone to laugh. Because Lord Masaie was big and obese he was not ordinarily able to be on his knees. After this event he thought it would not be fitting to be in attendance anymore and began refusing such duties.

Nakano Uemonnosuke Tadaaki was killed on the twelfth day of the eighth month in the sixth year of Eiroku, at the time of the fight between Master Goto and Master Hirai of Suko on the island of Kabashima in the Kishima district. When Uemonnosuke was leaving for the front lines, he embraced his son Shikibu (later called Jin'emon) in the garden and, although Shikibu was very young, said, "When you grow up, win honor in the Way of the Samurai!"

Even when the children in his family were very young, Yamamoto Jin'emon would draw near to them and say, "Grow up to be a great stalwart, and be of good use to your master." He said, "It is good to breathe these things into their ears even when they are too young to understand."

When Ogawa Toshikiyo's legitimate son Sahei Kiyoji died as a youth, there was one young retainer who galloped up to the temple and committed seppuku.

When Taku Nagato no kami Yasuyori passed away, Kola Yataemon said that he had been unable to repay the

*Opposite page: A Shinto priest offering sake to the kami. Baron Von Raimund Stillfried (1839–1911). Japan. 1880. Hand-tinted albumen print.*

# NAGINATA
## SWORD ON A SHAFT

The *naginata* was a pole arm fashioned by attaching a long sword blade to a wooden shaft. The length of the shaft varied and was useful for keeping an opponent at a distance. A *hirumaki*, or heavy iron butt, could be used as part of the weapon, and its positioning at the bottom of the pole counterbalanced the blade.

The naginata of warrior monk Saito Musashibo Benkei reportedly had a total length of more than twelve feet. This particular weapon is thought to have been made by a sword smith named Munenobu, who gave it a shaft of more than seven feet long and a blade more than four feet long. With this naginata, Benkei defended his master, the general Minamoto Yoshitsune (half-brother of Yoritomo, the first shogun), and in artwork the weapon is always depicted with retainer.

The scythe was probably the agricultural implement that inspired the creation of the naginata, but it was preceded in development by the *yari*, a type of straight-bladed spear. The point of the naginata, which had a strong curvature, and its side edges were all designed to be used to stab and to cut. Production of the naginata became popular in the latter part of the Heian period. Several centuries later, the Nambokucho period naginata were typically large and impressive, while the smaller size of naginata of the Muromachi period made them easier to use on the battlefield. The *nagamiki*, another type of pole arm, was similar to the naginata, but the blade was shaped more like a sword and was less curved. These three, the naginata, yari, and nagamiki, were the most common pole arms in ancient Japan.

During the Gempei Wars, foot soldiers typically used naginata as their main pole arm, and the *sohei*, the warrior monks, also used naginata as their preferred weapon.

Gochim no Tajima was a warrior monk who earned fame for his use of naginata on a bridge across the Uji in 1180 while battling the Heike clan, as related by the *Heiki monogatari*: "Gochim-no-Tajima, throwing away the sheath of his long naginata, strode forth alone onto the bridge, whereupon the Heike shot at him fast and furious. Tajima, not at all perturbed, ducking to avoid the higher ones and leaping over those that flew low, cut through those that flew straight with his whirling halberd, so that even the enemy looked on with admiration. Thus it was that he was dubbed Tajima the arrow-cutter."

Another episode of the use of a naginata in battle is related in the *Taiheiki*, a chronicle of medieval Japan: "Just then a monk kicked over the shield in front of him and sprang forward, whirling his naginata like a water wheel. It was Kajitsu of Harima. Kaito received him with his right arm, meaning to cut down into his helmet bowl, but the glancing sword struck down lightly from Kajitsu's shoulder-plate to the cross stitching at the bottom of his armour. Again Kaito struck forcefully, but his left foot broke through its stirrup, and he was likely to fall from his horse. As he straightened his body, Kajitsu thrust up his naginata, and two or three times drove its point quickly into his helmet. Kaito fell off his horse, pierced cleanly through the throat. Swiftly Kajitsu put down his foot on Kaito's armour, seized his side hair, and cut off his head, that he might fix it to this naginata. Rejoicing, he mocked the enemy."

The warrior monks also used the naginata against the samurai in Kyoto, where this account was recorded: "So they spoke, whirling their great four-shaku-long naginata like water wheels. Again and again they leaped and attacked with flying sparks of fire. Many were the warriors whose horses' legs were cut when they sought to smite these two. Many were those who fell to the ground and perished with smashed helmets!"

Samurai and warrior monks used both the naginata and the yari. This comment by Miyamoto Musashi in *The Book of Five Rings* explains the limitations he saw in using these pole arms: "The naginata is inferior to the yari on the battlefield. With the yari you can take the initiative; the naginata is defensive. In the hands of one of two men of equal ability, the yari gives a little extra strength. Yari and naginata both have their uses but neither is very beneficial in confined spaces. They cannot be used for taking a prisoner. They are essentially weapons for the field."

The biography of Toyotomi Hideyoshi, the *Taikoki,* recorded this account of the victorious use of naginata at the siege of Ulsan in Korea in 1598: "The Ming army divided up and attacked Motomitsu, who was accompanied by soldiers under his command to right and left. They shouted and fought desperately. They fought hard for several hours but gradually grew weary from fighting and there were few of them that did not meet death in battle. The enemy joined in for a victory and attacked increasingly. Reizei Motomitsu wielded his naginata like a water wheel, slaying fifteen or sixteen enemy nearby, and Asanuma Buzen no Kami received death in battle. To their right and left over twenty men under his command fell fighting together."

As battles involving the samurai and sohei decreased, the use of the naginata faded from the battlefield. However, they were still used in processions or remounted without their long tangs to become the dagger-like *tanto* or the short *wakizashi* swords. The modern-day practice of *naginatajutsu* uses both the wooden and the steel pole arm as martial arts weapons. But these naginata typically have a smaller pole and are actually more similar to those wielded by samurai women in Japanese art.

*Opposite page, left: Straight yari. Masatoshi. Japan. Circa 1650.*
*Opposite page, right: Jumonji yari. Shimosaka. Circa 1600.*
*Above: Naginata. Mounted on lacquered pole and decorated with gold paint. Japan. Circa 1800.*
*Below: Ornately lacquered naginata saya. Japan. 19th century.*

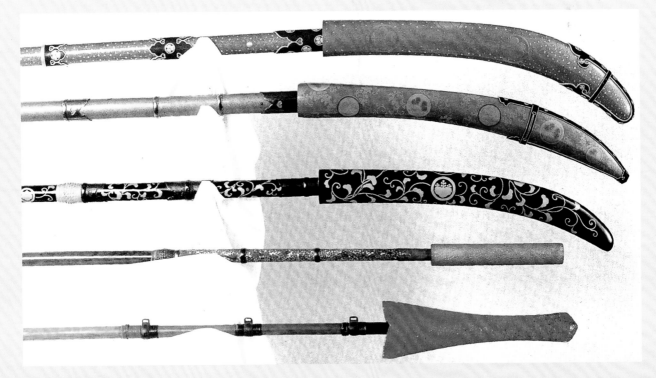

# From the Seventh Chapter

Narutomi Hyogo said, "What is called winning is defeating one's allies. Defeating one's allies is defeating oneself, and defeating oneself is vigorously overcoming one's own body.

"It is as though a man were in the midst of ten thousand allies but not a one were following him. If one hasn't previously mastered his mind and body, he will not defeat the enemy."

During the Shimabara Rebellion, his armor being still at the encampment, Shugyo Echizen no kami Tanenao participated in the fight dressed only in *hakama* and *haori*. It is said that he died in battle in this attire.

At the time of the attack on the castle at Shimabara, Tazaki Geki was wearing very resplendent armor. Lord Katsushige was not pleased by this, and after that every time he saw something showy he would say, "That's just like Geki's armor."

In the light of this story, military armor and equipment that are showy can be seen as being weak and having no strength. By them one can see through the wearer's heart.

When Nabeshima wizen no kami Tadanao died, his attendant Ezoe Kinbei took his remains and had them consecrated at Mount Koya. Then, confining himself in a hermitage, he carved a statue of his master and another of himself doing reverence before the master. On the first anniversary of Tadanao's death, he returned to his home and committed *tsuifuku*. Later the statue was taken from Mount Koya and was placed at the Kodenji.

In the generation of Lord Mitsushige, Oishi Kosuke was at first a foot soldier serving at the side of his master. Whenever Lord Mitsushige was making the trip for his alternate-year residence in Edo, Kosuke would make the rounds around the sleeping quarters of his master, and if he thought a certain area to be insecure, he would spread a straw mat and pass through the night awake by himself. In rainy weather he would simply wear a bamboo hat and an oilpaper raincoat and would stand watch while being pelted by the rain. It is said that to the end he never spent a single night in negligence.

When Oishi Kosuke was an *uchitonin*, a mysterious person sneaked into the area of the maids' chambers late at night. There was a great commotion from upstairs to down and men and women of all ranks were running about; only Kosuke was not to be seen. While the senior ladies-in-waiting were searching about, Kosuke yanked his sword from its scabbard and waited quietly in the room next to the master's bedchamber. As all was in confusion, he had felt apprehension for the master and was there to protect him. Because of this it was said that his viewpoint was quite different.

The man who had sneaked in was Narutomi Kichibei. He and his accomplice Hamada Ichizaemon were condemned to death for adultery.

Once when Lord Katsushige was hunting at Nishime, for some reason he got very angry. He drew his sword from his obi, scabbard and all, and began beating Soejima Zennojo with it, but his hand slipped and his sword fell into a ravine. Zennojo, in order to stay with the sword, fumbled down into the ravine and picked it up. This done, he stuck the sword in his lapel, crawled up the precipice, and just as he was, offered the sword to his master. In terms of quick-mindedness and reserve this was matchless resource.

Once when Master Sane Ukyo was crossing over the Takao River, the bridge was being repaired and there was one large piling that could not be pulled up. Master Ukyo dismounted, grasped the piling firmly, gave a shout, and began to pull it up. There was a tremendous sound, and although he was able to pull it up to his own height, it

> Narutomi Hyogo said, "What is called winning is defeating one's allies. Defeating one's allies is defeating oneself, and defeating oneself is vigorously overcoming one's own body."

*Opposite page: Head of a temple guard. Japan. Carved wood.*

would go no further and thereupon sank. After he returned home he became sick and suddenly died.

At the time of the funeral at the temple in Jobaru, when the funeral procession crossed the Takao Bridge, the corpse leapt from the casket and fell into the river. A sixteen-year-old acolyte from the Shufukuji immediately jumped into the river and took hold of the dead body. Everyone then ran down into the river and pulled up the corpse. The head monk was very impressed and instructed the other acolytes to be guided by this young man. It is said that he later became a very famous monk.

Yamamoto Kichizaemon was ordered by his father Jin'emon to cut down a dog at the age of five, and at the age of fifteen he was made to execute a criminal. Everyone, by the time they were fourteen or fifteen, was ordered to do a beheading without fail. When Lord Katsushige was young, he was ordered by Lord Naoshige to practice killing with a sword. It is said that at that time he was made to cut down more than ten men successively.

A long time ago this practice was followed, especially in the upper classes, but today even the children of the lower classes perform no executions, and this is extreme negligence. To say that one can do without this sort of thing, or that there is no merit in killing a condemned man, or that it is a crime, or that it is defiling, is to make excuses. In short, can it not be thought that because a person's martial valor is weak, his attitude is only that of trimming his nails and being attractive?

If one investigates into the spirit of a man who finds these things disagreeable, one sees that this person gives himself over to cleverness and excuse-making not to kill because he feels unnerved. But Naoshige made it his orders exactly because this is something that must be done.

Last year I went to the Kase Execution Grounds to try my hand at beheading, and I found it to be an extremely good feeling. To think that it is unnerving is a symptom of cowardice.

Among the pageboys in forelocks in Lord Mitsushige's retinue, one Tomoda Shozaemon was in attendance. A rather wanton fellow, he fell in love with a leading actor of the theater by the name of Tamon Shozaemon and changed both his name and his crest to that of the actor. Completely abandoning himself to this affair, he spent everything he had and lost all his clothing and furnishings. And at length, when he had exhausted all his means, he stole Mawatari Rokubei's sword and had a spearman take it to a pawnshop.

The spearman, however, spoke up about this matter, and in the investigation both he and Shozaemon were condemned to death. The investigator was Yamamoto Gorozaemon. When he read the report, he spoke in a loud voice and said, "The man who accuses the defendant is Spearman so-and-so."

Mitsushige responded quickly, "Put him to death."

When it came time to announce his fate to Shozaemon, Gorozaemon came in and said, "There is now nothing left to be done for you. Prepare yourself for your place of death."

Shozaemon settled himself and said, "Very well. I understand what you have said and am grateful for your

*Masterful small sculpted ivory figurines, or okimono, like this one were produced in exquisite detail during the Meiji period. It was at this time that the emperor's power was restored after the fall of the shoguns. With the advent of U.S. Navy Commodore Matthew Perry, the country opened quickly to the Western world. Okimono of rice sellers. Japan. Circa 1900.*

words." Due to somebody's trickery, however, while a *kaishaku* was introduced to Shozaemon, it was arranged that a foot soldier, Naozuka Rokuuemon, was to step from the side and decapitate him.

Repairing to the execution grounds, where the kaishaku stood opposite him, Shozaemon saluted him with extreme calm. But just then, seeing Naozuka drawing his sword, he jumped up and said, "Who are you? I'll never let you cut off my head!" From that point on his peace of mind was shattered, and he showed terrible cowardice. Finally he was brought to the ground, stretched out, and decapitated.

Gorozaemon later said secretly, "If he hadn't been deceived, he would have probably met his death well."

Noda Kizaemon said about the function of kaishaku, "When a man who has come to his place of death loses his wits and is crawling about, it is likely some damage will be done when it comes time to perform kaishaku. At such a time first wait a bit and by some means gather your strength. Then if you cut by standing firm and not missing the chance, you will do well."

In the generation of Lord Katsushige there were retainers who, regardless of high or low rank, were requested to work before the master from the time they were young. When Shiba Kizaemon was doing such service, once the master was clipping his nails and said, "Throw these away." Kizaemon held them in his hand but did not stand up, and the master said, "What's the matter?" Kizaemon

said, "There's one missing." The master said, "Here it is," and handed over the one that he had hidden.

Sawabe Heizaemon was ordered to commit *seppuku* on the eleventh day of the eleventh month in the second year of Tenna. As this became known to him on the night of the tenth, he sent a request to Yamamoto Gonnojo [Tsunetomo] to be kaishaku. The following is a copy of Yamamoto's reply. (Tsunetomo was twenty-four years old at this time.)

"I am in accord with your resolution and accept your request for me to function as kaishaku. I instinctively felt that I should decline, but as this is to take place tomorrow, there is no time for making excuses, and I will undertake the job. The fact that you have chosen me from among many people is a great personal satisfaction to me. Please set your mind at ease concerning all that must follow. Although it is now late at night, I will come to your house to talk over the particulars."

When Heizaemon saw this reply, it is said that he remarked, "This is a matchless letter."

From ages past it has been considered ill-omened by samurai to be requested as kaishaku. The reason for this is that one gains no fame even if the job is well done. And if by chance one should blunder, it becomes a lifetime disgrace.

Once when Tanaka Yahei was attending to affairs in Edo, one of his menials was rather insolent, and Yahei scolded him severely. Late that night Yahei heard the noise of someone coming up the stairs. He felt this to be suspicious and quietly got up. With short sword in hand he asked who was there, and it turned out to be the menial whom he had scolded previously, secretly holding a short sword. Yahei leapt down and with a single stroke cut the man down. I heard many people later state that he had had good luck.

A certain Master Tokuhisa was born quite different from other people and looked to be a bit moronic. Once, a guest was invited, and mudfish salad was served. At that time everyone said, "Master Tokuhisa's mudfish salad," and laughed. Later when he was in attendance and a certain person made fun of him by quoting the above remark, Tokuhisa pulled out his sword and cut the man down. This event was investigated, and it was stated to Lord Naoshige, "Seppuku is recommended because this was a matter of rashness within the palace."

When Lord Naoshige heard this, he said, "To be made fun of and remain silent is cowardice. There is no reason to overlook this fact because one is within the palace. A man who makes fun of people is himself a fool. It was his own fault for being cut down."

Once when Nakano Mokunosuke boarded a small boat on the Sumida River to enjoy the coolness, a rogue got in too and committed all manner of rude acts. When Mokunosuke saw that the rogue was relieving himself over the side of the boat, he cut the man's head off, and it fell into the river. So that people would not notice this, he quickly covered the body with various things. He then said to the boatman, "This matter should not become known. Row up to the upper reaches of the river and bury the corpse. I shall naturally pay you well."

The boatman did as he was told, but in the lagoon where the body was buried, Mokunosuke cut off the head of the boatman and returned directly. It is said that this fact never became known publicly.

At that time there was also one young homosexual male prostitute riding in the boat. Mokunosuke said, "That fellow was a man too. It is best to learn how to cut a man while one is still young," and so the man cut the corpse once. Because of that the young man said nothing later on.

It is said that every time Oki Hyobu's group gathered and after all their affairs were finished, he would say, "Young men should discipline themselves rigorously in intention and courage. This will be accomplished if only courage is fixed in one's heart. If one's sword is broken, he will strike with his hands. If his hands are cut off, he will press the enemy down with his shoulders. If his shoulders are cut away, he will bite through ten or fifteen enemy necks with his teeth. Courage is such a thing."

Shida Kichinosuke said, "At first it is an oppressive thing to run until one is breathless. But it is an extraordinarily good feeling when one is standing around after the running. More than that, it is even better to sit down. More than that, it is even better to lie down. And more than that, to put down a pillow and sleep soundly is even better. A man's whole life should be like this. To exert oneself to a great extent when one is young and then to sleep when he is old or at the point of death is the way it should be. But to first sleep and then exert oneself.... To exert oneself to the end, and to end one's whole life in toil is regrettable." Shimomura Rokurouemon told this story.

A saying of Kichinosuke's that is similar to this is, "A man's life should be as toilsome as possible."

When Ueno Rihei was overseer of accounting in Edo, he had a young assistant whom he treated

*Meiji period okimono went out of fashion for a time, after the opening of Japan to the West. The intricate carvings were considered old-fashioned and busy, as tastes in art gave way to the modern. However the reverse is true today, and okimono are prized for the delicate artistry present in every minute carved detail. Okimono figure of a poulterer. Okawa Shizumune. Japan. Circa 1900. Ivory.*

in a very intimate way. On the first night of the eighth month, he went drinking with Hashimoto Taemon, an overseer of foot soldiers, and got so drunk that he lost good sense. He accompanied his young assistant back home, babbling on in a drunken manner, and when they arrived there, Rihei said that he was going to cut the assistant down. The assistant pushed away the tip of Rihei's scabbard. They grappled and both fell into the gutter with the assistant on top, pushing Rihei down. At this time, Rihei's servant ran up and asked, "Is Master Rihei on the top or on the bottom?"

When Rihei replied, "I'm on the bottom!" the servant stabbed the assistant once. The assistant got up and, as his wound was light, ran away.

When the affair was brought under investigation, Rihei was put into confinement at the Naekiyama prison and was condemned to capital punishment by beheading. Before this, when he was positioned in Edo and living in a rented house in the merchants' district, a servant had opposed him, and he had cut him down. But he had acted in a good way at that time, and people said that he had acted like a man. This time, however, his actions were outrageous and were certainly unnecessary.

If one thinks about this well from beginning to end, to get so drunk as to draw one's sword is both cowardice and lack of resolve. Rihei's servant was a man from Taku, but his name is not remembered. Though he was a member of the

*Right: Gunpowder flask. Japan. 19th century. Lacquered with bamboo spout and measure. Opposite page: Battle of Nagashino and Himeji Castle. Dan Escott. 1928–1987. Gouache on paper.*

lower classes, he was a brave man. It is said that Taemon committed suicide during the investigation.

In the twelfth section of the fifth chapter of the Ryoankyo there is this story:

In the province of Wizen there was a certain man from Take who, although he had contracted smallpox, was considering joining the forces attacking the castle at Shimabara. His parents earnestly tried to get him to desist, saying, "With such a grave illness, even if you should get there, how could you be of any use?"

He replied, "It would be to my satisfaction to die on the way. After having received the warm benevolence of the master, should I tell myself that I will be of no use to him now?" And he left for the front. Although it was winter camp and the cold was extreme, he did not pay any attention to his health, and neither put on many layers of clothing nor took off his armor day or night. Moreover, he did not avoid uncleanliness, and in the end recovered quickly and was able to fulfill his loyalty completely. So to the contrary of what you would expect, it cannot be said that one is to despise uncleanliness.

When the teacher, Suzuki Shozo, heard this, he said, "Was it not a cleansing act to throw away his life for his master? For a man who will cut off his life for the sake of righteousness, there is no need to call upon the god of smallpox. All the gods of heaven will protect him."

Lord Katsushige said, "Whether a man of Hizen holds death in regret or not is not a matter of concern. What I worry about is that people will not take to heart the command to keep the rules of manners and etiquette correctly. I am afraid that the entire clan, our relatives and elders, out of too much earnestness, will feel that the command to keep correct etiquette is an exaggeration. Up to now there have existed men who were used to these things, and even if etiquette was slightly wrong, they could remember the correct way, and the matter was settled. I have given this command because people are negligent in affairs of this sort."

During the Genroku period there was a samurai of low rank from the Province of Ise by the name of Suzuki Rokubei. He was ill with a severe fever, and his consciousness became dim. At that time a certain male nurse was unexpectedly stricken with greed and was about to open up the inkbox and steal the money that was kept in it. Just then the sick man suddenly stirred, took the sword from the base of his pillow, and in a sudden attack cut the man down with one blow. With that, the sick man fell back and died. By this act, Rokubei seemed to be a man of principled disposition.

I heard this story in Edo, but later when I was serving in the same province with a Dr. Nagatsuka, who was also from the province of Ise, I asked him about it, and indeed he knew the story and said that it was true.

# JAPANESE CASTLES

The form and function of Japanese castles was an important aspect of warfare. Castle size and detail demonstrated the wealth of the *daimyo*, and the castle's strength as a fortification served to preserve the daimyo's wealth and his life, as well as the lives of his subjects, including his samurai.

Strategic defensive placement of the castle, which typically consisted of a main structure and its annexes, was a matter of life and death during times of war. Castles built during the early half of the sixteenth century, such as Iwakuni-jo and Gifu-jo, were built at high elevations. These mountaintop castles, or *yamajiro*, were not usually the main residences of the daimyo but were occupied primarily during war, because the view gave notice of potential attackers. Attackers also had more difficulty reaching the yamajiro as a result of the difficult terrain. These castles were usually about three stories high. Mountaintop castles were difficult to build and supply because of limited access. They were safe during earthquakes but susceptible to the typhoon winds.

Himeji-jo is an example of the so-called flatland-mountain castle, the *hirayamajiro*, which began to appear during the Sengoku period, between 1392 and 1603. They were easier to access than the mountaintop castle because of their placement on large hills or low mountains adjacent to a plain. The daimyo of these castles could more easily bring in supplies and could communicate more effectively with the

rest of the world. Because potential attackers could not be seen as easily as from the mountaintop castles, the castle had a higher tower, and for fortification, the castle more heavily relied on walls, moats, and other defensive measures.

The moats and walls of the *hirajiro*, the flatland castles, were built stronger and larger than those of mountaintop or flatland-mountain castles to offset their lack of defensive positioning. The daimyo of the hirajiro built their castles during the end of the Sengoku period and the beginning of the Edo period (1600 to 1867) to aid them in their governmental responsibilities. Toyotomi Hideyoshi, who unified Japan and served as its leader, built Osaka-jo, which was the first castle of this type. Flooding was a challenge of maintaining flatland castles, especially those surrounded by water, which were called *ukishiro*, "floating castles."

Moats served as a first line of defense as the castle was approached. Water or fine mud filled the moat, or sometimes it was left dry. The core of the castle walls was usually built from the earth excavated during the moat-digging process. The earth was mounded to create freestanding walls or embankments, depending on the topography of the castle site, and stone would then be added to further fortify the

*Above: Matsumoto castle in Japan.*
*Left: Himeji, Japan's best preserved castle.*
*Opposite page: Detail of Japanese castle wall in Fukuoka, Japan. Dates back almost 600 years.*

walls. Various methods of stone placement were devised, including random stone piling *(ranseki-zumi)*, fieldstone piling *(nozura-zumi)*, beaten and inserted masonry *(uchikomi-hagi)*, and cut and inserted masonry *(kirikomihagi)*. Random stone piling was the least expensive and most common method of construction, while cut and inserted masonry involved a different type of expertise and was more costly. Mortar was not used in wall construction.

Fire was a constant threat to the wooden castles. Design elements, such as dolphins and rain symbols, frequently decorated the castle to spiritually protect them from fire. But mud and plaster walls were the most common structural deterrent to fire. Earth, sand, and straw were combined to create a strong mud coating for the typically cypress wooden walls. Once the mud had dried, a combination of seaweed, shell lime, and water was plastered in layers to create walls with strength comparable to that of concrete.

The castle compound varied in design but usually included a tower. The *tenshukaku*, "high heavenly protector," served as a lookout post, arsenal, and command center and was heavily protected. The tower was placed on the highest elevation on the complex and could be from two to eight stories high. Thick, blue-gray tiles covered tower roofs, and that and the combination of triangular and curved gables gave most of these castles a temple-like appearance.

To prevent access to the tower, a series of gates, mud walls, storehouses, and wall towers were also part of the castle compound. These were designed like a maze, which prevented easy access to the interior of the compound and slowed down attackers. The walls were punctuated with shooting holes and special windows designed to protect soldiers as they dropped heavy stones, boiling water, or other objects on attackers below. Cone-shaped shooting holes, designed to allow for maximum maneuverability on the inside of the wall, had only a small opening, which ingeniously prevented enemy fire from entering. The shape of the shooting hole designated the weapon to be used. Gun shooting holes were circular, square, and triangular, while arrow shooting holes were rectangular.

The decorating styles of castles illustrate the building fashions of the time. Simple natural designs reflect a Zen aesthetic, while gold and intricate detailing were indicative of the more flamboyant tastes characterizing the reigns of both Oda Nobunaga and Toyotomi Hideyoshi. Family crests often adorned roof tiles, gates, and other structural elements of the castles, which usually had black-and-white exteriors.

Castles and the accompanying land were sometimes confiscated by Japanese rulers and given as rewards to loyal samurai. During the Edo period, castle building, additions, and remodeling were restricted, which resulted in the destruction of many burned or damaged buildings that may have otherwise been preserved.

During peacetime, maintenance on the castle was constant. Guards were posted night and day. The offices and domestic rooms of the daimyo and his family were in a separate building called a *yashiki*. Sliding screens, or *shoji*, divided the large rooms of the compound buildings, and interiors included alcoves, or *tokonoma*. Wooden paneling covered the walls and ceiling; straw mats, or *tatami*, covered the floors.

## Japanese Castles Today

The castles listed below are limited to those select few that have retained their original structures.

*Bitchu Matsuyama Castle*, Takahashi, Okayama prefecture, 1683, National Historic Site, Important Cultural Properties.

*Hikone Castle*, Hikone, Shiga prefecture, 1603 to 1622, Special Historic Site, National Treasures, Important Cultural Properties.

*Himeji Castle*, Himeji, Hyogo prefecture, 1580 (conversion of fort to castle), 1601 to 1609 (completion of castle complex), UNESCO World Heritage Site, Special Historic Site, National Treasures, Important Cultural Properties.

*Hirosaki Castle*, Hirosaki, Aomori prefecture, 1611, Important Cultural Properties.

*Inuyama Castle*, Inuyama, Aichi prefecture, 1537, National Treasures.

*Iyo Matsuyama Castle*, Matsuyama, Ehime prefecture, 1603, National Historic Site, Important Cultural Properties.

*Kochi Castle*, Kochi, Kochi prefecture, 1603, National Historic Site, Important Cultural Properties.

*Marugame Castle*, Marugame, Kagawa prefecture, 1597, National Historic Site, Important Cultural Properties.

*Maruoka Castle*, Kanazawa, Fukui prefecture, 1576, Important Cultural Properties.

*Matsue Castle*, Matsue, Shimane prefecture, 1611, National Historic Site, Important Cultural Properties.

*Matsumoto Castle*, Kyoto-Osaka, Nagano prefecture, ca. 1590, National Historic Site, National Treasures.

*Uwajima Castle*, Uwajima, Ehime prefecture, 1596, National Historic Site, Important Cultural Properties.

# From the Eighth Chapter

On the night of the thirteenth day of the ninth month in the fourth year of Teikyo, there was a group of ten Noh actors moon-viewing at the house of Nakayama Mosuke, a foot soldier, in Sayanomoto. Beginning with Naotsuka Kanzaemon they all began to make fun of the foot soldier Araki Kyozaemen because he was so short. Araki became angry, killed Kanzaemon with his sword, and then began striking at the others.

Though he suffered a severed hand, Matsumoto Rokuzaemon came down into the garden, seized Araki from behind with his other hand, and said, "As for the likes of you, I'll twist your head off with one hand!" Grabbing away Araki's sword, he pushed him to the doorsill and pressed him down with his knee, but as he seized him by the neck he became faint and was quickly overpowered.

Araki quickly sprang back and again began to strike at those around him, but now Master Hayata (later known as Jirozaemon) met him with a spear. In the end he was overpowered by a number of men. Following this, Araki was made to commit *seppuku*, and the others who were involved were all made *ronin* on account of their indiscretion, but Hayata was later pardoned.

As Tsunetomo does not remember this story clearly, one should ask around about it.

Some years ago there was a sutra reading at the Jissoin in Kawakami. Five or six men from Kon'yamachi and the area of Tashiro had gone to the service, and on their way home passed some time drinking. Among them was one of Kizuka Kyuzaemon's retainers who, having some reason for doing so, turned down his companions' invitation to join them and returned home before nightfall. The others, however, later got into a fight with some men and cut them all down.

Kyuzaemon's retainer heard of this late that night and went quickly to his companions' quarters. He listened to the details and then said, "In the end I suppose you will have to submit a statement. When you do, you should say that I was there also and assisted in cutting down those men. When I return, I will say as much to Kyuzaemon. Since a fight is a matter involving all concerned, I should meet the same death sentence as you. And that is my deepest desire. The reason is that, even if I were to explain to my master that I had returned home early, he would never accept it as the truth. Kyuzaemon has always been a severe man, and even if I were cleared by the investigators, he would probably have me executed as a coward right before his eyes. In such a case, dying with the bad reputation of having run away from a place would be extremely regretful.

"Since the fate of dying is the same, I would like to die being blamed for having killed a man. If you are not in agreement with this, I will cut my stomach open right here."

Having no alternative, his companions spoke as he had requested. Presently, during the inquiry, although the circumstances were explained in the above manner, it became known that the retainer had returned home early. All the investigators were impressed and in fact praised the man.

Yamamoto Jin'emon always said to his retainers, "Go ahead and gamble and lie. A person who will not tell you seven lies within a hundred yards is useless as a man." Long ago people spoke in this fashion because they were only concerned with a man's attitude toward military matters and considered that a man who was "correct" would never do great works. They also ignored the misconduct of men and dismissed such matters by saying, "They do good works, too..."

Men like Sagara Kyoma also excused retainers who had committed theft and adultery and trained them gradually. He said, "If it weren't for such persons, we would have no useful men at all."

Ikumo Oribe said, "If a retainer will just think about what he is to do for the day at hand, he will be able to do anything. If it is a single day's work, one should be able to put up with it. Tomorrow, too, is but a single day."

At the time when Lord Nabeshima Tsunashige had still not taken over as heir, he was converted by the Zen priest

*Opposite page: Matsumoto Koshiro V in the role of Matsuomaru, from the Tokaido Road series. Utagawa Kunisada (1786–1864). Japan. 19th century. Color lithograph.*

Kurotakiyama Choon and learned Buddhism from him. Since he had had an enlightenment, the priest was going to confer the seal upon him, and this became known throughout the mansion. At that time Yamamoto Gorozaemon had been ordered to be both Tsunashige's attendant and overseer. When he heard of this, he knew that it absolutely would not do and planned to make a request to Choon, and if he did not assent, kill him. He went to the priest's house in Edo and entered; the priest, thinking that he was someone on a pilgrimage, met him in a dignified manner.

Gorozaemon drew near him and said, "I have some secret thing to tell you directly. Please send out your attendant priests.

"It is said that you will soon award Tsunashige the seal because of his cleverness in Buddhism. Now as you are from Hizen, you should know in large part the customs of the Ryuzoji and Nabeshima clans. Our country is ruled with harmony between high and low because, unlike others, it has had continuous heirs for successive generations. There has never been the taking of a Buddhist seal by the *daimyo* for ages past. If you present the seal now, Tsunashige will probably think of himself as enlightened and regard what his retainers say as so much dirt. A great man will become vain. Absolutely do not give this award. If you do not agree to this, I too am resolved." This he said with determination.

The priest's color changed, but he said, "Well, well. You have trustworthy intentions, and I see that you understand the affairs of your clan well. You are a loyal retainer."

But Gorozaemon said, "No! I understand that ploy. I didn't come here to be praised. Without adding anything else, let me hear clearly whether you plan to cancel the seal or not."

Choon said, "What you say is reasonable. I will definitely not award the seal."

Gorozaemon made sure of this and returned.

A group of eight samurai all took the same road for some merrymaking. Two of them, Komori Eijun and Otsubo Jin'emon, went into a teahouse in front of the Kannon temple at Asakusa, got into an argument with the male employees there, and were soundly beaten. This could be heard by the others, who were in an excursion boat, and Mute Rokuemen said, "We should go back and take revenge." Yoshii Yoichiemon and Ezoe Jinbei both agreed to this.

The others, however, dissuaded them, saying, "This will cause trouble for the clan," and they all returned home. When they arrived at the mansion, Rokuemon again said, "We should definitely take revenge!" but the others dissuaded him. Although they sustained heavy wounds on

*The Uji Bridge, from Tale of Heike, one of a pair. Japan. 1650–1700. Ink, color, and gold on paper.*

their arms and legs, Eijian and Jin'emon cut the teahouse men down, and those who had returned were taken to task by the master.

In due course some thought was given to the details of this event. One person said, "By waiting to get the agreement of others, a matter like taking revenge will never be brought to a conclusion. One should have the resolution to go alone and even to be cut down. A person who speaks vehemently about taking revenge but does nothing about it is a hypocrite. Clever people, by using their mouths alone, are taking care of their reputations for a later date. But a real stalwart is a man who will go out secretly, saying nothing, and die. It is not necessary to achieve one's aim; one is a stalwart in being cut down. Such a person will most likely achieve his purpose."

527

Ichiyuken was a low-class servant in the kitchen of Lord Takanobu. Because of some grudge he had over a matter of wrestling, he cut down seven or eight men and was hence ordered to commit suicide. But when Lord Takanobu heard of this he pardoned the man and said, "In these strife-torn times of our country, brave men are important. This man would seem to be a man of bravery."

Consequently, at the time of the action around the Uji River, Lord Takanobu took Ichiyuken along, and the latter earned unrivaled fame, advancing deep into the lead and plundering the enemy every time.

At the battle of Takagi, Ichiyuken went so far into the enemy lines that Lord Takanobu felt regret and called him back. Since the vanguard had been unable to advance, only by quickly dashing out was he able to grab

Ichiyuken by the sleeve of his armor. At that time Ichiyuken's head had suffered many wounds, but he had stopped them up with green leaves that he bound with a thin towel.

On the first day of the attack on Hara Castle, Tsuruta Yashichibei went as a messenger from Lord Mimasaka to Oki Hyobu, but as he was delivering the message, he was shot through the pelvic region by a bullet fired from the castle and instantly fell on his face. He got up again and delivered the rest of the message, was felled a second time, and died. Yashichibei's body was carried back by Taira Chihyoei. When Chihyoei was returning to Hyobu's camp, he too was struck by a rifle ball and died.

Denko was born in Taku, and the members of his family living at this time were his elder brother Jirobei, his younger brother, and his mother. Around the ninth month Denko's mother took Jirobei's son with her to hear a sermon. When it was time to go home, the child, as he was putting on his straw sandals, accidentally stepped on the foot of the man next to him. The man rebuked the child, and in the end they got into a vehement argument and the man unsheathed his short sword and killed him. Jirobei's mother was dumbstruck. She clung to the man, and he killed her too. Having done this, the man returned to his house.

This man's name was Gorouemon, and he was the son of a ronin by the name of Nakajima Moan. His younger brother was the mountain ascetic, Chuzobo. Moan was an advisor to Master Mimasaka, and Gorouemon had been given a stipend also.

When the circumstances became known at Jirobei's home, his younger brother set out for Gorouemon's place. Finding that the door was locked from within and that no one would come out, he disguised his voice, pretending to be a visitor. When the door was opened, he shouted his real name and crossed swords with his enemy. Both men fumbled into the rubbish heap, but in the end Gorouemon was killed. At this point, Chuzobo dashed in and cut down Jirobei's younger brother.

Hearing of this incident, Denko went immediately to Jirobei's place and said, "Of our enemies only one has been killed, while we have lost three. This is extremely regrettable, so why don't you strike at Chuzobo?" Jirobei, however, would not comply.

*Helmet with design of an orc. Japan. Mixed media.*

Denko felt that this was indeed shameful, and although a Buddhist priest, he decided on striking at the enemy of his mother, younger brother, and nephew. He knew, nevertheless, that since he was simply an ordinary priest, there was likely to be a reprisal from Master Mimasaka and therefore worked hard, finally gaining eminence as the chief priest of the Ryuunji. He then went to the sword-maker Iyonojo and asked him to make both a long and a short sword, offered to be his apprentice, and was even allowed to take part in the work.

By the twenty-third day of the ninth month of the following year, he was ready to make his departure. By chance a guest had come at this time. Giving orders for food to be served, Denko secretly slipped out of the chief priest's headquarters disguised as a layman. He then went to Taku and, upon asking about Chuzobo, learned that he was with a large group of people who had gathered to watch the moonrise, and that therefore nothing much could be done. Unwilling to let time pile up, he felt that it would be fulfilling his basic desire to strike at the father, Moan. Going to Moan's house, he forced his way into the sleeping chambers, announced his name, and when the man began to get up, stabbed and killed him. When the people of the neighborhood came running and surrounded him, he explained the situation, threw away both long and short swords, and returned home. News of this preceded him to Saga, and a good number of Denko's parishioners came out quickly and accompanied him on his return.

Master Mimasaka was quite outraged, but as Denko was the chief priest of a Nabeshima clan temple, there was nothing to be done. Finally, through the offices of Nabeshima Toneri, he sent word to Tannen, the chief priest of the Kodenji, saying, "When a priest has killed a man, he should be given a sentence of death." Tannen's reply was, "The punishment for one within the religion will be in accordance with the feelings of the Kodenji. Kindly do not interfere."

Master Mimasaka became even angrier and asked, "What sort of punishment will this be?" Tannen replied, "Although it is profitless for you to know, you are forcing the question, so I will give you an answer. The [Buddhist] Law is that an apostate priest is deprived of his robes and driven out."

Denko's robes were taken from him at the Kodenji, and when he was to be driven out, some novices put on their long and short swords, and a great number of parishioners came to protect him, accompanying him as far as Todoroki. On the road a number of men who looked like hunters

appeared and asked if the party had come from Taku. Thereafter Denko lived in Chikuzen, was well received by all, and was on friendly terms with samurai as well. This story was widely circulated, and it is said that he was treated kindly everywhere.

Horie San'emon's misdeed was robbing the Nabeshima warehouse in Edo of its money and fleeing to another province. He was caught and confessed.

Thus it was pronounced, "Because this is a grave crime he should be tortured to death," and Nakano Daigaku was ordered to be the official who verified the execution.

At first all the hairs on his body were burned off and his fingernails were pulled out. His tendons were then cut; he was bored with drills and subjected to various other tortures. Throughout, he did not flinch once, nor did his face change color. In the end his back was split, he was boiled in soy sauce, and his body was bent back in two.

Once when Fukuchi Rokurouemon was leaving the castle, the palanquin of what appeared to be a rather upper-class woman was passing in front of Master Taku's mansion, and a man who was standing there made the proper salutation. A halberd carrier who was with the palanquin procession, however, said to the man, "You didn't bow low enough," and struck him on the head with the handle of his halberd. When the man wiped his head, he found that he was bleeding. In just that condition he stood up and said, "You have committed an outrageous act, even though I was courteous. A regrettable piece of luck." So saying, he cut the halberd carrier down with a single blow. The palanquin continued on to wherever it was going, but Rokurouemon unsheathed his spear, stood before the man, and said, "Put away your sword. Within the castle grounds it is forbidden to go about holding a naked blade." The man said, "What happened now was unavoidable, and I was compelled by the circumstances. Certainly you could see that this was so. Although I would like to sheathe my sword, it is difficult to do so due to the tone of your words. It is unpleasant, but I shall be glad to accept your challenge."

Rokurouemon immediately threw down his spear and said courteously, "What you have said is reasonable. My name is Fukuchi Rokurouemon. I will bear witness that your conduct was quite admirable. Moreover, I will back you up even if it

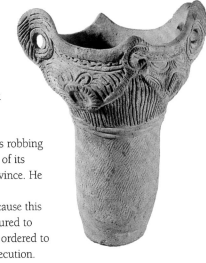

*Jomon vase from the Kanto province. Japan. Earthenware.*

*Do-maru-type parade armor. Black-lacquered zunari-kabuto with short fukugaesh, and wakidate formed as a Buddhist ken. Japan. 18th century.*

means forfeiting my life. Now put away your sword."

"With pleasure," the man said, and sheathed his sword. On being asked where he was from, the man replied that he was a retainer of Taku Nagato no kami Yasuyori. Therefore Rokurouemon accompanied him and explained the circumstances. Knowing that the woman in the palanquin was the wife of a nobleman, however, Lord Nagato ordered his retainer to commit seppuku.

Rokurouemon came forward and said, "Because I have given the promise of a samurai, if this man is ordered to commit seppuku, then I will commit seppuku first."

It is said that the affair was thus finished without mishap.

Lord Shima sent a messenger to his father, Lord Aki, saying, "I would like to make a pilgrimage to the Atago Shrine in Kyoto." Lord Aki asked, "For what reason?" and the messenger replied, "Since Atago is the god of archery, my intentions are for the sake of fortune in war." Lord Aki became angry and answered, "That is absolutely worthless! Should the vanguard of the Nabeshimas be making requests to Atago? If the incarnation of Atago were fighting on the enemy's side, the vanguard should be equal to cutting him neatly in two."

Dohaku lived in Kurotsuchibaru. His son was named Gorobei. Once when Gorobei was carrying a load of rice, a ronin of Master Kumashiro Sakyo's by the name of Iwamura Kyunai was coming from the other direction. There was a grudge between the two of them from some former incident, and now Gorobei struck Kyunai with his load of rice, started an argument, beat him and pushed him into a ditch, and then returned home. Kyunai yelled some threat at Gorobei and returned to his home where he related this event to his older brother Gen'emon. The two of them then went off to Gorobei's to take revenge.

When they got there the door was open just a bit, and Gorobei was waiting behind it with drawn sword. Not knowing this, Gen'emon entered and Gorobei struck at him with a sweep from the side. Having received a deep wound, Gen'emon used his sword as a staff and hobbled back outside. Then Kyunai rushed in and struck at Dohaku's son-in-law Katsuemon, who was sitting by the hearth. His sword glanced off the pot hanger, and he cut off half of Katsuemon's face. Dohaku, together with his wife, grabbed the sword away from Kyunai.

Kyunai apologized and said, "I have already

achieved my purpose. Please give me back my sword, and I will accompany my brother home. But when Dohaku handed it back to him, Kyunai cut him once in the back and severed his neck halfway through. He then crossed swords with Gorobei again, and both went outside and fought an even match until he cut off Gorobei's arm.

At this point Kyunai, who also suffered many wounds, shouldered his elder brother Gen'emon and returned home. Gen'emon, however, died on the way back.

Gorobei's wounds were numerous. Although he stopped the bleeding, he died on account of drinking some water. Dohaku's wife suffered some severed fingers. Dohaku's wound was a severed neck bone, and since only his throat remained intact, his head hung down in front. Now boosting his head up with his own hands, Dohaku went off to the surgeon's.

The surgeon's treatment was like this: First he rubbed a mixture of pine resin and oil on Dohaku's jaw and bound it in ramie. He then attached a rope to the top of his head and tied it to a beam, sewed the open wound shut, and buried his body in rice so that he would not be able to move.

Dohaku never lost consciousness, nor did he change from his everyday attitude, nor did he even drink ginseng. It is said that only on the third day when there was a hemorrhage did he use a little medicinal stimulant. In the end the bones mended, and he recovered without incident.

When Lord Mitsushige contracted smallpox at Shimonoseki, Ikushima Sakuan gave him some medicine. It was an exceptionally heavy case of smallpox, and his attendants both high and low were rather tense. Suddenly his scabs turned black. The men who were nursing him lost heart and secretly informed Sakuan, who came immediately. He said, "Well, this is something to be thankful for. The scabs are healing. He should soon make a complete recovery with no complications. I give you my guarantee."

The people who were at Lord Mitsushige's side heard this and thought, "Sakuan looks a little deranged. This has become all the more hopeless." Sakuan then set folding screens around, came out after a while, and fed Lord Mitsushige one packet of medicine. Very quickly the patient's scabs healed, and he made a complete recovery. Sakuan later confided to someone, "I gave the master that one packet of medicine, resolved that, as I was undertaking this treatment alone, if he did not recover I would quickly cut open my stomach and die with him."

When Nakano Takumi was dying, his whole house gathered and he said, "You should understand that there are three conditions to the resolution of a retainer. They are the condition of the master's will, the condition of vitality, and the condition of one's death."

Once when a number of men had gathered on the platform of the inner citadel of the castle, a certain man said to Uchida Shouemon, "It is said that you are a teacher of the sword, but judging by your everyday attitude, your teaching must be very wild indeed. If you were requested to perform *kaishaku*, I can imagine that instead of cutting the neck you'd probably cut the top of the man's head."

Shouemon rejoined, "Such is not the case. Draw a little ink spot on your own neck, and I'll show you that I can cut without being off by a hair."

Nagayama Rokurozaemon was going down the Tokaido and was at Hamamatsu. As he passed by an inn, a beggar faced his palanquin and said, "I am a ronin from Echigo. I am short of money and in difficulties. We are both warriors. Please help me out."

Rokurozaemon got angry and said, "It is a discourtesy to mention that we are both warriors. If I were in your state of

*Left: Zatoichi stick/sword. Japan.*
*Below: Iron tsuba with Sukushi dragonfly. Japan. 19th century.*

531

affairs, I'd cut my stomach open. Rather than being out of money for the road and exposing yourself to shame, cut your stomach open right where you are!" It is said that the beggar moved off.

At the time of a certain person's seppuku, when the kaishaku cut off his head, a little bit of skin was left hanging, and the head was not entirely separated from the body. The official observer said, "There's some left." The kaishaku got angry, took hold of the head, and cutting it completely off, held it above eye level and said, "Take a look!" It is said that it was rather chilling. This is a story of Master Sukeemon.

In the practice of past times, there were instances when the head flew off. It was said that it is best to cut leaving a little skin remaining so that it doesn't fly off in the direction of the verifying officials. However, at present it is best to cut clean through.

A man who had cut off fifty heads once said, "According to the head, there are cases when even the trunk of a body will bring some reaction to you. Cutting off just three heads, at first there is no reaction and you can cut well. But when you get to four or five, you feel quite a bit of reaction. At any rate, since this is a very important matter, if one always plans on bringing the head to the ground, there should be no mistakes."

When Lord Nabeshima Tsunashige was a child, Iwamura Kuranosuke was ordered to the position of elder. On one occasion Kuranosuke saw that there were gold coins before the young Tsunashige and asked the attending retainer, "For what reason have you brought these out

*Kusonuki Masashige prepares to do battle for the imperial cause. Behind, his helmet and standard bearers attend him.*

before the young master?" The attendant replied, "The master just now heard that a gift had been brought for him. He said that he had not yet seen it, so I brought it out for him." Kuranosuke scolded the man severely, saying, "To place such base things before a person of importance is the extremity of carelessness. You may also consider them something not to be put before the lord's son. Attending retainers should henceforth be very mindful of this."

Another time, when Lord Tsunashige was about twenty years old, he once went to the mansion at Naekiyama for some diversion. As the party neared the mansion, he asked for a walking stick. His sandal carrier, Miura Jibuzaemon, fashioned a stick and was about to give it to the young lord. Kuranosuke saw this, quickly took the stick from Jibuzaemon, and scolded him severely, saying, "Will you make our important young lord a sluggard? Even if he should ask for a stick, it should not be given to him. This is carelessness on the part of the attending retainer."

Jibuzaemon was later promoted to the rank of teakiyari, and Tsunetomo heard this story directly from him.

# MARTIAL ARTS TODAY

Though it represents many forms, the term *martial arts* can be defined as any discipline that involves training for combat. Further defined, martial arts are established systems designed to either defeat an opponent or to defend oneself from physical harm. The very first form of martial arts began millions of years ago, the first time two men practiced the basic skills necessary for winning in hand-to-hand combat, moves that may have been as simple as grappling or wielding sticks. Martial arts training is practiced frequently among young males in the animal kingdom, in the form of wrestling or butting heads.

The term *martial arts* is often associated with Asian culture, in large part because of the widespread awareness of the success of *karate* combat over the past half-century. While karate is the most widely known of all combat arts worldwide, the scope of such disciplines is broad, ranging from unarmed tactics such as boxing and wrestling to armed tactics such as fencing and archery. There are distinct forms of martial arts

from all continents, each with its own unique style, but these forms are universally made up of one or a combination of combat techniques such as punching, striking, wrestling, throwing, kicking, locking, pinning, and wielding weapons.

## Asian Martial Arts

The roots of Asian martial arts can be traced to a hybrid of Chinese and Indian philosophies during the first century BCE, when trade and commerce began to flourish along the Silk Road traversing the north and southwestern sections of China. In his famous treatise on military strategy, *The Art of War*, Sun Tzu spoke of the importance of training and discipline among soldiers in order to achieve peak readiness in battle. In addition to the physical training, the practice of meditation is also an integral part of many Asian martial arts. This is a direct influence of the dominance of the Buddhist religion throughout the region. China's impact on the cultures of Korea and Japan in every aspect of daily life is well

documented, and the martial arts represent one link in a long chain of influences.

Although the combat discipline of karate is often attributed to Japan, it actually originated in China, from which it supposedly spread to Japan through the island of Okinawa, where it was refined into the practices known today.

Karate and several other styles of Asian martial arts, such as *jujitsu, judo, taekwondo,* and *aikido,* found their way to United States shores in the late nineteenth century, a result of men, first railroad workers and engineers and then soldiers, returning home from tours of duty in eastern Asia and on the islands adjacent to the continent. The unarmed disciplines are now viewed as sports, and two of them, judo and taekwondo, are official competitions in the modern Olympic games.

## Samurai Sword Disciplines

Training in the use of the sword flourished for centuries during Japan's long period of unrest in the time of the samurai. Although the sword was one of the least-used weapons during battle, the two long swords, the *tachi* and the *katana,* were, and are today, considered the holy grail of samurai weaponry. Sword training was a vital part of the samurai order, and *dojo,* or schools of training, dotted the islands of Japan.

The original method for teaching the proper two-handed sword technique was *kendo,* "way of the sword." Once a samurai had become a master swordsman in kendo, he could be subsidized by a *daimyo* (feudal lord) and then set up his own school. Many schools, which varied in name and instruction according to the founder, were established during the Muromachi era (1337 to 1573), including those of Nagahide Chujo, Bunguro Hukida, Choisai Iizasa, and In-Ei. Also appearing later in this period was *kata-kenjutsu,* which involved practice between two opponents who spar in a predetermined set of steps using wooden swords. In these early days, even with wooden swords, death or serious injury often occurred during practice sessions. To permit safer practice, a *shinai* practice sword was invented in 1750 by Chuzo Nakanishi, who pieced four bamboo sections together in a way that eliminated splinters and dangerous edges. After the Meiji restoration in 1868, several of these earliest schools continued, including *iaaijutsu, kenjutsu,* and *battojutsu,* which went on to spawn other schools in the modern era.

The most famous school of sword training and practice was *shinkage ryu,* made popular by noted samurai and author Yagyu Munenori, who penned one of the most famous treatises on swordsmanship, *The Sword and the Mind.* Munenori learned the practice of shinkage ryu from his father, who operated a dojo that specialized in the techniques of this style of sword fighting.

Blending swordsmanship with Zen mind-thought, Munenori, who gained the position of sword master for the powerful Tokugawa shogunate in the early seventeenth century, is credited with defining the true heart of the samurai warrior and elevating Japanese swordsmanship to a high art (an accomplishment he possibly shares with contemporary swordsman and fellow author Miyamoto Musashi through his own work, *The Book of Five Rings.* Shinkage ryu is still practiced today in modern dojo, though not with the popularity it experienced during Munenori's time. Munenori's philosophy can be best summed up in his own words, "First see with your mind, then with your eyes, and finally with your body."

A modern version of Japanese sword training, *shinkendo,* has been developed over the past few decades. Its *kaiso* (founder), Toshishiro Obata, created a blend of many Asian martial arts disciplines, including shikage ryu and *aikido.* Students of shinkendo are initially trained in a rigid discipline of swordsmanship using wooden swords (referred to as *bokuto* or *bokken*) before they are allowed to use the official Japanese long sword that is required for the pinnacle discipline of *tameshigiri,* or sword testing. Shinkendo practitioners use only swords made in Japan.

Though swords have gone the way of the samurai, edged-weapon combat is commonly taught in most military institutions worldwide. The United States military teaches both manual self-defense and knife combat to prepare troops for real-world scenarios. As long as wars are fought with soldiers on the ground, there will always be a need for martial arts training.

*Opposite page: Sumo wrestlers. Japan. 19th century. Hand-tinted wood engraving on paper.*
*Above: Okimono of wrestlers. Japan. 19th century. Ivory.*

# FORTIFIED TEMPLES

Though overlooked in favor of the more glamorous role of the samurai, Japan's *sohei,* or warrior monks, were valiant fighters in their own right. Based in the numerous Buddhist temples and monasteries throughout Japan, the sohei were aggressive in battle either alongside the samurai or against each other. The earliest accounts of monks fighting monks date to the eighth century CE between two factions from Kofukuji and Todaiji over land disputes around Kyoto. But by the twelfth century, the sohei were being recruited by their former enemies, the samurai, to fight in major battles during one of Japan's most violent periods.

Buddhist temples (*ji*) included sacred spaces for prayer, dormitories, eating areas, and administrative work. These multipurpose facilities were often buildings of three and four floors. They were situated on high or strategic ground for the purpose of protection against invasion, a necessary fact given the long history of war in Japan, especially during the turbulent Sengoku period. Most of the fortified temples were

erected during this battle-scarred era, and an influential monk named Rennyo Shonin of the Jodo Shinshu sect is credited as the builder or restorer of many of these defensive structures. The first true fortified temple, Yoshizaki Gobo, was built under Rennyo Shonin's direction at a location on the border between Echizen and Kaga provinces overlooking Lake Kitagana near the Sea of Japan.

As these temples became more sophisticated, homes and workspaces were built on the grounds around the temples, as were strong defensive walls for added safety in an attack. A formal main gateway into the courtyard area was typical, often flanked by a pair of large statues of the *Nio*, the Buddhist deities offering spiritual protection. The main building, the *hondo*, contained, but was not limited to, the main hall of worship, depending on the design of the temple. Temples were built to last with massive timbers and had steep roof eaves that extended over the main door leading into the temple.

Doors of the *shoji* type, which consisted of a wooden frame inset with translucent paper, either hinged or sliding, were situated at the main entrance to the temple. Within, daily and funerary services were performed in the sanctuary or sacred area, and a main altar for performing rites was opposite the main entrance to the sanctuary. Flooring was of wood-plank design, and common *tatami*, or straw mats, were used as prayer rugs to make it more comfortable on the knees. A bell tower outside the main hall was a common fixture used for the calling of services but also served as a defensive alarm, and as fighting became more pervasive, watchtowers were erected to serve as lookouts for advancing military threats.

The introduction of the gunpowder firearm in the sixteenth century led to modifications to both castles and fortified temples. The walled grounds surrounding the main complexes had to be expanded to compensate for the greater range of firearms, and virtually all structures were reinforced with sturdier building materials. Structures were also built or revised to adjust for factors such as firing angles, and moats were added to slow down fast-moving troops with superior weapons. Buildings were modified to include strategically located windows and hatches for firing on incoming combatants.

The largest defensive structure of its type is the fortified cathedral of Ishiyama Honganji. This was the official headquarters of the *ikko-ikki*, a ragtag league of peasant farmers, Buddhist monks, Shinto priests, and local nobility who followed the beliefs of the Jodo Shinshu, the so-called Pure Land religion. The ikko-ikki, which had grown to a powerful force, rebelled against the repressive samurai in the fifteenth and sixteenth centuries. Their biggest adversary was the powerful and legendary samurai Oda Nobunaga. The ikko-ikki were able to repel Nobunaga

for an entire decade at Ishiyama Honganji before finally succumbing in 1580.

Initially built in 1496, Ishiyama Honganji is located at the entrance of the Yodo River on the coast of Seto Inland Sea near the early capital of Naniwa (now Osaka), Settsu province. Located at the site that is now called Osaka castle, the Honganji complex was so large it consisted of several layers of stone-surface moats with isolated islands, which held as many as eighty to one hundred domestic and occupational structures each. Only the moats of Ishiyama Honganji remain today, but Osaka castle, scene of one of the last great battles of the Sengoku period, stands as one of Japan's most popular tourist attractions. Many of Japan's fortified temples are open for visitation, including Yoshizaki Gobo, Shorenji, Kofukuji, and Todaiji.

*Above: Oriental Buddha. Kita-Kamakura, Japan.*
*Opposite page: Golden Temple, Kyoto, Japan.*

# From the Ninth Chapter

When Shimomura Shoun was on service at the castle, Lord Naoshige said, "How wonderful it is that Katsushige is so vigorous and powerful for his age. In wrestling with his peers he even beat those who are older than he is."

Shoun replied, "Even though I'm an old man, I'll bet I'm best at seated wrestling." So saying, he jerked up Katsushige and threw him so forcefully that it hurt. He then said, "To be prideful about your strength while your mettle is not yet established is likely to bring you shame in the midst of people. You are weaker than you look." Then he withdrew.

At the time when Matsuda Yohei was an intimate friend of Ishii Jinku's, there developed some bad feelings between the former and Nozoe Jinbei. Yohei sent word to Jinbei saying, "Please come and I will settle this matter once and for all." Then he and Jinku set out together and, coming to the Yamabushi mansion at Kihara, they crossed the only bridge there was and destroyed it. Talking over the circumstances of the discord, they examined them from all sides and found no reason to fight. But when they decided to turn around and go home, there was, of course, no bridge.

While they were looking for an appropriate way of crossing the moat, the men whom the two had challenged could be seen approaching stealthily. Yohei and Jinku saw this and said, "We have passed the point of no return, and may as well fight rather than be disgraced at a later date." The battle lasted for some time. Seriously wounded, Yohei fell down between two fields. Jinbei also received a deep wound, and with blood flowing into his eyes was unable to find Yohei. While Jinbei thus searched about blindly, Yohei was able to hold him off from his prone position and in the end cut him down. But when he attempted to deliver the finishing blow, having no strength left in his hand, he pierced Jinbei's neck by pushing the sword with his foot.

*Carved panel representing the Empress Jingo Kogo and her prime minister Takemonchi. Japan. 3rd century.*

At this point, friends arrived and accompanied Yohei back. After his wounds healed he was ordered to commit *seppuku*. At that time he called his friend Jinku, and they drank a farewell cup together.

Okubo Toemon of Shioda ran a wine shop for Nabeshima Kenmotsu. Lord Okura, the son of Nabeshima Kai no kami, was a cripple and confined indoors in a place called Mine. He harbored wrestlers and liked rowdies. The wrestlers would often go to nearby villages and cause disturbances. One time they went to Toemon's place, drank sake, and talked unreasonably, bringing Toemon into an argument. He met them with a halberd, but as there were two of them, he was cut down.

His son, Kannosuke, was fifteen years old and was in the midst of studies at the Jozeiji when he was informed of the incident. Galloping off, he took a short sword about sixteen inches in length, joined combat with the two big men, and in a short time finished them both off. Although Kannosuke received thirteen wounds, he recovered. Later he was called Doko and is said to have become very adept at massage.

It is said that Tokunaga Kichizaemon repeatedly complained, "I've grown so old that now, even if there were to be a battle, I wouldn't be able to do anything. Still, I would like to die by galloping into the midst of the enemy and being struck down and killed. It would be a shame to do nothing more than to die in one's bed."

It is said that the priest Gyojaku heard this when he was an acolyte. Gyojaku's master was the priest Yemen, who was Kichizaemon's youngest child.

When Sagara Kyuma was requested to become a chief retainer, he said to Nabeshima Heizaemon, "For some reason I have been increasingly well treated by the master and now have been requested to take a high rank. Not having a good retainer, my affairs are liable to be in disorder. It is my request that you give me your retainer, Takase Jibusaemon." Heizaemon listened to him and consented, saying, "It is very gratifying that you have kept an eye on my retainer. I will therefore do as you ask."

But when he related this to Jibusaemon, the latter said, "I should reply directly to Master Kyuma." He then went to

*Above: Saigetaka on kake (sword stand). Inlaid wood. Japan.*

appeared by the hundreds of thousands, the Japanese troops were amazed and watched with bated breath. Lord Naoshige said, "Well, well. That's a great number of men! I wonder how many hundreds of thousands there are?"

Jin'emon said, "In Japan, for something that's numberless we say 'as many as the hairs on a three-year-old calf.' This would certainly live up to the number of hairs on a three-year-old calf!" It is said that everybody laughed and regained their spirits.

Later, Lord Katsushige was hunting at Mount Shiroishi and told Nakano Matabei about this. "Except for your father who spoke in such a way, there was no one who said even a word."

Nakano Jin'emon constantly said, "A person who serves when treated kindly by the master is not a retainer. But one who serves when the master is being heartless and unreasonable is a retainer. You should understand this principle well."

When Yamamoto Jin'emon was eighty years old, he became ill. At one point, he seemed to be on the verge of groaning, and someone said to him, "You'll feel better if you groan. Go ahead."

Kyuma's place and talked with him. Jibusaemon told Kyuma, "I know it is a great honor that you have thought well of me and have made this request. But a retainer is a person who cannot change masters. As you are of high rank, if I were to become your retainer my life would be replete, but that repleteness would be a vexation to me. Because Heizaemon is of low rank and is hard pressed, we live by eating cheap rice gruel. Yet that is sweet enough. Please think this over."

Kyuma was extremely impressed.

A certain man went off somewhere and, on returning home late at night, found that a strange man had slipped into the house and was committing adultery with his wife. He thereupon killed the man. He then broke down a wall and propped up a bale of rice, and by this arrangement submitted to the authorities that he had killed a thief. Thus it went without mishap. After some time had passed he divorced his wife and the affair was finished.

At New Year's in the third year of Keicho at a place in Korea called Yolsan, when the armies of the Ming

But he replied, "Such is not the case. The name of Yamamoto Jin'emon is known by everyone, and I have shown up well throughout a whole lifetime. To let people hear my groaning voice in my last moments would never do." It is said that he did not let out a groan to the very end.

A certain son of Mori Monbei got into a fight and returned home wounded. Asked by Monbei, "What did you do to your opponent?" his son replied, "I cut him down."

*Left: Praying mantis katana.*

When Monbei asked, "Did you deliver the coup de grâce?" his son replied, "Indeed I did."

Then Monbei said, "You have certainly done well, and there is nothing to regret. Now, even if you fled you would have to commit seppuku anyway. When your mood improves, commit seppuku, and rather than die by another's hand, you can die by your father's." And soon after he performed kaishaku for his son.

A man in the same group as Aiura Genzaemon committed some nefarious deed, and so the group leader gave him a note, condemning him to death, which was to be taken to Genzaemon's place. Genzaemon perused the note and then said to the man, "It says here that I should kill you, so I will do away with you on the eastern bank. Previously you have practiced such things as swordsmanship. Now fight with all you've got."

The man replied, "I will do as you say," and with Genzaemon alone accompanying him, they left the house. They had gone about twenty yards along the edge of the moat when a retainer of Genzaemon's yelled out, "Hey, Hey!" from the other side. As Genzaemon was turning around, the condemned man attacked him with his sword. Genzaemon ducked backward, drew his sword, and cut the man down. He then returned home.

He put the clothes he had been wearing at that time into a chest and locked them up, never showing them to anyone for the rest of his life. After he died the clothes were examined, and it was seen that they were rent. This was told by his son, Genzaemon.

While Fukahori Magoroku was still living as a dependent second son, he once went hunting at Fukahori, and his retainer, mistaking him for a wild boar in the darkness of the undergrowth, fired the rifle, wounding him in the knee and causing him to fall from a great height. The retainer, greatly upset, stripped himself to the waist and was about to commit seppuku. Magoroku said, "You can cut your stomach open later. I don't feel well, so bring me some water to drink." The retainer ran about and obtained some water for his master to drink and in the process calmed down. After that the retainer was again about to commit seppuku, but Magoroku forcibly stopped him. Upon returning they checked in with the man on guard, and Magoroku asked his father, Kanzaemon, to forgive the retainer.

Kanzaemon said to the retainer, "It was an unexpected mistake, so do not be worried. There is no need for reservation. Continue with your work."

A man by the name of Takagi got into an argument with three farmers in the neighborhood, was soundly beaten out in the fields, and returned home. His wife said to him, "Haven't you forgotten about the matter of death?" "Definitely not!" he replied.

His wife then retorted, "At any rate, a man dies only once. Of the various ways of dying—dying of disease, being cut down in battle, seppuku, or being beheaded—to die ignominiously would be a shame," and went outside. She soon returned, carefully put the two children to bed, prepared some torches, dressed herself for battle after nightfall, and then said, "When I went out to survey the scene a bit earlier, it seemed that the three men went into one place for a discussion. Now is the right time. Let's go quickly!" So saying, they went out with the husband in the lead, burning torches and wearing short swords. They broke into their opponents' place and dispersed them, both husband and wife slashing about and killing two of the men and wounding the other. The husband was later ordered to commit seppuku.

# MODERN-DAY SAMURAI
## TOSHISHIRO OBATA

Living samurai are rare in modern times, but there are still traditionally trained swordsmen who carry on the discipline. One such "living samurai" is Toshishiro Obata, the founder of the modern-day martial arts style known as *shinkendo*. Born in Gunma prefecture in 1948 of samurai family lineage, Obata was raised in the countryside, where he gained an understanding of body mechanics at a young age through outdoor activities such as chopping firewood, climbing trees, and running through nearby mountains.

At the age of eighteen, Obata left his home and moved to Tokyo where he began his quest for expertise in the Japanese martial arts. It was at this time that he applied and was accepted as an *uchideshi* (live-in student) and stayed for seven years at the Yoshinkan *dojo* under its founder, Shioda Gozo. Over the following years, Obata studied many disciplines in both full-contact and weapon-oriented martial arts, including *aikido* and *shinkage ryu*. Extensive training in a multitude of martial arts disciplines led Obata to establish the International Shinkendo Federation, one of the world's largest swordsmanship-based organizations.

### Shinkendo's Samurai Roots

Obata descibes Shinkendo as a modern martial art inspired by more than 1,200 years of samurai history and *bushi damashii*, "warrior spirit." From a physical standpoint, shinkendo's techniques are taken from the practical methods once used by the samurai. However, in addition to this catalog of techniques, there are also a myriad of deeper teachings that can be discovered through a *shugyo* (serious or austere) approach to practice.

In feudal times swordsmanship was considered the core of the samurai martial arts, just as the body's torso is the core of a person. Other military arts such as spearing, archery, and unarmed combat were subsets of this core art, in the same way that legs, arms, and fingers are subsets of the body. With the exception of foot soldiers (usually recruited from villages and given minimal training), all persons of the samurai class were trained in swordsmanship and would also specialize in archery or some other art.

The goal of shinkendo is to develop the mind and body while learning a significant cultural art, and then to apply these teachings and philosophies in everyday life. Serious training can enable one to discover the correct and proper path, using life skills found in the deeper levels of instruction. The study of swordsmanship in modern times focuses not on simply "ways of killing" but, rather, serves as the founding principle and path to understanding Japan's samurai mindset, spirit, and *bushido*, "way of the warrior." In the study of shinkendo, the philosophy and strategy of the art is of paramount importance.

Practitioners are divided into *seito* (regular student level), *deshi* (certain serious, direct students), and *kyakubun* (senior-ranked instructors of other styles who would like to study). Students are first trained in the basics of swordsmanship using wooden practice swords before they are allowed to adopt the official Japanese long sword, which

*Toshishiro Obata (below and right) trained in shinkage ryu, aikido, toyama ryu, and a host of other martial arts fields before developing and founding the International Shinkendo Federation. Students are trained using wooden swords until they reach the top level, when they are allowed to practice tameshigiri (sword-testing) with a live sword.*

Basic shinkendo training and practice, or tachiuchi, is done with wooden swords called bokuto. Shown here is the jodan kamae attack position, at right, and the sei gedan guard position at left.

At right the aggressor executes a jodan tate kiri strike, while the figure at left blocks with a kasumi position.

The aggressor executes a straight thrust tsuki, and the figure at left defends with a downward gedan suppressing block.

The figure at right is attacking with a straight thrust, or tsuki, move; the combatant on the left counters with a chudan side block.

is used in the advanced discipline of sword testing, known as *tameshigiri*.

The teaching of shinkendo involves five subdisciplines, the *gorin goho gogyo*, which must be accomplished by the student to become a master of the art: *suburi* (swinging and body movement), *battoho* (drawing methods), *tanrengata* (solo body form), *tachiuchi* (sparring), and *tameshigiri* (test-cutting).

The highlights of any shinkendo event are the tameshigiri demonstrations, where rolled straw mats are deftly sliced in quick swings of the sword in multiple or consecutive cuts. The International Shinkendo Federation, headquartered in Los Angeles, California, has *dojo* in many states, as well as branches in Canada, Europe, and Singapore.

Swordmaster Toshishiro Obata executes a left nitoken kesa cut using two swords simultaneously.

*Training in shinkendo is a highly regimented process in which students learn on practice swords before they are allowed to handle a full-fledged Japanese sword with a sharp metal blade. Because safety is of utmost importance, special practice swords have been designed to minimize the danger of a student becoming injured during training. For initial and intermediate training students practice using wooden bokuto or bokken practice swords. Regular and heavyweight katana-shaped versions are made of Japanese white oak, and some are fitted with a leather tsuba to protect the hand and fingers. Another style of practice sword, the tachi uchi, is made of Chinese waxwood, which is dense and facilitates vigorous sparring exercises. Advanced shinkendo practitioners also use wooden swords to practice advanced techniques.*

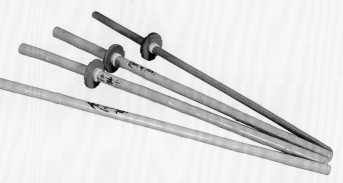

# *From the Tenth Chapter*

There was a certain retainer of Ikeda Shingen's who started an argument with a man, grappled him to the ground, thrashed him soundly, and trampled on him until his companions ran up and pulled them apart. The elders conferred over this and said, "The man who was trampled should be punished." Shingen heard this and said, "A fight is something that goes to the finish. A man who forgets the Way of the Samurai and does not use his sword will be forsaken by the gods and Buddhas. As an example to subsequent retainers, both men should be crucified." The men who had pulled them apart were banished.

In Yui Shosetsu's military instructions, "The Way of the Three Ultimates," there is a passage on the character of karma. He received an oral teaching of about eighteen chapters concerning the Greater Bravery and the Lesser Bravery. He neither wrote them down nor committed them to memory but rather forgot them completely. Then, in facing real situations, he acted on impulse and the things that he had learned became wisdom of his own. This is the character of karma.

When faced with a crisis, if one puts some spittle on his earlobe and exhales deeply through his nose, he will overcome anything at hand. This is a secret matter. Furthermore, when experiencing a rush of blood to the head, if one puts spittle on the upper part of one's ear, it will soon go away.

Tzu Ch'an was on the point of death when someone asked him how to govern the country. He replied:

"There is nothing that surpasses ruling with benevolence. However, to put into practice enough benevolent governing to rule the country is difficult. To do this lukewarmly will result in neglect. If governing with benevolence is difficult, then it is best to govern strictly. To govern strictly means to be strict before things have arisen, and to do things in such a way that evil will not arise. To be strict after the evil has arisen is like laying a snare. There are few people who will make mistakes with fire after having

*Opposite page: Cavalry in Winter, in the style of Yoshitoshi (1839–1892). Japan. 19th century. Woodblock print.*

once been burned. Of people who regard water lightly, many have been drowned."

Fukae Angen accompanied an acquaintance of his to the priest Tesshu of Osaka, and at first said privately to the priest, "This man aspires to study Buddhism and hopes to receive your teaching. He is a man of rather high determination."

Soon after the interview the priest said, "Angen is a man who does harm to others. He said that this man is a good man, but wherein is his goodness?" There was no goodness visible to Tesshu's eyes. It is not a good idea to praise people carelessly. When praised, both wise and foolish become prideful. To praise is to do harm.

A certain person said, "When a castle is being surrendered, as long as there are one or two men within it who are determined to hold on, the defending forces will not be of one accord, and in the end no one will hold the castle.

"In the taking of the castle, if when the man who is to receive it approaches and the one or two men who are determined to hold on to it lightly fire on him from the shadows, the man will be alarmed and the battle will be on. In such a case, even though it is unwillingly done, the castle will have to be stormed. This is called being forced to besiege a castle by those besieged."

The Buddhist priest Ryozan wrote down some generalities concerning Takanobu's battles. A certain priest saw this and criticized him, saying, "It is inappropriate for a priest to write about a military commander. No matter how successful his writing style may be, since he is not acquainted with military things, he is liable to be mistaken in understanding a famous general's mind. It is irreverent to pass on misconceptions concerning a famous general to later generations."

A certain person said, "In the Saint's mausoleum there is a poem that goes:

If in one's heart
He follows the path of sincerity,
Though he does not pray
Will not the gods protect him?
What is this path of sincerity?"

A man answered him by saying, "You seem to like poetry. I will answer you with a poem:

As everything in this world is but a shame,
Death is the only sincerity.

It is said that becoming as a dead man in one's daily living is the following of the path of sincerity."

If you cut a face lengthwise, urinate on it, and trample on it with straw sandals, it is said that the skin will come off. This was heard by the priest Gyojaku when he was in Kyoto. It is information to be treasured.

One of Matsudaira Sagami no kami's retainers went to Kyoto on a matter of debt collection and took up lodgings by renting living quarters in a townhouse. One day while standing out front watching the people go by, he heard a passerby say, "They say that Lord Matsudaira's men are involved in a fight right now." The retainer thought, "How worrisome that some of my companions are involved in a fight. There are some men to relieve those at Edo staying here. Perhaps these are the men involved." He asked the passerby of the location, but when he arrived out of breath, his companions had already been cut down and their adversaries were at the point of delivering the coup de grâce. He quickly let out a yell, cut the two men down, and returned to his lodgings.

This matter was made known to an official of the shogunate, and the man was called up before him and questioned. "You gave assistance in your companions' fight and thus disregarded the government's ordinance. This is true beyond a doubt, isn't it?"

The man replied, "I am from the country, and it is difficult for me to understand everything that Your Honor is saying. Would you please repeat that?"

The official got angry and said, "Is there

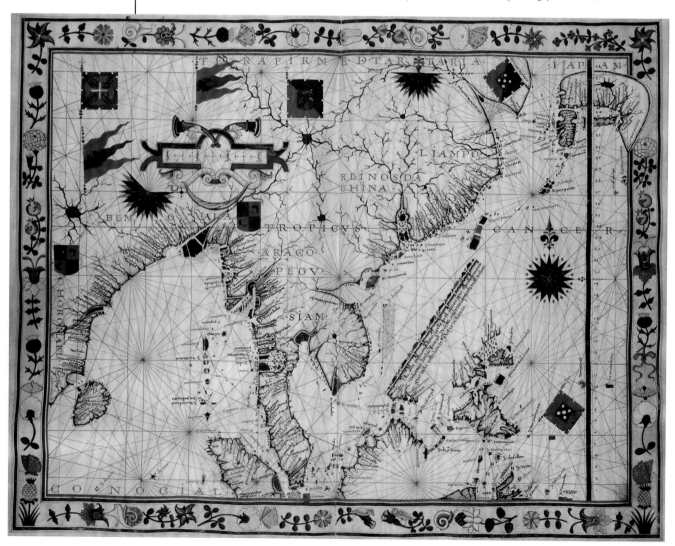

something wrong with your ears? Didn't you abet a fight, commit bloodshed, disregard the government's ordinance, and break the law?"

The man then replied, "I have at length understood what you are saying. Although you say that I have broken the law and disregarded the government's ordinance, I have by no means done so. The reason for this is that all living things value their lives, and this goes without saying for human beings. I, especially, value my life. However, I thought that to hear a rumor that one's friends are involved in a fight and to pretend not to hear this is not to preserve the Way of the Samurai, so I ran to the place of action. To shamelessly return home after seeing my friends struck down would surely have lengthened my life, but this too would be disregarding the Way. In observing the Way, one will throw away his own precious life. Thus, in order to preserve the Way of the Samurai and not to disregard the samurai Ordinances, I quickly threw away my life at that place. I beg that you execute me immediately."

The official was very impressed and later dismissed the matter, communicating to Lord Matsudaira, "You have a very able samurai in your service. Please treasure him."

This is among the sayings of the priest Banker. "Not to borrow the strength of another, nor to rely on one's own strength; to cut off past and future thoughts, and not to live within the everyday mind...then the Great Way is right before one's eyes."

Lord Soma's family genealogy, called the *Chiken marokashi*, was the best in Japan. One year when his mansion suddenly caught fire and was burning to the ground, Lord Soma said, "I feel no regret about the house and all its furnishings, even if they burn to the very last piece, because they are things that can be replaced later on. I only regret that I was unable to take out the genealogy, which is my family's most precious treasure."

There was one samurai among those attending him who said, "I will go in and take it out."

Lord Soma and the others all laughed and said, "The house is already engulfed in flames.

How are you going to take it out?"

Now this man had never been loquacious, nor had he been particularly useful, but being a man who did things from beginning to end, he was engaged as an attendant. At this point he said, "I have never been of use to my master because I'm so careless, but I have lived resolved that someday my life should be of use to him. This seems to be that time." And he leapt into the flames.

After the fire had been extinguished the master said, "Look for his remains. What a pity!"

Looking everywhere, they found his burnt corpse in the garden adjacent to the living quarters. When they turned it over, blood flowed out of the stomach. The man had cut open his stomach and placed the genealogy inside, and it was not damaged at all. From this time on it was called the "Blood Genealogy."

According to a certain person's story, "In the tradition of the I Ching, it is a mistake to think that it is something for divination. Its essence is non-divination. This can be seen by the fact that the Chinese character 'I' is read as 'change.' Although one divines good fortune, if he does evil it will become bad fortune. And although he divines bad fortune, if he does good it will become good fortune.

"Confucius' saying 'By setting myself to the task for many years and in the end learning change [I], I should make no big mistakes' is not a matter of learning the I Ching. It means by studying the essence of change and conducting oneself for many years in the Way of Good, one should make no mistakes."

Hirano Gonbei was one of the Men of Seven Spears who advanced straight up the hill at the battle of Shizugadake. At a later date he was invited to become one of Lord Ieyasu's hatamoto. Once he was being entertained at Master Hosekawa's. The master said, "Master Gonbei's bravery is not a hidden matter in Japan. It is truly a shame that such a man of bravery has been placed in a low rank such as you are in now. This must be contrary to your wishes. If you were to become a retainer of mine, I would give you half the domain."

*Left: This shallow circular hat (jingasa) was worn by samurai on official outings. On the crown are inscribed three characters that read "Move slowly like a forest," a passage from the classic military tactics treatise written by Sun Mu of ancient China. Samurai's shallow hat. Japan. 1615–1868. Lacquer on leather and paper.*

*Iron Sukashi tsuba with butterfly design. Japan. 19th century.*

# ZEN BUDDHISM AND REINCARNATION

The samurai monk Yamamoto Tsunetomo, in the final paragraphs of *Hagakure,* affirms his belief in reincarnation; after dying, he asserts, he prefers "not to become a Buddha," a level of existence higher than his current status. Instead, he intends to use his own will to return "to help manage the affairs" of his lord's clan, the Nabeshima, coming back at his same level of existence even as many as "seven times" over, if necessary. His faith in this aspect of his own spiritual journey appears unwavering.

Tsunetomo's eighteenth-century version of Zen Buddhism had evolved from a point more than a millennium earlier, when an Indian-based form of Buddhism crossed from China into Japan. From within this complex belief system, which focused on self-knowledge through meditation, the theory of reincarnation may have been one facet that the common folk of an unrefined time could grasp, becasuse it contained a powerful lesson in ethics and morality. An uneducated villager would find it easy to understand and to fear the notion, in its most simplistic terms, that if he persisted in animal-like behavior, he would be reborn into the animal world. This example shows why it is said that Buddha left tens of thousands of teachings to reflect the diversity of the people he encountered, so that his message could be tailored to the spiritual and mental capabilities of his followers.

However, the premise of reincarnation was not that elementary. The idea of the transmigration of the soul (the soul leaving one physical entity to enter another) did not have a place in Zen Buddhism. Instead, reincarnation was built around an intricate design of karmic order. The law of *karma,* from a Sanskrit word meaning "act," was the law of cause and effect. In essence, what a person does in this life would determine his next life; all of a person's acts were causes, and all that he experienced were actually effects arising from those causes. The moral energy of any action would be sustained until manifested as an influence on the present life or accumulated among other similar influences to reappear in a later life. In this way, the sum of the actions he projected and the influences and experiences he received represented the whole of his karma.

As Buddha or his disciples might have approached it metaphorically, a person's thoughts, words, and deeds might be considered as sown seeds, with good acts sowing seeds of future happiness and bad acts sowing seeds of future misery. If a person was suffering, it wasn't because he was being punished; it was because he had amassed the moral energy of many unrighteous acts in earlier lives, or he had sown too many bad seeds. However, he could be confident that he had the freedom to reverse his karma over a series of lifetimes by purifying his acts in an attempt to gain enlightenment. But even more immediately, by changing his present ways, he could improve his prospects of happiness in the limbic state between the end of his current life and the beginning of his next.

As the words of Tsunetomo imply, the traditions of Zen Buddhism offered a hierarchical feature in its promotion of six distinct realms of existence. If Buddha himself were thought to solely occupy the topmost realm, with lesser Buddhas or demigods below him, then humans would fall midway among the rankings, above animals, the "hungry ghosts," and (in the most basic sense) hellions. The more learned Buddhists of older times would have known that these realms stood not for physical entities but for psychological states of mind, a subtlety that might have been lost on a less educated individual. To further indicate the perplexing quality of reincarnation for the typical peasant of feudal Japan, any one of the six realms was thought to hold within itself the other five, so that a human would at once be capable of both selfless and selfish acts, and even a Buddha would be capable of identifying with and thus understanding the most depraved being in existence. Again, perhaps Yamamoto Tsunetomo felt certain that he had gathered enough untainted moral energy to propel himself into a higher realm of existence, but he just chose not to do so.

Regardless of the nuances of reincarnation, the concept was a vividly potent one for medieval Japanese minds. The end of the Gempei War between the Minamoto and Taira clans came around 1185, when the two fought in an extraordinary sea battle that resulted in the defeat of the Taira, also known as the Heiki. In what amounted to a mass suicide, all of the remaining Heiki nobles jumped into the sea to drown themselves and avoid being taken as captives. (Even grandmother of the young Heiki emperor flung herself and the child overboard.) In the waters where the battle occurred,

in the straits between the islands of Kyushu and Honshu, was a type of shellfish that would come to be called the Heiki crab or mask crab. When the locals realized that the body of this particular crab had a pattern of bumps and ridges that produced what to them seemed a samurai-like scowl, they deemed the species to be the sacred reincarnation of the Heiki warriors and would no longer eat it. Even today, a fisherman who captures a Heiki crab will bow respectfully to it as he pulls it from his traps and tosses it back into the sea.

*Opposite page: Sazai Hall, Five Hundred Raken [Temple], from the series One Hundred Views of Famous Places In Edo. Ando Hiroshige (1797–1858). Above: The War-Lords of Japan: Prince Morinaga leads soldier monks into battle. Dan Escott. 1928–1987. 20th century.*

*Face mask (mempo), Masanobu or Nara style. Japan. The mempo was an essential component of the samurai suit of armor and protected the lower face and neck. Other pieces, called shikoro or nowdawa, were additionally used to protect the vulnerable neck area.*

Giving no answer at all, Gonbei suddenly got up from his seat, went out to the veranda, stood facing the house, and urinated. Then he said, "If I were the master's retainer, it would never do to urinate from here."

When the priest Daiyu from Sanshu was making a sick call at a certain place, he was told, "The man has just now died." Daiyu said, "Such a thing shouldn't have happened at this time. Didn't this occur from insufficient treatment? What a shame!"

Now the doctor happened to be there at that time and heard what was said from the other side of the *shoji*. He got extraordinarily angry and came out and said, "I heard Your Reverence say that the man died from insufficient treatment. Since I am a rather bungling doctor, this is probably true. I have heard that a priest embodies the power of the Buddhist Law. Let me see you bring this dead man back to life, for without such evidence Buddhism is worthless."

Daiyu was put out by this, but he felt that it would be unpardonable for a priest to put a blemish on Buddhism, so he said, "I will indeed show you how to bring his life back by prayer. Please wait a moment. I must go prepare myself," and returned to the temple. Soon he came back and sat in meditation next to the corpse. Pretty soon the dead man began to breathe and then completely revived. It is said that he lived on for another half a year. As this was something told directly to the priest Tannen, there is nothing mistaken about it.

When telling of the way he prayed, Daiyu said, "This is something not practiced in our sect, so I didn't know of any way of prayer. I simply set my heart for the sake of the Buddhist Law, returned to the temple, sharpened a short sword that had been given as an offering to the temple, and put it in my robe. Then I faced the dead man and prayed, 'If the strength of the Buddhist Law exists, come back to life immediately.' Since I was thus committed, if he hadn't come back to life, I was resolved to the point of cutting open my stomach and dying, embracing the corpse."

When Yamamoto Gorozaemon went to the priest Tetsugyo in Edo wanting to hear something about Buddhism, Tetsugyo said, "Buddhism gets rid of the discriminating mind. It is nothing more than this. I can give you an illustration in terms of the warrior. The Chinese character for 'cowardice' is made by adding the character for 'meaning' to the character radical for 'mind.' Now 'meaning' is 'discrimination,' and when a man attaches discrimination to his true mind, he becomes a coward. In the Way of the Samurai can a man be courageous when discrimination arises? I suppose you can get the idea from this."

According to what one of the elders said, taking an enemy on the battlefield is like a hawk taking a bird. Even though it enters into the midst of a thousand of them, it gives no attention to any bird other than the one that it has first marked.

Moreover, what is called a *tezuke no kubi* is a head that one has taken after having made the declaration, "I will take that warrior wearing such and such armor."

In the Kiyogunkan one person said, "When facing the enemy, I feel as if I have just entered darkness. Because of this I get heavily wounded. Although you have fought with many famous men, you have never been wounded. Why is that?"

The other man answered, "When I have faced the enemy, of course it is like being in the dark. But if at that time I tranquilize my mind, it becomes like a night lit by a pale moon. If I begin my attack from that point, I feel as though I will not be wounded." This is the situation at the moment of truth.

In order to study medicine Eguchi Toan went to old Yoshida Ichian's place in the Bancho area of Edo. At that time, there was in the neighborhood a teacher of swordsmanship, to whom he used to go for training from time to time. There was a *ronin* pupil there who one day came up to Toan and said as a parting remark, "I am now going to realize a long-cherished ambition, one I have had for many years. I am informing you of this because you have always been friendly to me." Then he walked away. Toan felt uneasy about this, and when he followed him, he could see a man wearing a braided hat coming from the opposite direction.

Now the sword teacher was about eight or ten yards ahead of the ronin, and in passing by the man with the hat, he soundly struck the man's scabbard with his own. When the man looked around, the ronin knocked off the man's hat and announced in a loud voice that his purpose was revenge. With the man's attention being distracted by the confusion, he was easily cut down. A tremendous amount of congratulations came from the nearby mansions and townhouses. It is said that they even brought out money for him. This was a favorite story of Toan's.

Once when the priest Ungo of Matsushima was passing through the mountains at night, he was set upon by mountain bandits. Ungo said, "I am a man of this area, not a pilgrim. I have no money at all, but you can have these clothes if you like. Please spare my life."

The bandits said, "Well, our efforts have been in vain. We don't need anything like clothes," and passed on. They had gone about two hundred yards when Ungo turned back and called to them, "I have broken the commandment against lying. In my confusion I forgot that I had one piece of silver in my moneybag. I am truly regretful I said that I had nothing at all. I have it here now, so please take it." The mountain bandits were deeply impressed, cut off their hair right there, and became his disciples.

In Edo four or five hatamoto gathered together one night for a game of go. At one point one of them got up to go to the toilet, and while he was gone an argument broke out. One man was cut down, the lights were extinguished, and the place was in an uproar. When the man came running back, he yelled, "Everybody calm down! This is really over nothing at all. Put the lamps back on and let me handle this." After the lamps had been relighted and everyone had calmed down, the man suddenly struck off the head of the other man involved in the argument. He then said, "My luck as a samurai having run out, I was not present at the fight. If this were seen as cowardice, I would be ordered to commit *seppuku*. Even if that didn't happen, I would have no excuse if it were said that I had fled to the toilet, and I would still have no recourse other than seppuku. I have done this thing because I thought I would die having cut down an adversary rather than die having shamed myself alone." When the shogun heard of this matter, he praised the man.

Once a group of ten blind masseuses were traveling together in the mountains, and when they began to pass along the top of a precipice, they all became very cautious, their legs shook, and they were in general struck with terror. Just then the leading man stumbled and fell of the cliff. Those that were left all wailed, "Ahh, ahh! How piteous!" But the masseuse who had fallen yelled up from below, "Don't be afraid. Although I fell, it was nothing. I am now rather at ease. Before falling I kept thinking 'What will I do if I fall?' and there was no end to my anxiety. But now I've settled down. If the rest of you want to be at ease, fall quickly!"

Hojo Awa no kami once gathered together his disciples in the martial arts and called in a physiognomist, who was popular in Edo at the time, to have him determine whether they were brave men or cowards. He had them see the man one by one, telling them, "If he determines 'bravery,' you should strive all the more. If it is 'cowardice,' you should strive by throwing away your life. It's something that you're born with, so there's no shame in it."

Hirose Denzaemon was then about twelve or thirteen years old. When he sat down in front of the physiognomist, he said in a bristling voice, "If you read cowardice in me, I'll cut you down with a single blow!"

When there is something to be said, it is better if it is said right away. If it is said later, it will sound like an excuse. Moreover, it is occasionally good to really overwhelm your opponent. Also, in addition to having spoken sufficiently, it is the highest sort of victory to teach your opponent something that will be to his benefit. This is in accordance with the Way.

The priest Ryoi said: The samurai of old were mortified by the idea of dying in bed; they hoped only to die on the battlefield. A priest, too, will be unable to fulfill the Way unless he is of this disposition. The man who shuts himself away and avoids the company of men is a coward. Only evil thoughts allow one to imagine that something good can be done by shutting oneself away. For even if one does some good thing by shutting himself away, he will be unable to keep the way open for future generations by promulgating the clan traditions.

Takeda Shingen's retainer, Amari Bizen no kami, was killed in action, and his son, Tozo, at the age of eighteen took over his father's position as an armed horseman attached to a general. Once a certain man in his group received a deep wound, and since the blood would not clot, Tozo ordered him to drink the feces of a red-haired horse mixed with water. The wounded man said, "Life is dear to me. How can I drink horse feces?" Tozo heard this and said, "What an admirably brave warrior! What you say is reasonable. However, the basic meaning of loyalty requires us to preserve our lives and gain victory for our master on the battlefield. Well, then, I'll drink some for you." Then he drank some himself and handed over the cup to the man who took the medicine gratefully and recovered.

Cast-iron helmet inlaid with gold and silver, a technique known as komai. Japan. 19th century. The precious metals incorporated into the helmet design were indicative of the rank and power of its wearer.

# THE BUDDHIST SAMURAI'S COMMITMENT TO DEATH

The mind of the early Japanese warrior still presents something of a puzzle. Aside from the two oldest chronicles, the more mythical *Kojiki* of the seventh century CE and the more factual *Nihongi* of the next century, the *Hagakure,* which appeared a full millennium later, stands as one of the first personalized accounts of the warrior. Produced between those writings were the *gunki monogatari,* the "war tales" of the Kamakura and Muromachi periods. Based on historical records, oral narratives, and diaries, these tales invested the samurai with distinctive traits, including thoughts and feelings that reflected individual worldviews. However, in spite of what has been gathered from the outside stories of all of these original sources, one looming question remains unanswered: how was the samurai able to accommodate the contradictory dictates of both *bushido* and Buddhism?

The answer might be found in a look at the warrior's mindset regarding death. Within that mindset was lodged a resolution to die instead of just a willingness to die. If the meaning of life was simply death, as Yamamoto Tsunetomo suggested in *Hagakure,* accepting that fact required a hardened resolve, which could only be accomplished through daily contemplative examination of the self, or the meditation that is characteristic of Zen Buddhism. In correlation with the acceptance of death would have come another Zen precept, that of the need to live in the moment as necessitated by the very impermanence of life *(mujo)*. This precept is symbolized by the cherry blossom, whose petals fall at the peak of their beauty, the height of their existence.

These ideas are not as dark as they seem. Resigned to the prospect of being cut down at any given moment, the samurai, in his intention to die, was actually liberated—in action, in attachments, and in responsibility.

In action, the samurai, trained to the point of No-Mind in technique and toughened in resolve, found himself free of

calculation; with no conscious decision-making called for, his methods in battle were instinctive and impulsive. In direct opposition to this was the deliberative warrior, who was thought to be a coward because he presumably was torn between life and death, knowing that death was the only true option for a *bushi*. Such spontaneity of action, with disinclination toward deductive reasoning, was part of the essential Zen experience.

Regarding attachments, much discussion has been given to the warrior's loyalty to his lord (although little has been said about a lord's reciprocal obligation to his retainer). In fact, the samurai's devotion to his lord, because it was an inescapable given, could also be another type of freedom. According to his own conscience, he was at liberty to speak his mind and was even encouraged to oppose a ruler whose ideas and plans might be detrimental to that ruler's interests. As for the samurai and his own interests, he strove to hold personal desires and relationships secondary to his death resolve. And in holding himself in reserve from human attachments, he, like the Zen monk, would be in keeping with the principle of repudiation as a step toward enlightenment.

In terms of responsibility, the death resolve extricates the samurai from any blame for the outcome of his missions. Whether the results of his actions were deemed to be a success or a failure was of little importance; what was of primary importance was whether his actions were carried out with strength of intention and in accepted form. Why he fought or why he died would not have been judged, even

were he known to be of inferior skill and intelligence, but the quality of his fighting or his dying would have been examined unrelentingly. Such a mission, carried out with determination and with a certain refinement, would have been consistent with the Zen aesthetic sensibility.

The samurai may have been liberated to some extent by Zen Buddhism, which has been described as a religion of the will. But when truth is based on an intuitive and individualistic sense of what is right, as this definition implies, that rightness has no social or ethical standard by which it is held accountable. In other words, the samurai was perhaps free to attach himself to whatever purpose he might choose, according to his own sense of rightness.

One war tale from the *Heike monogatari* illustrates this point of ambiguity. During the Gempei War, the life of Yukishige, a young Minamoto samurai, was spared by an older Taira warrior, who thought the boy resembled the warrior's own son. Unmoved by the display of fatherly affection, Yukishige showed no mercy when he cold-bloodedly murdered the man who had refrained from killing him. In this case, the boy's sense of clan loyalty outweighed his sense of ethical behavior; so in the end, the traditional bushido code trumped the Buddhist code of compassion.

*Above: A stone statue at a temple in Misho, Japan.*
*Opposite page: Stone Road to a Shrine. Ioki Bunsai (1863–1906). Japan. Watercolor on paper.*

# From the Eleventh Chapter

In the "Notes on Martial Laws" it is written that:

The phrase "Win first, fight later" can be summed up in two words, "Win beforehand." The resourcefulness of times of peace is the military preparation for times of war. With five hundred allies one can defeat an enemy force of ten thousand.

When advancing on the enemy's castle and then pulling back, do not retreat by the main road, but rather by the side roads.

One should lay one's dead and wounded allies face down in the direction of the enemy.

It is a matter of course that a warrior's attitude should be to be in the vanguard during an attack and in the rear during a retreat. In approaching for the attack he does not forget to wait for the right moment. In waiting for the right moment he never forgets the attack. A helmet is usually thought to be very heavy, but when one is attacking a castle or something similar, and arrows, bullets, large rocks, great pieces of wood, and the like are coming down, it will not seem the least bit so.

Once when Master Yagyu was before the shogun on some business, a number of bamboo swords fell from the ceiling. He quickly clasped his hands above his head and was not struck.

Again, at a certain time when he was summoned, the shogun was waiting behind cover with a bamboo sword ready to strike him. Master Yagyu called out in a loud voice, "This is for your own discipline. Don't look!" As the shogun turned around, Master Yagyu stepped up and took the sword out of his hand.

A person who does not want to be struck by the enemy's arrows will have no divine protection. For a man who does not wish to be hit by the arrows of a common soldier, but rather by those of a warrior of fame, there will be the protection for which he has asked.

Wind-bells are things that are used during campaigns in order to know the direction of the wind. For night attacks, fire can be set windward while the attack can be carried out from the opposite direction. Your allies should be mindful of this also. One should always hang wind-bells in order to know the direction of the wind.

Lord Aki declared that he would not have his descendants learn military tactics. He said, "On the battlefield, once discretion starts it cannot be stopped. One will not break through to the enemy with discretion. Indiscretion is most important when in front of the tiger's den. Therefore, if one were informed of military tactics, he would have many doubts, and there will be no end to the matter. My descendants will not practice military tactics."

According to Lord Naoshige's words:

There is something to which every young samurai should pay attention. During times of peace when listening to stories of battle, one should never say, "In facing such a situation, what would a person do?" Such words are out of the question. How will a man who has doubts even in his own room achieve anything on the battlefield? There is a saying that goes, "No matter what the circumstances might be, one should be of the mind to win. One should be holding the first spear to strike." Even though you have put your life on the line, there is nothing to be done when the situation doesn't go as planned.

Takeda Shingen once said, "If there was a man who could kill Lord Ieyasu, I would give him a handsome reward." Hearing this, a boy of thirteen entered into the service of Lord Ieyasu and one night when he saw that Ieyasu had retired, took a stab at his bedding. Lord Ieyasu was actually in the next room silently reading a sutra, but he quickly grabbed the boy.

When the investigation was held, the boy related the facts honestly, and Lord Ieyasu said, "You seemed to be an excellent young man, so I employed you on friendly terms. Now, however, I am even more impressed by you." He then sent the lad back to Shingen.

One night some samurai from Karatsu gathered together and were playing go. Master Kitabatake was watching the game, and when he offered a suggestion, one man attacked

*Below: Benevolent protectors typically stood on either side of the entrance to a Japanese temple. Often the figures were devised to represent birth and death. Another convention has them representing latent power and overt power. Either way, the guardian figures represented the spectrum of being and completeness of the circle of life. Fragment of a guardian of a temple. Dakkatsu Kanshitsu. Japan.*

him with a sword. After the people around them had stopped the man, Master Kitabatake pinched out the light of the candle and said, "It was nothing more than my own indiscretion, and I apologize. The sword hit the go case; I was not the least bit wounded."

Then the candle was relighted, but when the man came to reconcile and offer him a sake cup, Kitabatake cut the man's head off with one blow. Presently he said, "My thigh having been cut through, it was difficult to offer any resistance, but by binding my leg with my coat and supporting myself with the go board, I have done this thing." Having said this, he expired.

There is nothing so painful as regret. We would all like to be without it. However, when we are very happy and become elated, or when we habitually jump into something thoughtlessly, later we are distraught, and it is for the most part because we did not think ahead and are now regretful. Certainly we should try not to become dejected, and when very happy should calm our minds.

These are teachings of Yamamoto Jin'emon:

*Single-mindedness is all-powerful.*
*Tether even a roasted chicken.*
*Continue to spur a running horse.*
*A man who will criticize you openly carries no connivance.*
*A man exists for a generation, but his name lasts to the end of time.*
*Money is a thing that will be there when asked for. A good man is not so easily found.*
*Walk with a real man one hundred yards and he'll tell you at least seven lies.*
*To ask when you already know is politeness.*
*To ask when you don't know is the rule.*
*Wrap your intentions in needles of pine.*
*One should not open his mouth wide or yawn in front of another. Do this behind your fan or sleeve.*
*A straw hat or helmet should be worn tilted toward the front.*

It is a principle of the art of war that one should simply lay down his life and strike. If one's opponent also does the same, it is an even match. Defeating one's opponent is then a matter of faith and destiny.

One should not show his sleeping quarters to other people. The times of deep sleep and dawning are very important. One should be mindful of this. This is from a story by Nagahama Inosuke.

When one departs for the front, he should carry rice in a bag. His underwear should be made from the skin of a badger. This way he will not have lice. In a long campaign, lice are troublesome.

When meeting with the enemy, there is a way to determine his strength. If he has his head cast down, he will appear black and is strong. If he is looking upward, he will appear white and is weak. This is from a story by Natsume Toneri.

If a warrior is not unattached to life and death, he will be of no use whatsoever. The saying that "All abilities come from one mind" sounds as though it has to do with sentient matters, but it is in fact a matter of being unattached to life and death. With such non-attachment one can accomplish any feat. Martial arts and the like are related to this insofar as they can lead to the Way.

To calm one's mind, one swallows his saliva. This is a secret matter. When one becomes angry, it is the same. Putting spittle on one's forehead is also good. In the Yoshida school of archery, swallowing one's spittle is the secret principle of the art.

A certain general said, "For soldiers other than officers, if they would test their armor, they should test only the front. Furthermore, while ornamentation on armor is unnecessary, one should be very careful about the appearance of his helmet. It is something that accompanies his head to the enemy's camp."

Nakano Jin'emon said, "Learning such things as military tactics is useless. If one does not strike out by simply closing his eyes and rushing into the enemy, even if it is only one step, he will be of no use." This was also the opinion of Iyanaga Sasuke.

In Natsume Toneri's "Military Stories" it is written: "Look at the soldiers of recent times! Even in long battles there are hardly one or two occasions when blood is washed with blood. One should not be negligent." Toneri was a *ronin* from the Kamigata area.

To have execution grounds in a place where travelers come and go is useless. The executions in Edo and the Kamigata area are meant to be an example for the whole country. But the executions in one province are only for an example in that province. If crimes are many, it is a province's shame. How would this look to other provinces?

With the passing of time, the criminal will forget the reason for his crime; it is best to execute him on the spot.

Matsudaira Izu no kami said to Master Mizuno Kenmotsu, "You're such a useful person, it's a shame that you're so short."

Kenmotsu replied, "That's true. Sometimes things in this world don't go the way we would like. Now if I were to cut off your head and attach it to the bottom of my feet, I would be taller. But that's something that couldn't be done."

A certain person was passing by the town of Yae when suddenly his stomach began to hurt. He stopped at a house on a side street and asked to use the toilet. There was only a young woman there, but she took him to the back and showed him where it was. Just as he was taking off his *hakama* and going into the toilet, the woman's husband came home and accused them both of adultery. In the end, it became a public matter.

Lord Naoshige heard the case and said, "Even if this is not a matter of adultery, it is the same as adultery to take off one's hakama without hesitation in a place where there is an unaccompanied woman, and in the woman's case to allow someone to disrobe while her husband is absent from home."

It is said that they were both condemned to death for this act.

In assessing the enemy's castle there is a saying that goes, "Smoke and mist are like looking at a spring mountain. After the rain is like viewing a clear day." There is weakness in perfect clarity.

People who have an intelligent appearance will not be outstanding even if they do something good, and if they do something normal, people will think them lacking. But if a person who is thought of as having a gentle disposition does even a slightly good thing, he will be praised by people.

On the fourteenth day of the seventh month in the third year of Shotoku, there were some cooks in the midst of preparations for the Ben Festival in the outer citadel of the castle. One of them, Hara Jurozaemon, unsheathed his sword and cut off the head of Sagara Genzaemon. Mawatari Rokuuemon, Aiura Tarobei, Kola Kinbei, and Kakihara Riemen all ran away in confusion. When Jurozaemon sighted Kinbei and started chasing him, the latter fled to the foot soldiers' gathering area. There, the daimyo's palanquin attendant, Tanaka Takeuemon, stood against Jurozaemon and took away his still drawn sword. Ishirnaru San'emon chased Jurozaemon, and when they came to the foot soldiers' area, assisted Takeuemon.

The punishment was given on the twenty-ninth day of the eleventh month in the same year. Jurozaemon was bound with rope and beheaded. Rokuuemon, Tarobei, Kinbei, and Riemon were banished, and San'emon was ordered to retire. Takeuemon was rewarded with three pieces of silver.

It was later said that Takeuemon had been slow to act, for he had not bound the man at that time.

Among Takeda Shingen's retainers there were men of matchless courage, but when Katsuyori was killed in the fight at Tenmokuzan, they all fled. Tsuchiya Sozo, a warrior who had been in disfavor for many years, came out alone, however, and said, "I wonder where all the men are who spoke so bravely every day? I shall return the master's favors to me." And he fell alone in battle.

The essentials of speaking are in not speaking at all. If you think that you can finish something without speaking, finish it without saying a single word. If there is something that cannot be accomplished without speaking, one should speak with few words, in a way that will accord well with reason.

To open one's mouth indiscriminately brings shame, and there are many times when people will turn their backs on such a person.

A devotee of the *Nembutsu* recites the Buddha's name with every incoming and outgoing breath in order never to forget the Buddha. A retainer, too, should be just like this in thinking of his master. Not to forget one's master is the most fundamental thing for a retainer.

*From before the dawn of recorded history, masks have been used in Japanese in rituals and theatrical performances. Masks of young women from the era of the one above are particularly common because male actors were called upon to play so many female roles. Top: Mask of an old man trying to whistle. Japan. Bottom: Noh theater mask of a young woman. Japan. 19th century.*

# THE MOUNTED SAMURAI
## SCOURGE OF THE BATTLEFIELD

The samurai battle scenes in paintings and woodblock prints commonly depict mounted warriors leading foot soldiers. Horses played an integral part in bushi warfare. They were used as pack animals, for scouting missions, and small raids, as well as in battle. Even though packhorses, usually led by nonarmored grooms, were needed in campaigns for transporting bulky loads, such as food supplies and additional weaponry, the samurai found the horse an indispensable accessory to war.

Samurai during the Gempei War were proficient in riding horses and wore gathered trousers that could accommodate this activity. In the sleeveless, rounded style of armor with solid breastplate, the *do-maru*, the warrior balanced atop a saddle typically made of lacquered wood, with the girth strap fastened on top of the horse's back. With the force of his *yari* (spear) or his *katana* (long sword), in conjunction with the horse's momentum, the samurai was in a strong position to inflict substantial damage to an opponent.

Documentation from the era is explicit in regards to the use of the horse. The *Tanki yoriaku*, which was written in 1735 to explain armor wearing, says "When you desire to march noiselessly in the case of a night attack, wrap your knee protectors with the lower part of the hakama, put a gag in the mouth of your horse, and bind the bridle with a piece of cotton cloth."

The *Koyo gunkan*, the record of the Takeda family, documents the 1548 defeat of Takeda Shingen by Murakami Yoshikiyo. Yoshikiyo explains his preparation against the

Takeda cavalry advance: "As defense against the horsemen, I chose 200 skilled shooters out of the army and to 150 soldiers I gave five well-made arrows and a bow; and to the rest gave matchlocks imported in the seventh year of Eisho with three bullets. They were ordered to shoot when they were told and to throw them away later and fight with swords. And for the gun shooters, I ordered to shoot the guns after the arrows were shot, and placed an officer for each five shooters." The *Koyo gunkan* also lists the fighting inventory of the Takeda army of 1573, which included 9,121 horsemen with two followers each, as well as a veterinarian for the horses.

The battle of Nagashino in 1575, between the Takeda army and the forces of Oda Nobunaga, illustrates the effective use of cavalry in battle. Nobunaga's troops included a unit of matchlock gunmen numbering 3,000. Takeda believed that many of his opponents' matchlocks were unusable because of a heavy rain that had occurred the previous night, and he planned for his horsemen to attack Nobunaga's armed *ashigaru* (foot soldiers) between the first and second rounds of fire as they reloaded their matchlocks. Takeda's horsemen were slowed in the crossing of a riverbed, and many were cut down in the second round of

*Above: Stirrups. Iijima Seizaemon. Japan. 1615–1868. Iron with silver inlay and lacquer.*
*Left: Stirrup. Japan. 19th century. Leather, metal copper alloy, and lacquer.*
*Opposite page: Surimono of an armed warrior on horseback. Toyota Hokkei (1780–1850). Japan. Circa 1822. Color woodblock print.*

matchlock fire or by spears, a situation that left Takeda in retreat with a casualty rate of two-thirds of his army.

The *Zohyo monogatari*, a text on warfare written in 1649, gives tactical considerations for the use of horses in raids and in battle: "When taking horses on a raid, you must be very careful. Young horses may break free and will get excited. Because of this an army could be defeated, so this must be strictly forbidden. Keep them well tied up to avoid this." It also urges warriors to immediately attack the horses in battle: "As for the enemy, after beginning with the horses it is good to attack the riders. On these occasions fire at those riding the horses so that they fall off and also at the horses. It will disturb many of the enemy." The text also recommends spearing the belly of the horse to render it useless and cause its rider to fall.

The author of *Hojo godaiki* describes the use of horses during a scouting mission in 1575. In this account, Hojo Ujinao's envoy dramatically escapes the enemy horsemen from Satake Yoshinobu's camp. The author praises the two participating scouts and also mentions the bravery of their horses as matching the level of bravery exhibited by the samurai themselves.

*Horse Jumping, one of a pair. Soga Shohaku (1730–1781). Japan. Circa 18th century. Ink on paper.*

Men who did well at the time of their deaths were men of real bravery. There are many examples of such. But people who talk in an accomplished fashion every day yet are agitated at the time of their deaths can be known not to have true bravery.

In the secret principles of Yagyu Tajima no kami Munenori, there is the saying "There are no military tactics for a man of great strength." As proof of this, there was once a certain vassal of the shogun who came to Master Yagyu and asked to become a disciple. Master Yagyu said, "You seem to be a man who is very accomplished in some school of martial art. Let us make the master-disciple contract after I learn the name of the school."

But the man replied, "I have never practiced one of the martial arts."

Master Yagyu said, "Have you come to make sport of Tajima no kami? Is my perception amiss in thinking that you are a teacher to the shogun?" But the man swore to it, and Master Yagyu then asked, "That being so, do you not have some deep conviction?"

The man replied, "When I was a child, I once became suddenly aware that a warrior is a man who does not hold his life in regret. Since I have held that in my heart for many years, it has become a deep conviction, and today I never think about death. Other than that I have no special conviction."

Master Yagyu was deeply impressed and said, "My perceptions were not the least bit awry. The deepest principle of my military tactics is just that one thing. Up until now, among all the many hundreds of disciples I have had, there is not one who is licensed in this deepest principle. It is not necessary for you to take up the wooden sword. I will initiate you right now." And it is said that he promptly handed him the certified scroll. This is a story of Muragawa Soden's.

Meditation on inevitable death should be performed daily. Every day when one's body and mind are at peace, one should meditate upon being ripped apart by arrows, rifles, spears, and swords, being carried away by surging waves, being thrown into the midst of a great fire, being struck by lightning, being shaken to death by a great earthquake, falling from thousand-foot cliffs, dying of disease, or committing *seppuku* at the death of one's master. And every day without fail one should consider himself as dead.

There is a saying of the elders that goes, "Step from under the eaves and you're a dead man. Leave the gate and the enemy is waiting." This is not a matter of being careful. It is to consider oneself as dead beforehand.

People will become your enemies if you become eminent too quickly in life, and you will be ineffectual. Rising slowly in the world, people will be your allies, and your happiness will be assured.

In the long run, whether you are fast or slow, as long as you have people's understanding there will be no danger. It is said that fortune that is urged upon you from others is the most effective.

The warriors of old cultivated mustaches. As proof that a man had been slain in battle, his ears and nose would be cut off and brought to the enemy's camp. So that there would be no mistake as to whether the person was a man or a woman, the mustache was also cut off with the nose. At such a time the head was thrown away if it had no mustache, for it might be mistaken for that of a woman. Therefore, growing a mustache was one of the disciplines of a samurai so that his head would not be thrown away upon his death.

Tsunetomo said, "If one washes his face with water every morning, if he is slain his complexion will not change."

The word "person of the north" comes from a tradition of the correct way of upbringing. A couple will put their pillows in the west, and the man, lying on the south side, will face the north, while the woman, lying on the north side, will face the south.

In bringing up a boy, one should first encourage a sense of valor. From the time he is young the child should liken his parents to the master, and learn everyday politeness and etiquette, the serving of other people, the ways of speech, forbearance, and even the correct way of walking down the street. The elders were taught in the same fashion. When he does not put effort into things, he should be scolded and made to go the entire day without eating. This is also one of the disciplines of a retainer.

As for a girl, it is most important to teach her chastity from the time she is a child. She should not be in the company of a man at a distance of less than six feet, nor should she meet them eye to eye, nor should she receive things from them directly from hand to hand. Neither should she go sightseeing or take trips to temples. A woman who has been brought up strictly and has endured suffering at her own home will suffer no ennui after she is married.

In dealing with younger children one should use rewards and punishments. If one is lax in being sure that they do as they are told, young children will become self-interested and will later be involved in wrongdoings. It is something about which one should be very careful.

*Iron Tsuba with wire (brass and copper inlay), Shingen Mukade style. 19th century.*

*Stone bracelet (ishikushiro). Japan. 300–400 CE. Jasper.*

# SAMURAI AFTER THE MEIJI RESTORATION

The Meiji restoration (1868 to 1912), a period of great transition for Japan, was named after the Emperor Meiji, who became ruler in 1868. He took power at the age of fifteen following the 1867 overthrow of the shogunate. With imperial power back in the hands of the emperor, Japan experienced a renewal of the type of government it had claimed some 700 years earlier. The feudal structure and isolationist ideas of the Edo period were changed dramatically, particularly for the samurai, who expanded their interests and vocations to include many subjects other than warfare, though the code of loyalty, honor, and service continued to be maintained by many of the class.

The exchange of knowledge with the rest of the world was demonstrated through the science, technology, and education acquired by Japanese students abroad and shared by foreign professionals within Japan. The words of Sakuma Shozan seemed to summarize the goal of the new government, which he felt was to blend "eastern ethics and western science."

The need for a warrior class of society had changed, and the Meiji restoration saw the end of the samurai class, beginning with a law prohibiting their wearing a *katana* in public. Soon, many samurai were being killed in Meiji conflicts over the governance of the new regime. One such conflict was the battle of Ueno in July 1868, which brought about the defeat of thousands of *ronin* who occupied a temple there as they tried to provoke the new government's soldiers and officials by shouting insults. The imperial forces subsequently eliminated the rebels.

Many of the samurai class supported the new emperor during the overthrow of the shogunate and became his advisors. For example, Saigo Takamori, who had been exiled for five years by the Tokugawa shogunate, returned to train warriors and fought in support of Meiji's

ascension to the throne. In spite of that support he advocated Japanese expansion through the conquest of Korea. His plan was to travel to Korea as a Japanese envoy to propose ridiculous demands and thereby provoke the Koreans into executing him, a plot that would secure an excuse for Japan to declare war and conquer the offending Koreans. He resigned when his plan was rejected. In 1877, he led an army of sword-wielding samurai dissidents against the modern firepower of the government army in a conflict known as the Satsuma rebellion. The government triumphed after a bloody battle. Saigo was badly wounded and committed *seppuku* to avoid capture. The emperor pardoned him posthumously, and his reputation for bravery and for loyalty to his principles has become symbolic of the samurai ethic. Among some scholars, he is commonly referred to as the "last of the samurai."

Samurai who opposed Saigo in the Satsuma rebellion and moved Japan toward an electoral form of government included Aritomo Yamagata, Taisuke Itagaki, and Hirobumi Ito. Yamagata favored military expansion abroad and founded the modern Japanese army. He also served as home minister, premier, and president of the privy council, which gave him enormous political power. Itagaki worked to set up a party form of government and served as home minister, while Ito studied foreign governments abroad and served in several high-level government positions, including that of prime minister and first president of the Seiyukai political party.

*Below: The "battle" at Ueno in July 1868.*
*Bottom: Detail from an Illustrated Manuscript Depicting 44 Varieties of Bugaku Dances. Japan. Early 18th century. Sumi, color, and gofun on paper.*

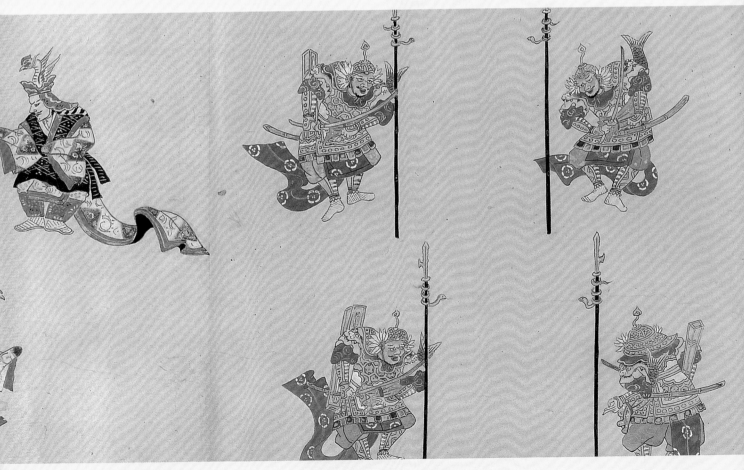

# Late Night Idle Talk

As a retainer of the Nabeshima clan, one should have the intention of studying our province's history and traditions, but provincial studies are made light of nowadays.

The basic reason for this study is to understand the foundation of our clan, and to know that the clan's forefathers established its perpetuity by means of their suffering and compassion. The fact that our clan has perpetually continued in an unrivaled manner up to this very day is due to the humanity and martial valor of Master Ryuzoji Iekane, the charity and faith of Master Nabeshima Kiyohisa, and the appearance of Lord Ryuzoji Takanobu and Lord Nabeshima Naoshige and their might.

I am at a complete loss when it comes to understanding why people of this generation have forgotten these things and respect the Buddhas of other places. Neither the Shakyamuni Buddha, nor Confucius, nor Kusunoki, nor Shingen were ever retainers of the Ryuzoji or the Nabeshima; hence it cannot be said that they are in harmony with our clan's customs.

In times of war or in times of peace it would be sufficient if both the upper and lower classes would worship our ancestors and study their teachings. One worships the head of whatever clan or discipline to which he belongs. Outside learning for retainers of our clan is worthless.

One may think that it is fine to study other disciplines as a diversion after his provincial studies are replete. Yet if a person has a good understanding of provincial studies, he will see that there is nothing lacking in them.

Today, if someone from another clan were to ask about the origin of the Ryuzoji and the Nabeshima, or why the fief was transferred from the former to the latter, or if they were to ask something like, "I have heard that the Ryuzoji and the Nabeshima are the greatest in Kyushu for deeds of martial valor, but can you tell me some of the particulars?" I suppose that the man with no knowledge of provincial studies would not be able to answer a word.

For a retainer there should be nothing other than doing his own job. For the most part people dislike their own jobs, find those of others more interesting, cause misunderstanding, and bring on utter disasters. Good models of men who performed their duty in their work are Lord Naoshige and Lord Katsushige. The retainers of those times all performed their duties. From the upper classes, men who would be of good use were searched out, while from the lower classes men desired to be useful. The minds of the two classes were of mutual accord, and the strength of the clan was secure.

In all our generations of masters there has never been a bad or foolish one, and in the end there has never been one who ranked second or third among the *daimyo* of Japan. It is truly a wonderful clan; this is due to the faith of its founders. Moreover, they did not send the clan's retainers to other provinces. Nor did they invite men from other provinces in. Men who were made *ronin* were kept within the province, as were the descendants of those who were made to commit *seppuku*.

The wonder of being born into a clan with such a deep pledge between master and servant is an inexpressible blessing, passed down through the ages, for both farmer and townsman. This goes without saying for the retainer.

The foundation of a Nabeshima samurai should be in knowing this fact; in being deeply resolved to return this blessing by being useful; in serving more and more selflessly when treated kindly by the master; in knowing that being made a ronin or being ordered to commit seppuku are also forms of service; and in aiming to be mindful of the clan forever, whether one is banished deep in the mountains or buried under the earth.

Although it is unfitting for someone like me to say this, in dying it is my hope not to become a Buddha. Rather, my will is permeated with the resolution to help manage the affairs of the province, though I be reborn as a Nabeshima samurai seven times. One needs neither vitality nor talent.

*Opposite page: Japanese court official or Samurai. Japan. Circa 1870s. Hand-colored albumen print.*

*Below: A white-laced do-maru of 18th-century manufacture. The 62-plate suji-bachi is signed by Saotome Iehisa, who was working in the mid-17th century and lived in Hitachi. The gold-colored crest is in the form of a ken or ancient straight sword, with a vraja hilt. The Saotome are thought to be related to the Miochin.*

In a word, it is a matter of having the will to shoulder the clan by oneself.

How can one human being be inferior to another? In all matters of discipline, one will be useless unless he has great pride. Unless one is determined to move the clan by himself, all his discipline will come to naught. Although, like a teakettle, it is easy for one's enthusiasm to cool, there is a way to keep this from happening. My own vows are the following:

Never to be outdone in the Way of the Samurai.

To be of good use to the master.

To be filial to my parents.

To manifest great compassion, and to act for the sake of Man.

If one dedicates these four vows to the gods and Buddhas every morning, he will have the strength of two men and will never slip backward. One must edge forward like the inchworm, bit by bit. The gods and Buddhas, too, first started with a vow.

# SAMURAI MUSEUMS

The samurai tradition has been richly preserved in its weaponry and armor and in artistic forms, including, among others, calligraphy, paintings, woodblock prints, writing boxes, scrolls, religious items, and many additional personal items. Museums worldwide exhibit many of these artifacts, which may be visited in person or online. This listing is in no way comprehensive but is a sample of the magnificent collections available to the viewing public. Note that exhibitions and collections are often changed and loaned to other museums, so before you plan a visit, verify the availability of objects of interest, as well as hours and admissions fees.

*Aoyagi Samurai Manor Museum*, Akita, Japan. The museum and its collections are housed in a complex of buildings previously inhabited by the Aoyagi family and include weaponry, scrolls, documents, and items from daily life from the seventeenth to twentieth centuries. Facilities include the main house, the *Akita Folk Museum*, the *Samurai Tools and Utensils Museum*, the *Antiques Museum* and *Tea Room*, the *Armory*, and the *Seiryu-an Gallery*. www.samurai world.com

*Asia Society*, 725 Park Avenue at 70th Street, New York, NY 10021. www.asiasociety.org

*Asian Art Museum of San Francisco*, 200 Larkin Street, San Francisco, CA. www.asianart.org

*British Museum*, Great Russell Street, London, England WC1B 3DG. www.britishmuseum.org

*Edo Tokyo Museum*, 1-4-1 Yokoami, Sumida-ku, Tokyo 130-0015, Japan. www.edo-tokyo-museum.or.jp

*Kyoto National Museum*, Higashiyama district, Kyoto, Japan. www.kyohaku.go.jp

*Los Angeles County Museum of Art*, 5905 Wilshire Boulevard, Los Angeles, CA 90036. www.lacma.org

*Morikami Museum and Japanese Gardens*, 4000 Morikami Park Road, Delray Beach, FL 33446. www.morikami.org

*National Gallery of Australia*, Parkes Place, Parkes ACT 2600, Canberra, Australia. www.nga.gov.au

*Philadelphia Museum of Art*, main building, 26th Street and Benjamin Franklin Parkway, Philadelphia, PA 19130; Perelman Building, Fairmount and Pennsylvania avenues, also in Philadelphia. www.philamuseum.org

*Smithsonian Institute's Freer Gallery of Art and Arthur M. Sackler Gallery*, Washington, D.C. www.asia.si.edu/collections/japaneseHome.htm

*Tikotin Museum of Japanese Art*, 89 Hanassi Avenue, Haifa, Israel. ilmuseums.com/museum_eng.asp?id=5

*Tokyo Fuji Art Museum*, 492-1, Yano-machi, Hachioji-shi, Tokyo 192-0016, Japan. www.fujibi.or.jp

*Tokyo Metropolitan Art Museum*, 8-36 Ueno Park, Taito-ku, Tokyo 110-0007, Japan. www.tobikan.jp/english/main.html

*Tokyo National Museum*, Tokyo, Japan. tnm.go.jp/en/index.html

# Glossary

## A

**Ainu** – Early ethnic group of Japan, with strong Caucasian features.

**Ashigaru** – Foot soldiers, usually farmers and manual laborers; the light field troops that did much of the frontline fighting in samurai-led battles.

## B

**Bakufu** – Regional government; another term for *shogunate*.

**Beijing** – Present-day capital of China; see also *Ji* and *Dadu*.

**Bishamon** – Buddhist god of war and one of the religion's Seven Deities of Good Fortune.

**Bodhisattva** – Buddhist practitioner who has attained enlightenment and helps others achieve the same goal.

**Bokuto** – Wooden sword used in training.

**Bronze** – Metal made from a mixture of copper and tin; used widely in China for both utilitarian and decorative purposes.

**Bronze Age** – Period between 2000 and 771 BCE, when bronze was the predominant metal used in China.

**Buddhism** – Primary religion of Asia, having migrated from India to China and spread to other countries, such as Korea and Japan.

**Budo** – Literally, "martial arts," used in a broad sense.

**Bushi** – Literally, "warrior."

**Bushido** – Literally, "way of the warrior," as an extension of the word *bushi*; the title of a classic samurai literary work by Inazo Nitobe.

## C

**Cha** – Japanese tea.

**Cha-no-yu** – Japanese tea ceremony; one of the most important ceremonies practiced by both samurai and nobles and still in practice today.

**Chosen** – Korea, Japan's closest neighbor.

**Confucianism** – Widespread philosophy and practice developed by Confucius, whose tenets stressed proper lifestyle and social behavior.

**Crossbow** – Bow developed in China and designed to shoot arrows from a horizontally held position, either with single or multiple arrows.

## D

**Dadu** – Name Kublai Khan gave his capital (present-day Beijing) during the Yuan dynasty, when China was under Mongol rule.

**Dagger-axe** – Handled weapon with a pointed, axelike head on the end, typically made of bronze and popularized in China; known as a *ko*.

**Daimyo** – Sovereign warlord exerting control over several provinces or smaller fiefs.

**Daisho** – Pair of swords worn by a samurai; most commonly included the katana and the wakizashi.

**Dao** – Short single-edge Chinese sword developed during the Shang dynasty, such as the curved "oxtail" sword.

**Dojo** – Martial arts training center or school, often centered on a specific type of combat.

**Dynasty** – Period of reign by one dominating faction or clan, often in a long string of Chinese emperors and often lasting hundreds of years.

## E

**Edo** – Capital of the Tokugawa clan, renamed Tokyo in 1868, during the Meiji period.

**Edo period** – Last era of the samurai, from 1600 to 1867.

## F

**Forbidden City** – Main hall of the Imperial Palace in Beijing.

**Fuchi** – Collar below the guard on a Japanese sword; usually decorated to match other sword furniture; see *Kashira*.

## G

**Gempei War** – Series of battles lasting from 1180 to 1185, in which the Taira clan was defeated by the Minamoto clan.

*Gorinso (Go rin no sho)* – *The Book of Five Rings*, a famous literary work on swordsmanship by Miyamoto Musashi.

**Great Wall of China** – Series of large walls and lookouts, erected in China as a means of defense and stretching from the Korean border into the Gobi Desert.

**Guard** – Upper portion of a sword handle that protects the hand and prevents it from slipping forward onto the blade; see *tsuba*.

**Gun-sen** – Folding war fan, typically of metal, commonly used to signal troops and less frequently as a weapon.

## H

**Habaki** – Collar above the guard on a Japanese sword.

**Hamon** – The clay-tempering line that runs along the length of a Japanese sword blade.

**Hara-kiri** – Another term for *seppuku*, a form of suicide in which a sword is plunged into the left midsection and dragged across to the right.

**Heian period** – Major Japanese period, from 794 to 1192 CE.

**Huang He** – Yellow River, one of China's two largest rivers, located in the northeastern section of the country.

## I

**Ikko-ikki** – Militant force of Japanese peasant farmers, Buddhist monks, Shinto priests, and local nobility, who followed the beliefs of the Jodo Shinshu sect and were prevalent around the sixteenth century.

## J

**Jade** – Highly prized stone in ancient China, more so than gold; commonly thought of as being green but can also be brown, tan, beige, or black.

**Jadeite** – One of the two types of jade; typically green, white, or yellow but occasionally reddish brown.

**Ji** – Original name for the capital of China (present-day Beijing), named during the Warring States period.

**Jia** – Chinese soldier's armor, translating literally as "shell."

**Jian** – Double-edge sword used by Chinese soldiers, developed during the Spring and Autumn period during the seventh century BCE.

**Jingasa** – Iron helmet used by Japanese foot soldiers in the sixteenth century; could also be used as a cooking pot.

**Jitte** – Thin batonlike fighting tool providing a modicum of protection and used primarily for disarming a swordsman.

**Jodo Shinshu** – Popular Japanese Buddhist sect of the sixteenth century, led by the powerful monk Rennyo Shonin; worshipped the god Amida; also known as the Pure Land sect.

**Jomon** – First settled culture in Japan, lasting from 14,000 to 300 BCE.

## K

**Kabuto** – Helmet worn by the samurai, often decorated to a high degree of conspicuousness.

# Glossary

**Kaiso** – Founding headmaster of a school of martial arts.

**Kamikaze** – Literally, "divine wind," a term given to the typhoons that destroyed the Mongol fleet as it tried to invade Japan in 1274 and then again in 1281; events possibly apocryphal in nature.

**Kamon** – Official family crest.

**Kashira** – Pommel or base of a Japanese sword, often decorated to match other pieces of sword furniture; see *fuchi*.

**Katana** – Long sword, the "soul" of the samurai; measuring twenty-four inches and over.

**Kenjutsu** – Art of Japanese swordsmanship.

**Kimono** – Common Japanese garment resembling a short robe.

**Ko** – See *dagger-axe*.

**Kozuka** – Small knife that fits inside the sheath of a Japanese sword.

**Kublai Khan** – Grandson of Genghis Khan, who conquered China in 1279.

**Kyoto** – Capital of Japan from 794 to 1868 CE; main battleground of the Onin War.

## M

**Mempo** – Frontispiece or mask worn with Japanese armor, often with unusual facial expressions, ranging from evil to humorous.

**Menuki** – Diminutive decorative ornament placed on the handle of a Japanese sword; either completely or partially covered by cord wrappings.

**Mon** – Crest or badge, used for identification.

**Mongols** – Natives of Mongolia, the only country ever to rule China; Kublai Khan, grandson of Genghis Khan, was the ruler of the Yuan dynasty from 1279 to 1368.

## N

**Naginata** – Pole arm ending in a curved blade; one of the most common weapons used by the warrior monks (*sohei*).

**Neolithic period** – Earliest era of Chinese culture, from circa 5000 to 1500 BCE; characterized by the use of stone tools, development of agriculture, and domestication of farm animals.

**Nephrite** – One of the two types of jade; occurs in a wide range of colors including white, black, gray, green, yellow, and tan/beige.

**Nu** – See *crossbow*.

**Nichiren** – Buddhist sect founded in the thirteenth century by a monk of the same name.

**Ninja** – Japanese spy or assassin.

## O

**Oni** – Angry ogrelike person often depicted in Japanese paintings and carvings.

**Otemon** – Main gate of a Japanese castle.

## P

**Pang pai** – A large square shield used by Chinese foot soldiers.

**Pole arm** – Shaft with a blade or pronged device on the end, used for thrusting, slashing, or otherwise disabling an opponent.

## Q

**Qiang** – Spear used by Chinese soldiers.

## R

**Ronin** – Samurai who served no master, often traveling the countryside as warriors for hire or for provoking combat to prove their skills.

**Ryu** – Japanese school for martial arts.

## S

**Sake** – Rice wine; not only popular during samurai times but also still the most common wine among the Japanese today.

**Samurai** – Literally, "one who serves;" the legendary warriors of Japan whose class flourished between the tenth century and the mid-nineteenth century.

**Saya** – Scabbard used to house a Japanese sword.

**Sengoku jidai** – Long era of war and unrest between 1477 and 1600; more commonly known as the Sengoku period or the Warring States period.

**Seppuku** – Ritual act of suicide performed by slitting open one's belly using a sword, most often a wakizashi.

**Shingon** – Buddhist sect founded in the early ninth century; shrouded in individualistic thought, mysticism, and ritual.

**Shinkage ryu** – Type of sword training taught by samurai Yagyu Menenori, author of *The Sword and the Mind*.

**Shinkendo** – Type of modern sword training developed by Toshishiro Obata.

**Shinto** – Japan's first indigenous religion, which included the worship of spirit gods.

**Shogun** – Japanese military ruler; leader of the samurai.

**Shogunate** – Government and holdings of a shogun; also referred to as bakufu.

**Silk Road** – Series of trade routes spanning the Middle East and Asia; also contributed to the spread of technology and religious thought across the area.

**Sohei** – Buddhist warrior monks who fought first against each other and then in association with the ikko-ikki (revolutionary Japanese peasants) in the fifteenth century; often fought alongside the samurai in the sixteenth century.

## T

**Tachi** – Original Japanese long sword used by the samurai; similar to the katana, the two differing mainly in their lengths and in the way they were worn.

**Taisho** – Japanese general or commander.

**Tanegashima** – Japanese matchlock rifle, closely copied from the Portugese harquebus in the mid-sixteenth century; also called teppo.

**Tanto** – The short sword or daggerlike knife, similar in design to a katana or a wakizashi; measuring a maximum of twelve inches.

**Taoism** – Buddhist sect guided by Chinese scholar Lao Tzu, whose philosophical teachings emphasized passive resistance.

**Teppo** – Another term for matchlock rifle; see *tanegashima*.

**Tsuba** – The guard on a Japanese sword, often decorated.

## U

**Uma** – Japanese word for horse.

**Utsubo** – Archer's quiver for holding arrows.

## W

**Wa** – Early Chinese name for the country of Japan.

**Wakizashi** – Japanese short sword, carried with the tachi or katana, as part of the daisho set; measuring twelve to twenty-four inches; the preferred sword for committing ritual suicide.

**Warring States period** – Most turbulent period in China's history, lasting from 480 to 221 BCE.

## Y

**Yabusame** – Form of archery practice conducted from horseback.

**Yakuza** – Criminals or gangsters of the Edo period, especially prevalent in the old Kozuke province.

**Yamabushi** – Members of the Shugendo sect of Buddhism; thought to have mysterious powers, such as the ability to cast out demons.

**Yamashiro** – A province of Japan.

**Yangtze River** – One of the two largest rivers of China, running midway through the eastern half of the country.

**Yari** – Lance or spear.

**Yashima** – Renowned Noh play composed by Zeami, its plot involving Minamoto Yoshitsune and the battle of Yashima.

**Yojimbo** – Bodyguard, especially during the Edo period.

**Yoriki** – Police official of the Edo period.

**Yoroi hitatare** – Set of silk shirt and pants worn under armor, primarily in the Heian period.

**Yu** – Chinese jade; also known as "the loin stone" because of its use in protective armor.

**Yumi** – Laminated bamboo bow with a wooden core; originally the primary weapon of the samurai but later relegated to the common foot soldier, who functioned as a skirmisher in battle.

**Yumiya no michi** – Literally, "way of the bow and arrow."

## Z

**Zen** – Sect of Buddhism that became highly popular in China and Japan because of its special emphasis on meditating to find inner peace.

**Zi dun** – A light shield used by Chinese infantry.

# Index

# Index

# Index

# Index

# Image Sources

End sheets: Copyright © 2008 Christie's Images Ltd. All rights reserved. CHP030687020_01. Page 6: Copyright © 2008 Christie's Images Ltd. All rights reserved. TEX021096058_01. Page 7: (top) istockphoto.com. (center) From the collection of Stephen Selby. Page 8: (left and right) From the collection of Stephen Selby. (bottom) Photo by Karim Shamsi-Basha. Page 9: From the collection of Clive Sinclair. Page 10–11: Chen Rong, Chinese, first half of the 13th century / Nine dragons (detail) / Chinese, Southern Song dynasty, dated 1244 / Ink and color on paper / 46.3 x 1096.4 cm (18 1/4 x 431 5/8 in.) / Museum of Fine Arts, Boston / Francis Gardner Curtis Fund, 17.1697. Page 12: Emperor Wu Ti (156-87 BC, r. 141-87 BC) welcoming a man of letters, from a history of Chinese emperors (colour on silk), Chinese School, (17th century) / Bibliotheque Nationale, Paris, France, Lauros / Giraudon / The Bridgeman Art Library International. Page 14: The Capture of the Mountain at Ko Hu Chu So Lung, from a series depicting scenes from the Quinlong Campaign in Sichuan, 1772–76 (engraving) / Private Collection, Photo © Bonhams, London, UK / The Bridgeman Art Library International. Page 16–17: Traditionally attributed to: Li Zanhua, Chinese, 899–936 / Nomads with a tribute horse (detail) / Chinese, Northern Song dynasty, 11th–12th century / Ink, color, and gold on silk / 27.8 x 125.1 cm (10 15/16 x 49 1/4 in.) / Museum of Fine Arts, Boston / Keith McLeod Fund, 52.1380. Page 18: The Avery Brundage Collection, B60P12+. © Asian Art Museum of San Francisco. Used by permission. Page 19: Gift of Chauncey Peter Lowe. 2001.31. © Asian Art Museum of San Francisco. Used by permission. Page 20: Attributed to: Yan Liben, Chinese, about 600–673 / The thirteen emperors (detail) / Chinese, Tang dynasty, second half of the 7th century A.D. / Ink and color on silk / 51.3 x 531 cm (20 3/16 x 209 1/16 in.) / Museum of Fine Arts, Boston / Denman Waldo Ross Collection, 31.643. Page 21: Gift of R.W. Winskill in Memory of Lionel H. Pries, B86J15. © Asian Art Museum of San Francisco. Used by permission. Page 22: The Avery Brundage Collection, B60S17. © Asian Art Museum of San Francisco. Used by permission. Page 23: The Second Sui Emperor, Yangdi (569–618) with his fleet of sailing craft, from a history of Chinese emperors (colour on silk), Chinese School, (17th century) / Bibliotheque Nationale, Paris, France, / The Bridgeman Art Library International. Page 25: Copyright © 2008 Christie's Images Ltd. All rights reserved. CHD230395288_01. Page 28–29: istockphoto.com. Page 30: (top left) istockphoto.com. (bottom right) The Avery Brundage Collection. B60J509. © Asian Art Museum of San Francisco. Used by permission. Page 31: Lan Ying, Chinese, 1585–after 1664 / The lofty Mount Song / Chinese, Ming dynasty, 1627 / Ink and color on silk / 193 x 97.4 cm (76 x 38 3/8 in.) / Museum of Fine Arts, Boston / Julia Bradford Huntington James Fund, 08.105. Page 33: Sun Tzu (6th–5th Century BC), Chinese School / Private Collection / The Bridgeman Art Library International. Page 34: The Avery Brundage Collection. B60P302. © Asian Art Museum of San Francisco. Used by permission. Page 35: From the collection of Stephen Selby. Page 36: Transfer from the Fine Arts Museums of San Francisco, Gift of Mrs. G. West and S. Bruce. B68P24. © Asian Art Museum of San Francisco. Used by permission. Page 37: The Avery Brundage Collection. B60B764. © Asian Art Museum of San Francisco. Used by permission. Page 38: (top left) The Avery Brundage Collection. B60J226. © Asian Art Museum of San Francisco. Used by permission. (top right) The Avery Brundage Collection. B60J8+. © Asian Art Museum of San Francisco. Used by permission. (bottom left) The Avery Brundage Collection. B60J521.a-.b. © Asian Art Museum of San Francisco. Used by permission. Page 39: (top) Gift of R.W. Winskill in Memory of Lionel H. Pries. B86J16. © Asian Art Museum of San Francisco. Used by permission. (middle) The Avery Brundage Collection. B60J608. © Asian Art Museum of San Francisco. Used by permission. (bottom) The Avery Brundage Collection. B62J63. © Asian Art Museum of San Francisco. Used by permission. Page 40–41: The Art Archive / Private Collection. AA335431. Page 42–43: istockphoto.com. Page 43: The Avery Brundage Collection. B60J132. © Asian Art Museum of San Francisco. Used by permission. Page 44: istockphoto.com. Page 46–47: The Art Archive / Alfredo Dagli Orti. AA328907. Page 48: istockphoto.com. Page 49: Or.2780 fol.49 v. Genghis Khan (c.1162-1227) Fighting a Battle in a Mountain Pass (ink on vellum), Chinese School / British Museum, London, UK / The Bridgeman Art Library International. Page 51: The Avery Brundage Collection. B60J513. © Asian Art Museum of San Francisco. Used by permission. Page 52: Portrait of Confucius (c. 551–479 BC) (gouache on paper scroll), Chinese School, (17th century) / Bibliotheque Nationale, Paris, France / The Bridgeman Art Library International. Page 53: Lao-Tzu (c. 604–531) on his buffalo, followed by a disciple (w/c on paper), Chinese School, (18th century) / Bibliotheque Nationale, Paris, France, Archives Charmet / The Bridgeman Art Library International. Page 54: istockphoto.com. Page 55: Portrait of Posou Fairy, Yuan Dynasty, 1279–1368 (wall painting) / Mogao Caves, Dunhuang, Gansu Province, NW China / The Bridgeman Art Library International. Page 56–57: Copyright © 2008 Christie's Images Ltd. All rights reserved. CHN220491101_01. Page 59: The Avery Brundage Collection. B60B1024. © Asian Art Museum of San Francisco. Used by permission. Page 60: Arthur M. Sackler Gallery, Smithsonian Institution, Washington, D.C. / Gift of Arthur M. Sackler, S1987.26. Page 62: The Avery Brundage Collection. B60S551. © Asian Art Museum of San Francisco. Used by permission. Page 63: The Avery Brundage Collection. B60B828. © Asian Art Museum of San Francisco. Used by permission. Page 64: The Avery Brundage Collection. B60B1026. © Asian Art Museum of San Francisco. Used by permission. Page 65: (bottom) The Avery Brundage Collection. B60B1+. © Asian Art Museum of San Francisco. Used by permission. (top right) The Avery Brundage Collection. B60B782. © Asian Art Museum of San Francisco. Used by permission. Page 67: Copyright © 2008 Christie's Images Ltd. All rights reserved. CHD301001651B_01. Page 68: The Avery Brundage Collection. B60J907. © Asian Art Museum of San Francisco. Used by permission. Page 69: (top) The Avery Brundage Collection. B60J756. © Asian Art Museum of San Francisco. Used by permission. (bottom) The Avery Brundage Collection. B62B145. © Asian Art Museum of San Francisco. Used by permission. Pages 70–71: National Palace Museum, Taipei, Taiwan, Republic of China. Page 72: Arthur M. Sackler Gallery, Smithsonian Institution, Washington, D.C. / Gift of Benjamin Chou in memory of Wang Yachen, S2000.90. Page 73: (top left) istockphoto.com. (top right) The Avery Brundage Collection. B60P141+. © Asian Art Museum of San Francisco. Used by permission. (bottom right) Transfer from the Fine Arts Museums of San Francisco, Gift of the M.H. de Young Endowment Fund. B81P75. © Asian Art Museum of San Francisco. Used by permission. Page 74: Horse / Chinese, Tang dynasty, first half of 8th century / Earthenware with three-color glaze and applied motifs / 73 cm (28 3/4 in.) / Museum of Fine Arts, Boston / John Gardner Coolidge Collection, 46.478. Page 75: (top right) Asian Art Museum. B60B834_B60B835. © Asian Art Museum of San Francisco. Used by permission. (center) Terracotta Army, Qin Dynasty, 210 BC; horses and carriage / Tomb of Qin shi Huang Di, Xianyang, China / The Bridgeman Art Library International. Page 76: Zhang Yichao, Governor of Western Gansu on Excursion to Fight the Tibetans, Tang Dynasty, 850-907 (wall painting) / Mogao Caves, Dunhuang, Gansu Province, NW China / The Bridgeman Art Library International. Page 77: The Avery Brundage Collection. B60P522. © Asian Art Museum of San Francisco. Used by permission. Page 78: Emperor Yang Ti (581–618) strolling in his gardens with his wives, from a history of Chinese emperors (color on silk) (see also 176855), Chinese School, (17th century) / Bibliotheque Nationale, Paris, France, Archives Charmet / The Bridgeman Art Library International. Page 79: The Avery Brundage Collection. B60J825. © Asian Art Museum of San Francisco. Used by permission. Page 81: The First Battle between the Chinese Army and that of the Eleuths in 1759, detail of fighting across the river, plate 10 from a series of prints representing the conquests of Qianlong, the Emperor of China, engraved by Nicolas Delaunay (1739–92) 1772 (eng, Damascene, Jean (An Tai) (d.1781) (after) / Private Collection, The Stapleton Collection / The Bridgeman Art Library International. Page 82: (top) The Avery Brundage Collection. B60J603. © Asian Art Museum of San Francisco. Used by permission. (bottom) The Avery Brundage Collection. B60B869. © Asian Art Museum of San Francisco. Used by permission. Page 83: From the collection of Stephen Selby. Page 84: The Avery Brundage Collection. B60B762. © Asian Art Museum of San Francisco. Used by permission. Page 85: istockphoto.com. Pages 86–87: From the collection of Stephen Selby. Page 87: (top) The Avery Brundage Collection. B60J736. © Asian Art Museum of San Francisco. Used by permission. (bottom) The Avery Brundage Collection. B60J799. © Asian Art Museum of San Francisco. Used by permission. Pages 88–89: Courtesy of CAS Hanwei. Pages 90–91: Courtesy of CAS Hanwei. Page 93: The Art Archive / National Palace Museum, Taiwan. AA335422. Page 94–95: istockphoto.com. Page 96: (top) The Avery Brundage Collection. B62P164. © Asian Art Museum of San Francisco. Used by permission. (bottom) The Avery Brundage Collection. B76M48. © Asian Art Museum of San Francisco. Used by permission. Page 97: istockphoto.com. Page 98: The Art Archive / Genius of China Exhibition. AA373791. Page 99: (top) From the collection of Stephen Selby. (bottom) The Avery Brundage Collection. B60B678. © Asian Art Museum of San Francisco. Used by permission. Page 100: (top left) The Avery Brundage Collection. B60J561. © Asian Art Museum of San Francisco. Used by permission. (right) From the collection of Stephen Selby. (middle, left) The Avery Brundage Collection. B60B763. © Asian Art Museum of San Francisco. Used by permission. (bottom left) The Avery Brundage Collection. B60B11. © Asian Art Museum of San Francisco. Used by permission.

Page 101: (top) The Avery Brundage Collection. B60B992. © Asian Art Museum of San Francisco. Used by permission. (bottom) From the collection of Stephen Selby. Page 102: An archery contest, late 18th century, (colour on silk), Chinese School, (18th century) / Victoria & Albert Museum, London, UK / The Bridgeman Art Library International. Page 104: Copyright © 2008 Christie's Images Ltd. All rights reserved. CHP270396101_01. Page 106: The Avery Brundage Collection. B60D87. © Asian Art Museum of San Francisco. Used by permission. Page 107: (top) The Avery Brundage Collection. B60J759. © Asian Art Museum of San Francisco. Used by permission. (middle) The Avery Brundage Collection. B60S74+. © Asian Art Museum of San Francisco. Used by permission. (bottom) The Avery Brundage Collection. B60J583. © Asian Art Museum of San Francisco. Used by permission. Page 108: istockphoto.com. Page 109: The Avery Brundage Collection. B60S77. © Asian Art Museum of San Francisco. Used by permission. Page 110: istockphoto.com. Page 111: istockphoto.com. Page 112: istockphoto.com. Page 113: istockphoto.com. Page 115: Copyright © 2008 Christie's Images Ltd. All rights reserved. CHN260498565_01. Page 116–117: istockphoto.com. Page 118–119: istockphoto.com. Page 121: istockphoto.com. Page 122: (top) Copyright © 2008 Christie's Images Ltd. All rights reserved. TOP260901050_01. (bottom) istockphoto.com. Page 123: (top and bottom) istockphoto.com. Page 124: The Avery Brundage Collection. B60B779. © Asian Art Museum of San Francisco. Used by permission. Page 126: The Avery Brundage Collection. B60B804. © Asian Art Museum of San Francisco. Used by permission. Page 127: Transfer from the Fine Arts Museums of San Francisco, Gift of Albert M. Bender. B81M29. © Asian Art Museum of San Francisco. Used by permission. Page 128: Gift of M. Jean-Pierre Dubosc. B77M24. © Asian Art Museum of San Francisco. Used by permission. Page 129: Sino Korean world map, c. 1800 (hand-coloured print), Korean School (19th Century) / British Library, London, UK / The Bridgeman Art Library International. Pages 130–131: Gift of Robert Raphael, B70D9. © Asian Art Museum of San Francisco. Used by permission. Page 132: Copyright © 2008 Christie's Images Ltd. All rights reserved. JPN111191045_01. Page 135: Ray Deadman Collection. Birmingham Museum of Art. Page 136: Yoshiie Ason: "The Barrier at Nakoso," from the series "Gekko's Idle Brush," 1892 (colour woodblock print), Gekko, Ogata (1859–1920) /UCL Art Collections, University College London, UK / The Bridgeman Art Library International. Page 138: The Avery Brundage Collection, B60S222. © Asian Art Museum of San Francisco. Used by permission. Page 139: Wikipedia Commons. Page 140: istockphoto.com. Page 142: istockphoto.com. Page143: istockphoto.com. Pages 144–145: istockphoto.com. Page 144: Bequest of Joseph M. Bransten, B80S1. ©Asian Art Museum of San Francisco. Used by permission. Page 145: (top) The Avery Brundage Collection, B69S31. © Asian Art Museum of San Francisco. Used by permission. (bottom) The Avery Brundage Collection, B62S56+. © Asian Art Museum of San Francisco. Used by permission. Page 146: Shogun touring in spring, Edo Period (1603–1867) (ink on paper) (screen, Japanese School / Private Collection, Photo © Boltin Picture Library / The Bridgeman Art Library International. Page 148: Transfer from the Fine Arts Museums of San Francisco, 1988.38. © Asian Art Museum of San Francisco. Used by permission. Page 149: istockphoto.com. Page 151: (left) Library of Congress. C-DIG-jpd-00043. (right) Ray Deadman Collection. Birmingham Museum of Art. Page 152: Ray Deadman Collection. Birmingham Museum of Art. Page 153: From the collection of Clive Sinclair. Page 154: Acquisition made possible by participants on the Jade Circle Trip to Santa Fe, August 2003, 2003.26. © Asian Art Museum of San Francisco. Used by permission. Page 155: Copyright © 2008 Christie's Images Ltd. All rights reserved. PHO191094059B_01. Pagse 156–157: Gift of Fernande May Lazarus, 1989.21. © Asian Art Museum of San Francisco. Used by permission. Page 158: The Actor Ichikawa Danjuro VII as a Samurai Warrior (surimono-woodblock print), Kunisada, Utagawa (1786–1864) / Fitzwilliam Museum, University of Cambridge, UK / The Bridgeman Art Library International. Page 159: istockphoto.com. Page 160: Ray Deadman Collection. Birmingham Museum of Art. Page 160–161: The Avery Brundage Collection, B69D24 B. © Asian Art Museum of San Francisco. Used by permission. Page 161: (bottom) Museum puchase, B74P4. © Asian Art Museum of San Francisco. Used by permission. Page 162: Night Attack on the Sanjô Palace, from the Illustrated Scrolls of the Events of the Heiji Era (Heiji monogatari emaki) / Japanese, Kamakura period, second half of the 13th century / Handscroll; ink and color on paper / 41.3 x 699.7 cm (16 1/4 x 275 1/2 in.) / Museum of Fine Arts, Boston / Fenollosa-Weld Collection, 11.4000 / © 2008 Museum of Fine Arts, Boston. All rights reserved. / The Bridgeman Art Library International. Page 163: (top) Gift of Dr. and Mrs. William Wedemeyer, 2004.38. © Asian Art Museum of San Francisco. Used by permission. (niddle) Ray Deadman Collection. Birmingham Museum of Art. (bottom) Copyright © 2008 Christie's Images Ltd. All rights reserved. KSJPN150698004F_01. Page 164: (top) The Avery Brundage Collection, B70Y28. © Asian Art Museum of San Francisco. Used by permission. (bottom) istockphoto.com. Page 165: Gift of the Tang Foundation, B87D9.1. © Asian Art Museum of San Francisco. Used by permission. Page 166: The Poet, Ariwara Narihira (825–880) from "The Kokka," September 1910 (colour litho), Japanese School, (20th century) / Bibliotheque des Arts Decoratifs, Paris, France, Archives Charmet / The Bridgeman Art Library International. Page 168: (top) Gift of Col. and Mrs. Samuel R. Dows, B72M1. © Asian Art Museum of San Francisco. Used by permission. (bottom) The Avery Brundage Collection, B70Y688. © Asian Art Museum of San Fransisco. Page 169: istockphoto.com. Pages 170–171: istockphoto.com. Page 171: istockphoto.com. Page 172: istockphoto.com. Pages 174–175: Copyright © 2008 Christie's Images Ltd. All rights reserved. JPN131195008_01. Page 176: "Fuji in Clear Weather," from the series "36 Views of Mount Fuji" (Fugaku sanjurokkei) (woodblock print). Hokusai, Katsushika (1760–1849) / Musee Guimet, Paris, France, Lauros / Giraudon / The Bridgeman Art Library International. Page 177: istockphoto.com. Page 178: Ichikawa Danjuro and Ichikawa Monnosuke as Jagekiyo and Iwai Kumesaburo, 1824 (woodblock engraving), Hokusai, Katsushika (1760–1849) / Fitzwilliam Museum, University of Cambridge, UK / The Bridgeman Art Library International. Page 180: (top) Tales of Yamato, from the series "Ten Designs of Old Tales," 1818–1830 (woodblock engraving), Harunobu, Gakutei (fl.1818–30) / Fitzwilliam Museum, University of Cambridge, UK / The Bridgeman Art Library International. (bottom) Models of late 16th century Japanese warriors (mixed media), Japanese School, (20th century) / Private Collection / The Bridgeman Art Library International. Page 181: (top) Sake flask inlaid with mother of pearl, Japanese, probably 19th century / Private Collection / The Bridgeman Art Library International. (bottom) The Avery Brundage Collection, B60B14+. © Asian Art Museum of San Fransisco. Used by permission. Page 182: Rice Planting, c. 1890s–1900s (colour woodblock print), Gekko, Ogata (1859–1920) / UCL Art Collections, University College London, UK / The Bridgeman Art Library International. Page 183: The Avery Brundage Collection, B70Y1176. © Asian Art Museum of San Francisco. Used by permission. Page 184: istockphoto.com. Page 185: (top) The Avery Brundage Collection, B65B54. © Asian Art Museum of San Francisco. Used by permission. (middle) Courtesy of The Morikami Museum and Japanese Gardens. 1994.027.008. (bottom) The Avery Brundage Collection, B64M13 (detail). © Asian Art Museum of San Francisco. Used by permission. Page 186: Library of Congress. LC-DIG-JPD-01799. Page 188: Kojima Takanori Writing a Poem on a Cherry Tree, from the series, "Pictures of Flowers of Japan," 1895 (woodblock print), Gekko, Ogata (1859–1920) / Fitzwilliam Museum, University of Cambridge, UK / The Bridgeman Art Library International. Page 189: (top right) Copyright © 2008 Christie's Images Ltd. All rights reserved. JPN231192461_01. (right) The Avery Brundage Collection, B60S561. © Asian Art Museum of San Francisco. Used by permission. (bottom left) Gift of Dr. and Mrs. Roger S. Spang, B81M1. © Asian Art Museum of San Francisco. Used by permission. Page 190: istockphoto.com. Page 191: The Avery Brundage Collection, B60D114. © Asian Art Museum of San Francisco. Used by permission. Page 192: istockphoto.com. Page 193: Freer Gallery of Art, Smithsonian Institution, Washington, D.C. / Gift of Charles Lang Freer, F1911.421. Page 194: Bishamonten, the Guardian of the North with his Retinue / Japanese, Kamakura period, late 12th to early 13th century / Panel; ink, color, gold, and silver on silk / 119.1 x 68.1 cm (46 7/8 x 26 13/16 in.) (height x width) / Museum of Fine Arts, Boston / Special Chinese and Japanese Fund, 05.202. / © 2008 Museum of Fine Arts, Boston. All rights reserved. / The Bridgeman Art Library International. Page 195: Ray Deadman Collection. Birmingham Museum of Art. Page 196: istockphoto.com. Page 198: From the collection of Paul Couch. Page 198–199: Ray Deadman Collection. Birmingham Museum of Art. Page 199: Teabowl, Japanese, 16th/17th century (stoneware pottery) / Private Collection, Paul Freeman / The Bridgeman Art Library International. Page 200: Yorimasa shooting at the monster Nuye, pub. c. 1845, (colour woodblock print). Kuniyoshi, Utagawa (1798–1861) / Private Collection / The Bridgeman Art Library International. Page 201: Samurai Armour, Muromachi Period (1333–1571) c. 1384 (mixed media), Japanese School (14th century) / American Museum of Natural History, New York, USA / Photo © Boltin Picture Library / The Bridgeman Art Library International. Page 202: From the collection of Clive Sinclair. Page 204: Onoe Kikugoro III as Nagoya in Sato no haru meibutsu amigasa, c. 1827 (coloured woodblock print), Kunisada, Utagawa (1786–1864) / Fitzwilliam Museum, University of Cambridge, UK / The Bridgeman Art

# Image Sources

Library International. Page 205: (top) Ray Deadman Collection. Birmingham Museum of Art. (bottom) Ray Deadman Collection. Birmingham Museum of Art. Page 206: Hero of a Monogatari by Ariwara no Narimira (825–880) 17th–19th century (woodblock print) (b/w photo), Japanese School / Private Collection, Lauros. Giraudon / The Bridgeman Art Library International. Page 207: (top) Inro depicting the Courtesan Morokoshi of Echizen-ya writing a letter, Japanese (polished lacquers and inlaid gold foil on a lacquer ground), Eishi, Hosada (1756–1829) (after) / © Ashmolean Museum, University of Oxford, UK / The Bridgeman Art Library International. (bottom) Helmet with the crest of Tokugawa (mixed media), Japanese School / © Tokyo Fuji Art Museum, Tokyo, Japan / The Bridgeman Art Library International. Page 208–209: The Tea House at Edo, by Kunishand (c. 1827), (woodblock print) / Victoria & Albert Museum, London, UK / The Bridgeman Art Library International. Page 209: Takigawa from the Tea-House, Ogi (colour woodblock print), Utamaro, Kitagawa (1753–1806) / Pushkin Museum, Moscow, Russia / The Bridgeman Art Library International. Page 210–211: Copyright © 2008 Christie's Images Ltd. All rights reserved. JPN251094199_01. Page 212: From the collection of Clive Sinclair. Page 213: From the collection of Paul Couch. Page 214: (top) Tsuba, 19th century (iron), Natsuo, Kano (1828–1898) / © Ashmolean Museum, University of Oxford, UK / The Bridgeman Art Library International. (bottom) istockphoto.com. Page 215: istockphoto.com. Page 216: istockphoto.com. Page 217: Courtesy of CAS Hanwei. Page 218: Statue of a Japanese warrior (ivory) / Private Collection / The Bridgeman Art Library International. Page 220: Moronao, the villain of "Chushingura" (the story of the forty-seven ronin, masterless samurai), made in 1852, (colour woodblock print), Kunisada, Utagawa (1786–1864) / © Maidstone Museum and Art Gallery, Kent, UK / The Bridgeman Art Library International. Page 221: istockphoto.com. Page 222: Ray Deadman Collection. Birmingham Museum of Art. Page 223: From the collection of Clive Sinclair. Pages 224–225: Ray Deadman Collection. Birmingham Museum of Art. Pages 225: Ray Deadman Collection. Birmingham Museum of Art. Pages 226–227: Courtesy of CAS Hanwei. Page 228: Minamoto Yorimasa sitting on a chair in formal court dress, from, "Famous Generals of Japan" / © School of Oriental & African Studies Library, University of London / The Bridgeman Art Library International. Page 230: Heiji Uprising of 1159. Momoyama Period / Japanese School / Private Collection / © Boltin Picture Library / The Bridgeman Art Library International. Page 231: (left) Courtesy of CAS Hanwei. (top right) From the collection of Paul Couch. (bottom right) From the collection of Paul Couch. Page 232: (top) Gift of Norma C. and Jack D. Tomlinson, B85M7. © Asian Art Museum of San Francisco. Used by permission. (bottom) Writing case decorated with a cockerel, writing case with a bamboo design and a kobako attributed to Ogata Korin (1658–1716) and a message box by the Kajikawa Family, 16th–18th century (lacquered gold & silver), Japanese School / Galerie Janette Ostier, Paris, France, Giraudon / The Bridgeman Art Library International. Page 233: (top) istockphoto.com. (bottom) Photo by Karim Shamsi-Basha. Page 234: B64W16. © Asian Art Museum of San Francisco. Used by permission. Page 235: Wikepedia Commons. Page 236: Samurai Combat (colour woodblock print), Japanese School, (19th century) / Bibliotheque des Arts Decoratifs, Paris, France, Archives Charmet / The Bridgeman Art Library International. Pages 238–239: Ray Deadman Collection. Birmingham Museum of Art. Page 240: From the collection of Clive Sinclair. Page 241: (top and bottom) From the collection of Clive Sinclair. Page 242: From the collection of Clive Sinclair. Page 243: Ray Deadman Collection. Birmingham Museum of Art. Page 244: (top) Copyright © 2008 Christie's Images Ltd. All rights reserved. JPN150698060_01. (bottom) Copyright © 2008 Christie's Images Ltd. All rights reserved. JPN160697086_01. Page 245: Copyright © 2008 Christie's Images Ltd. All rights reserved. JPN150698020_01. Page 247: From the collection of Stephen Selby. Page 248: Ray Deadman Collection. Birmingham Museum of Art. Page 249: From the collection of Clive Sinclair. Page 250: Copyright © 2008 Christie's Images Ltd. All rights reserved. JPN071088257_01. Pages 252–253: The Avery Brundage Collection, D62D9+. © Asian Art Museum of San Francisco. Used by permission. Page 254: The Poetess, Bijin, at her Calligraphy Table (colour woodblock print), Gakutei, Yashima (c. 1786–1868) / Private Collection, Archives Charmet / The Bridgeman Art Library International. Page 255: The Avery Brundage Collection, B62D15. © Asian Art Museum of San Francisco. Used by permission. Page 256: Transfer from the Fine Arts Museums of San Francisco, Gift of Mrs. Herbert Fleishacker, B69S36. © Asian Art Museum of San Francisco. Used by permission. Page 257: (left) Copyright © 2008 Christie's Images Ltd. All rights reserved. JPN050690634_01. (right) istockphoto.com. Page 258: Utagawa, Kuniyoshi, Japanese, 1797–1861/ Publisher: Yamamotoya Heikichi, Japanese / Tomoe Gozen / Japanese, Edo period, about 1840 (Tenpo 11) / Woodblock print (mishiki-e); ink and color on paper / Vertical oban / Museum of Fine Arts, Boston / William Sturgis Bigelow Collection, 11.41277. Page 260–261: Tea Time in Japan, c. 1900 (coloured photo), Japanese School, (20th century) / Bibliotheque des Arts Decoratifs, Paris, France, Archives Charmet / The Bridgeman Art Library International. Page 262: The Avery Brundage Collection, B62B2. © Asian Art Museum of San Francisco. Used by permission. Page 263: Copyright © 2008 Christie's Images Ltd. All rights reserved. JPN210389026_01. Page 265: Ronin Attacking the Kiras Gate, scene from Act XI of '"Chiushingura" or, "The Loyal League: A Japanese Romance," by Monzayemon Chikamatsu, 18th century (verso) (woodblock print) (see 144579 for recto), Kuniyoshi, Utagawa (1798–1861) / © Leeds Museums and Galleries (City Art Gallery) U.K. / The Bridgeman Art Library International. Page 266: (top) Depiction of Spiritual and Material Worlds (pen & ink and gold leaf on panel), Japanese School, (15th century) / American Museum of Natural History, New York, USA, Photo © Boltin Picture Library / The Bridgeman Art Library International. (bottom) Photo by Karim Shamsi-Basha. Page 267: (left) and Copyright © 2008 Christie's Images Ltd. All rights reserved. JPN011196415A_01 (right) Copyright © 2008 Christie's Images Ltd. All rights reserved. JPN011196415A. (bottom) Photo by Karim Shamsi-Basha. Page 268: Sake cup, depicting a landscape with boats and a bridge under Mount Fuji, Japanese, 19th century (lacquers and inlay of gold foil on lacquer ground) / © Ashmolean Museum, University of Oxford, UK / The Bridgeman Art Library International. Page 269: Three Women Preparing a Meal, 19th century (woodblock), Koriusai, (19th century) / Victoria & Albert Museum, London, UK / The Bridgeman Art Library International. Pages 270–271: The Avery Brundage Collection, B60D77+. © Asian Art Museum of San Francisco. Used by permission. Page 272: Copyright © 2008 Christie's Images Ltd. All rights reserved. JPN200391090_01. Page 273: (top) Inro decorated with a carp in a waterfall, Japanese (lacquer), Japanese School / © Leeds Museums and Art Galleries (City Museum) UK / The Bridgeman Art Library International. (left) A 315 Circular Buckler or Target, decorated with a shield charged with three bugle-horns surmounted by a foliated helmet all surrounded with a band of flowing scrolls, in gold on a black ground (wood and gesso), Japanese School (16th century) / © Wallace Collection, London, UK / The Bridgeman Art Library International. Page 274: The House of the Shogun (ink on silk), Japanese School, (18th century) / Private Collection, Photo © Boltin Picture Library / The Bridgeman Art Library International. Page 275: Shogun rulers (woodblock print), Japanese School, (19th century) / Cragside House, Northumberland, UK, National Trust Photographic Library/Derrick E. Witty / The Bridgeman Art Library International. Pages 276–277: From the collection of Clive Sinclair. Page 278: (left) Courtesy of The Morikami Museum and Japanese Gardens. 1984.013.001. (right) Shinagawa: departure of a Daimyo, in later editions called Sunrise, No.2 from the series "53 Stations of the Tokaido" ("Tokaido gojusan tsugi no uchi"), pub. by Hoeido, 1833 (oban size, yoko-e-horizontal format, colour woodblock print), Hiroshige, Ando or Utagawa (1797–1858) / Fitzwilliam Museum, University of Cambridge, UK / The Bridgeman Art Library International. Page 278: (top) Courtesy of The Morikami Museum and Japanese Gardens. 1983.004.002. (bottom) Sixty-two ribbed Suji Helmet (mixed media), Japanese School / © Tokyo Fuji Art Museum, Tokyo, Japan / The Bridgeman Art Library International. Page 280: From the collection of Paul Couch. Page 281: (all) From the collection of Paul Couch. Page 282: Wikimedia Commons. Page 283: Wikimedia Commons. Page 284: The Tale of Musashibo Benkei (ink, pigment, silver and gold on paper), Tosa, Mitsuhiro (fl.c.1430-45) (after) / © The Trustees of the Chester Beatty Library, Dublin / The Bridgeman Art Library International. Page 286: A Soldier in Full Armour (woodblock print), Japanese School, (19th century) / Florence Court, County Fermanagh, Northern Ireland, National Trust Photographic Library/John Hammond / The Bridgeman Art Library International. Page 288: Hideyoshi (c. 1536–98) Blowing a Conch Shell, from "100 Phases of the moon," (colour litho), Yoshitoshi, Tsukioka (1839–92) / © Ashmolean Museum, University of Oxford, UK / The Bridgeman Art Library International. Page 289: Copyright © 2008 Christie's Images Ltd. All rights reserved. PHO191094061A_01. Page 290: Copyright © 1997 Dianne Skoss/Koryu Books. Page 292: Courtesy CAS Hanwei. Page 293: (top) The Avery Brundage Collection, B70Y816. © Asian Art Museum of San Francisco. Used by permission. (middle) Copyright © 2008 Christie's Images Ltd. All rights reserved. JPN231091601_01. (bottom) The Avery Brundage Collection, B62M37. © Asian Art Museum of San Francisco. Used by permission. Page 294: Photos by Karim Shamsi-Basha. Page 295: Photos by Karim Shamsi-Basha. Page 296: Lance point, Yayoi Period, 200 BC–AD 100 (bronze), Japanese School / Musee Guimet, Paris, France, Lauros / Giraudon / The Bridgeman Art Library International. Page 296–297: Ray Deadman Collection. Birmingham Museum of Art. Page 297: Ray Deadman Collection. Birmingham Museum of Art. Page 298: Arms and Armament, B64W2. © Asian Art Museum of San Francisco. Used by permission. Page 299: From the collection of Clive Sinclair. Page 300–301: Ray Deadman Collection. Birmingham Museum of Art. Page 300: From the collection of Paul Couch. Page 301: (top and bottom) From the collection of Paul Couch. Page 302: Ray Deadman Collection. Birmingham Museum of Art. Page 303: Photo by Karim Shamsi-Basha. Page 304: Photos by Karim Shamsi-Basha. Page 305: Photos by Karim Shamsi-Basha. Page 306: Asahina, from the series 3 designs of breaking gates, 1827 (woodblock engraving), Harunobu, Gakutei (fl.1818–30) / Fitzwilliam Museum, University of Cambridge, UK / The Bridgeman Art Library International. Page 307: (top and bottom) Ray Deadman Collection. Birmingham Museum of Art. Page 308–309: The Avery Brundage Collection, B60D54+, © Asian Art Museum of San Francisco. Used by permission. Page 310: Portrait of Tokugawa Ieyasu (1543-1616), Japanese, 17th century, Japanese School, (17th century) / Private Collection / The Bridgeman Art Library International. Page 311: Ray Deadman Collection. Birmingham Museum of Art. Page 312: (top) istockphoto.com. (bottom) Ray Deadman Collection. Birmingham Museum of Art. Page 313: Copyright © 2008 Christie's Images Ltd. All rights reserved. PHO100591155B_01. Page 314: Ray Deadman Collection. Birmingham Museum of Art. Page 314–315: Ray Deadman Collection. Birmingham Museum of Art. Page 315: Ray Deadman Collection. Birmingham Museum of Art. Page 316–317: istockphoto.com. Page 316: (bottom left and bottom right) Photos by Karim Shamsi-Basha. Page 317: (bottom left and bottom right) Photos by Karim Shamsi-Basha. Page 318: (all) Ray Deadman Collection. Birmingham Museum of Art. Page 319: istockphoto.com. Page 320: Copyright © 2008 Christie's Images Ltd. All rights reserved. JPN231192060_01. Page 321: Copyright © 2008 Christie's Images Ltd. All rights reserved. JPN210390462_01. Page 322: Copyright © 2008 Christie's Images Ltd. All rights reserved. JPN090686665_01. Page 323: Rokuban hidara-Gempei, 1825 (coloured woodblock print), Kunisada, Utagawa (1786–1864) / Fitzwilliam Museum, University of Cambridge, UK / The Bridgeman Art Library International. Page 324: From the collection of Paul Couch. Page 325: Ray Deadman Collection. Birmingham Museum of Art. Page 326: (top left, top right, middle left, middle right) From the collection of Paul Couch. (bottom left) Ray Deadman Collection. Birmingham Museum of Art. Page 327: (all) From the collection of Paul Couch. Page 328: Sword Pommel, early Japanese, c. 6th century (gilt bronze) / Private Collection, Paul Freeman / The Bridgeman Art Library International. Page 329: (top left) Copyright © 2008 Christie's Images Ltd. All rights reserved. JPN181185617_01. (bottom left) Ray Deadman Collection. Birmingham Museum of Art. (bottom right) The Avery Brundage Collection, B70Y427, © Asian Art Museum of San Francisco. Used by permission. Page 330: B77D3.A. © Asian Art Museum of San Francisco. Used by permission. Page 331: Copyright © 2008 Christie's Images Ltd. All rights reserved. JPN060389462_01. Page 332: Gift of Dr. William A. Galeno, 2001.53. © Asian Art Museum of San Francisco. Used by permission. Page 333: istockphoto.com. Page 334–335: From the collection of Clive Sinclair. Page 337: From the collection of Clive Sinclair. Page 338: From the collection of Clive Sinclair. Page 339: Courtesy of CAS Hanwei. Page 340: (top) Sake bottle, from Oribe (ceramic), Japanese School / Musee Guimet, Paris, France, Lauros / Giraudon / The Bridgeman Art Library International. (middle) Sake bottle, 17th century (kyoto earthenware with overglaze enamels), Japanese School, (17th century) / © Ashmolean Museum, University of Oxford, UK / The Bridgeman Art Library International. (bottom) Museum purchase, 1990.18. © Asian Art Museum of San Francisco. Used by permission. Page 342: Copyright © 2008 Christie's Images Ltd. All rights reserved. JPN231092288B_01. Page 343: Copyright © 2008 Christie's Images Ltd. All rights reserved. JPN131189450_01. Page 344: (top) Tsuba with cut-out dragon (iron), Kinai of Echizen (18th century) / Fitzwilliam Museum, University of Cambridge, UK / The Bridgeman Art Library International. (bottom) Battle of Hogen in 1156, Momoyama Period (1568–1615) (ink on paper), Japanese School / Private Collection, Photo © Boltin Picture Library / The Bridgeman Art Library International. Page 345: Courtesy of CAS Hanwei. Page 346: istockphoto.com. Page 347: (top right) Gift of William A. Galeno, M.D., B87M22. © Asian Art Museum of San Francisco. Used by permission. (bottom) Copyright © 2008 Christie's Images Ltd. All rights reserved. JPN160699284_01. Page 348: (left) From the collection of Clive Sinclair. (right) Ray Deadman Collection. Birmingham Museum of Art. Page 349: Copyright © 2008 Christie's Images Ltd. All rights reserved. JPN150698054_01. Page 350: (top) Copyright © 2008 Christie's Images Ltd. All rights reserved. JPN210390171_01. (bottom) Copyright © 2008 Christie's Images Ltd. All rights reserved. JPN290396448_01. Page 351: Inro decorated with Nio, Edo period (1615–1868) Japanese (lacquer), Japanese School / Private Collection, Paul Freeman / The Bridgeman Art Library International. Page 352–353: Copyright © 2008 Christie's Images Ltd. All rights reserved. JPN020785495_01. Page 354: Haniwa Warrior, late 6th century (red earthenware), Japanese School / Museum of Fine Arts, Houston, Texas, USA, A. C. Arnold Endowment Fund & McAshan Charitable Trust / The Bridgeman Art Library International. Page 355: Copyright © 2008 Christie's Images Ltd. All rights reserved. JPN021196557_01. Page 356: istockphoto.com. Page 357: (top) istockphoto.com. (bottom) Copyright © 2008 Christie's Images Ltd. All rights reserved. JPN131189456_01. Page 358: istockphoto.com. Page 359: istockphoto.com. Page 360: The Avery Brundage Collection, B70Y54. © Asian Art Museum of San Francisco. Used by permission. Page 362–363: (bottom) Katsushika Hokusai, Japanese, 1760–1849 / Phoenix / Japanese, Edo period, 1835 (Tenpô 6) / Eight-panel folding screen; ink, color, cut gold-leaf, and sprinkled gold on paper / Image: 35.8 x 233.2 cm (14 1/8 x 91 13/16 in.) / Overall: 44.7 x 248 cm (17 5/8 x 97 5/8 in.) / Museum of Fine Arts, Boston / William Sturgis Bigelow Collection, 11.7433 / © 2008 Museum of Fine Arts, Boston. All rights reserved. / The Bridgeman Art Library International. Page 363: Parasol Maker, Okinomo, Edo Period (1600–1868) (ivory), Japanese School, (19th century) / Private Collection, Photo © Boltin Picture Library / The Bridgeman Art Library International. Page 364: Man's Kimono, Edo period (1600–1868) (silk), Japanese School, (19th century) / Indianapolis Museum of Art, USA, The Eliza M. and Sarah L. Niblack Collection / The Bridgeman Art Library International. Page 365: Copyright © 2008 Christie's Images Ltd. All rights reserved. JPN270391472_01. Page 366: (top) Photo by Karim Shamsi-Basha. Page 366–367: (bottom) From the collection of Paul Couch. Page 367: (left and right) From the collection of Paul Couch. Page 368: Library of Congress. LC-DIG-jpd-00507. Page 370: Wikipedia Commons. Page 372: Wikipedia Commons. Page 373: Ichikawa Danjuro VII Overpowering an Officer of the Law, c. 1830–44 (woodblock print), Kuniyoshi, Utagawa (1798–1861) / Fitzwilliam Museum, University of Cambridge, UK / The Bridgeman Art Library International. Page 374: Model of a 16th century Japanese warrior, Japanese School, (20th century) / Private Collection / The Bridgeman Art Library International. Page 375: Tea Bowl with Mt. Fuji (stoneware with black glaze), Japanese School, (19th century) / Indianapolis Museum of Art, USA, Gift of Mrs. Anna J. Brownell / The Bridgeman Art Library International. (middle) Courtesy of The Morikami Museum and Japanese Gardens. 2004.019.056. (bottom) The Avery Brundage Collection, B70Y133. © Asian Art Museum of San Francisco. Used by permission. Page 376: The Sadaijin in ceremonial costume, Muromachi Period (polychrome wood), Japanese School, (15th century) / Musee Historique des Tissus, Lyon, France, Giraudon / The Bridgeman Art Library International. Page 377: Library of Congress. LC-DIG-jpd-01793. Page 378: (top and bottom) istockphoto.com. Page 379: istockphoto.com. Page 380: (top left) Plate underneath incense burner bearing names of the makers and workshop seals, Meiji period, late 19th century (metal) (see 270967), Japanese School, (19th century) / Private Collection, Paul Freeman / The Bridgeman Art Library International. (top right, bottom left, bottom right) Ray Deadman Collection. Birmingham Museum of Art. Page 381: (all) From the collection of Paul Couch. Page 382–383: Wikipedia Commons. Page 384: Tsuba decorated with fans (copper with enamel), Japanese School / Fitzwilliam Museum, University of Cambridge, UK / The Bridgeman Art Library International. Page 385: Ivory okimono of people playing Go by Sei, Japanese, 19th century / Private Collection / The Bridgeman Art Library International. Page 386–387: Courtesy of The Morikami Museum and Japanese Gardens. 1984.006.016. Page 388: (right) From the collection of Paul Couch. Page 389: (top left, bottom right) From the collection of Paul Couch. Page 391: Ray Deadman Collection. Birmingham Museum of Art. Page 392: Copyright © 2008 Christie's Images Ltd. All rights reserved. JPN150698023_01. Page 394: Utagawa Yoshitora, Japanese, 1836–1887 / Publisher: Daikokuya Kinnosuke (Kinjiro), Japanese / The Syllable Wo: Hayami Sozaemon Fujiwara no Mitsutaka, from the series Biographies of the Faithful Samurai (Seichu gishi meimeiden) / Japanese, Edo period, 1866 (Keio 2), 5th month / Woodblock print (nishiki-e); ink and color on paper / Vertical oban / Museum of Fine Arts, Boston / William Sturgis Bigelow Collection, 11.41277. Page 395: Copyright © 2008 Christie's Images Ltd. All rights reserved. JPN151286037_01. Pages 396–397: Utagawa Kuniyoshi, Japanese, 1797–1861 / Publisher: Kagiya Hanjiro, Japanese / The Battle of Kurikaradani / Japanese, Edo period, about 1845 (Koka 2) / Woodblock print (nishiki-e); ink and color on paper / Vertical oban triptych / Museum of Fine Arts, Boston / Bequest of William

Perkins Babcock, 00.1089-91. Page 398: (top) Ray Deadman Collection. Birmingham Museum of Art. (bottom) 2004.39. © Asian Art Museum of San Francisco. Used by permission. Page 399: Courtesy of CAS Hanwei. Page 400: The Art Archive / Oriental Art Museum Genoa / Alfredo Dagli Orti. AA356167. Page 401: (top right) Copyright © 2008 Christie's Images Ltd. All rights reserved. JPN150698002F_01. (middle left) Bando Mitsugoro III, 1820 (woodblock engraving), Kunisada, Utagawa (1786–1864) / Fitzwilliam Museum, University of Cambridge, UK / The Bridgeman Art Library International. (middle right) Courtesy of The Morikami Museum and Japanese Gardens. 1989.00.017. (bottom right) istockphoto.com. Page 402: Courtesy of The Morikami Museum and Japanese Gardens. 1984.006.009. Page 403: Minamoto no Muneyuki Ason, from the series "100 Poems by 100 Poets Explained by a Nurse," c. 1835 (woodblock print), Hokusai, Katsushika (1760–1849) / Fitzwilliam Museum, University of Cambridge, UK / The Bridgeman Art Library International. Page 405: Copyright © 2008 Christie's Images Ltd. All rights reserved. JPN111191132_01. Page 407: Wikipedia Commons. Page 408: Wikipedia Commons. Page 410: (top) Ray Deadman Collection. Birmingham Museum of Art. (bottom) Three Aikichi Tanto (swords) of the Meiji period, late 19th century / Private Collection / The Bridgeman Art Library International. Page 411: Courtesy of CAS Hanwei. Page 412: The Actor Bando Tokuke as Takahastu Yajuro, a Samurai (woodblock print), Kunisada, Utagawa (1786–1864) / © Leeds Museums and Galleries (City Art Gallery) U.K. / The Bridgeman Art Library International. Page 413: istockphoto.com. Page 414–415: Ray Deadman Collection. Birmingham Museum of Art. Page 416: The Avery Brundage Collection, B60D36+. © Asian Art Museum of San Francisco. Used by permission. Page 418: Ray Deadman Collection. Birmingham Museum of Art. Page 420: istockphoto.com. Page 421: (top and bottom) istockphoto.com. (middle) Courtesy of The Morikami Museum and Japanese Gardens. 1989.023.012. Pages 422–423: From the collection of Clive Sinclair. Page 424: Wikipedia Commons. Page 425: B60D60+. © Asian Art Museum of San Francisco. Used by permission. Page 426–427: B60D61+. © Asian Art Museum of San Francisco. Used by permission. Page 427: Wikipedia Commons. Page 428: Ray Deadman Collection. Birmingham Museum of Art. Page 429: The Avery Brundage Collection, B60D5. © Asian Art Museum of San Francisco. Used by permission. Page 430: Courtesy of The Morikami Museum and Japanese Gardens. 1995.004.006. Page 431: Ray Deadman Collection. Birmingham Museum of Art. Page 432: The Avery Brundage Collection, B70Y1521. © Asian Art Museum of San Francisco. Used by permission. Page 433: (top left) The Avery Brundage Collection, B70Y1622. © Asian Art Museum of San Francisco. Used by permission. (top right) The Avery Brundage Collection, B70Y1530. © Asian Art Museum of San Francisco. Used by permission. (bottom left) The Avery Brundage Collection, B70Y1500. © Asian Art Museum of San Francisco. Used by permission. (bottom right) The Avery Brundage Collection, B70Y1501. © Asian Art Museum of San Francisco. Used by permission. Pages 434–435: B60D79+. © Asian Art Museum of San Francisco. Used by permission. Page 436: Wikipedia Commons. Page 437: Courtesy of The Morikami Museum and Japanese Gardens. 1995.004.007. Page 438: Portrait of a Ronin, from "Seichin Gushi Shozo" (woodblock print) (b/w print), Kuniyoshi, Utagawa (1798–1861) / Galerie Janette Ostier, Paris, France, Giraudon / The Bridgeman Art Library International. Page 439: Ronin Attacking the Kiras Gate, scene from Act XI of "Chushingura," or "The Loyal League: A Japanese Romance," by Monzayemon Chikamatsu (recto) (woodblock print) (see 144580 for verso), Kuniyoshi, Utagawa (1798–1861) / © Leeds Museums and Galleries (City Art Gallery) U.K. / The Bridgeman Art Library International. Page 440: The "Chushingura" (the story of the forty seven ronin—masterless samurai); a scene from act II when the ronin attack Moronao's castle, pub. c. 1854, (colour woodblock print), Kuniyoshi, Utagawa (1798–1861) / © Maidstone Museum and Art Gallery, Kent, UK / The Bridgeman Art Library International. Page 441: Shojiro with a sword by Natori Shunsen, 1924, (colour woodblock print) / Private Collection / The Bridgeman Art Library International. Pages 442–446: Photos by Karim Shamsi-Basha. Page 447: (top left, top right) Photos by Karim Shamsi-Basha. (bottom left) From the collection of Paul Couch. Page 448–449: The Avery Brundage Collection, B63D8. © Asian Art Museum of San Francisco. Used by permission. Page 451: Copyright © 2008 Christie's Images Ltd. All rights reserved. JPN231091405B_01. Page 452: Yoshitsune, with Benkei and Other Retainers in their Ship Beset by the Ghosts of Taira, 1853 (woodblock print), Kuniyoshi, Utagawa (1798–1861) / Fitzwilliam Museum, University of Cambridge, UK / The Bridgeman Art Library International. Pages 454–455: Samurai (gouache on paper), Nicolle, Pat (Patrick) (1907–95) / Private Collection, © Look and Learn / The Bridgeman Art Library International. Page 456: Wikipedia Commons. Page 457: istockphoto.com. Page 459: Wikipedia Commons. Pages 460–461: Photos by Karim Shamsi-Basha. Page 462: Library of Congress. LC-DIG-jpd-01785. Page 463: (top right) Courtesy of The Morikami Museum and Japanese Gardens. 2001.024.011. (bottom left) Courtesy of The Morikami Museum and Japanese Gardens. 1983.004.003. (bottom right) Courtesy of The Morikami Museum and Japanese Gardens. 1991.009.020. Page 464: Japanese Samurai, including Yoritomo, founder of the Bakafu Code, Escott, Dan (1928–87) / Private Collection, © Look and Learn / The Bridgeman Art Library International. Page 465: (top, bottom) istockphoto.com. Page 466: Copyright © 2008 Christie's Images Ltd. All rights reserved. PHO191094059D_01. Page 467: Copyright © 2008 Christie's Images Ltd. All rights reserved. PHO191094059C_01. Page 468: Copyright © 2008 Christie's Images Ltd. All rights reserved. PHO100591155C_01. Page 469: (all) Courtesy of The Morikami Museum and Japanese Gardens. 1989.021.056. Page 470–471: Night Attack on the Sanjô Palace, from the Illustrated Scrolls of the Events of the Heiji Era (Heiji monogatari emaki) / Japanese, Kamakura period, second half of the 13th century / Handscroll; ink and color on paper / 41.3 x 699.7 cm (16 1/4 x 275 1/2 in.) / Museum of Fine Arts, Boston / Fenollosa-Weld Collection, 11.4000 / © 2008 Museum of Fine Arts, Boston. All rights reserved. / The Bridgeman Art Library International. Page 472: 2005.100.121. © Asian Art Museum of San Francisco. Used by permission. Page 474: istockphoto.com. Page 475: (left) Wikipedia Commons. (right) Photo by Karim Shamsi-Basha. Pages 476–477: Night Attack on the Sanjô Palace, from the Illustrated Scrolls of the Events of the Heiji Era (Heiji monogatari emaki) / Japanese, Kamakura period, second half of the 13th century / Handscroll; ink and color on paper / 41.3 x 699.7 cm (16 1/4 x 275 1/2 in.) / Museum of Fine Arts, Boston / Fenollosa-Weld Collection, 11.4000 / © 2008 Museum of Fine Arts, Boston. All rights reserved. / The Bridgeman Art Library International. Page 478: Fan with maple design (paper), Hoitsu, Sakai (1761–1828) / © Ashmolean Museum, University of Oxford, UK / The Bridgeman Art Library International. Page 479: (top) Courtesy of The Morkami Museum and Japanese Gardens. 1990.013.002a-b. (bottom) Frat Bowl with chrysanthemum and water design, Kokutani Style, Early Edo Period (ceramic), Japanese School / © Tokyo Fuji Art Museum, Tokyo, Japan / The Bridgeman Art Library International. Page 480: (top) Courtesy of The Morikami Museum and Japanese Gardens. 1994.027.007. (bottom) F1998.40.25. © Asian Art Museum of San Francisco. Used by permission. Page 481: Palanquin of the Date Family with arabesque design, Middle Edo Period (Maki-e lacquer), Japanese School / © Tokyo Fuji Art Museum, Tokyo, Japan / The Bridgeman Art Library International. Page 482: Copyright © 2008 Christie's Images Ltd. All rights reserved. JPN240497291_01. Page 483: (top) Transfer from the Fine Arts Museums of San Francisco, Gift of Mr. R. P. Schwerin, B74M7. © Asian Art Museum of San Francisco. Used by permission. (bottom) The Last Stand of the Kusanoki Clan, the Battle of Shijo Nawate, 1348, c. 1851 (woodblock print), Kuniyoshi, Utagawa (1798–1861) / Victoria & Albert Museum, London, UK / The Bridgeman Art Library International. Page 484: Copyright © 2008 Christie's Images Ltd. All rights reserved. JPN0906886662_01. Page 485: (top) Two musicians (ivory), Japanese School / Musee Marmottan, Paris, France, Giraudon / The Bridgeman Art Library International. (bottom) Three masks (ivory), Japanese School / Musee Marmottan, Paris, France, Giraudon / The Bridgeman Art Library International. Page 486: Copyright © 2008 Christie's Images Ltd. All rights reserved. JPN270391494B_01. Page 487: (top left) Copyright © 2008 Christie's Images Ltd. All rights reserved. JPN 27039149F_01. (top, second) Copyright © 2008 Christie's Images Ltd. All rights reserved. JPN 27039149G_01. (top, third) Copyright © 2008 Christie's Images Ltd. All rights reserved. JPN 27039149I_01. (top right) Copyright © 2008 Christie's Images Ltd. All rights reserved. JPN 27039149H_01. (bottom) Memorial Portrait of Ando Hiroshige (1797–1858) (woodblock print), Kunisada, Utagawa (1786–1864) / © Leeds Museums and Galleries (City Art Gallery) U.K. / The Bridgeman Art Library International. Page 489: Wikipedia Commons. Page 490: (top) Courtesy of The Morikami Museum and Japanese Gardens. 1989.016.017a-c. (bottom) Courtesy of The Morikami Museum and Japanese Gardens. 1984.006.018. Page 491: (top) Courtesy of The Morikami Museum and Japanese Gardens. 2004.019.065. (bottom) Courtesy of The Morikami Museum and Japanese Gardens. 1995.018.052. Page 492: The Morikami Museum and Japanese Gardens. 2004.019.191. Page 492–493: Sixty-two ribbed Suji Helmet (mixed media), Japanese School / © Tokyo Fuji Art Museum, Tokyo, Japan / The Bridgeman Art Library International. Page 493: Courtesy of The Morikami Museum and Japanese Gardens. 1989.021.077. Page 494: istockphoto.com. Page 495: (top) Jomon figurine (earthenware), Japanese School / Musee Guimet, Paris, France, Lauros / Giraudon / The Bridgeman Art Library International. (bottom) Courtesy of The Morikami Museum and Japanese Gardens. 1989.008.003. Page 496: Transfer from the Fine Arts Museums of San Francisco, Gift of Mr. R. P. Schwerin, B74M7 B. © Asian Art Museum of San Francisco. Used by permission. Page 497: Courtesy of CAS Hanwei. Page 498: (left) Courtesy of CAS Hanwei. (right) Ray Deadman Collection. Birmingham Museum of Art. Page 499: (top) Ray Deadman Collection. Birmingham Museum of Art. (bottom) Courtesy of CAS Hanwei. (right) Ray Deadman Collection. Birmingham Museum of Art. Page 500: Samurai with raised sword, c. 1860 (albumen print), Beato, Felice (Felix) (1825–c. 1908) / Private Collection, The Stapleton Collection / The Bridgeman Art Library International. Page 501: Artist Unknown, Japanese / Mirror / Japanese, Tumuli period, 5th century / Bronze / 23.5 cm / Museum of Fine Arts, Boston / Museum purchase with funds donated by contribution, 08.160 / © 2008 Museum of Fine Arts, Boston. All rights reserved. / The Bridgeman Art Library International. Page 502: P.62-1938 Painting and calligraphy party at the Manpachiro teahouse, 1827 (colour woodblock print) (for companion print see 69775), Kunisada, Utagawa (1786–1864) / Fitzwilliam Museum, University of Cambridge, UK / The Bridgeman Art Library International. Page 503: (top) Wikipedia Commons. (bottom) Writing Box, c. 1830 (lacquer), Japanese School, (19th century) / Private Collection / The Bridgeman Art Library International. Page 504: Scenes of urban life under the "Bakufu," Tosa School, 1800 (from a six-fold screen), (for detail see 67713), (colour woodblock print) / Private Collection, Photo © Bonhams, London, UK / The Bridgeman Art Library International. Page 505: A Japanese Man Converted to Christianity (oil on panel), Japanese School, (17th century) / Museu do Caramulo, Portugal / The Bridgeman Art Library. Page 506--507: From the collection of Paul Couch. Page 508: (top) Inro, decorated with the figures of the Buddha, Confucius and Lao Tzu, by Serizawa Ryumin and Kajikawa Hogetsu, Japanese, 19th century (gold lacquer) (for reverse see 121555) / Private Collection, Paul Freeman / The Bridgeman Art Library International. (bottom) Inro, decorated with the three figures of the Buddha, Confucius and Lao Tzu, by Serizawa Ryumin and Kajikawa Hogetsu, Japanese, 19th century (gold lacquer) (for obverse see 121554) / Private Collection, Paul Freeman / The Bridgeman Art Library International. Page 509: (left) 1991.58. © Asian Art Museum of San Francisco. Used by permission. (right) The Avery Brundage Collection, B60D41+. © Asian Art Museum of San Francisco. Used by permission. Page 510: Kabuki Actor, c. 1859 (woodblock on paper), Kunisada, Utagawa (1786–1864) / Museum of Fine Arts, Houston, Texas, USA, Gift of Mrs Eleanor Freed / The Bridgeman Art Library International. Page 511: Sliding doors depicting a thunder god, Late Edo Period, Kiitsu, Suzuki (1796–1858) / © Tokyo Fuji Art Museum, Tokyo, Japan / The Bridgeman Art Library International. Page 513: Copyright © 2008 Christie's Images Ltd. All rights reserved. PHO191094952_01. Page 514: Ray Deadman Collection. Birmingham Museum of Art. Page 515: (top) Photo by Karim Shamsi-Basha. (bottom) Image from the collection of Clive Sinclair. Page 517: Head of a Temple Guard (carved wood), Japanese School / Daigoji Temple, Kyoto, Japan, Bildarchiv Steffens / The Bridgeman Art Library International. Page 518: Okimono of rice Sellers signed "Sei," Japan, c. 1900 / Private Collection / The Bridgeman Art Library International. Page 519: Ivory figure of a poulterer by Okawa Shizumune, c. 1900 / Private Collection / The Bridgeman Art Library International. Page 520: From the collection of Paul Couch. Page 521: Battle of Nagashino and Himeji Castle, Escott, Dan (1928–87) / Private Collection, © Look and Learn / The Bridgeman Art Library International. Page 522: (top and bottom) istockphoto.com. Page 523: istockphoto.com. Page 525: Matsumoto Koshiro V in the role of Matsuomaru, from the "Tokaido Road" series, (colour litho), Kunisada, Utagawa (1786–1864) / © Ashmolean Museum, University of Oxford, UK / The Bridgeman Art Library International. Page 526–527: Gift of Robert Raphael, B70D8. © Asian Art Museum of San Francisco. Used by permission. Page 528: Helmet with design of an Orc (mixed media), Japanese School / © Tokyo Fuji Art Museum, Tokyo, Japan / The Bridgeman Art Library International. Page 529: Jomon vase from the Kanto province (earthenware), Japanese School / Musee Guimet, Paris, France, Lauros / Giraudon / The Bridgeman Art Library International. Page 530: Copyright © 2008 Christie's Images Ltd. All rights reserved. JPN171292135_01. Page 531: (top) Courtesy of CAS Hanwei. (bottom) From the collection of Paul Couch. Page 532–533: From the collection of Clive Sinclair. Page 534: Sumo wrestlers (hand tinted wood engraving on paper), Japanese School, (19th century) / Royal Albert Memorial Museum, Exeter, Devon, UK / The Bridgeman Art Library International. Page 535: Ivory Okimono of Wrestlers, Japanese, 19th century / Private Collection / The Bridgeman Art Library International. Page 536: istockphoto.com. Page 537: istockphoto.com. Page 538: Carved panel representing the Empress Jingo Kogo and her Prime Minister Takemonchi, 3rd century / Private Collection / The Bridgeman Art Library International. Page 540: (top) Ray Deadman Collection. Birmingham Museum of Art. Page 540–541: Photo courtesy of CAS Hanwei. Page 542–545: Photos by Karim Shamsi-Basha. Page 546: Cavalry in Winter, in the style of Yoshitoshi (1839–92) (woodblock print), Japanese School, (19th century) / Cragside House, Northumberland, UK, National Trust Photographic Library/Derrick E. Witty / The Bridgeman Art Library International. Page 548: HM 41 (12) The Far East, from a portolan atlas, by Fernao vaz Dourado (1520–c. 1580) 1570 (coloured engraving), Portuguese School, (16th century) / Huntington Library and Art Gallery, San Marino, CA, USA / The Bridgeman Art Library International. Page 549: (top) Museum purchase, 1989.24. © Asian Art Museum of San Francisco. Used by permission. (bottom) From the collection of Paul Couch. Page 550: Copyright © 2008 Christie's Images Ltd. All rights reserved. JPN021196723_01. Page 551: The War-Lords of Japan: Prince Morinaga leads soldier monks into battle, Escott, Dan (1928–87) / Private Collection, © Look and Learn / The Bridgeman Art Library International. Page 552: Mempo face mask, Masanobu or Nara style, Japanese / © Leeds Museums and Art Galleries (City Museum) UK / The Bridgeman Art Library International. Page 553: Cast iron helmet inlaid with gold and silver, technique known as Komai, Japanese, 19th century / Private Collection / The Bridgeman Art Library International. Page 554: Copyright © 2008 Christie's Images Ltd. All rights reserved. JPN231091858_01. Page 555: istockphoto.com. Pages 556–557: Sixth Korean Embassy to Japan in Meireki 1 at the time of Tokugawa Ietsuna's succession in 1651, possibly by Kano Masunobu (1625–94) (scroll painting) (detail) (see also 79778), Japanese School, (17th century) / School of Oriental & African Studies Library, Uni. of London / The Bridgeman Art Library International. Page 558: Three Actors in a Scene from "Snow-Covered Bamboo: Genji in Long Sleeves," 1785 (woodblock print), Shunsho, Yushido (1726–92) / Fitzwilliam Museum, University of Cambridge, UK / The Bridgeman Art Library International. Page 560: Fragment of a guardian of a temple, Dakkatsu Kanshitsu, Japan / Musee Guimet, Paris, France / The Bridgeman Art Library International. Page 561: (top) Mask of an old man trying to whistle, Japanese, Japanese School / © Leeds Museums and Art Galleries (City Museum) UK / The Bridgeman Art Library International. (bottom) Noh theatre mask of a young woman, Japanese, Japanese School, (19th century) / © Leeds Museums and Art Galleries (City Museum) UK / The Bridgeman Art Library International. Page 562: (top) Transfer from the Fine Arts Museums of San Francisco, B69M51. © Asian Art Museum of San Francisco. Used by permission. (bottom) The Avery Brundage Collection, B70Y568. © Asian Art Museum of San Francisco. Used by permission. Page 563: Surimono of an Armed Warrior on Horseback, c. 1822 (colour woodblock print), Hokkei, Toyota (1780–1850) / Brooklyn Museum of Art, New York, USA, Gift of Eleanor Z. Wallace in memory of Stanley L. Wallace / The Bridgeman Art Library International. Page 564: Horse Jumping, Japanese, Edo period, c. 18th century (ink on paper) (one of a pair) (see also 121396), Shohaku, Soga (1730–81) / Private Collection, Paul Freeman / The Bridgeman Art Library International. Page 565: (top) From the collection of Paul Couch. (bottom) The Avery Brundage Collection, B62S57+. © Asian Art Museum of San Francisco. Used by permission. Page 566–567: (bottom) Copyright © 2008 Christie's Images Ltd. All rights reserved. JPN131189170_01. Page 567: (top) From the collection of Clive Sinclair. Page 568: Japanese Court Official or Samurai, c. 1870s (hand-coloured albumen print), English Photographer, (19th century) / Private Collection, The Stapleton Collection / The Bridgeman Art Library International. Page 570: From the collection of Clive Sinclair.

Maps
Pages 26–27, 45, 113, 120: Pat Covert.
Pages 32, 173: Mapping Specialists.